The SBL Handbook of Style

SECOND EDITION

The SBL Handbook of Style

SECOND EDITION

For Biblical Studies
and Related Disciplines

SBL Press
Atlanta, Georgia

Library of Congress Cataloging-in-Publication Data

The SBL handbook of style / Billie Jean Collins, project director ; Bob Buller, publishing director ; John F. Kutsko, executive director. —
Second edition.
pages cm
Includes index.
ISBN 978-1-58983-964-9 (hardcover binding)
1. Middle East—History—Authorship—Style manuals. 2. Bible—Historiography—Authorship—Style manuals. 3. Church history—Authorship—Style manuals. 4. History, Ancient—Authorship—Style manuals. 5. Middle East—Civilization—To 622—Historiography—Handbooks, manuals, etc. I. Collins, Billie Jean. II. Society of Biblical Literature. III. Title: Society of Biblical Literature handbook of style.
PN147.S26 2014
808'.027—dc23

2014034989

Cover redesign by Kathie Klein
Cover photo by Marek Uliasz/iStock

Printed in the United States of America on acid-free, recycled paper conforming to ANSI/NISO Z39.48-1992 (R1997) and ISO 9706:1994 standards for paper permanence.

TABLE OF CONTENTS

PREFACE TO THE SECOND EDITION

Fifteen years after the appearance of the first edition of *The SBL Handbook of Style*, the second edition continues its original goal: "To collect information as much as to dispense it; and more than dictating rules of conformity, it seeks to identify those stylistic points where the disciplines already intersect." The primary purpose of the handbook was modest, intending not to prescribe a universal standard but to help save time for scholars writing in the many related and intersecting fields of biblical studies. In so doing, it benefited publishers, as they began to expect such stylistic consistency from members of these fields and thereby relied on the handbook as a starting point for their own house rules. The handbook arrived at an especially opportune time, when consistency aided research in digital reference works, aggregated databases, and search engines. The appearance of the handbook in the digital revolution certainly contributed to its wide adoption, but largely it experienced this reception because of its original and modest goal.

The careful reader of *The SBL Handbook of Style* will have noticed "stealth" corrections over the course of the first edition's seven printings. Through a decade and half, as the handbook became the standard style for biblical studies and as many publishers and scholarly projects adopted it as their style guide or conformed their publications to it, the resource improved in accuracy as errors and inconsistencies were identified. Owners of the original printing, which likely has a cracked binding and loose pages, will find these corrections throughout the second edition.

In addition to corrections, the revisions to the second edition of *The SBL Handbook of Style* are fivefold. First, this edition includes carefully selected stylistic changes based on the review and recommendation of the editorial board members and consultants. The consultants and editorial board members consisted of scholars and academic publishers, and they, too, consulted with others in their areas of contribution and specialization. The introduction to the second edition of *The SBL Handbook of Style* alerts the reader to the most significant rule changes. Second, the new edition supplements and updates several areas. Third, the handbook has filled in gaps of coverage or added new sections. Fourth, the handbook has reordered chapters and moved the appendixes into the body of the handbook. Fifth, the second edition continues the practice of supplementing *The Chicago Manual of Style*. On the one hand, this edition reduces some differences between the two guides. On the other hand, while the first edition tended toward minimal duplication, relying on users referring to *The Chicago Manual of Style*, feedback from users noted that it would be more efficient to have style guidance in one place. Consequently, the second edition contains more complete information and requires less consultation of *The Chicago Manual of Style*.

It is worth restating that the field of biblical studies is remarkably diverse. It is not one field but many, including ancient Near Eastern studies, Jewish studies and rabbinics, Christian studies and late antiquity, and reception history. Members of the Society of Biblical Literature teach in departments of religion, biblical and theological studies, Near Eastern studies, Jewish and Judaic studies, history, anthropology, and literature. For this wide-ranging discipline, the Society of Biblical Literature will continue to evolve, and changes will be reflected in future editions of *The SBL Handbook of Style*.

The SBL Handbook of Style has always been a community resource, crowd-sourced by members of the guild and its many subdisciplines. Its contents reflect this diversity, and the publication is a result of a collaboration of individuals and organizations. Consequently, it would be impossible to thank all those who have contributed to it. The new edition no longer reflects a finite number of named editors. The second edition is a combination of many contributions from readers who submitted corrections and observations, as well as the editorial board and consultants. However, we want to acknowledge the commitment of the original publisher, Hendrickson Publishers, and to thank them for their service to SBL in conceiving the original and offering to SBL this resource. Further, the publisher would like to mention four individuals who were most involved in development of this revision. James Ernest, who was among the original editors, remained insightfully active. Allan Emery maintained the project notes at Hendrickson and delivered to SBL the files in as neat a package as humanly possible. Bob Buller and Billie Jean Collins, among SBL Press's publication staff, bore the weight of managing the revision and adjudicating opinions. Their editorial skill and good judgment are evident throughout.

—John F. Kutsko, SBL Executive Director

PREFACE TO THE FIRST EDITION

Nearly two years in the making, not counting the fifteen years of countless prototypes, *The SBL Handbook of Style* reflects a collaborative effort between Hendrickson Publishers and the Society of Biblical Literature. This collaboration came upon the heels of a conversation about Hendrickson's style manual with Rex Matthews, then editorial director at Scholars Press, who suggested that Hendrickson Publishers contact SBL associate director Gregory Glover. To Greg belongs much of the credit for working out the details and for putting Hendrickson in touch with David L. Petersen of Iliff School of Theology, in Denver. David reviewed the heart of the work, making suggestions about SBL's style preferences and offering sage editorial input. His patience, expertise, and care for certitude were most appreciated. Typesetting the project posed unique challenges; issues of extraordinary character sets, demanding designs, and constant tweaking by the obsessed editors were handled with great proficiency by Phil Frank, senior production editor, and Darren Hurlburt (who designed the book) and Doug LaBudde, production editors, of Communication Ink, Peabody, Massachusetts. The three set records in skill, endurance, and good humor. Thanks are due as well to Joe Carey for his sharp eye and helpful input. Appreciation is also due Emanuel Tov, the J. L. Magnes Professor of Bible at Hebrew University, Jerusalem. Professor Tov graciously provided the comprehensive list of the Dead Sea Scrolls in Appendix F. The generosity of Professor Tov gave the volume an added dimension of usability.

Mark Twain once remarked that he didn't give a damn for someone who could spell a word only one way; he would have hated this book. Precision—spelling that word only one way—is to editors what the Holy Grail was to Arthur's knights. This volume reflects nearly forty years of the editors' collective quests for precision, at least when it comes to everyday decisions associated with publishing in the academic fields of ancient Near Eastern, biblical, and early Christian studies. As most scholars have discovered, trying to maintain consistency in matters of style can be frustrating at best. Often it appears that there are as many ways to do something as there are scholars. Furthermore, the kinds of fine points scholars need resolved are not always addressed in the available resources, and when they are, styles may vary among books, journals, societies, and projects. *The SBL Handbook of Style* attempts to collect information as much as to dispense it; and more than dictating rules of conformity, it seeks to identify those stylistic points where the disciplines already intersect. Thus, *The SBL Handbook of Style* endeavors both to become a resource for making stylistic decisions and to be a basis for future judgments about editing and writing in these fields. Although the volume aspires to be comprehensive within its parameters, the editors realize that total comprehensiveness and consistency remain elusive. It is hoped that this volume will save writers, editors, proofreaders, and students time and energy. Should their effort be taken seriously and scholarly writing enhanced, the time required to make this happen will have been well spent.

—The Editors
Patrick H. Alexander
John F. Kutsko
James D. Ernest
Shirley Decker-Lucke
David L. Petersen

1 INTRODUCTION

The SBL Handbook of Style has been created to help scholars, students, editors, and proofreaders of ancient Near Eastern studies, biblical studies, early Christianity, and rabbinic studies.

Three principles have informed the selection of material and guided the contents of the handbook. First, *The SBL Handbook of Style* should as much as possible reflect usage and not make new law. Therefore it has not imposed an artificial consistency on the different areas of specialization in a multifaceted field such as biblical studies. If an area of specialization had a relatively standard and stable convention, it was adopted. Consequently, for example, the handbook includes several conventions for citing different categories of texts. Reflecting conventions within subdisciplines has its advantages and, of course, its disadvantages, particularly when many are used side by side in a single reference work. A second principle is that the handbook should supplement *The Chicago Manual of Style* (*CMS*), except in cases when the field very consciously and authoritatively adopts a different standard. Third, scholars and publishers will and should make decisions that trump standard styles. The spelling conventions, for example, have been intended only as a starting point for an author-editor style sheet, although this list includes the type of terminology that should remain consistent throughout any individual work, keeping in mind that consistency enhances discoverability in the digital age.

The second edition has been thoroughly updated to reflect the latest practices among scholars, editors, and publishers as well as to take into account current trends in scholarly publishing. This edition has been meticulously supplemented with important new subject matter that fills gaps in the first edition. Chapters and sections have been reorganized and restructured to be more intuitive and logical. The following list is a selection of the most significant rule changes in this edition, in order of appearance.

Rule Changes in the Second Edition

Following *The Chicago Manual of Style*, all names form the possessive with an apostrophe *s*. Jesus's and Moses's are not an exception to this rule (4.1.6). In the academic transliteration style for Hebrew, SBL now specifies upside-down *e* (*ə*) for a vocal *shewa*, to distinguish it from *khatef segol* (*ĕ*) (5.1.1). For the stems/*binyanim*, SBL now uses a consistent general-purpose style of transliteration: *qal, niphal, piel, pual, hiphil, hophal, hithpael*. The previous version was a mix of academic for consonants and general-purpose for vowels (5.1.1.3). Titles of unattributed ancient works are no longer italicized even when they represent a direct transliteration of the ancient language. This rule applies to nonbiblical ancient Near Eastern texts, Old Testament pseudepigraphical texts, Dead Sea Scrolls, apostolic fathers, New Testament apocrypha and pseudepigrapha, and Nag Hammadi codices (4.3.3.1, 8.3). In bibliographies and notes, the basic facts of publication (city, publisher, and date) are set within parentheses, while all secondary publication information is now placed outside of the parentheses (6.2–6.4). Series and journal titles are now abbreviated in both bibliography and notes (6). SBL now recommends using two-letter postal abbreviations rather than traditional state abbreviations (8.1.1). SBL now uses all caps without periods for BCE and CE rather than B.C.E. and C.E. (8.1.2). Small caps are no longer recommended for abbreviations of versions or texts of the Bible: NRSV, MT, etc. (8.2).

2 RESPONSIBILITIES OF AN AUTHOR

Apart from the obvious task of writing, authors who are preparing a manuscript for publication have other, related responsibilities before and after submitting their work. Developments in publishing technology have introduced new authorial responsibilities, even though the reality is that authors are no more computer wizards, editors, or publishers than editors and publishers are typically specialists in each author's particular field. For the forseeable future, therefore, authors will continue to benefit from close and respectful working relationships with editors, proofreaders, indexers, and production experts who are, to a greater degree than many people recognize, responsible for attractive books that bring their authors alone credit.

Publishers can and will provide detailed guidelines whenever an author is expected to submit a printer-ready file. Thus the following guidelines focus primarily on the traditional publication process, presuming that most books will continue to require collaboration between the author and various members of a publication team.

2.1 Before Submitting a Book Manuscript

2.1.1 Adherence to a Style

To speed publication and reduce editorial costs (and, therefore, book prices), authors should conform their manuscripts to the style and format detailed in this volume or in other guidelines supplied by their particular publisher. While proper style and format often concern apparently trivial details, the consequences of inconsistency can be far-reaching. Thus, for example, authors often cite primary sources inconsistently and incorrectly. Consider this: Within a work a scholar could conceivably cite a passage from Josephus's *Antiquities* as *Ant.* X,xiii.1 §258; *Antiq.* X,13,1; *Ant.* X.13.1 §258; *Antiq.* X.xiii, 1; *Ant.* X.13.1; *Antiq.* 10.13.1 §258; *Ant.* 10.258; *Ant.* X.xiii.1; *Antiq.* 10.13, 1 §258; and so on. Rather than creating unnecessary problems for a copy editor, who must standardize all these references, it is much easier for an author to follow a consistent style conscientiously from the beginning.

A book style sheet need not and often should not await preparation by a project editor (see §3.1). Careful authors will benefit from deliberately noting usages they follow and referring to their lists as writing progresses, and the publication process will be markedly facilitated if authors are able to consult with their editor about the publisher's standards and needs. An author who prepares a style sheet should submit it to the editor along with the manuscript. For guidelines on style-sheet preparation, see *CMS* §2.52.

2.1.2 Preliminary Technical Matters

Before beginning to write, make sure that your electronic files will be acceptable to the anticipated publisher. Production editors are able to translate files from many formats, but do not assume anything. Especially if you are using obsolete—or even very new or specialized—hardware or software, or if your manuscript will include non-Latin fonts, verify ahead of time that the production department will be able to read your files by sending a sample file and a corresponding PDF.

2.1.2.1 Fonts

Any manuscript prepared today should be typed using Unicode fonts, particularly if it includes non-Latin alphabets such as Hebrew, Greek, Coptic, or Arabic. Earlier (ASCII) fonts for non-Latin alphabets often assigned different keystrokes to the same character (e.g., a Hebrew *aleph* might be assigned to the "a" key or the ")" key), which greatly complicated file transfers from one computer platform to another (e.g., PC to Mac) and from one font to another (e.g., SPIonic to LaserGreek). Unicode fonts, on the other hand, assign each character in a given alphabet to a universally accepted "location," so that the character remains the same even though the font or typeface is changed from one Unicode font to another. The universality of the character location enables files from one platform and font (e.g., SBLHebrew on a PC) to be transferred seamlessly to a different platform and font (e.g., Ezra SIL on a Mac) with no change in the coding or display of the text.

In order to use Unicode for a non-Latin alphabet, an author will need both a font containing that alphabet and a keyboard to enter text in that language. To download the SBL Greek and Hebrew fonts, see http://www.sbl-site.org/educational/biblicalfonts.aspx. All recent computer operating systems have various keyboards already installed; all that remains is for a user to enable whichever keyboard is needed. For further information, see http://www.sbl-site.org/educational/BiblicalFonts_FAQ.aspx. Even though learning to switch to and use keyboard layouts for other languages takes a little bit of time, the benefits of using Unicode more than make up for this small initial investment of time and effort.

The publisher will determine in what font(s) a manuscript is published. Authors should use Unicode fonts to save time as well as minimize the introduction of errors.

2.1.2.2 Global Changes

Be especially careful when making global changes. An improper search-and-replace string can introduce errors. Keep backup copies so that if global changes go wrong you can restore your work with minimal effort.

2.1.3 Formatting Dos and Don'ts

Use the same font and point size throughout the manuscript (except that a different font may be used for each non-Latin alphabet). Otherwise, do not be too concerned about document formatting. Typesetting is the production team's job, not the author's. Just be sure the manuscript is complete, legible, and easily edited. Do not use your word processor's style option to mark different elements of the text (body text, headings, subheads). Do not use the indexing features of your word processor, as these may be lost in the production process.

2.1.3.1 Headings

Type all headings in uppercase and lowercase letters; do not use the "caps lock" key on your keyboard. The appropriate formatting will be done during typesetting. Do not attach footnote or endnote callouts to any headings (chapter heads, subheads). Try not to begin a chapter with a subheading, such as "Introduction." Use a maximum of three levels of subheading; more can be confusing and overly complicated.

2.1.3.2 Indenting Paragraphs

Do not use tabs to indent paragraphs; use your word processor's paragraph formatting to set indents. Depending upon how you control paragraph formatting, it can often be useful to indicate explicitly whether material following an extract is a continuation of the previous paragraph or should be indented as a new paragraph. The most effective method is to mark the beginning of an intentionally unindented line following an extract with a code such as <NO INDENT>.

2.1.3.3 Block Quotes

Quotations of five or more lines in any language should be formatted as separate paragraphs with all lines indented on the left, without opening and closing quotation marks. Such quotations should use the same font and point size as normal text.

2.1.3.4 Hyphens and Dashes

Please distinguish between hyphens (e.g., first-century writer), en dashes (e.g., Ps 1:1–3; 1972–1983), and em dashes (e.g., "I know who you are—the Holy One of God!"). All

Unicode fonts offer separate characters for each. Note that there is no space on either side of the hyphen, en dash, or em dash.

Do not use any automatic hyphenation capability that your word-processing software may have; that is, turn off auto-hyphenation so that words will not be broken by "soft hyphens" at line endings.

2.1.3.5 Spaces after Punctuation

Only one space is needed after any punctuation, whether within or at the end of a sentence.

2.1.3.6 Tables

Authors should use the table feature in their word processor to format tables rather than tabs and line breaks. As with all other text, do not use spaces to indent or align text within tables. Do not use boxes, shading, or other visual table features. Give each table a title and a number (tables should be numbered separately from figures) and provide sources and notes as needed; keep notes that pertain to information in the table with the respective table, separate from the notes to the running text. Such notes are generally best placed in a separate row at the end of the table. Mention each table in the text by number (e.g., table 3, table 6.2, etc.).

It is important to be mindful of the final size of the printed page. Complex tables with many columns and rows may not be usable in a standard trim size such as 6 × 9 inches. *CMS* §§3.46–85 provides extensive guidlines for the formatting of tables.

2.1.3.7 References

Authors are responsible for providing reference lists that conform to the designated style and for making sure that they are complete and correct. See §6 of this handbook for detailed instructions on notes and bibliographies.

2.1.3.8 Notes

Use your word processor's automatic footnote feature. Whether the book will have footnotes or endnotes, it is better to leave the notes where your word processor automatically stores them within the chapter files than to number notes manually and type footnote text in separate files. Production editors can move automatically footnoted material to the appropriate place.

Notes pertaining to information in tables should be kept with the respective table; do not include them with the notes to the running text. Do not attach any notes to chapter titles or subtitles. Acknowledgments, prior publication data, or other information not directly related to the subject matter of the work may be placed in an unnumbered note at the beginning of the chapter or article.

2.1.4 Verification of Quotations and Facts

Primary and ultimate responsibility for fact-checking and for verification of quotations (including primary-text references) lies with the author. This includes ensuring that bibliographic citations are accurate, complete, and in proper form and that quotations are accurate not only verbally but also in orthography and punctuation. No matter how many words are cited, they must reproduce the original work exactly. Errors or odd forms of expression in the original may be noted with *sic* ("so, thus, in this manner"; used without an exclamation point) in brackets following the error, but small typographical errors may also be silently corrected without the distraction of calling attention to someone else's inadvertent mistakes.

2.1.5 Permissions and "Fair Use"

It is the author's responsibility to obtain any necessary permissions for the use of text or illustrative material from other publications. Ideally the author should obtain all required permissions in writing in advance. Authors (especially those who are inexperienced in requesting permission) may ask their editor for a standard form letter that they can fill out and print on their own letterhead, or they may consult *CMS* §4.92–93. In most cases, the author must pay any fees associated with obtaining permissions.

Authors are sometimes unsure about how to determine whether permission is required in a particular instance. Under the common-law practice known as "fair use," authors are permitted under many circumstances to cite other published works without securing formal permission. As a quick rule of thumb, we estimate that "fair use" permits the quotation of about five hundred words, or if the work is small, proportionately fewer; but a word count is only a crude tool in judging fair use. Authors who wish fuller guidance may seek it in *CMS* §4.77–91 and in official publications of the United States Copyright Office, as well as on the SBL website at http://www.sbl-site.org/publications/publishing_fairuse.aspx. Editors may at any point in the publication process require authors to obtain written permission for uses that in their judgment exceed what is allowed by current copyright law.

In all cases, whether or not permission to quote is required, quoted material should be precisely documented. Copies of permission letters you have received should be submitted along with the manuscript; if you are still awaiting permission on any materials, submit copies of your letters requesting it.

2.2 Submitting a Manuscript

Submit all parts of the manuscript in electronic form. PDFs have rendered print copy obsolete; however, a PDF copy that is identical to the electronic files is essential so that the publisher can refer to it should questions arise as to the author's intent.

2.2.1 Preparation of Files

Authors should provide a file for each discrete unit of text, although the various parts of the front matter may be assembled into a single file: half-title page, title page, dedication or epigraph, table of contents, list of illustrations, list of tables, foreword, preface, acknowledgments, and abbreviations. (The publisher will supply the copyright page.) Units of the main text include the several chapters; if you have any chapters that are too large for your word processor to handle as single files, you may break such chapters into two or more files. Back matter should include any appendix(es) or glossary, the bibliography, and any list of contributors. (For notes, see §2.1.3.8. Authors must normally wait for page proofs before creating indexes.)

Give files names that correspond to the chapter number or other content: 00a_front .doc, 00b_introduction.doc, 01_chapter1.doc, 02_chapter2.doc ... 09_appendixA.doc, 10_bibliography.doc, 11_contributors.doc, and so on. (The extension should indicate the file format.)

Special material, such as charts or figures, should be produced and stored separate from the main text and files. The location of such material in the main text should be indicated clearly, for example, "insert here chart 1 (chart1.doc)."

2.2.2 Figures and Illustrations

The author is responsible for providing the publisher with all artwork, drawings, diagrams, and photographs. The original drawings should be submitted when possible, and photographic prints should be suitable for reproduction. Most publishers will provide specific guidelines for the preparation and submission of artwork. See also §2.1.5 regarding permissions.

2.2.3 Submission Checklist

A complete manuscript submission will include all the parts of the manuscript listed in §2.2.1 as well as all artwork with captions and copies of permission letters.

Please spellcheck all files before printing and submitting your manuscript, but take care lest your word processor beguile you into making incorrect substitutions for words not in its database. Make sure that your PDF represents the final form of your word-processing files.

2.3 After Submitting a Manuscript

2.3.1 Revisions

Before the manuscript is passed along to a copy editor, the project editor must be satisfied that it conforms to the terms of the contract; if not, it will be returned for revision. Sections 2.1 and 2.2 of this handbook should be understood as describing some of the technical conditions of acceptability. In addition, the editor may find that certain structural modifications, including major deletions, additions, or revisions, are required to produce the book envisioned. It is the responsibility of the author to work with the editor to produce a manuscript that is acceptable to both. After that, a copy editor will work on the manuscript. Purely stylistic changes will not be negotiated, but where the copy editor suggests changes that could alter meaning, it is the responsibility of the author either to approve the copy editor's suggestions or to provide alternatives that better suit the author's meaning. Those alternatives will be reviewed by a project editor.

2.3.2 Proofreading

After the editing process is complete and the book has been typeset, a proofreader should inspect the results. Two observations may be made. First, authors are frequently their own worst proofreaders because they tend to be too familiar with the material and subconsciously "read" a text as saying what they know it should say rather than for what it actually says. Thus, there is no substitute for an extra, critical set of eyes on the material. But second, no proofreader catches every error, so authors who proofread their books carefully are usually able to improve the final product.

For the sake of clarity, use standard proofreading marks such as those described in *CMS* fig. 2.6 (p. 101).

2.3.3 Indexing

Most scholarly books in biblical studies and related fields include subject indexes, indexes of citations of Scripture and other ancient texts, and some may include a modern author index. Such indexing is the author's responsibility. In some cases, especially for multivolume reference works and other books containing many thousands of Scripture references, it is a good idea to discuss indexing with the project editor ahead of time.

Indexing—especially subject indexing—is a very technical exercise and is sometimes best left to professional indexers, whom publishers can usually recommend and authors can hire. On the other hand, no one knows a book better than its author, and authors who are willing to spend time on an index can often do quite well. Inexperienced indexers are encouraged to read chapter 16 of *CMS* (16th ed.) and then consult the project editor before beginning. Chapter 7 of this handbook provides specific guidelines for the preparation of indexes.

Other resources for indexing include Nancy C. Mulvany, *Indexing Books* (Chicago: University of Chicago Press, 1994), Hans H. Wellisch, *Indexing from A to Z*, 2nd ed. (New York: Wilson, 1996), Larry S. Bonura, *The Art of Indexing* (New York: Wiley, 1994), and Linda K. Fetters, *Handbook of Indexing Techniques: A Guide for Beginning Indexers*, 3rd ed. (Corpus Christi, TX: Fetters InfoManagement, 2001). For suggestions on indexing for e-books and treatment of indexing in relation to newer technologies, see Diane Brenner and Marilyn Rowland, eds., *Beyond Book Indexing* (Phoenix: American Society of Indexers, 2000).

Indexes are normally prepared from page proofs, after final pagination has been established.

3 RESPONSIBILITIES OF AN EDITOR

Editors and proofreaders strive to ensure that a given book both adheres to a specific style and respects the unique demands of each volume. To achieve both goals, editors and proofreaders rely on "authorities." The most important authorities are, in descending order:

(1) Book style sheet (§3.1)
(2) *The SBL Handbook of Style*, 2nd ed. (§3.2)
(3) *Chicago Manual of Style*, 16th ed. (§3.3)
(4) Other authorities (§3.4)

3.1 Book Style Sheet

One mark of a well-edited volume is internal coherence. Such coherence begins, of course, with the selection and arrangement of the chapters or essays, but it does not end there. Rather, one should seek to enhance the coherence of the volume during the editing process by striving for internal consistency in conformity to an accepted standard. For this reason, chief among the arbiters of editorial problems is the book style sheet. Inevitably, each book will present unique issues. If enough issues arise, the project editor will need to create a book style sheet. These issues, often concerning capitalization, spelling of unique terms, hyphenation, and so on, should be documented in the book style sheet.

Internal consistency enhances the reader's sense of a volume's overall coherence. So, for example, careful editors do not allow the same word to be spelled in several different ways (even if both are acceptable) or some essays to use footnotes for bibliographical citations and others to use the author-date system or still others to be lax in citing their references at all. Furthermore, volumes will appear more consistent if the chapters or essays are consistent in the use of subheads (always helpful) and in the way they are labeled (e.g., numbered or unnumbered but not both; using arabic numerals consistently, rather than arabic in some essays and roman numerals in others). For the most part, style guides seek not to mandate the "right way" as opposed to the "wrong way" but to assist publishing professionals, editors included, in enforcing consistency and thus enhancing the coherence of a given volume. Conformity to the style sheet will not only simplify the editor's task (many decisions have already been made) but also improve the overall appearance of a volume, so that readers can focus on the volume's content, not be distracted by its uneven presentation.

3.2 *The SBL Handbook of Style*, 2nd ed.

The SBL Handbook of Style is designed to address editorial and stylistic issues that are not specific to a particular book manuscript. See in particular §4 for general matters of style.

3.3 *The Chicago Manual of Style*, 16th ed.

Currently in its 16th edition, *The Chicago Manual of Style* remains the most comprehensive general authority on editorial style and publishing practices. Answers to questions not addressed in this handbook may be found there.

3.4 Other Authorities

Questions of style that are not covered by the book style sheet, this handbook, or *CMS* may be resolved by other authorities. For the orthography of proper names, we follow the works listed below.

3.4.1 Biblical Names and Terms

For biblical names and terms, follow the version of the Bible used in your book, which should be specified in the book style sheet. If the translations are your own, indicate that. In general, we prefer the names and terms found in the NRSV or *The New Interpreter's Dictionary of the Bible*, 5 vols. (Nashville: Abingdon, 2006–2009).

3.4.2 Nonbiblical Ancient Near Eastern Names

For nonbiblical ancient Near Eastern names of persons, places, and deities, consult the following reference works: Erich Ebeling et al., eds., *Reallexikon der Assyriologie* (Berlin: de Gruyter, 1928– [= *RlA*]); Wolfgang Helck et al., eds., *Lexikon der Ägyptologie*, 7 vols. (Wiesbaden: Harrassowitz, 1972–1992 [= *LÄ*]); Donald B. Redford, ed., *The Oxford Encyclopedia of Ancient Egypt*, 3 vols. (Oxford: Oxford University Press, 2001); and Jack M. Sasson, ed., *Civilizations of the Ancient Near East*, 4 vols. (New York: Scribner's Sons, 1995; repr., 4 vols. in 2; Peabody, MA: Hendrickson, 2000).

For the titles of ancient Near Eastern texts and compositions, follow *RlA* and *LÄ*, as mentioned in the previous paragraph, as well as works such as Carl S. Ehrlich, ed., *From an Antique Land: An Introduction to Ancient Near Eastern Literature* (Lanham, MD: Rowman & Littlefield, 2009), James B. Pritchard, ed., *Ancient Near Eastern Texts Relating to the Old Testament*, 3rd ed. (Princeton: Princeton University Press, 1969 [= *ANET*]), William W. Hallo, ed., *The Context of Scripture*, 3 vols. (Leiden: Brill, 1997–2002 [= *COS*]), and the various volumes in the Society of Biblical Literature series Writings from the Ancient World (= WAW).

3.4.3 Names of Deceased Persons

Consult *Merriam-Webster's Biographical Dictionary* (Springfield, MA: Merriam-Webster, 1997).

3.4.4 Place Names

For place names in general, consult *Merriam-Webster's Geographical Dictionary*, 3rd ed. (Springfield, MA: Merriam-Webster, 1997). For ancient Near Eastern toponyms in particular, consult the series Répertoire géographique des textes cunéiformes (Wiesbaden: Reichert, 1974– [= RGTC]), and its parent series, Tübinger Atlas des Vorderen Orients (Wiesbaden: Reichert, 1977– [= TAVO]).

Concerning the names of temples and shrines, an essential resource is Andrew S. George, *House Most High: The Temples of Ancient Mesopotamia* (Winona Lake, IN: Eisenbrauns, 1993).

For modern toponyms, their spelling, and their geographical coordinates, consult the online database of the GEOnet Names Server (GNS) maintained by the National Geospatial-Intelligence Agency: http://earth-info.nga.mil/gns/html/index.html. For the spelling of archaeological site names and their corresponding ancient names, see §4.3.3.4 below.

4 GENERAL STYLE

This section, addressed to authors, copy editors, and proofreaders, sets forth standards concerning stylistic issues that commonly cause difficulties in the main text of books.

4.1 Punctuation

4.1.1 Commas

Commas should enable fluent reading. That is, they should *not* be used where they make for gratuitous lurches in reading; they *should* be used where owing to syntactical ambiguity (even such as would be resolved by the end of the sentence) the reader might not otherwise construe the text correctly in one pass. The following discussions of commas indicate those uses of commas that are most problematic. Fuller discussions of the proper use of commas can be found in *CMS* §§6.16–53.

4.1.1.1 Commas in Series

When three or more elements appear in series in running text, a serial comma ("Oxford comma") should precede the final conjunction. Thus, in phrases like "Sarah, Rebekah, and Rachel," always include the comma after "Rebekah." For more on series punctuation, see §4.1.8.

4.1.1.2 Commas in Essential and Nonessential Clauses

Essential (defining) clauses should *not* be set off with commas:

> Paul was an apostle who proclaimed Christ crucified.
> Bruce Metzger's book *The Text of the New Testament* was first published in 1964.
> Walter Brueggemann's *Theology of the Old Testament* bears the subtitle *Testimony, Dispute, Advocacy.*

Nonessential clauses (clauses that could be omitted without affecting the meaning of the sentence) *should* be set off with commas:

> Paul, who was one of the primary missionaries to the gentiles, studied under Gamaliel.
> Bruce Metzger's introduction to textual criticism, *The Text of the New Testament,* was first published in 1964.

Theology of the Old Testament: Testimony, Dispute, Advocacy, by Walter Brueggemann, approaches the subject using "the metaphor and imagery of a courtroom trial."

4.1.1.3 Other Uses of Commas

Be careful not to omit the second in a pair of commas in cases such as the following:

Judas returned on Nisan 21, 164 BCE, from his trip to ...
The emperor's behavior offended even Roman sensibilities when, for example, he immolated scores of innocent Christians.
Scholars are, generally speaking, inclined to dismiss such appeals.

Note that no commas are used around the year when the day precedes the month or is omitted; following *CMS* §6.47, no commas are used with Jr. or Sr.

Judas returned on 21 Nisan 164 BCE from his trip to ...
He published the second edition in March 1932.
Walter Wangerin Jr. spoke at the conference.

The comma before Sr., Jr., or III is retained in bibliographies and indexes, in which the surname precedes the given name (see *CMS* §6.47):

Walker, William O., Jr.

Commas are customarily used with abbreviations for religious orders and academic degrees following proper names:

The Reverend Joseph Fitzmyer, S.J., delivered a lecture.

For more on the uses of the comma, see *CMS* §§6.16–53.

4.1.2 Quotation Marks

SBL practice, in keeping with long-standing American style and *CMS*, calls for placing quotation marks, whether double or single, outside periods and commas. The most common exceptions involve close textual studies, in which it may be important to signal that the punctuation is not part of the quoted material (*CMS* §6.9), and linguistic or phonetic studies, where a foreign term is printed in italics, its definition follows within single quotation marks, and any punctuation is kept outside of the quotation marks (*CMS* §7.50).

Single quotation marks should be used to indicate quotations within double quotation marks.

Note the following examples:

"Correct punctuation is vital."
I am not a "pedant."
"He says he's not a 'pedant.'"
This man, who claims he is not a "pedant," nonetheless likes making rules about commas.

Question marks and exclamation points may be placed inside or outside of quotation marks, depending on whether they are part of the quoted or parenthetical material (*CMS* §6.70).

Thus:

Why had he said, "I'm too tired to respond"?
Do you understand the word "pedant"?
"Never!" he insisted, "How should a loyal subject rise up against his queen?"

Colons and semicolons belong outside quotation marks:

S. Westerholm wrote the article "'Letter' and 'Spirit': The Foundation of Pauline Ethics."

Quotation marks should not be used around block quotations; for a quotation within a block quotation, use double rather than single quotation marks.

4.1.3 Ellipses

An ellipsis, which consists of three evenly spaced periods, is most often used to signify that material has been omitted from a quotation. SBL Press recommends that authors use the precomposed ellipsis character (OPTION + ; on a standard Macintosh keyboard; CTRL + ALT + . or ALT 0133 on a Windows-based computer) rather than three typed periods.

When an ellipsis is used within a sentence, it should be preceded and followed by a space.

Correct:	"You shall not … let your voice be heard."
Incorrect:	"You shall not…let your voice be heard."

When a grammatically complete sentence is followed by an ellipsis, the punctuation for the sentence (period, question mark, or exclamation point) comes first, followed immediately (no space) by the ellipsis. As usual, a space is used before the following sentence begins.

Correct:	"You shall not … let your voice be heard.… Then you shall shout."
Incorrect:	"You shall not … let your voice be heard. … Then you shall shout."
	"You shall not … let your voice be heard.…Then you shall shout."

Punctuation may follow an ellipsis in the middle of a quotation when the material omitted precedes that punctuation. In this case, there should be no space between the last word of the quotation and the ellipsis or between the ellipsis and the original punctuation. When the ellipsis follows the original punctuation, it should be preceded and followed by a space (example 4).

Correct:	"Potiphar, an officer…, bought him from the Ishmaelites."
Incorrect:	"Potiphar, an officer …, bought him from the Ishmaelites."
	"Potiphar, an officer… , bought him from the Ishmaelites."
Correct:	"Potiphar, an officer of Pharaoh, … bought him from the Ishmaelites."

SBL Press discourages the use of an ellipsis at the beginning of a quotation, even if the quotation begins mid-sentence; readers will readily enough infer that the quoted material had a fuller context. Likewise, it is usually unnecessary to include an ellipsis at the end of a quotation. The most common exception to this is when a quotation is intentionally left incomplete (example 3 below).

Incorrect:	"... Potiphar, an officer of Pharoah, bought him from the Ishmaelites."
Incorrect:	"Potiphar, an officer of Pharoah, bought him from the Ishmaelites...."
Correct:	Israel's Little Credo begins "A wandering Aramean..." (Deut 26:5–9).

It is permissible to change the capitalization of the original to conform it to the quoted context, for example, capitalizing the first word of a quotation even though it originally appeared uncapitalized within the sentence. Although it is not necessary to signal this change (see *CMS* §13.16), one may do so by placing the changed letter in brackets.

Correct:	"You shall not let your voice be heard.... You shall shout."
Correct:	"You shall not let your voice be heard.... [Y]ou shall shout."

For additional discussion of ellipses, see *CMS* §§13.48–56.

4.1.4 Punctuation following Italics

Punctuation should be set in the same font style—roman or italic—as the main or surrounding text except when the punctuation belongs to a title or word that is presented in a different font style, such as italics. See *CMS* §6.2 for the standard practice and a fuller explanation with examples.

4.1.5 Final Punctuation for Block Quotations

Block quotations should conclude with punctuation, followed by the citation in parentheses:

> Thus says the Lord God: In the first month, on the first day of the month, you shall take a young bull without blemish, and purify the sanctuary. The priest shall take some of the blood of the sin offering and put it on the doorposts of the temple, the four corners of the ledge of the altar, and the posts of the gate of the inner court. You shall do the same on the seventh day of the month for anyone who has sinned through error or ignorance; so you shall make atonement for the temple. (Ezek 45:18–20 NRSV)

4.1.6 Possessives

The possessives of almost all singular and irregular plural English nouns (those that do not end in an *s*) are formed by the addition of an apostrophe and an *s*; normally, they create no problem, for example, *a day's march, the church's founding, Noah's vineyard, the journal's "experimental" nature*. The possessives of regular plural nouns are similarly simple, adding only an apostrophe following the *s* or *es* that has already made the noun plural, for example, *the prophets' oracles, the women's portion, the dresses' beauty*. More troublesome are instances where the possessive is applied to proper nouns, and this is in part because some rules have changed over the years. The following special cases warrant comment (for more extensive discussions and for allowed differences, see *CMS* §§7.15–21):

1) Most names ending in sibilants or in a silent *s*, *z*, or *x* should now be treated according to the general rule for common nouns. E.g., Lazarus's home, Achilles Tatius's supposed conversion, Cambyses's conquest, Achilles's fury.
2) SBL recommends following *CMS* in making no exception for the possessives of Moses and Jesus. E.g., Jesus's tunic, Moses's staff. As a matter of tradition, however,

some authors and publishers may still prefer to use only an apostrophe, not an additional *s*.

3) Like compound nouns, names and phrases that form a unit add the possessive to the final element, but the possessive is added to each unit if they really function independently. E.g., C. Black III's study of Mark, the king of Judea's authority, Jannes and Jambres's rebellion, James and John's mother, Jesus's and Lazarus's resurrections.
4) When the possessive is applied to an italicized title, the ending remains in roman font. E.g., the *Iliad*'s themes, motifs, and symbols....

With minor rewriting, troublesome possessives can often be avoided.

4.1.7 Citing Editions of Original Ancient Near Eastern Sources

When citing editions of original sources (copies of tablets, inscriptions, papyri, and the like), (1) avoid blank spaces without punctuation between volume, text, and page numbers, (2) try to distinguish obverse (obv.) from reverse (rev.), and (3) indicate columns with lowercase roman numerals. Thus,

> MVN 21: 200 obv. iii 21

When giving a series abbreviation followed by a volume number, insert a colon ":" followed by a space between the volume number and the text number. Thus,

> OIP 99: 256 obv. i 6

Distinguish between text number and page number; in the latter case, insert ", p." between the abbreviation and the number. Thus,

> MEE 3, p. 45 (as opposed to MEE 3: 45, which would refer to text no. 45)

When the abbreviation refers to a specific (single-volume) title and not a series, write the text number after the abbreviation with a space in between. Thus,

> LKA 118 rev. 1–2

Use the same system when giving museum or excavation numbers. Thus,

> UM 29-15-155 obv. i 1–10; 3N-T868 obv. 2.

4.1.8 Punctuation for a Series of Ancient Texts

Punctuation separating a series of ancient references should seek to present clearly both the references and their relationship to one another with the least amount of interruption. Thus, choosing which punctuation to use should take into account the context in which the references appear and the complexity of the series of references.

4.1.8.1 Similar Citations in Main Text

Within the context of normal prose, similar or parallel references are best separated by commas.

The prophetic messenger formula appears in Jer 26, 28, 30, and 31.
The prophetic messenger formula appears in Jer 26:2, 28:11, 30:5, and 31:15.
The temple incident is recounted in Matt 21, Mark 11, Luke 19, and John 2.
Epictetus addresses "courage" at *Disc.* 1.24, 2.1, 2.2, 3.24, 3.25, and 4.1.

Although some would use semicolons in examples 2–4, SBL Press prefers commas in simple series such as these.

4.1.8.2 Dissimilar Citations in Main Text

Dissimilar references within a prose sentence often require semicolons for clarity.

Most scholars assign Exod 31:12–18; 34:29–32; and 35–40 to the Priestly source.
Epictetus addresses "courage" at *Disc.* 1.24; 2.1, 2; 3.24, 25; and 4.1.

The semicolons in example 1 make it clear that the final reference is to chapters 35–40, not verses 35–40 of Exod 34. The semicolons in example 2 enable readers to distinguish books and chapters at a glance.

4.1.8.3 Citations within Parentheses

References set off from the rest of the sentence (e.g., within parentheses) should follow the same principles as found in §§4.1.8.1–2: use commas to separate similar or parallel references, semicolons to separate mixed or dissimilar references.

The messenger formula appears throughout Jeremiah (e.g., 26:2, 4, 18; 28:11; 30:5; 31:15).
All four canonical Gospels recount the temple incident (Matt 21, Mark 11, Luke 19, John 2).
Josephus refers to the Jerusalem temple in three of his works (e.g., *A.J.* 8.95, 11.297; *B.J.* 5.215; *C. Ap.* 1.228).

4.1.8.4 Citation of a Series of Primary Ancient Near Eastern Texts

When listing several texts from the same volume, separate them with semicolons (;).

OSP 1: 41 rev. i 2; 84 rev. 5.

When listing several lines from the same text, use commas to separate the line numbers.

OIP 99: 278 obv. vi 7, 12, 16; 328 ix 2; 504 obv. ii 2.

4.2 Numbers

4.2.1 When to Spell Out Numbers

As a general rule, whole numbers zero through one hundred and round multiples of those numbers should be spelled out. If whole numbers occur in an immediate context with numbers that by this rule would not be spelled out, then for the sake of consistency numerals should be used for all. Note, however, that items in one category may be given as numerals and items in another category spelled out (see, e.g., the third and fifth examples).

In nontechnical contexts measurements should be spelled out unless they occur in tables or charts. If an abbreviation or a symbol is used for the unit of measure, the quantity is always expressed by a numeral. Percentages are expressed in numerals and the word *percent* spelled out.

For more on numerals versus words, see *CMS* §§9.2–53.

Examples:

The fifth and sixth stanzas of this 239-line poem are remarkable for their use of puns.
At this nine-hectare site, only around ten Anatolian archives come from Level II, and only some 5 percent of the textual material recovered from this level stems from Anatolian archives.
Fragment 1 measures 4 × 10 cm and contains twelve partial lines of text.
The figurine is twelve and a half centimeters high and weighs three ounces.
In this analysis I examine 2,437 dog remains representing a minimum of 67 dog individuals from nine sites. A total of 53 canines were excavated, and of these 5 (or 9.5%) were broken.

4.2.2 Arabic Numbers

Our style generally requires arabic (1, 10) rather than roman (I, X) numerals. This rule is especially to hold true in bibliographic forms (e.g., volume numbers). It also concerns the citing of primary sources (3 John, not III John). Some exceptions to this rule are page numbers in the front matter of a book, column numbers in Qumran documents (see §8.3.5) and in many other ancient Near Eastern texts (see §4.1.7), manuscript numbers of the Greek Magical Papyri (§6.4.3.3), works in which roman numerals are an actual part of the title, and series numbers in Discoveries in the Judean Desert (see appendix C). The project editor will point out in the instructions to the copy editor any other instances (such as in archaeological periods or in certain catalogs of ancient Near Eastern texts) in which roman numerals are required.

4.2.3 Commas in Numbers

Numbers of four or more digits, except for four-digit page numbers and four-digit years, require commas. Thus:

3,795 pages
148,397 words
page 1021
1296 BCE
10,000 BCE

4.2.4 Inclusive Numbers: General

Inclusive numbers are represented by the first and last numbers in a continuous series. Such inclusive numbers most commonly refer to pages or sections of a work. See the general discussion of this topic in *CMS* §§9.58–63.

Inclusive numbers may be related verbally, as in the constructions "from/to" or "between/and," in which case all digits of each number should be used and the en dash is never used (see *CMS* §9.59). Examples:

Right: from 156 to 163
between 1797 and 1812

Wrong:	from 156–163
	between 1797–1812

When inclusive numbers are joined by an en dash, as is most often the case, the last number may be abbreviated by omitting certain repeated digits. SBL Press style follows the abbreviation system recommended in *CMS* §9.60. Examples:

3–9, 11–17, 53–55, 94–113
100–103, 500–508, 502–8, 1100–1187
285–89, 306–23, 809–902, 1003–7
327–35, 448–503, 1465–89, 1698–1703

4.2.5 Inclusive Numbers: Dates

Like many publishers, SBL Press prefers to use all digits for all years in all inclusive dates, CE as well as BCE. Examples:

Right:	502–500 BCE
	327–321 BCE
	31 BCE–14 CE
	154–157 CE
	the years 1939–1945
	from 1856 to 1857
	between 1850 and 1860
	during the 1960s and 1970s
Wrong:	327–21 BCE (if the last date is intended to be 321 BCE)
	154–57 CE
	from 1857–68
	between 1850–60
	in the 1960s and '70s

All digits should normally be used when inclusive dates appear in titles (including in chapter and section headings) unless one is citing a source whose title shortens a range of years; in that case, fidelity to the original overrides a concern for consistency. For the abbreviations for chronological eras, see §8.1.2.

4.2.6 Inclusive Numbers: Ancient Works

Like many publishers, SBL Press prefers that references to inclusive sections or parts of ancient works always use all digits. Examples:

Josephus, *J.W.* 1.321–329
Josephus, *Ant.* 2.233–235
Philo, *Migr.* 178–180
Philo, *Spec.* 1.13–20
Philo, *Spec.* 4.155–156
Plato, *Pol.* 271e–272b

Hesiod, *Op.* 100–191
Hesiod, *Op.* 119–191

4.2.7 Inclusive Numbers: Roman Numerals

To avoid possible ambiguity, inclusive references using roman numerals should always be given in full and never abbreviated.

Benoit, *DJD* II (1961), pls. XCVI–XCVIII

4.3 Terminology

4.3.1 Bias-Free Language

The generic use of masculine nouns and pronouns is increasingly unacceptable in current English usage. Historians must obviously be sensitive to the requirements of their sources, but in many cases the assignment of gender to God is best avoided. Consistent use of gender-inclusive language is primarily the author's responsibility. Editors are, of course, willing to help in this regard as in other stylistic matters. Especially in discussions of ancient texts and cultures, it can be difficult for copy editors to discern whether particular instances of masculine language were meant to be generic or really masculine, so authors should be especially attentive to potential problems.

Bias-free writing respects all cultures, peoples, and religions. Uncritical use of biblical characterizations such as *the Jews* or *the Pharisees* can perpetuate religious and ethnic stereotypes. Also be aware of the connotations of alternative expressions such as the following pairs:

Hebrew Bible, Old Testament
Second Temple period, intertestamental period
deuterocanonical literature, Apocrypha

For writers and editors who need help in finding language that avoids sexual, racial, and other types of bias, we recommend *The Handbook of Nonsexist Writing*, by Casey Miller and Kate Swift, 2nd ed. (New York: Harper & Row, 1988), or *Guidelines for Bias-Free Writing*, by Marilyn Schwartz and the Task Force on Bias-Free Language of the Association of American University Presses (Bloomington: Indiana University Press, 1995).

4.3.2 Principles

Many technical terms, foreign words, proper names, and so forth require definition or special treatment. The goal in these instances is always to provide the book's intended audience with the information necessary to understand the author's meaning and argument. When authors use words that may not be well known to readers at all levels of the book's intended audience, they should explain them at the first occurrence. In some books, especially textbooks, it may also be a good idea to put them in a glossary in the back matter.

4.3.2.1 Spelling

Our hierarchy of authorities for spelling, hyphenation, and capitalization is given in §3. These norms apply even to those authors who are accustomed to using British spellings. For words other than proper nouns, *Merriam-Webster's Collegiate Dictionary* is the preferred authority; where multiple spellings are listed, use the first. Thus, in general, a final consonant is doubled before a verbal ending only if the final syllable is accented: *worshiping, worshiped, repelled, repelling.* For spelling examples, see §4.3.6 below.

4.3.2.2 Open, Hyphenated, and Closed Compounds

If a compound word does not appear in the resources listed in §3.4 (and sometimes even if it does), we follow the general principles in *CMS* §§7.77–85 and the rules and specific examples given in the tables in *CMS* §7.85. In brief: generally accepted compounds tend to be closed rather than hyphenated or open; compound adjectives tend to be left open except when ambiguity would otherwise result (which normally is the case only when the compound adjective precedes the noun it modifies—e.g., a *half-baked cake*).

Some prefixes generally form closed compounds (*ante-, anti-, co-, neo-, post-, pre-, semi-,* and quite a few others; see the list in *CMS* pp. 383–84). As a general rule, any hyphenated compound in which the second component is a proper noun or adjective capitalizes the second term and leaves the prefix lowercase (*pre-Davidic, post-Pauline, non-Pauline*). But even these hyphenated forms sometimes become closed, in which case the whole word may be capitalized (Neoplatonism, Neoplatonic). Not infrequently in ancient Near Eastern studies, style sheets permit compound forms in which both the prefix and the noun are capitalized, especially if it is a proper noun (e.g., Neo-Assyrian, Neo-Hittite). Note that *quasi-* forms hyphenated compound adjectives and open compound nouns.

Sometimes compounds that should be closed because they are formed with one of the prefixes mentioned above are left open because the closed form would be awkward. So *CMS* lists *anti-intellectual, pro-life,* and we agree. Usage varies in the case of compounds in which a prefix ends with the same vowel as begins the base. Thus *CMS* and *Merriam-Webster's Collegiate Dictionary* accept the form *neoorthodox* but retain a hyphen for *co-opt.*

Some examples:

anti	antilegalistic, antimonarchic; but anti-Semitic
counter	counterintuitive, counterproductive
extra	extrabiblical, extramural
inter	internecine, interfaith
macro	macrostructure
meta	metalanguage; but meta-analysis
mid	midcareer, midcentury; but mid-first century
multi	multiauthor, multiperspectival
non	noncanonical, nonidolatrous, nonnative; but non-Christian
over	overemphasize, overread
post	postexilic, postbiblical
pre	preexilic, premonarchic
pro	promonarchic
proto	protolanguage, prototext

pseudo	pseudointellectual, pseudolegal
quasi	quasi-scientific (adj.), quasi contract (noun)
re	reread, reedit; but re-creation/re-create to signify creating again
semi	semitechnical; but semi-independent
socio	sociohistorical, sociorhetorical, sociocultural, socioeconomic
sub	subheading, substandard
super	superabundant, superstructure
trans	transhistorical, translegal
un	unchristian, unattested, uncorroborated
under	underrepresented, undervalued

4.3.2.3 Capitalization (Other Than Titles of Works)

A measure of the difficulties posed by capitalization is the fact that *CMS* devotes most of a chapter (7) to the topic. The first edition of this handbook endorsed the tendency toward *down* style (the use of fewer initial capital letters) but implemented it incompletely, perhaps owing to the weight of tradition and the diversity of the ancient literatures covered. Moreover, different publishers have different preferences, and individual publications may need to vary from accepted patterns for particular reasons. In all cases, the book style sheet (see §3.1) should record the preferences.

For our hierarchy of authorities concerning the spelling of proper names, see §3.4. For capitalization of names with particles, however, see §7.2.2 and the examples in §7.2.2.3, and for capitalization examples see §4.3.6.

4.3.2.4 Italics

Specific terms being discussed are best set in italics rather than quotation marks (see *CMS* §7.54). Thus, "*Hope* occurs three times in this verse." If the term is repeated, the italics need not be continued. On using italics for foreign words, see §4.3.2.5. For punctuation following italics, see §4.1.4.

4.3.2.5 Treatment of Foreign Words

Principles

1. Foreign words and phrases used within an English context are typically italicized (e.g., *imago Dei*).
2. Quotations of foreign words, phrases, and sentences are set roman and enclosed within quotation marks (e.g., "Ein umherirrender Aramäer war mein Vater").
3. Foreign words and phrases that have passed into common English usage are set roman (e.g., locus classicus). Any word or phrase listed in the main body of *Merriam-Webster's Collegiate Dictionary* (11th ed.) is considered to have passed into common English usage (e.g., ad hoc).
4. Similar or related words and phrases should be treated similarly (e.g., "ipsissima verba" is roman in *Merriam-Webster's*, so "ipsissima vox" should also be roman, even though it is not listed).
5. Transliterated foreign terms are italicized (e.g., *agapē*).
6. Foreign proper nouns are set roman (e.g., Aelia Capitolina, Tel Yinʿam).

7. Abbreviations for common foreign terms are set roman even if the foreign term itself would be italicized (e.g., et al. but *et alii*).
8. German nouns lowercased in *Merriam-Webster's* are lowercased (e.g., weltanschauung).

Common examples:

a priori
ad hoc
ad nauseam
Aelia Capitolina
agape (but transliterated *agapē*)
agora
amphora
anno mundi
apparatus criticus
archon (transliterated *archōn*)
atrium
bamah (transliterated *bāmâ*)
basilica
bema (but transliterated *bēma*)
boustrophedon
ca. (circa)
caveat lector
chiasm, chiasmus
contra
coup d'état
demos (transliterated *dēmos*)
de novo
e.g. (*exempli gratia*)
en masse
eros
et al. (*et alii*)
etc.
ex nihilo
ex novo
ex officio
fait accompli
faux pas
favissa (pl. *favissae*)
Festschrift (pl. Festschriften)
ff. (use is discouraged)
fibula (pl. fibulae)
floruit
glacis
Grundlage (pl. *Grundlagen*)
haggadah, haggadic
halakah, halakic
hapax legomenon (pl. *legomena*)
Haustafel (pl. *Haustafeln*)
Heilsgeschichte, heilsgeschichtliche
hic et nunc
ibid.
i.e. (*id est*)
imago Dei
in situ
inclusio
inter alia
ipsissima verba
ipsissima vox
kabbalah
kerygma
ketiv
koine (but Koine Greek [proper noun])
lectio brevior
lectio difficilior
lectio facilior
lex talionis
loc. cit. (use is discouraged)
loculus (pl. loculi)
locus
locus classicus
longue durée
maʿat (concept), Maat (deity)
masorah
mater lectionis (pl. *matres lectionis*)
materfamilias
merkabah
midrash
mise-en-scène
monde
mutatis mutandis
nomina sacra (sg. *nomen sacrum*)

pace
paraenesis, paraenetical
parallelismus membrorum
parousia
passim
paterfamilias
per se
pithos (pl. pithoi)
polis
qere
qinah
raison d'être
requiescat in pace
sans
scriptio continua
shalom
Shema
sic
sopherim
stadium (pl. stadia)
status quaestionis
supra
s.v. (but *sub verbo, sub voce*)
Tel Yin'am
Tendenz
terminus ante quem
terminus post quem
testimonium (pl. *testimonia*)
topos, topoi
tour de force
Übermensch
vaticinium ex eventu
vis-à-vis
Vorlage (pl. *Vorlagen*)
weltanschauung
Winkelhaken
Wissenschaft

4.3.3 Ancient Sources

4.3.3.1 Titles of Ancient Near Eastern Texts

A title should be set roman whether it is a conventional English-language title or a direct transliteration of the ancient language (see §4.3.2.5, principle 6). Titles should not be placed within quotation marks (except when citing the published translation of a text; see §6.4.1). Thus,

The Babylonian Story of Creation or Enuma Elish
The Stela of the Vultures
Code of Hammurabi
The Tale of Apopis and Seqenenre

Set in lowercase the plural generic description of archives and caches (e.g., inscriptions, letters, ostraca, papyri, texts) and in uppercase the individual references:

Lachish letters, Neo-Hittite inscriptions, genizahs

Lachish Letter 19, Moabite Inscription, Cairo Genizah

In those cases where texts have considerably different titles (not simply the difference, e.g., between Legend of Aqhat or Aqhat Epic), provide the reader with an explanatory comment. Thus,

The Birth of Dawn and Dusk (also known as The Birth of the Gracious Gods, or The Birth of Shahar and Shalim)

For spelling, see hierarchy of authorities in §3.4.

4.3.3.2 Ancient Persons

When a surname preceded by ben or ibn (meaning "son [of]") occurs in mid-sentence without a first name, the "ben" or "ibn" is capitalized ("the works of Ibn Ezra").

The first occurrence of an ancient personal name should be accompanied by the dates of that person's life. In many cases, of course, the best that can be offered is an indication of the century in which the person lived.

For spelling, see hierarchy of authorities in §3.4.

4.3.3.3 Ancient Places

Especially when a volume concerns ancient Near Eastern geography or archaeology, locations and dates of habitation should be given at the first occurrence of ancient place names. For sites that have multiple names (ancient, biblical, premodern, modern, Arabic), give all the names that are relevant:

> Mari (Tell Hariri), Ugarit (Ras Shamra), Shechem (Tell Balaṭah), Jericho (Tell es-Sultân), Hazor (Tell el-Qedah), Caesarea Philippi (Banias), Beit Shean (later Scythopolis, modern Tell el-Hisn), Samaria (Sebaste)

In some cases, it may be helpful to indicate which names are ancient, modern, and so on.

> Mari (modern Tell Hariri), Tel Dan (biblical Dan), Uruk (biblical Erech, present-day Warka), Akhetaten (modern Tell el-Amarna), Rabbath Ammon (later Philadelphia)

Alternatively, archaeological works may provide the modern name of a site followed by the ancient name, if known, separated by an en dash. Slashes are to be avoided.

> Tell Hariri–Mari, Boghazköy–Hattusa, Kültepe–Kanesh

Hebrew geographical names are, when needed, preceded by Tel (one *el*), Arabic by Tell (two *els*). If a mix of sites preceded by both *Tel* and *Tell* is being discussed collectively, or if used generically, *tell* is the default spelling. For names with the Arabic definite article *al*, follow *CMS* §11.99.

For spelling, see hierarchy of authorities in §3.4 and examples in §4.3.3.4.

4.3.3.4 Archaeological Site Names

The following is a selective list of archaeological sites in the ancient Near East and eastern Mediterranean. It is intended to provide guidance regarding the spelling of modern site names and their corresponding ancient place names. The modern site name is given first, followed by the ancient place name if known. In the absence of a modern name, the ancient place name alone is given. In some cases, the modern and ancient names are the same. Place names (ancient and modern) are given in roman font with the exception of Cypriot sites, for which it is traditional to use italics in the second, more precise, element of the toponym.

For additional guidance on the names, spelling, locations, and more of archaeological sites in the Greco-Roman world, consult Richard J. A. Talbert, ed., *Barrington Atlas of the*

Greek and Roman World (Princeton: Princeton University Press, 2000), and the Pleiades Project, http://pleiades.stoa.org/.

Cyprus

Akrotiri-*Vounarouthkia ton Lamnion* East
Alambra-*Mavroyi*
Alambra-*Mouttes*
Amathus
Ambelikou-*Aletri*
Apliki
Arsinoe. *See* Polikrusoko
Ayia Irini
Ayia Varvara-*Asprokremnos*
Ayios Andronikos
Ayios Athanasios
Ayios Epiktitos-*Vrysi*
Bellapais-*Vounous*
Cape Andreas-*Kastros*
Carpasia
Chytroi
Deneia-*Kafkalla*
Dhali-*Kafkalla*
Enkomi
Enkomi-*Ayios Iakovas*
Episkopi-*Bamboula*
Episkopi-*Kaloriziki*
Episkopi-*Phaneromeni*
Golgoi-*Ayios Photios*
Hala Sultan Tekke
Idalion
Kalavasos
Kalavasos-*Ayios Dhimitrios*
Kalavasos-*Ayious*
Kalavasos-*Tenta*
Kalopsidha
Kantou-*Kouphovounos*
Karmi
Kataliondas-*Kourvellos*
Khirokitia
Khirokitia-*Vounoi*
Kition
Kholetria-*Ortos*
Kissonerga-*Mosphilia*
Kissonerga-*Mylouthkia*
Klepini-*Troulli*
Kouklia-*Alonia*
Kouklia-*Palaepaphos*
Kourion
Kourion-*Kaloriziki*
Krini
Lapithos
Lapithos-*Vrysi tou Barbou*
Limassol-*Komissariato*
Maa-*Paleokastro*
Marion
Marki-*Alonia*
Maroni-*Vournes*
Morphou-*Toumba tou Skourou*
Nea Paphos
Nitoviklia
Palaepaphos-*Skales*
Paralimni-*Nissia*
Parekklisia-*Shillourokambos*
Philamoudi-*Melissa*
Philamoudi-*Vounari*
Philia-*Drakos*
Philia-*Vasiliko*
Phlamoudi-*Melissa*
Phlamoudi-*Vounari*
Polikrusoko (Arsinoe)
Prastio-*Mesorotsos*
Pyla-*Kokkinokremnos*
Pyla-*Koutsopetria*
Salamis
Salamis-*Cellarka*
Sanidha
Soloi
Sotira-*Arkolies*
Sotira-*Kaminoudhia*
Sotira-*Teppes*
Souskiou-*Vathyrkakas*
Tamassos
Vouni
Vounous

Egypt

modern (classical; Egyptian)

Abu Billo, Kom (Terenouthis)
Abu Ghurab
Abu Rawash
Abu Sefa, Tell (Sile)
Abu Simbel
Abu Sir Bana (Busiris Djedu)
Abusir (Busiris)
Abydos (Abedju)
Ahmar, al-Kom al- (Hierakonpolis; Nekhen)
Ahmar, Kom el- (Hebenu)
Akhmim (Panopolis; Khent-min)
Alexandria
Amarna, Tell el- (Akhetaten)
Araba el Madfuna, el-
Armant (Hermonthis; Iuny)
Ashmunein, El (Hermopolis Magna; Khmun)
Aswan (Syene; Swenet)
Asyut (Lykopolis; Zawty)
Atrib, Tell (Athribis)
Ausim (Letopolis; Khem)
Bahnasa, el- (Oxyrhynchus; Pe-Medjed)
Balamun, el- (Diospolis Inferior)
Baqliya, el- (Hermopolis Parva)
Basta, Tell (Bubastis; Bast)
Beit Khallaf
Beni Hasan
Arsinoe (Krokodilopolis; Shedet)
Dabʿa, Tell ed- (Avaris)
Dahshur
Damanhur (Hermopolis Parva)
Deir el-Bahri
Deir el-Bersha
Deir el-Gabrawi
Deir el-Medina
Dendera (Tentyris; Iunet)
Dishasha
Edfu (Apollinopolis Magna; Djeba)
Elephantine (Abu)
Esna (Latopolis; Iunyt)
Faiyum
Faqus (Phakussa)
Faraʿin, Tell el- (Buto)
Farama, Tell el- (Pelusium)
Fustat
Gebelein (Pathyris; Inerty)
Giʾeif, Kom (Naukratis)
Giza
Hawara (Arsinoiton Polis)
Hawawish, el-
Heliopolis (bibl. On)
Hiba, el (Ankyronopolis; Teudjo)
Hisn, Kom el- (Imu)
Ḥiṣn, Tall al- (Heliopolis; Unu)

Hiw (Diospolis Parva; Hut-Sekhem)
Hur (Herwer)
Hurbeit (Pharbaithos)
Ihnasya el-Medina (Herakleopolis Magna; Henen-Nesut)
Kab, el- (Eileithyiaspolis; Nekheb)
Karnak (Ipet-Isut)
Lahun, el- (Ptolemais Hormos)
Lisht, el-
Luxor (Ipet-Resyt)
Malqata, el-
Maskhuta, Tell el- (bibl. Pithom?; Tjeku)
Medinet Ghurab, Kom
Medinet Habu (Djeme)
Medinet Madi (Dja; Narmouthis)
Meidum
Meir (Mir)
Memphis (Inbu-Hedj, Men Nefer, and Mit Rahina)
Merimde
Moaʿalla, el- (Hefat)
Muqdam, Tell el- (Leontopolis)
Nabasha, Tell (Imet)
Nag Hammadi
Nagʿ el-Madamud (Kerameia; Petemout)
Naga ed-Der
Naqada (Ombo)
Nitria
Ombo, Kom (Ombos, Nubt)
Osireion
Oxyrhynchus. *See* Bahnasa, el-
Philae
Ptolemais
Qantir (Ramesses)
Qasr, el- (Khenoboskion)
Qasr el-Aguz
Qaw el-Kebir (Antaeopolis; Tjebu)
Qift (Koptos; Gebtu)
Qurna
Qus (Apollinopolis Parva; Gesa)
Rataba, Tell el-
Rubʾa, Tell el- (Mendes; Anpet)
Sa el-Hagar (Sais; Zau)
Saft el-Hinna (Per-Sopdu)
Sahaba, Tell el-
Sakha (Xois)
Salamuni, el-
Samannud (Sebennytos)
San el-Hagar (Tanis; Djnet)
Saqqara
Seila
Shanhur
Sharuna
Sheikh Ibada, el- (Antinoopolis)
Sheikh Saʿid, el-
Sedment el-Gebel
Sultan, Kom el-
Suwa
Tarkhan (Akanthopolis)
Tihna el-Gebel (Hakoris; Tenis)
Timai, Tell el- (Thmuis)
Tuna el-Gebel Hermopolis Magna)
Tura (Troikon Oros)
Umm el-Qaʿab
Yahudiya, Tell el- (Leontopolis)
Zawyet el-Maiyitin

Greece

Acrocorinth
Acropolis of Athens
Acropolis of Rhodes
Actium
Aiani
Akrotiri
Amphiareion of Oropos
Amphimalla
Amphipolis
Apollonia [Aetolia]
Apollonia [Athos]
Apollonia [Chalcidice]
Apollonia [Kavala]
Apollonia [north coast of Crete]
Apollonia [south coast of Crete]
Aptera
Areopagus
Argos
Arna
Arsinoe [Crete]
Asine
Assiros
Athens
Azoria
Bassae
Berea
Brauron
Corinth
Cytinium
Delphi
Dendra
Dimini
Diolkos
Dreros
Eleutherna
Epidaurus
Gla
Gortyn
Helike
Hephaistia
Heraion of Argos
Heraion of Perachora
Heraion of Samos
Iolcos
Kalapodi
Kalaureia
Kameiros
Kechries
Kerameikos
Kynos
Larissa [Argolis]
Lefkandi
Leibethra
Lerna
Lindos
Lyceum [classical, in Athens]
Lykaion, Mount
Midea [Argolid]
Mireou
Mycenae
Mytilene
Nemea
Nichoria
Odeon of Herodes Atticus
Olous
Olympia
Olynthus
Orchomenos [Arcadia]
Orchomenos [Boeotia]
Orestias
Patras
Pavlopetri
Pellana
Philippi

Phyle Cave
Pindus [city]
Pnyx
Pylos
Pythagoreion
Rhamnous
Rhithymna
Spartia temple
Thebes
Thermos [Aetolia]
Thoricus
Tiryns
Toumba
Trachis

Iran

Ali Kosh
Anshan
Asaak
Bastam
Bisitun
Chogha Mish
Chogha Zanbil
Ctesiphon
Deh Luran
Dinkha Tepe
Ecbatana
Farukhabad, Tepe
Ganj Dareh
Godin Tepe
Haft Tepe
Hajji Firuz
Hasanlu
Isfahan
Izeh
Malyan
Marlik
Mussian, Tepe
Naqsh-i Rustam
Nishapur
Pasargadae
Persepolis
Sialk, Tepe
Susa
Yahya, Tepe

Iraq

Abu Duwari, Tell (Mashkan-shapir)
Abu Habba, Tell (Sippar)
Abu Salabikh
Adab
ʿAqar Quf
Asmar, Tell (Eshnunna)
Assur. *See* Qalʿat Sherqat
Babylon
Baghdad
Balawat
Der, Tell ed-
Abu Shahrain, Tell (Eridu)
Eski Mosul Dam
Fara
Gawra, Tepe
Hassuna, Tell
Hiba, Tell al- (Lagash)
Isin
Jarmo
Jemdet Nasr
Kar-Tukulti-Ninurta
Khafaje (Tutub)
Khorsabad (Dur Sharrukin)
Kish
Larsa
Nimrud (Kalhu)
Nineveh
Nippur
Nuzi
ʾOueili, Tell el-
Qalʿat Sherqat (Assur)
Rimah, Tell er-
Samarra
Seleucia on the Tigris
Shanidar Cave
Taya, Tell
Telloh, Tell (Girsu)
Ubaid
Ur
Warka (Uruk)
Yorghan Tepe (Nuzi; Akk. Gasur)
Zurghul (Nigin)

Israel

Abu Hawam, Tell
Achziv
Ai
ʿAin es-Samiyeh
ʿAjjul, Tell el-
Akko
Anafa, Tel
Aphek
Arad
ʿAroʿer
Ashdod
Ashkelon
ʿAtlit Ram
Avdat
ʿAzekah
Barʿam
Balaṭah, Tell (Shechem)
Batash, Tel
Beʾer Resisim
Beersheba
Beit Mirsim, Tell
Beit Shean
Beth Alpha
Bethel
Beth-Gan
Bethlehem
Bethsaida
Beth-Sheʿarim
Beth-Shemesh
Beth-Yeraḥ
Beth-Zur
Bull Site
Caesarea
Caesarea Philippi (Banias)
Capernaum
Carmel Caves
Chorazin
Dan, Tel (Arabic Tell Qadi; Dan)
Decapolis
Deir el-Balaḥ
Dor
Dothan, Tell
Ebal, Mount
ʿEinan
ʿEin-Besor
ʿEin-Boqeq
ʿEin-Gedi
ʿEin-Gev
ʿEin-Shadud
ʿEin-Yaʾel
ʿEin-Zippori, Tel
Emmaus
ʿEn Ḥaṣeva
ʿErani, Tel
Esdar, Tel
Farʿah, Tell el- [North]
Farʿah, Tell el- [South]

Ful, Tell el-
Galilee
Gamla
Gerisa, Tel
Gezer
Gilat
Giloh
Golan
Gush Ḥalav
Hadar, Tel
Ḥaluṣa
Hammath Tiberias
Ḥammath-Gader
Haror, Tel
Harṭuv
Hatra
Hayonim
Hermon, Mount
Herodian Jericho
Herodium
Ḥesi, Tell el-
Hisn, Tell el- (Beit She'an, later Scythopolis, Arab Baysan)
ʿIra, Tel
ʿIzbet Ṣarṭah
Jaffa
Jebel Qaʿaqir
Jemmeh, Tell
Jerusalem
Jezreel, Tel
Jib, el (Gibeon)
Jotapata
Judeideh, Tell el-
Kabri, Tel
Kefar Ḥananyah
Kefar Veradim
Keisan, Tell
Ketef Hinnom
Kitan, Tel
Kurnub
Kursi
Lachish, Tel
Lahav, Tel
Maʿagan Mikhaʾel
Magdala
Malḥata, Tel
Maresha
Masada
Masos, Tel
Megiddo, Tel
Meiron
Meṣad Ḥashavyahu (near Yavneh-Yam)
Michal, Tel
Miqne, Tel (Ekron)
Mor, Tel
Munḥata
Nabratein
Naḥal Oren
Nami, Tel
Naṣbeh, Tell en- (Mispah)
Nazareth
Neṣṣana
Omrit, Ḥorvat
Qadesh-Barnea
Qasile, Tell
Qaṣrin
Qedah, Tell el- (Hazor)
Qiri, Tel
Qiryat Sepher
Qitmit, Ḥorvat
Qom, Khirbet el-
Qumran, Khirbet
Rabud, Khirbet
Radanna, Khirbet
Radum, Ḥorvat
Ramat Raḥel
Ramla
Ras, Tell er-
Reḥovot
Rosh Zayit, Ḥorvat
Rujm el-Hiri
Rumeide, Tell er- (Hebron)
Ṣafi, Tell eṣ- (Gath)
Sebaste (Samaria)
Sepphoris
Seraʿ, Tel
Shaʿar ha-Golan
Shavei-Zion
Shemaʿ, Khirbet
Shiloh
Shiqmim
Shiqmona
Sorek, Nahal
Subeita
Sultân, Tell es- (Jericho)
Susiya
Taʿanach
Tabgha
Tabor, Mount
Tabun
Teiman, Ḥorvat (Kuntillet ʿAjrud)
Tiberias
Timnaʿ
ʿUbeidiya
ʿUza, Ḥorvat
Wawiyat, Tell el-
Yarmut, Tel
Yavneh-Yam
Yiftaḥel
Yinʿam, Tel
Yaqneʿam
Zayit, Tel
Zeror, Tel

Jordan

Abila
Abu al-Kharaz, Tell
Abu Ḥamid, Tell
ʿAin Ghazal
ʿAjlun
Amman (Rabbath Ammon, later Philadelphia)
ʿAqaba
ʿAraʿir
Azraq
Bab edh-Dhraʿ
Badiat ash-Sham
Baluʿ
Baqʿah Valley
Basta
Beidha
Beit Ras
Buṣeirah
Decapolis
Deir ʿAlla, Tell
Dhraʿ
Dibon
Faris, Khirbet
Feinan
Ghrubba
Hasa, Wadi el-
Ḥayyat, Tell el-
Ḥesban (Heshbon)
Ḥumeima
Iktanu, Tell
ʿIraq el-Amir
Irbid
Iskander, Khirbet

Jawa
Jerash
Jilat, Wadi el-
Kafranja, Wadi
Karak
Kheleifeh, Tell el-
Lehun
Limes Arabicus
Machaerus
Madaba
Mafjar, Khirbat al-
Mazar, Tell el-
Medeineh, Khirbet el-
Nebo, Mount
Nimrin, Tell
Pella
Petra
Qaṣr al-Ḥallabat
Qaṣr al-Meshatta
Qaṣr Burquʿ
Quṣayr ʿAmra
Ras en-Naqb
Rumeith, Tell er-
Ṣafuṭ, Tell
Sahab
Saʿidiyeh, Tell es-
Samosata
Shuʿeib, Wadi
Tannur, Khirbet et-
Tawilan
Teleilat el-Ghassul
ʿUmayri, Tall al-
Umm el-Biyara
Umm el-Jimal
Umm er-Rasas
Umm Qeis
Yabis, Wadi el-
Zeraqun, Khirbet ez-
Ziqlab, Wadi

Syria and Lebanon

Afis, Tell
ʿAin Daraʿ
Atchana, Tell (Alalakh)
Aleppo (Halpa)
ʿAmrit
ʿAnjar
Antioch on Orontes
Apamea
Arwad
Baalbek (Rom. Heliopolis)
Bassit Beirut
Beydar, Tell (Nabada)
Bosra
Bouqras
Brak, Tell (Nagar)
Byblos
Chuera, Tell
Damascus
Douara
Dura-Europos
Fekheriye, Tell
Golan
Habuba Kabira
Hadidi, Tell
Ḥalaf, Tell
Hama
Hamoukar, Tell
Hariri, Tell (Mari)
Homs
Kamid el-Loz (Kumidi)
Kazel, Tell el-
Khabur
Khaldeh
Ksar ʾAkil
Latamne
Leilan, Tell (Shubat Enlil)
Maʿlula
Manbij
Mardikh, Tell (Ebla)
Meskene (Emar)
Minet el-Beida (Mahadu)
Mishrifeh
Mozan, Tell (Urkesh)
Mureybet
Nebi Mend, Tell
Palmyra
Qalʿat Simʿan
Qarqur, Tell
Qaṣr al-Ḥayr al-Gharbi
Qaṣr al-Ḥayr ash-Sharqi
Qinnishrin (Chalcis)
Qitar, el-
Raqqa, ar-
Ras Ibn Hani
Ras Shamra (Ugarit)
Rifaʿat, Tell
Rusafa
Said Naya
Sarepta
Sergilla
Sheikh Ḥamad, Tell
Sidon
Sukas, Tell
Suweida
Terqa
Til Barsip
Tyre

Turkey

Acemhöyük (Purushanda?)
Adana
Alişar Höyük (Ankuwa)
ʿAmuq
Aphrodisias
Arslantepe (Malatya)
Aspendos
Assos
Beycesultan
Boğazköy (Hattusa)
Çadır Höyük
Cape Gelidonya
Jerablous (Karkamis; Europos)
Çatal Höyük
Çayönü
Chalcedon
Didyma
Ephesus
Göbekli Tepe
Göltepe
Gordion
Gözlükule (Tarsus)
Hacılar
Halikarnassos
İkiztepe
Kaman-Kalehöyük
Karatepe (Azatiwada)
Kinet Höyük (Issos)
Kınık Höyük
Kültepe (Kanesh)
Kuşaklı (Sarissa)
Maraş
Maşat Höyük (Tapikka)
Mersin
Miletus
Nemrud Dağı
Nevalı Çori
Ortaköy (Sapinuwa)
Perga
Pergamon

Pessinus	Şeytan Deresi	Tille Höyük
Pinarbaşı Gölü	Side	Tyana
Priene	Sirkeli Höyük	Uluburun
Samsat (Kummuh)	Soli Höyük	Xanthos
Sardis	Tatarlı Höyük	Yazılıkaya
Serçe Limanı	Taʿyinat, Tell (Kinalua?)	Zincirli (Samʾal)

4.3.3.5 Other Geographical Terms and Names

For general reference, follow *Merriam-Webster's Geographical Dictionary*, 3rd ed. (Springfield, MA: Merriam-Webster, 1997).

The generic terms *delta, desert, gulf, island(s), lake, mount, mountain(s), nahal, nahr, river, sea, strait, tel, tell, valley, wadi* should be capitalized when used as part of a specific name (*CMS* §8.52):

> Kidron Valley, Lake Huleh, Lebanon Mountains, Ophel Ridge, Khirbet Qumran.

For spelling, see the hierarchy of authorities in §3.4; for capitalization, *CMS* (§8.52) recommends that in the plural a generic term "is capitalized when it is part of a single name (Hawaiian Islands) and when it is used of two or more names, whether beginning with the generic term (Mounts Washington and Rainier) or … when the generic term comes second and applies to two or more names." Thus:

> Tigris and Euphrates Rivers

Note political divisions, such as *Central Europe*, as distinct from geographical divisions, such as *central Asia* (*CMS* §§8.50, 52).

4.3.3.6 Events and Concepts

As a general rule, do not capitalize the names of biblical, religious, and theological (including eschatological) events and concepts:

> atonement (as a general concept or rite), body and blood, body of Christ, creation, crucifixion, day of judgment, exile, exodus (from Egypt), fall, first missionary journey, kingdom of God (or heaven), man of sin, nativity (of Jesus), new covenant, passion (of Christ), resurrection, tabernacle, temple, virgin birth.

4.3.4 Biblical Sources

4.3.4.1 Designations for the Bible

In general, a word or phrase used as a title of the whole or a specific part of the Bible is capitalized (as are titles of other ancient works); the name of a genre is not capitalized. Thus any ancient or modern designation for the Bible, a book of the Bible, a division of the biblical canon (e.g., Pentateuch), or a discrete section of a biblical book (e.g., Primeval History) may be a proper noun and so capitalized. But when the same words are used generically, they should remain in lowercase.

Many contentious debates can arise over correct usage on these matters, and authors will clearly encounter competing standards. While the best advice is to follow the preferences of your publisher and in any event to be consistent (keeping track of your preferences for the project editor; see §3.1), the following guidelines are offered with the hope that they will be found useful.

It is usually preferable to avoid designations like *book*, *letter*, and *epistle* when referring to the titles of biblical writings (e.g., *Psalms* is better than *book of Psalms*, and *James* than *Epistle of James*). While, again, authors must respect the preferences of their publishers, a general rule (followed, e.g., by *CMS* and *Merriam-Webster's Collegiate Dictionary*) is to capitalize words when they are used as titles of a specifically identifiable writing but lowercase them otherwise. Thus: "The Gospel of John begins with a prologue about the Logos," but "The Gospel of John's Prologue introduces the Logos."

SBL Press capitalizes *Gospel* when it is part of the title of a work and lowercases the term when it refers generically to the genre or to good news, message, or authoritative tradition.

Below are a few examples; for others, see §4.3.6.

Book of the Wars of the Lord; Book of Jashar (*but*: book of the law of Moses, the book of the covenant, the book of the prophet Ezra son of Seraiah)
book of Job; book of Jeremiah; Jeremiah's scroll
Law, Prophets, Writings (as canonical divisions; = Torah, Pentateuch, etc.); Mosaic law, Hebrew prophets, wisdom literature
Twenty-Third Psalm; Psalm 100; psalms of Asaph
the parable of the good Samaritan
four canonical gospels, the Gospel of John, the Fourth Gospel, Paul's gospel

4.3.4.2 Nouns Referring to God

Certain nouns traditionally used as alternative names of God or of one of the persons of the Trinity are capitalized when so used:

Bat Qol, Comforter, Creator, Father, G-d, Immanuel, King, King of kings, Lamb, Lamb of God, L-rd, Lord, Lord of lords, Maker, Messiah, Redeemer, Son, Son of God, Son of Man, Wisdom, Word

Nontraditional designations should also be capitalized (e.g., *Parent* used as a gender-neutral substitute for *Father*). Ordinarily, noun phrases are capitalized as if they were book titles (e.g., *Son of Man*), but when the point is to exalt the Divinity over lesser imitators, the phrases may contain capitals and lowercase (see, e.g., the NRSV and NIV usage of *God of gods*, *King of kings*, and *Lord of lords* in Deut 10:17 and Rev. 17:14 with the strictly human *king of kings* in Ezra 7:12; Dan 2:37). In an academic context the trend should be to lowercase. Other designations less often used outside of particular scriptural contexts are less often capitalized:

bread of life or Bread of Life, crucified one or Crucified One, man of sorrows or Man of Sorrows, light of the world or Light of the World

With all of these, and especially the latter category, usage varies. A book or journal should be internally consistent. If the author of a single-author volume has a preference and has been consistent, that preference should be allowed to stand. If not, SBL recommends lowercase. For biblical expressions, it can be helpful to consult the usage of a recent Bible translation such as the NRSV, the NIV, the REB, the NJB, or the CEB. In any event, the project editor should include all such items in the book's style sheet.

4.3.4.3 Pronouns Referring to God

Avoid using unnecessary gender-specific pronouns in reference to the Godhead (see §4.3.1). In those cases when such pronouns are unavoidable, they should not be capitalized (thus *he, him, his;* but for expressions like *Third Person of the Trinity,* see §4.3.4.2).

4.3.5 Qur'anic and Islamic Sources

4.3.5.1 Designation and Citation of the Qur'an

The title of the Islamic scripture, properly transliterated as *al-Qurʾān*, is rendered into English and other European languages in a variety of ways (e.g., Koran, Coran, Quran). The preferred form is "Qur'an" (with the medial glottal stop represented), with the adjective being "qur'anic." While "Koran" is the historical name for the scripture in the English language, this version of the title has come to seem old-fashioned and should be avoided. "Qur'an" and "qur'anic" with a single quote is preferred in most contexts, although works that render Arabic terms with full transliteration may choose to indicate the medial glottal stop with a proper *hamzah* (Qurʾan) for the sake of consistency.

The 114 chapters of the Qur'an (*suwar*, sg. *sūrah*; the plural *sūrah*s is also acceptable) are divided into verses (*āyāt*, sg. *āyah*; the plural *āyah*s is also acceptable).

Generally speaking, the first reference to a verse or verses in a single chapter should give the Arabic title of the *sūrah* first, followed by the numbers of the chapter and verse or verses separated by a colon, such as Q Baqarah 2:54, Q Maryam 19:20, Q ʿAlaq 96:1–5. In subsequent references to the same verse, or in other instances in which abbreviated reference is desirable, one may omit the title of the *sūrah*.

If one is citing a group of *sūrah*s to illustrate a point, it is not necessary to indicate the title of each. Thus, compare "The so-called Sword Verse (Q Tawbah 9:5) has historically occasioned much discussion..." with "Common themes link several of the *sūrah*s that tradition holds to be very early such as Q 96, 73, 74, 92, 89, et cetera."

When referring to a particular *sūrah* in its entirety, it is proper to use the construct form of *sūrah* as part of the title, as in "There has been significant debate as to whether long chapters such as Sūrat al-Baqarah should be considered unitary compositions."

It is not conventional to cite particular editions of the Qur'an, as modern printed Qur'ans are generally uniform regarding vocalization, division of verses, and the like. Most modern printed Qur'ans are derived from the Royal Cairo edition of 1924, produced under the supervision of a committee of scholars from Al-Azhar University. Due to the wide influence of this edition, the particular reading of the qur'anic text it represents (the transmission of Ḥafṣ from ʿĀṣim, one of fourteen generally recognized *qirāʾāt* or readings of the Qur'an) has become universally predominant, though alternative traditions of printing in India, Turkey, and elsewhere have led to printed versions that are slightly different in their vocalization and conventions. The alternative verse numberings found in the Flügel and older Indian editions of the Qur'an are seldom encountered these days, and it should be tacitly understood that the Cairo verse numbering is in use.

Casual reference to Muhammad as the author of the Qur'an, once conventional in Western scholarship, is now generally avoided. Discussion of the possibility of the authorship of the Qur'an by the historical Muhammad is acceptable in reasoned argument, however.

When possible, authors should also avoid ascribing agency to the Qur'an through expressions such as "The Qur'an argues that..."; a more neutral reference to the text itself and its contents is preferable, such as, "In many passages in the Qur'an, one finds the claim that..." or "Throughout the canonical scripture, stories familiar to Jews and Christians from their own sacred writings are portrayed." If an active subject is desired, "the text of the Qur'an" or "qur'anic discourse" may be acceptable depending on context. Ascribing intentionality, attitude, or belief to the Qur'an itself (or to the Deity) should be avoided.

4.3.5.2 Title and Author Conventions for Non-Qur'anic Texts

Titles of Arabic works other than the Qur'an should be given in full upon their first citation and in a shortened form thereafter. Only the first word should be capitalized, with the exception of book titles in which *kitāb* ("book") is the first word; in this case, the next word should be capitalized as well. Insofar as classical works in particular are commonly given ornamental rather than descriptive titles, translation of the title is to be avoided, except parenthetically upon first mention if it is deemed significant.

Al-Ṭabarī, *Jāmiʿ al-bayān ʿan taʾwīl āy al-Qurʾān* (first citation); *Jāmiʿ al-bayān* (subsequent citations)
Mālik b. Anas, *Al-Muwaṭṭaʾ li-Imām Mālik* (first citation); *Muwaṭṭaʾ* (subsequent citations)
Ibn Saʿd, *Kitāb al-Ṭabaqāt al-kubrā* (first citation); *Kitāb al-Ṭabaqāt* (subsequent citations)
Al-Zabīdī, *Tāj al-ʿarūs min jawāhir al-qāmūs* (first citation); *Tāj al-ʿarūs* (subsequent citations)
Due to its controversial subject matter, Ibn al-Kalbī's *Kitāb al-Aṣnām* (*Book of Idols*) was likely deliberately suppressed in early ʿAbbasid times.

Upon first mention, the name of a Muslim author, tradent, or other figure should be given in the fullest form possible, following the standard pattern: *kunyah* (progenitive); *ism* (proper name); *nasab* (patronymic); *nisbah* ("surname," that is, place of origin, tribal or professional association, etc.). The name should also be followed by the death date: for example, Abū Jaʿfar Muḥammad b. Jarīr al-Ṭabarī (d. 310/923). Subsequent mentions should use the *nisbah*, or otherwise the most commonly used term of reference, *ʿurf* (customary name): for example, al-Bukhārī, al-Bayḍāwī, al-Fīrūzābādī; but Muslim, Ibn Saʿd, Ibn al-Kalbī. For many medieval authors, a *laqab* (honorific) may be standard as well; further, the customary appellation or *ʿurf* may not be generated from the standard components of the name at all, for example, Shiḥab al-Dīn Abū'l-Faḍl Aḥmad b. ʿAlī al-ʿAsqalānī, universally known as Ibn Ḥajar al-ʿAsqalānī.

If two or more people are under discussion who have the same *nisbah*, they should be consistently distinguished at all times, for example, ʿAlī b. Rabbān al-Ṭabarī versus Abū Jaʿfar al-Ṭabarī; Abū Ḥātim al-Rāzī versus Fakhr al-Dīn al-Rāzī.

4.3.5.3 Divine Nomenclature

The name "Allah" (*Allāh*) is considered the proper name of the deity in the Qur'an and Islamic tradition, whereas the numerous other appellations applied to him by the Qur'an are understood as epithets. Because it is the main designation for the deity in Islamic tradition, the English "God" should consistently be used to render the word *Allāh*. The other appellations applied to God should be given in italics, with English translation indicated if desirable or contextually appropriate, for example:

> The epithet *al-Raḥmān*, "the Merciful One," is reminiscent of the South Arabian name *Raḥmanan*, which itself has an apparent parallel in talmudic usage as well.

> Islamic tradition assigns numerous epithets to God derived from adjectives used to describe him in the Qur'an; they indicate his power (*al-Qadīr* "the One Who Determines Affairs"), his might (*al-ʿAẓīm* "the Great," and *al-Muḥīṭ* "the Encompassing"), and his generosity (*al-Raḥīm* "the Merciful," and *al-Razzāq* "the Provider").

4.3.5.4 Common Names

The names of major figures associated with Islamic tradition such as Muhammad, ʿAli, ʿAʾisha, and Abu Bakr need not be subject to proper transliteration when they are cited, although ʿ*ayn* and *hamzah* should be included to assist correct pronunciation. When these names appear as part of the proper name of later figures, they should be fully transliterated. Thus, contrast "The Prophet Muhammad and his cousin ʿAli" and "Muḥammad b. ʿAlī al-Bāqir, recognized as the Fifth Imam of the Shiʿa."

The full spelling ʿAbd Allāh is to be preferred over ʿAbdallah, ʿAbdullah, and the like.

When characters from biblical, Jewish, and Christian tradition are discussed in the context of their appearance in the Qur'an or Islamic tradition, the familiar English version of the name should be used. However, when that name appears as part of the nomenclature of a specific historical individual from Islamic history or culture, it should appear in its Arabicized form, such as Jesus, but Abū ʿĪsā al-Warrāq; Aaron, but Hārūn al-Rashīd; Solomon, but Salmān Pak (and otherwise Sulaymān).

The rules of transliteration of Arabic names should not be applied to modern authors who have published in Western languages; rather, the authors' particular choice for representing their names should be respected, such as Maryam Jameelah, Ebrahim Moosa, and Nadia Maria El Cheikh.

While pious Muslims view the inclusion of benedictions upon Muhammad and major figures of the tradition as a religious requirement (e.g., "The Prophet Muhammad, prayers and peace of God upon him, migrated from Mecca to Medina in 632 CE"), this is generally to be avoided in scholarly usage.

4.3.5.5 Place Names

Common place names need not be subject to proper transliteration and should be rendered according to their familiar English form, such as Mecca, Medina, Damascus, Iraq, Syria, Hijaz, and so forth. When included as part of a proper name as an attributive adjective (*nisbah*), these names should be preserved in their Arabicized form. Compare "Muhammad's uncle Abu Talib was a major figure among the prominent leaders of tribes and clans in Mecca" and "The tenth-century jurist and mystic Abū Ṭālib al-Makkī interpreted these verses."

If the primary literary context of the discussion is a source in Arabic, *nisbahs* based on non-Arab locales should be given in their Arabicized forms (e.g., al-Nīsābūrī and not al-

Nīshāpūrī). If the primary literary context is Persian (especially with Persian text appearing in transliteration in the article), then the Persianate form is to be used.

4.3.5.6 Technical Terms in Islamicate Languages

There are three tiers of specialized terminology in use in scholarly discussions of the Qur'an and Islam in Western languages.

1. Some terms originating in Arabic or other Islamicate languages are so commonly encountered in English and other Western languages that they need not be formally transliterated nor glossed, such as bazaar, caliph, imam, Islam, jihad, ulama, and so on. This practice also extends to the names of major dynasties, political movements, philosophical and legal schools, and so forth, which should be given according to the most current and readily recognizable form: ʿAbbasids, Hanafis, Muʿtazila, Shiʿa (sg. Shiʿi; but cf. Sunni/Sunnis). Inclusion in the *Oxford English Dictionary* is a good indication of a first-tier Arabic term.
2. Some terms originating in Arabic or other Islamicate languages are not commonly encountered in English and other Western languages but are so well known to the probable audience of a scholarly work that they need not be glossed, although they should be italicized and properly transliterated, such as *fiqh*, *ḥadīth*, *muṣḥaf*, *qirāʾāt*, *tafsīr*.
3. All other specialized terms should be italicized and properly transliterated upon every occurrence, and glossed upon their first occurrence, such as *ʿiṣmah* (impeccability), *nubuwwah* (prophecy), and *taʿdīl* (validation).

4.3.6 Capitalization and Spelling Examples

A

a priori
Aaronide
Abba (but transliterated *abba*)
Abdi-Heba (not Abdi-Ḫepa, Abdu-Hepa, or Abdi-Hepa)
ʿabiru. See Habiru
ablative
abomination of desolation
Achaemenid
ad hoc
ad nauseam
Adad (Akkadian DN)
Adad-nirari (not Adad-Nirari)
Adapa
Adonai
Aelia Capitolina
affix (any prefix, suffix, or infix)
African American (noun and adj.)
Agade (Sumerian; = Akkad)
agape (but transliterated *agapē*)
age (church, classical, etc.)
Age (archaeological periods such as Bronze Age, Iron Age)
agora
agraphon, pl. agrapha
Ahhiyawa
Ahiqar or Aḥiqar (not Ahikar or ʾAḥiqar)
Ahiram or Aḥiram (not Ahirom or ʾAḥiram)
Ahmose (not Amosis)
Ahura Mazda (not Ahuramazda, Ahura Mazdā, or Ahura Mazdâ)
Akedah
Akhenaten (PN; = Amenhotep IV) (not Akhenaton)
Akiva (not Akiba or Aqiba)
Akitu festival (but transliterated *akītu*)

Akkad
Akkadian
Aktionsart
Aleppo Codex
Alpha and Omega (as titles of Christ)
Amarna age, letters, tablets
Amenemhet (not Amenemhat)
Amidah
amillennial(ism)
Ammisaduqa, Edict of
Amoraic period
Amoraim
amphictyony
amphora
Amun-Re (not Amun Re, Amun-Ra, or Amon-Ra)
Anat or ʿAnatu (not Anath)
ancient Near East (noun)
ancient Near Eastern (adj.)
angel of the Lord (an *or* the)
anno mundi (in the year of the world)
ante-Christian
antediluvian
ante-Nicene fathers
antichrist, the
anti-Christian
antimonarchic
anti-Semitic
anti-Semitism
Anu
ʿ*apiru*. See Habiru
Apocalypse, the (the book of Revelation)
apocalyptic
Apocrypha, the
apocryphal
Apology of Hattusili
apothegm
apostle(s), the (the twelve apostles)
apostle Paul (Paul the apostle, etc.)
Apostles' Creed
apostolic
apostolic age
apostolic council
apostolic fathers (individuals, authors)
Apostolic Fathers (corpus of writings)
apparatus criticus
Aqhat or Aqhatu (not ʾAqhatu)
Aramaean
archaeology
archbishop of Canterbury (but Archbishop Smith)
archon
Area *x* (archaeological reports; area followed by number)
ark (Noah's)
ark of the covenant
ascension, the
Ascension Day (as liturgical day)
Asclepius (not Asklepios, Asklēpios, or Aesculapius)
Asherah
ashlar masonry
Ashur. *See* Assur
Ashurbanipal. *See* Assurbanipal
Ashurnasirpal. *See* Assurnasirpal
Assur (not Ashur)
Assurbanipal (not Ashurbanipal)
Assurnasirpal (not Ashurnasirpal or Assurnaṣirpal)
Assyrian Empire
Assyrian King List
Astarte, Ashtoreth (HB), or Aštart
atheist
Athirat or ʾAtiratu
atonement, the
Atonement, Day of (Yom Kippur)
Atrahasis or Atraḫasis (not Atra-ḫasis or Atra-Ḫasis)
atrium

B

Baal or Baʿlu (not Ba'al or Baʿal)
Baalism
Baal-shamayn (not Baal Shamayn, Baal-Shamayn, or Baal-Shamaim)
Babylonian captivity
Babylonian Chronicle
Babylonian Empire
Babylonian King List

Babylonian Story of Creation (= Enuma Elish)
bamah (but transliterated *bâmâ*)
baptism (e.g., with the Holy Spirit, of Christ)
Bar Kokhba (= Simon ben Kosiba [actual name]; not Bar Kochba)
Bar Kokhba revolt
baraita (pl. baraitot)
basilica
Bat Qol (but transliterated *bat qôl*)
battle of Armageddon
battle of Carchemish, etc.
beast, the
Beatitudes, the
bedouin (singular and plural)
Beloved Disciple (as title)
Behistun. See Bisitun
bema (but transliterated *bēma*)
Ben Sira
Benedictus (Song of Zechariah)
Ben-hadad (per NRSV) or Ben-Hadad
Bible
biblical
Biblical Hebrew
bilingual
Birkat Haminim
bishop of Rome (but Bishop Smith)
Bisitun (not Behistun, Bisetun, or Bistun)
Black Obelisk
Bodmer papyri
Boghazköy (GN; = Hattusa)
body of Christ (= church)
book of Genesis (etc.)
Book of Noah
book of the covenant
book of the law
Book of the Twelve
boustrophedon
bridegroom, the (= Christ)
bulla (pl. bullae)
burnt offering

C

ca. (circa)
caesura
Cairo Genizah
call (of Amos, Jeremiah, etc.)
canon, the
captivity, the
cartouche
casuistic
catalog (verb or noun; not catalogue)
catena (pl. catenae)
catholic (meaning universal)
Catholic (when part of the name of a particular church or denomination)
Catholic Epistles (or Letters)
caveat lector
CD-ROM
central hill country
century (the first century; first-century *x* [adj.])
cereal offering
Chaldean
charismatic (noun and adj.)
charismatic movement
Chebar River (HB term for Khabur River)
Chester Beatty papyri
chiasm, chiasmus
chief priest
chosen people
Christian (noun and adj.)
Christian era
Christianize
Christlike
Christmas (Day, Eve, etc.)
Christocentric
christological (adj.)
Christology (noun)
Chronicler, the
church (general reference to worldwide or local group of Christians)
Church (when part of a name or title, e.g., Greek Orthodox Church)
church age
church father(s)

city of David
city of God
city-state
Classical Arabic
classical period
coastal plain
Code of Hammurabi
Codex Alexandrinus, Codex Vaticanus, etc.
colon (pl. cola; also bicola, tricola)
commandment (first, second, etc.; but Ten Commandments)
Community Rule (1QS) (see also Manual of Discipline)
conquest period
contra
coregency
coregent
cosmogony
council, apostolic
Council, Jerusalem
Council of Trent
counterintuitive
counterproductive
Counter-Reformation, the
coup d'état
covenant (Abrahamic, Mosaic, old, new)
Covenant Code (Exod 21–23)
creation, the
Creation Epic. See Babylonian Story of Creation
creedal (not credal)
crown prince
cross (object or synecdoche for the entire event)
Crucified One or crucified one, the
crucifixion, the
Crusades
cupbearer
curse, the
Cyrus Cylinder

D

D stem
Dagon (HB) or Dagan
dagesh forte
dagesh lene
Daliyeh, Wadi ed- (not Wādī d-Dāliya)
Damascus Document (CD) (not Damascus Covenant)
Danel or Daniʾilu (legendary king in Ugaritic text)
David's champions
Davidic (adj.)
Davidide (member of the royal house)
Day of Atonement (Yom Kippur)
day of judgment
day of Pentecost
day of the Lord (per NRSV)
de novo
Dead Sea Scrolls (but a Dead Sea scroll)
Decalogue (Ten Commandments)
Deity, the (but the deity of Christ)
demiurge
demos
demotic
deuterocanonical
Deutero-Isaiah
Deuteronomic
Deuteronomist
Deuteronomistic History/Historian
deutero-Pauline
Deutero-Zechariah
devil, the
diacritical mark
diaspora (the event or the dispersed community)
Diatessaron
différance, différence
diglot
diphthong
disciples
distich
divided kingdom
divided monarchy
divine
Divine Warrior
docetic
docetism
docetists
docetistic

Documentary Hypothesis
dolmen
dunam
dynasty (Omride, Davidic, etc.)
Dynasty (Egyptian) (e.g., Eighteenth Dynasty; pl. Dynasties)

E

E account/source
Ea
early Christianity, early Christian
early church
early church fathers
Easter
Eastern Orthodox Church
Eden
Edict of Ammisaduqa
editio princeps
e.g. (*exempli gratia*)
Egypt, Lower/Upper
Eighteen Benedictions
elect, God's elect
Elephantine papyri
Elohist source
e-mail
emperor, the (similar to the king, the pharoah, etc.)
emperor *x*, the (the emperor Constantine, the emperor Hadrian)
Emperor *x* (Emperor Constantine, Emperor Hadrian)
empire, the
Empire, Neo-Babylonian, Roman, etc.
en masse
end time, the (noun)
end-time (adj.)
Enheduanna
Enlil
Enuma Elish (not *Enuma Elish, Enuma elish, Enuma eliš, or Enūma Eliš*)
ephod
Epic of Creation. See Babylonian Story of Creation
epilogue
Epiphany (Christian holiday)
Epistle to the Romans (etc.)
Epistles, the (as canonical division distinct from Gospels, Acts, and Apocalypse)
Epistles, Paul's (as canonical division)
eponym
Ereshkigal
Eridu Genesis (Sumerian creation account)
Eros (DN); eros (common noun)
Erra (not Irra)
Erra, Poem of (not Epic of)
Esagila
eschatology
eschaton
Esdraelon Plain
Eshnunnu (not Ešnunnu)
et al. (*et alii*)
etc.
Etemenanki
etiological (not aetiological)
etiology (not aetiology)
etion (not aition)
etymology, etymological
Eucharist
eucharistic
evangelist (gospel writer, proclaimer of good news)
Evangelist (as part of a title: John the; the Fourth, etc.)
ex nihilo
ex novo
ex officio
Execration Texts
exile (general condition or the Babylonian captivity)
exilic
exodus, the
extispicy (the oracular reading of viscera)
extrabiblical

F

fait accompli
faith
fall, the (theological concept)

fall of humanity
fall of Jerusalem
Farewell Discourse(s) (John 13/14–17)
Father, the (referring to God)
fathers, church or early church (not the Fathers)
faux pas
favissa (pl. favissae) (pit for burying cult objects)
feast day
Feast of Firstfruits
Feast of the Nativity
Feast of Pentecost (etc.)
Feast of Tabernacles
feminist criticism, studies, theory
Fertile Crescent
fertility god(dess)
Festival of Weeks, Booths, Passover
Festschrift (pl. Festschriften)
fibula (pl. fibulae)
First Evangelist
First Gospel (= Matthew)
First Jewish Revolt
first missionary journey
First Temple period
firstborn
firstfruits
Fish Gate
flood, the
floruit
footwashing
form criticism (noun), form-critical (adj.)
Former Prophets
fosse (ditch, moat)
Four Document Hypothesis
Fourth Evangelist
Fourth Gospel (= John)
Fourth Philosophy
funerary offerings

G

G stem
gaon
gaonic
garden of Eden
gehenna
gematria
gender criticism (noun), gender-critical (adj.)
General Epistles (or General Letters)
genizah, a (but Cairo Genizah)
gentile(s) (noun and adj.)
geographical name
Gezer Calendar
Gilgamesh (not Gilgameš)
glacis (pl. glacis)
Gloria, the (or Gloria in Excelsis Deo)
Gloria Patri, the
gnosis (but transliterated *gnōsis*)
gnostic (noun and adj.)
Gnosticism
God Almighty
God Most High
Godfearer(s)
Godhead
godless
godlike
godly
golden calf, the
good news
gospel (the good news, the kerygma; the genre)
Gospel (as part of or substitute for a title of a work: Mark's Gospel)
Gospels, the (division of the canon)
goy (pl. goyim)
Great Commission, the
Great Rift Valley (= Jordan Valley)
Greco-Roman
Greek (noun and adj.)
Greek Testament
Grundlage (pl. *Grundlagen*)
guilt offering

H

Habiru (not *ḥabiru*, *ḥapiru*, *ḫabiru*, *ḫapiru*, *ʿabiru*, or *ʿapiru*)
Hadad (Northwest Semitic DN)

Hades
haftarah
haggadah (not aggadah)
haggadic (not aggadic)
hagiographa
halakah, halakic, halakist
half-brother
half-tribe
hallelujah
Hammurabi (not Hammurapi)
hanging gardens
Hanukkah
hapax legomenon (pl. *hapax legomena*)
ḥapiru or *ḫapiru*. See Habiru
haplography
Hasidic
Hasidim
Hasmonean
Hatti (not Ḫatti)
Hattusa (GN; = Boghazköy) (not Hattuša, Ḫattusa, or Ḫattuša)
Hattusili
Haustafel (pl. *Haustafeln*)
heaven
Hebraism
Hebrew Bible
hectare
Heilsgeschichte (noun); *heilsgeschichtlich* (adj.)
hekhalot
hell
Hellenism
Hellenistic
hellenize
he-locale
hendiadys
henotheism
Heptateuch
Herodian
Hexaemeron
Hexapla (noun); Hexaplaric (adj.)
hic et nunc
hieroglyph
high priest
hill country
Hillel the Elder
history of religions school
Hittite Law Code
Holiness Code (Lev 17–26)
Holy City
Holy Land
holy of holies
holy war
Horus (not Ḥorus)
house of David
humanity
Hurrian

I

ibid.
i.e. (*id est*)
idolaters
imago Dei
Immanuel (not Emmanuel)
Imperial Aramaic
in situ
Inanna's Descent to the Netherworld
incarnation
inclusio
Indo-European
infancy gospels
infix
Instruction of *x* (e.g., Amenemhet; Egyptian genre)
inter alia
interfaith
internecine
intertestamental
intertestamental period
ipsissima verba
ipsissima vox
Ishme-Dagan (not Išme-Dagan)
Ishtar (not Ištar)
Israelite settlement

J

Jacobian
Jamnia. See Yavneh

Jannaeus
JEDP
Jerusalem Council
Jew
Jewish
Jewish War
Johannine
John's Gospel (= Gospel of John)
Journey of Wen-Amon
Jubilee, Jubilee Year
Judah
Judah the Patriarch
Judahite (adj. for references to the kingdom of Judah)
Judaic
Judaism
Judaizer(s)
Judea
Judean
judgment day
judges, the

K

kabbalah
Kaddish
Karatepe inscription
Kassite
Keret. See Kirta
kerygma
ketiv
Ketuvim (division of the canon) (not Ketubim)
Khirbet *x* (not Ḫirbet or Ḫirbat)
Kimchi
king, the (similar to the emperor, the pharaoh, etc.)
King (referring to God)
King *x* (Herod, Omri, Solomon, etc.)
king list (generic; but Sumerian King List, etc.)
king of Israel
King of kings
King's Highway
kingdom, the
kingdom of God/heaven
Kirta (not Keret)
koine (common noun)
Koine Greek
Koran. See Qur'an

L

Lachish letters
Lachish Ostracon *x*
Lamb of God, the
Lamentation over the Destruction of *x* (Ur, Sumer and Ur, etc.)
land of Israel
lapidary
last day, the
last days
last judgment, the
Last Supper, the
Late period (Egypt)
Latter Prophets
law (Mosaic, Jewish, of Moses, of Israel)
Law, the (= Pentateuch; capitalize only as a division of the canon)
law book
law code
Laws of Ur-Nammu or Ur-Namma
lectio brevior
lectio difficilior
lectio facilior
Legend of King Kirta
Legend of Sargon
lemma
Leningrad Codex (or Leningradensis)
Letter of Aristeas
Letter to the Galatians (etc.)
Levant, the
Levantine
Level 4 (archaeological reports, level followed by number)
Leviathan
levirate
Levite
Levitical
lex talionis

liberation (theology, perspective, etc.)
light of the world (per NRSV)
limmu lists
lingua franca
Lipit-Eshtar (not Lipit-Ishtar)
literary criticism (noun), literary-critical
lithic
loanword
loc. cit. (use is discouraged)
loculus (pl. loculi)
locus
locus classicus
Locus *x* (archaeological reports, followed by number)
logion (pl. logia)
logogram
longue durée
Lord, the
Lord of Hosts
Lord of lords
Lord's Day
Lord's Prayer
Lord's Supper
lordship
Lower Egypt
lower Galilee
Lukan (not Lucan)
Luke-Acts (hyphen not en dash)
Luke's Gospel (= Gospel of Luke)

M

Maat (DN) or *maʿat* (concept)
Maccabean
macarism
Madeba Map
magi
Magnificat (Song of Mary)
mainland Greece
Major Prophets (division of the canon)
Manichaean
Manual of Discipline (1QS) (see also Community Rule)
Marduk (DN)
Mari (not Māri)
Mari letters, tablets
Mark Antony
Markan (not Marcan)
Mark's Gospel (= Gospel of Mark)
mashal (pl. *meshalim*)
masorah
Masoretes
masoretic (pronunciation, vocalization, etc.)
Masoretic Text
mater lectionis (pl. *matres lectionis*)
materfamilias
Matthean (not Matthaean)
Matthew's Gospel (= Gospel of Matthew)
medieval
Megillah (pl. Megilloth)
Memphite Theology (title of work)
menorah
mercy seat
Merenptah (not Merenptaḥ or Merneptah)
merkabah (not *merkevah* or *merkaba*)
Merodach-baladan (HB) (RN; = Marduk-apla-iddina II)
Mesha Stela (= Moabite Stone)
messiah (in general)
Messiah (in Christian contexts, as reference to Jesus Christ)
messiahship
messianic
messianic age
metheg
Mican
microliths
Middle Ages
Middle Assyrian Laws
Middle Assyrian period
Middle Babylonian period
middle Euphrates
middot (measures; exegetical principles)
midrash (pl. midrashim)
midrashic
midcentury
mid-second century (noun); mid-second-century *x* (adj.)
mighty men

mina
minor judges
Minor Prophets (division of the canon)
minuscule
miracle worker (noun); miracle-worker *x* (adj.)
mise-en-scène
Mishnah (noun), mishnaic (adj.)
Mishnaic Hebrew
Mitanni
Moabite Stone (= Mesha Stela)
modus operandi
monarchic period
monarchy, united/divided
monde
moon god (noun; general references)
moon-god (adj.) (moon-god worship, etc.)
Moon God of *x* (as title: Moon God of Harran, etc.)
Mosaic covenant
Mosaic law
Mot (DN)
Mount of Olives
Mount of Transfiguration
Mount Sinai
mud-brick (noun and adj.)
Muhammad (not Mohammed)
multiauthor
multivolume
Murabbaʿat, Wadi
Murashu archive
Muratorian Canon/Fragment
Mursili (not Mursilis)
Muslim (not Moslem)
mutatis mutandis
Mycenaean
myth and ritual school
mythopoeic

N

N stem
Nabatean
Nag Hammadi codices
Nahal *x* (not Naḥal)
Nahal Hever (not Nahal Ḥever)
name of God
Naram-Sin (not Naram-sin, Naramsin, or Narām-Sîn)
Narmer (RN), Narmer Palette
nation-state
nativity, the
nawamis (tomb type)
Nazirite
Near East
Nebiim. See Nevi'im
Nebuchadnezzar (not Nebuchadrezzar unless quoting HB)
Neco (not Necho)
Neferti, Prophecy of
Negev (not Negeb)
Neo-Assyrian period (but Neo-Assyrian Empire)
Neo-Babylonian period (but Neo-Babylonian Empire)
Neofiti
Neo-Hittite
neo-orthodoxy
Neoplatonic
Neoplatonism
Nergal (DN)
Nevi'im or Neviim (division of the canon) (not Nebiim)
new age
new covenant
new heaven and new earth
new Jerusalem
new moon (general use and festival)
New Testament (noun and adj.)
New World (as opposed to Old World)
New Year festival
Nicaea, Council of
Nicene Creed
Nile Delta
Nineveh
Ninevites
Noachian (covenant, flood, etc.) (not Noahide, Noachide, or Noachic)
nomina sacra (sg. *nomen sacrum*)

noncanonical
non-Christian (but unchristian)
nonidolatrous
nonnative
non-Pauline
north Arabia
North Galatian hypothesis
northern Israel
Northern Kingdom, the (as substitute for Israel)
Northwest Semitic
notariqon (not notarikon)
Nunc Dimittis, the
Nuzi texts (not Nuzu)

O

Official Aramaic
Old Assyrian period
Old Babylonian period
old covenant
Old Latin
Old South Arabic
Old Syriac
Old Testament (noun and adj.)
Old World (as opposed to New World)
Omride dynasty
Omrides
only begotten of the Father
only begotten Son
Onkelos (not Onqelos)
oral law (generic)
Oral Torah (proper noun)
oral tradition
Orient
oriental
orientalist
original sin
Orthodox (Judaism; Eastern Orthodox)
orthodoxy
orthostat
Osiris (not Usiris)
ostracon (pl. ostraca)
Our Father, the
Oxyrhynchus papyri (but P.Oxy. 250)

P

pace
pagan
palace complex
Paleo-Canaanite
paleography
palimpsest
papponymy
papyrus (pl. papyri)
parable of *x* (the good Samaritan, the wicked tenants, etc.)
paradise
paraenesis (noun), paraenetical (adj.)
parallelismus membrorum
parashah
parousia
paschal
passim
passion, the
passion narrative
Passover (noun and adj.)
Passover Seder
Pastoral Epistles
Pater Noster, the
paterfamilias
patriarchal narratives
patriarchal period/age
patriarchs, the
patristic, patristics
Pauline Epistles (or Letters)
Pentateuch
pentateuchal
Pentecost
Pentecostal (noun and adj.)
penult or penultima (noun)
penultimate (adj.)
people of Israel
per se
percent (spelled out in text; % in parentheses)
pericope (pl. pericopes)
period (Roman, Chalcolithic, First Intermediate, etc.)
period of the judges

Persian Empire
person of Christ
personal name
persons of the Trinity (but Third Person of the Trinity, as a title)
Pesach
pesher (pl. pesharim)
Peshitta (not Peshiṭṭa)
Petrine
petuhah
Phaistos Disk (not Phaestos)
pharoah, the (similar to the king, the emperor, etc.)
Pharaoh *x* (Pharoah Ramesses, Pharaoh Tutankhamun, etc.)
Pharisaic
Pharisees
pièce de résistance
pilgrim festivals
pithos (pl. pithoi)
Piye (not Piankhy or Piankhi)
place name
plain (as in Esdraelon plain)
Pleistocene
plene writing
polis
poetic(al) books (of the Hebrew Bible)
pope, the
Pope John XXIII
post hoc
postapostolic
postbiblical
postcolonial
postcritical
postdiluvian
postexilic
postmodern
post-Nicene
postresurrection
potsherd (not potshard)
pre-Christian
prediluvian
preexilic
premillennial(ism)
premonarchic
priesthood, the
priesthood of Christ
priestly (generic, not P below; priestly writings, theology, etc.)
Priestly (= P; source, redaction, code, document)
Prison Epistles
promised land
promonarchic
prooftext (noun and verb) (not proof text or proof-text)
Prophecy of Neferti
prophet (the prophet Jeremiah, Jeremiah the prophet, etc.)
prophetic(al) books (of the Bible)
prophets
Prophets (division of the canon)
Prophets, Former
Prophets, Latter
Protestant(ism)
Proto-Semitic
Proto-Sinaitic
Proto-Urban period
psalm, a
Psalm 23, the Twenty-Third Psalm
psalms of ascent (genre)
Psalms of Ascent (section of the book of Psalms = Pss 120–134)
psalms, royal
psalmist, the
psalter, a (volume containing a collection of psalms)
Psalter, the (= book of Psalms)
pseudepigrapha (in general)
Pseudepigrapha, the
pseudepigraphic (adj.)
Pyramid Texts

Q

qere
qinah
Qoheleth (not Qohelet)
Queen of Heaven (DN)

queen of Sheba
queen of the South
queer reading, theory, studies
quiescent letter
Qumran
Qumranic
Qur'an (not Koran)
qur'anic (not koranic)

R

rabbi(s)
Rabbi *x* (Rabbi Akiva, Rabbi Judah the Prince, etc.)
rabbinic (writings, school, thought, etc.)
raison d'être
Rameses (place)
Ramesses (person)
Ramesside
Re (not Ra)
reader-response criticism (noun)
Received Text
reception history (noun), reception-historical (adj.)
re-create, re-creation (= to create again)
redaction criticism (noun), redaction-critical (adj.)
reedit
Reformation, the
Reformers
reign of God, reign of heaven
requiescat in pace
reread
resurrection, the
return, the
risen Lord
Roman Empire
Roman Senate
root form
Rosh Hashanah
royal psalms
Rule of the Community. See Community Rule; Manual of Discipline

S

Sabbath, the (noun and adj.)
Sabbatical cycle
Sabbatical Year
Sadducees
salvation history
Samaritan (people, traditions, Pentateuch, Chronicle[s])
Sanhedrin, the
sans
Satan
satanic
satrap
satrapy (satrapy of Egypt, Abar Nahara satrapy, etc.)
Savior, the (referring to Jesus)
scarab
scholium (pl. scholia)
school, Tübingen (or Copenhagen or the like)
school of Hillel
school of Shammai
scribal
scribe
scriptio continua
scriptural
Scripture, Scriptures (when referring to the Bible as a canonical text)
Sea Peoples
Sealand (not Sea-Land)
Second Cataract (Nile)
Second Council of Nicea
second coming
Second Evangelist
Second Gospel (= Mark)
Second Isaiah
second missionary journey
Second Temple (period, literature, etc.)
Sed festival
Sefire Stela (not Sfire)
segolate
Seleucids
seminomadic
Semitic

Semitism(s)
sensus plenior
Septuagint
Sermon on the Mount (Matthew)
Sermon on the Plain (Luke)
servant of the Lord
servant passages
Servant Songs (in Second Isaiah)
settlement period
setumah
Shahar (not Shaḥar or Šaḥar)
Shalim (not Šalim)
Shalmaneser
shalom (but transliterated *šālôm*)
Shamash (not Šamaš)
sheikh
Shema, the
Shemoneh Esreh (= Amidah)
Sheol
shofar (pl. shofroth)
sic
siddur
Siloam Inscription
Siloam Pool (but pool of Siloam)
Sîn (moon god)
sin offering
Sinuhe
Sitz im Buch
Sitz im Leben (not *Sitz-im-Leben*)
social science(s)
social-scientific criticism
sociocultural
socioeconomic
sociohistorical
sociorhetorical
Son, the (referring to Jesus)
Son of God
son of man; except Son of Man as christological title
Song of Deborah
Song of Moses
Song of the Sea
sopherim
source criticism (noun), source-critical (adj.)
Southern Kingdom, the (as substitute for Judah)
South Galatian hypothesis
Spirit, the (as shorthand for Holy Spirit)
spirit of God
Spring, Gihon
stadium (pl. stadia)
status quaestionis
stela (pl. stelae)
stele. See stela
stich
Stoic(ism)
store cities
storm god (noun; general references)
storm-god (adj.) (storm-god worship, etc.)
Storm God, the (reference to supreme deity)
Storm God of *x* (as title: Storm God of Thunder, Storm God of Aleppo, etc.)
Stratum *x* (archaeological reports; stratum followed by number)
subheading
Succession Narrative (= 2 Sam 9–20; 1 Kgs 1–2)
suffering servant (in Isa 53)
Sumerian Law Code
sun god (noun; general references)
sun-god (adj.) (sun-god worship, etc.)
Sun God, the (reference to supreme deity)
Sun God of *x* (as title: Sun God of Heaven, Sun God of Hatti, etc.)
Sun Goddess of *x* (as title: Sun Goddess of Arinna, Sun Goddess of the Earth, etc.)
supersede (verb), supersession (noun), supersessionism (noun)
Suppiluliuma (not Shuppiluliuma or Šuppiluliuma)
supra
s.v. (*sub verbo, sub voce*)
syllabary
synagogue
synoptic (adj.) (a synoptic view, etc.)
Synoptic Gospels, the

Synoptic problem, the
Synoptics, the
Syria-Palestine (noun)
Syro-Palestinian (adj.)

T

tabernacle
tabula rasa
Table of Nations (= Gen 10)
Talmud
talmudic
Tanak
Tanakh (JPS edition)
Tannaim (noun)
Tannaitic (adj.)
targum, a (pl. targumim)
Targum Onkelos (etc.)
targumic (adj.)
targumist
Teacher of Righteousness (as title)
Telipinu Myth (not Telepinu)
tel (Hebrew)
tell (Arabic)
telos
temple, the
Temple, First
Temple, Herod's
Temple, Second
Temple, Solomon's
Temple Mount
Ten Commandments
Tendenz
terra-cotta (noun and adj.)
terminus ante quem
terminus post quem
Testaments, both
testimonium (pl. *testimonia*)
Tetragram or Tetragrammaton
Tetrateuch
textual criticism (noun), textual-critical or text-critical (adj.)
Textus Receptus
theophoric
Third Dynasty of Ur (or Ur III period)
Third Evangelist
Third Gospel (= Luke)
third missionary journey
Thomas's Gospel (= Gospel of Thomas)
threshing floor
throne name
Thummim
Thutmose (not Thutmosis, Tuthmose, Thothmes, or Tuthmosis)
Tiglath-pileser (RN; = Tukulti-apil-esharra) (not Tiglath-Pileser or Tiglathpileser)
titulary
Tjekker (not Tjeker)
topos (pl. topoi)
torah (general term for instruction) (but transliterated *tôrâ*)
Torah (division of the canon)
Tosefta (not Tosephta or Tosepta)
tour de force
Trans-Euphrates
transfiguration, the
transhistorical
Transjordan (noun) Transjordanian (adj.)
treaty form
Trinitarian (adj.; e.g., Trinitarian controversies)
Trinity (when referring to God)
Tudhaliya (not Tudḫaliya)
Tukulti-Ninurta Epic
Tutankhamun (not Tutankhamen or Tutankhamon)
tutelary deity (general references, e.g., tutelary deity of the city)
Tutelary Deity of *x* (as title: Tutelary Deity of Karahna, Tutelary Deity of the Countryside, etc.)
Twelve, the
twelve apostles
twelve tribes
twelve-tribe league
Twenty-First Psalm (etc.)

U

Übermensch
Ugarit (Ras Shamra)
Ugaritic
Ullikummi, Song of (not Ullikummis)
unchristian
uncial
underrepresented
underworld (noun and adj.)
united kingdom
united monarchy
Upper Egypt
upper Galilee
upper Mesopotamia
Ur III period (or Third Dynasty of Ur)
Urhi-Teshub (=Mursili III)
Ur-Nammu or Ur-Namma, Laws of
Urim
Ur-text
utopia

V

vassal treaties
vaticinium ex eventu
verb form
versions (Greek versions, Coptic versions, etc.)
vice versa
vice-regent
Virgin, the (Mary)
virgin birth, the
vis-à-vis
Vorlage (pl. *Vorlagen*)
Vulgate

W

wadi (pl. wadis) (general reference)
Wadi *x* (not Wādī)
Wailing Wall
War Scroll (1QM)
Way, the (in Acts)
Way of the Sea
weltanschauung
Wenamun (not Wenamon)
West Bank
West Semitic
Western church
Western text
Western Wall
whole burnt offering
whole offering
Wicked Priest (as title)
wilderness (wanderings, generation, etc.)
Wilderness of Zin
Winkelhaken
wisdom (literature, movement, quality, tradition)
Wisdom (personified)
wise men
Wissenschaft
womanist (noun and adj.)
wonderworker
Word, the (= Jesus)
word of God
wordplay
worldview
worship, worshiper, worshiping
Writings (division of the canon)
Written Torah

Y

Yahweh or YHWH (not Jahweh)
Yahwist (not Jahwist) source
Yam (DN) (not Yamm)
Yamhad (not Jamḫad, Jamhad, or Yamkhad)
Yarim-Lim (not Yarimlim)
Yavneh (not Jamnia)
Year of Jubilee
Yom Kippur (Day of Atonement)

Z

Zadokite Fragments. See Damascus Document
Zealots (first-century group)
ziggurat
Zimri-Lim
Ziusudra Myth
Zoroastrian(ism)

4.3.7 Dates

See §8.1.2 for treatment of eras.

4.3.7.1 Format

Dates are preferably presented in the day-month-year format, which now enjoys widest international acceptance and avoids interrupting punctuation. Because of the confusion that is introduced when dates are abbreviated by digits alone (does 3/12 refer to March 12 or 3 December?), such abbreviation is best avoided.

15 August 1979 (or, if the month-day-year system is used, August 15, 1979)
August 1979
August 20 CE (August AD 20)
August 20 BCE (August 20 BC)

4.3.7.2 Ancient Near Eastern Dates and Periods

For dates of ancient Near Eastern periods and rulers, consult the appropriate chapter in ed. Jack M. Sasson, ed., *Civilizations of the Ancient Near East*, 4 vols. (New York: Scribner's Sons, 1995; repr., 4 vols. in 2; Peabody, MA: Hendrickson, 2000), volume 2, part 5 ("History and Culture"). More detailed information may be found in the chronological tables included throughout Amélie Kuhrt, *The Ancient Near East c. 3000–330 BC*, 2 vols. (London: Routledge, 1995). Unless dates for rulers and dynasties are themselves the subject of discussion, it is convenient to use the Middle Chronology for citing dates for Egypt, Mesopotamia, and Anatolia, especially those before the first millennium BCE. Whichever chronology (High, Middle, or Low) is being used, the author should state it explicitly. All dates should be given in full: thus, 587–539 BCE. For Egypt, capitalize Dynasty but lowercase period: thus, Eighteenth Dynasty, Early Dynastic period, Middle Kingdom period, First Intermediate period, Late period, classical period, Hellenistic period; for Mesopotamia, use Akkadian period, Old Babylonian period, Ur III Dynasty, and so forth.

Ancient Near Eastern Periods

	Middle Chronology
Paleolithic	25,000–10,000 BCE
Mesolithic	10,000–8000 BCE
Neolithic	8000–3800 BCE
Prepottery Neolithic	
Pottery Neolithic	
Chalcolithic	3800–3400 BCE
Early Chalcolithic	
Late Chalcolithic	
Early Bronze Age (I–IV)	3400–2000 BCE
Middle Bronze Age (I–III)	2000–1550/1500 BCE

Late Bronze Age (I–II)	1550/1500–1200 BCE
Iron Age (I–III)	1200–539/500 BCE
Persian period	539/500–323 BCE
Hellenistic period	323–37 BCE
Roman period	37 BCE–324 CE
Byzantine period	324–1453 CE

4.3.7.3 Islamic Dates

It is preferable to indicate significant dates in premodern Islamic history (especially death dates) according to both the Hijri and the Gregorian calendars. The Hijri calendar began on Safar 26 (13 June 622) with Muhammad's departure from Mecca; as such, all events relevant to Islamic history after this point should be marked as 1/622, 2/623, and so on. In instances when the precise date in either calendar is known, authors are encouraged to convert dates accurately (easily done through any number of conversion programs or websites). In many instances, however, if only the year is known in one calendar, the range of possibility in the other should be acknowledged, for example, if an author is known to have died in 900 AH (*anno Hegirae*), this corresponds to 1494–1495 CE (Common Era).

Generally for dates after 1900, the year is given only according to the Western calendar and not the Hijri calendar.

5 TRANSLITERATING AND TRANSCRIBING ANCIENT TEXTS

The choice of how to present an ancient language in a given work will depend on the nature and purpose of the work. For example, a work that seeks to facilitate reading for a general readership may use a general-purpose transliteration style, while a work that includes comparisons of word formation in several Semitic languages will require a more precise transliteration style.

This section provides instructions for cases in which transliterations of ancient texts are to be used. Although some use "transliteration" to refer to both kinds of representation distinguished below, precisely understood transliteration is the conversion of a text from one script into another. It is not concerned with representing the phonology (pronunciation) of the original. Rather, it seeks to represent the characters accurately by presenting the most appropriate values of the individual signs. In contrast, transcription seeks to transcribe the phonology of a language.

The project editor will decide in consultation with the author whether Hebrew, Greek, and other ancient languages will be represented in their own alphabets or transliterated into the Latin alphabet. In general, there is rarely any reason to transliterate Greek in works intended for scholarly readers; for Semitic languages, transliteration may be preferable when it facilitates comparison of cognate forms.

In general, a work should be consistent in its use of transliteration over non-Latin characters and vice versa. If both transliteration and non-Latin characters are used in a single work, the rationale for doing so should be logical and easy to grasp. The project editor is responsible for ensuring that collected works conform to a single style.

5.1 Hebrew

The author should select a Hebrew transliteration convention that reflects the level of precision appropriate to the argumentation and the intended audience. An author may adopt one of two systems: (1) a fully reversible academic style that allows the reader to reproduce the Hebrew characters exactly (consonants and vowels); or (2) an essentially phonetic general-purpose style.[1]

5.1.1 Academic Style

5.1.1.1 Consonants

Character		Transliteration	Character		Transliteration
א	*aleph*	ʾ	מ ם	*mem*	*m*
ב	*bet*	*b*	נ ן	*nun*	*n*
ג	*gimel*	*g*	ס	*samek*	*s*
ד	*dalet*	*d*	ע	*ayin*	ʿ
ה	*he*	*h*	פ ף	*pe*	*p*
ו	*vav*	*w*	צ ץ	*tsade*	*ṣ*
ז	*zayin*	*z*	ק	*qoph*	*q*
ח	*khet*	*ḥ*	ר	*resh*	*r*
ט	*tet*	*ṭ*	שׂ	*sin*	*ś*
י	*yod*	*y*	שׁ	*shin*	*š*
כ ך	*kaph*	*k*	ת	*tav*	*t*
ל	*lamed*	*l*			

1. See further Werner Weinberg, "Transliteration and Transcription of Hebrew," *HUCA* 40–41 (1969–1970): 1–32; and idem, "On Hebrew Transliteration," *Bib* 56 (1975): 150–52. For the sake of simplicity and consistency between §5.1.1 and §5.1.2, this edition of the handbook recommends and uses general-purpose spellings for the names of Hebrew consonants, vowels, and *binyanim*.

5.1.1.2 Vowels

Character		Transliteration	Character		Transliteration
◌ַ	*patakh*	*a*	◌ִי	*hireq yod*	*î*
◌ַ	furtive *patakh*	*a*	◌ָ	*qamets khatuf*	*o*
◌ָ	*qamets*	*ā*	◌ֹ	*holem*	*ō*
◌ָה	final *qamets he*	*â*	וֹ	full *holem*	*ô*
◌ָיו	3ms suffix	*āyw*	◌ֻ	short *qibbuts*	*u*
◌ֶ	*segol*	*e*	◌ֻ	long *qibbuts*	*ū*
◌ֵ	*tsere*	*ē*	וּ	*shureq*	*û*
◌ֵי	*tsere yod*	*ê*	◌ֳ	*khatef qamets*	*ŏ*
◌ֶי	*segol yod*	*ê*	◌ֲ	*khatef patakh*	*ă*
◌ִ	short *hireq*	*i*	◌ֱ	*khatef segol*	*ĕ*
◌ִ	long *hireq*	*ī*	◌ְ	vocal *shewa*	*ə*

5.1.1.3 Stems (*Binyanim*)

Basic Hebrew Stems

qal G	*niphal* N	*piel* D	*pual* Dp
hiphil H	*hophal* Hp	*hithpael* HtD	

Basic Aramaic Stems

peal	*pael*	*peil*	*pual*
haphel	*huphal*	*hithpeel*	*hithpaal*
saphel			

Other Hebrew and Aramaic Stems

aphel	*ethpaal*	*ethpeel*	*histaphal*
hithpalel	*hithpalpel*	*hithpolel*	*istaphal*
ithpaal	*ithpeel*	*nithpael*	*pilpel*
polel	*yiphil*		

5.1.1.4 Notes

(1) The consonants *he*, *vav*, and *yod*, used to indicate long vowels (*matres lectionis*), are transliterated as a circumflex over the vowel: *â*, *ê*, *î*, *ô*, *û*; they are also taken into account when a transliteration reproduces an unpointed text (extrabiblical inscriptions, Qumran texts, *ketiv*, etc.) and for the purposes of alphabetization. With a final *he*, distinguish between the feminine singular possessive ending (*malkāh*, "her king") and the feminine ending *-â* (*malkâ*, "queen"): the הָּ (*hê* with a *mappîq*) should be written as *-āh*.

(2) Always transliterate quiescent *aleph* using ʾ: e.g., *lōʾ*, "not"; *hûʾ*, "he"; *rōʾš*, "head"; Aramaic *malkāʾ*, "the king."

(3) Transliterate short vowels that are written fully as *i*(*w*), *o*(*w*), *u*(*w*): e.g., *hu*(*w*)*kkâ* for הוּכָּה.

(4) Do not indicate *begadkepat* spirantization (absence of *dagesh forte*) unless it is important to the discussion. Exceptions may be shown by underlining the consonant: e.g., יָקְתְאֵל = *yoqṯĕʾēl* (see GKC §21).
(5) Indicate *dagesh forte* by doubling the consonant. A euphonic *dagesh* should not be doubled: e.g., מַה־שְּׁמוֹ = *mah-šĕmô* (see GKC §20).
(6) A silent *shewa* is not transliterated, including when it is the second of two *shewas* at the end of a word: e.g., *ʾatt* for אַתְּ; *yādalt* for יָדַלְתְּ.
(7) Do not mark stress unless it is relevant to a particular point. If stress is relevant, use an acute mark for the primary accent and a grave mark for secondary accent.
(8) Do not capitalize transliterated proper names, although every transliteration should be capitalized at the beginning of a sentence.
(9) Use a hyphen to indicate a *maqqep*.

5.1.2 General-Purpose Style

5.1.2.1 Consonants

Character		Transliteration	Character		Transliteration
א	*aleph*	ʾ or omit	מ ם	*mem*	*m*
ב	*bet*	*b, v*	נ ן	*nun*	*n*
ג	*gimel*	*g, gh*	ס	*samek*	*s*
ד	*dalet*	*d, dh*	ע	*ayin*	ʿ or omit
ה	*he*	*h*	פ ף	*pe*	*p, ph* or *f*
ו	*vav*	*v* or *w*	צ ץ	*tsade*	*ts*
ז	*zayin*	*z*	ק	*qoph*	*q*
ח	*khet*	*kh* or *h*	ר	*resh*	*r*
ט	*tet*	*t*	שׂ	*sin*	*s*
י	*yod*	*y*	שׁ	*shin*	*sh*
כ ך	*kaph*	*k, kh*	ת	*tav*	*t, th*
ל	*lamed*	*l*			

5.1.2.2 Vowels

Character		Transliteration	Character		Transliteration
ַ	*patakh*	*a*	ִי	*hireq yod*	*i*
ַ	furtive *patakh*	*a*	ָ	*qamets khatuf*	*o*
ָ	*qamets*	*a*	ֹ	*holem*	*o*
ָה	final *qamets he*	*ah*	וֹ	full *holem*	*o*
ָיו	3ms suffix	*ayw*	ֻ	short *qibbuts*	*u*
ֶ	*segol*	*e*	ֻ	long *qibbuts*	*u*
ֵ	*tsere*	*e*	וּ	*shureq*	*u*
ֵי	*tsere yod*	*e*	ֳ	*khatef qamets*	*o*
ֶי	*segol yod*	*e*	ֲ	*khatef patakh*	*a*
ִ	short *hireq*	*i*	ֱ	*khatef segol*	*e*
ִ	long *hireq*	*i*	ְ	vocal *shewa*	*e*

5.1.2.3 Notes

(1) For the names of the *binyanim* in the general-purpose style, see §5.1.1.3.
(2) When spelling Hebrew terms that begin with the definite article (*ha*), capitalize only the first letter of the word, and do not double the following consonant; thus, Birkat Hatorah (*not* Birkat HaTorah or Birkat haTorah or Birkat Hattorah).
(3) Spirant forms (*dagesh lene*) are optional, based upon convention and appearance. (In modern Hebrew, the presence or absence of the *dagesh lene* generally affects the pronunciation of only *bet*, *kaf*, and *pe* of the *begadkepat* letters.) The main guideline is that any given decision should remain consistent throughout a manuscript.
(4) Doubled forms (*dagesh forte*) should be doubled in transliteration (e.g., *hinneh*). The two exceptions to this doubling rule are צּ (*ts*) and שּׁ (*sh*); these two consonants should not be doubled (e.g., מַשָּׂא = *masha'*).

5.2 Aramaic

The systems described above for Hebrew are to be followed, even though *tsere* and *holem* are frequently not markers of long vowels in Aramaic.

5.3 Greek

Whereas for Hebrew both academic and general-purpose transliteration styles are provided, for Greek only a general-purpose style is provided; for academic readers, Greek should be given in Greek characters. (In books meant for a broad audience, editors may elect to use a Greek font only in notes and parentheses, transliterating Greek words that are necessary in the main text.) Thus no provision is made for transliteration of *iōta* subscript, diaeresis, digamma, accents, and the like; where these matter, use a Greek font.

5.3.1 Alphabet

Character		Transliteration	Character		Transliteration
Α α	*alpha*	*a*	Ν ν	*nu*	*n*
Β β	*bēta*	*b*	Ξ ξ	*xi*	*x*
Γ γ	*gamma*	*g* or *n*	Ο ο	*omicron*	*o*
Δ δ	*delta*	*d*	Π π	*pi*	*p*
Ε ε	*epsilon*	*e*	Ρ ρ	*rhō*	*r*
Ζ ζ	*zēta*	*z*	Σ σ, ς	*sigma*	*s*
Η η	*ēta*	*ē*	Τ τ	*tau*	*t*
Θ θ	*thēta*	*th*	Υ υ	*upsilon*	*u* or *y*
Ι ι	*iōta*	*i*	Φ φ	*phi*	*ph*
Κ κ	*kappa*	*k*	Χ χ	*chi*	*ch*
Λ λ	*lambda*	*l*	Ψ ψ	*psi*	*ps*
Μ μ	*mu*	*m*	Ω ω	*ōmega*	*ō*

5.3.2 Notes

(1) When a *gamma* appears before a γ, κ, ξ, or χ (*gamma* nasal), it is transliterated *n*.
(2) The vowels *ēta* and *ōmega* should be indicated with a macron.
(3) Initial ῥ is transliterated *rh*. The second *rhō* in medial double *rhō* is also transliterated *rh*: e.g., Πύρρος = *Pyrrhos*.
(4) When *upsilon* is part of a diphthong, it is transliterated *u* (*au, eu, ēu, ou, ui*). When it appears independently, it is transliterated *y*: e.g., κύριος = *kyrios*, not *kurios*.
(5) The rough breathing mark (ʽ) is transliterated *h* preceding an initial vowel or diphthong: e.g., ὕμνος = *hymnos*; αἵρεσις = *hairesis*.

5.4 Coptic

The transliteration of Coptic should follow Bentley Layton, *A Coptic Grammar: With Chrestomathy and Glossary: Sahidic Dialect*, 3rd ed. (Wiesbaden: Harrassowitz, 2011).

Character		Transliteration	Character		Transliteration
ⲁ	*alpha*	*a*	ⲡ	*pi*	*p*
ⲃ	*bēta*	*b*	ⲣ	*rhō*	*r*
ⲅ	*gamma*	*g*	ⲥ	*sigma*	*s*
ⲇ	*delta*	*d*	ⲧ	*tau*	*t*
ⲉ	*epsilon*	*e*	ⲩ	*upsilon*	*u*
ⲍ	*zēta*	*z*	ⲫ	*phi*	*ph*
ⲏ	*ēta*	*ē*	ⲭ	*khi*	*kh*
ⲑ	*thēta*	*th*	ⲯ	*psi*	*ps*
ⲓ	*iōta*	*i*	ⲱ	*ōmega*	*ō*
ⲕ	*kappa*	*k*	ϣ	*šai*	*š*
ⲗ	*lamda*	*l*	ϥ	*fai*	*f*
ⲙ	*mi*	*m*	ϩ	*hori*	*h*
ⲛ	*ni*	*n*	ϫ	*djandja*	*č*
ⲝ	*ksi*	*ks*	ϭ	*kyima*	*q*
ⲟ	*omicron*	*o*	ϯ	*ti*	*ti*

For the Achmimic and Boharic *ḫay*, use *ḫ*. For the supralinear stroke, use a superscripted italic *e* (e.g., ⲙ̄ⲡϫⲟⲉⲓⲥ, *ᵉmpčoeis*).

5.5 Akkadian

The transliteration of Akkadian should consistently follow either A. Leo Oppenheim et al., eds., *The Assyrian Dictionary of the Oriental Insititue of the University of Chicago*, 26 vols. (Chicago: The Oriental Institute, 1956–2010 [= *CAD*]) or Wolfram von Soden, *Akkadisches Handwörterbuch*, 3 vols. (Wiesbaden: Harrassowitz, 1965–1981 [= *AHw*]), with the following alphabetic representation.

Transliteration: *a, b, d, e, g, ḫ, ṭ, i, y, k, l, m, n, p, q, r, s, ṣ, š, t, ṭ, u, w, z*

Sumerian logograms should be set in small caps and, as opposed to Akkadian words, never in italics. If relying on von Soden's *AHw*, one should avoid the use of *j* when transliterating Akkadian in English articles; *y* should always be used instead. Determinatives should be set as superscript lowercase letters.

Whereas in Akkadian one should use acute and grave accents for the second and third homophonic signs (íl, ìl, ú, ù) and subscript numerical indexes for the fourth and following ones (u_4, u_5, etc.), in transliterating Sumerograms (or actual Sumerian from a Sumerian text) subscript numerical indexes should be used for all homophonic signs; thus, Sumerograms in Akkadian texts: U_2, U_3, U_4, U_5, U_6; Sumerian in Sumerian texts: u_2, u_3, u_4, u_5, u_6.

The rules for the Hebrew general-purpose style (§5.1.2) can be applied when transliterating in a nontechnical format (e.g., *misharum* instead of *mīšarum*).

When writing Assyrian names in English, always use Assur for both the city and the deity (not Ashur or Ashshur), Assurbanipal (not Ashurbanipal), and so on.

5.6 Egyptian

Egyptian transliteration follows either Alan H. Gardiner, *Egyptian Grammar*, 3rd ed. (London: Oxford University Press, 1957), 26–27; or Rainer Hannig, *Grosses Handwörterbuch Ägyptisch-Deutsch (2800–950 v. Chr.): Die Sprache der Pharaonen*, Kulturgeschichte der antiken Welt 64 (Mainz: von Zabern, 1995), xxxvii–xxxviii.

> Transliteration: *ȝ, ỉ* (*j* in Hannig), *y, ʿ, w, b, p, f, m, n, r, h, ḥ, ḫ, ẖ, s* (*z and s* in Hannig), *š, ḳ* (*q* in Hannig), *k, g, t, ṯ, d, ḏ*

In general, the sign *ḳ* should be avoided; use *q* instead.

For current treatment of the Egyptian language, see Antonio Loprieno, *Ancient Egyptian: A Linguistic Introduction* (Cambridge: Cambridge University Press, 1995); and Hannig's *Grosses Handwörterbuch Ägyptisch-Deutsch*, which includes an excellent discussion of various systems of Egyptian transliterations on pages xxxvi–xlii.

5.7 Ugaritic

Ugaritic transliteration generally follows Josef Tropper, *Ugaritische Grammatik*, 2nd ed. (Münster: Ugarit-Verlag, 2012), 11, 28, 90–91.

> Transliteration: *a, i, u, b, g, d, ḏ, h, w, z, ḥ, ḫ, ṭ, ẓ, y, k, l, m, n, s, ś, ʿ, ġ, p, ṣ, q, r, š, t, ṯ*

Note that *a*, *i*, and *u* do not indicate simple vowels but the variously vocalized glottal stop ʾ. Other conventions use the character *ǵ* for the voiced velar *ġ*, but the latter is preferable in the light of the standards employed for other Semitic languages.

5.8 Other Ancient Languages

5.8.1 Sumerian

There are currently several competing systems for transliterating Sumerian. For reasons of clarity and simplicity, one should follow the traditional system as established by Miguel Civil and others, which one can find in the first edition of Rykle Borger, *Mesopotamisches Zeichenlexikon* (Münster: Ugarit-Verlag, 2003): *a, e, i, u, b, d, g, ŋ, ḫ* (or *h*), *k, l, m, n, p, r, s, š, t, w, y, z*. The new readings introduced in the second edition of Borger's *Zeichenlexikon* (2010) are not preferred. When it occurs in running text, Sumerian should not be transliterated in italics but rather in e x p a n d e d f o n t (in MSWord set font spacing to "expanded" by "1 pt"; in InDesign set tracking to 100). As opposed to Akkadian, one should use a simple *h* rather than *ḫ*, and, if ever used, the nasal velar can be written *ŋ*. For the use of subscript numerical indexes, see §5.5.

5.8.2 Hittite

Hittite should be transliterated in italics. SBL Press recommends using a simple *h* rather than *ḫ*. However, if the author has a preference with regard to *s* versus *š* and *h* versus *ḫ* and has been consistent, that preference should be allowed to stand.

Transliteration: *a, e, i, h* (or *ḫ*), *g/k, l, m, n, o, b/p, r, s* (or *š*), *d/t, u, z*

For Sumerograms and Akkadograms in Hittite texts, use the current Hittitological standards, as in Harry A. Hoffner Jr. and H. Craig Melchert, *A Grammar of the Hittite Language* (Winona Lake, IN: Eisenbrauns, 2008), §§1.13–14.

When writing Hittite names in English, write Hattusa (not Hattusha, Hattushash, or Hattusas), Mursili (not Murshilish or Murshili), and so on; do not use *sh*, and drop the nominative case ending *-š*.

5.8.3 Ammonite, Edomite, and Moabite

Transcriptions of Ammonite, Edomite, and Moabite most often present consonants only in an unvocalized text. One should use the same transcription scheme as for academic Hebrew (§5.1.1.1), except that only *š* (not *ś*) is used in these languages.

5.8.4 Phoenician

For Phoenician, see Charles R. Krahmalkov, *A Phoenician-Punic Grammar*, HOS 1/54 (Leiden: Brill, 2001).

5.8.5 Old Persian and Other Ancient Iranian Languages

For Old Persian and ancient Iranian in general, follow Rüdiger Schmitt, in *Compendium linguarum iranicarum*, ed. Rüdiger Schmitt (Wiesbaden: Reichert, 1989), 62–65, 87–90.

5.8.6 Syriac and Mandaic

Depending on the nature of the text, Syriac and Mandaic may be transliterated either by rendering only the consonants or offering fully vocalized words. For transliteration of Syriac, see George A. Kiraz, *Tūrrāṣ Mamllā: A Grammar of the Syriac Language, 1: Orthography* (Piscataway, NJ: Gorgias, 2012), 31–90. For transliteration of Mandaic, one should follow Rudolf Macuch, *Handbook of Classical and Modern Mandaic* (Berlin: de Gruyter, 1965), 9–26.

5.8.6.1 Syriac Alphabet

Character		Transliteration	Character		Transliteration
ܐ	*ālap*	ʾ	ܠ	*lāmad*	*l*
ܒ	*bēth*	*b*	ܡ	*mīm*	*m*
ܓ	*gāmal*	*g*	ܢ	*nūn*	*n*
ܕ	*dālat*	*d*	ܣ	*semkat*	*s*
ܗ	*hē*	*h*	ܥ	*ʿē*	ʿ
ܘ	*waw*	*w*	ܦ	*pē*	*p*
ܙ	*zayn*	*z*	ܨ	*ṣādē*	*ṣ*
ܚ	*ḥēt*	*ḥ*	ܩ	*qop*	*q*
ܛ	*ṭēt*	*ṭ*	ܪ	*rīš*	*r*
ܝ	*yūd*	*y*	ܫ	*šīn*	*š*
ܟ	*kāp*	*k*	ܬ	*taw*	*t*

5.8.6.2 Mandaic Alphabet, or *Abāgāda*

Form	-ā	-ī	-ū	ă-	Transliteration Latin	Transliteration Hebrew
o (*halqa*)						
ࡀ	ࡀࡀ	ࡀࡉ	ࡀࡅ	ࡀ	*a*	א
ࡁ	ࡁࡀ	ࡁࡉ	ࡁࡅ	ࡁ	*b*	ב
ࡂ	ࡂࡀ	ࡂࡉ	ࡂࡅ	ࡂ	*g*	ג
ࡃ	ࡃࡀ	ࡃࡉ	ࡃࡅ	ࡃ	*d*	ד
ࡄ	ࡄࡀ	ࡄࡉ	ࡄࡅ	ࡄ	*h*	ה
ࡅ	ࡅࡀ	ࡅࡉ	ࡅࡅ	ࡅ	*w, u*	ו
ࡆ					*z*	ז
ࡇ	ࡇࡀ	ࡇࡉ	ࡇࡅ	ࡇ	*ḥ*	ח
ࡈ	ࡈࡀ	ࡈࡉ	ࡈࡅ	ࡈ	*ṭ*	ט
ࡉ	ࡉࡀ	ࡉࡉ	ࡉࡅ	ࡉ	*y, i*	י
ࡊ	ࡊࡀ	ࡊࡉ	ࡊࡅ	ࡊ	*k*	כ
ࡋ	ࡋࡀ	ࡋࡉ	ࡋࡅ	ࡋ	*l*	ל
ࡌ	ࡌࡀ	ࡌࡉ	ࡌࡅ	ࡌ	*m*	מ
ࡍ	ࡍࡀ	ࡍࡉ	ࡍࡅ	ࡍ	*n*	נ
ࡎ	ࡎࡀ	ࡎࡉ	ࡎࡅ	ࡎ	*s*	ס
ࡏ					ʿ	ע
ࡐ	ࡐࡀ	ࡐࡉ	ࡐࡅ	ࡐ	*p*	פ
ࡑ	ࡑࡀ	ࡑࡉ	ࡑࡅ	ࡑ	*ṣ*	צ
ࡒ	ࡒࡀ	ࡒࡉ	ࡒࡅ	ࡒ	*q*	ק
ࡓ	ࡓࡀ	ࡓࡉ	ࡓࡅ	ࡓ	*r*	ר
ࡔ	ࡔࡀ	ࡔࡉ	ࡔࡅ	ࡔ	*š*	ש
ࡕ	ࡕࡀ	ࡈ	ࡕࡅ	ࡕ	*t*	ת
ࡖ	ࡖࡀ	ࡖࡉ	ࡖࡅ	ࡖ	*ḏ*	ד

5.8.7 Ethiopic

For Ethiopic, consult Thomas O. Lambdin, *Introduction to Classical Ethiopic (Geʿez)* (Missoula, MT: Scholars Press, 1978; repr., HSS 24; Winona Lake, IN: Eisenbrauns, 2006).

Character							Transliteration
a	u	i	a	ē	ə	o	
ሀ	ሁ	ሂ	ሃ	ሄ	ህ	ሆ	*h*
ለ	ሉ	ሊ	ላ	ሌ	ል	ሎ	*l*
ሐ	ሑ	ሒ	ሓ	ሔ	ሕ	ሖ	*ḥ*
መ	ሙ	ሚ	ማ	ሜ	ም	ሞ	*m*
ሠ	ሡ	ሢ	ሣ	ሤ	ሥ	ሦ	*š*
ረ	ሩ	ሪ	ራ	ሬ	ር	ሮ	*r*
ሰ	ሱ	ሲ	ሳ	ሴ	ስ	ሶ	*s*
ቀ	ቁ	ቂ	ቃ	ቄ	ቅ	ቆ	*ḳ*
በ	ቡ	ቢ	ባ	ቤ	ብ	ቦ	*b*
ተ	ቱ	ቲ	ታ	ቴ	ት	ቶ	*t*
ኀ	ኁ	ኂ	ኃ	ኄ	ኅ	ኆ	*ḫ*
ነ	ኑ	ኒ	ና	ኔ	ን	ኖ	*n*
አ	ኡ	ኢ	ኣ	ኤ	እ	ኦ	ʾ
ከ	ኩ	ኪ	ካ	ኬ	ክ	ኮ	*k*
ወ	ዉ	ዊ	ዋ	ዌ	ው	ዎ	*w*
ዐ	ዑ	ዒ	ዓ	ዔ	ዕ	ዖ	ʿ
ዘ	ዙ	ዚ	ዛ	ዜ	ዝ	ዞ	*z*
የ	ዩ	ዪ	ያ	ዬ	ይ	ዮ	*y*
ደ	ዱ	ዲ	ዳ	ዴ	ድ	ዶ	*d*
ገ	ጉ	ጊ	ጋ	ጌ	ግ	ጎ	*g*
ጠ	ጡ	ጢ	ጣ	ጤ	ጥ	ጦ	*ṭ*
ጰ	ጱ	ጲ	ጳ	ጴ	ጵ	ጶ	*p̣*
ጸ	ጹ	ጺ	ጻ	ጼ	ጽ	ጾ	*ṣ*
ፀ	ፁ	ፂ	ፃ	ፄ	ፅ	ፆ	*ḍ*
ፈ	ፉ	ፊ	ፋ	ፌ	ፍ	ፎ	*f*
ፐ	ፑ	ፒ	ፓ	ፔ	ፕ	ፖ	*p*

5.8.8 Arabic

5.8.8.1 Arabic Alphabet

Character		Transliteration	Character		Transliteration
ا	*alif*	*a*	ط	*ṭāʾ*	*ṭ*
ب	*bāʾ*	*b*	ظ	*ẓāʾ*	*ẓ*
ت	*tāʾ*	*t*	ع	*ʿayn*	*ʿ*
ث	*thāʾ*	*th*	غ	*ghayn*	*gh*
ج	*jīm*	*j*	ف	*fāʾ*	*f*
ح	*ḥāʾ*	*ḥ*	ق	*qāf*	*q*
خ	*khāʾ*	*kh*	ك	*kāf*	*k*
د	*dāl*	*d*	ل	*lām*	*l*
ذ	*dhāl*	*dh*	م	*mīm*	*m*
ر	*rāʾ*	*r*	ن	*nūn*	*n*
ز	*zāy*	*z*	ه	*hāʾ*	*h*
س	*sīn*	*s*	و	*wāw*	*w*
ش	*shīn*	*sh*	ي	*yāʾ*	*y*
ص	*ṣād*	*ṣ*	ء	*hamzah**	*ʾ*
ض	*ḍād*	*ḍ*			

* *Hamzah* may be written on its own (ء) or on a letter "chair" (أ / إ / ؤ / ئ)

5.8.8.2 Vowels and Special Characters

ـَ	*fatḥah*	*a*
ـً	*tanwīn fatḥah*	*-an* (indefinite accusative ending)
ـَوْ	diphthong	*aw*
ـَيْ	diphthong	*ay*
ـُ	*ḍammah*	*u*
ـٌ	*tanwīn ḍammah*	*-un* (indefinite nominative ending)
ـِ	*kasrah*	*i*
ـٍ	*tanwīn kasrah*	*-in* (indefinite genitive ending)
ـّ	*shaddah*	geminate marker (doubled consonant)
ـْ	*sukūn*	unvoweled consonant marker
ـَا	*fatḥah alif*	long *a* (*ā*)
ـَى	*fatḥah alif maqṣūrah*	final *alif* (*ā*)
آ	*alif maddah*	long *alif* (*ā*)
ٱ	*hamzat al-waṣl*	elided *a*
ـِي	*kasrah yā*	long *i* (*ī*)
ـُو	*ḍammah wāw*	long *u* (*ū*)
ة / ـة	*tāʾ marbūṭah*	feminine ending

5.8.8.3 Notes

(1) Long vowels should be indicated with a macron (*ā*, *ī*, *ū*), and the so-called emphatic consonants need to be properly noted as well: *ṭ*, *ṣ*, *ḍ*, *ẓ*. Diphthongs may be indicated simply with a double letter (*aw*, *ay*).

(2) Instead of using underlined consonants, one should write *th* (not *ṯ*) for ث and *dh* (not *ḏ*) for ذ, even if the digraphs *th* and *dh* can create some ambiguities.
(3) One must distinguish between *hamzah* and *ʿayn*, but the former should not be indicated in transliteration when it occurs in initial position, thus *alif* rather than *ʾalif*, *amr* rather than *ʾamr*.
(4) Many archaeological sites of relevance to the history of the ancient Near East, the Greco-Roman world, late antiquity, and Islam are commonly known by their modern names in colloquial Arabic. These place names should not be fully transliterated but rather given according to their most recognizable form, such as Qalʿat Sherqat (ancient Assur), Abu Simbel, Bu Njem (ancient Golaia), Deir Simʿan or Qalʿat Simʿan, or Quṣayr ʿAmra. See the list at §4.3.3.4.
(5) The final feminine marker *tāʾ marbūṭah* should be explicitly indicated with a final –*h* and with a final –*t* in the construct state (*iḍāfah*) (e.g., *shīʿat ʿAlī*, Sūrat al-Māʾidah).
(6) Case endings should generally be omitted in transliteration unless they are germane to the discussion. Indicating *tanwīn* is optional. An exception must be made when the noun has a suffix attached, in which instance the case ending must be recognized, such as *fī ṣudūrihim*.
(7) Proper names in transliteration should not be capitalized: "Powers' theories concerning the development of early Muslim attitudes toward inheritance center on the interpretation of a well-known qur'anic verse, 'Muhammad is not the father of any of your men; rather, he is the Messenger of God and the Seal of the Prophets' (*mā kāna muḥammad abā aḥad min rijālikum wa-lakin rasūl allāh wa-khātim al-nabiyyīn*; Q Aḥzāb 33:40)."
(8) In indicating ligatures caused by elision, greater precision is preferable as long as the vocalized text being rendered remains readily recognizable. A short or long vowel eliding with the definite article *al-* should be indicated with an apostrophe, as should other elisions. Assimilation of the definite article to following "sun letters" (*ḥurūf shamsiyyah*) should be ignored in transliteration, for example, *al-nās* and not *an-nās*. Attached conjunctions (*wa-*, *fa-*) should be joined with a simple hyphen, except if elision occurs; attached prepositions should also be joined with a hyphen, unless they are joined to a pronomial suffix, in which case the hyphen is omitted. Note the following examples:

    fa-tūbū ilā bāriʾikum faʿqtulū anfusakum (Q Baqarah 2:54)

    a-lam taʿlam anna allāh lahu mulk al-samawāt waʾl-arḍ (Q Baqarah 2:107)

    tanazzaluʾl-malāʾikah waʾl-rūḥ fīhā bi-ithn rabbihim min kull amr (Q Qadr 97:4)

    wa-min sharr al-nafāthāt fīʾl-ʿuqad (Q Falaq 113:4)

To emphasize rhyme scheme or continuity of thought, multiple verses may be transcribed with a slash indicating the division, as follows:

    fa-ammā man thaqulat mawāzinuhu / fa-huwa fī ʿīshah rāḍiyah (Q Qāriʿah 101:6–7)

    a-lam tara kayf faʿala rabbuka bi-aṣḥāb al-fīl / a-lam tajʿal kaydahum fī taḍlīl (Q Fīl 105:1–2)

5.8.9 Turkish

With Turkish words, preserve *ğ*, *ç*, and *ş*, as well as the distinction between *ı* and *i* (and *I* versus *İ*). When providing Turkish place names in an English context, it is permissible to replace *ğ* with gh, as in Boghazköy.

5.9 Transcribing Ancient Texts

When citing or discussing ancient texts, the following symbols and conventions should be used:

[ ]	in both transliteration and translation, brackets indicate reconstructed text or gaps. [...] indicates a gap of indeterminate length; [x x] indicates a break of approximately x signs
⸢ ⸣	in both transliteration and translation, half brackets indicate characters, signs, or sequences that are only partly readable (damaged but recognizable)
( )	1. in English translations, parentheses are used for additions to improve the sense 2. in transcriptions, parentheses enclose signs restored from a duplicate when placed within square brackets
*	in discussions of grammatical and lexical items, asterisk preceding a term indicates an unattested form
§	section markers used to cite a natural division of a text (e.g., Code of Hammurabi §10) or a published division (e.g., *ARAB* 2 §808)
x or o	illegible sign/trace
< >	in cuneiform transliteration, encloses sign(s) inadvertently omitted by the scribe
« »	errant scribal insertion; enclosed sign(s) to be ignored
* *	encloses signs written over an erasure or over other sign traces
?	reading/restoration of sign uncertain
(?)	reading/restoration of word/phrase uncertain
א̊	in Hebrew, indicates a damaged letter
א̣	in Hebrew, deletion dots written by the scribe
•אאא•	in Hebrew, alternate word
{ }	in Hebrew, letter(s) erased by the scribe and space left on the leather; in English translation, word(s) indicated by scribe as alternative

However symbols are used, authors should provide a list in the front matter.

6 NOTES AND BIBLIOGRAPHIES

Authors are responsible for supplying complete, accurate, and stylistically correct notes and bibliographies (see §§2.1.3.7–8). This includes checking carefully to be certain that all the notes correctly match their reference numbers in the body text and that the body text contains no extra or duplicate reference numbers.

Some publishers, including SBL Press, prefer the traditional documentation style that uses footnotes and bibliographies, but other publishers use endnotes, and for some books author-date citations are appropriate. As the footnote-endnote issue is a production matter, authors normally need not be overconcerned with placement of notes (see §2.1.3.8); more fundamental are decisions about whether to use social-scientific or traditional humanities methods of documentation, and these decisions should be made (and agreed upon with the publisher) before a manuscript is prepared.

With the author-date format, the reference list (or "Works Cited") should include all the works, and only the works, referred to in text notes. For books using the traditional format, the bibliography may cite exactly the same books referred to in notes, or it may cite a subset of these (a "select bibliography"), or it may cite the books mentioned in the notes plus others. Including citations in both notes and bibliography facilitates the work of the reader.

For books and articles using the traditional format, complete publication data should be supplied in the first note referring to a given source. Subsequent notes in the same work referring to the same source should use the abbreviated note form exhibited in the examples in §§6.2–4, including a shortened form of the main title of the work cited. The shortened title should include key words occurring as close to the beginning of the title as possible and with the word order unchanged. Titles of four words or less are not shortened.

Standard abbreviations for journal titles and series (for which see §8.4) should be used in both the notes and the bibliography. A separate list of all abbreviations used should be included in the book (normally at the end of the book's front matter). It is our practice to abbreviate *ed.* and *trans.* in notes and in bibliographies when they do not begin a sentence and to spell out *edited by* and *translated by* when the words appear at the beginning of sentences in a bibliography.

6.1 Rules

6.1.1 Sequence of Information

As a general rule, the sequence of publication information is as follows:

Author(s) or, if there is no author, editor(s)
Title of chapter or journal article
Title of book (including subtitle) or periodical
Editor, compiler, and/or translator
Edition if not the first
Volumes: if citing the whole work, give the total number of volumes; if only a single volume is cited, list that volume number and the title of the volume
Series title and/or volume number
Details of publication: city, publisher, and/or date
Volume and/or page numbers (In bibliographical listings of chapters in a book, this information typically precedes the book title.)
Electronic source information if applicable

Generally, only a select portion of this material is necessary, depending in part on how thorough the bibliography is (the aim is mainly to provide readers sufficient information to allow them quickly to locate the precise volume in a library and secondarily to credit the people whose work has been most directly relied upon; for an illustration, see §6.2.14). Colons precede page numbers in journal articles, and colons separate volume and page numbers in books. Commas separate book titles (with their associated publishing information) from page numbers in book citations.

In a departure from the first edition of this handbook, we now follow *CMS* footnote style, which places the basic "facts of publication" (city, publisher, and date) in parentheses and all "secondary" publication information outside of the parentheses. The style is clear throughout §§6.2–6.4 below.

6.1.2 Author or Editor

6.1.2.1 Modern Authors

Whenever possible, the author's or editor's full first name and middle name or initial (not just a first initial) should be provided. But if an author has made a habit of using initials rather than full given names, there is no need to supply those names. (Thus, even if one consistently lists first names and middle initials, one would cite W. D. Davies, not William D. or William David Davies.) Initials should always be followed by a period, and a (preferably nonbreaking) word space should separate initials. Multiple references to the same author in a bibliography should be conformed to the same style; regardless of how names appear on title pages, authors should not be listed under one name for one work and under a different form of their name for another work. For issues of capitalization, names with particles, and the citing of non-English names, see §7.2 and *CMS* §§8.4–17.

6.1.2.2 Ancient Authors

Ancient works may be listed in bibliographies either under the name of the premodern author or under the name of the modern editor, but all premodern works should be treated the same. If works are listed by premodern author, the standard English spelling of the name should be used regardless of the spelling on the title page of the work being cited: Aristotle (not Aristote or Aristoteles), Sophocles (not Sophokles), Jerome (not Hieronymus), Augustine (not Augustinus or Augustin), and so on. The standard English spellings may be found as headings in library catalogs. Where necessary, fuller forms of names may be used: Eusebius of Caesarea, Cyril of Jerusalem, Athanasius of Alexandria, and so on.

6.1.2.3 Latinized Names

Similarly, when citing premodern Latin works, one should give the author's name in its native form, not in the artificially Latinized form that is likely to appear on the title page (and not in an even more artificial nominative version of the Latin). For example, in citing his *Demonstratio evangelica*, one would list Pierre-Daniel Huet rather than Petri Danielis Huetii (or Petrus Daniel Huetius). One may rely on the Library of Congress website (http://catalog.loc.gov) or WorldCat (http://www.worldcat.org) for standard cataloging information.

6.1.3 Title

6.1.3.1 Punctuation

Typefaces and design features on the title pages of books frequently allow punctuation to be omitted. In citing a book, therefore, punctuation must often be added and may even be altered: except when double punctuation would result (e.g., following a question mark or exclamation point), a colon (not a period, semicolon, comma, or dash) should separate the title and subtitle. This rule may be applied regardless of the punctuation or lack thereof on the title page and regardless of the language of the book. Use a comma before a range of years at the end of a title unless the title page uses parentheses. Use semicolons between titles of separate works published in the same binding. Retain any dashes that are present in the original title.

6.1.3.2 Format of Abbreviations, Foreign Terms, and Included Titles

When abbreviations such as BCE and CE are used in a book title, they should be set in full caps, not small caps, and italicized to agree with the rest of the title. When non-English words are used in an English title, they should ordinarily be italicized to match the rest of the title (see *CMS* §§8.171, 14.103). Titles within titles should be set off by quotation marks (even though they are titles of books) and should be capitalized in the same style as the title that includes them. See *CMS* §§8.163, 8.171, and 14.102.

Ampersands found in original titles should be changed to *and* in notes or bibliographical entries. Likewise, except in the case of foreign language titles, digits that would ordinarily be spelled out in running text should be spelled out in citations (e.g., 2nd Century becomes Second Century).

6.1.3.3 Capitalization of Titles in English

In English titles, all words should be capitalized except articles, coordinating conjunctions, and prepositions (the first and last words in the title or subtitle are, however, capitalized regardless of their part of speech). Even longer prepositions, including not only single words (such as *between* and *among*) but also phrases that are given their own entries and classed as prepositions in *Merriam-Webster's Collegiate Dictionary* (such as *according to, owing to,* and *due to*), are lowercased. Other phrases (such as *based on* or in *spite of*) that might seem analogous but are not given such entries in this dictionary are not treated as prepositions. Always capitalize the first of two or more full words connected by hyphens; capitalize subsequent words unless they are articles, coordinating conjnctions, or prepositions that are not used adverbially. Words following a prefix (as opposed to a full word) are capitalized only if they are proper nouns or proper adjectives. For examples, see *CMS* §8.159.

6.1.3.4 Capitalization of Titles Not in English

For titles in languages other than English, the general rule is to capitalize only the first word of the title or subtitle and any words that would be capitalized in a normal sentence. For most languages, only proper nouns (but not proper adjectives) are capitalized. In German, nouns are capitalized, and in Dutch, proper adjectives are capitalized. For more on titles in particular languages see §§6.1.3.7–9.

6.1.3.5 Series and Multivolume Works

Series titles are set roman; titles of multivolume works are set italic. Some works could be classified either way. SBL Press treats the following as series titles:

> Patrologia Graeca (for *Patrologiae Cursus Completus*. Series Graeca)
> Patrologia Latina (for *Patrologiae Cursus Completus*. Series Latina)
> Patrologia Orientalis
> Sources chrétiennes

SBL Press treats the following as multivolume works:

> *Ante-Nicene Fathers*
> *Aufstieg und Niedergang der römischen Welt*
> *Nicene and Post-Nicene Fathers*, First Series
> *Nicene and Post-Nicene Fathers*, Second Series

6.1.3.6 Primary Sources

In the body of a manuscript, cite primary sources, including biblical texts, parenthetically, inside the final punctuation. Thus,

> In Luke, for example, it is the lawyer who cites the double command, whereas in Matthew and Mark it is Jesus (Matt 22:37–40; Mark 12:29–31).

> All of this occurred "in the ninth year of King Zedekiah of Judah, in the tenth month" (Jer 39:1).

Examples of how to cite some specific texts such as *ANF*, *NPNF*, and LCL texts in parentheses and in notes and bibliographies appear in §6.4.

If indicating the translation is important, insert it following the reference.

> From Luke's point of view, "the kingdom of God is among you" (Luke 17:21 NRSV).

Likewise, if a longer passage is cited as an excerpt, the source should appear within parentheses, but this time outside the final punctuation. In excerpted material, the translator should be included unless an earlier statement has indicated the source of the translation for a given work or corpus. Thus,

> Therefore according to the circumstances and temper and even age of each is the delay of baptism more profitable, yet especially in the case of little children. For where is the need of involving sponsors also in danger? They too through mortality may fail to perform their promises, or may be deceived by the growth of an evil disposition. (Tertullian, *De baptismo* 18 [Gwatkin])

If the translation is referred to consistently, a note at the first instance indicating which edition and translation are used throughout the manuscript is appropriate.

For citing primary sources in notes and bibliographies, see §6.4.1.

6.1.3.7 French Titles

SBL style treats French like other modern languages, capitalizing titles according to the general rule given in §6.1.3.4 and retaining the accents on uppercase vowels.

6.1.3.8 Latin Titles

SBL style follows general convention (as concisely summarized in *CMS* §11.59) by treating premodern and modern Latin titles differently. In short, premodern Latin titles receive sentence-style capitalization, while modern Latin titles receive headline capitalization.

Latin titles of premodern works (in Latin, Greek, or other languages) are capitalized in accord with the general rule given in §6.1.3.4: capitalize only the first word of the title (or subtitle) and any proper nouns (but not proper adjectives) included in the title. In accord with the practice of the Stuttgart edition of the Vulgate, we include as proper nouns not only names of persons and places but also various appellations of God: Deus, Pater, Filius (and so Filioque), Trinitas, and other terms when they are clearly used as alternative names of the deity (Verbum, Creator, etc.).

> *De divinis officiis*
> *De incarnatione*
> *De glorificatione Trinitatis*
> *De Sancta Trinitate et operibus eius*
> *De vita Cuthberti*
> *In Aristotelis analyticorum priorum librum i commentarium*

When one book title occurs within another, the included title is capitalized as if it were standing alone.

When an adjective is so closely associated with a proper noun that the two form in effect a compound noun, both words are capitalized:

Sancta Trinitas, Sanctus Augustinus, Sanctus Spiritus, Beata Virgo Maria

"Modern works" for the purposes of this section includes Renaissance and later treatises and books. It also includes journals, series (including series of modern editions of ancient works), and Latin phrases used as modern designations of corpora of ancient works.

Printed editions of ancient and medieval works often have long Latin titles that are really complete sentences comprising the name of the ancient writer, the title of the work, and the name and contribution of each modern editor involved in the product. Library catalogers usually insert a colon between the main title and further descriptive information and then a slash before the part of the sentence that identifies the modern editor(s). In notes and bibliographies, the title may be truncated at the colon, but if it is not, this added punctuation (and the slash) should not be retained.

In a bibliography, if the works of St. Anselm are listed under the editor's name, then *Sancti Anselmi* would be retained as part of the title. If they are listed under Anselm's name, *Sancti Anselmi* should be deleted from the title.

Thus the title *Sancti Anselmi ex Beccensi abbate Cantuariensis archiepiscopi opera: nec non Eadmeri monachi Cantuariensis Historia novorum, et alia opuscula/labore ac studio d. Gabrielis Gerberon monachi congregationis S. Mauri ad mss. fidem expurgata et aucta* could be listed in either of the following ways:

Gerberon, Gabriel, ed. *Sancti Anselmi ex Beccensi Abbate Cantuariensis archiepiscopi Opera*. Paris, 1675.

Anselm of Canterbury. *Opera*. Edited by Gabriel Gerberon. Paris, 1675.

Latin terms for the Bible (roman if referring to the Bible itself, italic when used as the title for a particular published edition):

Biblia Hebraica, Biblia Vulgata, Novum Testamentum, Vetus Testamentum

Latin journal titles:

Vigiliae Christianae, Vetus Testamentum, Sacris Erudiri

Series titles:

Analecta Gregoriana
Compendia Rerum Iudaicarum ad Novum Testamentum
Corpus Christianorum: Continuatio Mediaevalis
Corpus Scriptorum Ecclesiasticorum Latinorum
Monumenta Germaniae Historica
Patrologia Latina
Patrologia Orientalis

Actual practice in books and in library catalogs varies widely; the rules given here are suggestions meant to help authors and editors who must decide what practice to follow in particular cases. There may be exceptions to the general rules delineated above for Latin titles. For example:

- Just as Latin titles of modern books written in English are capped headline style (Alfred North Whitehead and Bertrand Russell, *Principia Mathematica*), Latin titles of medieval or ancient works, when cited in contexts where most other titles are modern, may be capped headline style (e.g., a citation of Thomas Aquinas, *Summa Theologica*, in a context where the other works referenced are all or nearly all modern or are cited in modern English translations with English titles).
- Latin titles of works with subtitles in another foreign language may be capitalized in accord for the rule for that language (e.g., *Index scriptorum operumque latino-belgicorum medii aevi: Nouveau répertoire des oeuvres médiolatines belges*).

Latin series titles in bibliographic entries for books with titles in modern languages other than English should be capitalized in accord with the usual rules for Latin (e.g., still Monumenta Germaniae Historica when listed as the series for a German-titled book).

6.1.3.9 Titles in Other Languages; Non-Latin Alphabets

Titles of modern works in Hebrew and other languages that use non-Latin alphabets should ordinarily be given in translation only, and the original language should be indicated in parentheses. When for sufficient reason a title is given in the original language, we still recommend adding a translation in square brackets. Capitalize only the first word and proper nouns of translations and (as appropriate) of the original titles. If Hebrew is transliterated, use the general-purpose style given in §5.1.2.

Even titles in languages that use the Latin or modified Latin alphabet should be translated if authors anticipate that most of their readers will be unable to read the original. Whether one merely translates the title and specifies the original language in parentheses or cites the actual title followed by a translation will involve editorial judgment and consideration of the benefits to the target audience. In any case, one should be consistent in treating all titles that fall into this category. See *CMS* §§14.107–108. See §6.2.11 for an example.

6.1.4 Publication Information

6.1.4.1 Names of Presses

The publisher's name should be abbreviated in footnotes and bibliographies by the omission of *Press*, *Publishing Company*, and other such terms except in the case of university presses and wherever else ambiguity or awkwardness would result.

An ampersand should be used in a publisher's name rather than *and* (e.g., T&T Clark; Vandenhoeck & Ruprecht; Farrar, Straus & Giroux). Note that the serial comma is omitted before an ampersand.

Presses named after a founder or family member are generally identified by the founder's last name only (e.g., Brill rather than E. J. Brill; Eerdmans rather than Wm. B. Eerdmans). Presses named after a historical figure who was not a founder are identified by the full name (e.g., John Knox rather than Knox).

The following list provides the preferred bibliographical forms of publishers' names. The list also indicates the most common places of publication for the publishers. Although some entries include two or more locations, only the first place listed on the title or copyright page of the work being cited should be included in a bibliographical citation. Note further that the list indicates when a city needs to be identified further by adding a state, province, or country: if no state, province, or country is given for a publisher below, it may be omitted in all citations.

A. & C. Black. *See* Black
A. Töpelmann. *See* Töpelmann
A Turizm Yayınları (Istanbul)
Aarhus University Press (Aarhus)
Abingdon (Nashville; New York)
Åbo Akademi University (Åbo)
Academic Press (London; New York)
Acumen (Durham)
A.D.P.F. (Paris)
Agade (Warsaw)
Akademie (Berlin)
Akademische Verlagsbuchhandlung (Freiburg im Breisgau)
Alba House (New York)
Aldine (Chicago)
Alfred A. Knopf. *See* Knopf
Allen & Unwin (London)
Allenson (Naperville, IL)
Almond Press (Sheffield)
Almqvist & Wiksell (Uppsala; Stockholm)
Am Oved (Tel-Aviv)
American Oriental Society (New Haven)
American Schools of Oriental Research (Boston; Cambridge)
Anselm Academic (Winona, MN)
Apollos (Leicester)
Archaeopress (Oxford)
Archon Books (Hamden, CT)
Ares (Milan)
Aris & Phillips (Oxford)
Aschendorff (Münster)
Ashgate (Burlington, VT; Farnham, Surrey, UK)
Associació Bíblica de Catalunya (Catalonia, Spain)
Athlone Press (London)
Augsburg (Minneapolis)
Augsburg Fortress (Minneapolis)
Augustin (Locust Valley, NY)
AUSA (Sabadell)
B. G. Teubner Verlag. *See* Teubner
Baker Academic (Grand Rapids)
Baker Books (Grand Rapids)
Bamberger & Wahrmann (Jerusalem)
Banner of Truth Trust (London; Carlisle, PA)
B.A.R. (Oxford)
Basic Books (New York)
Basil Blackwell. *See* Blackwell
Baylor University Press (Waco, TX)
Beacon (Boston)
Beacon Hill (Kansas City)
Beauchesne (Paris)
Beck (Munich)
Ben Yehuda Press (Teaneck, NJ)
Ben-Gurion University of the Negev Press (Beer-Sheva)
Benzinger (Zurich)
Bertelsmann (Gütersloh)
Bialik Institute (Jerusalem)
Biblical Archaeology Society (Washington, DC)
Biblical Institute Press (Rome)
Black (Edinburgh; London)
Blackwell (Oxford; Malden, MA)
Bloomsbury (London; New Delhi; New York; Sydney)
Bohn (Haarlem)
Bouvier (Bonn)
Braziller (New York)
Brazos (Grand Rapids)
Brepols (Turnhout)
Brill (Leiden; Boston)
British Academy (London)
Broadman & Holman (Nashville)
Brockhaus (Wuppertal)
Browne & Nolan (Dublin)
Brown Judaic Studies (Providence, RI)

C. H. Beck. *See* Beck
Calwer (Stuttgart)
Cambridge University Press (Cambridge; New York)
Carl Winter. *See* Winter
Carta (Jerusalem)
Cascade (Eugene, OR)
Cassell (London)
Catholic Biblical Association of America (Washington, DC)
Catholic University of America Press (Washington, DC)
CDL (Bethesda, MD)
Cerf (Paris)
Chalice (Atlanta)
Charles Scribner's Sons. *See* Scribner's Sons
Chr. Kaiser Verlag. *See* Kaiser
Clarendon (Oxford)
Cokesbury (Nashville)
Collins (London)
Columbia University Press (New York)
Concordia (St. Louis)
Consejo Superior de Investigaciones Cientificas (Madrid)
Continuum (New York; London)
Cornell University Press (Ithaca, NY)
Crossroad (New York)
Crossway (Wheaton, IL)
Curtius (Berlin)
Darton, Longman & Todd (London)
de Boccard (Paris)
de Gruyter (Berlin)
Dehoniane (Bologna)
Deichert (Leipzig)
Dekker & Van de Vegt (Nijmegen)
Delachaux & Niestle (Neuchatel; Paris)
Deo (Dorset, UK)
Desclée (Paris)
Desclée de Brouwer (Paris)
Deutsche Bibelgesellschaft (Stuttgart)
Doubleday (Garden City, NY; New York)
Duckworth (London)
Duculot (Gembloux)
Duke University Press (Durham, NC)
Duquesne University Press (Pittsburgh)
Dura-Europos Publications (New Haven)
Dybwad (Oslo)
E. J. Brill. *See* Brill
Echter (Würzburg)
EDB (Edizioni Dehoniane Bologna). *See* Dehoniane
Edinburgh University Press (Edinburgh)
Éditions de Boccard. *See* de Boccard
Éditions Desclée de Brouwer. *See* Desclée de Brouwer
Editions du Cerf. *See* Cerf
Éditions Gallimard. *See* Gallimard
Éditions Rieder. *See* Rieder
Editorial Verbo Divina (Pamplona)
Editrice Anselmiana (Rome)
Editrice Pontificia Università Gregoriana (Rome)
Editrice Pontificio Istituto Biblico. *See* Pontifical Biblical Institute
Edizioni Dehoniane. *See* Dehoniane
Edizioni di Storia e Letteratura (Rome)
Eduard Pfeiffer. *See* Pfeiffer
Edwin Mellen. *See* Mellen
Eerdmans (Grand Rapids)
Ege (Istanbul)
Egypt Exploration Fund (London)
Eisenbrauns (Winona Lake, IN)
ELITE (Florence)
Epworth (London)
Equinox (Sheffield)
Evangelische Verlagsanstalt (Berlin)
Evangelischer Verlag (Zollikon-Zurich)
EVZ-Verlag (Zurich)
Finnish Exegetical Society (Helsinki)
Fortress (Philadelphia)
Franciscan Herald Press (Chicago)
Franciscan Institute Publications (St. Bonaventure, NY)
Franciscan Printing Press (Jerusalem)
Francke (Bern; Tübingen)
Franz Steiner Verlag. *See* Steiner
Free Press (Glencoe, IL; New York)

Friedrich Reinhardt. *See* Reinhardt
Funk & Wagnalls (New York)
Gabalda (Paris)
Gallimard (Paris)
Gebr. Mann (Berlin)
Gelbstverlag der Erben (Berlin)
George Braziller. *See* Braziller
Georg Olms. *See* Olms
Georg Reimer. *See* Reimer
Gerald Duckworth. *See* Duckworth
Gerd Mohn. *See* Mohn
Gerstenberg (Hildesheim)
Geuthner (Paris)
Gianni Iuculano. *See* Iuculano
Glazier (Wilmington, DE)
Gleerup (Lund)
Gorgias (Piscataway, NJ)
Gregorian University Press (Rome)
Gunter Narr Verlag. *See* Narr
Gütersloher Verlagshaus (Gütersloh)
Hanstein (Bonn; Cologne)
Harcourt, Brace (New York)
Harcourt Brace Jovanovich (New York)
Harcourt, Brace & World (New York)
Harcourt, Brace & Company. *See* Harcourt, Brace
Harper & Brothers (New York)
Harper & Row (New York; San Francisco)
HarperCollins (New York; San Francisco)
HarperOne (San Francisco)
HarperSanFrancisco (San Francisco)
Harrassowitz (Leipzig; Wiesbaden)
Hartford Seminary Foundation Press (Hartford, CT)
Harvard University Press (Cambridge)
Hebrew Union College Press (Cincinnati)
Heinemann (London)
Hendrickson (Peabody, MA)
Henry Holt. *See* Holt
Henry Regnery. *See* Regnery
Herald Press (Kitchener, ON)
Herder (Freiburg im Breisgau; Rome)
Hinrichs (Leipzig)
Hodder & Stoughton (London)
Holt (New York)
Holt, Rinehart & Winston (New York)
Huber (Munich)
Humanities Press (New York)
Imprimerie Nationale (Paris)
Indiana University Press (Bloomington)
Institut für Orientalistik der Universität Wien (Vienna)
Institut für Sprachwissenschaft der Universität Innsbruck (Innsbruck)
Institut Biblique Pontifical. *See* Pontifical Biblical Institute
InterVarsity Press (Downers Grove, IL)
Inter-Varsity Press (Leicester; London)
ISLET (Dresden)
Israel Antiquities Authority (Jerusalem)
Istituto Universitario Orientale (Naples)
Itzkowski (Berlin)
Iuculano (Pavia)
J. C. B. Mohr (Paul Siebeck). *See* Mohr Siebeck
J. Duculot. *See* Duculot
J. Kauffmann Verlag. *See* Kauffmann
Jacob Dybwad. *See* Dybwad
Jewish Publication Society of America (Philadelphia)
Jewish Theological Seminary of America (New York)
J. J. Augustin. *See* Augustin
John Knox (Atlanta; Richmond, VA)
John Murray. *See* Murray
John Wiley & Sons. *See* Wiley & Sons
Johns Hopkins University Press (Baltimore; London)
Josef Knecht. *See* Knecht
JSOT Press (Sheffield)
Judson (Pennsylvania)
K. G. Saur Verlag. *See* Saur
Kaiser (Munich)
Karl J. Trübner. *See* Trübner
Katholisches Bibelwerk (Stuttgart)
Kauffmann (Frankfurt am Main)
KBW (Stuttgart)

Kiryath Sepher (Jerusalem)
Klinksiek (Paris)
Knecht (Frankfurt am Main)
Knopf (New York)
Kohlhammer (Stuttgart)
Kok (Kampen)
Kok Pharos (Kampen)
Kosel (Munich)
Kregel (Grand Rapids)
Ktav (New York)
Labor et Fides (Geneva)
Lang (New York; Bern)
Librairie Lecoffre (Paris)
Leroux (Paris)
Letouzey et Ané (Paris)
Leuven University Press (Gembloux; Leuven)
Leykam (Graz)
LIT (Berlin)
Little, Brown (Boston)
Liturgical Press (Collegeville, MN)
Longmans, Green (London; New York)
Louisiana State University Press (Baton Rouge)
Lutterworth (London)
Macmillan (New York; London)
Magnes (Jerusalem)
Manchester University Press (Manchester)
Marshall, Morgan & Scott (London)
Massad Harav Kook (Jerusalem)
Max Niemeyer Verlag. *See* Niemeyer
McGill-Queens University Press (Montreal; Kingston, ON)
McGraw-Hill (New York)
Mellen (Lewiston, NY)
Mercer University Press (Macon, GA)
Meridian Books (New York)
Methuen (London; New York)
Michael Glazier. *See* Glazier
Minerva (Paris)
Mohn (Gütersloh)
Mohr Siebeck (Tübingen)
Mouton (The Hague)
Mowbrays (London)
Münz (Breslau)
Murray (London)
Narr (Tübingen)
Nederlands Historisch-Archaeologisch Instituut te Istanbul (Istanbul)
Nelson (Nashville; London)
Neo-Assyrian Text Corpus Project (Helsinki)
Neukirchener Verlag (Neukirchen-Vluyn)
Niemeyer (Halle)
Northern Illinois University Press (DeKalb)
Northwestern University Press (Evanston, IL)
Norton (New York)
Oliphants (London)
Oliver & Boyd (Edinburgh)
Olms (Hildesheim)
Open Book (Cambridge)
Orbis Books (Maryknoll, NY)
Oriental Institute of the University of Chicago (Chicago)
Ortsel (Jerusalem)
Österreichische Akademie der Wissenschaften (Vienna)
Otto Harrassowitz. *See* Harrassowitz
Otto Zeller. *See* Zeller
Oxbow (Oxford)
Oxford University Press (Oxford; London; New York)
Paideia (Brescia)
Pantheon (New York)
Paternoster (Exeter; Milton Keynes)
Patmos (Düsseldorf; Mannheim)
Paul Geuthner. *See* Geuthner
Paulist (New York; Mahwah, NJ)
Peeters (Leuven)
Penguin Books (Harmondsworth; London)
Pennsylvania State University Press (University Park)
Pergamon Press (New York)
Peter Hanstein. *See* Hanstein

Peter Lang. *See* Lang
Pfeiffer (Leipzig)
Pickwick (Pittsburgh; Eugene, OR)
Polebridge (Sonoma, CA)
Pontifical Biblical Institute (Rome)
Praeger (New York)
Prentice Hall (Englewood Cliffs, NJ; Upper Saddle River, NJ)
Presses Universitaires (Fribourg)
Presses Universitaires de France (Paris)
Presses Universitaires de Vincennes (Saint Denis)
Princeton University Press (Princeton)
Prometheus (Amherst, NY)
PUF. *See* Presses Universitaires de France
Purdue University Press (West Lafayette, IN)
Pustet (Regensburg)
Random House (New York)
Regnery (Chicago)
Reimer (Berlin)
Reinhardt (Basel)
Revell (New York)
Rieder (Paris)
Rivington (London)
Routledge (London; New York)
Routledge & Kegan Paul (London)
Rowman & Littlefield (Lanhan, MD)
Royal Asiatic Society (London)
Royal Irish Academy (Dublin)
Royal Scottish Museum (Edinburgh)
Saur (Munich)
SBL Press (Atlanta)
Schnell & Steiner (Munich)
Schocken Books (New York)
Scholars Press (Missoula, MT; Chico, CA; Atlanta)
School of Oriental and African Studies (London)
Scientia (Aalen)
SCM (London)
Scribner's Sons (New York)
Seabury (New York)
Sheffield Academic (Sheffield)
Sheffield Phoenix (Sheffield)
SIL International (Dallas)
Simon & Schuster (New York)
Smyth & Helwys (Macon, GA)
Societatis Litterariae Fennicae (Helsinki)
Society for Promoting Christian Knowledge. *See* SPCK
Society of Biblical Literature (Atlanta)
Soncino (Hindhead, Surrey, UK; Jerusalem; Brooklyn)
Southern Illinois University Press (Carbondale)
SPCK (London)
St. Benno (Leipzig)
Stanford University Press (Stanford, CA)
Stefan Münz. *See* Münz
Steiner (Stuttgart)
Styx (Groningen)
Suhrkamp (Frankfurt; Berlin)
Suomalainen Tiedeakatemia (Helsinki)
Swets & Zeitlinger (Amsterdam; Lisse)
T&T Clark (Edinburgh; London; New York)
Taylor & Francis (London)
Tel Aviv University Press (Tel Aviv)
Temple University Press (Philadelphia)
Teubner (Leipzig; Stuttgart; Berlin)
Thames & Hudson (London)
Theologischer Verlag. *See* TVZ
Theologischer Verlag Rudolf Brockhaus. *See* Brockhaus
Thomas Nelson. *See* Nelson
Töpelmann (Giessen; Berlin)
Trinity University Press (San Antonio, TX)
Trübner (Strassburg)
Truman State University Press (Kirksville, MO)
Türk Tarih Kurumu Basımevi (Ankara)
TVZ (Theologischer Verlag Zurich) (Zurich)
Tyndale House (Carol Stream, IL)
Tyndale Press (London)
Ugarit-Verlag (Münster)

Undena (Los Angeles; Malibu, CA)
United Bible Societies (London; New York; Stuttgart)
Universitätsverlag (Göttingen)
Universitetsforlaget (Oslo)
University of Birmingham Press (Birmingham)
University of California Press (Berkeley)
University of Chicago Press (Chicago)
University of Copenhagen (Copenhagen)
University of Exeter Press (Exeter)
University of Michigan Press (Ann Arbor)
University of Minnesota Press (Minneapolis)
University of Nebraska Press (Lincoln)
University of North Carolina Press (Chapel Hill)
University of Notre Dame Press (Notre Dame)
University of Pennsylvania Press (Philadelphia)
University of Pennsylvania Museum of Archaeology and Anthropology (Philadelphia)
University of Pittsburgh Press (Pittsburgh)
University of South Carolina Press (Columbia)
University of Texas Press (Austin)
University of Wales Press (Cardiff)
University Press of America (Lanham, MD)
Uppsala Universitet (Uppsala)
Van Gorcum (Assen)
Vandenhoeck & Ruprecht (Göttingen)
Verbo Divino (Estella, Navarra, Spain)
Verlag Philipp von Zabern. *See* von Zabern
Viking (New York)
Vintage Books (New York; London)
Vittorio Klostermann (Frankfurt am Main)
Voigtländer (Leipzig)
von Zabern (Mainz)
W. Heinemann. *See* Heinemann
W. W. Norton. *See* Norton
Wahrmann (Jerusalem)
Waisenhaus (Halle)
Walter de Gruyter. *See* de Gruyter
Wayne State University Press (Detroit)
Weidenfeld & Nicolson (London)
Weidmann (Berlin)
Westminster (Philadelphia)
Westminster John Knox (Louisville)
Wiley & Sons (New York)
Wiley-Blackwell (Malden, MA; Chichester)
Wilfrid Laurier University Press (Waterloo, ON)
William B. Eerdmans. *See* Eerdmans
Williams & Norgate (London)
Winter (Heidelberg)
Wipf & Stock (Eugene, OR)
Wissenschaftliche Buchgesellschaft (Darmstadt)
Word (Waco, TX; Dallas; Nashville)
Yale University Press (New Haven)
Zeller (Osnabruck)
Zondervan (Grand Rapids)
Zwingli-Verlag (Zurich)

6.1.4.2 Place of Publication

If the title or copyright page lists more than one city, only the first city should ordinarily be used in the bibliography and notes (see *CMS* §14.135). When the city or publisher is not well known, reference to the state or country should be included. Be careful to do this consistently; thus if you name "Grand Rapids, MI" in one citation, you must include the state in every other citation of a publisher in Grand Rapids. On the use of two-letter postal abbreviations for state/province references, see §8.1.1.

6.1.4.3 Translating Foreign-Language Publication Information

For foreign-language publications, authors should translate the details of publication (including city of publication and the roles of editors, translators, etc.) into English. When an author has not done so, the copy editor should either translate such information or query the project editor. For example:

Original	**Preferred**
Basilae	Basel
Berolini	Berlin
Bruxelles	Brussels
Cantabrigiae	Cambridge
Genève	Geneva
Lipsiae	Leipzig
Louvain	Leuven
Lugdunum	Lyon
Lugdunum Batavorum	Leiden
Lutetiae	Paris
München	Munich
Oxonii	Oxford
Wien	Vienna

For treatment of authors' names, see §§6.1.2.2–3.

6.1.4.4 Listing Multiple Publishers

Books are often published cooperatively by a pair of publishers. In such cases, it is necessary to cite both publishers; the two should be listed in their normal way and separated by a semicolon. Places of publication and publishers' names should not be combined and separated by slashes:

> Göttingen: Vandenhoeck & Ruprecht; Fribourg: Presses Universitaires
> Not: Göttingen/Fribourg: Vandenhoeck & Ruprecht/Presses Universitaires

6.1.4.5 Date

The use of *n.d.* (no date) in place of the year in the publication details should be avoided. In the case of unpublished manuscripts, use the date of the version consulted or the last-modified date in the case of electronic files. Use *forthcoming* for manuscripts under contract but not yet published (§6.2.19). Manuscripts not under contract are treated as unpublished manuscripts.

6.1.5 Page Numbers

Avoid using *f.* and *ff.* for "following" pages; give actual page ranges.

6.1.6 Electronic Sources Information

The last element in a citation will be information about the electronic format cited (PDF e-book; Kindle edition, etc.) or, for online publications, an electronic resource identifier such as a DOI (digital object identifier) or URL (uniform resource locator). DOIs are unique and permanent names assigned to an individual work that will resolve directly to the work regardless of changes in its online location. For this reason, DOIs are preferred to URLs. For more on electronic resource identifiers, see *CMS* §§14.4–7.

SBL Press no longer recommends including access dates—the date on which the author last consulted a source—as they are unreliable, unverifiable, and unnecessary. Authors should consult with their publisher early, however, as some publishers may require them.

URL addresses are never hyphenated at the end of a line and should be divided before the "dot" or at a "slash" if they must wrap to the next line.

6.2 General Examples: Books

The following examples define SBL style for notes and bibliographies more fully than the select rules in §6.1.

6.2.1 A Book by a Single Author

15. Charles H. Talbert, *Reading John: A Literary and Theological Commentary on the Fourth Gospel and the Johannine Epistles* (New York: Crossroad, 1992), 127.

19. Talbert, *Reading John*, 22.

Talbert, Charles H. *Reading John: A Literary and Theological Commentary on the Fourth Gospel and the Johannine Epistles*. New York: Crossroad, 1992.

6.2.2 A Book by Two or Three Authors

4. James M. Robinson and Helmut Koester, *Trajectories through Early Christianity* (Philadelphia: Fortress, 1971), 237.

12. Robinson and Koester, *Trajectories through Early Christianity*, 23.

Robinson, James M., and Helmut Koester. *Trajectories through Early Christianity*. Philadelphia: Fortress, 1971.

6.2.3 A Book by More Than Three Authors

If a work is by more than three authors, simply list one and "et al." to indicate additional authors (without comma following the first author's name). All names are generally listed in the bibliographical entry, but "et al." following the first author's name (and, in this case, a comma) is permitted.

7. Bernard Brandon Scott et al., *Reading New Testament Greek* (Peabody, MA: Hendrickson, 1993), 53.

9. Scott et al., *Reading New Testament Greek*, 42.

Scott, Bernard Brandon, Margaret Dean, Kristen Sparks, and Frances LaZar. *Reading New Testament Greek*. Peabody, MA: Hendrickson, 1993.

6.2.4 A Translated Volume

14. Wilhelm Egger, *How to Read the New Testament: An Introduction to Linguistic and Historical-Critical Methodology*, trans. Peter Heinegg (Peabody, MA: Hendrickson, 1996), 28.

18. Egger, *How to Read*, 291.

Egger, Wilhelm. *How to Read the New Testament: An Introduction to Linguistic and Historical-Critical Methodology*. Translated by Peter Heinegg. Peabody, MA: Hendrickson, 1996.

6.2.5 The Full History of a Translated Volume

Generally it is unnecessary to present the full history of a translated volume. But if you choose to do so, the following format may be used.

3. Julius Wellhausen, *Prolegomena to the History of Ancient Israel* (New York: Meridian Books, 1957), 296; repr. of *Prolegomena to the History of Israel*, trans. J. Sutherland Black and A. Enzies, with preface by W. Robertson Smith (Edinburgh: Black, 1885); trans. of *Prolegomena zur Geschichte Israels*, 2nd ed. (Berlin: Reimer, 1883).

Julius Wellhausen, *Prolegomena to the History of Ancient Israel*. New York: Meridian Books, 1957. Reprint of *Prolegomena to the History of Israel*. Translated by J. Sutherland Black and A. Enzies, with preface by W. Robertson Smith. Edinburgh: Black, 1885. Translation of *Prolegomena zur Geschichte Israels*. 2nd ed. Berlin: Reimer, 1883.

6.2.6 A Book with One Editor

5. Jeffrey H. Tigay, ed., *Empirical Models for Biblical Criticism* (Philadelphia: University of Pennsylvania Press, 1985), 35.

9. Tigay, *Empirical Models*, 38.

Tigay, Jeffrey H., ed. *Empirical Models for Biblical Criticism*. Philadelphia: University of Pennsylvania Press, 1985.

6.2.7 A Book with Two or Three Editors

44. John Kaltner and Steven L. McKenzie, eds., *Beyond Babel: A Handbook for Biblical Hebrew and Related Languages*, RBS 42 (Atlanta: Society of Biblical Literature, 2002), xii.

47. Kaltner and McKenzie, viii.

Kaltner, John, and Steven L. McKenzie, eds. *Beyond Babel: A Handbook for Biblical Hebrew and Related Languages*. RBS 42. Atlanta: Society of Biblical Literature, 2002.

6.2.8 A Book with Four or More Editors

The same rules apply as in §6.2.3.

4. John F. Oates et al., eds., *Checklist of Editions of Greek and Latin Papyri, Ostraca, and Tablets*, 5th ed., BASPSup 9 (Oakville, CT: American Society of Papyrologists, 2001), 10.

Oates, John F., William H. Willis, Roger S. Bagnall, and Klaas A. Worp, eds. *Checklist of Editions of Greek and Latin Papyri, Ostraca, and Tablets*. 5th ed. BASPSup 9. Oakville, CT: American Society of Papyrologists, 2001.

6.2.9 A Book with Both Author and Editor

45. Edward Schillebeeckx, *The Schillebeeckx Reader*, ed. Robert J. Schreiter (Edinburgh: T&T Clark, 1986), 20.

Schillebeeckx, Edward. *The Schillebeeckx Reader*. Edited by Robert J. Schreiter. Edinburgh: T&T Clark, 1986.

6.2.10 A Book with Author, Editor, and Translator

3. Friedrich Blass and Albert Debrunner, *Grammatica del greco del Nuovo Testamento*, ed. Friedrich Rehkopf, trans. Giordana Pisi (Brescia: Paideia, 1982), 40.

Blass, Friedrich, and Albert Debrunner. *Grammatica del greco del Nuovo Testamento*. Edited by Friedrich Rehkopf. Translated by Giordana Pisi. Brescia: Paideia, 1982.

6.2.11 A Title in a Modern Work Citing Words in a Non-Latin Alphabet

When citing a title containing non-Latin characters, it is permissible (although not SBL Press preference) to represent such characters as transliteration. Indicate to readers that the transliteration is not original by setting it within brackets, as in the following:

34. Stuart A. Irvine, "Idols [*ktbwnm*]: A Note on Hosea 13:2a," *JBL* 133 (2014): 509–17.

See also §6.1.3.9.

6.2.12 An Article in an Edited Volume

3. Harold W. Attridge, "Jewish Historiography," in *Early Judaism and Its Modern*

Interpreters, ed. Robert A. Kraft and George W. E. Nickelsburg (Philadelphia: Fortress; Atlanta: Scholars Press, 1986), 311–43.

6. Attridge, "Jewish Historiography," 314–17.

If subsequent references could be confused with another article by the same author, include the information concerning the editors with the short title.

6. Attridge, "Jewish Historiography" (Kraft and Nickelsburg), 314–17.

Additionally, if another article in the same edited volume has already been cited with the full bibliographic information, the short form including information concerning the editors may be used for all other articles in the edited volume cited subsequently:

9. Attridge, "Jewish Historiography," in Kraft and Nickelsburg, *Early Judaism*, 314–17.

Attridge, Harold A. "Jewish Historiography." Pages 311–43 in *Early Judaism and Its Modern Interpreters*. Edited by Robert A. Kraft and George W. E. Nickelsburg. Philadelphia: Fortress; Atlanta: Scholars Press, 1986.

6.2.13 An Article in a Festschrift

Bibliographies should use the full title.

8. John Van Seters, "The Theology of the Yahwist: A Preliminary Sketch," in *"Wer ist wie du, Herr, unter den Göttern?": Studien zur Theologie und Religionsgeschichte Israels für Otto Kaiser zum 70. Geburtstag*, ed. Ingo Kottsieper et al. (Göttingen: Vandenhoeck & Ruprecht, 1995), 219–28.

17. Van Seters, "Theology of the Yahwist," 222.

Van Seters, John. "The Theology of the Yahwist: A Preliminary Sketch." Pages 219–28 in *"Wer ist wie du, Herr, unter den Göttern?": Studien zur Theologie und Religionsgeschichte Israels für Otto Kaiser zum 70. Geburtstag*. Edited by Ingo Kottsieper et al. Göttingen: Vandenhoeck & Ruprecht, 1995.

6.2.14 An Introduction, Preface, or Foreword Written by Someone Other Than the Author

2. Hendrikus Boers, introduction to *How to Read the New Testament: An Introduction to Linguistic and Historical-Critical Methodology*, by Wilhelm Egger, trans. Peter Heinegg (Peabody, MA: Hendrickson, 1996), xi–xxi.

6. Boers, introduction, xi–xx.

Boers, Hendrikus. Introduction to *How to Read the New Testament: An Introduction to Linguistic and Historical-Critical Methodology*, by Wilhelm Egger. Translated by Peter Heinegg. Peabody, MA: Hendrickson, 1996.

6.2.15 Multiple Publishers for a Single Book

Birger Gerhardsson, *Memory and Manuscript: Oral Tradition and Written Transmission in Rabbinic Judaism and Early Christianity*. ASNU 22. Lund: Gleerup; Copenhagen: Munksgaard, 1961.

For treatment of multiple publishers, see §6.1.4.4.

6.2.16 A Revised Edition

87. James B. Pritchard, ed., *Ancient Near Eastern Texts Relating to the Old Testament*, 3rd ed. (Princeton: Princeton University Press, 1969), xxi.

Pritchard, James B., ed. *Ancient Near Eastern Texts Relating to the Old Testament*. 3rd ed. Princeton: Princeton University Press, 1969.

56. Joseph Blenkinsopp, *A History of Prophecy in Israel*, rev. and enl. ed. (Louisville: Westminster John Knox, 1996), 81.

Blenkinsopp, Joseph. *A History of Prophecy in Israel*. Rev. and enl. ed. Louisville: Westminster John Knox, 1996.

6.2.17 Reprint of a Recent Title

5. John Van Seters, *In Search of History: Historiography in the Ancient World and the Origins of Biblical History* (New Haven: Yale University Press, 1983; repr., Winona Lake, IN: Eisenbrauns, 1997), 35.

Van Seters, John. *In Search of History: Historiography in the Ancient World and the Origins of Biblical History*. New Haven: Yale University Press, 1983. Repr., Winona Lake, IN: Eisenbrauns, 1997.

6.2.18 Reprint of a Title in the Public Domain

See *CMS* §§4.19–21. When a work is in the public domain, one may omit all except the most relevant information (in the following instance, the translator and original publication date) and supply information about the source from which the book is now available.

5. Gustav Adolf Deissmann, *Light from the Ancient East: The New Testament Illustrated by Recently Discovered Texts of the Graeco-Roman World* (trans. Lionel R. M. Strachan; 1927; repr., Peabody, MA: Hendrickson, 1995), 55.

Deissmann, Gustav Adolf. *Light from the Ancient East: The New Testament Illustrated by Recently Discovered Texts of the Graeco-Roman World*. Translated by Lionel R. M. Strachan. 1927. Repr., Peabody, MA: Hendrickson, 1995.

6.2.19 A Forthcoming Book

When a book is under contract with a publisher and is already titled, but the date of publication is not yet known, *forthcoming* is used in place of the date. Books not under contract should be treated as unpublished manuscripts (for which see *CMS* §§14.224–31).

9. James R. Harrison and L. L. Welborn, eds., *The First Urban Churches 2: Roman Corinth*, WGRWSup (Atlanta: SBL Press, forthcoming).

12. Harrison and Welborn, *Roman Corinth*, 201.

Harrison, James R. and L. L. Welborn, eds. *The First Urban Churches 2: Roman Corinth*. WGRWSup. Atlanta: SBL Press, forthcoming.

6.2.20 A Multivolume Work

5. Adolf Harnack, *History of Dogma*, trans. Neil Buchanan, 7 vols. (Boston: Little, Brown, 1896–1905).

9. Harnack, *History of Dogma*, 2:126.

Harnack, Adolf. *History of Dogma*. Translated from the 3rd German ed. by Neil Buchanan. 7 vols. Boston: Little, Brown, 1896–1905.

6.2.21 A Titled Volume in a Multivolume Work

5. Bruce W. Winter and Andrew D. Clarke, eds., *The Book of Acts in Its Ancient Literary Setting*, vol. 1 of *The Book of Acts in Its First Century Setting*, ed. Bruce W. Winter (Grand Rapids: Eerdmans, 1993), 25.

16. Winter and Clarke, *Book of Acts*, 25.

Winter, Bruce W., and Andrew D. Clarke, eds. *The Book of Acts in Its Ancient Literary Setting*. Vol. 1 of *The Book of Acts in Its First Century Setting*. Edited by Bruce W. Winter. Grand Rapids: Eerdmans, 1993.

It is unnecessary when citing a single volume to give information about the total number of volumes in the series. If you need to cite the entire multivolume series, see §6.2.20.

6.2.22 A Chapter within a Multivolume Work

24. Steve Mason, "Josephus on Canon and Scriptures," in *Hebrew Bible/Old Testament: The History of Its Interpretation*, ed. Magne Saebø (Göttingen: Vandenhoeck & Ruprecht, 1996), 1.1:217–335.

28. Mason, "Josephus on Canon and Scriptures," 224.

Mason, Steve. "Josephus on Canon and Scriptures." Pages 217–35 in vol. 1, part 1 of *Hebrew Bible/Old Testament: The History of Its Interpretation*. Edited by Magne Saebø. Göttingen: Vandenhoeck & Ruprecht, 1996.

6.2.23 A Chapter within a Titled Volume in a Multivolume Work

66. David Peterson, "The Motif of Fulfilment and the Purpose of Luke-Acts," in *The Book of Acts in Its Ancient Literary Setting*, ed. Bruce W. Winter and Andrew D. Clarke, vol. 1 of *The Book of Acts in Its First Century Setting*, ed. Bruce W. Winter (Grand Rapids: Eerdmans, 1993), 83–104.

78. Peterson, "Motif of Fulfilment," 92.

David Peterson, "The Motif of Fulfilment and the Purpose of Luke-Acts." Pages 83–104 in *The Book of Acts in Its Ancient Literary Setting*. Edited by Bruce W. Winter and Andrew D. Clarke. Vol. 1 of *The Book of Acts in Its First Century Setting*. Edited by Bruce W. Winter. Grand Rapids: Eerdmans, 1993.

6.2.24 A Work in a Series

Volumes that appear in a series follow the standard note and bibliographic form.

12. Otfried Hofius, *Paulusstudien*, WUNT 51 (Tübingen: Mohr Siebeck, 1989), 122.

14. Hofius, *Paulusstudien*, 124.

Hofius, Otfried. *Paulusstudien*. WUNT 51. Tübingen: Mohr Siebeck, 1989.

When a series begins anew, distinguishing between the old and new series can be problematic. Slashes (e.g., SBT 2/18) are often used to denote the new series.

23. Joachim Jeremias, *The Prayers of Jesus*, SBT 2/6 (Naperville, IL: Allenson, 1967), 123–27.

32. Jeremias, *Prayers*, 126.

Jeremias, Joachim. *The Prayers of Jesus*. SBT 2/6. Naperville, IL: Allenson, 1967.

6.2.25 Electronic Book

Books available for download from a library or bookseller are generally available in two main formats: PDF e-books and editions for e-readers, such as Kindle, iPad, and Nook. If citing a PDF e-book that is identical in all respects to the print edition, it is not necessary to indicate the format consulted. However, because other electronic formats do not conform in all respects to the print edition, in those cases authors must indicate the format consulted. The indication of the format follows the publication information:

14. Henning Graf Reventlow, *From the Old Testament to Origen*. Vol. 1 of *History of Biblical Interpretation*, trans. Leo G. Perdue (Atlanta: Society of Biblical Literature, 2009), Nook edition, ch. 1.3.

18. Reventlow, *From the Old Testament to Origen*, ch. 1.3.

Reventlow, Henning Graf. *From the Old Testament to Origen*. Volume 1 of *History of Biblical Interpretation*. Translated by Leo G. Perdue. Atlanta: Society of Biblical Literature, 2009. Nook edition.

3. Jacob L. Wright, *David, King of Israel, and Caleb in Biblical Memory* (Cambridge: Cambridge University Press, 2014), Kindle edition, ch. 3, "Introducing David."

21. Wright, *David, King of Israel*, ch. 5, "Evidence from Qumran."

Jacob L. Wright, *David, King of Israel, and Caleb in Biblical Memory*. Cambridge: Cambridge University Press, 2014. Kindle edition.

Since e-reader formats do not have stable page numbers, it is preferable to cite the print edition. However, if an alternative format is consulted, in lieu of a page number, include a chapter or section number in the citation, as in the example footnotes above.

When citing an online version of a book, include the DOI. In the absence of a DOI, include the URL in the citation.

53. Ann E. Killebrew and Margreet Steiner, eds., *The Oxford Handbook of the Archaeology of the Levant: c. 8000–332 BCE* (Oxford: Oxford University Press, 2014), doi:10.1093/oxfordhb/9780199212972.001.0001.

55. Killebrew and Steiner, *Archaeology of the Levant*.

Killebrew, Ann E. and Margreet Steiner, eds. *The Oxford Handbook of the Archaeology of the Levant: c. 8000–332 BCE*. Oxford: Oxford University Press, 2014. doi:10.1093/oxfordhb/9780199212972.001.0001.

The format is the same for older works that have been made available freely online:

29. Stephen Kaufman. *The Akkadian Influences on Aramaic*, AS 19 (Chicago: The Oriental Institute of the University of Chicago, 1974), http://oi.uchicago.edu/pdf/as19.pdf.

32. Kaufman, *Akkadian Influences on Aramaic*, 123.

Kaufman, Stephen. *The Akkadian Influences on Aramaic*. AS 19. Chicago: The Oriental Institute of the University of Chicago, 1974. http://oi.uchicago.edu/pdf/as19.pdf.

6.3 General Examples: Journal Articles, Reviews, and Dissertations

6.3.1 A Journal Article

7. Blake Leyerle, "John Chrysostom on the Gaze," *JECS* 1 (1993): 159–74.

23. Leyerle, "John Chrysostom," 161.

Leyerle, Blake. "John Chrysostom on the Gaze." *JECS* 1 (1993): 159–74.

For articles written by more than one author, follow the examples above in §§6.2.2–3. It is unnecessary to include the issue number unless the journal volume is not paginated consecutively. See §6.3.9.

6.3.2 A Journal Article with Multiple Page Locations and Multiple Volumes

21. Hans Wildberger, "Das Abbild Gottes: Gen 1:26–30," *TZ* 21 (1965): 245–59, 481–501.

Wildberger, Hans. "Das Abbild Gottes: Gen 1:26–30." *TZ* 21 (1965): 245–59, 481–501.

24. Julius Wellhausen, "Die Composition des Hexateuchs," *JDT* 21 (1876): 392–450; 22 (1877): 407–79.

Wellhausen, Julius. "Die Composition des Hexateuchs." *JDT* 21 (1876): 392–450; 22 (1877): 407–79.

If a multiple-part article includes "Part 1," "Part 2," and the like as a part of the title, omit the "part" specification and cite only the primary title. Including a part number in the first reference complicates short-title citations for later references, since one would then need to include the part number as a part of the short-title reference.

6.3.3 A Journal Article Republished in a Collected Volume

It is generally necessary to cite only the version that you consulted, not the complete history.

20. David Noel Freedman, "Pottery, Poetry, and Prophecy: An Essay on Biblical Poetry," *JBL* 96 (1977): 20

Freedman, David Noel. "Pottery, Poetry, and Prophecy: An Essay on Biblical Poetry." *JBL* 96 (1977): 5–26.

or

20. David Noel Freedman. "Pottery, Poetry, and Prophecy: An Essay on Biblical Poetry," in *Pottery, Poetry, and Prophecy: Studies in Early Hebrew Poetry* (Winona Lake, IN: Eisenbrauns, 1980), 14.

Freedman, David Noel. "Pottery, Poetry, and Prophecy: An Essay on Biblical Poetry." Pages 1–22 in *Pottery, Poetry, and Prophecy: Studies in Early Hebrew Poetry*. Winona Lake, IN: Eisenbrauns, 1980.

but neither

20. David Noel Freedman, "Pottery, Poetry, and Prophecy: An Essay on Biblical

Poetry," *JBL* 96 (1977): 20; repr. in *Pottery, Poetry, and Prophecy: Studies in Early Hebrew Poetry* (Winona Lake, IN: Eisenbrauns, 1980).

Freedman, David Noel. "Pottery, Poetry, and Prophecy: An Essay on Biblical Poetry." *JBL* 96 (1977): 5–26. Repr. pp. 1–22 in *Pottery, Poetry, and Prophecy: Studies in Early Hebrew Poetry*. Winona Lake, IN: Eisenbrauns, 1980.

nor

20. David Noel Freedman. "Pottery, Poetry, and Prophecy: An Essay on Biblical Poetry," in *Pottery, Poetry, and Prophecy: Studies in Early Hebrew Poetry* (Winona Lake, IN: Eisenbrauns, 1980), 14; first publ. in *JBL* 96 (1977).

Freedman, David Noel. "Pottery, Poetry, and Prophecy: An Essay on Biblical Poetry." Pages 1–22 in *Pottery, Poetry, and Prophecy: Studies in Early Hebrew Poetry*. Winona Lake, IN: Eisenbrauns, 1980. First publ. in *JBL* 96 (1977): 5–26.

6.3.4 A Book Review

Untitled book reviews may be cited as follows.

8. Howard M. Teeple, review of *Introduction to the New Testament*, by André Robert and André Feuillet, *JBR* 34 (1966): 368–70.

21. Teeple, review of *Introduction to the New Testament* (by Robert and Feuillet), 369.

Teeple, Howard M. Review of *Introduction to the New Testament*, by André Robert and André Feuillet. *JBR* 34 (1966): 368–70.

Titled book reviews should be cited as normal journal articles.

9. Jaroslav Pelikan, "The Things That You're Liable to Read in the Bible," review of *The Anchor Bible Dictionary*, ed. David Noel Freedman. *New York Times Review of Books*, 20 December 1992, 3.

Pelikan, Jaroslav. "The Things That You're Liable to Read in the Bible," review of *The Anchor Bible Dictionary*, ed. David Noel Freedman. *New York Times Review of Books*, 20 December 1992, 3.

Review articles are treated like articles:

7. David Petersen, "Hebrew Bible Textbooks: A Review Article," *CRBR* 1 (1988): 1–18.

14. Petersen, "Hebrew Bible Textbooks," 8.

Petersen, David. "Hebrew Bible Textbooks: A Review Article." *CRBR* 1 (1988): 1–18.

6.3.5 An Unpublished Dissertation or Thesis

21. Lee E. Klosinski, "Meals in Mark" (PhD diss., The Claremont Graduate School, 1988), 22–44.

26. Klosinski, "Meals in Mark," 23.

Klosinski, Lee. E. "Meals in Mark." PhD diss., The Claremont Graduate School, 1988.

6.3.6 An Article in an Encyclopedia or a Dictionary

Individual articles in an encyclopedia or a dictionary should be included in the bibliography. The article form applies. It is not necessary to place a comma following the abbreviation preceding the volume and page number. This imitates the rule for journal volumes. Multivolume lexicons, collections of primary sources, and dictionaries are candidates for this special treatment. For examples, see here and in §6.3.7.

33. Krister Stendahl, "Biblical Theology, Contemporary," *IDB* 1:418–32.

36. Stendahl, "Biblical Theology," 1:419.

Stendahl, Krister. "Biblical Theology, Contemporary." *IDB* 1:418–32.

6.3.7 An Article in a Lexicon or a Theological Dictionary

For the discussion of a word or a family of words, give the entire title and page range of the article:

3. Karl Dahn and Walter L. Liefeld, "See, Vision, Eye," *NIDNTT* 3:511–21.

6. Hermann W. Beyer, "διακονέω, διακονία, κτλ," *TDNT* 2:81–93.

7. Ceslas Spicq, "ἀτακτέω, ἄτακτος, ἀτάκτως," *TLNT* 1:223–24.

143. Ceslas Spicq, "ἀμοιβή," *TLNT* 1:95–96.

For the discussion of a specific word in an article covering a larger group of words, name just the word discussed and those pages on which it is discussed:

23. Hermann W. Beyer, "διακονέω," *TDNT* 2:81–87.

26. Karl Dahn, "ὁράω," *NIDNTT* 3:511–18.

Subsequent entries need to include only the dictionary volume and page numbers.

25. Beyer, *TDNT* 2:83.

29. Dahn, *NIDNTT* 3:511.

147. Spicq, *TLNT* 1:95.

In the bibliography, cite only the theological dictionary.

Brown, Colin, ed. *New International Dictionary of New Testament Theology*. 4 vols. Grand Rapids: Zondervan, 1975–1985.

Kittel, Gerhard, and Gerhard Friedrich, eds. *Theological Dictionary of the New Testament*. Translated by Geoffrey W. Bromiley. 10 vols. Grand Rapids: Eerdmans, 1964–1976.

Spicq, Ceslas. *Theological Lexicon of the New Testament*. Translated and edited by James D. Ernest. 3 vols. Peabody, MA: Hendrickson, 1994.

6.3.8 A Paper Presented at a Professional Society

31. Susan Niditch, "Oral Culture and Written Documents" (paper presented at the Annual Meeting of the New England Region of the SBL, Worcester, MA, 25 March 1994), 13–17.

35. Niditch, "Oral Culture," 14.

Niditch, Susan. "Oral Culture and Written Documents." Paper presented at the Annual Meeting of the New England Region of the SBL. Worcester, MA, 25 March 1994.

6.3.9 An Article in a Magazine

8. Anthony J. Saldarini, "Babatha's Story," *BAR* 24.2 (1998): 28–33, 36–37, 72–74.

27. Saldarini, "Babatha's Story," 28.

Saldarini, Anthony J. "Babatha's Story." *BAR* 24.2 (1998): 28–33, 36–37, 72–74.

Note that issue numbers are included in the previous references because the issues of vol. 24 are paginated separately rather than consecutively; see §6.3.1. Traditionally, the issue numbers in the above examples have been introduced by a comma and the abbreviation "no." (e.g., *BAR* 24, no. 2). Unless your publisher objects, SBL Press recommends the simple period.

6.3.10 An Electronic Journal Article

As discussed in §6.1.6, electronic journal article citations should include a DOI (preferred) or a URL. The URL must resolve directly to the page on which the article appears. Both DOI and URL may be included if desired.

43. Carl P. E. Springer, "Of Roosters and *Repetitio*: Ambrose's *Aeterne rerum conditor*," *VC* 68 (2014): 155–77, doi:10.1163/15700720-12341158.

45. Springer, "Of Roosters and *Repetitio*," 158.

Springer, Carl P. E. "Of Roosters and *Repetitio*: Ambrose's *Aeterne rerum conditor*." *VC* 68 (2014): 155–77. doi:10.1163/15700720-12341158.

8. Charles Truehart, "Welcome to the Next Church," *Atlantic Monthly* 278 (August 1996): 37–58, http://www.theatlantic.com/past/docs/issues/96aug/nxtchrch/nxtchrch.htm.

12. Truehart, "Next Church," 37.

Truehart, Charles. "Welcome to the Next Church." *Atlantic Monthly* 278 (August 1996): 37–58. http://www.theatlantic.com/past/docs/issues/96aug/nxtchrch/nxtchrch.htm.

31. Alan Kirk, "Karl Polanyi, Marshall Sahlins, and the Study of Ancient Social Relations," *JBL* 126 (2007): 182–91, doi:10.2307/27638428, http://www.jstor.org/stable/27638428.

35. Kirk, "Karl Polanyi," 186.

Alan Kirk. "Karl Polanyi, Marshall Sahlins, and the Study of Ancient Social Relations," *JBL* 126 (2007): 182–91. doi:10.2307/27638428. http://www.jstor.org/stable/27638428.

For Internet publications without a print counterpart, see §6.4.15 on citing websites and blogs.

6.4 Special Examples

6.4.1 Texts from the Ancient Near East

Citing primary sources from the ancient Near East presents special problems for authors and editors. The written materials are diverse. The evidence is ever increasing. The publications of these texts are scattered throughout journals, series, and monographs. Principal editions are not always easy to find, and one may have to gather several volumes to locate the necessary transcriptions, transliterations, and translations. The diverse nature of these texts requires the author and publisher to use a variety of formats, abbreviations, numerations, and symbols. Even at the most basic level—for example, that of the titles of texts—no consistency prevails. Thus, we offer the following paragraphs only as basic guidelines.

6.4.1.1 Citing *COS*

A translated text from William W. Hallo, ed., *The Context of Scripture*, 3 vols. (Leiden: Brill, 1997–2002), is cited using the abbreviation *COS* (+ vol. no. + text no. + pages):

7. "The Great Hymn to the Aten," trans. Miriam Lichtheim (*COS* 1.26:44–46).

11. "Great Hymn to the Aten," *COS* 1.26:44–46.

Hallo, William W., ed. *Canonical Compositions from the Biblical World*. Vol. 1 of *The Context of Scripture*. Leiden: Brill, 1997.

6.4.1.2 Citing Other Texts

Citing a text can be as easy as citing a well-known translation:

16. "Suppiluliumas and the Egyptian Queen," trans. Albrecht Goetze (*ANET*, 319).

Pritchard, James B., ed. *Ancient Near Eastern Texts Relating to the Old Testament*. 3rd ed. Princeton: Princeton University Press, 1969.

5. "Erra and Ishum" (Stephanie Dalley, *Myths from Mesopotamia* [Oxford: Oxford University Press, 1991], 282–315).

Dalley, Stephanie. *Myths from Mesopotamia*. Oxford: Oxford University Press, 1991.

5. "Erra and Ishum" (Benjamin Foster, *Before the Muses: An Anthology of Akkadian Literature* [Bethesda, MD: CDL, 1993], 1:771–805).

Foster, Benjamin. *Before the Muses: An Anthology of Akkadian Literature*. Vol. 1. Bethesda, MD: CDL, 1993.

34. "The Doomed Prince" (Miriam Lichtheim, *Ancient Egyptian Literature* [Berkeley: University of California Press, 1976], 2:200–203).

36. "The Doomed Prince" (*AEL* 2:200–203).

Lichtheim, Miriam. *Ancient Egyptian Literature*. Vol. 2. Berkeley: University of California Press, 1976.

Follow the convention of whatever text edition or translation you cite in your notes and bibliography (for symbols common to ancient Near Eastern texts, see §5.9):

12. "The Disappearance of the Sun God," §3 (A I 11–17) (Harry A. Hoffner Jr., *Hittite Myths* [ed. Gary M. Beckman; WAW 2; Atlanta: Scholars Press, 1990], 26).

Hoffner, Harry A., Jr. *Hittite Myths*. Edited by Gary M. Beckman. WAW 2. Atlanta: Scholars Press, 1990.

Authors are encouraged to provide the reader with the most current edition, particularly if a transliterated text is cited:

32. Ashur Inscription, obv. lines 10–17 (Albert Kirk Grayson, *Assyrian Rulers of the Early First Millennium BC [1114–859 BC]*, RIMA 2 [Toronto: University of Toronto Press, 1991], 143–44).

34. Ashur Inscription, obv. lines 10–17 (RIMA 2:143–44).

Grayson, Albert Kirk. *Assyrian Rulers of the Early First Millennium BC (1114–859 BC)*. RIMA 2. Toronto: University of Toronto Press, 1991.

33. Esarhaddon Chronicle, lines 3–4 (Albert Kirk Grayson, *Assyrian and Babylonian Chronicles*, TCS [Locust Valley, NY: Augustin, 1975], 125).

33. Esarhaddon Chronicle, lines 3–4 (*ABC*, 125).

Grayson, Albert Kirk. *Assyrian and Babylonian Chronicles*. TCS. Locust Valley, NY: Augustin, 1975.

Some texts, especially letters, are conventionally cited by their number in the principal edition, without a page reference; for example, a letter from the Mari archive sent by Yasmah-Adad is cited as:

45. ARM 1.3.

Dossin, Georges. *Lettres*. ARM 1. 1946. Repr., Paris: Geuthner, 1967.

If citing it from the edited version:

45. ARMT 1.3.

Georges Dossin, *Correspondance de Šamši-Addu et de ses fils*. ARMT 1. Paris: Imprimerei nationale, 1950.

6.4.2 Loeb Classical Library (Greek and Latin)

Citing a volume or work in the Loeb Classical Library, especially if the work is well known, requires only the primary reference. Ordinarily these are cited in parentheses, just as any other primary source. (See §6.1.3.6 on conventions for citing primary sources.)

(Josephus, *Ant.* 2.233–235)

1. Josephus, *Ant.* 2.233–235.

4. Tacitus, *Ann.* 15.18–19

As in the case of all ancient works, if the translation is being quoted, it is appropriate to cite the translator:

(Josephus, *Ant.* 2.233–235 [Thackeray, LCL])

5. Josephus, *Ant.* 2.233–235 (Thackeray, LCL).

6. Tacitus, *Ann.* 15.18–19 (Jackson, LCL).

The bibliography provides the necessary information regarding the work.

Josephus. Translated by Henry St. J. Thackeray et al. 10 vols. LCL. Cambridge: Harvard University Press, 1926–1965.

Tacitus. *The Histories and The Annals*. Translated by Clifford H. Moore and J.ohn Jackson. 4 vols. LCL. Cambridge: Harvard University Press, 1937.

If a complete work within an ancient author's corpus is under consideration, the entry can reflect that.

14. Flavius Josephus, *The Jewish Antiquities, Books 1–19*, trans. Henry St. J. Thackeray et al., LCL (Cambridge: Harvard University Press, 1930–1965).

But the bibliography should reflect the entire collection.

Josephus. Translated by Henry St. J. Thackeray et al. 10 vols. LCL. Cambridge: Harvard University Press, 1926–1965.

6.4.3 Papyri, Ostraca, and Epigraphica

6.4.3.1 Papyri and Ostraca in General

When a papyrus or ostracon, or a translation thereof, is cited from the standard critical edition listed in the most recent edition of the *Checklist of Editions of Greek and Latin Papyri, Ostraca, and Tablets* (ed. John F. Oates et al., 5th ed., BASPSup 9 [Oakville, CT: American Society of Papyrologists], 2001; more current is the online version at http://scriptorium.lib.duke.edu/papyrus/texts/clist.html), it is sufficient to cite by abbreviation (using the abbreviation from the *Checklist*; note that there are no spaces within the abbreviation) and inventory number.

(P.Cair.Zen. 59003)

22. P.Cair.Zen. 59003.

Bibliographic information for all collections so abbreviated should be included in a list of abbreviations or short titles. If a papyrus, or a translation thereof, is quoted from a source other than the principal edition (such as Hunt and Edgar's *Select Papyri*), the source should be identified in parentheses. In such cases, it is nevertheless preferable to use the standard abbreviation from the *Checklist* and include that abbreviation in the list of abbreviations or short titles.

22. P.Cair.Zen. 59003 (Arthur S. Hunt and Campbell C. Edgar, *Select Papyri*, LCL [Cambridge: Harvard University Press, 1932], 1:96).

If *Select Papyri* or a similar collection is cited frequently, it should be abbreviated. In the case of *Select Papyri*, citation may be by selection number rather than volume and page number.

22. P.Cair.Zen. 59003 (Hunt and Edgar §31).

6.4.3.2 Epigraphica

Taking their cue from Oates et al., *Checklist of Editions* (see §6.4.3.1), G. H. R. Horsley and John A. L. Lee offer "A Preliminary Checklist of Abbreviations of Greek Epigraphic Volumes" in *Epigraphica: Periodico internazionale di epigrafia* 56 (1994): 129–69. This indispensable checklist seeks "to provide a list of coherent abbreviations for Greek epigraphic volumes which are both acceptable to specialist epigraphers and comprehensible in themselves to nonspecialists who have occasion to use and refer to inscriptions" (p. 130). Abbreviations for a few of the more common epigraphic resources are included in §8.4 (e.g., *BGU, MAMA, SIG*), but for a more comprehensive catalogue, see Horsley and Lee's checklist.

6.4.3.3 Greek Magical Papyri

The Greek Magical Papyri are abbreviated following Hans Dieter Betz, *The Greek Magical Papyri in Translation, including the Demotic Spells*, 2nd ed. (Chicago: University of Chicago Press, 1996). The roman numerals, even those with appended letters (e.g., *PGM* Va. 1–3), follow Preisendanz's catalog of manuscripts. Betz retains Preisendanz's Greek text numeration (until the end of Preisendanz's list, LXXX), except he creates his own system (still dependent on *PGM*) for the demotic spells (which he identifies as *PDM*). N.B.: Spaces separate roman numerals and arabic numerals, which "usually delineate the compass of individual spells within the papyrus manuscript" (ibid., xxxi).

(*PGM* III. 1–164)

22. *PGM* III. 1–164.

If the edition should be mentioned, cite it in parentheses following the reference, listing it in full in the bibliography.

22. *PGM* III. 1–164 (Betz).

Betz, Hans Dieter. *The Greek Magical Papyri in Translation, Including the Demotic Spells*. 2nd ed. Chicago: University of Chicago Press, 1996.

6.4.4 Ancient Epistles and Homilies

The edition of the Cynic epistles edited by Abraham Malherbe (*The Cynic Epistles: A Study Edition*, SBS 12 [Atlanta: Scholars Press, 1977]) provides a convenient model for citation. Citing the Cynic epistles or the several ancient collections of letters, homilies, and the like can be confusing on two fronts since the writings frequently bear both titles and numbers but sometimes only a number. For example, the *Epistles of Diogenes* include *Epistle 26: To Crates* and a simple numeric designation, *Epistle 28*. Since all the epistles have numbers but not all have titles, the numbers serve as the best identifiers of the pieces and are considered sufficient citation. Line numbers should be included in specific quotations, with a comma separating the work from the line number.

(Heraclitus, *Epistle 1*, 10)

34. Heraclitus, *Epistle 1*, 10.

A comma separates the epistle number (set in italic) from the line number (set in roman). If the translation itself requires notation, include it in parentheses.

36. Heraclitus, *Epistle 1*, 10 (Worley).

Heraclitus. *Epistle 1*. Translated by David Worley. Page 187 in *The Cynic Epistles: A Study Edition*. Edited by Abraham J. Malherbe. SBS 12. Atlanta: Scholars Press, 1977.

If several authors from the collection are cited, put the full work in the bibliography:

Malherbe, Abraham J., ed. *The Cynic Epistles: A Study Edition*. SBS 12. Atlanta: Scholars Press, 1977.

6.4.5 *ANF* and *NPNF*, First and Second Series

Citing the church fathers can be confusing and frustrating since often there are a variety of levels at which one can cite. Authors may elect to cite both the primary reference and the volume and page number within a given series. If this does not become cumbersome for the reader, it is helpful to include both. In either case, it is better to use arabic numbers rather than roman numerals and to put the *ANF* or *NPNF* reference in parentheses. It is not necessary to give a full citation if a bibliography is included and subsequent citations in the notes are identical to the first citation.

14. *The Clementine Homilies* 1.3 (*ANF* 8:223).

In this example, the title of the work appears in italics. The number 1 indicates the homily number, and 3 designates the chapter. The parenthetical information refers to the series, volume, and page number. In the bibliography, one need cite only the series information, unless the translation itself plays an integral role in the discussion. Thus:

The Ante-Nicene Fathers. Edited by Alexander Roberts and James Donaldson. 1885–1887. 10 vols. Repr., Peabody, MA: Hendrickson, 1994.

An example in which the translation itself needs to be documented follows:

44. Augustine, *Letters of St. Augustin* 28.3.5 (*NPNF*[1] 1:252).

Augustine. *The Letters of St. Augustin*. In vol. 1 of *The Nicene and Post-Nicene Fathers*, Series 1. Edited by Philip Schaff. 1886–1889. 14 vols. Repr., Peabody, MA: Hendrickson, 1994.

6.4.6 J.-P. Migne's Patrologia Latina and Patrologia Graeca

For this series, use the abbreviated form:

6. Gregory of Nazianzus, *Orationes theologicae* 4 (PG 36:12c).

Patrologia Latina. Edited by J.-P. Migne. 217 vols. Paris, 1844–1864.

Patrologia Graeca. Edited by J.-P. Migne. 162 vols. Paris, 1857–1886.

Regarding the use of roman type for these series names, see §6.1.3.5.

6.4.7 Strack-Billerbeck, *Kommentar zum Neuen Testament*

Citing Hermann Strack and Paul Billerbeck's *Kommentar zum Neuen Testament aus Talmud und Midrasch* is simplified by using the abbreviation for the work, Str-B and the volume and page number(s). Thus a note might read:

3. See the discussion of ἐκρατοῦντο in Str-B 2:271.

Strack, Hermann L., and Paul Billerbeck. *Kommentar zum Neuen Testament aus Talmud und Midrasch*. 6 vols. Munich: Beck, 1922–1961.

6.4.8 *Aufstieg und Niedergang der römischen Welt* (*ANRW*)

The multivolume *Aufstieg und Niedergang der römischen Welt: Geschichte und Kultur Roms im Spiegel der neueren Forschung* (*ANRW*) can be problematic because of the variety of levels, languages, and titles within this ongoing work. Articles appear in English, French, German, and Italian. Later volumes have the parallel English title *Rise and Decline of the Roman World*. Volumes of part 2, *Principat*, the material most commonly cited, have separate subtitles (e.g., *Religion, Politische Geschichte, Sprache und Literatur*, etc., with nearly thirty volumes in print). The note example below assumes that *ANRW* is listed properly in the bibliography and included in the list of abbreviations.

76. Graham Anderson, "The *pepaideumenos* in Action: Sophists and Their Outlook in the Early Empire," *ANRW* 33.1:80–208.

79. Anderson, "*Pepaideumenos*," *ANRW* 33.1:86.

Anderson, Graham. "The *pepaideumenos* in Action: Sophists and Their Outlook in the Early Empire." *ANRW* 33.1:80–208. Part 2, *Principat*, 33.1. Edited by H. Temporini and W. Haase. New York: de Gruyter, 1989.

As a strictly bibliographical entry, *ANRW* can be entered as follows.

Temporini, Hildegard, and Wolfgang Haase, eds. *Aufstieg und Niedergang der römischen Welt: Geschichte und Kultur Roms im Spiegel der neueren Forschung*. Part 2, *Principat*. Berlin: de Gruyter, 1972–.

6.4.9 Bible Commentaries

Properly citing Bible commentaries can be complex, especially when the commentaries are (1) multivolume or (2) in a series. Commentaries are normally cited just as any other book, with the commentary series name being the only significant addition. Since editors of commentary series usually acquire rather than edit, the names of general editors need not be included in bibliographic or note references. Thus:

8. Morna Hooker, *The Gospel according to Saint Mark*, BNTC 2 (Peabody, MA: Hendrickson, 1991), 223.

Hooker, Morna. *The Gospel according to Saint Mark*. BNTC 2. Peabody, MA: Hendrickson, 1991.

6.4.10 A Single Volume of a Multivolume Commentary in a Series

The style for citing a single volume of a multivolume commentary in a series is the same as for a titled volume in a multivolume edited work (§6.2.21). The style for citing the the entire work follows that for a multivolume work (§6.2.20).

6.4.11 SBL Seminar Papers

33. James L. Crenshaw, "Theodicy in the Book of the Twelve," *Society of Biblical Literature 2001 Seminar Papers*, SBLSPS 40 (Atlanta: Society of Biblical Literature, 2001), 1–18.

Crenshaw, James L. "Theodicy in the Book of the Twelve." Pages 1–18 in *Society of Biblical Literature 2001 Seminar Papers*. SBLSPS 40. Atlanta: Society of Biblical Literature, 2001.

6.4.12 A CD-ROM Reference (with a Corresponding Print Edition)

Books on CD-ROM should be cited according to the print edition. It is not necessary to indicate the medium in the citation.

6.4.13 Text Editions Published Online with No Print Counterpart

When citing original editions of primary texts that are published online (as opposed to electronic versions of texts published previously in print form), an electronic resource identifier (DOI or URL) must be included.

2. Gernot Wilhelm, ed., "Der Vertrag Šuppiluliumas I. von Ḫatti mit Šattiwazza von Mittani (CTH 51.I)," released 24 February 2013, doi:hethiter.net/: CTH 51.I (INTR 2013-02-24).

4. Wilhelm, "Der Vertrag Šuppiluliumas I."

Gernot Wilhelm, ed. "Der Vertrag Šuppiluliumas I. von Ḫatti mit Šattiwazza von Mittani (CTH 51.I)." doi:hethiter.net/: CTH 51.I (INTR 2013-02-24).

6.4.14 Online Database

Citations of databases containing formally published materials should identify the author of the content or the owner or sponsor of the site, and provide the title of the content and the name of the database, followed by the electronic resource identifier(s).

37. Cobb Institute of Archaeology. "The Figurines of Maresha, the Persian Era," DigMaster, http://www.cobb.msstate.edu/dignew/Maresha/index.html.

39. Cobb Institute of Archaeology, "The Figurines of Maresha."

Cobb Institute of Archaeology. "The Figurines of Maresha, the Persian Era." DigMaster. http://www.cobb.msstate.edu/dignew/Maresha/index.html.

15. William R. Caraher, ed., "Pyla-Koutsopetria Archaeological Project: (Overview)," Open Context, released 5 November 2013, http://opencontext.org/projects/3F6DCD13-A476-488E-ED10-47D25513FCB2, doi:10.6078/M7B56GNS.

17. Caraher, "Pyla-Koutsopetria Archaeological Project."

William R. Caraher, ed. "Pyla-Koutsopetria Archaeological Project: (Overview)." Open Context. Released 5 November 2013. http://opencontext.org/projects/3F6DCD13-A476-488E-ED10-47D25513FCB2. doi:10.6078/M7B56GNS.

6.4.15 Websites and Blogs

Material published informally online must nevertheless be included in notes and bibliography. (Blog entries, however, may be omitted from the bibliography.) In such citations, a URL alone is not sufficient. Rather, the material cited must be referred to by a descriptive phrase or title, followed by the author of the content if known, the owner or sponsor of the site, and the URL. SBL Press does not advocate including access dates (see §6.1.6).

10. "The One Hundred Most Important Cuneiform Objects," cdli:wiki, http://cdli.ox.ac.uk/wiki/doku.php?id=the_one_hundred_most_important_cuneiform_objects.

"The One Hundred Most Important Cuneiform Objects." cdli:wiki. http://cdli.ox.ac.uk/wiki/doku.php?id=the_one_hundred_most_important_cuneiform_objects.

Per *CMS* §14.246, citations of blog entries should include the author of the entry; the name of the entry, in quotation marks; the title or description of the blog; the date; and a URL.

3. Mark Goodacre, "Jesus' Wife Fragment: Another Round-Up," *NT Blog*, 9 May 2014, http://ntweblog.blogspot.com.

For further reference, see Janice R. Walker and Todd Taylor, *The Columbia Guide to Online Style*, 2nd ed. (New York: Columbia University Press, 2006).

6.5 Author-Date Citations

Authors writing in the social sciences may elect to use an author-date form of citation rather than the more traditional note-based system described above. The primary purpose of author-date style is to eliminate cumbersome notes while still facilitating source references that do not interrupt the flow of the main text to a major degree. Because the style eliminates duplicate listings in notes and bibliography, it can save considerable space. If one chooses, it can even be combined with strictly substantive notes to produce a clear and "streamlined" overall appearance.

In the author-date system, a reference list (often called "Works Cited") provides complete publication information on all the sources, and only the sources, referred to in the text; "select bibliographies" have no place here. As the style name implies, the source list is arranged according to each work's author(s) and date of publication, thus producing an author-date sequence that is used, along with page numbers, in text citations.

A bibliographical listing in the author-date reference list differs from the traditional system in several key ways: the date of publication follows the author's name rather than falling at the end of the citation, and multiple works by the same author are organized by publication date (oldest to most recent) rather than alphabetically by title of the work.

For a wealth of additional information, consult *CMS* §§15.1–55. Examples:

> An elaborate treatment can be found in Talbert 1992, 51.
> The explanation for this is not clear (Leyerle 1997, 61).
> Pfuhl (1980, 65–68) notes five possible techniques.

Two citations in the same sentence:

> An agrarian society is built upon agricultural production (Lenski and Lenski 1974, 207; Lenski 1966, 192).

When an author has more than one work in the bibliography, the entries should follow this order: (1) works authored, edited, or translated by author in chronological order from the oldest to the most recent; (2) works compiled, edited, or translated by that author and another. Thus, for books by the same author:

> Wilder, Amos. 1939. *Eschatology and Ethics in the Teaching of Jesus*. New York: Harper & Bros.
>
> ———. 1971. *Early Christian Rhetoric: The Language of the Gospel*. Cambridge: Harvard University Press.

When an author has two or more works in the same year, the entries should be arranged in alphabetical order and designated "a," "b," etc.

> (Pilch 1988a, 14)
>
> (Pilch 1988b, 60)
>
> Pilch, John J. 1988a. "Interpreting Scripture: The Social Science Method." *BTB* 18:13–19.
>
> ———. 1988b. "Understanding Biblical Healing: Selecting the Appropriate Model." *BTB* 18:60–66.

When multiple works by an author are cited together, they are separated by a semicolon when they include page references and by a comma in the absence of page references.

> (Pilch 1988a, 14; 1988b, 60) *but* (Pilch 1988a, 1988b)

6.5.1 A Book by a Single Author

> (Talbert 1992, 22)

Talbert, Charles H. 1992. *Reading John: A Literary and Theological Commentary on the Fourth Gospel and the Johannine Epistles*. New York: Crossroad.

6.5.2 A Book by Two or Three Authors

(Robinson and Koester 1971, 23)

Robinson, James M., and Helmut Koester. 1971. *Trajectories through Early Christianity*. Philadelphia: Fortress.

6.5.3 A Translated Volume

(Egger 1996, 291)

Egger, Wilhelm. 1996. *How to Read the New Testament: An Introduction to Linguistic and Historical-Critical Methodology*. Translated by Peter Heinegg. Peabody, MA: Hendrickson.

6.5.4 An Edited Volume

(Kraft and Nickelsburg 1986)

Kraft, Robert A., and George W. E. Nickelsburg, eds. 1986. *Early Judaism and Its Modern Interpreters*. Philadelphia: Fortress; Atlanta: Scholars Press.

6.5.5 An Article in a Festschrift

(Van Seters 1995, 222)

Van Seters, John. 1995. "The Theology of the Yahwist: A Preliminary Sketch." Pages 219–28 in *"Wer ist wie du, Herr, unter den Göttern?": Studien zur Theologie und Religionsgeschichte Israels für Otto Kaiser zum 70. Geburtstag*. Edited by Ingo Kottsieper et al. Göttingen: Vandenhoeck & Ruprecht.

6.5.6 A Reprint Title

(Moore 1997, 2:228)

Moore, George Foot. 1997. *Judaism in the First Three Centuries of the Christian Era: The Age of Tannaim*. 3 vols. Cambridge: Harvard University Press, 1927–1930. Repr., 3 vols. in 2, Peabody, MA: Hendrickson.

6.5.7 A Titled Volume in a Multivolume Work

(Winter 1993, 137)

Winter, Bruce W., and Andrew D. Clarke, eds. 1993. *The Book of Acts in Its Ancient Literary Setting*. Vol. 1 of *The Book of Acts in Its First Century Setting*. Edited by Bruce W. Winter. Grand Rapids: Eerdmans.

6.5.8 A Chapter within a Titled Volume in a Multivolume Work

(Bauckham 1993, 53)

Bauckham, Richard. 1993. "The *Acts of Paul* as a Sequel to Acts." Pages 105–52 in *The Book of Acts in Its Ancient Literary Setting.* Edited by Bruce W. Winter and Andrew D. Clarke. Vol. 1 of *The Book of Acts in Its First Century Setting.* Edited by Bruce W. Winter. Grand Rapids: Eerdmans.

6.5.9 A Work in a Series

(Hofius 1989, 124)

Hofius, Otfried. 1989. *Paulusstudien.* WUNT 51. Tübingen: Mohr Siebeck.

6.5.10 A Journal Article

(Leyerle 1993, 161)

Leyerle, Blake. 1993. "John Chrysostom on the Gaze." *JECS* 1:159–74.

6.5.11 An Article in an Encyclopedia or a Dictionary

(Stendahl 1962, 1:419)

Stendahl, Krister. 1962. "Biblical Theology, Contemporary." *IDB* 1:418–32.

6.5.12 An Article in a Lexicon or a Theological Dictionary

For the discussion of a specific word:

(Beyer 1965, 2:81–87)

Beyer, H. 1965. "διακονέω." Pages 81–87 in vol. 2 of *Theological Dictionary of the New Testament.* Edited by Gerhard Kittel and Gerhard Friedrich. Translated by Geoffrey W. Bromiley. 10 vols. Grand Rapids: Eerdmans, 1964–1976.

6.5.13 A Paper Presented at a Professional Society

(Niditch 1994, 14)

Niditch, Susan. 1994. "Oral Culture and Written Documents." Paper presented at the Annual Meeting of the New England Region of the SBL. Worcester, MA, March 25.

6.5.14 Loeb Classical Library (Greek and Latin)

Noting a volume or work in the Loeb Classical Library, especially if the work is well known, requires only the primary reference. See §6.4.2. (See §8.3.14 on abbreviating classical and early Christian works.)

(Josephus, *Ant.* 2.233–235)

(Tacitus, *Ann.* 15.18–19)

Or with a translation or excerpt:

(Josephus, *Ant.* 2.233–235 [Thackeray])

When citing the full work, with an emphasis on the translator:

Thackeray, H. St. J., et al., trans. 1926–1965. *Josephus.* 10 vols. LCL. Cambridge: Harvard University Press.

With an emphasis on the original author:

Tacitus, Cornelius. 1937. *The Histories and The Annals.* Translated by C. H. Moore and J. Jackson. 4 vols. LCL. Cambridge: Harvard University Press.

7 INDEXES

7.1 Types of Indexes

The author or editor of a volume is usually responsible for creating any indexes to be included. Authors and editors should consult with the publisher regarding the types of indexes to be included, as this will vary depending on the type of book.

At a minimum, most monographs and many multiauthor volumes will include a subject index. In biblical studies and related fields it is also a desideratum to include an ancient sources index. Some works may benefit from an author index as well.

7.1.1 Subject Index

The primary requisite of a subject index is usefulness to the reader. Entry headings should be concise and logical. In deciding what topics to include, the indexer must try to anticipate names or terms that readers are likely to look for as well as when they might look for them under an alternative term. It is not necessary to index names or terms that occur in passing and are not essential to the theme of the work.

7.1.1.1 Main Headings

As a rule, use nouns and noun phrases, rather than adjectives, for the main headings of a subject index (e.g., *holiness* rather than *holy*). A comprehensive subject index will often include proper nouns designating people and places as well as common nouns identifying objects and ideas. If a reader is likely to search by the second word in a noun phrase, invert the two words (e.g., *coherence, literary*). See *CMS* §16.9.

7.1.1.2 Subentries

Overly broad entries that list eight or more page numbers may frustrate readers searching for a specific passage. To prevent this, supply helpful subheadings detailing the various parts or aspects of a main entry. In some cases a subheading combines with the main entry to identify a narrower subject (e.g., *feminist* and *criticism* in §7.1.1.6); in others the subheading identifies a specific division within the main entry. If both kinds will assist readers, both should be used. See *CMS* §16.10.

7.1.1.3 Locators

To help readers locate passages quickly and accurately, an index should provide specific and clear locators, such as page numbers, paragraph or section numbers, note numbers, or text and line numbers. When a subject is discussed over multiple pages or sections, specify the beginning and ending pages (e.g., 34–36); if a subject is merely mentioned on a series of pages, list them separately (e.g., 34, 35, 36). See *CMS* §16.13.

7.1.1.4 Cross-References

Cross-references serve two purposes. *See* references guide readers from possible index terms to the terms actually used in the index (e.g., treaty. *See* covenant). *See also* cross-references direct readers to related topics that they may want to consider. Note that both *See* and *See also* are set in italics, and the latter generally appears after all the locators. For more on cross-references, see *CMS* §§16.15–23.

7.1.1.5 Capitalization of Index Entries

Capitalize only those index entries that would be capitalized in the middle of a sentence. See *CMS* §16.11.

7.1.1.6 Sample Subject Index

canon, 6, 143, 163, 173. *See also* Council of Carthage
coherence, literary, 165–66
concept formation, 129, 162, 170–76
criticism
    feminist, 33
    form. *See* form criticism
    historical, 34
    literary, 167
    philosophical, 146
crucifixion, 9, 132–34, 138, 142–43

7.1.2 Ancient Sources Index

Ancient sources indexes are essential tools in biblical studies and related fields. Thus, most scholarly works will include such an index, while works designed for a more general audience may omit it. It is helpful to boldface primary discussions of texts to aid the reader in navigating through the work.

7.1.2.1 Sorting Primary-Text References

Please pay particular attention to the following model regarding the ordering of references within indexes of primary-text references. Some general principles can be observed in the examples below: (1) When two ranges have the same starting point, the one with the earlier end point is listed first. (2) A simple reference (to a chapter, a verse, or part of a verse, rather than a range) precedes a range whose starting point is the same as the simple reference. (3) We strongly discourage the use of a reference to a range with no explicitly named end point (i.e., a reference using f. or ff.); but if used such a reference would follow any simple references and precede any references to ranges whose end points are explicitly given. (4) A reference to a specified portion of a verse (or a range beginning therewith) comes after a reference to the whole verse (or a range beginning therewith).

Acts	2	2:4a
	2–3	2:4b
	2:4	2:4b–6
	2:4–7	2:4b–7

7.1.2.2 Common Subdivisions of an Ancient Sources Index

Common subdivisions of an ancient sources index include the following, in order:

Hebrew Bible [if Hebrew Bible order is followed; otherwise, use "Old Testament"]
Ancient Near Eastern Texts
Deuterocanonical Books [preferred to "Apocryphal Books"]
Pseudepigrapha
Dead Sea Scrolls
Ancient Jewish Writers [e.g., Josephus and Philo]
New Testament
Rabbinic Works [or individually, in the following order: Mishnah; Tosefta; Talmuds; Targums; Midrash and Related Literature]
Early Christian Writings
Greco-Roman Literature

7.1.2.3 Sample Ancient Sources Index

Hebrew Bible/Old Testament
Genesis

1:2	70, 173, 204
1:7	113–15

7.1.3 Author Index

If an author and publisher determine that an author index will be of value to the reader, then one may be included. Author indexes may be included whether the book utilizes the traditional documentation style of citation or the author-date system (for which see §6). Unlike with the subject index and the ancient sources index, it is not necessary to specify when an author name appears in the footnotes; the page number alone is sufficient.

7.1.3.1 General

Only primary author(s) should be indexed. Do not index editors of a volume in which an essay appears unless the citation is to the edited work as a whole. Do not include note numbers when providing page listings; the page itself is sufficient.

7.1.3.2 Sample Author Index

7.2 Alphabetizing

The rules provided in this section apply equally to bibliographies.

7.2.1 General

The two main systems of alphabetizing are generally called letter-by-letter and word-by-word (for a full discussion of the two, see *CMS* §16.58–61). For those who are accustomed to the terminology, we use the word-by-word rule. A simple way of explaining this rule is: *proceed character by character, giving priority to word-units*. Letters, obviously enough, will go in alphabetical order: *a* ranks highest; *z* lowest; case and diacritics are ignored (o = ö = ø). Commas and spaces signal an interruption, and the material that follows is considered only in alphabetizing entries with an identical first word. (This is similar to the numerical system used in this handbook; each set of digits separated by a period constitutes a "word," and one takes into account only as many "digit-words" as are common to the numbers being sequenced.) If the same word is followed by a comma and by a space in two entries, the word with the comma is listed first (e.g., *New, Zoe* before *New Deal*). Hyphens, capital letters, and quotation marks are ignored. An apostrophe used in transliteration ranks before an a, but in names it is often ignored (see §§7.2.2.2–3). The following list gives a fuller hierarchy:

space] Signals a break in alphabetizing
' [apostrophe]
0
1
(etc.)
9
a, A, ä, á, å (etc.)
b
(etc.)
z
Ignored: - – . " " ' ' [hyphen, en dash, period, double and single quotation marks]

Thus, to borrow and modify the *CMS* §16.61 word-by-word example:

N stem
NEW (Now End War)
New, Arthur
New, Zoe
New Deal
new economics
New England
New Latin
new math
New Testament
New Word
New Year's Day
new years and old habits
newborn
newcomer
newel
"new-fangled notions"
newlyweds
news, lamentable
News, Networks, and the Arts
news conference
News of the World
news release
newsletter
newsprint
newt
Newton, Lady Anne
Newton, Isaac
Newton, Rev. Philip T.
Newtonian

7.2.2 Names with Particles and Titles

For surnames that begin with particles (i.e., prepositions and articles) we follow two general rules: (1) capitalize according to established usage; (2) alphabetize by the first capitalized part of the surname.

We do not conform Jewish and Arabic names with ben and ibn to the rules for particles because ben and ibn are not particles but nouns (meaning "son [of]"). *Abraham ibn Ezra* should be alphabetized as *Ibn Ezra, Abraham*. *Moses ben Maimon* would be alphabetized as *Ben Maimon, Moses* (or as *Maimonides*).

Since titles (such as "Lady" and "Rev." in the sample list of §7.2.1) can easily displace an author's name from its natural location, you may consider omitting the titles altogether or putting them in parentheses and ignoring them in alphabetizing. Such decisions will involve editorial judgment about the most recognizable form of a name and the form in which readers are most likely to search for it.

7.2.2.1 Capitalization

It is not always easy to know what constitutes established usage, since different rules apply to different particles in names of different nationalities; for example, names that have been Americanized are generally capitalized without regard to such rules. The table in §7.2.2.3 gives our usage for some names that occur commonly in biblical scholarship and related fields. Others may be treated by analogy with these (but be careful to follow the right model for the nationality at hand) or looked up in a standard reference work such as *Merriam-Webster's Biographical Dictionary*. If no print authority is available, consult WorldCat (http://WorldCat.org) or the Library of Congress (http://catalog.loc.gov).

A particle in a given person's name should have the same case in running text, footnotes, bibliographies, and indexes whether or not the surname is preceded by a first name or initials. Thus:

> In his earlier works, Gerhard von Rad said . . .
> In his earlier works, von Rad said . . .
> In his earlier works, François Du Bois said . . .
> In his earlier works, Du Bois said . . .

Any name with a particle at the beginning of a sentence is capitalized:

> Von Rad often said . . .

7.2.2.2 Alphabetization

John Van Seters should be alphabetized as *Van Seters, John,* because in this Americanized name *Van* is capitalized; *Hans von Campenhausen* should be alphabetized as *Campenhausen, Hans von,* because *von* is not capitalized. Follow this same rule even when a noncapitalized particle is separated from the main part of the surname by an apostrophe or hyphen rather than a space (as with *Jean Le Rond d'Alembert* and *Khalid Ahmad al-A'dami* in the following table).

For names beginning with *M', Mc, Mac,* or *O',* as well as names beginning with *St., Saint, Saint-, Sainte,* and the like, follow the general rule given above in §7.2.1. These names should be "sorted as they appear," not "sorted as if spelled out"; for this purpose, the apostrophes are ignored (see *CMS* §16.73–75). Remember that spaces are significant in sorting.

It is important to anticipate occasions when readers may not look up a particular name in the "right" place. In indexes containing only a few names with particles, judicious use of cross-references and even double entries is encouraged.

7.2.2.3 Examples

The following list is a guide for capitalization as well as alphabetization. Some names without particles have been included to demonstrate correct alphabetization.

A'dami, Khalid Ahmad al-
Aarde, Andries G. van
Alembert, Jean Le Rond d'
Balthasar, Hans Urs von
Ben Maimon, Moses. *See* Maimonides
Ben-Tor, Amnon

Berardino, Angelo di
Berchem, Denis van
Bickerman, Elias J.
Boer, Martinus C. de
Böhl, Franz Marius Theodor de Liagre
Born, Adrianus van den
Campenhausen, Hans von
Cranenburgh, Henri van
Dake, Finis J.
D'Angelo, Mary Rose
De Boer, Willis Peter
De Lacey, D. R.
De Vries, Simon J.
Des Places, Eduard
deSilva, David A.
Di Lella, Alexander A.
Díez Macho, Alejandro
Dobschütz, Ernst von
Du Buit, F. M.
Du Cange, Charles Du Fresne
Du Plessis, Paul Johannes
Dubarle, André M.
Fraine, Jean de
García Bachmann, Mercedes L.
Geus, C. H. J. de
Grobel, Kendrick
Grønbaek, J. H.
Gröndahl, Franke
Gross, Walter
Harnack, Adolf von, *or*
Harnack, Adolf
Hoek, Annewies van den
Horst, P. W. van der
Houwink ten Cate, Philo H. J.
Ibn Ezra, Abraham ben Meir
Imschoot, Paul van
Jonge, H. J. de
Jonge, Marinus de
Kooij, Gerrit van der
La Mésangère, Pierre de
La Potterie, Ignace de
Lacocque, André
Lagarde, Pierre de
Lagrange, Marie-Joseph
Langhe, Robert de
Laperrousaz, Ernest-Marie
LaSor, William Sanford
Le Boulluec, Alain
Le Déaut, R.
Le Moyne, J.
Le Nain de Tillemont, Louis-Sebastien
Loon, Maurits Nanning van
Lubac, Henri de
Maass, F.
MacDermot, Violet
Macdonald, John
Maimonides (Moses ben Maimon)
Markus, R. A.
McKenzie, J. L.
Medico, H. E. del
Meer, Frederik van der
Moor, Johannes C. de
Oakman, Douglas E.
O'Day, Gail R.
Odell, Margaret S.
Olmo Lete, G. del
O'Neil, Edward N.
Ortiz de Urbina, Ignacio
Osten-Sacken, Peter von der
Ploeg, J. P. M. van der
Rad, Gerhard von
Ranke, Leopold von
Rossum, J. van
Santos, Elmaro Camilo dos
Santos Otero, A. de
Saulcy, Louis Felicien Joseph Caignart de
Selms, Adrianus van
Smitten, Wilhelm T. in der
Soden, Hermann von
Soden, Wolfram von
Sola Pool, D. de
St. Ville, Susan M.
Strycker, Emile de
Teilhard de Chardin, Pierre
Tuya, Manuel de
Unnik, W. C. van
Van Dusen, Henry P.
Van Seters, John

Van Til, Cornelius
VanderKam, James C.
Vaux, Roland de
Vries, Benjamin de
Wette, W. M. L. de
Woude, A. S. van der

7.2.3 Compound Surnames

Most Spanish authors and some English-speaking authors use double surnames, which should be alphabetized according to the first element. It is often impossible to tell just from looking at such names how they should be treated, so authors and editors are encouraged to make use of WorldCat. With English-speaking authors, the absence of a hyphen does not necessarily mean that the two family names do not make a double surname—although it usually does. As for names with particles, we look to the Library of Congress for definitive guidance in individual cases. A few examples:

Alonso Schökel, Luis
Busto Saiz, José Ramon
Díez Macho, Alejandro
García Cordero, M.
García de la Fuente, Olegario
Fernández-Armesto, Felipe
Lane Fox, Robin
Payne Smith, Robert
Ruiz Bueno, Daniel
Santos Otero, Aurelio de
Schüssler Fiorenza, Elisabeth
Teilhard de Chardin, Pierre
Yarbro Collins, Adela
but:
Darr, Katheryn Pfisterer
Jones, Henry Stuart

As in the case of names with particles (see §7.2.2.2), appropriate use of cross-references is encouraged.

7.2.4 Asian Names

For indexing Asian names, see *CMS* §§16.77–78, 80–82, 85–87.

7.2.5 Arabic Names

For indexing Arabic names, see *CMS* §16.76.

8 ABBREVIATIONS

Authors' use of abbreviations will vary depending on the material and its intended readers. Abbreviations can be particularly useful in notes, parenthetical materials, tables, lists, and bibliographies, and in the right circumstances SBL Press encourages authors to make the most of them. Where abbreviations are frequent, it is helpful to list the uncommon ones (those that would not be found in a standard dictionary or universally known among the target audience) in the front matter; on the other hand, if technical abbreviations are infrequent, one could make a good case for eliminating them entirely.

In running text, it is much more common to spell terms out, but even there abbreviations can be used to advantage. Thus Old and New Testament books (particularly where specific passages are being cited), the different versions of the Scripture, conventional journal and dictionary titles, and numerous other common terms may be readily abbreviated—provided the audience is unlikely to be confused. If the term to be abbreviated appears at the beginning of a sentence, it should ordinarily be spelled out.

The following pages present abbreviations that are widely used in the pertinent academic disciplines. We acknowledge that many inconsistencies exist, both as a result of developments (sometimes reflected in major publications) in relatively independent and specialized fields and as a function of normal variations in English usage. Thus ours is not an attempt to prescribe inviolable rules but rather to provide an accessible reference for authors and to document SBL Press's own usage. Naturally, if our suggestions help bring about a greater consistency across the fields represented, we will not be unhappy; even though no one will love every abbreviation, their common use can have overriding benefits. Still, we wish to be quite clear that authors and publishers may freely choose to vary from the usages we describe, provided they appropriately document their chosen abbreviations for readers.

8.1 General Abbreviations

8.1.1 Postal Abbreviations

The names of states or other geographic entities should not be abbreviated in the body of a work when they stand alone, unless they occur in parentheses. SBL Press now prefers to use the two-letter postal codes over the traditional abbreviations (e.g., MA instead of Mass., CA instead of Calif., ON instead of Ont.) for US states and Canadian provinces. Authors should ascertain their publisher's preference and use one system or the other consistently.

Alabama	AL	Kentucky	KY	North Dakota	ND
Alaska	AK	Lousiana	LA	Ohio	OH
Arizona	AZ	Maine	ME	Oklahoma	OK
Arkansas	AR	Maryland	MD	Oregon	OR
California	CA	Massachusetts	MA	Pennsylvania	PA
Colorado	CO	Michigan	MI	Rhode Island	RI
Connecticut	CT	Minnesota	MN	South Carolina	SC
Delaware	DE	Mississippi	MS	South Dakota	SD
D.C.	DC	Missouri	MO	Tennessee	TN
Florida	FL	Montana	MT	Texas	TX
Georgia	GA	Nebraska	NE	Utah	UT
Hawaii	HI	Nevada	NV	Vermont	VT
Idaho	ID	New Hampshire	NH	Virginia	VA
Illinois	IL	New Jersey	NJ	Washington	WA
Indiana	IN	New Mexico	NM	West Virginia	WV
Iowa	IA	New York	NY	Wisconsin	WI
Kansas	KS	North Carolina	NC	Wyoming	WY

Canada:

Alberta	AB	New Brunswick	NB
British Columbia	BC	Newfoundland and Labrador	NL
Manitoba	MB	Nova Scotia	NS

Ontario	ON	Quebec	QC
Prince Edward Island	PE	Saskatchewan	SK

8.1.2 Eras

SBL style uses all caps without periods (see also *CMS* §§9.35, 10.39) in abbreviations of chronological eras. If you use AD and BC, remember that AD precedes the date (e.g., AD 325) and BC follows the date (e.g., 127 BC). For the use of these abbreviations in titles, see §6.1.3.2.

AD	*anno Domini* (in the year of our Lord) [precedes date]
AH	*anno Hegirae* (in the year of [Muhammad's] Hegira [622 CE]) [precedes date]
AM	*anno mundi* (in the year of the world) [precedes date]
AUC	*ab urbe condita* (from the founding of the city [Rome, 753 BCE]) [precedes date]
BC	before Christ
BCE	before the Common Era
BP	before the present
CE	Common Era

8.1.3 Technical Abbreviations

abl.	ablative
abs.	absolute
acc.	accusative
act.	active
ad loc.	*ad locum*, at the place discussed
adj.	adjective, adjectival
adv.	adverb
apocr.	apocryphon
Aram.	Aramaic
art.	article
Assyr.	Assyrian
b.	born
Bibl. Aram.	Biblical Aramaic
bibliog.	bibliography
bis	twice
bk.	book
c.	century; common (grammatical gender)
ca.	circa
Can.	Canaanite
cf.	[Lat.] *confer*, compare
ch(s).	chapter(s)
Chr	Chronicler
cj.	conjecture (regarding an uncertain reading)
cod.	codex
col(s).	column(s)
com.	common (also c.)
comm(s).	commentary, commentaries
conj.	conjunction
consec.	consecutive
const.	construct
cont.	continued
Copt.	Coptic
D	Deuteronomistic source (of the Pentateuch)
d.	died; dual (grammatical number)
dat.	dative
def.	definition
deriv.	derivative
dim.	diminutive
diss.	dissertation
Dtn	Deuteronomic (History; writer)
Dtr	Deuteronomistic (History; writer); Deuteronomist
Dyn.	Dynasty
E	Elohist source (of the Pentateuch)
ed(s).	editor(s), edited by, edition
e.g.	*exempli gratia*, for example
Eg.	Egyptian

emph.	emphatic
Eng.	English
ep(s).	episode(s); section of an inscription or section of a common narrated event extant in more than one inscription
ESem.	East Semitic (language group)
esp.	especially
ET	English translation
et al.	*et alii*, and others
etc.	*et cetera*, and so forth, and the rest
Eth.	Ethiopic
ex.	example
excl.	excluding
exp.	expanded
extrabibl.	extrabiblical
f(f).	and the following one(s)
fasc.	fascicle
f. or fem.	feminine
fig.	figurative, figuratively
flor.	floruit
fol(s).	folio(s)
Fr.	French
frag.	fragment
FS	Festschrift
fut.	future
gen.	genitive, genitival
Ger.	German
Gk.	Greek, referring to lexical forms, not translation
HB	Hebrew Bible
Heb.	Hebrew
Hitt.	Hittite
i.e.	*id est*, that is
ibid.	*ibidem*, in the same place
idem	the same
Imp. Aram.	Imperial Aramaic
imper.	impersonal
impf.	imperfect
impf. cons.	*imperfectum consecutivum*
impv.	imperative
incl.	inclusive; including
indic.	indicative
inf.	infinitive
inscr.	inscription
instr.	instrumental
intrans.	intransitive
Isr.	Israelite
J	Yahwist source (of the Pentateuch)
juss.	jussive
κτλ	καὶ τὰ λοιπά (= and the rest; etc.)
line(s)	[always spell out]
Lat.	Latin
lit.	literally
loc.	locative
loc. cit.	*loco citato*, in the place cited
LXX	Septuagint (the Greek OT)
m	meter (unit of measurement)
m. or masc.	masculine
Mand.	Mandaic
mg.	marginal
Mid. Assyr.	Middle Assyrian
Mid. Heb.	Middle Hebrew
Midr.	Midrash
Moab.	Moabite
mod.	modern
MS(S)	manuscript(s)
MT	Masoretic Text (of the HB)
N	Northern (source)
n(n).	note(s)
N.B.	*nota bene*, note carefully
n.d.	no date
n.p.	no place; no publisher; no page
Nab.	Nabatean
neg.	negative
neut.	neuter
NHC	Nag Hammadi Codices
no(s).	number(s)
nom.	nominal, nominative
NS	new series
NT	New Testament
NWSem.	Northwest Semitic
obj.	object
obs.	obsolete
obv.	obverse (front) of a tablet
OL	Old Latin
op. cit.	*opere citato*, in the work cited
orig.	original
OP	Old Persian
OT	Old Testament
P	Priestly source (of the Pentateuch)
p(p).	page(s)
Pal.	Palestinian
Palm.	Palmyrene

pap.	papyrus
par(r).	parallel(s); see §8.2.2
pass.	passive
passim	here and there
per.	person, persons
Pers.	Persia, Persian
pers. comm.	personal communication
pf.	perfect, perfective
Phoen.	Phoenician
PIE	Proto-Indo-European
pl(s).	plural; plate(s)
PN	personal name
poss.	possessive
postbibl.	postbiblical
prep.	preposition, prepositional
pres.	present
pron.	pronoun
ps.-	pseudo-
pt.	part
ptc.	participle
publ.	published (in)
Pun.	Punic
q.v.	*quod vide*, which see
R	Redactor
r	recto
re	regarding
rec(s).	recension(s)
reg.	register
repr.	reprinted
resp.	respectively
rev.	revised (by); reverse (of a tablet)
s	side (of an ostracon; often superscripted)
Sam.	Samaritan
sec.	section; *secundum*, according to
Sem.	Semitic
ser.	series
sg. or s.	singular
Skt.	Sanskrit
SSem.	South Semitic (language group)
subj.	subject
subst.	substantive, substantival
suf.	suffix
Sum.	Sumerian
superl.	superlative
suppl.	supplement
s.v.	*sub verbo*, under the word
SWSem.	Southwest Semitic (language group)
syn.	synonym (-ous)
Syr.	Syriac
theol.	theology; theological
trans.	translator, translated by; transitive
txt em	textual emendation
v	verso
v(v).	verse(s)
Vulg.	Vulgate
viz.	*videlicet*, namely
voc.	vocative
vol(s).	volume(s)
vs.	versus
WSem.	West Semitic

The above list is selective and is admittedly more descriptive than prescriptive. Thus it includes several abbreviations whose use we strongly discourage. The abbreviations *f.* and *ff.* (for references to ranges with no explicitly named end point) should be replaced by an exact range. Instead of using op. cit. and loc. cit. for note citations, an abbreviated citation (author's last name and a short title) is preferred.

8.2 Bible Texts and Versions

Books of the Bible cited without chapter (or chapter and verse) should ordinarily be spelled out in the main text. Books of the Bible cited with chapter are more commonly abbreviated unless they come at the beginning of the sentence. Authors citing more than one translation of the Bible must indicate which translation is used in a particular citation. When this citation is in parentheses, a comma is not needed between the reference and the abbreviation of the translation, as is indicated in the fourth example below.

Right:	The passage in 1 Cor 5 is often considered crucial.
	The passage, 1 Cor 5:6, is often considered crucial.
	First Corinthians 5:6 is a crucial text.
	"Do you not know that a little yeast leavens the whole batch of dough?" (1 Cor 5:6 NRSV).
Wrong:	1 Cor 5:6 is a crucial text.
	1 Corinthians 5:6 is a crucial text.

8.2.1 Divisions, Units, Texts, and Versions

In addition to the abbreviations for biblical books given below in §§8.3.1–3, the following abbreviations should be used:

Divisions of the canon:

HB	Hebrew Bible
NT	New Testament
OT	Old Testament

Units of text:

ch(s).	chapter(s)
v(v).	verse(s)
par(r).	and the parallel text(s); see §8.2.2

Ancient texts, text types, and versions:

Byz.	Byzantine
Copt.	Coptic
LXX	Septuagint
MT	Masoretic Text
SP	Samaritan Pentateuch
Syr.	Syriac
TR	Textus Receptus
Vulg.	Vulgate

Modern editions:

BF^{2}	British and Foreign Bible Societies, 2nd ed.
BHK	*Biblia Hebraica*, ed. R. Kittel
BHL	*Biblia Hebraica Leningradensia*, ed. A. Dotan
BHQ	*Biblia Hebraica Quinta*
BHS	*Biblia Hebraica Stuttgartensia*
HBCE	The Hebrew Bible: A Critical Edition
NA^{28}	*Novum Testamentum Graece*, Nestle-Aland, 28th ed.
SBLGNT	The Greek New Testament: SBL Edition
UBS^{5}	*The Greek New Testament*, United Bible Societies, 5th ed.
WH	Westcott-Hort

Modern versions:

ASV	American Standard Version
CEB	Common English Bible
CEV	Contemporary English Version
ESV	English Standard Version
GNB	Good News Bible

Goodspeed	*The New Testament: An American Translation,* by Edgar J. Goodspeed; *The Apocrypha: An American Translation,* by Edgar J. Goodspeed. For *The Complete Bible,* see Smith-Goodspeed.
HCSB	Holman Christian Standard Bible
JB	Jerusalem Bible
KJV	King James Version
Lamsa	*Holy Bible from Ancient Eastern Manuscripts … Translated from the Peshitta,* by George M. Lamsa
LB	Living Bible
MLB	Modern Language Bible
Moffatt	*The New Testament: A New Translation,* James Moffatt
NAB	New American Bible
NABR	New American Bible, Revised Edition
NASB	New American Standard Bible
NEB	New English Bible
NET	New English Translation
NETS	*A New English Translation of the Septuagint.* Edited by Albert Pietersma and Benjamin G. Wright. New York: Oxford University Press, 2007
NIV	New International Version
NIVI	New International Version, Inclusive Language Edition
NJB	New Jerusalem Bible
NJPS	*Tanakh: The Holy Scriptures: The New JPS Translation according to the Traditional Hebrew Text*
NKJV	New King James Version
NLT	New Living Translation
NRSV	New Revised Standard Version
Phillips	*The New Testament in Modern English,* J. B. Phillips
REB	Revised English Bible
RSV	Revised Standard Version
RV	Revised Version
Smith-Goodspeed	*The Complete Bible: An American Translation,* OT trans. J. M. Powis Smith et al.; Apocrypha and NT trans. Edgar J. Goodspeed
SV	*The Complete Gospels Annotated Scholars Version,* ed. Robert J. Miller
TEV	Today's English Version (= Good News Bible)
TNIV	Today's New International Version
Weymouth	*The New Testament in Modern Speech,* R. F. Weymouth

To specify that a reference is to a particular ancient version or modern translation, follow the format described for the Septuagint in §8.3.3, but substitute the appropriate version abbreviation for LXX.

8.2.2 Citations of Parallel Texts

In gospel research, and in some other areas, it is often useful to point readers to parallel texts. To refer to a parallel without citing chapter and verse, use the abbreviation *par.* (whose plural, like vv. for verses, is *parr.*). To cite specific texts, use twin slashes, set closely together (//), between the cited passages. Thus:

> Matt 11:2–6 par. means Matt 11:2–6 and an unspecified parallel text. Or more fully:
> Matt 11:2–6 // Luke 7:18–23

Mark 6:32–44; 8:1–10; and parr.
Gos. Thom. 26 // Q 6:41–42 (Luke 6:41–42, Matt 7:3–5)

8.3 Primary Sources: Ancient Texts

Abbreviations for the Hebrew Bible/Old Testament, New Testament, deuterocanonical works, and Dead Sea Scrolls and related texts do not use a period. All other abbreviations are marked by periods.

Patterns of punctuation around numbers in text references vary as noted below. In general, we prefer to separate chapter and verse references such as one finds in biblical materials with colons (see §8.3.1). With other ancient texts, where numbering may be by book, chapter, section, paragraph, or line, periods have become more common for separating the successive unit numbers. In some cases, by discipline-specific convention, other patterns may be used.

8.3.1 Hebrew Bible/Old Testament

In biblical references, a colon normally separates chapters and verses, a comma and a letter space separate verse designations within a chapter, and a semicolon followed by a letter space separates references to different chapters (or chapters and verses). Thus: Isa 1:8; 5:1–7, 10; Jer 2:21 (see further §4.1.8).

Gen	Genesis	Eccl (or Qoh)	Ecclesiastes (or Qoheleth)
Exod	Exodus	Song or (Cant)	Song of Songs (Song of Solomon, or Canticles)
Lev	Leviticus	Isa	Isaiah
Num	Numbers	Jer	Jeremiah
Deut	Deuteronomy	Lam	Lamentations
Josh	Joshua	Ezek	Ezekiel
Judg	Judges	Dan	Daniel
Ruth	Ruth	Hos	Hosea
1–2 Sam	1–2 Samuel	Joel	Joel
1–2 Kgdms	1–2 Kingdoms (LXX)	Amos	Amos
1–2 Kgs	1–2 Kings	Obad	Obadiah
3–4 Kgdms	3–4 Kingdoms (LXX)	Jonah	Jonah
1–2 Chr	1–2 Chronicles	Mic	Micah
Ezra	Ezra	Nah	Nahum
Neh	Nehemiah	Hab	Habakkuk
Esth	Esther	Zeph	Zephaniah
Job	Job	Hag	Haggai
Ps/Pss	Psalms	Zech	Zechariah
Prov	Proverbs	Mal	Malachi

8.3.2 New Testament

Matt	Matthew	John	John
Mark	Mark	Acts	Acts
Luke	Luke	Rom	Romans

1–2 Cor	1–2 Corinthians	Phlm	Philemon
Gal	Galatians	Heb	Hebrews
Eph	Ephesians	Jas	James
Phil	Philippians	1–2 Pet	1–2 Peter
Col	Colossians	1–2–3 John	1–2–3 John
1–2 Thess	1–2 Thessalonians	Jude	Jude
1–2 Tim	1–2 Timothy	Rev	Revelation
Titus	Titus		

8.3.3 Deuterocanonical Works and Septuagint

For abbreviations of LXX books that appear in the Hebrew Bible under different names, see §8.3.1. Add "LXX" to Hebrew Bible/Old Testament citations explicitly from the Septuagint; thus, 3 Kgdms 2:46h LXX (or 1 Kgs 2:46h LXX); Jer 28:1–4 LXX; Ps 80:8 (80:9 LXX). Otherwise, chapters and verses are cited as described in §8.3.1.

Tob	Tobit	Sus	Susanna
Jdt	Judith	Bel	Bel and the Dragon
Add Esth	Additions to Esther	1–2 Macc	1–2 Maccabees
Wis	Wisdom of Solomon	1 Esd	1 Esdras
Sir	Sirach/Ecclesiasticus	Pr Man	Prayer of Manasseh
Bar	Baruch	Ps 151	Psalm 151
Ep Jer	Epistle of Jeremiah	3 Macc	3 Maccabees
Add Dan	Additions to Daniel	2 Esd	2 Esdras
Pr Azar	Prayer of Azariah	4 Macc	4 Maccabees
Sg Three	Song of the Three Young Men		

8.3.4 Old Testament Pseudepigrapha

The names of authors whose works survive only in a small number of fragments should not normally be abbreviated. Abbreviations for them are included in this list (in roman type) mainly for the benefit of editors who may need to expand them.

Ahiqar	Ahiqar	Ascen. Isa.	Mart. Ascen. Isa. 6–11
Ant. bib.	Use LAB	2 Bar.	2 Baruch (Syriac Apocalypse)
Apoc. Ab.	Apocalypse of Abraham	3 Bar.	3 Baruch (Greek Apocalypse)
Apoc. Adam	Apocalypse of Adam	4 Bar.	4 Baruch (Paraleipomena Jeremiou)
Apoc. Dan.	Apocalypse of Daniel		
Apoc. El. (C)	Coptic Apocalypse of Elijah	Bib. Ant.	Use LAB
Apoc. El. (H)	Hebrew Apocalypse of Elijah	Bk. Noah	Book of Noah
Apoc. Ezek.	Use Apocr. Ezek.	Cav. Tr.	Cave of Treasures
Apoc. Mos.	Apocalypse of Moses	Cl. Mal.	Cleodemus Malchus
Apoc. Sedr.	Apocalypse of Sedrach	Dem.	Demetrius (the Chronographer)
Apoc. Zeph.	Apocalypse of Zephaniah		
Apoc. Zos.	Use Hist. Rech.	El. Mod.	Eldad and Modad
Apocr. Ezek.	Apocryphon of Ezekiel	1 En.	1 Enoch (Ethiopic Apocalypse)
Aris. Ex.	Aristeas the Exegete		
Aristob.	Aristobulus	2 En.	2 Enoch (Slavonic Apocalypse)
Artap.	Artapanus		
As. Mos.	Assumption of Moses	3 En.	3 Enoch (Hebrew Apocalypse)

Eup.	Eupolemus
Ezek. Trag.	Ezekiel the Tragedian
4 Ezra	4 Ezra
5 Apoc. Syr. Pss.	Five Apocryphal Syriac Psalms
Gk. Apoc. Ezra	Greek Apocalypse of Ezra
Hec. Ab.	Hecataeus of Abdera
Hel. Syn. Pr.	Hellenistic Synagogal Prayers
Hist. Jos.	History of Joseph
Hist. Rech.	History of the Rechabites
Jan. Jam.	Jannes and Jambres
Jos. Asen.	Joseph and Aseneth
Jub.	Jubilees
LAB	Liber antiquitatum biblicarum (Pseudo-Philo)
LAE	Life of Adam and Eve
Lad. Jac.	Ladder of Jacob
Let. Aris.	Letter of Aristeas
Liv. Pro.	Lives of the Prophets
Lost Tr.	The Lost Tribes
3 Macc.	3 Maccabees
4 Macc.	4 Maccabees
5 Macc.	5 Maccabees (Arabic)
Mart. Ascen. Isa.	Martyrdom and Ascension of Isaiah
Mart. Isa.	Mart. Ascen. Isa. 1–5
Odes Sol.	Odes of Solomon
PJ	Use 4 Bar.
Ph. E. Poet	Philo the Epic Poet
Pr. Jac.	Prayer of Jacob
Pr. Jos.	Prayer of Joseph
Pr. Man.	Prayer of Manasseh
Pr. Mos.	Prayer of Moses
Ps.-Eup.	Pseudo-Eupolemus
Ps.-Hec.	Pseudo-Hecataeus
Ps.-Orph.	Pseudo-Orpheus
Ps.-Philo	Use LAB
Ps.-Phoc.	Pseudo-Phocylides
Pss. Sol.	Psalms of Solomon
Ques. Ezra	Questions of Ezra
Rev. Ezra	Revelation of Ezra
Sib. Or.	Sibylline Oracles
Syr. Men.	Sentences of the Syriac Menander
T. 12 Patr.	Testaments of the Twelve Patriarchs
T. Ash.	Testament of Asher
T. Benj.	Testament of Benjamin
T. Dan	Testament of Dan
T. Gad	Testament of Gad
T. Iss.	Testament of Issachar
T. Jos.	Testament of Joseph
T. Jud.	Testament of Judah
T. Levi	Testament of Levi
T. Naph.	Testament of Naphtali
T. Reu.	Testament of Reuben
T. Sim.	Testament of Simeon
T. Zeb.	Testament of Zebulun
T. 3 Patr.	Testaments of the Three Patriarchs
T. Ab.	Testament of Abraham
T. Isaac	Testament of Isaac
T. Jac.	Testament of Jacob
T. Adam	Testament of Adam
T. Hez.	Testament of Hezekiah (Mart. Ascen. Isa. 3:13–4:22)
T. Job	Testament of Job
T. Mos.	Testament of Moses
T. Sol.	Testament of Solomon
Theod.	Theodotus, *On the Jews*
Treat. Shem	Treatise of Shem
Vis. Ezra	Vision of Ezra
Vis. Isa.	Use Ascen. Isa.

8.3.5 Dead Sea Scrolls and Related Texts

Certain conventions are used to cite texts from Qumran and the surrounding area. The name of the site is given, abbreviated according to the list below.

Q	Qumran
Ḥev	Naḥal Ḥever
Ḥev/Se	Used for documents earlier attributed to Seiyal
Mas	Masada
Mird	Khirbet Mird
Mur	Murabbaʿat

The different caves at each site are denoted with sequential numbers, for example, 1Q, 2Q, and so on. Different copies of the same composition from the same cave are indicated by the use of raised lowercase letters, for example, 1QIsa[a], 1QIsa[b].

There is considerable diversity in nomenclature in actual use for individual documents. In most cases, it is helpful to give the number of the document to avoid confusion. In addition to the number, the descriptive name should be given in the initial citation to permit ease of identification. The number of the text should not be put in italics or bold type, for example, 4Q520 or Mur 16.

The first seven scrolls removed from Cave 1, as well as the Cairo Genizah copy of the Damascus Document, are referred to customarily by name (not by number). The standard names and abbreviations are as follows:

1QapGen ar	Genesis Apocryphon
1QH[a]	Hodayot[a] or Thanksgiving Hymns[a]
1QIsa[a]	Isaiah[a]
1QIsa[b]	Isaiah[b]
1QM	Milḥamah *or* War Scroll
1QpHab	Pesher Habakkuk
1QS	Serek Hayaḥad *or* Rule of the Community
CD	Cairo Genizah copy of the Damascus Document

Common abbreviations for the classification of the scrolls are as follows:

apocr	apocryphon (e.g., 1QapGen)
ar	Aramaic (e.g., 4QMess ar)
gr	Greek (e.g., 4QpapParaExod gr)
hebr	Hebrew (e.g., 4QTob[e] hebr)
p	pesher (e.g., 1QpHab)
paleo	Paleo-Hebrew (e.g., 11QpaleoLev)
pap	papyrus (e.g., 4QpapParaExod gr)
tg	targum (e.g., 11QtgJob)

When a manuscript is referred to by column and line number, roman numerals are used for the column number, followed by a comma and space, with the line number set as an arabic numeral (e.g., 1QS III, 12; 1QpHab I, 2). Manuscripts of biblical texts can include the biblical citation of chapter and verse in parentheses: 4QpaleoExod[m] V, 4 (9:7).

When several fragments are numbered separately within a work, the fragments should be in arabic numerals. Thus, 1Q27 1 II, 25 means text 27 from Qumran Cave 1, fragment 1, column II, line 25; 4QpIsa[c] 4–7 II, 2–4 means the third copy (copy c) of a pesher on Isaiah from Qumran Cave 4, joined fragments 4 to 7, column II, lines 2 to 4. Fragments are sometimes identified by uppercase letters (e.g., 11Q1 A [Lev 4:24–26]). (While some scholars use lowercase column numbers, with or without the comma [e.g., 1Q27 1 ii, 25 or 1Q27 1 ii 25], the above conventions are recommended for the sake of simplicity.)

Some frequently cited texts, examples from various categories, and texts whose names have been changed since first publication are given below:

Number	Abbreviation	Name (and Alternative Names)
1Q28a	1QSa	Rule of the Congregation (appendix a to 1QS)
1Q28b	1QSb	Rule of the Blessings (appendix b to 1QS)
3Q15		Copper Scroll
4Q17	4QExod-Lev[f]	
4Q22	4QpaleoExod[m]	
4Q82	4QXII[g]	The Greek Minor Prophets Scroll
4Q120	4QpapLXXLev[b]	
4Q127	4QpapParaExod gr	ParaExodus
4Q174	4QFlor (MidrEschat[a])	Florilegium, also Midrash on Eschatology[a]
4Q175	4QTest	Testimonia
4Q177	4QCatena[a] (MidrEschat[b])	Catena[a], also Midrash on Eschatology[b]
4Q180	4QAgesCreat	Ages of Creation
4Q182	4QCatena[b] (MidrEschat[c])	Catena[b], also Midrash on Eschatology[c]
4Q242	4QPrNab ar	Prayer of Nabonidus
4Q246	4QapocrDan ar	Apocryphon of Daniel
4Q252	4QCommGen A	Commentary on Genesis A, formerly Patriarchal Blessings or Pesher Genesis
4Q265	4QSD	Serek Damascus
4Q266	4QD[a]	Damascus Document[a]
4Q274	4QToḥorot A	Toḥorot A
4Q285		Sefer Hamilḥamah
4Q299	4QMyst[a]	Mysteries[a]
4Q320	4QCalDoc A	Calendrical Document A, formerly Mishmarot A
4Q365	4QRP[c]	Reworked Pentateuch[c]
4Q378	4QapocrJosh[a]	Apocryphon of Joshua[a], formerly Psalms of Joshua[a]
4Q394	4QMMT[a]	Miqṣat Maʿaśê ha-Torah[a]
4Q400	4QShirShabb[a]	Songs of the Sabbath Sacrifice[a]
4Q414	4QRitPur A	Ritual Purity A, formerly Baptismal Liturgy
4Q418	4QInstruction[a]	Instruction[a], formerly Sapiential Work A[a]
4Q434	4QBarki Nafshi[a]	BarkhiNafshi[a]
4Q502	4QpapRitMar	Ritual of Marriage
4Q503	4QpapPrQuot	Prières quotidiennes or Daily Prayers
4Q504	4QDibHam[a]	Dibre Hameʾorot[a] or Words of the Luminaries[a]
4Q507	4QPrFêtes[a]	Prières pour les fêtes[a] or Festival Prayers[a]
4Q510	4QShir[a]	Shirot[a] or Songs of the Sage[a]
4Q512	4QpapRitPur B	Ritual Purity B
4Q521	4QMessAp	Messianic Apocalypse
4Q525	4QBeat	Beatitudes
11Q5	11QPs[a]	Psalms Scroll[a]
11Q10	11QtgJob	Targum of Job
11Q11	11QApPs[a]	Apocryphal Psalms[a]
11Q13	11QMelch	Melchizedek
11Q18	11QNJ ar	New Jerusalem
11Q19	11QT[a]	Temple Scroll[a]

Appendix C contains an exhaustive list of Dead Sea Scroll texts, numbers, and principal publications.

8.3.6 Philo

Latin and English titles are provided with their corresponding abbreviations. No priority is intended by our listing of the Latin titles first; authors should decide which they prefer and remain consistent.

Abr.	*De Abrahamo*
Abraham	*On the Life of Abraham*
Aet.	*De aeternitate mundi*
Eternity	*On the Eternity of the World*
Agr.	*De agricultura*
Agriculture	*On Agriculture*
Anim.	*De animalibus*
Animals	*Whether Animals Have Reason* (= *Alexander*)
Cher.	*De cherubim*
Cherubim	*On the Cherubim*
Conf.	*De confusione linguarum*
Confusion	*On the Confusion of Tongues*
Congr.	*De congressu eruditionis gratia*
Prelim. Studies	*On the Preliminary Studies*
Contempl.	*De vita contemplativa*
Contempl. Life	*On the Contemplative Life*
Decal.	*De decalogo*
Decalogue	*On the Decalogue*
Deo	*De Deo*
God	*On God*
Det.	*Quod deterius potiori insidari soleat*
Worse	*That the Worse Attacks the Better*
Deus	*Quod Deus sit immutabilis*
Unchangeable	*That God Is Unchangeable*
Ebr.	*De ebrietate*
Drunkenness	*On Drunkenness*
Exsecr.	*De exsecrationibus*
Curses	*On Curses* (= *Rewards* 127–172)
Flacc.	*In Flaccum*
Flaccus	*Against Flaccus*
Fug.	*De fuga et inventione*
Flight	*On Flight and Finding*
Gig.	*De gigantibus*
Giants	*On Giants*
Her.	*Quis rerum divinarum heres sit*
Heir	*Who Is the Heir?*
Hypoth.	*Hypothetica*
Hypothetica	*Hypothetica*
Ios.	*De Iosepho*
Joseph	*On the Life of Joseph*
Leg. 1, 2, 3	*Legum allegoriae* I, II, III
Alleg. Interp. 1, 2, 3	*Allegorical Interpretation* 1, 2, 3
Legat.	*Legatio ad Gaium*
Embassy	*On the Embassy to Gaius*
Migr.	*De migratione Abrahami*
Migration	*On the Migration of Abraham*
Mos. 1, 2	*De vita Mosis* I, II
Moses 1, 2	*On the Life of Moses* 1, 2
Mut.	*De mutatione nominum*
Names	*On the Change of Names*
Opif.	*De opificio mundi*
Creation	*On the Creation of the World*
Plant.	*De plantatione*
Planting	*On Planting*
Post.	*De posteritate Caini*
Posterity	*On the Posterity of Cain*
Praem.	*De praemiis et poenis*
Rewards	*On Rewards and Punishments*
Prob.	*Quod omnis probus liber sit*
Good Person	*That Every Good Person Is Free*
Prov. 1, 2	*De providentia* I, II
Providence 1, 2	*On Providence* 1, 2
QE 1, 2	*Quaestiones et solutiones in Exodum* I, II
QE 1, 2	*Questions and Answers on Exodus* 1, 2
QG 1, 2, 3, 4	*Quaestiones et solutiones in Genesin* I, II, III, IV
QG 1, 2, 3, 4	*Questions and Answers on Genesis* 1, 2, 3, 4
Sacr.	*De sacrificiis Abelis et Caini*
Sacrifices	*On the Sacrifices of Cain and Abel*

Sobr. *Sobriety*	*De sobrietate* *On Sobriety*	*Spec.* 1, 2, 3, 4 *Spec. Laws* 1, 2, 3, 4	*De specialibus legibus* I, II, III, IV *On the Special Laws* 1, 2, 3, 4
Somn. 1, 2 *Dreams* 1, 2	*De somniis* I, II *On Dreams* 1, 2	*Virt.* *Virtues*	*De virtutibus* *On the Virtues*

8.3.7 Josephus

On whether to cite Latin or English titles and abbreviations, see §8.3.6. Authors may follow the numbering scheme appropriate to their audience, utilizing the book and small-unit numbering scheme of Niese's edition (retained in the margin and running heads of the Loeb volumes; see §6.4.2); the book, chapter, and paragraph numbering of older editions (including the Whiston translation ubiquitously used by general readers, though some recent reprints now also include the Niese numbers); or a combination of the two. Thus, for example, if one needed to reference Josephus's little geographical excursus on the Lake of Gennesareth, the fertility of the region, and the course of the Jordan, one might use any of the following formats:

> Josephus, *J.W.* 3.506–521
> Josephus, *J.W.* 3.10.7–8
> Josephus, *J.W.* 3.10.7–8 §§506–521

Of course, one could cite the abbreviation *B.J.* instead of *J.W.* For the record, SBL Press uses the third option above. Note that whereas some printed versions number the paragraphs III.x.7–8, SBL Press encourages exclusive use of arabic numbers (see §4.2.2). With all these options, we stress the importance of consistency: as always, pick a style and stick with it throughout your book or essay.

Vita *Life*	*Vita* *The Life*	*A.J.* *Ant.*	*Antiquitates judaicae* *Jewish Antiquities*
C. Ap. *Ag. Ap.*	*Contra Apionem* *Against Apion*	*B.J.* *J.W.*	*Bellum judaicum* *Jewish War*

8.3.8 Mishnah, Talmud, and Related Literature

Abbreviations distinguish the versions of the talmudic tractates: y. for Jerusalem and b. for Babylonian. A prefixed t. denotes the tractates of the Tosefta and an m. those of the Mishnah. A prefixed bar. denotes a baraita (an authoritative Tannaitic rule external to the Mishnah). When citing the Mishnah, a colon separates the chapter from the paragraph (i.e., *mishnah*); thus, m. Ber. 1:1. The standard way to cite the Babylonian Talmud is by folio and side (a or b); thus, b. Ber. 2a. The Jerusalem Talmud combines elements of both styles, beginning with a chapter and paragraph reference and ending with reference to the folio and column (a–d); thus, y. B. Bat. 10:1, 17c. A colon separates chapter and paragraph (as with Mishnah references), followed by a comma and space, then the folio and column designation. Successive references are separated by semicolons. (Another common format is y. B. Bat. 10.1, 17c; if one uses it, consistency requires substituting a period for the colon in Mishnah references as well.)

The third column in the following list contains nontechnical transliterations following the general-purpose Hebrew transliteration style (§5.1.2).

ʿAbod. Zar.	ʿAbodah Zarah	Avodah Zarah
ʾAbot	ʾAbot	Avot
ʿArak.	ʿArakin	Arakhin
B. Bat.	Baba Batra	Bava Batra
B. Meṣ.	Baba Meṣiʿa	Bava Metzi'a
B. Qam.	Baba Qamma	Bava Qamma
Bek.	Bekorot	Bekhorot
Ber.	Berakot	Berakhot
Beṣah	Beṣah (=Yom Ṭob)	Betzah (= Yom Tov)
Bik.	Bikkurim	Bikkurim
Demai	Demai	Demai
ʿEd.	ʿEduyyot	Eduyyot
ʿErub.	ʿErubin	Eruvin
Giṭ.	Giṭṭin	Gittin
Ḥag.	Ḥagigah	Hagigah
Ḥal.	Ḥallah	Hallah
Hor.	Horayot	Horayot
Ḥul.	Ḥullin	Hullin
Kelim	Kelim	Kelim
Ker.	Keritot	Kerithot
Ketub.	Ketubbot	Ketubbot
Kil.	Kilʾayim	Kil'ayim
Maʿaś.	Maʿaśerot	Ma'aserot
Maʿaś. Š.	Maʿaśer Šeni	Ma'aser Sheni
Mak.	Makkot	Makkot
Makš.	Makširin	Makhshirin
Meg.	Megillah	Megillah
Meʿil.	Meʿilah	Me'ilah
Menaḥ.	Menaḥot	Menahot
Mid.	Middot	Middot
Miqw.	Miqwaʾot	Mikwa'ot
Moʿed	Moʿed	Mo'ed
Moʿed Qaṭ.	Moʿed Qaṭan	Mo'ed Qatan
Naš.	Našim	Nashim
Naz.	Nazir	Nazir
Ned.	Nedarim	Nedarim
Neg.	Negaʿim	Nega'im
Nez.	Neziqin	Neziqin
Nid.	Niddah	Niddah
ʾOhal.	ʾOhalot	Ohalot
ʿOr.	ʿOrlah	Orlah
Parah	Parah	Parah
Peʾah	Peʾah	Pe'ah
Pesaḥ.	Pesaḥim	Pesahim
Qidd.	Qiddušin	Qiddushin
Qinnim	Qinnim	Qinnim
Qod.	Qodašim	Qodashim

Roš Haš.	Roš Haššanah	Rosh Hashanah
Šabb.	Šabbat	Shabbat
Sanh.	Sanhedrin	Sanhedrin
Šeb.	Šebiʿit	Shevi'it
Šebu.	Šebuʿot	Shevu'ot
Seder	Seder	Seder
Šeqal.	Šeqalim	Sheqalim
Soṭah	Soṭah	Sotah
Sukkah	Sukkah	Sukkah
Ṭ. Yom	Ṭebul Yom	Tevul Yom
Taʿan.	Taʿanit	Ta'anit
Tamid	Tamid	Tamid
Ṭehar.	Ṭeharot	Teharot
Tem.	Temurah	Temurah
Ter.	Terumot	Terumot
ʿUq.	ʿUqṣin	Uqtzin
Yad.	Yadayim	Yadayim
Yebam.	Yebamot	Yevamot
Yoma	Yoma (= Kippurim)	Yoma
Zabim	Zabim	Zavim
Zebaḥ.	Zebaḥim	Zevahim
Zera.	Zeraʿim	Zera'im

8.3.9 Targumic Texts

Frg. Tg.	Fragmentary Targum
Sam. Tg.	Samaritan Targum
Tg. Esth. I, II	First or Second Targum of Esther
Tg. Isa.	Targum Isaiah
Tg. Ket.	Targum of the Writings
Tg. Neb.	Targum of the Prophets
Tg. Neof.	Targum Neofiti
Tg. Onq.	Targum Onqelos
Tg. Ps.-J.	Targum Pseudo-Jonathan
Tg. Yer. I	Targum Yerušalmi I
Tg. Yer. II	Targum Yerušalmi II
Yem. Tg.	Yemenite Targum

8.3.10 Other Rabbinic Works

The third column lists the titles according to the general-purpose style (§5.1.2).

ʿAbad.	ʿAbadim	Avadim
ʾAbot R. Nat.	ʾAbot de Rabbi Nathan	Avot of Rabbi Nathan
ʾAg. Ber.	ʾAggadat Berešit	Aggadat Bereshit
Bab.	Babylonian I (used alone)	Babylonian
Der. Er. Rab.	Derek Ereṣ Rabbah	Derekh Eretz Rabbah
Der. Er. Zuṭ	Derek Ereṣ Zuṭa	Derekh Eretz Zuta
Gem.	Gemara	Gemara
Gerim	Gerim	Gerim

Kallah	Kallah	Kallah
Kallah Rab.	Kallah Rabbati	Kallah Rabbati
Kutim	Kutim	Kutim
Mas. Qeṭ.	Massektot Qeṭannot	Massekhtot Qetannot
Mek.	Mekilta	Mekilta
Mez.	Mezuzah	Mezuzah
Midr.	Midrash I (+ biblical book)	Midrash
Pal.	Palestinian I (used alone)	Palestinian
Pesiq. Rab.	Pesiqta Rabbati	Pesiqta Rabbati
Pesiq. Rab Kah.	Pesiqta de Rab Kahana	Pesiqta of Rab Kahana
Pirqe R. El.	Pirqe Rabbi Eliezer	Pirqe Rabbi Eliezer
Rab. (e.g., Gen. Rab. = Genesis Rabbah)	Rabbah (+ biblical book)	Rabbah
S. Eli. Rab.	Seder Eliyahu Rabbah	Seder Eliyahu Rabbah
S. Eli. Zut.	Seder Eliyahu Zuta	Seder Eliyahu Zuta
Sem.	Semaḥot	Semahot
Sep. Torah	Seper Torah	Sefer Torah
Sipra	Sipra	Sifra
Sipre	Sipre	Sifre
Ṣiṣit	Ṣiṣit	Tzitzit
Sop.	Soperim	Soferim
S. ʿOlam Rab.	Seder ʿOlam Rabbah	Seder Olam Rabbah
Tanḥ.	Tanḥuma	Tanhuma
Tep.	Tepillin	Tefillin
Yal.	Yalquṭ	Yalqut

8.3.11 Apostolic Fathers

Recent scholarship appears quite divided over whether to cite these texts like biblical materials (by chapter and verse, with an intervening colon) or like later Christian writings (using a period between successive units). The numbering system for most of the writings is so simple (and the place some of them had in the early church was so close to that held by some of the canonical NT writings) that the tendency toward use of a colon is understandable. Complicating the picture slightly is the fact that two numbering systems are sometimes used for the Shepherd of Hermas. For all the Apostolic Fathers, we recommend a consistent use of periods rather than commas, and for the Shepherd we recommend composite references such as Herm. Vis. 4.1.4 (22.4). For a more complete explanation of citing the Shepherd, see appendix D.

Barn.	Barnabas
1–2 Clem.	1–2 Clement
Did.	Didache
Diogn.	Diognetus
Herm. Mand.	Shepherd of Hermas, Mandate(s)
Herm. Sim.	Shepherd of Hermas, Similitude(s)
Herm. Vis.	Shepherd of Hermas, Vision(s)
Ign. *Eph.*	Ignatius, *To the Ephesians*
Ign. *Magn.*	Ignatius, *To the Magnesians*
Ign. *Phld.*	Ignatius, *To the Philadelphians*

Ign. *Pol.*	Ignatius, *To Polycarp*
Ign. *Rom.*	Ignatius, *To the Romans*
Ign. *Smyrn.*	Ignatius, *To the Smyrnaeans*
Ign. *Trall.*	Ignatius, *To the Trallians*
Mart. Pol.	Martyrdom of Polycarp
Pol. *Phil.*	Polycarp, *To the Philippians*

8.3.12 Coptic Codices

8.3.12.1 Nag Hammadi

The names of individual treatises listed below follow the new standard translation *The Nag Hammadi Scriptures: The International Edition*, edited by Marvin Meyer (New York: HarperOne, 2007), 799–802.

Nag Hammadi codices (= NHC) are identified in the following list by the codex number (a roman numeral) and the tractate number (an arabic numeral). Specific text references designate the page and line numbering of the tractates, except that in the case of the Gospel of Thomas it is more common to use the saying number. By convention, page and line numbers are separated from each other by a period. Thus one might refer to Gos. Truth (NHC I 32.31–33.32) to designate page 32 line 31 through page 33 line 32 of the full "gospel" text as it stands in Nag Hammadi codex I (there is a fragmentary text in codex XII).

Pr. Paul	I 1 Prayer of the Apostle Paul
Ap. Jas.	I 2 Secret Book of James
Gos. Truth	I 3 Gospel of Truth
Treat. Res.	I 4 Treatise on the Resurrection
Tri. Trac.	I 5 Tripartite Tractate
Ap. John	II 1 Secret Book of John
Gos. Thom.	II 2 Gospel of Thomas
Gos. Phil.	II 3 Gospel of Philip
Nat. Rulers	II 4 Nature of the Rulers
Orig. World	II 5 On the Origin of the World
Exeg. Soul	II 6 Exegesis of the Soul
Bk. Thom.	II 7 Book of Thomas
Ap. John	III 1 Secret Book of John
Gos. Eg.	III 2 Gospel of the Egyptians
Eugnostos	III 3 Eugnostos the Blessed
Wis. Jes. Chr.	III 4 Wisdom of Jesus Christ
Dial. Sav.	III 5 Dialogue of the Savior
Ap. John	IV 1 Secret Book of John
Gos. Eg.	IV 2 Gospel of the Egyptians
Eugnostos	V 1 Eugnostos the Blessed
Apoc. Paul	V 2 Revelation of Paul
1 Apoc. Jas.	V 3 (First) Revelation of James
2 Apoc. Jas.	V 4 (Second) Revelation of James
Apoc. Adam	V 5 Revelation of Adam
Acts Pet. 12 Apos.	VI 1 Acts of Peter and the Twelve Apostles
Thund.	VI 2 Thunder: Perfect Mind
Auth. Disc.	VI 3 Authoritative Discourse

Great Pow.	VI 4 Concept of our Great Power
Plato Rep.	VI 5 Plato, *Republic* 588b–589b
Disc. 8–9	VI 6 Discourse on the Eighth and Ninth
Pr. Thanks.	VI 7 Prayer of Thanksgiving
Perf. Disc.	VI 8 Excerpt from the Perfect Discourse 21–29
Paraph. Shem	VII 1 Paraphrase of Shem
Disc. Seth	VII 2 Second Discourse of Great Seth
Apoc. Pet.	VII 3 Revelation of Peter
Teach. Silv.	VII 4 Teachings of Silvanus
Steles Seth	VII 5 Three Steles of Seth
Zost.	VIII 1 Zostrianos
Ep. Pet. Phil.	VIII 2 Letter of Peter to Philip
Melch.	IX 1 Melchizedek
Norea	IX 2 Thought of Norea
Testim. Truth	IX 3 Testimony of Truth
Marsanes	X Marsanes
Interp. Know.	XI 1 Interpretation of Knowledge
Val. Exp.	XI 2 A Valentinian Exposition
On Anointing	XI 2a On the Anointing
On Bap. A	XI 2b On Baptism A
On Bap. B	XI 2c On Baptism B
On Euch. A	XI 2d On the Eucharist A
On Euch. B	XI 2e On the Eucharist B
Allogenes	XI 3 Allogenes the Stranger
Hypsiph.	XI 4 Hypsiphrone
Sent. Sextus	XII 1 Sentences of Sextus
Gos. Truth	XII 2 Gospel of Truth
Frm.	XII 3 Fragments
Three Forms	XIII 1 Three Forms of First Thought
Orig. World	XIII 2 On the Origin of the World

8.3.12.2 Berlin Gnostic Codex

The Berlin Gnostic Papyrus uses the letters "BG" in place of the codex number.

Gos. Mary	BG 1 Gospel of Mary
Ap. John	BG 2 Secret Book of John
Wis. Jes. Chr.	BG 3 Wisdom of Jesus Christ
Act Pet.	BG 4 Act of Peter

8.3.12.3 Codex Tchacos

Ep. Pet. Phil.	Tchacos 1 Letter of Peter to Philip
James / 1 Rev. Jas.	Tchacos 2 First Revelation of James
Gos. Jud.	Tchacos 3 Gospel of Judas
Bk. Allog.	Tchacos 4 Book of Allogenes

8.3.13 New Testament Apocrypha and Pseudepigrapha

Acts Andr.	Acts of Andrew
Acts Andr. Mth.	Acts of Andrew and Matthias

Acts Andr. Paul	Acts of Andrew and Paul
Acts Barn.	Acts of Barnabas
Acts Jas.	Acts of James the Great
Acts John	Acts of John
Acts John Pro.	Acts of John (by Prochorus)
Acts Paul	Acts of Paul
Acts Pet.	Acts of Peter
Acts Pet. (Slav.)	Acts of Peter (Slavonic)
Acts Pet. Andr.	Acts of Peter and Andrew
Acts Pet. Paul	Acts of Peter and Paul
Acts Phil.	Acts of Philip
Acts Phil. (Syr.)	Acts of Philip (Syriac)
Acts Pil.	Acts of Pilate
Acts Thad.	Acts of Thaddaeus
Acts Thom.	Acts of Thomas
Apoc. Pet.	Apocalypse of Peter
Ap. John	Apocryphon of John
Apoc. Dosith.	Apocalypse of Dositheus
Apoc. Messos	Apocalypse of Messos
Apoc. Thom.	Apocalypse of Thomas
Apoc. Vir.	Apocalypse of the Virgin
(Apocr.) Ep. Tit.	Apocryphal Epistle of Titus
(Apocr.) Gos. John	Apocryphal Gospel of John
Apos. Con.	Apostolic Constitutions and Canons
Ps.-Abd.	Apostolic History of Pseudo-Abdias
(Arab.) Gos. Inf.	Arabic Gospel of the Infancy
(Arm.) Gos. Inf.	Armenian Gospel of the Infancy
Asc. Jas.	Ascents of James
Assum. Vir.	Assumption of the Virgin
Bk. Barn.	Book of the Resurrection of Christ by Barnabas the Apostle
Bk. Elch.	Book of Elchasai
Cerinthus	Cerinthus
3 Cor.	3 Corinthians
Ep. Alex.	Epistle to the Alexandrians
Ep. Apos.	Epistle to the Apostles
Ep. Chr. Abg.	Epistle of Christ and Abgar
Ep. Chr. Heav.	Epistle of Christ from Heaven
Ep. Lao.	Epistle to the Laodiceans
Ep. Lent.	Epistle of Lentulus
Ep. Paul Sen.	Epistles of Paul and Seneca
Gos. Barn.	Gospel of Barnabas
Gos. Bart.	Gospel of Bartholomew
Gos. Bas.	Gospel of Basilides
Gos. Bir. Mary	Gospel of the Birth of Mary
Gos. Eb.	Gospel of the Ebionites
Gos. Eg.	Gospel of the Egyptians
Gos. Eve	Gospel of Eve
Gos. Gam.	Gospel of Gamaliel
Gos. Heb.	Gospel of the Hebrews
Gos. Marcion	Gospel of Marcion

Gos. Mary	Gospel of Mary
Gos. Naass.	Gospel of the Naassenes
Gos. Naz.	Gospel of the Nazarenes
Gos. Nic.	Gospel of Nicodemus
Gos. Pet.	Gospel of Peter
Ps.-Mt.	Gospel of Pseudo-Matthew
Gos. Thom.	Gospel of Thomas
Gos. Trad. Mth.	Gospel and Traditions of Matthias
Hist. Jos. Carp.	History of Joseph the Carpenter
Hymn Dance	Hymn of the Dance
Hymn Pearl	Hymn of the Pearl
Inf. Gos. Thom.	Infancy Gospel of Thomas
Inf. Gos.	Infancy Gospels
Mart. Bart.	Martyrdom of Bartholomew
Mart. Mt.	Martyrdom of Matthew
Mart. Paul	Martyrdom of Paul
Mart. Pet.	Martyrdom of Peter
Mart. Pet. Paul	Martyrdom of Peter and Paul
Mart. Phil.	Martyrdom of Philip
Melkon	Melkon
Mem. Apos.	Memoria of the Apostles
Pre. Pet.	Preaching of Peter
Prot. Jas.	Protevangelium of James
Ps.-Clem.	Pseudo-Clementines
Rev. Steph.	Revelation of Stephen
Sec. Gos. Mk.	Secret Gospel of Mark
Vis. Paul	Vision of Paul

8.3.14 Classical and Ancient Christian Writings

When citing a particular work only once, spell it out rather than abbreviate it, especially if many readers might not be familiar with the work in question. If the same work is cited many times, or if many different works are cited, use abbreviations within notes or parentheses to avoid cluttering the book with spelled-out titles.

We have consulted a number of standard references: the various Oxford Greek and Latin lexicons and dictionaries, the *Dictionnaire latin-français des auteurs chrétiens* (Turnhout: Brepols, 1967), the *TLG Canon* (New York: Oxford University Press, 1990 [for titles; does not give abbreviations]), and others. We do not, however, follow any of these without exception for several reasons: none of them covers the whole field of ancient and late antique, Greek and Latin, Christian and non-Christian writers; most of them are inconsistent internally and with other complementary works; and most of them abbreviate at least some works too concisely for readers not specializing in classical studies or patristics.

We therefore provide not only the table below but also a set of rules. If the work you need to abbreviate is not in the table, similar titles may be; and if not, you can use the rules to devise an acceptable abbreviation of your own.

8.3.14.1 Rules for Abbreviating Latin Titles

(1) Abbreviate titles of works but not names of authors (except as in rule 12 below).

(2) Latin and Greek titles are capitalized according to the rules for Latin (see §6.1.3.8).
(3) The first letter of an abbreviation is always uppercase; otherwise, case in the abbreviation follows case in the spelled-out title.
(4) With regard to Latin orthography: we prefer *v* and *j* for consonantal *u* and *i*.
(5) Avoid acronymns. (In a monograph on Eusebius, the author may elect to use *HE* rather than *Hist. eccl.*, but otherwise *Hist. eccl.* is more helpful to readers.) Do not use acronym-abbreviation hybrids such as *DMort.* or *JTr.* Do not abbreviate by omitting vowels, as in *Phdr.* for *Phaedrus*. (An exception would be a standard biblical abbreviation, such as *Phlm* for *Philemon* [see §§8.3.2 and 8.3.15].)
(6) Rather, abbreviate words by truncating them and placing a period at the point of truncation. Don't truncate between consonants; truncate after a consonant rather than after a vowel where possible. The abbreviation should normally contain at least a whole syllable. Thus: use *Phaedr.* rather than *Phaed.* for *Phaedrus*, *Socr.* rather than *Soc.* for *Socrates*, *coll.* rather than *col.* for *collatio*, *parad.* rather than *para.* for *paradoxa*, and *Thras.* rather than *Thr.* for *Thrasonidis*.
(7) Do not double a final consonant in an abbreviation to indicate a plural; for example, use *Can. ap.* not *Cann. app.* for a reference in *Canones apostolicae*.
(8) For Latin titles that begin with prepositions (*De*, *In*, *Contra*, *Adversus*, *Pro*, *Ad*), the abbreviation includes the preposition (or its abbreviation) only if one of the following holds: (1) The work is a commentary, homily, and the like whose title consists of *In* plus the name of the primary text. (2) The preposition is followed by a noun too short to be abbreviated, so that omitting the preposition would result in an abbreviation beginning with a noun in a case other than the nominative. (3) Without the preposition, this work could be confused with another whose name is similarly abbreviated, as with the orations of Demosthenes for and against Phormio. Similarly, prepositions within a title are omitted in the absence of like complications: *Enarrationes in Psalmos* is abbreviated *Enarrat. Ps.*, not *Enarrat. in Ps.* (See rule 12 below.) Note that in the table we take into account initial prepositions in alphabetizing the abbreviations.
(9) Like prepositions, *et* is omitted from abbreviations.
(10) When a single author has several numbered works by the same name, we prefer in the abbreviation to place the numeral before the name and italicize it. This keeps the treatise number from being confused with a section, chapter, or paragraph number and is consistent with the usage for numbered biblical books. On the other hand, sometimes such works are commonly treated as books of a unified opus, in which case the number follows the name, is set roman, and is followed immediately by a period and a section number.
(11) Where different authors have works with the same title, use the same abbreviation for each author; where the same word occurs in different titles, try to use the same abbreviation for the same word. Here is a list of words that occur commonly in titles and their abbreviations:

adv.	*adversus*	*ap.*	*apostolicus*
an.	*anima; analytica; animal, animalia*	*apol.*	*apologia*
		Apoll.	*Apollo, Apollonius, etc.*
anth.	*anthologia*	*Arian.*	*Arianus*

bell.	*bellum*	*metam.*	*metamorphoses*
catech.	*catechesis*	*metaph.*	*metaphysica*
c.	*contra*	*mete.*	*meteorologica*
comm.	*commentarius, commentarium, commentariolum*	*od.*	*odae*
cor.	*corona*	*or.*	*orator, oratoria, oratio*
d.	*deus*	*orac.*	*oraculum*
Did. apost.	*Didascalia apostolorum*	*orig.*	*origo, originalis*
eccl.	*ecclesiasticus*	*Orig.*	*Origen*
enarrat.	*enarratio*	*pr.*	*prior*
ep.	*epistula*	*pol.*	*politicus, politeia*
epigr.	*epigrammata*	*post.*	*posterior*
eth.	*ethica*	*quaest.*	*quaestiones*
ev.	*evangelium, evangelicus*	*res.*	*resurrectio*
Ev.	*Evangelium*	*rhet.*	*rhetor, rhetorica*
exc.	*excerpta*	*sat.*	*satirae, saturae*
exp.	*expositio*	*schol.*	*scholia*
expl.	*explanatio*	*sel.*	*selecta*
fr.	*fragmentum, fragmenta*	*spir.*	*spiritus*
hist.	*historia*	*tract.*	*tractatus*
hom.	*homilia*	*virg.*	*virgo, virgines*
hymn.	*hymnus*	*virginit.*	*virginitas*
int.	*interpretatio*	*vit.*	*vita*

(12) Similarly, where the title of one work (e.g., a biblical book or a treatise of Aristotle) occurs in the title of another (such as a commentary or a translation), the abbreviation for the primary work should be incorporated (and capitalized) in the abbreviation of the secondary work. The abbreviation for the secondary work is not simply identical to the abbreviation for the primary work. Rather, if it is a translation, it should begin with an abbreviation for the name of the original author (for examples, see under Rufinus and Jerome for their translations of Origen; this is the only circumstance in which we abbreviate authors' names); if the secondary work is a commentary of some kind, its abbreviation should begin with *Comm.*, *Enarrat.*, *Hom.*, *Tract.*, or the like, or at least with *In*.

8.3.14.2 Citing Numbered Passages

The manner in which one cites numbered passages will depend to some degree upon the text one is referencing. In general, we recommend citing the numbering that is original to the work first, followed if appropriate by any secondary numerical identification supplied by the standard critical edition (or by another edition whose numbering is widely followed). In many cases, the secondary numbers will designate pages, but in other cases (see, e.g., §8.3.7 on Josephus) it will represent a more precise—but equally artificial—reference system. (If the secondary reference system is not almost universally recognizable, its source should be indicated by either an annotated bibliographical entry or an explanation in the list of abbreviations.) Since the numbering of a critical edition is usually the most helpful in identifying the precise passage one wants to cite, it is tempting to reference this number alone. We prefer the composite form described above because it helps readers who do not have access to the same edition or translation used by the author; they may still be able to find the passage in their own edition or translation. We prefer to separate book, chapter, and section numbers by periods, place references to particular critical editions in parentheses, and divide successive references with semicolons. As indicated elsewhere, we encourage use of arabic numbers, even in cases where the cited text uses roman numerals.

Examples:

Plutarch, *Is. Os.* 46 (369E) designates the paragraph from *Isis and Osiris* along with the page number used since the 1572 Stephanus edition of Plutarch's *Moralia*.
Plato, *Resp.* 5.4 (454D)
Clement of Alexandria, *Strom.* 2.10 (46.1)
Diogenes Laertius, *Lives* 7.1 Zeno (89)
Quintilian, *Inst.* 1.10.22

8.3.14.3 Greek and Latin Works and Their Abbreviations

Explanatory notes regarding the table:

(1) For Greek works as for Latin works, a Latin title and abbreviation are normally used; but if the work is well known under its Greek name, this may be provided in parentheses following the Latin title. In a few cases where scholars almost always use a Greek title instead, we give a Greek abbreviation and a Greek title, both transliterated. We do not use Greek abbreviations in Greek characters.

(2) For many better-known works, English as well as Latin titles are given. For Greek and Latin classical and patristic works, however, we prefer to use Latin abbreviations in notes even if English titles are used in the text of the book. If English abbreviations are used, the author should provide a list of these.

(3) Most of the works in this table are traditionally cited by author and title, the latter of which is presented in italics. Works traditionally cited by title alone (no author attribution) are presented in roman, following the same principle operative in §4.3.3.1 of italicizing the title of a work only if that work is typically cited by author and title. In the table below, works cited by title alone are alphabetized by their abbreviations, which are given in bold to distinguish them from works of the preceding author. Naturally, when such an abbreviation is used it should be set roman but not bold.

(4) Abbreviations of spurious works are bracketed.

(5) For the sake of completeness, some titles are included that are short enough that they need no abbreviation.

(6) The table is very selective in its choice of authors, but for authors that are included we have tried to offer complete lists of their works.

ABBREVIATIONS	LATIN (OR GREEK) TITLE	ENGLISH TITLE
Achilles Tatius		
Leuc. Clit.	*Leucippe et Clitophon*	*The Adventures of Leucippe and Cleitophon*
Aelian		
Nat. an.	*De natura animalium*	*Nature of Animals*
Var. hist.	*Varia historia*	
Aeschines		
Ctes.	*In Ctesiphonem*	*Against Ctesiphon*
Fals. leg.	*De falsa legatione*	*False Embassy*
Tim.	*In Timarchum*	*Against Timarchus*
Aeschylus		
Ag.	*Agamemnon*	*Agamemnon*
Cho.	*Choephori*	*Libation-Bearers*
Eum.	*Eumenides*	*Eumenides*
Pers.	*Persae*	*Persians*
Prom.	*Prometheus vinctus*	*Prometheus Bound*
Sept.	*Septem contra Thebas*	*Seven against Thebes*
Suppl.	*Supplices*	*Suppliant Women*
Aesop		
Fab.	*Fabulae*	*Fables*
Albinus		
Epit.	*Epitome doctrinae platonicae (Didaskalikos)*	*Handbook of Platonism*
Intr.	*Introductio in Platonem (Prologus* or *Eisagōge)*	*Introduction to Plato*
Alexander of Aphrodisias		
Comm. An. post.	*In Analytica posteriora commentariorum fragmenta*	
Comm. An. pr.	*In Aristotelis Analyticorum priorum librum i commentarium*	
Comm. Metaph.	*In Aristotelis Metaphysica commentaria*	
Comm. Mete.	*In Aristotelis Meteorologicorum libros commentaria*	
Comm. Sens.	*In librum De sensu commentarium*	
Comm. Top.	*In Aristotelis Topicorum libros octo commentaria*	
De an.	*De anima*	
Fat.	*De fato*	
Mixt.	*De mixtione*	
Probl.	*Problemata*	
Ambrose		
Abr.	*De Abraham*	
Apol. Dav.	*Apologia prophetae David*	
Aux.	*Sermo contra Auxentium de basilicis tradendis*	
Bon. mort.	*De bono mortis*	*Death as a Good*
Cain	*De Cain et Abel*	
Enarrat. Ps.	*Enarrationes in XII Psalmos Davidicos*	
Exc.	*De excessu fratris sui Satyri*	
Exh. virginit.	*Exhortatio virginitatis*	
Fid.	*De fide*	
Exp. Isa.	*Expositio Isaiae prophetae*	
Exp. Luc.	*Expositio Evangelii secundum Lucam*	
Exp. Ps. 118	*Expositio Psalmi CXVIII*	
Expl. symb.	*Explanatio symboli ad initiandos*	
Fid. Grat.	*De fide ad Gratianum*	
Fug.	*De fuga saeculi*	*Flight from the World*
Hel.	*De Helia et Jejunio*	
Hex.	*Hexaemeron libri sex*	*Six Days of Creation*
Hymn.	*Hymni*	
Incarn.	*De incarnationis dominicae sacramento*	*The Sacrament of the Incarnation of the Lord*
Instit.	*De institutione virginis*	
Isaac	*De Isaac vel anima*	*Isaac,* or *The Soul*
Jac.	*De Jacob et vita beata*	*Jacob and the Happy Life*
Job	*De interpellatione Job et David*	*The Prayer of Job and David*
Jos.	*De Joseph patriarcha*	
Myst.	*De mysteriis*	*The Mysteries*
Nab.	*De Nabuthae historia*	

ABBREVIATIONS	LATIN (OR GREEK) TITLE	ENGLISH TITLE
Noe	*De Noe et arca*	
Ob. Theo.	*De obitu Theodosii*	
Ob. Val.	*De obitu Valentianiani consolatio*	
Off.	*De officiis ministrorum*	
Paen.	*De paenitentia*	
Parad.	*De paradiso*	*Paradise*
Patr.	*De benedictionibus patriarcharum*	*The Patriarchs*
Sacr.	*De sacramentis*	*The Sacraments*
Sacr. regen.	*De sacramento regenerationis sive de philosophia*	
Spir.	*De Spiritu Sancto*	*The Holy Spirit*
Symb.	*Explanatio symboli*	
Tob.	*De Tobia*	
Vid.	*De viduis*	
Virg.	*De virginibus*	
Virginit.	*De virginitate*	
Anaximenes of Lampsacus		
Rhet. Alex.	*Rhetorica ad Alexandrum* (*Ars rhetorica*)	
Andronicus		
[*Pass.*]	*De passionibus*	*The Passions*
Anth. pal.	Anthologia palatina	Palatine Anthology
Anth. plan.	Anthologia planudea	Planudean Anthology
Antoninus Liberalis		
Metam.	*Metamorphōseōn synagōge*	
Apollonius of Rhodes		
Argon.	*Argonautica*	*Argonautica*
Apollonius Sophista		
Lex. hom.	*Lexicon homericum*	*Homeric Lexicon*
Appian		
Bell. civ.	*Bella civilia*	*Civil Wars*
Hist. rom.	*Historia romana*	*Roman History*
Apuleius		
Apol.	*Apologia* (*Pro se de magia*)	*Apology*
De deo Socr.	*De deo Socratico*	
Dogm. Plat.	*De dogma Platonis*	
Flor.	*Florida*	
Metam.	*Metamorphoses*	*The Golden Ass*
Aratus		
Phaen.	*Phaenomena*	
Archimedes		
Aequil.	*De planorum aequilibriis*	*The Equilibriums of Planes* or *Centers of Gravity of Planes*
Aren.	*Arenarius*	*The Sand-Reckoner*
Assumpt.	*Liber assumptorum*	
Bov.	*Problema bovinum*	
Circ.	*Dimensio circuli*	*Measurement of the Circle*
Con. sph.	*De conoidibus et sphaeroidibus*	*On Conoids and Spheroids*
Eratosth.	*Ad Eratosthenem methodus*	*To Eratosthenes on the Method of Mechanical Theorems*
Fluit.	*De corporibus fluitantibus*	*On Floating Bodies*
Quadr.	*Quadratura parabolae*	*Quadrature of the Parabola*
Sph. cyl.	*De sphaera et cylindro*	*On the Sphere and the Cylinder*
Spir.	*De lineis spiralibus*	*On Spirals*
Stom.	*Stomachion*	
Aretaeus		
Cur. acut.	*De curatione acutorum morborum*	
Cur. diut.	*De curatione diuturnorum morborum*	
Sign. acut.	*De causis et signis acutorum morborum*	
Sign. diut.	*De causis et signis diuturnorum morborum*	
Aristophanes		
Ach.	*Acharnenses*	*Acharnians*
Av.	*Aves*	*Birds*

ABBREVIATIONS	LATIN (OR GREEK) TITLE	ENGLISH TITLE
Eccl.	*Ecclesiazusae*	*Women of the Assembly*
Eq.	*Equites*	*Knights*
Lys.	*Lysistrata*	*Lysistrata*
Nub.	*Nubes*	*Clouds*
Pax	*Pax*	*Peace*
Plut.	*Plutus*	*The Rich Man*
Ran.	*Ranae*	*Frogs*
Thesm.	*Thesmophoriazusae*	
Vesp.	*Vespae*	*Wasps*
Aristotle		
An. post.	*Analytica posteriora*	*Posterior Analytics*
An. pr.	*Analytica priora*	*Prior Analytics*
Ath. pol.	*Athēnaīn politeia*	*Constitution of Athens*
[*Aud.*]	*De audibilibus*	*Sounds*
Cael.	*De caelo*	*Heavens*
Cat.	*Categoriae*	*Categories*
[*Col.*]	*De coloribus*	*Colors*
De an.	*De anima*	*Soul*
Div. somn.	*De divinatio per somnum*	*Prophesying by Dreams*
Ep.	*Epistulae*	*Letters*
Eth. eud.	*Ethica eudemia*	*Eudemian Ethics*
Eth. nic.	*Ethica nicomachea*	*Nicomachean Ethics*
Gen. an.	*De generatione anamalium*	*Generation of Animals*
Gen. corr.	*De generatione et corruptione*	*Generation and Corruption*
[*Gorg.*]	*De Gorgia*	
Hist. an.	*Historia animalium*	*History of Animals*
Inc. an.	*De incessu animalium*	*Gait of Animals*
Insomn.	*De insomniis*	
Int.	*De interpretatione*	*Interpretation*
Juv. sen.	*De juventute et senectute*	*Youth and Old Age*
[*Lin. ins.*]	*De lineis insecabilibus*	*Indivisible Lines*
Long. brev.	*De longitudine et brevitate vitae*	*Longevity and Shortness of Life*
[*Mag. mor.*]	*Magna moralia*	
[*Mech.*]	*Mechanica*	*Mechanics*
Mem. rem.	*De memoria et reminiscentia*	*Memory and Reminiscence*
Metaph.	*Metaphysica*	*Metaphysics*
Mete.	*Meteorologica*	*Meteorology*
[*Mir. ausc.*]	*De mirabilibus auscultationibus*	*On Marvelous Things Heard*
Mot. an.	*De motu animalium*	*Movement of Animals*
[*Mund.*]	*De mundo*	
[*Oec.*]	*Oeconomica*	*Economics*
Part. an.	*De partibus animalium*	*Parts of Animals*
Phys.	*Physica*	*Physics*
[*Physiogn.*]	*Physiognomonica*	*Physiognomonics*
[*Plant.*]	*De plantis*	*Plants*
Poet.	*Poetica*	*Poetics*
Pol.	*Politica*	*Politics*
[*Probl.*]	*Problemata*	*Problems*
Protr.	*Protrepticus*	
Resp.	*De respiratione*	*Respiration*
Rhet.	*Rhetorica*	*Rhetoric*
[*Rhet. Alex.*]	*Rhetorica ad Alexandrum* (see Anaximenes)	*Rhetoric to Alexander*
Sens.	*De sensu et sensibilibus*	*Sense and Sensibilia*
Somn.	*De somniis*	*Dreams*
Somn. vig.	*De somno et vigilia*	*Sleep and Waking*
Soph. elench.	*Sophistici elenchi* (*Top.* 9)	*Sophistical Refutations*
[*Spir.*]	*De spiritu*	
Top.	*Topica*	*Topics*
[*Vent.*]	*De ventorum situ et nominibus*	*Situations and Names of Winds*
[*Virt. vit.*]	*De virtutibus et vitiis*	*Virtues and Vices*
Vit. mort.	*De vita et morte*	*Life and Death*

ABBREVIATIONS	LATIN (OR GREEK) TITLE	ENGLISH TITLE
[Xen.]	*De Xenophane*	
[Zen.]	*De Zenone*	
Arrian		
Anab.	*Anabasis*	
Epict. diss.	*Epicteti dissertationes*	
Peripl. M. Eux.	*Periplus Maris Euxini*	
Tact.	*Tactica*	
Artemidorus Daldianus		
Onir.	*Onirocritica*	
Athanasius		
Apol. Const.	*Apologia ad Constantium*	*Defense before Constantius*
Apol. sec.	*Apologia secunda* (= *Apologia contra Arianos*)	*Defense against the Arians*
[*Apoll.*]	*De incarnatione contra Apollinarium*	*On the Incarnation against Apollinaris*
C. *Ar.*	*Orationes contra Arianos*	*Orations against the Arians*
Decr.	*De decretis*	*Defense of the Nicene Definition*
Dion.	*De sententia Dionysii*	*On the Opinion of Dionysius*
Ep. Adelph.	*Epistula ad Adelphium*	*Letter to Adelphius*
Ep. Aeg. Lib.	*Epistula ad episcopos Aegypti et Libyae*	*Letter to the Bishops of Egypt and Libya*
Ep. Afr.	*Epistula ad Afros episcopos*	*Letter to the Bishops of Africa*
Ep. Amun	*Epistula ad Amun*	*Letter to Ammoun*
Ep. cler. Alex.	*Epistula ad clerum Alexandriae*	*Letter to the Clergy of Alexandria*
Ep. cler. Mareot.	*Epistula ad clerum Mareotae*	*Letter to the Clergy of the Mareotis*
Ep. Drac.	*Epistula ad Dracontium*	*Letter to Dracontius*
Ep. encycl.	*Epistula encyclica*	*Circular Letter*
Ep. Epict.	*Epistula ad Epictetum*	*Letter to Epictetus*
Ep. fest.	*Epistulae festales*	*Festal Letters*
Ep. Jo. Ant.	*Epistula ad Joannem et Antiochum presbyteros*	*Letter to John and Antiochus*
Ep. Jov.	*Epistula ad Jovianum*	*Letter to Jovian*
Ep. Marcell.	*Epistula ad Marcellinum de interpretatione Psalmorum*	*Letter to Marcellinus on the Interpretation of the Psalms*
Ep. Max.	*Epistula ad Maximum*	*Letter to Maximus*
Ep. mon. 1	*Epistula ad monachos i*	*First Letter to Monks*
Ep. mon. 2	*Epistula ad monachos ii*	*Second Letter to Monks*
Ep. mort. Ar.	*Epistula ad Serapionem de more Arii*	*Letter to Serapion concerning the Death of Arius*
Ep. Ors. 1	*Epistula ad Orsisium i*	*First Letter to Orsisius*
Ep. Ors. 2	*Epistula ad Orsisium ii*	*Second Letter to Orsisius*
Ep. Pall.	*Epistula ad Palladium*	*Letter to Palladius*
Ep. Rufin.	*Epistula ad Rufinianum*	*Letter to Rufinianus*
Ep. Serap.	*Epistulae ad Serapionem*	*Letters to Serapion concerning the Holy Spirit*
Ep. virg. (Copt.)	*Epistula ad virgines* (Coptice)	*First* (*Coptic*) *Letter to Virgins*
Ep. virg. (Syr.)	*Epistula ad virgines* (Syriace)	*Second* (*Syriac*) *Letter to Virgins*
Ep. virg. (Syr./Arm.)	*Epistula ad virgines* (Syriace et Armeniace)	*Letter to Virgins*
Ep. virg. (Theod.)	*Epistula exhortatora ad virgines apud Theodoretum*	*Letter to Virgins*
Fug.	*Apologia de fuga sua*	*Defense of His Flight*
C. *Gent.*	*Contra gentes*	*Against the Pagans*
H. Ar.	*Historia Arianorum*	*History of the Arians*
Hen. sōm.	*Henos sōmatos*	*Encyclical Letter of Alexander concerning the Deposition of Arius*
Hom. Jo. 12:27	*In illud Nunc anima mea turbata est*	*Homily on John 12:27*
Hom. Luc. 12:10	*In illud Qui dixerit verbum in filium*	*Homily on Luke 12:10*
Hom. Matt. 11:27	*In illud Omnia mihi tradita sunt*	*Homily on Matthew 11:27*
Inc.	*De incarnatione*	*On the Incarnation*
Mor. et val.	*De morbo et valitudine*	*On Sickness and Health*
Narr. fug.	*Narratio ad Ammonium episcopum de fuga sua*	*Report of Athanasius concerning Theodorus*
Syn.	*De synodis*	*On the Councils of Ariminum and Seleucia*
Tom.	*Tomus ad Antiochenos*	*Tome to the People of Antioch*
Vit. Ant.	*Vita Antonii*	*Life of Antony*
Athenaeus		
Deipn.	*Deipnosophistae*	

ABBREVIATIONS	LATIN (OR GREEK) TITLE	ENGLISH TITLE
Athenagoras		
Leg.	*Legatio pro Christianis*	
Res.	*De resurrectione*	
Augustine		
Acad.	*Contra Academicos*	*Against the Academics*
Adim.	*Contra Adimantum*	*Against Adimantus*
Adnot. Job	*Adnotationum in Job liber I*	*Annotations on Job*
Adv. Jud.	*Tractatus adversus Judaeos*	*In Answer to the Jews*
Agon.	*De agone christiano*	*Christian Combat*
An. orig.	*De anima et eius origine*	*The Soul and Its Origin*
Arian.	*Contra sermonem Arianorum*	
Bapt.	*De baptismo contra Donatistas*	*Baptism*
Beat.	*De vita beata*	
Bon. conj.	*De bono conjugali*	*The Good of Marriage*
Brev. coll.	*Breviculus collationis cum Donatistis*	
C. du. ep. Pelag.	*Contra duas epistulas Pelagianorum ad Bonifatium*	*Against the Two Letters of the Pelagians*
C. Jul.	*Contra Julianum*	*Against Julian*
C. Jul. op. imp.	*Contra secundam Juliani responsionem imperfectum opus*	*Against Julian: Opus Imperfectum*
C. litt. Petil.	*Contra litteras Petiliani*	
C. mend.	*Contra mendacium*	*Against Lying (to Consentius)*
Catech.	*De catechizandis rudibus*	*Catechizing the Uninstructed*
Civ.	*De civitate Dei*	*The City of God*
Coll. Max.	*Collatio cum Maximino Arianorum episcopo*	
Conf.	*Confessionum libri XIII*	*Confessions*
Cons.	*De consensu evangelistarum*	*Harmony of the Gospels*
Contin.	*De continentia*	*Continence*
Corrept.	*De correptione et gratia*	*Admonition and Grace*
Cresc.	*Contra Cresconium Donatistam*	
Cur.	*De cura pro mortuis gerenda*	*The Care to Be Taken for the Dead*
De mend.	*De mendacio*	*On Lying*
Dial.	*Principia dialecticae*	
Disc.	*De disciplina christiana*	
Div.	*De divinitate daemonum*	*The Divination of Demons*
Div. quaest. LXXXIII	*De diversis quaestionibus LXXXIII*	*Eighty-three Different Questions*
Div. quaest. Simpl.	*De diversis quaestionibus ad Simplicianum*	
Doctr. chr.	*De doctrina christiana*	*Christian Instruction*
Don.	*Post collationem adversus Donatistas*	
Duab.	*De duabus animabus*	*Two Souls*
Dulc.	*De octo Dulcitii quaestionibus*	*The Eight Questions of Dulcitius*
Emer.	*De gestis cum Emerino*	
Enarrat. Ps.	*Enarrationes in Psalmos*	*Enarrations on the Psalms*
Enchir.	*Enchiridion de fide, spe, et caritate*	*Enchiridion on Faith, Hope, and Love*
Exp. Gal.	*Expositio in epistulam ad Galatas*	
Exp. quaest. Rom.	*Expositio quarumdam quaestionum in epistula ad Romanos*	
Faust.	*Contra Faustum Manichaeum*	*Against Faustus the Manichaean*
Fel.	*Contra Felicem*	*Against Felix*
Fid.	*De fide rerum quae non videntur*	*Faith in Things Unseen*
Fid. op.	*De fide et operibus*	*Faith and Works*
Fid. symb.	*De fide et symbolo*	*Faith and the Creed*
Fort.	*Contra Fortunatum*	*Against Fortunatus*
Fund.	*Contra epistulam Manichaei quam vocant Fundamenti*	*Against the Letter of the Manichaeans That They Call "The Basics"*
Gaud.	*Contra Gaudentium Donatistarum episcopum*	*Against Gaudentius the Donatist Bishop*
Gen. imp.	*De Genesi ad litteram imperfectus liber*	*On the Literal Interpretation of Genesis: An Unfinished Book*
Gen. litt.	*De Genesi ad litteram*	*On Genesis Literally Interpreted*
Gen. Man.	*De Genesi contra Manichaeos*	*On Genesis against the Manichaeans*
Gest. Pelag.	*De gestis Pelagii*	*Proceedings of Pelagius*

ABBREVIATIONS	LATIN (OR GREEK) TITLE	ENGLISH TITLE
Gramm.	*De grammatica*	
Grat.	*De gratia et libero arbitrio*	*Grace and Free Will*
Grat. Chr.	*De gratia Christi, et de peccato originali*	*The Grace of Christ and Original Sin*
Haer.	*De haeresibus*	*Heresies*
Immort. an.	*De immortalitate animae*	*The Immortality of the Soul*
Incomp. nupt.	*De incompetentibus nuptiis*	*Adulterous Marriages*
Leg.	*Contra adversarium legis et prophetarum*	
Lib.	*De libero arbitrio*	*Free Will*
Locut. Hept.	*Locutionum in Heptateuchum libri septem*	
Mag.	*De magistro*	
Man.	*De moribus Manichaeorum*	*The Morals of the Manichaeans*
Maxim.	*Contra Maximinum Arianum*	*Against Maximinus the Arian*
Mor. eccl.	*De moribus ecclesiae catholicae*	*The Way of Life of the Catholic Church*
Mor. Manich.	*De moribus Manichaeorum*	*The Way of Life of the Manichaeans*
Mus.	*De musica*	*Music*
Nat. bon.	*De natura boni contra Manichaeos*	*The Nature of the Good*
Nat. grat.	*De natura et gratia*	*Nature and Grace*
Nat. orig.	*De natura et origine animae*	*The Nature and Origin of the Soul*
Nupt.	*De nuptiis et concupiscentia ad Valerium comitem*	*Marriage and Concupiscence*
Oct. quaest. Vet. Test.	*De octo quaestionibus ex Veteri Testamento*	*Eight Questions from the Old Testament*
Op. mon.	*De opere monachorum*	*The Work of Monks*
Ord.	*De ordine*	
Parm.	*Contra epistulam Parmeniani*	
Pat.	*De patientia*	*Patience*
Pecc. merit.	*De peccatorum meritis et remissione*	*Guilt and Remission of Sins*
Pecc. orig.	*De peccato originali*	*Original Sin*
Perf.	*De perfectione justitiae hominis*	*Perfection in Human Righteousness*
Persev.	*De dono perseverantiae*	*The Gift of Perseverance*
Praed.	*De praedestinatione sanctorum*	*The Predestination of the Saints*
Priscill.	*Ad Orosium contra Priscillianistas et Origenistas*	*To Orosius against the Priscillianists and the Origenists*
Psal. Don.	*Psalmus contra partem Donati*	
Quaest. ev.	*Quaestionum evangelicarum libri II*	
Quaest. Hept.	*Quaestiones in Heptateuchum*	
Quaest. Matt.	*Quaestiones in evangelium Matthaei*	
Quant. an.	*De quantitate animae*	*The Magnitude of the Soul*
Reg.	*Regula ad servos Dei*	
Retract.	*Retractationum libri II*	*Retractations*
Rhet.	*De rhetorica, Rhetores Latini*	
Secund.	*Contra Secundinum Manichaeum*	
Serm.	*Sermones*	
Serm. Dom.	*De sermone Domini in monte*	*Sermon on the Mount*
Solil.	*Soliloquiorum libri II*	*Soliloquies*
Spec.	*De scriptura sancta speculum*	
Spir. et litt.	*De spiritu et littera*	*The Spirit and the Letter*
Symb.	*De symbolo ad catechumenos*	*The Creed: For Catechumens*
Tract. ep. Jo.	*In epistulam Johannis ad Parthos tractatus*	*Tractates on the First Epistle of John*
Tract. Ev. Jo.	*In Evangelium Johannis tractatus*	*Tractates on the Gospel of John*
Trin.	*De Trinitate*	*The Trinity*
Unic. bapt.	*De unico baptismo*	
Unit. eccl.	*De unitate ecclesiae*	*The Unity of the Church*
Util. cred.	*De utilitate credendi*	*The Usefulness of Believing*
Util. jej.	*De utilitate jejunii*	*The Usefulness of Fasting*
Ver. rel.	*De vera religione*	*True Religion*
Vid.	*De bono viduitatis*	*The Excellence of Widowhood*
Virginit.	*De sancta virginitate*	*Holy Virginity*
Vit. Christ.	*De vita christiana*	*The Christian Life*
Aulus Gellius		
Bell. afr.	*Bellum africum*	*African War*
Bell. alex.	*Bellum alexandrinum*	*Alexandrian War*
Noct. att.	*Noctes atticae*	*Attic Nights*

ABBREVIATIONS	LATIN (OR GREEK) TITLE	ENGLISH TITLE
Bion		
Epitaph. Adon.	*Epitaphius Adonis*	*Lament for Adonis*
[*Epith. Achil.*]	*Epithalamium Achillis et Deidameiae*	*Epithalamium to Achilles and Deidamea*
Caesar		
Bell. civ.	*Bellum civile*	*Civil War*
Bell. gall.	*Bellum gallicum*	*Gallic War*
Callimachus		
Aet.	*Aetia* (in P.Oxy. 2079)	*Causes*
Epigr.	*Epigrammata*	*Epigrams*
Hec.	*Hecala*	*Hecale*
Hymn.	*Hymni*	*Hymns*
Hymn. Apoll.	*Hymnus in Apollinem*	*Hymn to Apollo*
Hymn. Cer.	*Hymnus in Cererem*	*Hymn to Ceres* or *Demeter*
Hymn. Del.	*Hymnus in Delum*	*Hymn to Delos*
Hymn. Dian.	*Hymnus in Dianam*	*Hymn to Diana* or *Artemis*
Hymn. Jov.	*Hymnus in Jovem*	*Hymn to Jove* or *Zeus*
Hymn. lav. Pall.	*Hymnus in lavacrum Palladis*	*Hymn to the Baths of Pallas*
Can. ap.	Canones apostolicae	Apostolic Canons
Cato		
Agr.	*De agricultura* (*De re rustica*)	*Agriculture*
Orig.	*Origines*	*Origins*
Ceb. Tab.	Cebetis Tabula	
Chariton		
Chaer.	*De Chaerea et Callirhoe*	*Chaereas and Callirhoe*
Chrysostom	See *John Chrysostom*	
Cicero		
Acad.	*Academicae quaestiones*	
Acad. post.	*Academica posteriora* (*Lucullus*)	
Acad. pr.	*Academica priora*	
Agr.	*De Lege agraria*	
Amic.	*De amicitia*	
Arch.	*Pro Archia*	
Att.	*Epistulae ad Atticum*	
Aug.	*De auguriis*	
Balb.	*Pro Balbo*	
Brut.	*Brutus* or *De claris oratoribus*	
Caecin.	*Pro Caecina*	
Cael.	*Pro Caelio*	
Cat.	*In Catalinam*	
Clu.	*Pro Cluentio*	
Corn.	*Pro Cornelio de maiestate*	
De or.	*De oratore*	
Deiot.	*Pro rege Deiotaro*	
Div.	*De divinatione*	
Div. Caec.	*Divinatio in Caecilium*	
Dom.	*De domo suo*	
Ep. Brut.	*Epistulae ad Brutum*	
Epigr.	*Epigrammata*	
Fam.	*Epistulae ad familiares*	
Fat.	*De fato*	
Fin.	*De finibus*	
Flac.	*Pro Flacco*	
Font.	*Pro Fonteio*	
Har. resp.	*De haruspicum responso*	
Inv.	*De inventione rhetorica*	
Leg.	*De legibus*	
Leg. man.	*Pro Lege manilia* (*De imperio Cn. Pompeii*)	
Lig.	*Pro Ligario*	
Lim.	*Limon*	
Mar.	*Marius*	
Marcell.	*Pro Marcello*	

ABBREVIATIONS	LATIN (OR GREEK) TITLE	ENGLISH TITLE
Mil.	*Pro Milone*	
Mur.	*Pro Murena*	
Nat. d.	*De natura deorum*	
Off.	*De officiis*	
Opt. gen.	*De optimo genere oratorum*	
Or. Brut.	*Orator ad M. Brutum*	
Parad.	*Paradoxa Stoicorum*	
Part. or.	*Partitiones oratoriae*	
Phil.	*Orationes philippicae*	
Pis.	*In Pisonem*	
Planc.	*Pro Plancio*	
Prov. cons.	*De provinciis consularibus*	
Quinct.	*Pro Quinctio*	
Quint. fratr.	*Epistulae ad Quintum fratrem*	
Rab. Perd.	*Pro Rabirio Perduellionis Reo*	
Rab. Post.	*Pro Rabirio Postumo*	
Red. pop.	*Post reditum ad populum*	
Red. sen.	*Post reditum in senatu*	
Rep.	*De republica*	
Rosc. Amer.	*Pro Sexto Roscio Amerino*	
Rosc. com.	*Pro Roscio comoedo*	
Scaur.	*Pro Scauro*	
Sen.	*De senectute*	
Sest.	*Pro Sestio*	
Sull.	*Pro Sulla*	
Tim.	*Timaeus*	
Tog. cand.	*Oratio in senatu in toga candida*	
Top.	*Topica*	
Tull.	*Pro Tullio*	
Tusc.	*Tusculanae disputationes*	
Vat.	*In Vatinium*	
Verr.	*In Verrem*	
Clement of Alexandria		
Adumbr.	*Adumbrationes in epistulas canonicas*	*Adumbrations*
Ecl.	*Eclogae propheticae*	*Extracts from the Prophets*
Exc.	*Excerpta ex Theodoto*	*Excerpts from Theodotus*
Hyp.	*Hypotyposes*	
Paed.	*Paedagogus*	*Christ the Educator*
Protr.	*Protrepticus*	*Exhortation to the Greeks*
Quis div.	*Quis dives salvetur*	*Salvation of the Rich*
Strom.	*Stromateis*	*Miscellanies*
Cod. justin.	Codex justinianus	
Cod. theod.	Codex theodosianus	
Commodian		
Carm. apol.	*Carmen apologeticum*	*[Song of] Apology*
Columella		
Arb.	*De arboribus*	
Rust.	*De re rustica*	
Const. ap.	Constitutiones apostolicae	Apostolic Constitutions
Cornutus		
Nat. d.	*De natura deorum (Epidromē tōn kata tēn Hellēniken theologian paradedomenōn)*	*Summary of the Traditions concerning Greek Mythology*
Corp. herm.	Corpus hermeticum	
Cosmas Indicopleustes		
Top.	*Topographia christiana*	*Christian Topography*
Cyprian		
Demetr.	*Ad Demetrianum*	*To Demetrian*
Dom. or.	*De dominica oratione*	*The Lord's Prayer*
Don.	*Ad Donatum*	*To Donatus*
Eleem.	*De opere et eleemosynis*	*Works and Almsgiving*
Fort.	*Ad Fortunatum*	*To Fortunatus: Exhortation to Martyrdom*

ABBREVIATIONS	LATIN (OR GREEK) TITLE	ENGLISH TITLE
Hab. virg.	*De habitu virginum*	*The Dress of Virgins*
[Idol.]	*Quod idola dii non sint*	*That Idols Are Not Gods*
Laps.	*De lapsis*	*The Lapsed*
Mort.	*De mortalitate*	*Mortality*
Pat.	*De bono patientiae*	*The Advantage of Patience*
Sent.	*Sententiae episcoporum de haereticis baptizandis*	
Test.	*Ad Quirinum testimonia adversus Judaeos*	*To Quirinius: Testimonies against the Jews*
Unit. eccl.	*De catholicae ecclesiae unitate*	*The Unity of the Catholic Church*
Zel. liv.	*De zelo et livore*	*Jealousy and Envy*
Demetrius		
Eloc.	*De elocutione (Peri hermēneias)*	*Style*
Demosthenes		
Andr.	*Adversus Androtionem*	*Against Androtion*
[Apat.]	*Contra Apatourium*	*Against Apaturius*
1–3 Aphob.	*In Aphobum*	*1–3 Against Aphobus*
Aristocr.	*In Aristocratem*	*Against Aristocrates*
1–2 Aristog.	*In Aristogitonem*	*1–2 Against Aristogeiton*
1 [2] Boeot.	*Contra Boeotum i–ii*	*1–2 Against Boeotos*
C. Phorm.	*Contra Phormionem*	*Against Phormio*
Call.	*Contra Calliclem*	*Against Callicles*
[Callip.]	*Contra Callipum*	*Against Callipus*
Chers.	*De Chersoneso*	*On the Chersonese*
Con.	*In Cononem*	*Against Conon*
Cor.	*De corona*	*On the Crown*
Cor. trier.	*De corona trierarchiae*	*On the Trierarchic Crown*
De pace	*De pace*	*On the Peace*
[Dionys.]	*Contra Dionysodorum*	*Against Dionysodorus*
Epitaph.	*Epitaphius*	*Funeral Oration*
[Erot.]	*Eroticus*	*Eroticus*
Eub.	*Contra Eubulidem*	*Against Eubulides*
[Euerg.]	*In Evergum et Mnesibulum*	*Against Evergus and Mnesibulus*
Exord.	*Exordia (Prooemia)*	
Fals. leg.	*De falsa legatione*	*False Embassy*
Halon.	*De Halonneso*	*On the Halonnesus*
[Lacr.]	*Contra Lacritum*	*Against Lacritus*
[Leoch.]	*Contra Leocharem*	*Against Leochares*
Lept.	*Adversus Leptinem*	*Against Leptines*
[Macart.]	*Contra Macartatum*	*Against Macartatus*
Meg.	*Pro Megalopolitanis*	*For the Megalopolitans*
Mid.	*In Midiam*	*Against Meidias*
Naus.	*Contra Nausimachum et Xenopeithea*	*Against Nausimachus*
[Neaer.]	*In Neaeram*	*Against Neaera*
Nicostr.	*Contra Nicostratum*	*Against Nicostratus*
[Olymp.]	*In Olympiodorum*	*Against Olympiodorus*
1–3 Olynth.	*Olynthiaca i–iii*	*1–3 Olynthiac*
1–2 Onet.	*Contra Onetorem*	*1–2 Against Onetor*
Pro Phorm.	*Pro Phormione*	*For Phormio*
Pant.	*Contra Pantaenetum*	*Against Pantaenetus*
1–3 [4] Philip.	*Philippica i–iv*	*1–4 Philippic*
[Poly.]	*Contra Polyclem*	*Against Polycles*
Rhod. lib.	*De Rhodiorum libertate*	*On the Liberty of the Rhodians*
Spud.	*Contra Spudiam*	*Against Spudia*
1 [2] Steph.	*In Stephanum i–ii*	*1–2 Against Stephanus*
Symm.	*De symmoriis*	*On the Symmories*
[Syntax.]	*Peri syntaxeōs*	*On Organization*
[Theocr.]	*In Theocrinem*	*Against Theocrines*
[Tim.]	*Contra Timotheum*	*Against Timotheus*
Timocr.	*In Timocratem*	*Against Timocrates*
Zenoth.	*Contra Zenothemin*	*Against Zenothemis*
Didymus		
Comm. Eccl.	*Commentarii in Ecclesiasten*	

ABBREVIATIONS	LATIN (OR GREEK) TITLE	ENGLISH TITLE
Comm. Job	*Commentarii in Job*	
Comm. Oct. Reg.	*Commentarii in Octateuchum et Reges*	
Comm. Ps.	*Commentarii in Psalmos*	
Comm. Zach.	*Commentarii in Zachariam*	
Dial. haer.	*Dialogus Didymi Caeci cum haeretico*	
Enarrat. Ep. Cath.	*In Epistulas Catholicas brevis enarratio*	
Fr. Cant.	*Fragmentum in Canticum canticorum*	
Fr. 1 Cor.	*Fragmenta in Epistulam i ad Corinthios*	
Fr. 2 Cor.	*Fragmenta in Epistulam ii ad Corinthios*	
Fr. Heb.	*Fragmentum in Epistulam ad Hebraeos*	
Fr. Jer.	*Fragmenta in Jeremiam*	
Fr. Jo.	*Fragmenta in Joannem*	
Fr. Prov.	*Fragmenta in Proverbia*	
Fr. Ps.	*Fragmenta in Psalmos*	
Fr. Rom.	*Fragmenta in Epistulam ad Romanos*	
In Gen.	*In Genesim*	
Incorp.	*De incorporeo*	
Man.	*Contra Manichaeos*	
Philos.	*Ad philosophum*	
Trin.	*De Trinitate*	
Dig.	Digesta	
Dinarchus		
Aristog.	*In Aristogitonem*	*Against Aristogiton*
Demosth.	*In Demosthenem*	*Against Demosthenes*
Phil.	*In Philoclem*	*Against Philocles*
Dio Chrysostom		
Achill.	*Achilles* (*Or.* 58)	*Achilles and Cheiron*
Admin.	*De administratione* (*Or.* 50)	*His Past Record*
Aegr.	*De aegritudine* (*Or.* 16)	*Pain and Distress of Spirit*
Alex.	*Ad Alexandrinos* (*Or.* 32)	*To the People of Alexandria*
Apam.	*Ad Apamenses* (*Or.* 41)	*To the Apameians*
Aud. aff.	*De audiendi affectione* (*Or.* 19)	*Fondness for Listening*
Avar.	*De avaritia* (*Or.* 17)	*Covetousness*
Borysth.	*Borysthenitica* (*Or.* 36)	*Borysthenic Discourse*
Cel. Phryg.	*Celaenis Phrygiae* (*Or.* 35)	*At Celaenae in Phrygia*
Charid.	*Charidemus* (*Or.* 30)	
Chrys.	*Chryseis* (*Or.* 61)	
Compot.	*De compotatione* (*Or.* 27)	*Symposia*
Conc. Apam.	*De concordia cum Apamensibus* (*Or.* 40)	*On Concord with Apamea*
Consuet.	*De consuetudine* (*Or.* 76)	*Custom*
Consult.	*De consultatione* (*Or.* 26)	*Deliberation*
Cont.	*Contio* (*Or.* 47)	*In the Public Assembly at Prusa*
[*Cor.*]	*Corinthiaca* (*Or.* 37)	*Corinthian Discourse*
De lege	*De lege* (*Or.* 75)	*Law*
De pace	*De pace et bello* (*Or.* 22)	*Peace and War*
De philosophia	*De philosophia* (*Or.* 70)	*Philosophy*
De philosopho	*De philosopho* (*Or.* 71)	*The Philosopher*
Def.	*Defensio* (*Or.* 45)	*Defense*
Dei cogn.	*De dei cognitione* (*Or.* 12)	*Man's First Conception of God* (*Olympic Discourse*)
Dial.	*Dialexis* (*Or.* 42)	*In His Native City*
Dic. exercit.	*De dicendi exercitatione* (*Or.* 18)	*Training for Public Speaking*
Diffid.	*De diffidentia* (*Or.* 74)	*Distrust*
Diod.	*Ad Diodorum* (*Or.* 51)	*To Diodorus*
Divit.	*De divitiis* (*Or.* 79)	*Wealth*
Exil.	*De exilio* (*Or.* 13)	*Banishment*
Fel.	*De felicitate* (*Or.* 24)	*Happiness*
Fel. sap.	*De quod felix sit sapiens* (*Or.* 23)	*The Wise Man Is Happy*
Fid.	*De fide* (*Or.* 73)	*Trust*
1 Fort.	*De fortuna i* (*Or.* 63)	*Fortune 1*
2 Fort.	*De fortuna ii* (*Or.* 64)	*Fortune 2*

ABBREVIATIONS	LATIN (OR GREEK) TITLE	ENGLISH TITLE
3 Fort.	*De fortuna iii* (*Or.* 65)	*Fortune 3*
Gen.	*De genio* (*Or.* 25)	*The Guiding Spirit*
1 Glor.	*De gloria i* (*Or.* 66)	*Reputation*
2 Glor.	*De gloria ii* (*Or.* 67)	*Popular Opinion*
3 Glor.	*De gloria iii* (*Or.* 68)	*Opinion*
Grat.	*Gratitudo* (*Or.* 44)	*Friendship for His Native Land*
Hab.	*De habitu* (*Or.* 72)	*Personal Appearance*
Hom.	*De Homero* (*Or.* 53)	*Homer*
Hom. Socr.	*De Homero et Socrate* (*Or.* 55)	*Homer and Socrates*
In cont.	*In contione* (*Or.* 48)	*Political Address in the Assembly*
Invid.	*De invidia* (*Or.* 77/78)	*Envy*
Isthm.	*Isthmiaca* (*Or.* 9)	*Isthmian Discourse*
Lib.	*De libertate* (*Or.* 80)	*Freedom*
Lib. myth.	*Libycus mythos* (*Or.* 5)	*A Libyan Myth*
1 Melanc.	*Melancomas i* (*Or.* 29)	*Melancomas 1*
2 Melanc.	*Melancomas ii* (*Or.* 28)	*Melancomas 2*
Ness.	*Nessus* (*Or.* 60)	*Nessus*, or *Deianeira*
Nest.	*Nestor* (*Or.* 57)	*Homer's Portrayal of Nestor*
Nicaeen.	*Ad Nicaeenses* (*Or.* 39)	*To the Nicaeans*
Nicom.	*Ad Nicomedienses* (*Or.* 38)	*To the Nicomedians*
Philoct.	*Philoctetes* (*Or.* 59)	
Philoct. arc.	*De Philoctetae arcu* (*Or.* 52)	*Appraisal of the Tragic Triad*
Pol.	*Politica* (*Or.* 43)	*Political Address*
Pulchr.	*De pulchritudine* (*Or.* 21)	*Beauty*
Rec. mag.	*Recusatio magistratus* (*Or.* 49)	*Refusal of the Office of Archon*
Regn.	*De regno* (*Or.* 56)	*Kingship*
1 Regn.	*De regno i* (*Or.* 1)	*Kingship 1*
2 Regn.	*De regno ii* (*Or.* 2)	*Kingship 2*
3 Regn.	*De regno iii* (*Or.* 3)	*Kingship 3*
4 Regn.	*De regno iv* (*Or.* 4)	*Kingship 4*
Regn. tyr.	*De regno et tyrannide* (*Or.* 62)	*Kingship and Tyranny*
Rhod.	*Rhodiaca* (*Or.* 31)	*To the People of Rhodes*
Sec.	*De secessu* (*Or.* 20)	*Retirement*
Serv.	*De servis* (*Or.* 10)	*Servants*
1 Serv. lib.	*De servitute et libertate i* (*Or.* 14)	*Slavery and Freedom 1*
2 Serv. lib.	*De servitute et libertate ii* (*Or.* 15)	*Slavery and Freedom 2*
Socr.	*De Socrate* (*Or.* 54)	*Socrates*
1 Tars.	*Tarsica prior* (*Or.* 33)	*First Tarsic Discourse*
2 Tars.	*Tarsica altera* (*Or.* 34)	*Second Tarsic Discourse*
Troj.	*Trojana* (*Or.* 11)	*Trojan Discourse*
Tumult.	*De tumultu* (*Or.* 46)	*Protest against Mistreatment*
Tyr.	*De tyrannide* (*Or.* 6)	*Diogenes*, or *On Tyranny*
Ven.	*Venator* (*Or.* 7)	*The Hunter* (*Eubeoan Discourse*)
Virt. (*Or.* 8)	*De virtute* (*Or.* 8)	*Virtue*
Virt. (*Or.* 69)	*De virtute* (*Or.* 69)	*Virtue*
Dionysius of Halicarnassus		
1–2 Amm.	*Epistula ad Ammaeum i–ii*	
Ant. or.	*De antiquis oratoribus*	
Ant. rom.	*Antiquitates romanae*	
Comp.	*De compositione verborum*	
Dem.	*De Demosthene*	
Din.	*De Dinarcho*	
Is.	*De Isaeo*	
Isocr.	*De Isocrate*	
Lys.	*De Lysia*	
Pomp.	*Epistula ad Pompeium Geminum*	
[*Rhet.*]	*Ars rhetorica*	
Thuc.	*De Thucydide*	
Thuc. id.	*De Thucydidis idiomatibus*	
Dioscorides Pedanius		
[*Alex.*]	*Alexipharmaca*	

ABBREVIATIONS	LATIN (OR GREEK) TITLE	ENGLISH TITLE
Mat. med.	*De materia medica*	
Epictetus		
Diatr.	*Diatribai (Dissertationes)*	
Ench.	*Enchiridion*	
Gnom.	*Gnomologium*	
Epiphanius		
Pan.	*Panarion (Adversus haereses)*	*Refutation of All Heresies*
Euripides		
Alc.	*Alcestis*	
Andr.	*Andromache*	
Bacch.	*Bacchae*	*Bacchanals*
Cycl.	*Cyclops*	
Dict.	*Dictys*	
El.	*Electra*	
Hec.	*Hecuba*	
Hel.	*Helena*	*Helen*
Heracl.	*Heraclidae*	*Children of Hercules*
Herc. fur.	*Hercules furens*	*Madness of Hercules*
Hipp.	*Hippolytus*	
Hyps.	*Hypsipyle*	
Iph. aul.	*Iphigenia aulidensis*	*Iphigeneia at Aulis*
Iph. taur.	*Iphigenia taurica*	*Iphigeneia at Tauris*
Med.	*Medea*	
Orest.	*Orestes*	
Phoen.	*Phoenissae*	*Phoenician Maidens*
Rhes.	*Rhesus*	
Suppl.	*Supplices*	*Suppliants*
Tro.	*Troades*	*Daughters of Troy*
Eusebius		
Chron.	*Chronicon*	*Chronicle*
Coet. sanct.	*Ad coetum sanctorum*	*Oration of the Emperor Constantine Which He Addressed to the Assembly of the Saints*
Comm. Isa.	*Commentarius in Isaiam*	*Commentary on Isaiah*
Comm. Ps.	*Commentarius in Psalmos*	*Commentary on the Psalms*
Dem. ev.	*Demonstratio evangelica*	*Demonstration of the Gospel*
Eccl. theol.	*De ecclesiastica theologia*	*Ecclesiastical Theology*
Ecl. proph.	*Eclogae propheticae*	*Extracts from the Prophets*
Hier.	*Contra Hieroclem*	*Against Hierocles*
Hist. eccl.	*Historia ecclesiastica*	*Ecclesiastical History*
Laud. Const.	*De laudibus Constantini*	*Praise of Constantine*
Marc.	*Contra Marcellum*	*Against Marcellus*
Mart. Pal.	*De martyribus Palaestinae*	*The Martyrs of Palestine*
Onom.	*Onomasticon*	
Praep. ev.	*Praeparatio evangelica*	*Preparation for the Gospel*
Theoph.	*Theophania*	*Divine Manifestation*
Vit. Const.	*Vita Constantini*	*Life of Constantine*
Firmicus Maternus		
Err. prof. rel.	*De errore profanarum religionum*	
Math.	*Mathesis*	
Gaius		
Inst.	*Institutiones*	
Gorgias		
Hel.	*Helena*	
Pal.	*Palamedes*	
Gregory of Nazianzus		
Ep.	*Epistulae*	
Or. Bas.	*Oratio in laudem Basilii*	
Gregory of Nyssa		
Deit.	*De deitate Filii et Spiritus Sancti*	
Gregory the Great		
Moral.	*Expositio in Librum Job, sive Moralium libri xxv*	*Moralia*

ABBREVIATIONS	LATIN (OR GREEK) TITLE	ENGLISH TITLE
Gregory the Wonderworker (Thaumaturgus)		
Orat. paneg.	*Oratio panegyrica in Origenem*	*Address of Gratitude to Origen [Panergyric on Origen]*
Heliodorus		
Aeth.	*Aethiopica*	
Heraclitus		
All.	*Allegoriae (Quaestiones homericae)*	
Herodotus		
Hist.	*Historiae*	*Histories*
Hesiod		
Op.	*Opera et dies*	*Works and Days*
[*Scut.*]	*Scutum*	*Shield*
Theog.	*Theogonia*	*Theogony*
Hieronymus	See *Jerome*	
Hippocrates		
Acut.	*De ratione victus in morbis acutis* (Περὶ διαίτης ὀξέων)	*Regimen in Acute Diseases*
Aff.	*De affectionibus* (Περὶ παθῶν)	*Affections*
Alim.	*De alimento* (Περὶ τροφῆς)	*Nutriment*
Aph.	*Aphorismata* (Ἀφορισμοί)	*Aphorisms*
Artic.	*De articulis reponendis* (Περὶ ἄρθρων ἐμβολῆς)	*Joints*
Carn.	*De carne* (Περὶ σαρκῶν)	*Fleshes*
Coac.	*Praenotiones coacae* (Κωακαὶ προγνώσεις)	
De arte	*De arte* (Περὶ τέχνης)	*The Art*
Decent.	*De habitu decenti* (Περὶ εὐσχημοσύνης)	*Decorum*
Dent.	*De dentitione* (Περὶ ὀδοντοφυΐης)	*Dentition*
Epid.	*Epidemiae* (Ἐπιδημίαι)	*Epidemics*
Fist.	*Fistulae* (Περὶ συρίγγων)	*Fistulas*
Fract.	*De fracturis* (Περὶ ἀγμῶν)	*Fractures*
Genit.	*Genitalia* (Περὶ γονῆς)	*Genitals*
Int.	*De affectionibus internis* (Περὶ τῶν ἐντὸς παθῶν)	*Internal Affections*
Jusj.	*Jus jurandum* (Ὅρκος)	*The Oath*
Lex	*Lex* (Νόμος)	*Law*
Liq.	*De liquidorum usu* (Περὶ ὑγρῶν χρήσιος)	*Use of Liquids*
Loc. hom.	*De locis in homine* (Περὶ τόπων τῶν κατὰ ἀνθρώπων)	*Places in Man*
Med.	*De medico* (Περὶ ἰητροῦ)	*The Physician*
Mochl.	*Mochlichon*	*Instruments of Reduction*
Morb.	*De morbis* (Περὶ νούσων)	*Diseases*
Morb. sacr.	*De morbo sacro* (Περὶ ἱερῆς νούσου)	*The Sacred Disease*
Mul.	*De morbis mulierum* (Γυναικεῖα)	*Female Diseases*
Nat. hom.	*De natura hominis* (Περὶ φύσιος ἀνθρώπου)	*Nature of Man*
Nat. mul.	*De natura muliebri* (Περὶ γυναικείης φύσιος)	*Nature of Woman*
Nat. puer.	*De natura pueri* (Περὶ φύσιος παιδίου)	*Nature of the Child*
Oct.	*De octimestri partu* (Περὶ ὀκταμήνου)	
Off.	*De officina medici* (Κατ' ἰητρεῖον)	*In the Surgery*
Praec.	*Praeceptiones* (Παραγγελίαι)	*Precepts*
Progn.	*Prognostica* (Προγνωστικόν)	*Prognostic*
Prorrh.	*Prorrhetica* (Προρρητικόν)	*Prorrhetic*
Septim.	*De septimestri partu* (Περὶ ἑπταμήνου)	
Steril.	*De sterilitate* (Περὶ ἀφόρων)	*Sterility*
Vet. med.	*De vetere medicina* (Περὶ ἀρχαίης ἰητρικῆς)	*Ancient Medicine*
Vict.	*De victu* (Περὶ διαίτης)	*Regimen*
Vict. salubr.	*De ratione victus salubris* (Περὶ διαίτης ὑγιεινῆς)	*Regimen in Health*
Hippolytus		
Antichr.	*De antichristo*	
Ben. Is. Jac.	*De benedictionibus Isaaci et Jacobi*	
Can. pasch.	*Canon paschalis*	
Cant. Mos.	*In canticum Mosis*	
Chron.	*Chronicon*	

ABBREVIATIONS	LATIN (OR GREEK) TITLE	ENGLISH TITLE
Comm. Dan.	*Commentarium in Danielem*	
Fr. Prov.	*Fragmenta in Proverbia*	
Fr. Ps.	*Fragmenta in Psalmos*	
Haer.	*Refutatio omnium haeresium (Philosophoumena)*	*Refutation of All Heresies*
Helc. Ann.	*In Helcanam et Annam*	
In Cant.	*In Canticum canticorum*	
Noet.	*Contra haeresin Noeti*	
Trad. ap.	*Traditio apostolica*	*The Apostolic Tradition*
Univ.	*De universo*	
Hippolytus of Rome		
Haer.	*Refutatio omnium haeresium (Philosophoumena; Elenchus)*	*Refutation of All Heresies*
Homer		
Il.	*Ilias*	*Iliad*
Od.	*Odyssea*	*Odyssey*
Horace		
Ars	*Ars poetica*	
Carm.	*Carmina*	*Odes*
Ep.	*Epistulae*	*Epistles*
Epod.	*Epodi*	*Epodes*
Saec.	*Carmen saeculare*	
Sat.	*Satirae*	*Satires*
Irenaeus		
Epid.	*Epideixis tou apostolikou kērygmatos*	*Demonstration of the Apostolic Preaching*
Haer.	*Adversus haereses (Elenchos)*	*Against Heresies*
Isocrates		
Ad Nic.	*Ad Nicoclem* (*Or.* 2)	
Aeginet.	*Aegineticus* (*Or.* 19)	
Antid.	*Antidosis* (*Or.* 15)	
Archid.	*Archidamus* (*Or.* 6)	
Areop.	*Areopagiticus* (*Or.* 7)	
Big.	*De bigis* (*Or.* 16)	*On the Team of Horses*
Bus.	*Busiris* (*Or.* 11)	
Callim.	*In Callimachum* (*Or.* 18)	*Against Callimachus*
De pace	*De pace* (*Or.* 8)	
Demon.	*Ad Demonicum* (*Or.* 1)	
Ep.	*Epistulae*	
Euth.	*In Euthynum* (*Or.* 21)	
Evag.	*Evagoras* (*Or.* 9)	
Hel. enc.	*Helenae encomium* (*Or.* 10)	
Loch.	*In Lochitum* (*Or.* 20)	
Nic.	*Nicocles* (*Or.* 3)	
Panath.	*Panathenaicus* (*Or.* 12)	
Paneg.	*Panegyricus* (*Or.* 4)	
Phil.	*Philippus* (*Or.* 5)	
Plat.	*Plataicus* (*Or.* 14)	
Soph.	*In sophistas* (*Or.* 13)	
Trapez.	*Trapeziticus* (*Or.* 17)	*On the Banker*
Jerome		
Chron.	*Chronicon Eusebii a Graeco Latine redditum et continuatum*	
Comm. Abd.	*Commentariorum in Abdiam liber*	
Comm. Agg.	*Commentariorum in Aggaeum liber*	
Comm. Am.	*Commentariorum in Amos libri III*	
Comm. Eccl.	*Commentarii in Ecclesiasten*	
Comm. Eph.	*Commentariorum in Epistulam ad Ephesios libri III*	
Comm. Ezech.	*Commentariorum in Ezechielem libri XVI*	
Comm. Gal.	*Commentariorum in Epistulam ad Galatas libri III*	
Comm. Habac.	*Commentariorum in Habacuc libri II*	
Comm. Isa.	*Commentariorum in Isaiam libri XVIII*	
Comm. Jer.	*Commentariorum in Jeremiam libri VI*	
Comm. Joel.	*Commentariorum in Joelem liber*	

ABBREVIATIONS	LATIN (OR GREEK) TITLE	ENGLISH TITLE
Comm. Jon.	*Commentariorum in Jonam liber*	
Comm. Mal.	*Commentariorum in Malachiam liber*	
Comm. Matt.	*Commentariorum in Matthaeum libri IV*	
Comm. Mich.	*Commentariorum in Michaeum libri II*	
Comm. Nah.	*Commentariorum in Nahum liber*	
Comm. Os.	*Commentariorum in Osee libri III*	
Comm. Phlm.	*Commentariorum in Epistulam ad Philemonem liber*	
Comm. Ps.	*Commentarioli in Psalmos*	
Comm. Soph.	*Commentariorum in Sophoniam libri III*	
Comm. Tit.	*Commentariorum in Epistulam ad Titum liber*	
Comm. Zach.	*Commentariorum in Zachariam libri III*	
Did. Spir.	*Liber Didymi de Spiritu Sancto*	
Epist.	*Epistulae*	
Expl. Dan.	*Explanatio in Danielem*	
Helv.	*Adversus Helvidium de Mariae virginitate perpetua*	
Hom. Matth.	*Homilia in Evangelium secundum Matthaeum*	
Interp. Job	*Libri Job versio, textus hexaplorum*	
Jo. Hier.	*Adversus Joannem Hierosolymitanum liber*	
Jov.	*Adversus Jovinianum libri II*	
Lucif.	*Altercatio Luciferiani et orthodoxi seu dialogus contra Luciferianos*	
Mon. Pachom.	*Monitorum Pachomii versio latina*	
Monogr.	*Tractatus de monogrammate*	
Nom. hebr.	*De nominibus hebraicis (Liber nominum)*	
Orig. Hom. Cant.	*Homiliae II Origenis in Canticum canticorum Latine redditae*	
Orig. Hom. Luc.	*In Lucam homiliae XXXIX ex Graeco Origenis Latine conversae*	
Orig. Jer. Ezech.	*Homiliae XXVIII in Jeremiam et Ezechielem Graeco Origenis Latine redditae*	
Orig. Princ.	*De principiis*	
Pelag.	*Adversus Pelagianos dialogi III*	
Psalt. Hebr.	*Psalterium secundum Hebraeos*	
Qu. hebr. Gen.	*Quaestionum hebraicarum liber in Genesim*	
Reg. Pachom.	*Regula S. Pachomii, e Graeco*	
Ruf.	*Adversus Rufinum libri III*	
Sit.	*De situ et nominibus locorum Hebraicorum (Liber locorum)*	
Tract. Isa.	*Tractatus in Isaiam*	
Tract. Marc.	*Tractatus in Evangelium Marci*	
Tract. Ps.	*Tractatus in Psalmos*	
Tract. var.	*Tractatus varii*	
Vigil.	*Adversus Vigilantium*	
Vir. ill.	*De viris illustribus*	
Vit. Hil.	*Vita S. Hilarionis eremitae*	
Vit. Malch.	*Vita Malchi monachi*	
Vit. Paul.	*Vita S. Pauli, primi eremitae*	
John Chrysostom		
Adfu.	*Adversus eos qui non adfuerant*	
Adv. Jud.	*Adversus Judaeos*	*Discourses against Judaizing Christians*
Aeg.	*In martyres Aegyptios*	
Anna	*De Anna*	
Anom.	*Contra Anomoeos*	
Ant. exsil.	*Sermo antequam iret in exsilium*	
Ascens.	*In ascensionem domini nostri Jesu Christi*	
Bab.	*De sancto hieromartyre Babyla*	*Babylas the Martyr*
Bab. Jul.	*De Babyla contra Julianum et gentiles*	
Bapt.	*De baptismo Christi*	
Barl.	*In sanctum Barlaam martyrem*	
Bern.	*De sanctis Bernice et Prosdoce*	
Catech. illum.	*Catecheses ad illuminandos*	
Catech. jur.	*Catechesis de juramento*	
Catech. ult.	*Catechesis ultima ad baptizandos*	
Cath.	*Adversus Catharos*	
Coemet.	*De coemeterio et de cruce*	

ABBREVIATIONS	LATIN (OR GREEK) TITLE	ENGLISH TITLE
Comm. Isa.	*Commentarius in Isaiam*	
Comm. Job	*Commentarius in Job*	
Comp. reg. mon.	*Comparatio regis et monachi*	
Compunct. Dem.	*Ad Demetrium de compunctione*	
Compunct. Stel.	*Ad Stelechium de compunctione*	
Cruc.	*De cruce et latrone homiliae II*	
Cum exsil.	*Sermo cum iret in exsilium*	
Dav.	*De Davide et Saule*	
Delic.	*De futurae vitae deliciis*	
Diab.	*De diabolo tentatore*	
Diod.	*Laus Diodori episcopi*	
Dros.	*De sancta Droside martyre*	
Educ. lib.	*De educandis liberis*	
El. vid.	*In Eliam et viduam*	
Eleaz. puer.	*De Eleazaro et septem pueris*	
Eleem.	*De eleemosyna*	
Ep. carc.	*Epistula ad episcopos, presbyteros et diaconos in carcere*	
Ep. Cyr.	*Epistula ad Cyriacum*	
1 Ep. Innoc.	*Ad Innocentium papam epistula I*	
2 Ep. Innoc.	*Ad Innocentium papam epistula II*	
Ep. Olymp.	*Epistulae ad Olympiadem*	
Ep. Theod.	*Letter to Theodore*	
Eust.	*In sanctum Eustathium Antiochenum*	
Eutrop.	*In Eutropium*	
Exp. Ps.	*Expositiones in Psalmos*	
Fat. prov.	*De fato et providentia*	
Fem. reg.	*Quod regulares feminae viris cohabitare non debeant*	
Fr. Ep. Cath.	*Fragmenta in Epistulas Catholicas*	
Freq. conv.	*Quod frequenter conveniendum sit*	
Goth. concin.	*Homilia habita postquam presbyter Gothus concionatus fuerat*	
Grat.	*Non esse ad gratiam concionandum*	
Hom. Act.	*Homiliae in Acta apostolorum*	
Hom. Act. 9:1	*De mutatione nominum*	
Hom. Col.	*Homiliae in epistulam ad Colossenses*	
Hom. 1 Cor.	*Homiliae in epistulam i ad Corinthios*	
Hom. 1 Cor. 7:2	*In illud: Propter fornicationes autem unusquisque suam uxorem habeat*	
Hom. 1 Cor. 10:1	*In dictum Pauli: Nolo vos ignorare*	
Hom. 1 Cor. 11:19	*In dictum Pauli: Oportet haereses esse*	
Hom. 2 Cor.	*Homiliae in epistulam ii ad Corinthios*	
Hom. 2 Cor. 4:13	*In illud: Habentes eundem spiritum*	
Hom. 2 Cor. 11:1	*In illud: Utinam sustineretis modicum*	
Hom. Eph.	*Homiliae in epistulam ad Ephesios*	
Hom. Gal.	*Homiliae in epistulam ad Galatas commentarius*	
Hom. Gal. 2:11	*In illud: In faciem ei restiti*	
Hom. Gen.	*Homiliae in Genesim*	
Hom. Heb.	*Homiliae in epistulam ad Hebraeos*	
Hom. Isa. 6:1	*In illud: Vidi Dominum*	
Hom. Isa. 45:7	*In illud Isaiae: Ego Dominus Deus feci lumen*	
Hom. Jer. 10:23	*In illud: Domine, non est in homine*	
Hom. Jo.	*Homiliae in Joannem*	
Hom. Jo. 5:17	*In illud: Pater meus usque modo operatur*	
Hom. Jo. 5:19	*In illud: Filius ex se nihil facit*	
Hom. Matt.	*Homiliae in Matthaeum*	
Hom. Matt. 9:37	*In illud: Messis quidem multa*	
Hom. Matt. 18:23	*De decem millium talentorum debitore*	
Hom. Matt. 26:39	*In illud: Pater, si possibile est, transeat*	
Hom. Phil.	*Homiliae in epistulam ad Philippenses*	
Hom. Phlm.	*Homiliae in epistulam ad Philemonem*	
Hom. princ. Act.	*In principium Actorum*	
Hom. Ps. 48:17	*In illud: Ne timueris cum dives factus fuerit homo*	
Hom. Rom.	*Homiliae in epistulam ad Romanos*	

ABBREVIATIONS	LATIN (OR GREEK) TITLE	ENGLISH TITLE
Hom. Rom. 5:3	*De gloria in tribulationibus*	
Hom. Rom. 8:28	*In illud: Diligentibus deum omnia cooperantur in bonum*	
Hom. Rom. 12:20	*In illud: Si esurierit inimicus*	
Hom. Rom. 16:3	*In illud: Salutate Priscillam et Aquilam*	
Hom 1 Thess.	*Homiliae in epistulam i ad Thessalonicenses*	
Hom. 2 Thess.	*Homiliae in epistulam ii ad Thessalonicenses*	
Hom. 1 Tim.	*Homiliae in epistulam i ad Timotheum*	
Hom. 1 Tim. 5:9	*In illud: Vidua eligatur*	
Hom. 2 Tim.	*Homiliae in epistulam ii ad Timotheum*	
Hom. 2 Tim. 3:1	*In illud: Hoc scitote quod in novissimis diebus*	
Hom. Tit.	*Homiliae in epistulam ad Titum*	
Hom. Tit. 2:11	*In illud: Apparuit gratia dei omnibus hominibus*	
Ign.	*In sanctum Ignatium martyrem*	
Inan. glor.	*De inani gloria*	
Iter. conj.	*De non iterando conjugio*	
Jud. gent.	*Contra Judaeos et gentiles quod Christus sit deus*	
Jul.	*In sanctum Julianum martyrem*	
Juv.	*In Juventinum et Maximum martyres*	
Kal.	*In Kalendas*	
Laed.	*Quod nemo laeditur nisi a se ipso*	*No One Can Harm the Man Who Does Not Injure Himself*
Laud. Max.	*Quales ducendae sint uxores* (=*De laude Maximi*)	
Laud. Paul.	*De laudibus sancti Pauli apostoli*	
Laz.	*De Lazaro*	
Lib. repud.	*De libello repudii*	
Liturg.	*Liturgia*	
Lucian.	*In sanctum Lucianum martyrem*	
Macc.	*De Maccabeis*	
Mart.	*De sanctis martyribus; Homilia in martyres* (must give vol./pg. ref.)	
Melet.	*De sancto Meletio Antiocheno*	
Natal.	*In diem natalem Christi*	
Non desp.	*Non esse desperandum*	
Oppugn.	*Adversus oppugnatores vitae monasticae*	
Ordin.	*Sermo cum presbyter fuit ordinatus*	
Paenit.	*De paenitentia*	
Paralyt.	*In paralyticum demissum per tectum*	
Pasch.	*In sanctum pascha*	
Pecc.	*Peccata fratrum non evulganda*	*Against Publicly Exposing the Sins of the Brethren*
Pelag.	*De sancta Pelagia virgine et martyre*	
Pent.	*De sancta pentecoste*	
Phoc.	*De sancto hieromartyre Phoca*	
Praes. imp.	*Homilia dicta praesente imperatore*	
Prod. Jud.	*De proditione Judae*	
Prof. evang.	*De profectu evangelii*	*Lowliness of Mind*
Proph. obscurit.	*De prophetarum obscuritate*	
Quatr. Laz.	*In quatriduanum Lazarum*	
1 Redit.	*Post reditum a priore exsilio sermo I*	
2 Redit.	*Post reditum a priore exsilio sermo II*	
Regr.	*De regressu*	
Reliq. mart.	*Homilia dicta postquam reliquiae martyrum*	
Res. Chr.	*Adversus ebriosos et de resurrectione domini nostri Jesu Christi*	
Res. mort.	*De resurrectione mortuorum*	
Rom. mart.	*In sanctum Romanum martyrem*	
Sac.	*De sacerdotio*	*Priesthood*
Sanct. Anast.	*Homilia dicta in templo sanctae Anastasiae*	
Saturn.	*Cum Saturninus et Aurelianus acti essent in exsilium*	
Scand.	*Ad eos qui scandalizati sunt*	
Serm. Gen.	*Sermones in Genesim*	
Stag.	*Ad Stagirium a daemone vexatum*	

ABBREVIATIONS	LATIN (OR GREEK) TITLE	ENGLISH TITLE
Stat.	*Ad populum Antiochenum de statuis*	
Stud. praes.	*De studio praesentium*	
Subintr.	*Contra eos qui subintroductas habent virgines*	
Terr. mot.	*De terrae motu*	
Theatr.	*Contra ludos et theatra*	
Theod. laps.	*Ad Theodorum lapsum*	*Exhortation to Theodore after His Fall*
Vid.	*Ad viduam juniorem*	*To a Young Widow*
Virginit.	*De virginitate*	
John Malalas		
Chron.	*Chronographia*	
John Philoponus		
Comm. De an.	*In Aristotelis De anima libros commentaria*	
Josephus	See §8.3.7	
Justin		
1 Apol.	*Apologia i*	*First Apology*
2 Apol.	*Apologia ii*	*Second Apology*
Dial.	*Dialogus cum Tryphone*	*Dialogue with Trypho*
Justinian		
Edict.	*Edicta*	
Nov.	*Novellae*	
Juvenal		
Sat.	*Satirae*	*Satires*
Lactantius		
Epit.	*Epitome divinarum institutionum*	*Epitome of the Divine Institutes*
Inst.	*Divinarum institutionum libri VII*	*The Divine Institutes*
Ir.	*De ira Dei*	*The Wrath of God*
Mort.	*De mortibus persecutorum*	*The Death of the Persecutors*
Opif.	*De opificio Dei*	*The Workmanship of God*
Longinus		
[*Subl.*]	*De sublimitate*	*On the Sublime*
Longus		
Daphn.	*Daphnis and Chloe*	
Lucian		
Abdic.	*Abdicatus*	*Disowned*
Alex.	*Alexander (Pseudomantis)*	*Alexander the False Prophet*
[*Am.*]	*Amores*	*Affairs of the Heart*
Anach.	*Anacharsis*	
[*Asin.*]	*Asinus (Lucius)*	*Lucius*, or *The Ass*
Astr.	*Astrologia*	*Astrology*
Bis acc.	*Bis accusatus*	*The Double Indictment*
Cal.	*Calumniae non temere credendum*	*Slander*
Cat.	*Cataplus*	*The Downward Journey*, or *The Tyrant*
Char.	*Charon*	
Demon.	*Demonax*	
Deor. conc.	*Deorm concilium*	*Parliament of the Gods*
Dial. d.	*Dialogi deorum*	*Dialogues of the Gods*
Dial. meretr.	*Dialogi meretricii*	*Dialogues of the Courtesans*
Dial. mort.	*Diologi mortuorum*	*Dialogues of the Dead*
Dom.	*De domo*	*The Hall*
Electr.	*De electro*	*Amber*, or *The Swans*
[*Encom. Demosth.*]	*Demosthenous encomium*	*Praise of Demosthenes*
Eunuch.	*Eunuchus*	*The Eunuch*
Fug.	*Fugitivi*	*The Runaways*
Gall.	*Gallus*	*The Dream*, or *The Cock*
Hermot.	*Hermotimus (De sectis)*	*Hermotimus*, or *Sects*
Icar.	*Icaromenippus*	
Imag.	*Imagines*	*Essays in Portraiture*
Ind.	*Adversus indoctum*	*The Ignorant Book-Collector*
Jud. voc.	*Judicium vocalium*	*The Consonants at Law*
Jupp. conf.	*Juppiter confutatus*	*Zeus Catechized*
Jupp. trag.	*Juppiter tragoedus*	*Zeus Rants*

ABBREVIATIONS	LATIN (OR GREEK) TITLE	ENGLISH TITLE
Laps.	*Pro lapsu inter salutandum*	*A Slip of the Tongue in Greeting*
Lex.	*Lexiphanes*	
Luct.	*De luctu*	*Funerals*
Men.	*Menippus (Necyomantia)*	*Menippus*, or *Descent into Hades*
Merc. cond.	*De mercede conductis*	*Salaried Posts in Great Houses*
Musc. laud.	*Muscae laudatio*	*The Fly*
Nav.	*Navigium*	*The Ship*, or *The Wishes*
Nigr.	*Nigrinus*	
Par.	*De parasito*	*The Parasite*
Peregr.	*De morte Peregrini*	*The Passing of Peregrinus*
Phal.	*Phalaris*	
[*Philopatr.*]	*Philopatris*	*The Patriot*
Philops.	*Philopseudes*	*The Lover of Lies*
Pisc.	*Piscator*	*The Dead Come to Life*, or *The Fisherman*
Pro imag.	*Pro imaginibus*	*Essays in Portraiture Defended*
Pseudol.	*Pseudologista*	*The Mistaken Critic*
Rhet. praec.	*Rhetorum praeceptor*	*A Professor of Public Speaking*
Sacr.	*De sacrificiis*	*Sacrifices*
Salt.	*De saltatione*	*The Dance*
Sat.	*Saturnalia*	*Conversation with Cronus*
Scyth.	*Scytha*	*The Scythian*, or *The Consul*
Somn.	*Somnium (Vita Luciani)*	*The Dream*, or *Lucian's Career*
Symp.	*Symposium*	*The Carousal*, or *The Lapiths*
Syr. d.	*De syria dea*	*The Goddess of Syria*
Tim.	*Timon*	
Tox.	*Toxaris*	
Tyr.	*Tyrannicida*	*The Tyrannicide*
Ver. hist.	*Vera historia*	*A True Story*
Vit. auct.	*Vitarum auctio*	*Philosophies for Sale*
Menander		
Dysk.	*Dyskolos*	
Epitr.	*Epitrepontes*	
Georg.	*Georgos*	
Mis.	*Misoumenos*	
Mon.	*Monostichoi*	
Perik.	*Perikeiromenē*	
Phasm.	*Phasma*	
Sam.	*Samia*	
Sik.	*Sikyonios*	
Thras.	*Thrasonidis*	
Methodius of Olympus		
Lib. arb.	*De libero arbitrio*	
Res.	*De resurrectione*	
Symp.	*Symposium (Convivium decem virginum)*	
Minucius Felix		
Oct.	*Octavius*	
Nepos		
Ag.	*Agesilaus*	
Alc.	*Alciabiades*	
Arist.	*Aristides*	
Att.	*Atticus*	
Cat.	*Cato*	
Chabr.	*Chabrias*	
Cim.	*Cimon*	
Con.	*Conon*	
Dat.	*Datames*	
Di.	*Dion*	
Epam.	*Epaminondas*	
Eum.	*Eumenes*	
Ham.	*Hamilcar*	
Han.	*Hannibal*	

ABBREVIATIONS	LATIN (OR GREEK) TITLE	ENGLISH TITLE
Iph.	*Iphicrates*	
Lys.	*Lysander*	
Milt.	*Miltiades*	
Paus.	*Pausanias*	
Pel.	*Pelopidas*	
Phoc.	*Phocion*	
Reg.	*De regibus*	
Them.	*Themistocles*	
Thras.	*Thrasybulus*	
Timol.	*Timoleon*	
Timoth.	*Timotheus*	
Nicander		
Alex.	*Alexipharmaca*	
Ther.	*Theriaca*	
Nicolaus of Damascus		
Hist. univ.	*Historia universalis*	*Universal History* (*in Athenaeus*)
Vit. Caes.	*Vita Caesaris*	
Nonnus		
Dion.	*Dionysiaca*	
Paraphr. Jo.	*Paraphrasis sancti evangelii Joannei*	
Orac. chald.	De oraculis chaldaicis	Chaldaean Oracles
Origen		
Adnot. Deut.	*Adnotationes in Deuteronomium*	
Adnot. Exod.	*Adnotationes in Exodum*	
Adnot. Gen.	*Adnotationes in Genesim*	
Adnot. Jes. Nav.	*Adnotationes in Jesum filium Nave*	
Adnot. Judic.	*Adnotationes in Judices*	
Adnot. Lev.	*Adnotationes in Leviticum*	
Adnot. Num.	*Adnotationes in Numeros*	
Cant. (*Adulesc.*)	*In Canticum canticorum* (libri duo quos scripsit in adulescentia)	
Cels.	*Contra Celsum*	*Against Celsus*
Comm. Cant.	*Commentarius in Canticum*	
Comm. Gen.	*Commentarii in Genesim*	
Comm. Jo.	*Commentarii in evangelium Joannis*	
Comm. Matt.	*Commentarium in evangelium Matthaei*	
Comm. Rom.	*Commentarii in Romanos*	
Comm. ser. Matt.	*Commentarium series in evangelium Matthaei*	
Dial.	*Diologus cum Heraclide*	*Dialogue with Heraclides*
Enarrat. Job	*Enarrationes in Job*	
Engastr.	*De engastrimytho*	*Witch of Endor*
Ep. Afr.	*Epistula ad Africanum*	
Ep. Greg.	*Epistula ad Gregorium Thaumaturgum*	
Ep. ign.	*Epistula ad ignotum (Fabianum Romanum)*	
Exc. Ps.	*Excerpta in Psalmos*	
Exp. Prov.	*Expositio in Proverbia*	
Fr. Act.	*Fragmentum ex homiliis in Acta apostolorum*	
Fr. Cant.	*Libri x in Canticum canticorum*	
Fr. 1 Cor.	*Fragmenta ex commentariis in epistulam i ad Corinthios*	
Fr. Eph.	*Fragmenta ex commentariis in epistulam ad Ephesios*	
Fr. Exod.	*Fragmenta ex commentariis in Exodum*	
Fr. Ezech.	*Fragmenta ex commentariis in Ezechielem*	
Fr. Heb.	*Fragmenta ex homiliis in epistulam ad Hebraeos*	
Fr. Jer.	*Fragmenta in Jeremiam*	
Fr. Jo.	*Fragmenta in evangelium Joannis*	
Fr. Lam.	*Fragmenta in Lamentationes*	
Fr. Luc.	*Fragmenta in Lucam*	
Fr. Matt.	*Fragmenta ex commentariis in evangelium Matthaei*	
Fr. Os.	*Fragmentum ex commentariis in Osee*	
Fr. Prin.	*Fragmenta de principiis*	
Fr. Prov.	*Fragmenta ex commentariis in Proverbia*	

ABBREVIATIONS	LATIN (OR GREEK) TITLE	ENGLISH TITLE
Fr. Ps.	*Fragmenta in Psalmos 1–150*	
Fr. 1 Reg.	*Fragmenta in librum primum Regnorum*	
Fr. Ruth	*Fragmentum in Ruth*	
Hex.	*Hexapla*	
Hom. Cant.	*Homiliae in Canticum*	
Hom. Exod.	*Homiliae in Exodum*	
Hom. Ezech.	*Homiliae in Ezechielem*	
Hom. Gen.	*Homiliae in Genesim*	
Hom. Isa.	*Homiliae in Isaiam*	
Hom. Jer.	*Homiliae in Jeremiam*	
Hom. Jes. Nav.	*In Jesu Nave homiliae xxvi*	
Hom. Job	*Homiliae in Job*	
Hom. Judic.	*Homiliae in Judices*	
Hom. Lev.	*Homiliae in Leviticum*	
Hom. Luc.	*Homiliae in Lucam*	
Hom. Num.	*Homiliae in Numeros*	
Hom. Ps.	*Homiliae in Psalmos*	
Hom. 1 Reg.	*Homiliae in I Reges*	
Mart.	*Exhortatio ad martyrium*	*Exhortation to Martyrdom*
Or.	*De oratione (Peri proseuchēs)*	*Prayer*
Pasch.	*De pascha*	*The Pascha*
Philoc.	*Philocalia*	
Princ.	*De principiis (Peri archōn)*	*First Principles*
Res.	*De resurrectione libri ii*	
Schol. Apoc.	*Scholia in Apocalypsem*	
Schol. Cant.	*Scholia in Canticum canticorum*	
Schol. Luc.	*Scholia in Lucam*	
Schol. Matt.	*Scholia in Matthaeum*	
Sel. Deut.	*Selecta in Deuteronomium*	
Sel. Exod.	*Selecta in Exodum*	
Sel. Ezech.	*Selecta in Ezechielem*	
Sel. Gen.	*Selecta in Genesim*	
Sel. Jes. Nav.	*Selecta in Jesum Nave*	
Sel. Job	*Selecta in Job*	
Sel. Judic.	*Selecta in Judices*	
Sel. Lev.	*Selecta in Leviticum*	
Sel. Num.	*Selecta in Numeros*	
Sel. Ps.	*Selecta in Psalmos*	
Ovid		
Am.	*Amores*	
Ars	*Ars amatoria*	
Fast.	*Fasti*	
Hal.	*Halieutica*	
Her.	*Heroides*	
Ib.	*Ibis*	
Med.	*Medicamina faciei femineae*	
Metam.	*Metamorphoses*	
Pausanias		
Descr.	*Graeciae descriptio*	*Description of Greece*
Peripl. M. Rubr.	Periplus Maris Rubri	The Periplus of the Erythraean Sea
Persius		
Sat.	*Satirae*	
Philo	See §8.3.6	
Philodemus of Gadara		
Adv. Soph.	*Adversus sophistas*	
D.	*De diis*	
Hom.	*De bono rege secundum Homerum*	
Ir.	*De ira*	
Lib.	*De libertate dicendi*	
Mort.	*De morte*	
Mus.	*De musica*	

ABBREVIATIONS	LATIN (OR GREEK) TITLE	ENGLISH TITLE
Piet.	*De pietate*	
Rhet.	*Volumina rhetorica*	
Sign.	*De signis*	
Vit.	*De vitiis X*	
Philostratus		
Ep.	*Epistulae*	
Gymn.	*De gymnastica*	
Imag.	*Imagines*	
Vit. Apoll.	*Vita Apollonii*	
Vit. soph.	*Vitae sophistarum*	
Photius		
Lex.	*Lexicon*	
Pindar		
Isthm.	*Isthmionikai*	*Isthmian Odes*
Nem.	*Nemeonikai*	*Nemean Odes*
Ol.	*Olympionikai*	*Olympian Odes*
Paean.	*Paeanes*	*Hymns*
Pyth.	*Pythionikai*	*Pythian Odes*
Thren.	*Threnoi*	*Dirges*
Plato		
[*Alc. maj.*]	*Alcibiades major*	*Greater Alcibiades*
Apol.	*Apologia*	*Apology of Socrates*
[*Ax.*]	*Axiochus*	
Charm.	*Charmides*	
Crat.	*Cratylus*	
[*Def.*]	*Definitiones*	*Definitions*
Ep.	*Epistulae*	*Letters*
[*Epin.*]	*Epinomis*	
Euthyd.	*Euthydemus*	
Euthyphr.	*Euthyphro*	
Gorg.	*Gorgias*	
Hipparch.	*Hipparchus*	
Hipp. maj.	*Hippias major*	*Greater Hippias*
Hipp. min.	*Hippias minor*	*Lesser Hippias*
Lach.	*Laches*	
Leg.	*Leges*	*Laws*
Menex.	*Menexenus*	
[*Min.*]	*Minos*	
Parm.	*Parmenides*	
Phaed.	*Phaedo*	
Phaedr.	*Phaedrus*	
Phileb.	*Philebus*	
Pol.	*Politicus*	*Statesman*
Prot.	*Protagoras*	
Resp.	*Respublica*	*Republic*
Soph.	*Sophista*	*Sophist*
Symp.	*Symposium*	
Theaet.	*Theaetetus*	
Tim.	*Timaeus*	
Plautus		
Amph.	*Amphitruo*	
Asin.	*Asinaria*	
Aul.	*Aulularia*	
Bacch.	*Bacchides*	
Capt.	*Captivi*	
Cas.	*Casina*	
Cist.	*Cistellaria*	
Curc.	*Curculio*	
Epid.	*Epidicus*	
Men.	*Menaechmi*	
Mil. glor.	*Miles gloriosus*	

ABBREVIATIONS	LATIN (OR GREEK) TITLE	ENGLISH TITLE
Most.	*Mostellaria*	
Pers.	*Persae*	
Poen.	*Poenulus*	
Pseud.	*Pseudolus*	
Rud.	*Rudens*	
Stic.	*Sticus*	
Trin.	*Trinummus*	
Truc.	*Truculentus*	
Vid.	*Vidularia*	
Pliny the Elder		
Nat.	*Naturalis historia*	*Natural History*
Pliny the Younger		
Ep.	*Epistulae*	
Ep. Tra.	*Epistulae ad Trajanum*	
Pan.	*Panegyricus*	
Plotinus		
Enn.	*Enneades*	
Plutarch		
Adol. poet. aud.	*Quomodo adolescens poetas audire debeat*	
Adul. am.	*De adulatore et amico*	
Adul. amic.	*Quomodo adulator ab amico internoscatur*	
Adv. Col.	*Adversus Colotem*	
Aem.	*Aemilius Paullus*	
Ag. Cleom.	*Agis et Cleomenes*	
Ages.	*Agesilaus*	
Alc.	*Alcibiades*	
Alex.	*Alexander*	
Alex. fort.	*De Alexandri magni fortuna aut virtute*	
Am. prol.	*De amore prolis*	
Amat.	*Amatorius*	
[*Amat. narr.*]	*Amatoriae narrationes*	
Amic. mult.	*De amicorum multitudine*	
An. corp.	*Animine an corporis affectiones sint peiores*	
[*An ignis*]	*Aquane an ignis utilior*	
An. procr.	*De animae procreatione in Timaeo*	
An. procr. epit.	*Epitome libri de procreatione in Timaeo*	
An seni	*An seni respublica gerenda sit*	
An virt. doc.	*An virtus doceri possit*	
An vit.	*An vitiositas ad infelicitatem sufficiat*	
Ant.	*Antonius*	
[*Apoph. lac.*]	*Apophthegmata laconica*	
Arat.	*Aratus*	
Arist.	*Aristides*	
Art.	*Artaxerxes*	
Brut.	*Brutus*	
Brut. an.	*Bruta animalia ratione uti*	
Caes.	*Caesar*	
Cam.	*Camillus*	
Cat. Maj.	*Cato Major*	*Cato the Elder*
Cat. Min.	*Cato Minor*	*Cato the Younger*
Cic.	*Cicero*	
Cim.	*Cimon*	
Cleom.	*Cleomenes*	
Cohib. ira	*De cohibenda ira*	
Comm. not.	*De communibus notitiis contra stoicos*	
Comp. Aem. Tim.	*Comparatio Aemilii Paulli et Timoleontis*	
Comp. Ag. Cleom. cum Ti. Gracch.	*Comparatio Agidis et Cleomenis cum Tiberio et Gaio Graccho*	
Comp. Ages. Pomp.	*Comparatio Agesilai et Pompeii*	
Comp. Alc. Cor.	*Comparatio Alcibiadis et Marcii Coriolani*	
Comp. Arist. Cat.	*Comparatio Aristidis et Catonis*	

ABBREVIATIONS	LATIN (OR GREEK) TITLE	ENGLISH TITLE
Comp. Arist. Men. compend.	*Comparationis Aristophanis et Menandri compendium*	
Comp. Cim. Luc.	*Comparatio Cimonis et Luculli*	
Comp. Dem. Cic.	*Comparatio Demosthenis et Ciceronis*	
Comp. Demetr. Ant.	*Comparatio Demetrii et Antonii*	
Comp. Dion. Brut.	*Comparatio Dionis et Bruti*	
Comp. Eum. Sert.	*Comparatio Eumenis et Sertorii*	
Comp. Lyc. Num.	*Comparatio Lycurgi et Numae*	
Comp. Lys. Sull.	*Comparatio Lysandri et Sullae*	
Comp. Nic. Crass.	*Comparatio Niciae et Crassi*	
Comp. Pel. Marc.	*Comparatio Pelopidae et Marcelli*	
Comp. Per. Fab.	*Comparatio Periclis et Fabii Maximi*	
Comp. Phil. Flam.	*Comparatio Philopoemenis et Titi Flaminini*	
Comp. Sol. Publ.	*Comparatio Solonis et Publicolae*	
Comp. Thes. Rom.	*Comparatio Thesei et Romuli*	
Conj. praec.	*Conjugalia Praecepta*	
[*Cons. Apoll.*]	*Consolatio ad Apollonium*	
Cons. ux.	*Consolatio ad uxorem*	
Cor.	*Marcius Coriolanus*	
Crass.	*Crassus*	
Cupid. divit.	*De cupiditate divitiarum*	
Curios.	*De curiositate*	
De esu	*De esu carnium*	
De laude	*De laude ipsius*	
Def. orac.	*De defectu oraculorum*	
Dem.	*Demosthenes*	
Demetr.	*Demetrius*	
Dion	*Dion*	
E Delph.	*De E apud Delphos*	
Eum.	*Eumenes*	
Exil.	*De exilio*	
Fab.	*Fabius Maximus*	
Fac.	*De facie in orbe lunae*	
Flam.	*Titus Flamininus*	
Fort.	*De fortuna*	
Fort. Rom.	*De fortuna Romanorum*	
Frat. amor.	*De fraterno amore*	
Galb.	*Galba*	
Garr.	*De garrulitate*	
Gen. Socr.	*De genio Socratis*	
Glor. Ath.	*De gloria Atheniensium*	
Her. mal.	*De Herodoti malignitate*	
Inim. util.	*De capienda ex inimicis utilitate*	
Inv. od.	*De invidia et odio*	
Is. Os.	*De Iside et Osiride*	
Lat. viv.	*De latenter vivendo*	
Lib. aegr.	*De libidine et aegritudine*	
[*Lib. ed.*]	*De liberis educandis*	
Luc.	*Lucullus*	
Lyc.	*Lycurgus*	
Lys.	*Lysander*	
Mar.	*Marius*	
Marc.	*Marcellus*	
Max. princ.	*Maxime cum principibus philosophiam esse disserendum*	
Mor.	*Moralia*	
Mulier. virt.	*Mulierum virtutes*	
[*Mus.*]	*De musica*	
Nic.	*Nicias*	
Num.	*Numa*	
Oth.	*Otho*	
Parsne an fac.	*Parsne an facultas animi sit vita passiva*	

ABBREVIATIONS	LATIN (OR GREEK) TITLE	ENGLISH TITLE
Pel.	*Pelopidas*	
Per.	*Pericles*	
Phil.	*Philopoemen*	
Phoc.	*Phocion*	
[*Plac. philos.*]	*De placita philosophorum*	
Pomp.	*Pompeius*	
Praec. ger. rei publ.	*Praecepta gerendae rei publicae*	
Prim. frig.	*De primo frigido*	
Princ. iner.	*Ad principem ineruditum*	
Publ.	*Publicola*	
Pyrrh.	*Pyrrhus*	
Pyth. orac.	*De Pythiae oraculis*	
Quaest. conv.	*Quaestionum convivialum libri IX*	
Quaest. nat.	*Quaestiones naturales* (*Aetia physica*)	
Quaest. plat.	*Quaestiones platonicae*	
Quaest. rom.	*Quaestiones romanae et graecae* (*Aetia romana et graeca*)	
Rect. rat. aud.	*De recta ratione audiendi*	
[*Reg. imp. apophth.*]	*Regum et imperatorum apophthegmata*	
Rom.	*Romulus*	
Sept. sap. conv.	*Septem sapientium convivium*	
Sera	*De sera numinis vindicta*	
Sert.	*Sertorius*	
Sol.	*Solon*	
Soll. an.	*De sollertia animalium*	
Stoic. abs.	*Stoicos absurdiora poetis dicere*	
Stoic. rep.	*De Stoicorum repugnantiis*	
Suav. viv.	*Non posse suaviter vivi secundum Epicurum*	
Sull.	*Sulla*	
Superst.	*De superstitione*	
Them.	*Themistocles*	
Thes.	*Theseus*	
Ti. C. Gracch.	*Tiberius et Caius Gracchus*	
Tim.	*Timoleon*	
Tranq. an.	*De tranquillitate animi*	
Trib. r. p. gen.	*De tribus rei publicae generibus*	
Tu. san.	*De tuenda sanitate praecepta*	
Un. rep. dom.	*De unius in republica dominatione*	
Virt. mor.	*De virtute morali*	
Virt. prof.	*Quomodo quis suos in virtute sentiat profectus*	
Virt. vit.	*De virtute et vitio*	
Vit. aere al.	*De vitando aere alieno*	
[*Vit. poes. Hom.*]	*De vita et poesi Homeri*	
Vit. pud.	*De vitioso pudore*	
[*Vit. X orat.*]	*Vitae decem oratorum*	
Pollux		
Onom.	*Onomasticon*	
Porphyry		
Abst.	*De abstinentia*	
Agalm.	*Peri agalmatōn*	
Aneb.	*Epistula ad Anebonem*	
Antr. nymph.	*De antro nympharum*	
Christ.	*Contra Christianos*	
Chron.	*Chronica*	
Comm. harm.	*Eis ta harmonika Ptolemaiou hypomnēma*	
Comm. Tim.	*In Platonis Timaeum commentaria*	
Exp. Cat.	*In Aristotelis Categorias expositio per interrogationem et responsionem*	
Isag.	*Isagoge sive quinque voces*	
Marc.	*Ad Marcellam*	
Philos. orac.	*De philosophia ex oraculis*	
Quaest. hom.	*Quaestiones homericae*	
Quaest. hom. Odd.	*Quaestionum homericarum ad Odysseam pertinentium reliquiae*	

ABBREVIATIONS	LATIN (OR GREEK) TITLE	ENGLISH TITLE
Sent.	*Sententiae ad intelligibilia ducentes*	
Vit. Plot.	*Vita Plotini*	
Vit. Pyth.	*Vita Pythagorae*	
Ptolemy (the Gnostic)		
Flor.	*Epistula ad Floram*	*Letter to Flora*
Quintilian		
Decl.	*Declamationes*	
Inst.	*Institutio oratoria*	
Res gest. divi Aug.	Res gestae divi Augusti	
Rhet. Her.	Rhetorica ad Herennium	
Rufinus		
Adam. Haer.	*Adamantii libri Contra haereticos*	
Adult. libr. Orig.	*De adulteratione librorum Origenis*	*On the Falsification of Origen's Books*
Anast.	*Apologia ad Anastasium papam*	
Apol. Hier.	*Apologia adversus Hieronymum*	
Apol. Orig.	*Eusebii et Pamphyli Apologia Origenis*	
Basil. hom.	*Homiliae S. Basilii*	
Ben. patr.	*De benedictionibus patriarcharum*	
Clem. Recogn.	*Clementis quae feruntur Recognitiones*	
Greg. Orat.	*Gregorii Orationes*	
Hist.	*Eusebii Historia ecclesiastica a Rufino translata et continuata*	
Hist. mon.	*Historia monachorum in Aegypto*	
Orig. Comm. Cant.	*Origenis Commentarius in Canticum*	
Orig. Comm. Rom.	*Origenis Commentarius in epistulam ad Romanos*	
Orig. Hom. Exod.	*Origenis in Exodum homiliae*	
Orig. Hom. Gen.	*Origenis in Genesism homiliae*	
Orig. Hom. Jos.	*Origenis Homiliae in librum Josua*	
Orig. Hom. Judic.	*Origenis in librum Judicum homiliae*	
Orig. Hom. Lev.	*Origenis Homiliae in Leviticum*	
Orig. Hom. Num.	*Origenis in Numeros homiliae*	
Orig. Hom. Ps.	*Origenis Homiliae in Psalmos*	
Orig. Princ.	*Origenis Libri Peri archōn seu De principiis libri IV*	
Sent. Sext.	*Sexti philosophi Sententiae a Rufino translatae*	
Symb.	*Commentarius in symbolum apostolorum*	
Sallust		
Bell. Cat.	*Bellum catalinae*	
Bell. Jug.	*Bellum jugurthinum*	
Hist.	*Historiae*	
Rep.	*Epistulae ad Caesarem senem de re publica*	
Seneca (the Younger)		
Ag.	*Agamemnon*	
Apol.	*Apolocyntosis*	
Ben.	*De beneficiis*	
Clem.	*De clementia*	
Dial.	*Dialogi*	
Ep.	*Epistulae morales*	
Helv.	*Ad Helviam*	
Herc. fur.	*Hercules furens*	
Herc. Ot.	*Hercules Otaeus*	
Ira	*De ira*	
Lucil.	*Ad Lucilium*	
Marc.	*Ad Marciam de consolatione*	
Med.	*Medea*	
Nat.	*Naturales quaestiones*	
Phaed.	*Phaedra*	
Phoen.	*Phoenissae*	
Polyb.	*Ad Polybium de consolatione*	
Thy.	*Thyestes*	
Tranq.	*De tranquillitate animi*	
Tro.	*Troades*	
Vit. beat.	*De vita beata*	

ABBREVIATIONS	LATIN (OR GREEK) TITLE	ENGLISH TITLE
Sextus Empiricus		
Math.	*Adversus mathematicos*	*Against the Mathematicians*
Pyr.	*Pyrrhoniae hypotyposes*	*Outlines of Pyrrhonism*
Sophocles		
Aj.	*Ajax*	
Ant.	*Antigone*	
El.	*Elektra*	
Ichn.	*Ichneutae*	
Oed. col.	*Oedipus coloneus*	
Oed. tyr.	*Oedipus tyrannus*	
Phil.	*Philoctetes*	
Trach.	*Trachiniae*	
Stobaeus		
Ecl.	*Eclogae*	
Flor.	*Florilegium*	
Strabo		
Geogr.	*Geographica*	*Geography*
Suetonius		
Aug.	*Divus Augustus*	
Cal.	*Gaius Caligula*	
Claud.	*Divus Claudius*	
Dom.	*Domitianus*	
Galb.	*Galba*	
Gramm.	*De grammaticis*	
Jul.	*Divus Julius*	
Nero	*Nero*	
Otho	*Otho*	
Poet.	*De poetis*	
Rhet.	*De rhetoribus*	
Tib.	*Tiberius*	
Tit.	*Divus Titus*	
Vesp.	*Vespasianus*	
Vit.	*Vitellius*	
Tacitus		
Agr.	*Agricola*	
Ann.	*Annales*	
Dial.	*Dialogus de oratoribus*	
Germ.	*Germania*	
Hist.	*Historiae*	
Tatian		
Diatesseron	*Diatesseron (Evangelion de Mehallete)*	*Harmony of the Gospels*
Or. Graec.	*Oratio ad Graecos (Pros Hellēnas)*	
Terence		
Ad.	*Adelphi*	
Andr.	*Andria*	
Eun.	*Eunuchus*	
Haut.	*Hauton timorumenos*	
Hec.	*Hecyra*	
Phorm.	*Phormio*	
Tertullian		
Adv. Jud.	*Adversus Judaeos*	*Against the Jews*
An.	*De anima*	*The Soul*
Apol.	*Apologeticus*	*Apology*
Bapt.	*De baptismo*	*Baptism*
Carn. Chr.	*De carne Christi*	*The Flesh of Christ*
Cor.	*De corona militis*	*The Crown*
Cult. fem.	*De cultu feminarum*	*The Apparel of Women*
Exh. cast.	*De exhortatione castitatis*	*Exhortation to Chastity*
Fug.	*De fuga in persecutione*	*Flight in Persecution*
Herm.	*Adversus Hermogenem*	*Against Hermogenes*
Idol.	*De idololatria*	*Idolatry*

ABBREVIATIONS	LATIN (OR GREEK) TITLE	ENGLISH TITLE
Jejun.	*De jejunio adversus psychicos*	*On Fasting, against the Psychics*
Marc.	*Adversus Marcionem*	*Against Marcion*
Mart.	*Ad martyras*	*To the Martyrs*
Mon.	*De monogamia*	*Monogamy*
Nat.	*Ad nationes*	*To the Heathen*
Or.	*De oratione*	*Prayer*
Paen.	*De paenitentia*	*Repentance*
Pall.	*De pallio*	*The Pallium*
Pat.	*De patientia*	*Patience*
Praescr.	*De praescriptione haereticorum*	*Prescription against Heretics*
Prax.	*Adversus Praxean*	*Against Praxeas*
Pud.	*De pudicitia*	*Modesty*
Res.	*De resurrectione carnis*	*The Resurrection of the Flesh*
Scap.	*Ad Scapulam*	*To Scapula*
Scorp.	*Scorpiace*	*Antidote for the Scorpion's Sting*
Spect.	*De spectaculis*	*The Shows*
Test.	*De testimonio animae*	*The Soul's Testimony*
Ux.	*Ad uxorem*	*To His Wife*
Val.	*Adversus Valentinianos*	*Against the Valentinians*
Virg.	*De virginibus velandis*	*The Veiling of Virgins*
Theocritus		
Id.		*Idylls*
Theodoret		
Car.	*De caritate*	
Haer. fab.	*Haereticarum fabularum compendium*	*Compendium of Heretical Falsehoods*
Hist. eccl.	*Historia ecclesiastica*	*Ecclesiastical History*
Phil. hist.	*Philotheos historia*	*History of the Monks of Syria*
Theon of Alexandria		
Comm. Alm.	*Commentarium in Almagestum*	*Commentary on the Almagest*
Theophilus		
Autol.	*Ad Autolycum*	*To Autolycus*
Theophrastus		
Caus. plant.	*De causis plantarum*	
Char.	*Characteres*	
Hist. plant.	*Historia plantarum*	
Sens.	*De sensu*	
Tyconius		
Reg.	*Liber regularum*	
Varro		
Ling.	*De lingua latina*	
Rust.	*De re rustica*	
Vergil		
Aen.	*Aeneid*	
Ecl.	*Eclogae*	
Georg.	*Georgica*	
Xenophon		
Ages.	*Agesilaus*	
Anab.	*Anabasis*	
Apol.	*Apologia Socratis*	
[Ath.]	*Respublica atheniensium*	
Cyn.	*Cynegeticus*	
Cyr.	*Cyropaedia*	
Eq.	*De equitande ratione*	
Eq. mag.	*De equitum magistro*	
Hell.	*Hellenica*	
Hier.	*Hiero*	
Lac.	*Respublica Lacedaemoniorum*	
Mem.	*Memorabilia*	
Oec.	*Oeconomicus*	
Symp.	*Symposium*	

8.3.15 Latin Names of Biblical Books

The following table provides abbreviations for the Latin names of biblical books. For the benefit of those not familiar with the Latin Bible, the English name of each book is also given. These abbreviations for the Latin names of the books of the Bible follow the *Dictionnaire latin-français des auteurs chrétiens* (Turnhout: Brepols, 1967) except as modified according to the following hierarchy of rules: (1) unabbreviated forms are used only for short, uninflected forms; (2) where possible, these Latin abbreviations conform to the abbreviations given below for the English book names, except that the Latin abbreviations are italicized and followed by a period; (3) otherwise, these Latin abbreviations conform to the rules given above. For numbered books, the abbreviation should use arabic numbers set italic; for example, a patristic commentary on 1 Chronicles, if such had been written, might be titled *Commentarii in primum Paralipomenorum librum* and abbreviated *Comm. 1 Par.*[1]

	LATIN TITLE	ENGLISH TITLE
	Vetus Testamentum	**Old Testament**
Abd.	*Abdias*	Obadiah
Agg.	*Aggaeus*	Haggai
Am.	*Amos*	Amos
Bar.	*Baruch*	Baruch
Cant.	*Canticum canticorum*	Song of Songs
Dan.	*Daniel*	Daniel
Deut.	*Deuteronomium*	Deuteronomy
Eccl.	*Ecclesiastes*	Ecclesiastes
Ecclesiastic.	*Ecclesiasticus*	Sirach
Esdr.	*Esdras*	Esdras and Ezra
Esth.	*Esther*	Esther
Exod.	*Exodus*	Exodus
Ezech.	*Ezechiel*	Ezekiel
Gen.	*Genesis*	Genesis
Hab.	*Habacuc*	Habakkuk
Isa.	*Isaias*	Isaiah
Jer.	*Jeremias*	Jeremiah
Jes. Nav.	*Jesus Nave* (= *Josue*)	Joshua
Job	*Job*	Job
Joel	*Joel*	Joel
Jon.	*Jonas*	Jonah
Jos.	*Josue*	Joshua
Judic.	*Judices*	Judges
Judith	*Judith*	Judith
Lam.	*Lamentationes*	Lamentations
Lev.	*Leviticus*	Leviticus
Macc.	*Macchabaei*	Maccabees

[1] Some writers use inflected forms of Hebrew names that other writers leave uninflected. When inflected names are used, abbreviated forms must have a period. For example, Commentarius in Joel would be abbreviated *Comm. Joel* (no period after Joel); but *Commentarius in Joelem* is abbreviated *Comm. Joel.*, since in this case an accusative ending is being dropped.

Mal.	*Malachias*	Malachi
Mich.	*Michaeas*	Micah
Nah.	*Nahum*	Nahum
Num.	*Numeri*	Numbers
Or. Man.	*Oratio Manasse*	Prayer of Manasseh
Os.	*Osee*	Hosea
Par.	*Paralipomena*	Chronicles
Prov.	*Proverbia Salomonis*	Proverbs
Ps.	*Psalmi*	Psalms
Reg.	*Reges*	Kings
Ruth	*Ruth*	Ruth
Sap.	*Sapientia*	Wisdom
Soph.	*Sophonias*	Zephaniah
Tob.	*Tobias*	Tobit
Zach.	*Zacharias*	Zechariah
	Novum Testamentum	**New Testament**
Act.	*Actus apostolorum*	Acts
Apoc.	*Apocalypsis*	Revelation
Col.	*Pauli epistula ad Colossenses*	Colossians
Cor.	*Pauli epistulae ad Corinthios*	Corinthians
Eph.	*Pauli epistula ad Ephesios*	Ephesians
Gal.	*Pauli epistula ad Galatas*	Galatians
Heb.	*Pauli epistula ad Hebraeos*	Hebrews
Jac.	*Epistula Jacobi*	James
Jo.	*Euangelium Joannis*	John
Jo. ep.	*Johannis epistulae*	Letters of John
Jud.	*Epistula Judae*	Jude
Laod.	*Epistula ad Laodicenses*	Laodiceans
Luc.	*Evangelium Lucae*	Luke
Marc.	*Evangelium Marci*	Mark
Matt.	*Evangelium Matthaei*	Matthew
Pet.	*Epistulae Petri*	Peter
Phil.	*Pauli epistula ad Philippenses*	Philippians
Phlm.	*Pauli epistula ad Philemonem*	Philemon
Rom.	*Pauli epistula ad Romanos*	Romans
Thess.	*Pauli epistulae ad Thessalonicenses*	Thessalonians
Tim.	*Pauli epistulae ad Timotheum*	Timothy
Tit.	*Pauli epistula ad Titum*	Titus

8.3.16 Papyri, Ostraca, and Epigraphical Citations

The standard resource for abbreviating Greek papyri, ostraca, and tablets is the *Checklist of Editions of Greek and Latin Papyri, Ostraca and Tablets*, ed. John F. Oates et al., 4th ed., BASPSup 7 (Atlanta: Scholars Press, 1992); an online edition is available at http://library.duke.edu/rubenstein/scriptorium/papyrus/texts/clist.html. When collections or selections of papyri are given, include the source of the citation. Thus,

4. P.Ryl. 77.32–47 (ed. Hunt and Edgar, 2:154–59).

Select Papyri. Translated by Arthur S. Hunt and Campbell C. Edgar. 5 vols. LCL. Cambridge: Harvard University Press.

See §6.4.3.

8.3.17 Ancient Near Eastern Texts

For standard abbreviations of editions of Akkadian and Sumerian cuneiform texts and compositions, see Rykle Borger, *Handbuch der Keilschrift Literatur*, 3 vols. (Berlin: de Gruyter: 1967–1975), as well as the lists of abbreviations in *CAD* and *AHw* (see §§3.4.2, 5.5). For Hittite and Anatolian studies, follow Silvin Košak, *Konkordanz der hethitischen Keilschrifttafeln* 1 (Wiesbaden: Harrassowitz, 2005), xliii–lxxii. Researchers may also consult lists of abbreviations available online through the Cuneiform Digital Library Initiative (CDLI) at http://cdli.ox.ac.uk/wiki/doku.php?id=abbreviations_for_assyriology and the Hethitologie Portal Mainz at http://www.hethport.uni-wuerzburg.de/hetkonk/hetkonkabkrz.html. For abbreviations of Egyptological sources, follow the *Annual Egyptological Bibliography* (*AEB*), published by Brill between 1947 and 2001 and now updated online at http://oeb.griffith.ox.ac.uk.

8.4 Secondary Sources: Journals, Major Reference Works, and Series

Abbreviations for works not listed below should follow Siegfried M. Schwertner, *Internationales Abkürzungsverzeichnis für Theologie und Grenzgebiete*, 3rd ed. (Berlin: de Gruyter, 2014 [=IATG³]). Abbreviations use superscripted numbers to indicate multiple editions. Superscripted numbers should not be used in bibliographic or note citations.

8.4.1 Alphabetized by Source

ABAW	Abhandlungen der Bayerischen Akademie der Wissenschaften
ADOG	Abhandlungen der deutschen Orientgesellschaft
AHAW	Abhandlungen der Heidelberger Akademie der Wissenschaften
ADPV	Abhandlungen des Deutschen Palästina-Vereins
AKM	Abhandlungen für die Kunde des Morgenlandes
ALASP	Abhandlungen zur Literatur Alt-Syren-Palästinas und Mesopotamiens
ASAW	Abhandlungen der Sächsischen Akademie der Wissenschaften
ATANT	Abhandlungen zur Theologie des Alten und Neuen Testaments
ANTC	Abingdon New Testament Commentaries
AOTC	Abingdon Old Testament Commentaries
AbrN	*Abr-Nahrain*
AbrNSup	Abr-Nahrain Supplements
AcBib	Academia Biblica
ActAnt	Acta Antiqua Academiae Scientiarum Hungaricae
Acta Iranica	Acta Iranica
AAS	*Acta Apostolicae Sedis*
ACO	*Acta Conciliorum Oecumenicorum*. Edited by Eduard Schwartz. Berlin: de Gruyter, 1914–1984
AMS	*Acta Martyrum et Sanctorum Syriace*. Edited by Paul Bedjan. 7 vols.

	Paris, Leipzig: Harrassowitz, 1890–1897. Repr., Hildesheim: Olms, 1968
AcOr	*Acta Orientalia*
ASS	*Acta Sanctae Sedis*
AASS	*Acta Sanctorum Quotquot Toto Orbe Coluntur.* Antwerp, 1643–
ASNU	Acta Seminarii Neotestamentici Upsaliensis
ASSF	Acta Societatis Scientiarum Fennicae
ASJ	*Acta Sumerologica*
AcT	*Acta Theologica*
ATDan	Acta Theologica Danica
BGU	*Aegyptische Urkunden aus den Königlichen Staatlichen Museen zu Berlin, Griechische Urkunden.* 15 vols. Berlin: Weidmann, 1895–1937
Aeg	*Aegyptus*
Aev	*Aevum: Rassegna de scienze, storiche, linguistiche, e filologiche*
AJBS	*African Journal of Biblical Studies*
ÄAT	Ägypten und Altes Testament
AeL	Ägypten und Levante
ÄHK	*Die ägyptisch-hethitische Korrespondenz aus Boghazköi in babylonischer und hethitischer Sprache.* Elmar Edel. Opladen: Westdeutscher Verlag, 1994
ÄgAbh	Ägyptologische Abhandlungen
ÄF	Ägyptologische Forschungen
Akkadica	*Akkadica*
AHw	*Akkadisches Handwörterbuch.* Wolfram von Soden. 3 vols. Wiesbaden, 1965–1981
Altaner	Altaner, Berthold. *Patrologie: Leben, Schriften und Lehre der Kirchenväter.* 8th ed. Freiburg: Herder, 1978
AbB	*Altbabylonische Briefe in Umschrift und Übersetzung.* Edited by Fritz R. Kraus. Leiden: Brill, 1964–
AO	*Der Alte Orient*
ATD	Das Alte Testament Deutsch
AOAT	Alter Orient und Altes Testament
AOBib	Altorientalische Bibliothek
ABAT2	*Altorientalische Bilder zum Alten Testament.* Edited by Hugo Gressmann. 2nd ed. Berlin: de Gruyter, 1927
AoF	*Altorientalische Forschungen*
AOTAT	*Altorientalische Texte zum Alten Testament.* Edited by Hugo Gressmann. 2nd ed. Berlin: de Gruyter, 1926
AoN	*Altorientalistische Notizen*
ATA	Alttestamentliche Abhandlungen
AARAS	American Academy of Religion Academy Series
AARASR	American Academy of Religion Aids for the Study of Religion
AARCRS	American Academy of Religion Classics in Religious Studies
AARCCS	American Academy of Religion Cultural Criticism Series

AARRTSR	American Academy of Religion Reflection and Theory in the Study of Religion
AARRCH	American Academy of Religion Religion, Culture, and History Series
AARRT	American Academy of Religion Religion in Translation Series (formerly Texts and Translations Series)
AARSR	American Academy of Religion Studies in Religion
AARTRSS	American Academy of Religion Teaching Religious Studies Series
AARTTS	American Academy of Religion Texts and Translations Series
AARTS	American Academy of Religion Thematic Studies
AARRS	American Academy of Religion The Religions Series
ABQ	*American Baptist Quarterly*
AER	*American Ecclesiastical Review*
AHR	*American Historical Review*
AJAS	*American Journal of Arabic Studies*
AJA	*American Journal of Archaeology*
AJP	*American Journal of Philology*
AJSL	*American Journal of Semitic Languages and Literatures*
AmJT	*American Journal of Theology*
AOS	American Oriental Series
AOSTS	American Oriental Society Translation Series
APSP	*American Philosophical Society Proceedings*
ASOR	American Schools of Oriental Research
ASP	*American Studies in Papyrology*
ATLA	American Theological Library Association
ACEBT	*Amsterdamse Cahiers voor Exegese en bijbelse Theologie*
AAeg	*Analecta Aegyptiaca*
AnBib	Analecta Biblica
AnBoll	Analecta Bollandiana
ALBO	Analecta Lovaniensia Biblica et Orientalia
AnOr	Analecta Orientalia
Anám	*Anámnesis*
AnAnt	*Anatolia Antiqua*
AnSt	*Anatolian Studies*
Anatolica	*Anatolica*
AB	Anchor Bible
ABD	*Anchor Bible Dictionary*. Edited by David Noel Freedman. 6 vols. New York: Doubleday, 1992
ABRL	Anchor Bible Reference Library
ACCS	Ancient Christian Commentary on Scripture
ACW	Ancient Christian Writers
AEL	*Ancient Egyptian Literature*. Miriam Lichtheim. 3 vols. Berkeley: University of California Press, 1971–1980
AEO	*Ancient Egyptian Onomastica*. Alan H. Gardiner. 3 vols. London: Oxford University Press, 1947

AIL	Ancient Israel and Its Literature
AMD	Ancient Magic and Divination
ANEM	Ancient Near East Monographs/Monografías sobre el Antiquo Cercano Oriente
ANEP[2]	*The Ancient Near East in Pictures Relating to the Old Testament*. 2nd ed. Edited by James B. Pritchard. Princeton: Princeton University Press, 1994
ANESTP	*The Ancient Near East: Supplementary Texts and Pictures Relating to the Old Testament*. Edited by James B. Pritchard. Princeton: Princeton University Press, 1969
ANESSup	Ancient Near Eastern Studies Supplement Series
ANET	*Ancient Near Eastern Texts Relating to the Old Testament*. Edited by James B. Pritchard. 3rd ed. Princeton: Princeton University Press, 1969
ARAB	*Ancient Records of Assyria and Babylonia*. Daniel David Luckenbill. 2 vols. Chicago: University of Chicago Press, 1926–1927. Repr., New York: Greenwood, 1968
ARE	*Ancient Records of Egypt*. Edited by James Henry Breasted. 5 vols. Chicago: University of Chicago Press, 1906–1907. Repr., New York: Russell & Russell, 1962
ATASMS	American Translators Association Scholarly Monograph Series
AUS	American University Studies
AUSTR	American University Studies, Series 7: Theology and Religion
AUSCLL	American University Studies, Series 17: Classical Languages and Literature
AYBRL	Anchor Yale Bible Reference Library
ANES	Ancient Near Eastern Studies
ANES	*Ancient Near Eastern Studies*
ASH	Ancient Society and History
Andalus	*Al-Andalus: Revista de la Escuela de Estudios Árabes de Madrid y Granada*
ANQ	*Andover Newton Quarterly*
AUCT	Andrews University Cuneiform Texts
AUSS	*Andrews University Seminary Studies*
Ang	*Angelicum*
ATbR	*Anglican Theological Review*
AASF	Annales Academiae Scientiarum Fennicae
ASAE	*Annales du Service des antiquités de l'Egypte*
AT	*Annales Theologici*
AION	*Annali dell'Istituto Orientale di Napoli*
AAA	Annals of Archaeology and Anthropology
AE	*Année épigraphique*
AnPhil	*L'année philologique*
AIPHOS	*Annuaire de l'Institut de philologie et d'histoire orientales et slaves*
AEB	*Annual Egyptological Bibliography*
Bar-Ilan	*Annual of Bar-Ilan University*

ALUOS	*Annual of Leeds University Oriental Society*
AASOR	Annual of the American Schools of Oriental Research
ABSA	Annual of the British School at Athens
ADAJ	*Annual of the Department of Antiquities of Jordan*
AJBI	*Annual of the Japanese Biblical Institute*
ASTI	*Annual of the Swedish Theological Institute*
ARRIM	Annual Review of the Royal Inscriptions of Mesopotamia Project
ANF	*Ante-Nicene Fathers*
AnthLyrGraec	*Anthologia Lyrica Graeca*. Edited by Ernst Diehl. Leipzig: Teubner, 1954–
AnL	*Anthropological Linguistics*
Antichthon	*Antichthon: Journal of the Australian Society for Classical Studies*
AW	*Antike Welt*
AJ	*Antiquaries Journal*
Anton	*Antonianum*
Anuari	*Anuari de filología*
AÖAW	Anzeiger der Österreichischen Akademie der Wissenschaften
AAHG	*Anzeiger für die Altertumswissenschaft*
AMWNE	*Apocalypticism in the Mediterranean World and the Near East. Proceedings of the International Colloquium on Apocalypticism, Uppsala, Aug. 12–17, 1979*. Edited by David Hellholm. 2nd ed. Tübingen: Mohr Siebeck, 1989
APOT	*The Apocrypha and Pseudepigrapha of the Old Testament*. Edited by Robert H. Charles. 2 vols. Oxford: Clarendon, 1913
AOT	*The Apocryphal Old Testament*. Edited by Hedley F. D. Sparks. Oxford: Clarendon, 1984
APAT	*Die Apokryphen und Pseudepigraphen des Alten Testaments*. Translated and edited by Emil Kautzsch. 2 vols. Tübingen: Mohr Siebeck, 1900
ApOTC	Apollos Old Testament Commentary
AMEL	*Arabic and Middle Eastern Literatures*
Arabica	*Arabica: Journal of Arabic and Islamic Studies/Revue d'études arabes et islamiques*
ArBib	The Aramaic Bible
AS	*Aramaic Studies*
Aramazd	*Aramazd: Armenian Journal of Near Eastern Studies*
AJSUFS	*Arbeiten aus dem Juristischen Seminar der Universität Freiburg* (Switzerland)
ANTJ	Arbeiten zum Neuen Testament und Judentum
ASKA	Arbeiten zum spätantiken und koptischen Ägypten
AGJU	Arbeiten zur Geschichte des antiken Judentums und des Urchristentums
AGSU	Arbeiten zur Geschichte des Spätjudentums und Urchristentums
ALGHJ	Arbeiten zur Literatur und Geschichte des hellenistischen Judentums
ANTF	Arbeiten zur neutestamentlichen Textforschung

AzTh	Arbeiten zur Theologie
Arch	*Archaeology*
ABS	Archaeology and Biblical Studies
ABW	*Archaeology in the Biblical World*
AA	*Archäologischer Anzeiger*
AfK	*Archiv für Keilschriftforschung*
AfO	*Archiv für Orientforschung*
AfOB	Archiv für Orientforschung: Beiheft
APF	*Archiv für Papyrusforschung*
ARG	*Archiv für Reformationsgeschichte*
AR	*Archiv für Religionswissenschaft*
ArOr	*Archív orientální*
AAM	Archives administrativs de Mari
ASSR	*Archives de sciences sociales des religions*
AEM	Archives épistolaires de Mari
ARMT	Archives royales de Mari, transcrite et traduite
ARES	Archivi reali di Ebla, Studi
ARET	Archivi reali di Ebla, Testi
ATG	*Archivo teológico granadino*
ArsOr	*Ars Orientalis*
Assur	Assur: Monographic Journals of the Near East
AsTJ	*Asbury Theological Journal*
ATJ	*Ashland Theological Journal*
AsJT	*Asia Journal of Theology*
Asp	*Asprenas: Rivista di scienze teologiche*
AsSeign	*Assemblées du Seigneur*
AJSR	*Association for Jewish Studies Review*
ABC	*Assyrian and Babylonian Chronicles.* Albert K. Grayson. TCS 5. Locust Valley, NY: Augustin, 1975
ABL	*Assyrian and Babylonian Letters Belonging to the Kouyunjik Collections of the British Museum.* Edited by Robert F. Harper. 14 vols. Chicago: University of Chicago Press, 1892–1914
ADD	*Assyrian Deeds and Documents.* Claude Herman Walter Johns. 4 vols. Cambridge: Deighton, Bell, 1898–1923
CAD	*The Assyrian Dictionary of the Oriental Institute of the University of Chicago.* Chicago: The Oriental Institute of the University of Chicago, 1956–2006
ARI	*Assyrian Royal Inscriptions.* Albert K. Grayson. 2 vols. Wiesbaden: Harrasowitz, 1972–1976
AS	Assyriological Studies
AB	*Assyriologische Bibliothek*
ABZ	*Assyrisch-babylonische Zeichenliste.* Rykle Borger. 3rd ed. Neukirchen-Vluyn: Neukirchener Verlag, 1986
Athenaeum	Athenaeum: Studi Periodici di Letteratura e Storia dell'Antichità

Atiqot	*'Atiqot*
AVTRW	Aufsätze und Vorträge zur Theologie und Religionswissenschaft
ANRW	*Aufstieg und Niedergang der römischen Welt: Geschichte und Kultur Roms im Spiegel der neueren Forschung.* Part 2, *Principat.* Edited by Hildegard Temporini and Wolfgang Haase. Berlin: de Gruyter, 1972–
ACNT	Augsburg Commentary on the New Testament
AugStud	*Augustinian Studies*
Aug	*Augustinianum*
AuOr	*Aula Orientalis*
AGLB	*Aus der Geschichte der lateinischen Bibel* (= *Vetus Latina: Die Reste der altlateinischen Bibel: Aus der Geschichte der lateinischen Bibel*). Freiburg: Herder, 1957–
ACR	*Australasian Catholic Record*
ATR	*Australasian Theological Review*
ABR	*Australian Biblical Review*
ANZSTR	Australian and New Zealand Studies in Theology and Religion
AJBA	*Australian Journal of Biblical Archaeology*
Bab	*Babyloniaca*
BOR	*Babylonian and Oriental Record*
BIN	Babylonian Inscriptions in the Collection of James B. Nies
BWL	*Babylonian Wisdom Literature.* Wilfred G. Lambert. Oxford: Clarendon, 1960
BaF	*Baghdader Forschungen*
BaM	*Baghdader Mitteilungen*
BBMS	Baker Biblical Monograph Series
BCOTWP	Baker Commentary on the Old Testament Wisdom and Psalms
BECNT	Baker Exegetical Commentary on the New Testament
BEB	*Baker Encyclopedia of the Bible.* Edited by Walter A. Elwell. 2 vols. Grand Rapids: Baker, 1988
BARIS	BAR (British Archaeological Reports) International Series
BAGD	Bauer, Walter, William F. Arndt, F. Wilbur Gingrich, and Frederick W. Danker. *Greek-English Lexicon of the New Testament and Other Early Christian Literature.* 2nd ed. Chicago: University of Chicago Press, 1979 (Bauer-Arndt-Gingrich-Danker)
BDAG	*See under* Danker, Frederick W.
Bayan	*Al-Bayan: Journal of Quran and Hadith Studies*
BegC	*The Beginnings of Christianity.* Part 1: *The Acts of the Apostles.* Edited by Frederick J. Foakes-Jackson and Kirsopp Lake. 5 vols. London: Macmillan, 1922. Repr. under the subtitle, Grand Rapids: Baker, 1977.
BZABR	Beihefte zur Zeitschrift für altorientalische und biblische Rechtsgeschichte
BZAW	Beihefte zur Zeitschrift für die alttestamentliche Wissenschaft
BZNW	Beihefte zur Zeitschrift für die neutestamentliche Wissenschaft
BZRGG	Beihefte zur Zeitschrift für Religions- und Geistesgeschichte

BAP	*Beiträge zum altbabylonischen Privatrecht*. Bruno Meissner. Leipzig: Hinrichs, 1893
BzA	Beiträge zur Assyriologie
BBET	Beiträge zur biblischen Exegese und Theologie
BEATAJ	Beiträge zur Erforschung des Alten Testaments und des antiken Judentum
BEvT	Beiträge zur evangelischen Theologie
BFCT	Beiträge zur Förderung christlicher Theologie
BGBE	Beiträge zur Geschichte der biblischen Exegese
BHT	Beiträge zur historischen Theologie
BzN	Beiträge zur Namenforschung
BNL	Beiträge zur neueren Literaturgeschichte
BWA(N)T	Beiträge zur Wissenschaft vom Alten (und Neuen) Testament
Belleten	*Belleten*
BSGW	Berichte der Sächsischen Gesellschaft der Wissenschaften
BerMatÖAI	Berichte und Materialien des Österreichischen archäologischen Instituts
BBVO	Berliner Beiträge zum Vorderer Orient Texte
BBVF	Berliner Beiträge zur Vor- und Frühgeschichte
BJVF	*Berliner Jahrbuch für Vor- und Frühgeschichte*
BTZ	*Berliner Theologische Zeitschrift*
Berytus	*Berytus: Archaeological Studies*
BeO	*Bibbia e oriente*
BK	*Bibel und Kirche*
BibLeb	*Bibel und Leben*
BL	*Bibel und Liturgie*
BibleInt	The Bible and Its Interpretation
BMI	The Bible and Its Modern Interpreters
BibleRec	The Bible and Its Reception
BLS	Bible and Literature Series
BW	Bible and Women
BiBh	*Bible Bhashyam*
BTS	*Bible et terre sainte*
BVC	*Bible et vie chrétienne*
BRev	*Bible Review*
BSC	Bible Student's Commentary
TBT	*The Bible Today*
BT	*The Bible Translator*
BHK	*Biblia Hebraica*. Edited by Rudolf Kittel. Leipzig: Hinrichs, 1905–1906
BHQ	*Biblia Hebraica Quinta*. Edited by Adrian Schenker et al. Stuttgart: Deutsche Bibelgesellschaft, 2004–
BHS	*Biblia Hebraica Stuttgartensia*. Edited by Karl Elliger and Wilhelm Rudolph. Stuttgart: Deutsche Bibelgesellschaft, 1983
ByF	Biblia y fe

BiPa	*Biblia Patristica: Index des citations et allusions bibliques dans la littérature.* Paris: CNRS, 2000
Bib	*Biblica*
BibOr	Biblica et Orientalia
BJSUCSD	Biblical and Judaic Studies from the University of California, San Diego
BA	*Biblical Archaeologist*
BAR	*Biblical Archaeology Review*
BibEnc	Biblical Encyclopedia
BFT	Biblical Foundations in Theology
BI	*Biblical Illustrator*
BibInt	*Biblical Interpretation*
BibInt	Biblical Interpretation Series
BR	*Biblical Research*
BSNA	Biblical Scholarship in North America
BibSem	The Biblical Seminar
BTB	*Biblical Theology Bulletin*
BTS	Biblical Tools and Studies
BV	*Biblical Viewpoint*
BW	*The Biblical World: A Dictionary of Biblical Archaeology.* Edited by Charles F. Pfeiffer. Grand Rapids: Baker, 1966
BAC	Biblioteca de autores cristianos
BCBO	Biblioteca de Ciencias Bíblicas y Orientales
BPOA	*Biblioteca del Proximo Oriente Antiguo*
BCR	Biblioteca di cultura religiosa
BRLF	Biblioteca di ricerche linguistiche e filologiche
HumTeo	Biblioteca humanística e teológica
BETL	Bibliotheca Ephemeridum Theologicarum Lovaniensium
BHG	*Bibliotheca Hagiographica Graeca.* Edited by François Halkin. 3rd ed. 3 vols. Brussels: Société des Bollandistes, 1986
BHLAMA	*Bibliotheca Hagiographica Latina Antiquae et Mediae Aetatis.* 2 vols. Brussels: Socii Bollandiani, 1898–1901
BHO	*Bibliotheca Hagiographica Orientalis.* Brussels, 1910
BMes	Bibliotheca Mesopotamica
BO	*Bibliotheca Orientalis*
BSac	*Bibliotheca Sacra*
BSGRT	Bibliotheca Scriptorum Graecorum et Romanorum Teubneriana
BEHEH	Bibliothèque de l'École des hautes études: Sciences historiques et philologiques
BEHER	Bibliothèque de l'École des hautes études: Sciences religieuses
BLit	*Bibliothèque liturgique*
BibB	Biblische Beiträge
BN	*Biblische Notizen*
BibS(F)	Biblische Studien (Freiburg, 1895–)
BibS(N)	Biblische Studien (Neukirchen, 1951–)

BZ	*Biblische Zeitschrift*
BKAT	Biblischer Kommentar, Altes Testament
BRL2	*Biblisches Reallexikon*. 2nd ed. Edited by Kurt Galling. HAT 1/1. Tübingen: Mohr Siebeck, 1977
BHH	*Biblisch-historisches Handwörterbuch: Landeskunde, Geschichte, Religion, Kultur*. Edited by Bo Reicke and Leonhard Rost. 4 vols. Göttingen: Vandenhoeck & Ruprecht, 1962–1966. Republished electronically, Berlin: Directmedia, 2003
Bijdr	*Bijdragen: Tijdschrift voor filosofie en theologie*
BNTC	Black's New Testament Commentaries
BDF	Blass, Friedrich, Albert Debrunner, and Robert W. Funk. *A Greek Grammar of the New Testament and Other Early Christian Literature*. Chicago: University of Chicago Press, 1961
BoHa	Boğazköy-Ḫattuša
Böhl	Böhl, F. M. Th. de Liagre. *Opera minora: Studies en bijdragen op Assyriologisch en Oudtestamentisch terrein*. Groningen: Wolters, 1953
BAEO	*Boletín de la Asociación Española de Orientalistas*
BBB	Bonner biblische Beiträge
BJ	*Bonner Jahrbücher*
BAFCS	The Book of Acts in Its First Century Setting
B&R	*Books and Religion*
BAT	Die Botschaft des Alten Testaments
BRLA	Brill Reference Library of Judaism
BNP	*Brill's New Pauly: Encyclopaedia of the Ancient World*. Edited by Hubert Cancik. 22 vols. Leiden: Brill, 2002–2011
BSJS	Brill's Series in Jewish Studies
BSIEL	Brill's Studies in Indo-European Languages and Linguistics
BMQ	*British Museum Quarterly*
BJS	Brown Judaic Studies
BDB	Brown, Francis, S. R. Driver, and Charles A. Briggs. *A Hebrew and English Lexicon of the Old Testament*
BBB	*Bulletin de bibliographie biblique*
BCH	*Bulletin de correspondance hellénique*
BEO	*Bulletin d'études orientales de l'Institut Français de Damas*
BAGB	*Bulletin de l'Association G. Budé*
BHEAT	*Bulletin d'histoire et d'exégèse de l'Ancien Testament*
BIFAO	*Bulletin de l'Institut français d'archéologie orientale*
BSAA	*Bulletin de la Société archéologique d'Alexandrie*
BSAC	*Bulletin de la Société d'archéologie copte*
BSL	*Bulletin de la Société de Linguistique de Paris*
BLE	*Bulletin de littérature ecclésiastique*
BThAM	*Bulletin de théologie ancienne et médiévale*
BCPE	*Bulletin du Centre protestant d'études*
BBR	*Bulletin for Biblical Research*

BBRSup	*Bulletin for Biblical Research, Supplements*
BBS	*Bulletin of Biblical Studies*
BSA	*Bulletin of Sumerian Agriculture*
BASOR	*Bulletin of the American Schools of Oriental Research*
BASORSup	Bulletin of the American Schools of Oriental Research Supplements
BASP	*Bulletin of the American Society of Papyrologists*
BASPSup	Bulletin of the American Society of Papyrologists Supplements
BAIAS	*Bulletin of the Anglo-Israel Archeological Society*
BCSMS	*Bulletin of the Canadian Society for Mesopotamian Studies*
BCSR	*Bulletin of the Council on the Study of Religion*
BIOSCS	*Bulletin of the International Organization for Septuagint and Cognate Studies*
BIES	*Bulletin of the Israel Exploration Society* (= *Yediot*)
BJPES	*Bulletin of the Jewish Palestine Exploration Society*
BJRL	*Bulletin of the John Rylands University Library of Manchester*
BMECCJ	*Bulletin of the Middle Eastern Culture Center in Japan*
BSOAS	*Bulletin of the School of Oriental and African Studies*
BSR	*Bulletin for the Study of Religion* (formerly *CSSRB*)
Burg	*Burgense*
BurH	*Buried History: Quarterly Journal of the Australian Institute of Archaeology*
ByzF	*Byzantinische Forschungen*
ByzZ	*Byzantinische Zeitschrift*
Byzantion	*Byzantion*
CahRB	Cahiers de la Revue biblique
CRTL	Cahiers de la Revue théologique de Louvain
CaE	*Cahiers évangile*
CahT	Cahiers Théologiques
CBTJ	*Calvary Baptist Theological Journal*
CTJ	*Calvin Theological Journal*
CAH	Cambridge Ancient History
CBC	Cambridge Bible Commentary
CCTC	Cambridge Classical Texts and Commentaries
CGTC	Cambridge Greek Testament Commentary
CGTSC	Cambridge Greek Testament for Schools and Colleges
CHJ	*Cambridge History of Judaism*. Edited by William D. Davies and Louis Finkelstein. 4 vols. Cambridge: Cambridge University Press, 1984–2006
CML	*Canaanite Myths and Legends*. Edited by Godfrey R. Driver. Edinburgh: T&T Clark, 1956. 2nd ed. edited by John C. L. Gibson, 1978, e-book 2004
CTAED	*Canaanite Toponyms in Ancient Egyptian Documents*. Shmuel Ahituv. Jerusalem, 1984
CJT	*Canadian Journal of Theology*
CNIP	Carsten Niebuhr Institute Publications
Car	*Carthagiensia*

CTH	*Catalogue des textes hittites*. Emmanuel Laroche. Paris: Klincksieck, 1971
CBQMS	Catholic Biblical Quarterly Monograph Series
CBQ	*Catholic Biblical Quarterly*
CHR	*Catholic Historical Review*
CBM	Chester Beatty Monographs
CSHJ	Chicago Studies in the History of Judaism
Chiron	*Chiron: Mitteilungen der Kommission für Alte Geschichte und Epigraphik des Deutschen Archäologischen Instituts*
ChrCent	*Christian Century*
ChrLit	*Christianity and Literature*
CdE	*Chronique d'Égypte*
CH	*Church History*
CQ	*Church Quarterly*
CQR	*Church Quarterly Review*
Chm	Churchman
CClCr	*Civilità classica e cristiana*
CANE	*Civilizations of the Ancient Near East*. Edited by Jack M. Sasson. 4 vols. New York, 1995. Repr. in 2 vols. Peabody, MA: Hendrickson, 2006
ClAnt	*Classical Antiquity*
CF	*Classical Folia*
CJ	*Classical Journal*
CP	*Classical Philology*
ClQ	*Classical Quarterly*
CW	*Classical World*
CWS	Classics of Western Spirituality
CPG	*Clavis Patrum Graecorum*. Edited by Maurice Geerard. 5 vols. Turnhout: Brepols, 1974–1987
CPL	*Clavis Patrum Latinorum*. Edited by Eligius Dekkers. 2nd ed. Steenbrugis: Abbatia Sancti Petri, 1961
CAA	Codices Arabici Antiqui
Coll	*Collationes*
ColT	*Collectanea Theologica*
CAGN	*Collected Ancient Greek Novels*. Edited by Bryan P. Reardon. Berkeley, 1989
CÉFR	Collection de l'École française de Rome
Budé	Collection des universités de France, publiée sous le patronage de l'Association Guillaume Budé
CDOG	Colloquien der Deutschen Orient-Gesellschaft
Colloq	*Colloquium*
COut	Commentaar op het Oude Testament
CAT	Commentaire de l'Ancien Testament
CNT	Commentaire du Nouveau Testament
CEJL	Commentaries on Early Jewish Literature
CSEANT	Commentario storico ed esegetico all'Antico e al Nuovo Testamento

Comm	*Communio*
Cmio	*Communio: Commentarii Internationales de Ecclesia et Theología*
CV	*Communio Viatorum*
CIS	Comparative Islamic Studies
CRINT	Compendia Rerum Iudaicarum ad Novum Testamentum
Comp	*Compostellanum*
CRAI	Comptes rendus de l'Académie des inscriptions et belles-lettres
CDME	*A Concise Dictionary of Middle Egyptian*. Edited by Raymond O. Faulkner. Oxford: Griffith Institute, 1962
CUL	*A Concordance of the Ugaritic Literature*. Richard E. Whitaker. Cambridge: Harvard University Press, 1972
ConcC	Concordia Commentary
CTM	*Concordia Theological Monthly*
CTQ	*Concordia Theological Quarterly*
ConBOT	Coniectanea Biblica: Old Testament Series
ConBNT	Coniectanea Neotestamentica or Coniectanea Biblica: New Testament Series
COS	*The Context of Scripture*. Edited by William W. Hallo. 3 vols. Leiden: Brill, 1997–2002
CC	Continental Commentaries
Cont	*Continuum*
CBET	Contributions to Biblical Exegesis and Theology
CA	*Convivium Assisiense*
CCath	Corpus Catholicorum
CCCM	Corpus Christianorum: Continuatio Mediaevalis
CCT	Corpus Christianorum in Translation
CCSG	Corpus Christianorum: Series Graeca
CCSL	Corpus Christianorum: Series Latina
CTA	*Corpus des tablettes en cunéiformes alphabétiques découvertes à Ras Shamra-Ugarit de 1929 à 1939*. Edited by Andrée Herdner. Paris: Geuthner, 1963
CIC	*Corpus Inscriptionum Chaldicarum*
CIG	*Corpus Inscriptionum Graecarum*. Edited by August Boeckh. 4 vols. Berlin, 1828–1877
CIJ	*Corpus Inscriptionum Judaicarum*. Edited by Jean-Baptiste Frey. 2 vols. Rome: Pontifical Biblical Institute, 1936–1952
CIL	*Corpus Inscriptionum Latinarum*. Berlin, 1862–
CIS	*Corpus Inscriptionum Semiticarum*. Paris, 1881–
CPJ	*Corpus Papyrorum Judaicarum*. Edited by Victor A. Tcherikover. 3 vols. Cambridge: Harvard University Press, 1957–1964
CSCO	Corpus Scriptorum Christianorum Orientalium. Edited by Jean Baptiste Chabot et al. Paris, 1903
CUSAS	Cornell University Studies in Assyriology and Sumerology
ChS	Corpus der hurritischen Sprachdenkmäler

CCTMMA	Corpus of Cuneiform Texts in the Metropolitan Museum of Art
CSEL	Corpus Scriptorum Ecclesiasticorum Latinorum
CSHB	Corpus Scriptorum Historiae Byzantinae
CSSRB	*Council of Societies for the Study of Religion Bulletin*
CAP	Cowley, Arthur E. *Aramaic Papyri of the Fifth Century B.C.* Oxford: Clarendon, 1923
CNS	*Cristianesimo nella storia*
CTR	*Criswell Theological Review*
CRBR	*Critical Review of Books in Religion*
Crux	*Crux*
CB	*Cultura Bíblica*
CHANE	Culture and History of the Ancient Near East
CTU	*The Cuneiform Alphabetic Texts from Ugarit, Ras Ibn Hani, and Other Places.* Edited by Manfried Dietrich, Oswald Loretz, and Joaquín Sanmartín. Münster: Ugarit-Verlag, 1995
CDLB	Cuneiform Digital Library Bulletin
CDLI	Cuneiform Digital Library Initiative
CDLJ	*Cuneiform Digital Library Journal*
CDLN	Cuneiform Digital Library Notes
RawlCu	*The Cuneiform Inscriptions of Western Asia.* Edited by H. C. Rawlinson. London, 1891
CM	Cuneiform Monographs
CT	*Cuneiform Texts from Babylonian Tablets in the British Museum*
CCT	*Cuneiform Texts from Cappadocian Tablets in the British Museum*
CurBR	*Currents in Biblical Research* (formerly *Currents in Research: Biblical Studies*)
CurBS	*Currents in Research: Biblical Studies*
CurTM	*Currents in Theology and Mission*
DamM	Damaszener Mitteilungen
BDAG	Danker, Frederick W., Walter Bauer, William F. Arndt, and F. Wilbur Gingrich. *Greek-English Lexicon of the New Testament and Other Early Christian Literature.* 3rd ed. Chicago: University of Chicago Press, 2000 (Danker-Bauer-Arndt-Gingrich)
DTT	*Dansk teologisk tidsskrift*
DSD	*Dead Sea Discoveries*
DSSC	*The Dead Sea Scrolls Concordance.* Martin G. Abegg Jr., James E. Browley, and Edward M. Cook. 3 vols. Leiden: Brill, 2003–
DSSR	*The Dead Sea Scrolls Reader.* Edited by Donald W. Parry and Emanuel Tov. 6 vols. Leiden: Brill, 2004–2005
Der Islam	*Der Islam: Journal of the History and Culture of the Middle East*
DCLS	Deuterocanonical and Cognate Literature Studies
Di	*Dialog*
DHA	*Dialogues d'histoire ancienne*

DBI	*Dictionary of Biblical Interpretation*. Edited by John Hayes. 2 vols. Nashville: Abingdon, 1999
DBT	*Dictionary of Biblical Theology*. Edited by Xavier Léon-Dufour. 2nd ed. New York, Seabury, 1972
DCG	*Dictionary of Christ and the Gospels*. Edited by James Hastings. 2 vols. Edinburgh: T&T Clark, 1908
DCB	*Dictionary of Christian Biography*. Edited by William Smith and Henry Wace. 4 vols. London: Murray, 1877–1887
DCH	*Dictionary of Classical Hebrew*. Edited by David J. A. Clines. 9 vols. Sheffield: Sheffield Phoenix Press, 1993–2014
DDD	*Dictionary of Deities and Demons in the Bible*. Edited by Karel van der Toorn, Bob Becking, and Pieter W. van der Horst. Leiden: Brill, 1995. 2nd rev. ed. Grand Rapids: Eerdmans, 1999
DGWE	*Dictionary of Gnosis and Western Esotericism*. Edited by Wouter J. Hanegraaff et al. 2 vols. Leiden: Brill, 2005
DJG	*Dictionary of Jesus and the Gospels*. Edited by Joel B. Green, Jeannine K. Brown, and Nicholas Perrin. 2nd ed. Downers Grove, IL: InterVarsity Press, 2013
DLE	*Dictionary of Late Egyptian*. Edited by Leonard H. Lesko and Barbara S. Lesko. 4 vols. Berkeley: B.C. Scribe, 1982–1989
DMBI	*Dictionary of Major Biblical Interpreters*. Edited by Donald K. McKim. 2nd ed. Downers Grove, IL: Intervarsity Press, 2007
DNTB	*Dictionary of New Testament Background*. Edited by Craig A. Evans and Stanley E. Porter. Downers Grove, IL: InterVarsity Press, 2000
DLNT	*Dictionary of the Later New Testament and Its Developments*. Edited by R. P. Martin and P. H. Davids. Downers Grove, IL: InterVarsity Press, 1997
DNWSI	*Dictionary of the North-West Semitic Inscriptions*. Jacob Hoftijzer and Karen Jongeling. 2 vols. Leiden: Brill, 1995
DPL	*Dictionary of Paul and His Letters*. Edited by Gerald F. Hawthorne and Ralph P. Martin. Downers Grove, IL: InterVarsity Press, 1993
DACL	*Dictionnaire d'archéologie chrétienne et de liturgie*. Edited by Fernand Cabrol. 15 vols. Paris: Letouzey et Ané, 1907–1953
DB	*Dictionnaire de la Bible*. Edited by Fulcran Vigouroux. 5 vols. Paris: Letouzey et Ané, 1895–1912
DBSup	*Dictionnaire de la Bible: Supplément*. Edited by Louis Pirot and André Robert. Paris: Letouzey et Ané, 1928–
DTC	*Dictionnaire de théologie catholique*. Edited by Alfred Vacant et al. 15 vols. Paris: Letouzey et Ané, 1908–1950
DISO	*Dictionnaire des inscriptions sémitiques de l'ouest*. Edited by Charles François Jean and Jacob Hoftijzer. Leiden: Brill, 1965
Did	*Didaskalia*
DBAT	*Dielheimer Blätter zum Alten Testament und seiner Rezeption in der Alten Kirche*

DJD — Discoveries in the Judaean Desert
DissAb — Dissertation Abstracts
DivThom — *Divus Thomas*
DPAC — *Dizionario patristico e di antichità cristiane*. Edited by Angelo di Berardino. 3 vols. 2nd ed. Genoa: Marietti 2006–2008
DA — Documenta Asiana
DMOA — Documenta et Monumenta Orientis Antiqui
DOTT — *Documents from Old Testament Times*. Edited by D. Winton Thomas, London: Nelson, 1958
DRev — *Downside Review*
DBH — Dresdner Beiträge zur Hethitologie
DrewG — *Drew Gateway*
Duchesne — Duchesne, Louis, ed. *Le Liber pontificalis*. 2 vols. Paris: Thorin, 1886, 1892. Repr. with 3rd vol. by Cyrille Vogel. Paris: de Boccard, 1955–1957, 1981
DOP — *Dumbarton Oaks Papers*
DunRev — *Dunwoodie Review*
ECL — Early Christianity and Its Literature
ECF — Early Church Fathers
EJL — Early Judaism and Its Literature
ECR — *Eastern Churches Review*
EMC — *Echos du monde classique/Classical Views*
EB — Echter Bibel
ECC — Eerdmans Critical Commentary
EDB — *Eerdmans Dictionary of the Bible*. Edited by David Noel Freedman. Grand Rapids: Eerdmans, 2000
EfMex — *Efemerides mexicana*
EgT — *Eglise et théologie*
ECT — *The Egyptian Coffin Texts*. Edited by Adriaan de Buck and Alan H. Gardiner. Chicago: University of Chicago Press, 1935–1947
EA — El-Amarna tablets. According to the edition of Jørgen A. Knudtzon. *Die el-Amarna-Tafeln*. Leipzig: Hinrichs, 1908–1915. Repr., Aalen: Zeller, 1964. Continued in Anson F. Rainey, *El-Amarna Tablets*, 359–379. 2nd rev. ed. Kevelaer: Butzon & Bercker, 1978
ETCSL — *Electronic Text Corpus of Sumerian Literature*
Elenchus — *Elenchus Bibliographicus Biblicus of Biblica*. Rome: Biblical Institute Press, 1985–
EnchBib — *Enchiridion Biblicum*
Enc — *Encounter*
EIr — *Encyclopaedia Iranica*. Edited by Ehsan Yarshater. London: Routledge & Kegan Paul, 1982–
EIs — *Encyclopaedia Islamica*. Edited by Wilferd Madelung and Farhad Daftary. Leiden: Brill, 2008–

EQ	*Encyclopædia of the Qurʾān*. Edited by Jane Dammen McAuliffe. 6 vols. Leiden: Brill, 2001–2006
EncJud	*Encyclopedia Judaica*. Edited by Fred Skolnik and Michael Berenbaum. 2nd ed. 22 vols. Detroit: Macmillan Reference USA, 2007
EAEHL	*Encyclopedia of Archaeological Excavations in the Holy Land*. Edited by Michael Avi-Yonah. 4 vols. Jerusalem: Israel Exploration Society and Massada Press, 1975
EEC	*Encyclopedia of Early Christianity*. Edited by Everett Ferguson. 2nd ed. New York: Garland, 1997
EI²	*Encyclopedia of Islam*. Edited by Clifford E. Bosworth et al. 2nd ed. 12 vols. Leiden: Brill, 1954–2005
EI³	*Encyclopedia of Islam Three*. Edited by Marc Gaborieau et al. 3rd ed. Leiden: Brill, 2007–
EJIW	*Encyclopedia of Jews in the Islamic World*. Edited by Norman A. Stillman. 5 vols. Leiden: Brill, 2010
EJud	*The Encyclopedia of Judaism*. Edited by Jacob Neusner, Alan J. Avery-Peck, and William Scott Green. 2nd ed. 5 vols. Leiden: Brill, 2005
ER	*Encyclopedia of Religion*. Edited by Lindsay Jones. 2nd ed. 15 vols. Detroit: Macmillan Reference USA, 2005.
ERE	*Encyclopedia of Religion and Ethics*. Edited by James Hastings. 13 vols. New York: Scribner's Sons, 1908–1927. Repr., 7 vols. 1951
EBR	*Encyclopedia of the Bible and Its Reception*. Edited by Hans-Josef Klauck et al. Berlin: de Gruyter, 2009–
EDSS	*Encyclopedia of the Dead Sea Scrolls*. Edited by Lawrence H. Schiffman and James C. VanderKam. 2 vols. New York: Oxford University Press, 2000
EECh	*Encyclopedia of the Early Church*. Edited by Angelo di Berardino. Translated by Adrian Walford. New York: Oxford University Press, 1992
ETL	*Ephemerides Theologicae Lovanienses*
EEA	*L'epigrafia ebraica antica*. Sabatino Moscati. Rome: Pontifical Biblical Institute, 1951
Epiph	*Epiphany*
ERAS	*Epithètes royales akkadiennes et sumériennes*. M.-J. Seux. Paris: Letouzey et Ané, 1967
ErJb	*Eranos-Jahrbuch*
ErIsr	*Eretz-Israel*
ETS	Erfurter theologische Studien
EdF	Erträge der Forschung
EstAg	*Estudio Agustiniano*
EstBib	*Estudios bíblicos*
EFN	Estudios de filología neotestamentaria
EstEcl	*Estudios eclesiásticos*
EstMin	*Estudios mindonienses*

EstTeo	*Estudios teológicos*
EBib	*Etudes bibliques*
EPap	*Etudes de papyrologie*
EM	Etudes musulmanes
EPRO	Etudes préliminaires aux religions orientales dans l'empire romain
ETR	*Etudes théologiques et religieuses*
EuroJTh	*European Journal of Theology*
EvJ	*Evangelical Journal*
EvQ	*Evangelical Quarterly*
EvK	Evangelische Kommentare
EvT	*Evangelische Theologie*
EKL	*Evangelisches Kirchenlexikon*. Edited by Erwin Fahlbusch et al. 4 vols. 3rd ed. Göttingen: Vandenhoeck & Ruprecht, 1985–1996
EKKNT	Evangelisch-katholischer Kommentar zum Neuen Testament
ELKZ	*Evangelisch-Lutherische Kirchenzeitung*
ExAud	*Ex Auditu*
Exeg	*Exegetica* [Japanese]
EDNT	*Exegetical Dictionary of the New Testament*. Edited by Horst Balz and Gerhard Schneider. ET. 3 vols. Grand Rapids: Eerdmans, 1990–1993
EHAT	Exegetisches Handbuch zum Alten Testament
Expedition	*Expedition: Bulletin of the University Muesum of the University of Pennsylvania*
EANEC	*Explorations in Ancient Near Eastern Civilizations*
ExpTim	*Expository Times*
FBBS	Facet Books, Biblical Series
FC	Fathers of the Church
FCB	Feminist Companion to the Bible
FCNTECW	Feminist Companion to the New Testament and Early Christian Writings
FJTC	Flavius Josephus: Translation and Commentary
FoiVie	*Foi et vie*
FO	*Folia Orientalia*
FT	*Folia Theologica*
FSBP	Fontes et Subsidia ad Bibliam Pertinentes
FIOTL	Formation and Interpretation of Old Testament Literature
FCIW	Formation of the Classical Islamic World
FOTL	Forms of the Old Testament Literature
FB	Forschung zur Bibel
FiE	*Forschungen in Ephesos*
FuB	Forschungen und Berichte
FF	*Forschungen und Fortschritte*
FARG	Forschungen zur Anthropologie und Religionsgeschichte
FAT	Forschungen zum Alten Testament

FRLANT	Forschungen zur Religion und Literatur des Alten und Neuen Testaments
ForFasc	*Forum Fascicles*
FBE	Forum for Bibelsk Eksegese
Foster, *Muses*	Foster, Benjamin R. *Before the Muses: An Anthology of Akkadian Literature*. 3rd ed. 2 vols. Bethesda, MD: CDL, 2005
FF	Foundations and Facets
FGH	*Die Fragmente der griechischen Historiker*. Edited by Felix Jacoby. Leiden: Brill, 1954–1964
FHG	Fragmenta Historicorum Graecorum. Paris, 1841–1870
Fran	*Franciscanum*
FAOS	Freiburger altorientalische Studien
FZPhTh	*Freiburger Zeitschrift für Philosophie und Theologie*
FMSt	Frühmittelalterliche Studien
Fund	*Fundamentum*
GTR	Gender, Theory, and Religion
GTTOT	*The Geographical and Topographical Texts of the Old Testament*. Edited by Jan Josef Simons. Leiden: Brill, 1959
GP	*Géographie de la Palestine*. Félix-Marie Abel. 2 vols. Paris, 1933
GTT	*Gereformeerd theologisch tijdschrift*
GS	*Gesammelte Studien*
GKC	*Gesenius' Hebrew Grammar*. Edited by Emil Kautzsch. Translated by Arther E. Cowley. 2nd ed. Oxford: Clarendon, 1910
GPBS	Global Perspectives on Biblical Scholarship
Gn	*Gnomon*
GNS	*Good News Studies*
GAAL	Göttinger Arbeitshefte zur altorientalischen Literatur
GTA	Göttinger theologischer Arbeiten
GHL	*A Grammar of the Hittite Language*. Harry A. Hoffner Jr., and H. Craig Melchert. 2 vols. Winona Lake, IN: Eisenbrauns, 2008
GCDS	*Graphic Concordance to the Dead Sea Scrolls*. Edited by James H. Charlesworth et al. Tübingen: Mohr Siebeck; Louisville: Westminster John Knox, 1991
GR	*Greece and Rome*
GELS	*A Greek-English Lexicon of the Septuagint*. Takamitsu Muraoka. Leuven: Peeters, 2009
GOTR	*Greek Orthodox Theological Review*
GRBS	*Greek, Roman, and Byzantine Studies*
Greg	*Gregorianum*
GCS	Die griechischen christlichen Schriftsteller der ersten [drei] Jahrhunderte
GAG	*Grundriss der akkadischen Grammatik*. Wolfram von Soden. 2nd ed. Rome: Pontifical Biblical Institute, 1969
GVG	*Grundriss der vergleichenden Grammatik der semitischen Sprachen*. Carl

	Brockelmann, 2 vols. Berlin: Reuther & Reichard; New York: Lemcke & Buechne, 1908–1913. Repr., Hildesheim: Olms, 1961
GAT	Grundrisse zum Alten Testament
GNT	Grundrisse zum Neuen Testament
GBS	Guides to Biblical Scholarship
GMTR	Guides to the Mesopotamian Textual Record
HdA	Handbuch der Archäologie
HKL	*Handbuch der Keilschriftliteratur*. Rykle Borger. 3 vols. Berlin: de Gruyter, 1967–1975
NE	*Handbuch der nordsemitischen Epigraphik*. Edited by Mark Lidzbarski. Weimar: Felber, 1898. Repr., Hildesheim: Olms, 1962
HdO	Handbuch der Orientalistik
HAT	Handbuch zum Alten Testament
HNT	Handbuch zum Neuen Testament
HKAT	Handkommentar zum Alten Testament
HKNT	Handkommentar zum Neuen Testament
HBD	*HarperCollins Bible Dictionary*. Edited by Mark Allan Powell et al. 3rd ed. San Francisco: HarperOne, 2011
HBC	*Harper's Bible Commentary*. Edited by James L. Mays et al. San Francisco: Harper & Row, 1988
HNTC	Harper's New Testament Commentaries
Harris	Harris, Zelig S. *A Grammar of the Phoenician Language*. New Haven: American Oriental Society, 1936. Repr., 1990
HDR	Harvard Dissertations in Religion
HSM	Harvard Semitic Monographs
HSS	Harvard Semitic Studies
HSCP	*Harvard Studies in Classical Philology*
HTR	*Harvard Theological Review*
HTS	Harvard Theological Studies
HRCS	Hatch, Edwin, and Henry A. Redpath. *Concordance to the Septuagint and Other Greek Versions of the Old Testament*. 2 vols. Oxford: Clarendon, 1897. 2nd ed. Grand Rapids: Baker, 1998
HAL	*Hebräisches und aramäisches Lexikon zum Alten Testament*. Ludwig Koehler, Walter Baumgartner, and Johann J. Stamm. 3rd ed. Leiden: Brill, 1995, 2004
HALOT	*The Hebrew and Aramaic Lexicon of the Old Testament*. Ludwig Koehler, Walter Baumgartner, and Johann J. Stamm. Translated and edited under the supervision of Mervyn E. J. Richardson. 4 vols. Leiden: Brill, 1994–1999
HAR	*Hebrew Annual Review*
HBAI	Hebrew Bible and Ancient Israel
HBCE	The Hebrew Bible: A Critical Edition
HS	*Hebrew Studies*
HUCA	*Hebrew Union College Annual*

HSAO	Heidelberger Studien zum Alten Orient
HSAT	*Die Heilige Schrift des Alten Testaments*. Edited by Emil Kautzsch and Alfred Bertholet. 4th ed. Tübingen: Mohr Siebeck, 1922–1923
Hell	*Hellenica: Recueil d'épigraphie, de numismatique et d'antiquités grecques*
HCS	Hellenistic Culture and Society
Hen	*Henoch*
HThKAT	Herders Theologischer Kommentar zum Alten Testament
HThKNT	Herders Theologischer Kommentar zum Neuen Testament
Herm	*Hermanthena*
HUT	Hermeneutische Untersuchungen zur Theologie
HvTSt	*Hervormde teologiese studies*
Hesperia	*Hesperia: Journal of the American School of Classical Studies at Athens*
Hethitica	*Hethitica*
HZL	*Hethitisches Zeichenlexikon: Inventar und Interpretation der Keilschriftzeichen aus den Bogazköy-Texten*. Christel Rüster and Erich Neu. Wiesbaden: Harrassowitz, 1989
HPMM	Hethitologie Portal Mainz–Materialien
HeyJ	*Heythrop Journal*
HibJ	*Hibbert Journal*
HTB	Histoire du texte biblique. Lausanne, 1996–
Historia	*Historia: Zeitschrift für alte Geschichte*
HCOT	Historical Commentary on the Old Testament
HistTh	*History and Theory*
HACL	History, Archaeology, and Culture of the Levant
HHBS	History of Biblical Studies
CMR	History of Christian-Muslim Relations
HANE/M	History of the Ancient Near East/Monographs
HR	*History of Religions*
HT	*History Today*
CHD	*The Hittite Dictionary of the Oriental Institute of the University of Chicago*. Edited by Hans G. Güterbock, Harry A. Hoffner Jr., and Theo P. J. van den Hout. Chicago: The Oriental Institute of the University of Chicago, 1980–
HED	*Hittite Etymological Dictionary*. Jaan Puhvel. Berlin: Mouton, 1984–
HTh	*Ho Theológos*
Hok	*Hokhma*
HolBD	*Holman Bible Dictionary*. Edited by Trent C. Butler. Nashville: Holman Bible Publishers, 1991
HSem	*Horae semiticae*. Margaret Dunlop Gibson et al. 9 vols. London: Clay; Cambridge: Cambridge University Press, 1903–1916
Hor	*Horizons*
HBT	*Horizons in Biblical Theology*
Hug	*Hugoye: Journal of Syriac Studies*
Imm	*Immanuel*

IDS	*In die Skriflig*
IJT	*Indian Journal of Theology*
ISBL	Indiana Studies in Biblical Literature
IF	*Indogermanische Forschungen*
ICUR	*Inscriptiones christianae urbis Romae*. Edited by Giovanni B. de Rossi. Rome: Officina Libraria Pontificia, 1857–1888
IG	*Inscriptiones Graecae. Editio Minor*. Berlin: de Gruyter, 1924–
ILCV	*Inscriptiones Latinae Christianae Veteres*. Edited by Ernst Diehl. 2nd ed. Berlin: Druckerei Hildebrand, 1961
IEQ	*Integrated Encyclopedia of the Qurʾān*. Edited by Muzaffar Iqbal et al. Sherwood Park, AB: Center for Islamic Sciences, 2013–
ICAANE	International Congress on the Archaeology of the Ancient Near East
ICC	International Critical Commentary
IESS	*International Encyclopedia of the Social Sciences*. Edited by David L. Sills and Robert K. Merton. New York: Macmillan, 1968–
IECOT	International Exegetical Commentary on the Old Testament
IGNTP	International Greek New Testament Project
IJMES	*International Journal of Middle East Studies*
ISBE	*International Standard Bible Encyclopedia*. Edited by Geoffrey W. Bromiley. 4 vols. Grand Rapids: Eerdmans, 1979–1988
ITC	International Theological Commentary
IVBS	International Voices in Biblical Studies
IKaZ	*Internationale katholische Zeitschrift*
IKZ	*Internationale kirchliche Zeitschrift*
IZBG	*Internationale Zeitschriftenschau für Bibelwissenschaft und Grenzgebiete*
IATG^3	*Internationales Abkürzungsverzeichnis für Theologie und Grenzgebiete*. Siegfried M. Schwertner. 3rd ed. Berlin: de Gruyter, 2014
Int	*Interpretation*
IBC	Interpretation: A Bible Commentary for Teaching and Preaching
IB	*Interpreter's Bible*. Edited by George A. Buttrick et al. 12 vols. New York: Abingdon, 1951–1957
IDB	*The Interpreter's Dictionary of the Bible*. Edited by George A. Buttrick. 4 vols. New York: Abingdon, 1962
IDBSup	*Interpreter's Dictionary of the Bible: Supplementary Volume*. Edited by Keith Crim. Nashville: Abingdon, 1976
IBHS	*An Introduction to Biblical Hebrew Syntax*. Bruce K. Waltke and Michael O'Connor. Winona Lake, IN: Eisenbrauns, 1990
Iran	*Iran: Journal of the British Institute of Persian Studies*
IrAnt	*Iranica Antiqua*
Iraq	*Iraq*
IAR	Iraq Archaeological Reports
Irén	*Irénikon*
IBS	*Irish Biblical Studies*
ITQ	*Irish Theological Quarterly*

Isd	*Isidorianum*
ICMR	*Islam and Christian-Muslim Relations*
IHC	Islamic History and Civilization: Studies and Texts
ILS	*Islamic Law and Society*
IPTS	Islamic Philosophy, Theology, and Science: Studies and Texts
IQ	*Islamic Quarterly*
IS	*Islamic Studies*
IU	Islamkundliche Untersuchungen
IHS	Ismaili Heritage Studies
ITT	Ismaili Texts and Translations
IEJ	*Israel Exploration Journal*
INJ	*Israel Numismatic Journal*
IOS	*Israel Oriental Studies*
IPN	*Die israelitischen Personennamen*. Martin Noth. Stuttgart: Kohlhammer, 1928. Repr., Hildesheim: Olms, 1980
IRT	Issues in Religion and Theology
IstMitt	*Istanbuler Mitteilungen*
Istina	*Istina*
Itala	*Itala: Das Neue Testament in altlateinischer Überlieferung*. Adolf Jülicher, Walter Matzkow, and Kurt Aland. 4 vols. Berlin: de Gruyter, 1938–1963
Iter	*Iter*
Itin (Portugal)	*Itinerarium* (Portugal)
Itin (Italy)	*Itinerarium* (Italy)
JEOL	*Jaarbericht van het Vooraziatisch-Egyptisch Gezelschap (Genootschap) Ex oriente lux*
Jahnow	Jahnow, Hedwig. *Das hebräische Leichenlied im Rahmen der Völkerdichtung*. Giessen: Töpelmann, 1923
JdI	*Jahrbuch des deutschen archäologischen Instituts*
JAC	*Jahrbuch für Antike und Christentum*
JDT	*Jahrbuch für deutsche Theologie*
JET	*Jahrbuch für Evangelische Theologie*
JÖAI	*Jahreshefte des Österreichischen archäologischen Instituts*
Jeev	*Jeevadhara*
JBC	*Jerome Biblical Commentary*. Edited by Raymond E. Brown et al. Englewood Cliffs, NJ: Prentice-Hall, 1968
JB	Jerusalem Bible
JBS	Jerusalem Biblical Studies
JSAI	*Jerusalem Studies in Arabic and Islam*
JAL	Jewish Apocryphal Literature Series
JBQ	*Jewish Bible Quarterly*
JE	*The Jewish Encyclopedia*. Edited by Isidore Singer. 12 vols. New York: Funk & Wagnalls, 1925
JLA	*Jewish Law Annual*

JQR	*Jewish Quarterly Review*
JQRMS	Jewish Quarterly Review Monograph Series
JSQ	*Jewish Studies Quarterly*
JWSTP	*Jewish Writings of the Second Temple Period: Apocrypha, Pseudepigrapha, Qumran Sectarian Writings, Philo, Josephus*. Edited by Michael E. Stone. Assen: Van Gorcum: Philadelphia Fortress, 1984
Jian Dao	*Jian Dao*
JHNES	*The Johns Hopkins Near Eastern Studies*
JLCRS	Jordan Lectures in Comparative Religion Series
JJT	*Josephinum Journal of Theology*
Joüon	Joüon, Paul. *A Grammar of Biblical Hebrew*. Translated and revised by T. Muraoka. 2 vols. Rome: Pontifical Biblical Institute, 1991
JA	*Journal Asiatique*
JSSR	*Journal for the Scientific Study of Religion*
JSJ	*Journal for the Study of Judaism in the Persian, Hellenistic, and Roman Periods*
JSNT	*Journal for the Study of the New Testament*
JSNTSup	Journal for the Study of the New Testament Supplement Series
JSOT	*Journal for the Study of the Old Testament*
JSOTSup	Journal for the Study of the Old Testament Supplement Series
JSP	*Journal for the Study of the Pseudepigrapha*
JSPSup	Journal for the Study of the Pseudepigrapha Supplement Series
JTISup	Journal for Theological Interpretation, Supplements
JTC	*Journal for Theology and the Church*
JAAL	*Journal of Afroasiatic Languages*
ZAC	*Journal of Ancient Christianity/Zeitschrift für Antikes Christentum*
JACiv	*Journal of Ancient Civilizations*
JANER	*Journal of Ancient Near Eastern Religions*
JArSt	*Journal of Arabian Studies*
JAIS	*Journal of Arabic and Islamic Studies*
JAL	*Journal of Arabic Literature*
JAS	*Journal of Asian Studies*
JBR	*Journal of Bible and Religion*
JBL	*Journal of Biblical Literature*
JCTR	*Journal of Christian Theological Research*
JCoptS	*Journal of Coptic Studies*
JCS	*Journal of Cuneiform Studies*
JECS	*Journal of Early Christian Studies*
JEH	*Journal of Ecclesiastical History*
JES	*Journal of Ecumenical Studies*
JEA	*Journal of Egyptian Archaeology*
JFSR	*Journal of Feminist Studies in Religion*
JFA	*Journal of Field Archaeology*
JGRChJ	*Journal of Greco-Roman Christianity and Judaism*

JHebS	*Journal of Hebrew Scriptures*
JHS	*Journal of Hellenic Studies*
JIES	*Journal of Indo-European Studies*
JIS	*Journal of Islamic Studies*
JJA	*Journal of Jewish Art*
JJS	*Journal of Jewish Studies*
JJP	*Journal of Juristic Papyrology*
JMedHist	*Journal of Medieval History*
JMES	*Journal of Middle Eastern Studies*
JMS	*Journal of Mithraic Studies*
JNES	*Journal of Near Eastern Studies*
JNSL	*Journal of Northwest Semitic Languages*
JPJ	*Journal of Progressive Judaism*
JQS	*Journal of Qur'anic Studies*
JR	*Journal of Religion*
JRE	*Journal of Religious Ethics*
JRH	*Journal of Religious History*
JRelS	*Journal of Religious Studies*
JRT	*Journal of Religious Thought*
JRitSt	*Journal of Ritual Studies*
JRA	*Journal of Roman Archaeology*
JRS	*Journal of Roman Studies*
JSS	*Journal of Semitic Studies*
JSem	*Journal of Semitics*
JAAR	*Journal of the American Academy of Religion*
JAARSup	Journal of the American Academy of Religion Supplements
JAOS	*Journal of the American Oriental Society*
JANESCU	*Journal of the Ancient Near Eastern Society of Columbia University*
JBRec	*Journal of the Bible and Its Reception*
JCSCS	*Journal of the Canadian Society for Coptic Studies*
JESHO	*Journal of the Economic and Social History of the Orient*
JETS	*Journal of the Evangelical Theological Society*
JHI	*Journal of the History of Ideas*
JISMOR	*Journal of the Interdisciplinary Study of Monotheistic Religions*
JPOS	*Journal of the Palestine Oriental Society*
JRAS	*Journal of the Royal Asiatic Society*
JSSEA	*Journal of the Society for the Study of Egyptian Antiquities*
JSOR	*Journal of the Society of Oriental Research*
JTS	*Journal of Theological Studies*
JTSA	*Journal of Theology for Southern Africa*
JOTT	*Journal of Translation and Textlinguistics*
Jud	*Judaica* (Buenos Aires)
Judaica	*Judaica: Beiträge zum Verständnis des jüdischen Schicksals in Vergangenheit und Gegenwart* (Zurich: Zwingli)

JudChr	Judaica et Christiana
Judaism	*Judaism*
JDS	Judean Desert Studies
JSHRZ	*Jüdische Schriften aus hellenistisch-römischer Zeit*
Kairós	*Kairós*
KI	*Kanaanäische Inschriften (Moabitisch, Althebraisch, Phonizisch, Punisch).* Edited by Mark Lidzbarski. Giessen: Töpelmann, 1907
KAI	*Kanaanäische und aramäische Inschriften.* Herbert Donner and Wolfgang Röllig. 2nd ed. Wiesbaden: Harrassowitz, 1966–1969
KK	*Katorikku Kenkyu*
K&D	Keil, Carl Friedrich, and Franz Delitzsch. *Biblical Commentary on the Old Testament.* Translated by James Martin et al. 25 vols. Edinburgh, 1857–1878. Repr., 10 vols., Peabody, MA: Hendrickson, 1996
KTU	*Die keilalphabetischen Texte aus Ugarit.* Edited by Manfried Dietrich, Oswald Loretz, and Joaquín Sanmartín. Münster: Ugarit-Verlag, 2013. 3rd enl. ed. of *KTU: The Cuneiform Alphabetic Texts from Ugarit, Ras Ibn Hani, and Other Places.* Edited by Manfried Dietrich, Oswald Loretz, and Joaquín Sanmartín. Münster: Ugarit-Verlag, 1995 (= *CTU*)
KB	*Keilinschriftliche Bibliothek.* Edited by Eberhard Schrader. 6 vols. Berlin: Reuther & Reichard, 1889–1915
KAH 1	*Keilschrifttexte aus Assur historischen Inhalts.* Leopold Messerschmidt. Vol. 1. Leipzig: Hinrichs, 1911
KAH 2	*Keilschrifttexte aus Assur historischen Inhalts.* Ootto Schroeder. Vol. 2. Leipzig: Hinrichs, 1922
KAR	*Keilschrifttexte aus Assur religiösen Inhalts.* Edited by Erich Ebeling. Leipzig: Hinrichs, 1919–1923
KBo	*Keilschrifttexte aus Boghazköi.* Leipzig: Hinrichs, 1916–1923; Berlin: Gebr. Mann, 1954–
KUB	*Keilschrifturkunden aus Boghazköi.* Berlin: Akademie, 1921–
Kerux	*Kerux*
KD	*Kerygma und Dogma*
KTAH	Key Themes in Ancient History
KS	*Kirjath-Sepher*
KlF	*Kleinasiatische Forschungen*
KlPauly	*Der kleine Pauly*
KlT	Kleine Texte
Klio	*Klio: Beiträge zur Alten Geschichte*
KBL	Koehler, Ludwig, and Walter Baumgartner. *Lexicon in Veteris Testamenti libros.* 2nd ed. Leiden, 1958
KVRG	Kölner Veroffentlichungen zur Religionsgeschichte
KAT	Kommentar zum Alten Testament
KBANT	Kommentare und Beiträge zum Alten und Neuen Testament
Konk.	*Konkordanz der hethitischen Keilschrifttafeln.* Košak, Silvin. Wiesbaden: Harrassowitz, 2005–

Ktèma	*Ktèma: Civilisations de l'Orient, de la Grèce et de Rome antiques*
KEK	Kritisch-exegetischer Kommentar über das Neue Testament (Meyer-Kommentar)
Kuhn	Kuhn, Karl G. *Konkordanz zu den Qumrantexten*. Göttingen: Vandenhoeck & Ruprecht, 1960
KHC	Kurzer Hand-Commentar zum Alten Testament
Lane	Lane, Edward W. *An Arabic-English Lexicon*. 8 vols. London: Williams & Norgate, 1863. Repr., Beirut: Libr. du Liban, 1980
LANE	*Languages of the Ancient Near East*
Laur	*Laurentianum*
LTP	*Laval théologique et philosophique*
LD	Lectio Divina
LSS	*Leipziger semitische Studien*
Leö	*Leöonénu*
Levant	*Levant*
LCI	*Lexikon der christlichen Ikonographie*. Edited by Engelbert Kirschbaum and Günter Bandmann. 8 vols. Rome: Herder, 1968–1976
LTK	*Lexicon für Theologie und Kirche*
LIMC	*Lexicon Iconographicum Mythologiae Classicae*. Edited by H. Christoph Ackerman and Jean-Robert Gisler. 8 vols. Zurich: Artemis, 1981–1997
LexSyr	*Lexicon Syriacum*. Carl Brockelmann. 2nd ed. Halle: Niemeyer, 1928
LÄ	*Lexikon der Ägyptologie*. Edited by Wolfgang Helck, Eberhard Otto, and Wolfhart Westendorf. Wiesbaden: Harrassowitz, 1972
LTQ	*Lexington Theological Quarterly*
LASBF	*Liber Annuus Studii Biblici Franciscani*
LAI	Library of Ancient Israel
LCC	Library of Christian Classics
LEC	Library of Early Christianity
LHBOTS	The Library of Hebrew Bible/Old Testament Studies
LNTS	The Library of New Testament Studies
LSTS	The Library of Second Temple Studies
LSJ	Liddell, Henry George, Robert Scott, Henry Stuart Jones. *A Greek-English Lexicon*. 9th ed. with revised supplement. Oxford: Clarendon, 1996
LSAWS	*Linguistic Studies in Ancient West Semitic*
LB	*Linguistica Biblica*
List	*Listening: Journal of Religion and Culture*
LJPSTT	Literature of the Jewish People in the Period of the Second Temple and the Talmud
LAPO	Littératures anciennes du Proche-Orient
LW	*Living Word*
LCL	Loeb Classical Library
LS	*Louvain Studies*
L&N	Louw, Johannes P., and Eugene A. Nida, eds. *Greek-English Lexicon of the*

	New Testament: Based on Semantic Domains. 2nd ed. New York: United Bible Societies, 1989
Lum	*Lumen*
LumVie	*Lumière et vie*
LUÅ	Lunds universitets årsskrift
LEH	Lust, Johan, Erik Eynikel, and Katrin Hauspie, eds. *Greek-English Lexicon of the Septuagint*. Rev. ed. Stuttgart: Deutsche Bibelgesellschaft, 2003
LQ	*Lutheran Quarterly*
LR	*Lutherische Rundschau*
Maarav	*Maarav*
MCuS	*Manchester Cuneiform Studies*
MCS	Manchester Cuneiform Studies
MARI	*Mari: Annales de recherches interdisciplinaires*
Masāq	*Al-Masāq: Journal of the Medieval Mediterranean*
MasS	Masoretic Studies
MSJ	*The Master's Seminary Journal*
MEE	Materiali epigrafici de Ebla
MSL	*Materialien zum sumerischen Lexikon/Materials for the Sumerian Lexikon. 17 vols. Rome: Pontifical Biblical Institute, 1937–2004*
MAD	Materials for the Assyrian Dictionary
McCQ	*McCormick Quarterly*
Med	*Medellin*
MS	*Mediaeval Studies*
ME	*Medieval Encounters: Jewish, Christian and Muslim Culture in Confluence and Dialogue*
MEFR	*Mélanges d'archéologie et d'histoire de l'école français de Rome*
MFOB	*Mélanges de la faculté orientale de l'Université St. Joseph de Beyrouth*
MIDEO	*Mélanges de l'institut dominicain d'études orientales du Caire*
MUSJ	*Mélanges de l'Université Saint-Joseph*
MScRel	*Mélanges de science religieuse*
MelT	*Melita Theologica*
MPAIBL	Mémoires présentés à l'Academie des inscriptions et belles-lettres
MAAR	Memoirs of the American Academy in Rome
MDB	*Mercer Dictionary of the Bible*. Edited by Watson E. Mills. Macon, GA: Mercer University Press, 1990
MC	Mesopotamian Civilizations
MZL	*Mesopotamisches Zeichenlexikon*. Rykle Borger. Münster: Ugarit-Verlag, 2003
MBS	Message of Biblical Spirituality
MTSR	*Method and Theory in the Study of Religion*
Mid-Stream	*Mid-Stream*
MilS	*Milltown Studies*
MCom	*Miscelánea Comillas*

MEAH	*Miscelánea de estudios arabes y hebraicos*
MRS	Mission de Ras Shamra
MAOG	Mitteilungen der Altorientalischen Gesellschaft
MDOG	Mitteilungen der Deutschen Orient-Gesellschaft
MVAG	Mitteilungen der Vorderasiatisch-ägyptischen Gesellschaft
MDAI	*Mitteilungen des Deutschen archäologischen Instituts*
MIOF	*Mitteilungen des Instituts für Orientforschung*
MSU	Mitteilungen des Septuaginta-Unternehmens
Mnemosyne	*Mnemosyne: A Journal of Classical Studies*
MNTC	Moffatt New Testament Commentary
MGWJ	*Monatschrift für Geschichte und Wissenschaft des Judentums*
MdB	*Le Monde de la Bible*
HUCM	Monographs of the Hebrew Union College
MAMA	*Monumenta Asiae Minoris Antiqua. Manchester and London, 1928–1993*
MBE	Monumenta Biblica et Ecclesiastica
MM	Moulton, James H., and George Milligan. *The Vocabulary of the Greek Testament*. London, 1930. Repr. Peabody, MA: Hendrickson, 1997
MBPF	Münchener Beiträge zur Papyrusforschung und antiken Rechtsgeschichte
MSS	Münchener Studien zur Sprachwissenschaft
MTZ	*Münchener theologische Zeitschrift*
MW	*Muslim World* (formerly *Moslem World*)
Musurillo	Musurillo, Herbert, ed. and trans. *The Acts of the Christian Martyrs*. Oxford: Clarendon, 1972
Mus	*Muséon: Revue d'études orientales*
MH	*Museum Helveticum*
NAWG	*Nachrichten (von) der Akademie der Wissenschaften in Göttingen*
NHC	Nag Hammadi Codices
NHL	*Nag Hammadi Library in English*. Edited by James M. Robinson. 4th rev. ed. Leiden: Brill, 1996
NHScr	*The Nag Hammadi Scriptures: The International Edition*. Edited by Marvin Meyer. New York: HarperOne, 2007
NHS	Nag Hammadi Studies
NEA	*Near Eastern Archaeology* (formerly *Biblical Archaeologist*)
NETR	*Near East School of Theology Theological Review* (Beirut)
NGTT	*Nederduitse gereformeerde teologiese tydskrif*
NedTT	*Nederlands theologisch tijdschrift*
Nem	*Nemalah*
Neot	*Neotestamentica*
NEchtB	Neue Echter Bibel
NJahrb	*Neue Jahrbücher für das klassiche Altertum (1898–1925); Neue Jahrbücher für Wissenschaft und Jugendbildung (1925–1936)*
NKZ	*Neue kirchliche Zeitschrift*
NTD	Das Neue Testament Deutsch

DNP	*Der neue Pauly: Enzyklopädie der Antike*. Edited by Hubert Cancik and Helmuth Schneider. Stuttgart: Metzler, 1996–
NSKAT	Neuer Stuttgarter Kommentar, Altes Testament
NTAbh	Neutestamentliche Abhandlungen
NTF	Neutestamentliche Forschungen
NAC	New American Commentary
NBD[3]	*New Bible Dictionary*. Edited by D. R. W. Wood, Howard Marshall, J. D. Douglas, and N. Hillyer. 3rd ed. Downers Grove, IL: InterVarsity Press, 1996
NBf	*New Blackfrairs*
NCE	*New Catholic Encyclopedia*. Edited by William J. McDonald et al. 15 vols. New York: McGraw-Hill, 1967
NCB	New Century Bible
NewDocs	*New Documents Illustrating Early Christianity*. Edited by Greg H. R. Horsley and Stephen Llewelyn. North Ryde, NSW: The Ancient History Documentary Research Centre, Macquarie University, 1981–
NEAEHL	*The New Encyclopedia of Archaeological Excavations in the Holy Land*. Edited by Ephraim Stern. 4 vols. Jerusalem: Israel Exploration Society & Carta ; New York: Simon & Schuster, 1993
NFT	New Frontiers in Theology
NIBCNT	New International Biblical Commentary on the New Testament
NIBCOT	New International Biblical Commentary on the Old Testament
NICNT	New International Commentary on the New Testament
NICOT	New International Commentary on the Old Testament
NIDBA	*New International Dictionary of Biblical Archaeology*. Edited by E. M. Blaiklock and R. K. Harrison. Grand Rapids: Zondervan, 1983
NIDNTT	*New International Dictionary of New Testament Theology*. Edited by Colin Brown. 4 vols. Grand Rapids: Zondervan, 1975–1978
NIDOTTE	*New International Dictionary of Old Testament Theology and Exegesis*. Edited by Willem A. VanGemeren. 5 vols. Grand Rapids: Zondervan, 1997
NIGTC	New International Greek Testament Commentary
NIB	*The New Interpreter's Bible*. Edited by Leander E. Keck. 12 vols. Nashville: Abingdon, 1994–2004
NIDB	*New Interpreter's Dictionary of the Bible*. Edited by Katharine Doob Sakenfeld. 5 vols. Nashville: Abingdon, 2006–2009
NJBC	*The New Jerome Biblical Commentary*. Edited by Raymond E. Brown et al. Englewood Cliffs, NJ: Prentice-Hall, 1990
NTA	*New Testament Abstracts*
NTSI	New Testament and the Scriptures of Israel
NTApoc	*New Testament Apocrypha*. 2 vols. Revised ed. Edited by Wilhelm Schneemelcher. English trans. ed. Robert McL. Wilson. Cambridge: Clarke; Louisville: Westminster John Knox, 2003
NTG	New Testament Guides

NTGF	New Testament in the Greek Fathers
NTL	New Testament Library
NTM	New Testament Message
NTS	*New Testament Studies*
NTTS	New Testament Tools and Studies
NTTSD	New Testament Tools, Studies, and Documents
NPNF^1	*Nicene and Post-Nicene Fathers*, Series 1
NPNF^2	*Nicene and Post-Nicene Fathers*, Series 2
TDNTW	*The NIV Theological Dictionary of New Testament Words*. Edited by Verlyn D. Verbrugge. Grand Rapids: Zondervan, 2000
NTT	*Norsk Teologisk Tidsskrift*
Notes	*Notes on Translation*
NRTh	*La nouvelle revue théologique*
NABU	*Nouvelles assyriologiques brèves et utilitaires*
NV	*Nova et Vetera*
NovT	*Novum Testamentum*
NTOA	Novum Testamentum et Orbis Antiquus
NuMu	*Nuevo mundo*
Numen	*Numen: International Review for the History of Religions*
NumC	*Numismatic Chronicle*
ÖTK	Ökumenischer Taschenbuch-Kommentar
OTA	*Old Testament Abstracts*
OTE	*Old Testament Essays*
OTG	Old Testament Guides
OTL	Old Testament Library
OTP	*Old Testament Pseudepigrapha*. Edited by James H. Charlesworth. 2 vols. New York: Doubleday, 1983, 1985
OTM	Old Testament Message
OTR	Old Testament Readings
OTS	Old Testament Studies
OiC	*One in Christ*
OBO	Orbis Biblicus et Orientalis
OBO.SA	Orbis Biblicus et Orientalis, Series Archaeologica
OrAnt	*Oriens Antiquus*
OrChr	*Oriens Christianus*
OeO	Oriens et Occidens
OrSyr	*L'orient syrien*
OIC	*Oriental Institute Communications*
OIMP	Oriental Institute Museum Publications
OIP	Oriental Institute Publications
OIS	Oriental Institute Seminars
OrChrAn	Orientalia Christiana Analecta
OCP	*Orientalia Christiana Periodica*
OLA	Orientalia Lovaniensia Analecta

OLP	Orientalia Lovaniensia Periodica
Or	*Orientalia* (NS)
OLZ	*Orientalistische Literaturzeitung*
OrA	Orient-Archäologie
Orient	*Orient: Report of the Society for Near Eastern Studies in Japan*
OAC	Orientis Antiqui Collectio
OGIS	*Orientis Graeci Inscriptiones Selectae*. Edited by Wilhelm Dittenberger. 2 vols. Leipzig: Hirzel, 1903–1905
Orita	*Orita*
ÖBS	Österreichische biblische Studien
OtSt	*Oudtestamentische Studiën*
OBT	Overtures to Biblical Theology
OCD	*Oxford Classical Dictionary*. Edited by Simon Hornblower and Antony Spawforth. 4th ed. Oxford: Oxford University Press, 2012
OCM	Oxford Classical Monographs
OCT	Oxford Classical Texts / Scriptorum classicorum bibliotheca oxoniensis
ODCC	*The Oxford Dictionary of the Christian Church*. Edited by Frank L. Cross and Elizabeth A. Livingstone. 3rd ed. rev. Oxford: Oxford University Press, 2005
OECS	Oxford Early Christian Studies
OECT	Oxford Early Christian Texts
OCuT	Oxford Editions of Cuneiform Texts
OEAE	*The Oxford Encyclopedia of Ancient Egypt*. Edited by Donald Redford. 3 vols. Oxford: Oxford University Press, 2001
OEANE	*The Oxford Encyclopedia of Archaeology in the Near East*. Edited by Eric M. Meyers. 5 vols. New York: Oxford University Press, 1997
OJA	*Oxford Journal of Archaeology*
OSHT	Oxford Studies in Historical Theology
Pacifica	Pacifica
Palamedes	*Palamedes: A Journal of Ancient History*
PRU	*Le palais royal d'Ugarit*
PJ	*Palästina-Jahrbuch*
PEFQS	Palestine Exploration Fund Quarterly Statement
PEQ	*Palestine Exploration Quarterly*
PDM	*Papyri Demoticae Magicae*. Demotic texts in PGM corpus as collated in Hans Dieter Betz, ed. *The Greek Magical Papyri in Translation, including the Demotic Spells*. Chicago: University of Chicago Press, 1996
PGM	*Papyri Graecae Magicae: Die griechischen Zauberpapyri*. Edited by Karl Preisendanz. 2nd ed. Stuttgart: Teubner, 1973–1974
PapyCast	*Papyrologica Castroctaviana, Studia et Textus*
Parab	*Parabola*
ParOr	*Parole de l'orient*
PaVi	*Parole di vita*

PGL	*Patristic Greek Lexicon*. Edited by Geoffrey W. H. Lampe. Oxford: Clarendon, 1961
PTS	Patristische Texte und Studien
PG	Patrologia Graeca [= *Patrologiae Cursus Completus*: Series Graeca]. Edited by Jacques-Paul Migne. 162 vols. Paris, 1857–1886
PL	Patrologia Latina [= *Patrologiae Cursus Completus*: Series Latina]. Edited by Jacques-Paul Migne. 217 vols. Paris, 1844–1864
PO	Patrologia Orientalis
PS	*Patrologia Syriaca*. Rev. ed. Ignatio Ortiz de Urbina. Rome: Pontifical Biblical Institute, 1965
PW	*Paulys Real-Encyclopädie der classischen Altertumswissenschaft*. New edition by Georg Wissowa and Wilhelm Kroll. 50 vols. in 84 parts. Stuttgart: Metzler and Druckenmüller, 1894–1980
PNTC	Pelican New Testament Commentaries
PSTJ	*Perkins (School of Theology) Journal*
PerTeol	*Perspectiva teológica*
Per	*Perspectives*
PRSt	*Perspectives in Religious Studies*
PHSC	Perspectives on Hebrew Scriptures and Its Contexts
Phasis	*Phasis, Greek and Roman Studies*
PACS	Philo of Alexandria Commentary Series
Phil	*Philologus*
PhA	Philosophia Antiqua
Phon	*Phonetica*
PTMS	Pittsburgh Theological Monograph Series
Pneuma	*Pneuma: Journal for the Society of Pentecostal Studies*
PLO	Porta Linguarum Orientalium
POuT	De Prediking van het Oude Testament
Presb	*Presbyterion*
PSB	*Princeton Seminary Bulletin*
PTSDSSP	Princeton Theological Seminary Dead Sea Scrolls Project
ProEccl	*Pro Ecclesia*
PAAJR	*Proceedings of the American Academy of Jewish Research*
PIBA	Proceedings of the Irish Biblical Association
PIASH	Proceedings of the Israel Academy of Sciences and Humanities
Proof	*Prooftexts: A Journal of Jewish Literary History*
PAe	Probleme der Ägyptologie
PMLA	*Proceedings of the Modern Language Association*
Protest	*Protestantesimo*
PzB	*Protokolle zur Bibel*
Proy	*Proyección*
PVTG	Pseudepigrapha Veteris Testamenti Graece
PIHANS	Publications de l'Institut historique-archéologique néerlandais de Stamboul

Qad	*Qadmoniot*
Qanṭara	*Al-Qanṭara: Revista de estudios árabes*
QD	Quaestiones Disputatae
QDAP	*Quarterly of the Department of Antiquities in Palestine*
QR	*Quarterly Review*
Quasten	Quasten, Johannes *Patrology*. 4 vols. Westminster, MD: Newman, 1953–1986
QC	*Qumran Chronicle*
RS	Ras Shamra
RSP	*Ras Shamra Parallels*
RdT	*Rassegna di teologia*
RE	*Realencyklopädie für protestantische Theologie und Kirche*
RÄR	*Reallexikon der ägyptischen Religionsgeschichte*. Hans Bonnet. Berlin: de Gruyter, 1952
RlA	*Reallexikon der Assyriologie*. Edited by Erich Ebeling et al. Berlin: de Gruyter, 1928–
RLV	*Reallexikon der Vorgeschichte*. Edited by Max Ebert. Berlin: de Gruyter, 1924–1932
RAC	*Reallexikon für Antike und Christentum*. Edited by Theodor Klauser et al. Stuttgart: Hiersemann, 1950–
RBK	*Reallexikon zur byzantinischen Kunst*. Edited by Klaus Wessel and Marcell Restle. Stuttgart: Hiersemann, 1966–
RechBib	Recherches bibliques
RechPap	*Recherches de papyrologie*
RSR	*Recherches de science religieuse*
RTAM	*Recherches de théologie ancienne et médiévale*
RANE	Records of the Ancient Near East
RefLitM	*Reformed Liturgy and Music*
RefR	*Reformed Review*
RTR	*Reformed Theological Review*
RNT	Regensburger Neues Testament
RST	Regensburger Studien zur Theologie
RelSoc	*Religion and Society*
RelArts	Religion and the Arts
R&T	*Religion and Theology*
RC	*Religion Compass*
RGG	*Religion in Geschichte und Gegenwart*. Edited by Hans Dieter Betz. 4th ed. Tübingen: Mohr Siebeck, 1998–2007
RPP	*Religion Past and Present: Encyclopedia of Theology and Religion*. Edited by Hans Dieter Betz et al. 14 vols. Leiden: Brill, 2007–2013
RGRW	Religions in the Graeco-Roman World
RVV	Religionsgeschichtliche Versuche und Vorarbeiten
RelEd	*Religious Education*
RelS	*Religious Studies*

RelStTh	*Religious Studies and Theology*
RelSRev	*Religious Studies Review*
RAI	Rencontre assyriologique internationale
RES	*Répertoire d'épigraphie sémitique*
RGTC	Répertoire géographique des textes cunéiformes
ResOr	Res Orientales
RBS	Resources for Biblical Study
RAIS	Resources in Arabic and Islamic Studies
ResQ	*Restoration Quarterly*
RevExp	*Review and Expositor*
RBL	*Review of Biblical Literature*
RR	*Review of Religion*
RRelRes	*Review of Religious Research*
RevistB	*Revista bíblica*
RBB	*Revista biblica brasileira*
RCT	*Revista catalana de teología*
RCB	*Revista de cultura bíblica*
RIBLA	*Revista de interpretación bíblica latino-americana*
REB	*Revista eclesiástica brasileira*
RET	*Revista española de teología*
RAr	*Revue archéologique*
RBPH	*Revue belge de philologie et d'histoire*
RBén	*Revue bénédictine*
RB	*Revue biblique*
RA	*Revue d'assyriologie et d'archéologie orientale*
REg	*Revue d'égyptologie*
RHE	*Revue d'histoire ecclésiastique*
RHPR	*Revue d'histoire et de philosophie religieuses*
RHR	*Revue de l'histoire des religions*
RUO	*Revue de l'université d'Ottawa*
RevPhil	*Revue de philologie*
RevQ	*Revue de Qumran*
RSém	*Revue de sémitique*
RTP	*Revue de théologie et de philosophie*
REA	*Revue des études anciennes*
REAug	*Revue des études augustiniennes*
REG	*Revue des études grecques*
REI	*Revue des études islamiques*
REJ	*Revue des études juives*
RES	Revue des études sémitiques
RSPT	*Revue des sciences philosophiques et théologiques*
RevScRel	*Revue des sciences religieuses*
RHA	*Revue hittite et asianique*
RIDA	*Revue internationale des droits de l'antiquité*

RRef	*La revue réformée*
RTL	*Revue théologique de Louvain*
RThom	*Revue thomiste*
RStB	*Ricerche storico bibliche*
RivB	*Rivista biblica italiana*
RSO	*Rivista degli studi orientali*
RivSR	*Rivista di scienze religiose*
RSC	*Rivista di studi classici*
RSF	*Rivista di studi fenici*
RocT	*Roczniki teologiczne*
RomBarb	*Romanobarbarica*
RQ	*Römische Quartalschrift für christliche Altertumskunde und Kirchengeschichte*
RoMo	Rowohlts Monographien
RIMA	The Royal Inscriptions of Mesopotamia, Assyrian Periods
RIMB	The Royal Inscriptions of Mesopotamia, Babylonian Periods
RIME	The Royal Inscriptions of Mesopotamia, Early Periods
RIM	The Royal Inscriptions of Mesopotamia Project. Toronto
RIMS	The Royal Inscriptions of Mesopotamia Supplements
RISA	*Royal Inscriptions of Sumer and Akkad*. Edited by George A. Barton. New Haven: Yale University Press, 1929
RINAP	Royal Inscriptions of the Neo-Assyrian Period
LSB	La Sacra Bibbia
SP	Sacra Pagina
SacEr	*Sacris erudiri: Jaarboek voor Godsdienstwetenschappen*
Salm	*Salmanticensis*
SB	*Sammelbuch griechischer Urkunden aus Aegypten*. Edited by Friedrich Preisigke et al. Vols. 1–21. Wiesbaden: Harrassowitz, 1915–2002
SAQ	Sammlung ausgewählter Kirchen- und dogmen-geschichtlicher Quellenschriften
Sap	*Sapienza*
SJOT	*Scandinavian Journal of the Old Testament*
Schol	*Scholastik*
SQAW	Schriften und Quellen der alten Welt
SThU	*Schweizerische theologische Umschau*
SThZ	*Schweizerische theologische Zeitschrift*
ScEs	*Science et esprit*
ScEccl	*Sciences ecclésiastiques*
SJT	*Scottish Journal of Theology*
SFulg	*Scripta fulgentina*
ScrHier	Scripta Hierosolymitana
ScrTh	*Scripta Theologica*
ScrVict	*Scriptorium Victoriense*
Scr	*Scripture*

ScrB	*Scripture Bulletin*
ScrC	*Scripture in Church*
ScC	*La scuola cattolica*
SecCent	*Second Century*
Sef	*Sefarad*
Semeia	*Semeia*
SemeiaSt	Semeia Studies
SemeiaSup	Semeia Supplements
SSS	Semitic Study Series
Sem	*Semitica*
SCS	Septuagint and Cognate Studies
SMBen	Série monographique de Benedictina: Section paulinienne
STRev	*Sewanee Theological Review*
Shofar	*Shofar*
SIDIC	*SIDIC (Journal of the Service internationale de documentation judeo-chrétienne)*
SDAW	Sitzungen der deutschen Akademie der Wissenschaften zu Berlin
SHAW	Sitzungen der heidelberger Akademie der Wissenschaften
SÖAW	Sitzungen der österreichischen Akademie der Wissenschaften in Wien
SBAW	Sitzungsberichte der bayerischen Akademie der Wissenschaften
SPAW	Sitzungsberichte der preussischen Akademie der Wissenschaften
SK	*Skrif en kerk*
SHBC	Smyth & Helwys Bible Commentary
Sobornost	*Sobornost*
SWBA	Social World of Biblical Antiquity
SNTSMS	Society for New Testament Studies Monograph Series
SOTSMS	Society for Old Testament Studies Monograph Series
SBL	Society of Biblical Literature
SBLHS	*Society of Biblical Literature Handbook of Style*. 2nd ed. Atlanta, GA: SBL Press, 2014
SBLBAC	Society of Biblical Literature The Bible and American Culture
SBLCS	Society of Biblical Literature Commentary on the Septuagint
SBLDS	Society of Biblical Literature Dissertation Series
SBLMS	Society of Biblical Literature Monograph Series
SBLSP	Society of Biblical Literature Seminar Papers
SBLSBS	Society of Biblical Literature Sources for Biblical Study
SBLStBL	Society of Biblical Literature Studies in Biblical Literature
SBLTT	Society of Biblical Literature Texts and Translations
Sound	*Soundings*
SB	Sources bibliques
SC	Sources chrétiennes. Paris: Cerf, 1943–
SANE	Sources of the Ancient Near East
SFSHJ	South Florida Studies in the History of Judaism
SwJT	*Southwestern Journal of Theology*

Spec	*Speculum*
SSL	Spicilegium sacrum Lovaniense: Études et documents
SLJT	*St. Luke's Journal of Theology*
SVTQ	*St. Vladimir's Theological Quarterly*
SAA	State Archives of Assyria
SAAB	*State Archives of Assyria Bulletin*
SAACT	State Archives of Assyria Cuneiform Texts
SAALT	State Archives of Assyria Literary Texts
SAAS	State Archives of Assyria Studies
StZ	Stimmen der Zeit
SVF	*Stoicorum Veterum Fragmenta*. Hans Friedrich August von Arnim. 4 vols. Leipzig: Teubne, 1903–1924
Str-B	Strack, Hermann Leberecht and Paul Billerbeck. *Kommentar zum Neuen Testament aus Talmud und Midrasch*. 6 vols. Munich: Beck, 1922–1961
Str	*Stromata*
SCO	Studi classici e orientali
SMSR	*Studi e materiali di storia delle religioni*
SEVO	Studi egei e vicinorientali
SEL	*Studi epigrafici e linguistici sul Vicino Oriente antico*
SMEA	*Studi Micenei ed Egeo-Anatolici*
StSem	Studi semitici
StudStor	*Studi storici: Rivista trimestrale dell'Istituto Gramsci*
SCHNT	Studia ad Corpus Hellenisticum Novi Testamenti
SOA	Studia ad Orientem Antiquum
SAeg	*Studia Aegyptiaca*
SA	Studia Anselmiana
StudBib	Studia Biblica
StC	Studia Catholica
SEAug	Studia Ephemeridis Augustinianum
SE	*Studia Evangelica I, II, III* (= TU 73 [1959], 87 [1964], 88 [1964], etc.)
SVTP	Studia in Veteris Testamenti Pseudepigraphica
SIr	*Studia Iranica*
SIs	*Studia Islamica*
SJ	Studia Judaica
StMed	Studia Mediterranea
StudMon	Studia Monastica
StudNeot	Studia Neotestamentica
StOr	Studia Orientalia
SPap	*Studia Papyrologica*
StPat	*Studia Patavina*
StPatr	Studia Patristica
SPhilo	*Studia Philonica*
SPhiloA	Studia Philonica Annual

SPhiloM	Studia Philonica Monograph Series
StPohl	Studia Pohl
StPB	Studia Post-biblica
SSN	Studia Semitica Neerlandica
StSin	Studia Sinaitica
ST	*Studia Theologica*
Su	*Studia Theologica Varsaviensia*
StT	Studi e Testi, Biblioteca apostolica vaticana
STSA	Studi e testi di storia antica
StBoT	Studien zu den Boğazköy-Texten
SANT	Studien zum Alten und Neuen Testaments
SNT	Studien zum Neuen Testament
SNTSU	Studien zum Neuen Testament und seiner Umwelt
SUNT	Studien zur Umwelt des Neuen Testaments
SD	Studies and Documents
StABH	Studies in American Biblical Hermeneutics
SAOC	Studies in Ancient Oriental Civilizations
SAC	Studies in Antiquity and Christianity
SBA	Studies in Biblical Archaeology
StBibLit	Studies in Biblical Literature (Lang)
SBT	Studies in Biblical Theology
SCH	Studies in Church History
SCR	*Studies in Comparative Religion*
SHT	Studies in Historical Theology
SILS	Studies in Islamic Law and Society
SJC	Studies in Jewish Civilization
SJLA	Studies in Judaism in Late Antiquity
SLAEI	Studies in Late Antiquity and Early Islam
StOR	Studies in Oriental Religions
SPhA	Studies in Philo of Alexandria
SPhAMA	Studies in Philo of Alexandria and Mediterranean Antiquity
SR	*Studies in Religion*
STI	Studies in Theological Interpretation
SSEJC	Studies in Scripture in Early Judaism and Christianity
SHAJ	Studies in the History and Archaeology of Jordan
SHR	Studies in the History of Religions (supplements to Numen)
SHANE	Studies in the History of the Ancient Near East
SNTW	Studies of the New Testament and Its World
SCCNH	Studies on the Civilization and Culture of Nuzi and the Hurrians
STDJ	Studies on the Texts of the Desert of Judah
SBFLA	*Studii Biblici Franciscani Liber Annus*
SMT	*Studii Montis Regii*
SNTA	Studiorum Novi Testamenti Auxilia
St	*Studium*

SBFA	Studium Biblicum Franciscanum Analecta
SBFCMa	Studium Biblicum Franciscanum, Collectio major
SBFCMi	Studium Biblicum Franciscanum, Collectio minor
STJ	*Stulos Theological Journal*
SBS	Stuttgarter Bibelstudien
SBAB	Stuttgarter biblische Aufsatzbände
SBB	Stuttgarter biblische Beiträge
SBM	Stuttgarter biblische Monographien
SKKNT	Stuttgarter kleiner Kommentar, Neues Testament
SubBi	Subsidia Biblica
Sumer	*Sumer: A Journal of Archaeology and History in Iraq*
PSD	*The Sumerian Dictionary of the University Museum of the University of Pennsylvania*. Edited by Åke W. Sjöberg with the collaboration of Hermann Behrens. Philadelphia: Babylonian Section of the University Museum, 1884–. Restructured into an online endeavor.
SL	*Sumerisches Lexikon*. Edited by Anton Deimel. 8 vols. Rome: Pontifical Biblical Institute, 1928–1950
PWSup	Supplement to PW
NovTSup	Supplements to Novum Testamentum
VTSup	Supplements to Vetus Testamentum
SEG	Supplementum epigraphicum graecum
SEÅ	*Svensk exegetisk årsbok*
STK	*Svensk teologisk kvartalskrift*
SIG	*Sylloge Inscriptionum Graecarum*. Edited by Wilhelm Dittenberger. 4 vols. 3rd ed. Leipzig: Hirzel, 1915–1924
SymBU	Symbolae Biblicae Upsalienses
SO	Symbolae Osloenses
SymS	Symposium Series
SMS	Syro-Mesopotamian Studies
Tarbiz	*Tarbiz*
TDV-EI	*TDV Encyclopedia of Islam* (*İslâm Ansiklopedisi*). Ahmet Topaloğlu, ed. Istanbul: Türkiye Diyanet Vakfı, 1988–
TA	*Tel Aviv*
SMNIA	Tel Aviv University Sonia and Marco Nadler Institute of Archaeology Monograph Series
Teol	*Teología*
TI	*Teologia iusi*
TV	*Teología y vida*
TGST	Tesi Gregoriana, Serie Teologia
TRSR	Testi e ricerche di scienze religiose
THB	Text of the Hebrew Bible
TGI	*Textbuch zur Geschichte Israels*. Edited by Kurt Galling. 2nd ed. Tübingen: Mohr Siebeck, 1968

TUAT	*Texte aus der Umwelt des Alten Testaments*. Edited by Otto Kaiser. Gütersloh: Mohn, 1984–
THeth	Texte der Hethiter
TK	Texte und Kommentare
T&K	*Texte & Kontexte*
TSAJ	Texte und Studien zum antiken Judentum
TSO	Texte und Studien zur Orientalistik
TU	Texte und Untersuchungen
TUGAL	Texte und Untersuchungen zur Geschichte der altchristlichen Literatur
TCL	Textes cunéiformes. Musée du Louvre
TENTS	Texts and Editions for New Testament Study
TS	Texts and Studies
TSQ	Texts and Studies on the Qurʾān
TCSt	Text-Critical Studies
TCS	Texts from Cuneiform Sources
Text	*Textus*
Them	*Themelios*
TdT	Themen der Theologie
TBN	Themes in Biblical Narrative
Thf	*Theoforum*
ThViat	*Theologia Viatorum*
Theol	*Theologica*
TDNTW	*The NIV Theological Dictionary of New Testament Words*. Edited by Verlyn D. Verbrugge. Grand Rapids: Zondervan, 2000
TDNT	*Theological Dictionary of the New Testament*. Edited by Gerhard Kittel and Gerhard Friedrich. Translated by Geoffrey W. Bromiley. 10 vols. Grand Rapids: Eerdmans, 1964–1976
TDOT	*Theological Dictionary of the Old Testament*. Edited by G. Johannes Botterweck and Helmer Ringgren. Translated by John T. Willis et al. 8 vols. Grand Rapids: Eerdmans, 1974–2006
TTE	*The Theological Educator*
TLNT	*Theological Lexicon of the New Testament*. Ceslas Spicq. Translated and edited by James D. Ernest. 3 vols. Peabody, MA: Hendrickson, 1994
TLOT	*Theological Lexicon of the Old Testament*. Edited by Ernst Jenni, with assistance from Claus Westermann. Translated by Mark E. Biddle. 3 vols. Peabody, MA: Hendrickson, 1997
TS	*Theological Studies*
TWOT	*Theological Wordbook of the Old Testament*. Edited by R. Laird Harris, Gleason L. Archer Jr., and Bruce K. Waltke. 2 vols. Chicago: Moody Press, 1980
ThH	Théologie historique
TGl	*Theologie und Glaube*
TP	*Theologie und Philosophie*
Theo	*Theologika*

TPQ	*Theologisch-praktische Quartalschrift*
ThT	*Theologisch tijdschrift*
TBei	*Theologische Beiträge*
TBl	*Theologische Blätter*
TB	Theologische Bücherei: Neudrucke und Berichte aus dem 20. Jahrhundert
TF	Theologische Forschung
TLZ	*Theologische Literaturzeitung*
TQ	*Theologische Quartalschrift*
TRE	*Theologische Realenzyklopädie*. Edited by Gerhard Krause and Gerhard Müller. Berlin: de Gruyter, 1977–
TRev	*Theologische Revue*
TRu	*Theologische Rundschau*
ThSt	Theologische Studiën
TSK	*Theologische Studien und Kritiken*
TVM	Theologische Verlagsgemeinschaft: Monographien
TWNT	*Theologische Wörterbuch zum Neuen Testament*. Edited by Gerhard Kittel and Gerhard Friedrich. Stuttgart, 1932–1979
TZ	*Theologische Zeitschrift*
THKNT	Theologischer Handkommentar zum Neuen Testament
THAT	*Theologisches Handwörterbuch zum Alten Testament*. Edited by Ernst Jenni, with assistance from Claus Westermann. 2 vols. Munich: Chr. Kaiser Verlag; Zürich: Theologischer Verlag, 1971–1976
ThWAT	*Theologisches Wörterbuch zum Alten Testament*. Edited by G. Johannes Botterweck and Helmer Ringgren. Stuttgart: Kohlhammer, 1970–
ThPQ	*Theologisch-praktische Quartalschrift*
TD	*Theology Digest*
ThTo	*Theology Today*
TLG	*Thesaurus Linguae Graecae: Canon of Greek Authors and Works*. Edited by Luci Berkowitz and Karl A. Squitier. 3rd ed. New York: Oxford University Press, 1990
TLL	*Thesaurus Linguae Latinae*
Payne Smith	*Thesaurus Syriacus*. Edited by R. Payne Smith et al. Oxford: Clarendon, 1879–1901
TTKi	*Tidsskrift for Teologi og Kirke*
TvT	*Tijdschrift voor theologie*
TimesLitSupp	*Times Literary Supplement*
TBC	Torch Bible Commentaries
TJT	*Toronto Journal of Theology*
TPINTC	TPI New Testament Commentaries
TAPA	*Transactions of the American Philological Association*
TAPS	Transactions of the American Philosophical Society
TGUOS	Transactions of the Glasgow University Oriental Society
Transeu	*Transeuphratène*

TThSt	Trierer theologische Studien
TTZ	*Trierer theologische Zeitschrift*
TJ	*Trinity Journal*
TTJ	*Trinity Theological Journal*
TUMSR	Trinity University Monograph Series in Religion
Trumah	Trumah
TAVO	Tübinger Atlas des Vorderen Orients
TTKY	Türk Tarih Kurumu Yayinları
TCW	*Tydskrif vir Christelike Wetenskap*
TynBul	*Tyndale Bulletin*
TNTC	Tyndale New Testament Commentaries
TOTC	Tyndale Old Testament Commentaries
UF	*Ugarit-Forschungen*
UHP	*Ugaritic-Hebrew Philology*. Mitchell J. Dahood. 2nd ed. Rome: Pontifical Biblical Institute, 1989
UNP	*Ugaritic Narrative Poetry*. Edited by Simon B. Parker. WAW 9. Atlanta: Society of Biblical Literature, 1997
UT	*Ugaritic Textbook*. Cyrus H. Gordon. Rome: Pontifical Biblical Institute, 1965
UBL	Ugaritisch-biblische Literatur
USQR	*Union Seminary Quarterly Review*
UJEnc	*The Universal Jewish Encyclopedia*. Edited by Isaac Landman. 10 vols. New York: Universal Jewish Encyclopedia, 1939–1943
UCPCP	University of California Publications in Classical Philology
UCPNES	University of California Publications, Near Eastern Studies
UCPSP	University of California Publications in Semitic Philology
UCOP	University of Cambridge Oriental Publications
PBS	University of Pennsylvania, Publications of the Babylonian Section
USFSJH	University of South Florida Studies in the History of Judaism
UNT	Untersuchungen zum Neuen Testament
UUA	Uppsala Universitetsårskrift
UrE	Ur Excavations
UET	Ur Excavations: Texts
VCS	Variorum Collected Studies (formerly Variorum Reprints)
VCaro	*Verbum Caro*
VD	*Verbum Domini*
VS	*Verbum Salutis*
VF	*Verkündigung und Forschung*
VDI	*Vestnik drevnej istorii*
VL	Vetus Latina: Die Reste der altlateinischen Bibel
VT	*Vetus Testamentum*
Vid	*Vidyajyoti*
VSpir	*Vie spirituelle*
VC	*Vigiliae Christianae*

VH	*Vivens Homo*
VAT	Vorderasiatische Abteilung Tontafel. Vorderasiatisches Museum, Berlin
VAB	Vorderasiatische Bibliothek
VAS	Vorderasiatische Schriftdenkmaler
VS	Vorderasiatische Schriftdenkmäler der (Königlichen) Museen zu Berlin
VE	*Vox Evangelica*
VR	*Vox Reformata*
VoxS	*Vox Scripturae*
Wehr	Wehr, Hans. *A Dictionary of Modern Written Arabic.* Edited by J. Milton Cowan. 3rd ed. Ithaca: Spoken Languages Services, 1976. Repr., 4th enlarged and amended ed., Wiesbaden: Harrassowtiz, 1979
WI	*Die Welt des Islams*
WO	*Die Welt des Orients*
WC	Westminster Commentaries
WDB	*Westminster Dictionary of the Bible*
WHAB	*The Westminster Historical Atlas to the Bible.* George Ernest Wright and Floyd Vivian Filson. Rev. ed. Philadelphia: Westminster, 1974
WTJ	*Westminster Theological Journal*
WOO	Wiener Offene Orientalistik
WZKM	*Wiener Zeitschrift für die Kunde des Morgenlandes*
WZKSO	*Wiener Zeitschrift für die Kunde Süd- und Ostasiens*
Wilbour Studies	Wilbour Studies in Egyptology and Ancient Western Asia
WLAW	Wisdom Literature from the Ancient World
WMANT	Wissenschaftliche Monographien zum Alten und Neuen Testament
WUANT	Wissenschaftliche Untersuchungen zum Alten und Neuen Testament
WUNT	Wissenschaftliche Untersuchungen zum Neuen Testament
WVDOG	Wissenschaftliche Veröffentlichungen der deutschen Orient-Gesellschaft
WZ	*Wissenschaftliche Zeitschrift*
WZJ	*Wissenschaftliche Zeitschrift der Friedrich-Schiller-Universität Jena*
WBC	*The Women's Bible Commentary.* Edited by Carol A. Newsom, Sharon H. Ringe, and Jacqueline E. Lapsley. 3rd ed. Louisville: Westminster John Knox, 2012
WW	*Word and World*
WBC	Word Biblical Commentary
WHJP	World History of the Jewish People
WD	*Wort und Dienst*
WÄS	*Wörterbuch der ägyptischen Sprache.* Adolf Erman and Hermann Grapow. 5 vols. Leipzig: Hinrichs; Berlin: Akademie, 1926–1931. Repr., 1963
WKAS	*Wörterbuch der klassischen arabischen Sprache.* Edited by Jörg Kraemer, et al. Wiesbaden: Deutsche Morgenländische Gesellschaft, 1970–.
WUS	*Das Wörterbuch der ugaritischen Sprache.* Joseph Aistleitner. Edited by Otto Eissfeldt. 4th ed. Berlin: Akademie, 1974

WTM	*Das Wörterbuch über die Talmudim und Midraschim*. Jacob Levy. 2nd ed. Berlin: Harz, 1924. Repr., 1963
WAW	Writings from the Ancient World
WAWSup	Writings from the Ancient World Supplement Series
WGRW	Writings from the Greco-Roman World
WGRWSup	Writings from the Greco-Roman World Supplement Series
WIW	Writings from the Islamic World
Xenia	Xenia, Konstanzer Althistorische Vorträge und Forschungen
YCS	Yale Classical Studies
YJS	Yale Judaica Series
YNER	Yale Near Eastern Researches
YOSR	Yale Oriental Series, Researches
YOS	Yale Oriental Series, Texts
ZBA	Zaberns Bildbände zur Archäologie
ZDMG	*Zeitschrift der deutschen morgenländischen Gesellschaft*
ZDMGSup	Zeitschrift der deutschen morgenländischen Gesellschaft Supplementbände
ZSS	*Zeitschrift der Savigny-Stiftung für Rechtsgeschichte*
ZDPV	*Zeitschrift des deutschen Palästina-Vereins*
ZÄS	*Zeitschrift für ägyptische Sprache und Altertumskunde*
ZAH	*Zeitschrift für Althebräistik*
ZABR	*Zeitschrift für altorientalische und biblische Rechtgeschichte*
ZAC	*Zeitschrift für Antikes Christentum*
ZAL	*Zeitschrift für arabische Linguistik*
ZA	*Zeitschrift für Assyriologie*
ZABeih	Zeitschrift für Assyriologie: Beihefte
ZAW	*Zeitschrift für die alttestamentliche Wissenschaft*
ZKM	*Zeitschrift für die Kunde des Morgenlandes*
ZNW	*Zeitschrift für die neutestamentliche Wissenschaft und die Kunde der älteren Kirche*
ZEE	*Zeitschrift für evangelische Ethik*
ZHT	*Zeitschrift für historische Theologie*
ZIF	*Zeitschrift für Indogermanische Forschungen*
ZKT	*Zeitschrift für katholische Theologie*
ZK	*Zeitschrift für Keilschriftforschung*
ZKG	*Zeitschrift für Kirchengeschichte*
ZKunstG	*Zeitschrift für Kunstgeschichte*
ZPE	*Zeitschrift für Papyrologie und Epigraphik*
ZRGG	*Zeitschrift für Religions- und Geistesgeschichte*
ZS	*Zeitschrift für Semitistik und verwandte Gebiete*
ZST	*Zeitschrift für systematische Theologie*
ZTK	*Zeitschrift für Theologie und Kirche*
ZVS	*Zeitschrift für vergleichende Sprachforschung auf dem Gebiet der indogermanischen Sprachen*

ZWKL	*Zeitschrift für Wissenschaft und kirchliches Leben*
ZWT	*Zeitschrift für wissenschaftliche Theologie*
Zion	*Zion*
ZPEB	*Zondervan Pictorial Encyclopedia of the Bible.* Edited by Merrill C. Tenney. 5 vols. Grand Rapids: Zondervan, 1975
Zorell	Zorell, Franz. *Lexicon Hebraicum et Aramaicum Veteris Testamenti.* Rome: Pontifical Biblical Institute, 1968
ZB	Zürcher Bibel
ZBK	Zürcher Bibelkommentare

8.4.2 Alphabetized by Abbreviation

AA	*Archäologischer Anzeiger*
AAA	Annals of Archaeology and Anthropology
AAeg	*Analecta Aegyptiaca*
AAHG	*Anzeiger für die Altertumswissenschaft*
AAM	Archives administrativs de Mari
AARAS	American Academy of Religion Academy Series
AARASR	American Academy of Religion Aids for the Study of Religion Series
AARCC	American Academy of Religion Cultural Criticism Series
AARCRS	American Academy of Religion Classics in Religious Studies Series
AARRTSR	American Academy of Religion Reflection and Theory in the Study of Religion Series
AARSR	American Academy of Religion Studies in Religion Series
AARTR	American Academy of Religion The Religions Series
AARTRS	American Academy of Religion Teaching Religious Studies Series
AARTS	American Academy of Religion Thematic Studies
AARTT	American Academy of Religion Texts and Translations
AAS	*Acta Apostolicae Sedis*
AASF	Annales Academiae Scientiarum Fennicae
AASOR	Annual of the American Schools of Oriental Research
AASS	*Acta Sanctorum Quotquot Toto Orbe Coluntur. Antwerp,* 1643–
ÄAT	Ägypten und Altes Testament
AB	Anchor Bible
AB	*Assyriologische Bibliothek*
ABAT2	*Altorientalische Bilder zum Alten Testament.* Edited by Hugo Gressmann. 2nd ed. Berlin: de Gruyter, 1927
ABAW	Abhandlungen der Bayerischen Akademie der Wissenschaften
AbB	*Altbabylonische Briefe in Umschrift und Übersetzung.* Edited by Fritz R. Kraus. Leiden: Brill, 1964–
ABC	*Assyrian and Babylonian Chronicles.* Albert K. Grayson. TCS 5. Locust Valley, NY: Augustin, 1975
ABD	*Anchor Bible Dictionary.* Edited by David Noel Freedman. 6 vols. New York: Doubleday, 1992
ABL	*Assyrian and Babylonian Letters Belonging to the Kouyunjik Collections*

	of the British Museum. Edited by Robert F. Harper. 14 vols. Chicago: University of Chicago Press, 1892–1914
ABQ	*American Baptist Quarterly*
ABR	*Australian Biblical Review*
ABRL	Anchor Bible Reference Library
AbrN	*Abr-Nahrain*
AbrNSup	Abr-Nahrain Supplements
ABS	Archaeology and Biblical Studies
ABSA	Annual of the British School at Athens
ABW	*Archaeology in the Biblical World*
ABZ	*Assyrisch-babylonische Zeichenliste*. Rykle Borger. 3rd ed. Neukirchen-Vluyn: Neukirchener Verlag, 1986
AcBib	Academia Biblica
ACCS	Ancient Christian Commentary on Scripture
ACEBT	*Amsterdamse Cahiers voor Exegese en bijbelse Theologie*
ACNT	Augsburg Commentaries on the New Testament
ACO	*Acta Conciliorum Oecumenicorum*. Edited by Eduard Schwartz. Berlin: de Gruyter, 1914–1984
AcOr	*Acta Orientalia*
ACR	*Australasian Catholic Record*
AcT	*Acta Theologica*
Acta Iranica	Acta Iranica
ActAnt	Acta Antiqua Academiae Scientiarum Hungaricae
ACW	Ancient Christian Writers
ADAJ	*Annual of the Department of Antiquities of Jordan*
ADD	*Assyrian Deeds and Documents*. Claude Herman Walter Johns. 4 vols. Cambridge: Deighton, Bell, 1898–1923
ADOG	Abhandlungen der deutschen Orientgesellschaft
ADPV	Abhandlungen des Deutschen Palästina-Vereins
AE	*Année épigraphique*
AEB	*Annual Egyptological Bibliography*
Aeg	*Aegyptus*
AeL	Ägypten und Levante
AEL	*Ancient Egyptian Literature*. Miriam Lichtheim. 3 vols. Berkeley: University of California Press, 1971–1980
AEM	Archives épistolaires de Mari
AEO	*Ancient Egyptian Onomastica*. Alan H. Gardiner. 3 vols. London: Oxford University Press, 1947
AER	*American Ecclesiastical Review*
Aev	*Aevum: Rassegna de scienze, storiche, linguistiche, e filologiche*
AfK	*Archiv für Keilschriftforschung*
AfO	*Archiv für Orientforschung*
AfOB	Archiv für Orientforschung: Beiheft
ÄF	Ägyptologische Forschungen

ÄgAbh	Ägyptologische Abhandlungen
AGJU	Arbeiten zur Geschichte des antiken Judentums und des Urchristentums
AGLB	*Aus der Geschichte der lateinischen Bibel* (= *Vetus Latina: Die Reste der altlateinischen Bibel: Aus der Geschichte der lateinischen Bibel*). Freiburg: Herder, 1957–
AGSU	Arbeiten zur Geschichte des Spätjudentums und Urchristentums
AHAW	Abhandlungen der Heidelberger Akademie der Wissenschaften
ÄHK	*Die ägyptisch-hethitische Korrespondenz aus Boghazköi in babylonischer und hethitischer Sprache*. Elmar Edel. Opladen: Westdeutscher Verlag, 1994
AHR	*American Historical Review*
AHw	*Akkadisches Handwörterbuch*. Wolfram von Soden. 3 vols. Wiesbaden, 1965–1981
AIL	Ancient Israel and Its Literature
AION	*Annali dell'Istituto Orientale di Napoli*
AIPHOS	Annuaire de l'Institut de philologie et d'histoire orientales et slaves
AJ	*Antiquaries Journal*
AJA	*American Journal of Archaeology*
AJAS	*American Journal of Arabic Studies*
AJBA	*Australian Journal of Biblical Archaeology*
AJBI	Annual of the Japanese Biblical Institute
AJBS	*African Journal of Biblical Studies*
AJP	*American Journal of Philology*
AJSL	*American Journal of Semitic Languages and Literatures*
AJSR	*Association for Jewish Studies Review*
AJSUFS	Arbeiten aus dem Juristischen Seminar der Universität Freiburg (Switzerland)
Akkadica	*Akkadica*
AKM	Abhandlungen für die Kunde des Morgenlandes
AmJT	*American Journal of Theology*
AsJT	*Asia Journal of Theology*
ALASP	Abhandlungen zur Literatur Alt-Syrien-Palästinas und Mesopotamiens
ALBO	Analecta Lovaniensia Biblica et Orientalia
ALGHJ	Arbeiten zur Literatur und Geschichte des hellenistischen Judentums
Altaner	Altaner, Berthold. *Patrologie: Leben, Schriften und Lehre der Kirchenväter*. 8th ed. Freiburg: Herder, 1978
ALUOS	*Annual of Leeds University Oriental Society*
AMD	Ancient Magic and Divination
AMEL	*Arabic and Middle Eastern Literatures*
AMS	*Acta Martyrum et Sanctorum Syriace*. Edited by Paul Bedjan. 7 vols. Paris, Leipzig: Harrassowitz, 1890–1897. Repr., Hildesheim: Olms, 1968
AMWNE	*Apocalypticism in the Mediterranean World and the Near East. Proceedings*

	of the International Colloquium on Apocalypticism, Uppsala, Aug. 12–17, 1979. Edited by David Hellholm. 2nd ed. Tübingen: Mohr Siebeck, 1989
Anám	*Anámnesis*
AnAnt	*Anatolia Antiqua*
Anatolica	*Anatolica*
AnBib	Analecta Biblica
AnBoll	Analecta Bollandiana
Andalus	*Al-Andalus: Revista de la Escuela de Estudios Árabes de Madrid y Granada*
ANEM	Ancient Near East Monographs/Monografías sobre el Antiguo Cercano Oriente
ANEP	*The Ancient Near East in Pictures Relating to the Old Testament.* 2nd ed. Edited by James B. Pritchard. Princeton: Princeton University Press, 1994
ANES	Ancient Near Eastern Studies
ANES	*Ancient Near Eastern Studies*
ANESSup	Ancient Near Eastern Studies Supplement Series
ANESTP	*The Ancient Near East: Supplementary Texts and Pictures Relating to the Old Testament.* Edited by James B. Pritchard. Princeton: Princeton University Press, 1969
ANET	*Ancient Near Eastern Texts Relating to the Old Testament.* Edited by James B. Pritchard. 3rd ed. Princeton: Princeton University Press, 1969
ANF	*Ante-Nicene Fathers*
Ang	*Angelicum*
AnL	*Anthropological Linguistics*
AnOr	*Analecta Orientalia*
AnPhil	*L'année philologique*
ANQ	*Andover Newton Quarterly*
ANRW	*Aufstieg und Niedergang der römischen Welt: Geschichte und Kultur Roms im Spiegel der neueren Forschung.* Part 2, *Principat.* Edited by Hildegard Temporini and Wolfgang Haase. Berlin: de Gruyter, 1972–
AnSt	*Anatolian Studies*
ANTC	Abingdon New Testament Commentaries
ANTF	Arbeiten zur neutestamentlichen Textforschung
Antichthon	*Antichthon: Journal of the Australian Society for Classical Studies*
AnthLyrGraec	*Anthologia Lyrica Graeca.* Edited by Ernst Diehl. Leipzig: Teubner, 1954–
ANTJ	Arbeiten zum Neuen Testament und Judentum
Anton	*Antonianum*
Anuari	*Anuari de filología*
ANZSTR	Australian and New Zealand Studies in Theology and Religion
AO	Der Alte Orient
AOAT	Alter Orient und Altes Testament
AÖAW	Anzeiger der Österreichischen Akademie der Wissenschaften

AOBib	Altorientalische Bibliothek
AoF	Altorientalische Forschungen
AoN	*Altorientalistische Notizen*
AOS	American Oriental Series
AOSTS	American Oriental Society Translation Series
AOT	*The Apocryphal Old Testament*. Edited by Hedley F. D. Sparks. Oxford: Clarendon, 1984
AOTAT	*Altorientalische Texte zum Alten Testament*. Edited by Hugo Gressmann. 2nd ed. Berlin: de Gruyter, 1926
AOTC	Abingdon Old Testament Commentaries
APAT	*Die Apokryphen und Pseudepigraphen des Alten Testaments*. Translated and edited by Emil Kautzsch. 2 vols. Tübingen: Mohr Siebeck, 1900
APF	*Archiv für Papyrusforschung*
APOT	*The Apocrypha and Pseudepigrapha of the Old Testament*. Edited by Robert H. Charles. 2 vols. Oxford: Clarendon, 1913
ApOTC	Apollos Old Testament Commentary
APSP	*American Philosophical Society Proceedings*
AR	*Archiv für Religionswissenschaft*
ARAB	*Ancient Records of Assyria and Babylonia*. Daniel David Luckenbill. 2 vols. Chicago: University of Chicago Press, 1926–1927. Repr., New York: Greenwood, 1968
Arabica	*Arabica: Journal of Arabic and Islamic Studies/Revue d'études arabes et islamiques*
Aramazd	*Aramazd: Armenian Journal of Near Eastern Studies*
ArBib	The Aramaic Bible
Arch	*Archaeology*
ARE	*Ancient Records of Egypt*. Edited by James Henry Breasted. 5 vols. Chicago: University of Chicago Press, 1906–1907. Repr., New York: Russell & Russell, 1962
ARES	Archivi reali di Ebla, Studi
ARET	Archivi reali di Ebla, Testi
ARG	*Archiv für Reformationsgeschichte*
ARI	*Assyrian Royal Inscriptions*. Albert K. Grayson. 2 vols. Wiesbaden: Harrasowitz, 1972–1976
ARMT	Archives royales de Mari, transcrite et traduite
ArOr	*Archív orientální*
ARRIM	Annual Review of the Royal Inscriptions of Mesopotamia Project
ArsOr	*Ars Orientalis*
AS	*Aramaic Studies*
AS	Assyriological Studies
ASAE	*Annales du service des antiquités de l'Egypte*
ASAW	Abhandlungen der Sächsischen Akademie der Wissenschaften
ASH	Ancient Society and History
ASJ	*Acta Sumerologica*

ASKA	Arbeiten zum spätantiken und koptischen Ägypten
ASNU	Acta Seminarii Neotestamentici Upsaliensis
ASOR	American Schools of Oriental Research
ASP	*American Studies in Papyrology*
Asp	*Asprenas: Rivista di scienze teologiche*
ASS	*Acta Sanctae Sedis*
AsSeign	*Assemblées du Seigneur*
ASSF	Acta Societatis Scientiarum Fennicae
ASSR	Archives de sciences sociales des religions
Assur	Assur: Monographic Journals of the Near East
ASTI	Annual of the Swedish Theological Institute
AsTJ	Asbury Theological Journal
AT	Annales Theologici
ATA	Alttestamentliche Abhandlungen
ATANT	Abhandlungen zur Theologie des Alten und Neuen Testaments
ATASMS	American Translators Association Scholarly Monograph Series
ATD	Das Alte Testament Deutsch
ATDan	Acta Theologica Danica
ATG	*Archivo teológico granadino*
Athenaeum	Athenaeum: Studi Periodici di Letteratura e Storia dell'Antichità
AThR	*Anglican Theological Review*
Atiqot	*'Atiqot*
ATJ	*Ashland Theological Journal*
ATLA	American Theological Library Association
ATR	*Australasian Theological Review*
AUCT	Andrews University Cuneiform Texts
Aug	*Augustinianum*
AugStud	*Augustinian Studies*
AuOr	*Aula Orientalis*
AUS	American University Studies
AUSCLL	American University Studies, Series 17: Classical Languages and Literature
AUSS	*Andrews University Seminary Studies*
AUSTR	American University Studies, Series 7: Theology and Religion
AVTRW	Aufsätze und Vorträge zur Theologie und Religionswissenschaft
AW	*Antike Welt*
AYBRL	Anchor Yale Bible Reference Library
AzTh	Arbeiten zur Theologie
B&R	*Books and Religion*
BA	*Biblical Archaeologist*
Bab	*Babyloniaca*
BAC	Biblioteca de autores cristianos
BAEO	*Boletín de la Asociación Española de Orientalistas*
BaF	*Baghdader Forschungen*

BAFCS	The Book of Acts in Its First Century Setting
BAGB	*Bulletin de l'Association G. Budé*
BAGD	Bauer, Walter, William F. Arndt, F. Wilbur Gingrich, and Frederick W. Danker. *Greek-English Lexicon of the New Testament and Other Early Christian Literature.* 2nd ed. Chicago: University of Chicago Press, 1979 (Bauer-Arndt-Gingrich-Danker)
BaghM	*Baghdader Mitteilungen*
BAIAS	*Bulletin of the Anglo-Israel Archeological Society*
BAP	*Beiträge zum altbabylonischen Privatrecht.* Bruno Meissner. Leipzig, 1893
BAR	*Biblical Archaeology Review*
Bar-Ilan	*Annual of Bar-Ilan University*
BARIS	BAR (British Archaeological Reports) International Series
BASOR	*Bulletin of the American Schools of Oriental Research*
BASORSup	Bulletin of the American Schools of Oriental Research Supplements
BASP	Bulletin of the American Society of Papyrologists
BASPSup	Bulletin of the American Society of Papyrologists Supplements
BAT	Die Botschaft des Alten Testaments
Bayan	*Al-Bayan: Journal of Quran and Hadith Studies*
BBB	Bonner biblische Beiträge
BBB	*Bulletin de bibliographie biblique*
BBET	Beiträge zur biblischen Exegese und Theologie
BBMS	Baker Biblical Monograph Series
BBR	*Bulletin for Biblical Research*
BBRSup	*Bulletin for Biblical Research, Supplements*
BBS	*Bulletin of Biblical Studies*
BBVF	Berliner Beiträge zur Vor- und Frühgeschichte
BBVO	Berliner Beiträge zum Vorderer Orient Texte
BCBO	Biblioteca de Ciencias Bíblicas y Orientales
BCH	*Bulletin de correspondance hellénique*
BCOTWP	Baker Commentary on the Old Testament Wisdom and Psalms
BCPE	*Bulletin du Centre protestant d'études*
BCR	Biblioteca di cultura religiosa
BCSMS	*Bulletin of the Canadian Society for Mesopotamian Studies*
BCSR	*Bulletin of the Council on the Study of Religion*
BDAG	Danker, Frederick W., Walter Bauer, William F. Arndt, and F. Wilbur Gingrich. *Greek-English Lexicon of the New Testament and Other Early Christian Literature.* 3rd ed. Chicago: University of Chicago Press, 2000 (Danker-Bauer-Arndt-Gingrich)
BDB	Brown, Francis, S. R. Driver, and Charles A. Briggs. *A Hebrew and English Lexicon of the Old Testament*
BDF	Blass, Friedrich, Albert Debrunner, and Robert W. Funk. *A Greek Grammar of the New Testament and Other Early Christian Literature.* Chicago: University of Chicago Press, 1961

BEATAJ	Beiträge zur Erforschung des Alten Testaments und des antiken Judentum
BEB	*Baker Encyclopedia of the Bible.* Edited by Walter A. Elwell. 2 vols. Grand Rapids: Baker, 1988
BECNT	Baker Exegetical Commentary on the New Testament
BegC	*The Beginnings of Christianity.* Part 1: *The Acts of the Apostles.* Edited by Frederick J. Foakes-Jackson and Kirsopp Lake. 5 vols. London: Macmillan, 1922. Repr. under the subtitle, Grand Rapids: Baker, 1977
BEHEH	Bibliothèque de l'École des hautes études: Sciences historiques et philologiques
BEHER	Bibliothèque de l'École des hautes études: Sciences religieuses
Belleten	*Belleten*
BeO	*Bibbia e oriente*
BEO	*Bulletin d'études orientales de l'Institut Français de Damas*
BerMatÖAI	Berichte und Materialien des Österreichischen archäologischen Instituts
Berytus	*Berytus: Archaeological Studies*
BETL	Bibliotheca Ephemeridum Theologicarum Lovaniensium
BEvT	Beiträge zur evangelischen Theologie
BFCT	Beiträge zur Förderung christlicher Theologie
BFT	Biblical Foundations in Theology
BGBE	Beiträge zur Geschichte der biblischen Exegese
BGU	*Aegyptische Urkunden aus den Königlichen Staatlichen Museen zu Berlin, Griechische Urkunden.* 15 vols. Berlin: Weidmann, 1895–1937
BHEAT	*Bulletin d'histoire et d'exégèse de l'Ancien Testament*
BHG	*Bibliotheca Hagiographica Graeca.* Edited by François Halkin. 3rd ed. 3 vols. Brussels: Société des Bollandistes, 1986
BHH	*Biblisch-historisches Handwörterbuch: Landeskunde, Geschichte, Religion, Kultur.* Edited by Bo Reicke and Leonhard Rost. 4 vols. Göttingen: Vandenhoeck & Ruprecht, 1962–1966. Republished electronically, Berlin: Directmedia, 2003
BHK	*Biblia Hebraica.* Edited by Rudolph Kittel. Liepzig: Hinrichs, 1905–1906
BHLAMA	*Bibliotheca Hagiographica Latina Antiquae et Mediae Aetatis.* 2 vols. Brussels, 1898–1901
BHO	*Bibliotheca Hagiographica Orientalis.* Brussels, 1910
BHQ	*Biblia Hebraica Quinta.* Edited by Adrian Schenker et al. Stuttgart: Deutsche Bibelgesellschaft, 2004–
BHS	*Biblia Hebraica Stuttgartensia.* Edited by Karl Elliger and Wilhelm Rudolph. Stuttgart: Deutsche Bibelgesellschaft, 1983
BHT	Beiträge zur historischen Theologie
BI	*Biblical Illustrator*
Bib	*Biblica*
BibB	Biblische Beiträge
BibEnc	Biblical Encyclopedia

BiBh	*Bible Bhashyam*
BibInt	*Biblical Interpretation*
BibInt	Biblical Interpretation Series
BibLeb	*Bibel und Leben*
BibleInt	The Bible and Its Interpretation
BibleRec	The Bible and Its Reception
BibOr	Biblica et Orientalia
BibSem	The Biblical Seminar
BibS(F)	Biblische Studien (Freiburg, 1895–)
BibS(N)	Biblische Studien (Neukirchen, 1951–)
BIES	*Bulletin of the Israel Exploration Society* (= *Yediot*)
BIFAO	*Bulletin de l'Institut français d'archéologie orientale*
Bijdr	*Bijdragen: Tijdschrift voor filosofie en theologie*
BIN	Babylonian Inscriptions in the Collection of James B. Nies
BIOSCS	*Bulletin of the International Organization for Septuagint and Cognate Studies*
BiPa	*Biblia Patristica: Index des citations et allusions bibliques dans la littérature.* Paris: CNRS, 2000
BJ	*Bonner Jahrbücher*
BJPES	*Bulletin of the Jewish Palestine Exploration Society*
BJRL	*Bulletin of the John Rylands University Library of Manchester*
BJS	Brown Judaic Studies
BJSUCSD	Biblical and Judaic Studies from the University of California, San Diego
BJVF	*Berliner Jahrbuch für Vor- und Frühgeschichte*
BK	*Bibel und Kirche*
BKAT	Biblischer Kommentar, Altes Testament
BL	*Bibel und Liturgie*
BLE	*Bulletin de littérature ecclésiastique*
BLit	*Bibliothèque liturgique*
BLS	Bible and Literature Series
BMECCJ	Bulletin of the Middle Eastern Culture Center in Japan
BMes	Bibliotheca Mesopotamica
BMI	The Bible and Its Modern Interpreters
BMQ	*British Museum Quarterly*
BN	*Biblische Notizen*
BNL	Beiträge zur neueren Literaturgeschichte
BNP	*Brill's New Pauly: Encyclopaedia of the Ancient World*. Edited by Hubert Cancik. 22 vols. Leiden: Brill, 2002–2011
BNTC	Black's New Testament Commentaries
BO	Bibliotheca Orientalis
BoHa	Boğazköy-Ḫattuša
Böhl	Böhl, F. M. Th. de Liagre. *Opera minora: Studies en bijdragen op Assyriologisch en Oudtestamentisch terrein*. Groningen: Wolters, 1953
BOR	*Babylonian and Oriental Record*

BPOA	*Biblioteca del Proximo Oriente Antiguo*
BR	*Biblical Research*
BRev	*Bible Review*
BRL2	*Biblisches Reallexikon*. 2nd ed. Edited by Kurt Galling. HAT 1/1. Tübingen: Mohr Siebeck, 1977
BSAA	*Bulletin de la Société archéologique d'Alexandrie*
BRLA	Brill Reference Library of Judaism
BRLF	Biblioteca di ricerche linguistiche e filologiche
BSA	*Bulletin of Sumerian Agriculture*
BSac	*Bibliotheca Sacra*
BSAC	*Bulletin de la Société d'archéologie copte*
BSC	Bible Student's Commentary
BSGRT	Bibliotheca Scriptorum Graecorum et Romanorum Teubneriana
BSGW	Berichte der Sächsischen Gesellschaft der Wissenschaften
BSIEL	Brill's Studies in Indo-European Languages and Linguistics
BSJS	Brill's Series in Jewish Studies
BSL	*Bulletin de la Société de Linguistique de Paris*
BSNA	Biblical Scholarship in North America
BSOAS	*Bulletin of the School of Oriental and African Studies*
BSR	*Bulletin for the Study of Religion* (formerly *CSSRB*)
BT	*The Bible Translator*
BTB	*Biblical Theology Bulletin*
BThAM	*Bulletin de théologie ancienne et médiévale*
BTS	*Bible et terre sainte*
BTS	Biblical Tools and Studies
BTZ	*Berliner Theologische Zeitschrift*
Budé	Collection des universités de France, publiée sous le patronage de l'Association Guillaume Budé
Burg	*Burgense*
BurH	*Buried History: Quarterly Journal of the Australian Institute of Archaeology*
BV	*Biblical Viewpoint*
BVC	*Bible et vie chrétienne*
BW	*The Biblical World: A Dictionary of Biblical Archaeology*. Edited by Charles F. Pfeiffer. Grand Rapids: Baker, 1966
BW	Bible and Women
BWA(N)T	Beiträge zur Wissenschaft vom Alten (und Neuen) Testament
BWL	*Babylonian Wisdom Literature*. Wilfred G. Lambert. Oxford, Clarendon, 1960
ByF	*Biblia y fe*
Byzantion	*Byzantion*
ByzF	*Byzantinische Forschungen*
ByzZ	*Byzantinische Zeitschrift*
BZ	*Biblische Zeitschrift*
BzA	Beiträge zur Assyriologie

BZABR	Beihefte zur Zeitschrift für altorientalische und biblische Rechtsgeschichte
BZAW	Beihefte zur Zeitschrift für die alttestamentliche Wissenschaft
BzN	*Beiträge zur Namenforschung*
BZNW	Beihefte zur Zeitschrift für die neutestamentliche Wissenschaft
BZRGG	Beihefte zur Zeitschrift für Religions- und Geistesgeschichte
CA	*Convivium Assisiense*
CAA	Codices Arabici Antiqui
CAD	*The Assyrian Dictionary of the Oriental Institute of the University of Chicago*. Chicago: The Oriental Institute of the University of Chicago, 1956–2006
CaE	*Cahiers évangile*
CAGN	*Collected Ancient Greek Novels*. Edited by B. P. Reardon. Berkeley, 1989
CAH	Cambridge Ancient History
CahRB	Cahiers de la Revue biblique
CahT	Cahiers Théologiques
CANE	*Civilizations of the Ancient Near East*. Edited by Jack M. Sasson. 4 vols. New York, 1995. Repr. in 2 vols. Peabody, MA: Hendrickson, 2006
CAP	Cowley, Arthur E. *Aramaic Papyri of the Fifth Century B.C.* Oxford: Clarendon, 1923
Car	*Carthagiensia*
CAT	Commentaire de l'Ancien Testament
CB	*Cultura Bíblica*
CBC	Cambridge Bible Commentary
CBET	Contributions to Biblical Exegesis and Theology
CBM	Chester Beatty Monographs
CBQ	*Catholic Biblical Quarterly*
CBQMS	Catholic Biblical Quarterly Monograph Series
CBTJ	*Calvary Baptist Theological Journal*
CC	Continental Commentaries
CCath	Corpus Catholicorum
CCCM	Corpus Christianorum: Continuatio Mediaevalis. Turnhout: Brepols, 1969–
CClCr	*Civilità classica e cristiana*
CCSG	Corpus Christianorum: Series Graeca. Turnhout: Brepols, 1977–
CCSL	Corpus Christianorum: Series Latina. Turnhout: Brepols, 1953–
CCT	*Cuneiform Texts from Cappadocian Tablets in the British Museum*
CCTC	Cambridge Classical Texts and Commentaries
CCTMMA	Corpus of Cuneiform Texts in the Metropolitan Museum of Art
CdE	*Chronique d'Égypte*
CDLB	*Cuneiform Digital Library Bulletin*
CDLI	Cuneiform Digital Library Initiative
CDLJ	*Cuneiform Digital Library Journal*
CDLN	*Cuneiform Digital Library Notes*

CDME	*A Concise Dictionary of Middle Egyptian.* Edited by Raymond O. Faulkner. Oxford: Griffith Institute, 1962
CDOG	Colloquien der Deutschen Orient-Gesellschaft
CÉFR	Collection de l'École française de Rome
CEJL	Commentaries on Early Jewish Literature
CF	*Classical Folia*
CGTC	Cambridge Greek Testament Commentary
CGTSC	Cambridge Greek Testament for Schools and Colleges
CH	Church History
CHANE	Culture and History of the Ancient Near East
CHD	*The Hittite Dictionary of the Oriental Institute of the University of Chicago.* Edited by Hans G. Güterbock, Harry A. Hoffner Jr., and Theo P. J. van den Hout. Chicago: The Oriental Institute of the University of Chicago, 1980–
Chiron	*Chiron: Mitteilungen der Kommission für Alte Geschichte und Epigraphik des Deutschen Archäologischen Instituts*
CHJ	*Cambridge History of Judaism.* Edited by William D. Davies and Louis Finkelstein. 4 vols. Cambridge: Cambridge University Press, 1984–2006
Chm	Churchman
ChS	Corpus der hurritischen Sprachdenkmäler
CHR	*Catholic Historical Review*
ChrCent	*Christian Century*
ChrLit	*Christianity and Literature*
CIC	*Corpus Inscriptionum Chaldicarum*
CIG	*Corpus Inscriptionum Graecarum.* Edited by August Boeckh. 4 vols. Berlin, 1828–1877
CIJ	*Corpus Inscriptionum Judaicarum.* Edited by Jean-Baptiste Frey. 2 vols. Rome: Pontifical Biblical Institute, 1936–1952
CIL	*Corpus Inscriptionum Latinarum.* Berlin, 1862–
CIS	Comparative Islamic Studies
CIS	*Corpus Inscriptionum Semiticarum.* Paris, 1881–
CJ	*Classical Journal*
CJT	*Canadian Journal of Theology*
ClAnt	*Classical Antiquity*
CM	Cuneiform Monographs
Cmio	*Communio: Commentarii Internationales de Ecclesia et Theología*
CML	*Canaanite Myths and Legends.* Edited by Godfrey R. Driver. Edinburgh: T&T Clark, 1956. 2nd ed. edited by John C. L. Gibson, 1978, e-book 2004
CNIP	Carsten Niebuhr Institute Publications
CNS	*Cristianesimo nella storia*
CNT	Commentaire du Nouveau Testament
Coll	*Collationes*
Colloq	*Colloquium*

ColT	*Collectanea Theologica*
Comm	*Communio*
Comp	*Compostellanum*
ConBNT	Coniectanea Neotestamentica or Coniectanea Biblica: New Testament Series
ConBOT	Coniectanea Biblica: Old Testament Series
ConcC	Concordia Commentary
Cont	*Continuum*
COS	*The Context of Scripture*. Edited by William W. Hallo. 3 vols. Leiden: Brill, 1997–2002
COuT	*Commentaar op het Oude Testament*
CP	*Classical Philology*
CPG	*Clavis Patrum Graecorum*. Edited by Maurice Geerard. 5 vols. Turnhout: Brepols, 1974–1987
CPJ	*Corpus Papyrorum Judaicarum*. Edited by Victor A. Tcherikover. 3 vols. Cambridge: Harvard University Press, 1957–1964
CPL	*Clavis Patrum Latinorum*. Edited by Eligius Dekkers. 2nd ed. Steenbrugis: Abbatia Sancti Petri, 1961
CQ	*Church Quarterly*
ClQ	*Classical Quarterly*
CQR	*Church Quarterly Review*
CRAI	Comptes rendus de l'Académie des inscriptions et belles-lettres
CRBR	*Critical Review of Books in Religion*
CRINT	Compendia Rerum Iudaicarum ad Novum Testamentum
CRTL	Cahiers de la Revue théologique de Louvain
Crux	*Crux*
CSCO	Corpus Scriptorum Christianorum Orientalium. Edited by Jean Baptiste Chabot et al. Paris, 1903
CSEANT	Commentario storico ed esegetico all'Antico e al Nuovo Testamento
CSEL	Corpus Scriptorum Ecclesiasticorum Latinorum
CSHB	Corpus Scriptorum Historiae Byzantinae
CSHJ	Chicago Studies in the History of Judaism
CSSRB	*Council of Societies for the Study of Religion Bulletin*
CT	*Cuneiform Texts from Babylonian Tablets in the British Museum*
CTA	*Corpus des tablettes en cunéiformes alphabétiques découvertes à Ras Shamra-Ugarit de 1929 à 1939*. Edited by Andrée Herdner. Paris: Geuthner, 1963
CTAED	*Canaanite Toponyms in Ancient Egyptian Documents*. Shmuel Ahituv. Jerusalem, 1984
CTH	*Catalogue des textes hittites*. Emmanuel Laroche. Paris: Klincksieck, 1971
CTJ	*Calvin Theological Journal*
CTM	*Concordia Theological Monthly*
CTQ	*Concordia Theological Quarterly*
CTR	*Criswell Theological Review*

CTU	*The Cuneiform Alphabetic Texts from Ugarit, Ras Ibn Hani, and Other Places*. Edited by Manfried Dietrich, Oswald Loretz, and Joaquín Sanmartín. Münster: Ugarit-Verlag, 1995
CUL	*A Concordance of the Ugaritic Literature*. Richard E. Whitaker. Cambridge: Harvard University Press, 1972
CurBR	*Currents in Biblical Research* (formerly *Currents in Research: Biblical Studies*)
CurBS	*Currents in Research: Biblical Studies*
CurTM	*Currents in Theology and Mission*
CUSAS	Cornell University Studies in Assyriology and Sumerology
CV	*Communio Viatorum*
CW	*Classical World*
CWS	Classics of Western Spirituality
DA	Documenta Asiana
DACL	*Dictionnaire d'archéologie chrétienne et de liturgie*. Edited by Fernand Cabrol. 15 vols. Paris: Letouzey et Ané, 1907–1953
DamM	Damaszener Mitteilungen
DB	*Dictionnaire de la Bible*. Edited by Fulcran Vigouroux. 5 vols. Paris: Letouzey et Ané, 1895–1912
DBAT	*Dielheimer Blätter zum Alten Testament und seiner Rezeption in der Alten Kirche*
DBH	Dresdner Beiträge zur Hethitologie
DBI	*Dictionary of Biblical Interpretation*. Edited by John Hayes. 2 vols. Nashville: Abingdon, 1999.
DBSup	*Dictionnaire de la Bible: Supplément*. Edited by Lous Pirot and André Robert. Paris: Letouzey & Ané, 1928–
DBT	*Dictionary of Biblical Theology*. Edited by Xavier Léon-Dufour. 2nd ed. New York, Seabury, 1972
DCB	*Dictionary of Christian Biography*. Edited by William Smith and Henry Wace. 4 vols. London: Murray, 1877–1887
DCG	*Dictionary of Christ and the Gospels*. Edited by James Hastings. 2 vols. Edinburgh: T&T Clark, 1908
DCH	*Dictionary of Classical Hebrew*. Edited by David J. A. Clines. 9 vols. Sheffield: Sheffield Phoenix Press, 1993–2014
DCLS	Deuterocanonical and Cognate Literature Studies
DDD	*Dictionary of Deities and Demons in the Bible*. Edited by Karel van der Toorn, Bob Becking, and Pieter W. van der Horst. Leiden: Brill, 1995. 2nd rev. ed. Grand Rapids: Eerdmans, 1999
Der Islam	*Der Islam: Journal of the History and Culture of the Middle East*
DGWE	*Dictionary of Gnosis and Western Esotericism*. Edited by Wouter J. Hanegraaff et al. 2 vols. Leiden: Brill, 2005
DHA	*Dialogues d'histoire ancienne*
Di	*Dialog*
Did	*Didaskalia*

DISO	*Dictionnaire des inscriptions sémitiques de l'ouest*. Edited by Charles François Jean and Jacob Hoftijzer. Leiden: Brill, 1965
DissAb	Dissertation Abstracts
DivThom	*Divus Thomas*
DJD	Discoveries in the Judaean Desert
DJG	*Dictionary of Jesus and the Gospels*. Edited by Joel B. Green, Jeannine K. Brown, and Nicholas Perrin. 2nd ed. Downers Grove, IL: InterVarsity Press, 2013
DLE	*Dictionary of Late Egyptian*. Edited by Leonard H. Lesko and Barbara S. Lesko. 4 vols. Berkeley: B.C. Scribe, 1982–1989
DLNT	*Dictionary of the Later New Testament and Its Developments*. Edited by Ralph P. Martin and Peter H. Davids. Downers Grove, IL: InterVarsity Press, 1997
DMBI	*Dictionary of Major Biblical Interpreters*. Edited by Donald K. McKim. 2nd ed. Downers Grove, IL: Intervarsity Press, 2007
DMOA	Documenta et Monumenta Orientis Antiqui
DNP	*Der neue Pauly: Enzyklopädie der Antike*. Edited by Hubert Cancik and Helmuth Schneider. Stuttgart: Metzler, 1996–
DNTB	*Dictionary of New Testament Background*. Edited by Craig A. Evans and Stanley E. Porter. Downers Grove, IL: Inter-Varsity, 2000
DNWSI	*Dictionary of the North-West Semitic Inscriptions*. Jacob Hoftijzer and Karen Jongeling. 2 vols. Leiden: Brill, 1995
DOP	*Dumbarton Oaks Papers*
DOTT	*Documents from Old Testament Times*. Edited by D. Winton Thomas, London: Nelson, 1958
DPAC	*Dizionario patristico e di antichità cristiane*. Edited by Angelo di Berardino. 3 vols. 2nd ed. Genoa: Marietti 2006–2008
DPL	*Dictionary of Paul and His Letters*. Edited by Gerald F. Hawthorne and Ralph P. Martin. Downers Grove, IL: InterVarsity Press, 1993
DRev	*Downside Review*
DrewG	*Drew Gateway*
DSD	*Dead Sea Discoveries*
DSSC	*The Dead Sea Scrolls Concordance*. Martin G. Abegg Jr., James E. Browley, and Edward M. Cook. 3 vols. Leiden: Brill, 2003–
DSSR	*The Dead Sea Scrolls Reader*. Edited by Donald W. Parry and Emanuel Tov. 6 vols. Leiden: Brill, 2004–2005
DTC	*Dictionnaire de théologie catholique*. Edited by Alfred Vacant et al. 15 vols. Paris: Letouzey et Ané, 1908–1950
DTT	*Dansk teologisk tidsskrift*
Duchesne	Duchesne, Louis, ed. *Le Liber pontificalis*. 2 vols. Paris: Thorin, 1886, 1892. Repr. with 3rd vol. by Cyrille Vogel. Paris: de Boccard, 1955–1957, 1981
DunRev	*Dunwoodie Review*
EA	El-Amarna tablets. According to the edition of Jørgen A. Knudtzon. *Die*

	el-Amarna-Tafeln. Leipzig: Hinrichs, 1908–1915. Repr., Aalen: Zeller, 1964. Continued in Anson F. Rainey, *El-Amarna Tablets, 359–379*. 2nd rev. ed. Kevelaer: Butzon & Bercker, 1978
EAEHL	*Encyclopedia of Archaeological Excavations in the Holy Land*. Edited by Michael Avi-Yonah. 4 vols. Jerusalem: Israel Exploration Society and Massada Press, 1975
EANEC	*Explorations in Ancient Near Eastern Civilizations*
EB	Echter Bibel
EBib	*Etudes bibliques*
EBR	*Encyclopedia of the Bible and Its Reception*. Edited by Hans-Josef Klauck et al. Berlin: de Gruyter, 2009–
ECC	Eerdmans Critical Commentary
ECF	Early Church Fathers
ECR	*Eastern Churches Review*
ECT	*The Egyptian Coffin Texts*. Edited by Adriaan de Buck and Alan H. Gardiner. Chicago: University of Chicago Press, 1935–1947EdF Erträge der Forschung
EDB	*Eerdmans Dictionary of the Bible*. Edited by David Noel Freedman. Grand Rapids: Eerdmans, 2000
EDNT	*Exegetical Dictionary of the New Testament*. Edited by Horst Balz and Gerhard Schneider. ET. 3 vols. Grand Rapids: Eerdmans, 1990–1993
EDSS	*Encyclopedia of the Dead Sea Scrolls*. Edited by Lawrence H. Schiffman and James C. VanderKam. 2 vols. New York: Oxford University Press, 2000
EEA	*L'epigrafia ebraica antica*. Sabatino Moscati. Rome: Pontifical Biblical Institute, 1951
EEC	*Encyclopedia of Early Christianity*. Edited by Everett Ferguson. 2nd ed. New York: Garland, 1997
EECh	*Encyclopedia of the Early Church*. Edited by Angelo di Berardino. Translated by Adrian Walford. New York: Oxford University Press, 1992
EfMex	*Efemerides mexicana*
EFN	Estudios de filología neotestamentaria
EgT	*Eglise et théologie*
EHAT	Exegetisches Handbuch zum Alten Testament
EI^2	*Encyclopedia of Islam*. Edited by Clifford E. Bosworth et al. 2nd ed. 12 vols. Leiden: Brill, 1954–2005
EI^3	*Encyclopedia of Islam Three*. Edited by Marc Gaborieau et al. 3rd ed. Leiden: Brill, 2007–
EIr	*Encyclopaedia Iranica*. Edited by Ehsan Yarshater. London: Routledge & Kegan Paul, 1982–
EIs	*Encyclopaedia Islamica*. Edited by Wilferd Madelung and Farhad Daftary. Leiden: Brill, 2008–

EJIW	*Encyclopedia of Jews in the Islamic World*. Edited by Norman A. Stillman. 5 vols. Leiden: Brill, 2010
EJL	Early Judaism and Its Literature
EJud	*The Encyclopedia of Judaism*. Edited by Jacob Neusner, Alan J. Avery-Peck, and William Scott Green. 2nd ed. 5 vols. Leiden: Brill, 2005
EKKNT	Evangelisch-katholischer Kommentar zum Neuen Testament
EKL	*Evangelisches Kirchenlexikon*. Edited by Erwin Fahlbusch et al. 4 vols. 3rd ed. Göttingen: Vandenhoeck & Ruprecht, 1985–1996
Elenchus	*Elenchus Bibliographicus Biblicus of Biblica*. Rome: Biblical Institute Press, 1985–
ELKZ	*Evangelisch-Lutherische Kirchenzeitung*
EM	Etudes musulmanes
EMC	*Echos du monde classique/Classical Views*
Enc	*Encounter*
EnchBib	*Enchiridion Biblicum*
EncJud	*Encyclopedia Judaica*. Edited by Fred Skolnik and Michael Berenbaum. 2nd ed. 22 vols. Detroit: Macmillan Reference USA, 2007
EPap	*Etudes de papyrologie*
Epiph	*Epiphany*
EPRO	Etudes préliminaires aux religions orientales dans l'empire romain
EQ	*Encyclopædia of the Qurʾān*. Edited by Jane Dammen McAuliffe. 6 vols. Leiden: Brill, 2001–2006
ER	*Encyclopedia of Religion*. Edited by Lindsay Jones. 2nd ed. 15 vols. Detroit: Macmillan Reference USA, 2005
ERAS	*Epithètes royales akkadiennes et sumériennes*. M.-J. Seux. Paris: Letouzey et Ané, 1967
ERE	*Encyclopedia of Religion and Ethics*. Edited by James Hastings. 13 vols. New York: Scribner's Sons, 1908–1927. Repr., 7 vols. 1951
ErIsr	*Eretz-Israel*
ErJb	*Eranos-Jahrbuch*
EstAg	*Estudio Agustiniano*
EstBib	*Estudios bíblicos*
EstEcl	*Estudios eclesiásticos*
EstMin	*Estudios mindonienses*
EstTeo	*Estudios teológicos*
ETCSL	Electronic Text Corpus of Sumerian Literature
ETL	*Ephemerides Theologicae Lovanienses*
ETR	*Etudes théologiques et religieuses*
ETS	Erfurter theologische Studien
EuroJTh	European Journal of Theology
EvJ	*Evangelical Journal*
EvK	Evangelische Kommentare
EvQ	*Evangelical Quarterly*
EvT	*Evangelische Theologie*

ExAud	*Ex Auditu*
Exeg	*Exegetica* [Japanese]
Expedition	*Expedition: Bulletin of the University Muesum of the University of Pennsylvania*
ExpTim	*Expository Times*
FAOS	Freiburger altorientalische Studien
FARG	Forschungen zur Anthropologie und Religionsgeschichte
FAT	Forschungen zum Alten Testament
FB	Forschung zur Bibel
FBBS	Facet Books, Biblical Series
FBE	Forum for Bibelsk Eksegese
FC	Fathers of the Church
FCB	Feminist Companion to the Bible
FCIW	Formation of the Classical Islamic World
FCNTECW	Feminist Companion to the New Testament and Early Christian Writings
FF	*Forschungen und Fortschritte*
FF	Foundations and Facets
FGH	*Die Fragmente der griechischen Historiker*. Edited by Felix Jacoby. Leiden: Brill, 1954–1964
FHG	Fragmenta Historicorum Graecorum. Paris, 1841–1870
FiE	*Forschungen in Ephesos*
FIOTL	Formation and Interpretation of Old Testament Literature
FJTC	Flavius Josephus: Translation and Commentary
FMSt	Frühmittelalterliche Studien
FO	*Folia Orientalia*
FoiVie	*Foi et vie*
ForFasc	*Forum Fascicles*
Foster, *Muses*	Foster, Benjamin R. *Before the Muses: An Anthology of Akkadian Literature*. 3rd ed. 2 vols. Bethesda, MD: CDL, 2005
FOTL	Forms of the Old Testament Literature
Fran	*Franciscanum*
FRLANT	Forschungen zur Religion und Literatur des Alten und Neuen Testaments
FSBP	Fontes et Subsidia ad Bibliam Pertinentes
FT	*Folia Theologica*
FuB	Forschungen und Berichte
Fund	*Fundamentum*
FZPhTh	*Freiburger Zeitschrift für Philosophie und Theologie*
GAAL	Göttinger Arbeitshefte zur altorientalischen Literatur
GAG	*Grundriss der akkadischen Grammatik*. Wolfram von Soden. 2nd ed. Rome: Pontifical Biblical Institute, 1969
GAT	Grundrisse zum Alten Testament
GBS	Guides to Biblical Scholarship

GCDS	*Graphic Concordance to the Dead Sea Scrolls*. Edited by James H. Charlesworth et al. Tübingen, 1991
GCS	Die griechischen christlichen Schriftsteller der ersten [drei] Jahrhunderte
GELS	*A Greek-English Lexicon of the Septuagint*. Takamitsu Muraoka. Leuven: Peeters, 2009
GHL	*A Grammar of the Hittite Language*. Harry A. Hoffner Jr., and H. Craig Melchert. 2 vols. Winona Lake, IN: Eisenbrauns, 2008
GKC	*Gesenius' Hebrew Grammar*. Edited by Emil Kautzsch. Translated by Arther E. Cowley. 2nd ed. Oxford: Clarendon, 1910
GMTR	Guides to the Mesopotamian Textual Record
Gn	*Gnomon*
GNS	*Good News Studies*
GNT	Grundrisse zum Neuen Testament
GOTR	*Greek Orthodox Theological Review*
GP	*Géographie de la Palestine*. Félix-Marie Abel. 2 vols. Paris, 1933
GPBS	Global Perspectives on Biblical Scholarship
GR	*Greece and Rome*
GRBS	*Greek, Roman, and Byzantine Studies*
Greg	*Gregorianum*
GS	*Gesammelte Studien*
GTA	Göttinger theologischer Arbeiten
GTR	Gender, Theory, and Religion
GTT	*Gereformeerd theologisch tijdschrift*
GTTOT	*The Geographical and Topographical Texts of the Old Testament*. Edited by Jan Josef Simons. Leiden: Brill, 1959
GVG	*Grundriss der vergleichenden Grammatik der semitischen Sprachen*. Carl Brockelmann, 2 vols. Berlin: Reuther & Reichard; New York: Lemcke & Buechne, 1908–1913. Repr., Hildesheim: Olms, 1961
HACL	History, Archaeology, and Culture of the Levant
HAL	*Hebräisches und aramäisches Lexikon zum Alten Testament*. Ludwig Koehler, Walter Baumgartner, and Johann J. Stamm. 3rd ed. Leiden: Brill, 1995, 2004
HALOT	*The Hebrew and Aramaic Lexicon of the Old Testament*. Ludwig Koehler, Walter Baumgartner, and Johann J. Stamm. Translated and edited under the supervision of Mervyn E. J. Richardson. 4 vols. Leiden: Brill, 1994–1999
HANE/M	History of the Ancient Near East/Monographs
HAR	*Hebrew Annual Review*
Harris	Harris, Zelig S. *A Grammar of the Phoenician Language*. New Haven: American Oriental Society, 1936. Repr., 1990
HAT	Handbuch zum Alten Testament
HBAI	*Hebrew Bible and Ancient Israel*

HBC	*Harper's Bible Commentary*. Edited by James L. Mays et al. San Francisco: Harper & Row, 1988
HBCE	The Hebrew Bible: A Critical Edition
HBD	*HarperCollins Bible Dictionary*. Edited by Mark Allan Powell et al. 3rd ed. San Francisco: HarperOne, 2011
HBS	History of Biblical Studies
HBT	*Horizons in Biblical Theology*
HCMR	History of Christian-Muslim Relations
HCOT	Historical Commentary on the Old Testament
HCS	Hellenistic Culture and Society
HdA	Handbuch der Archäologie
HDR	Harvard Dissertations in Religion
HED	*Hittite Etymological Dictionary*. Jaan Puhvel. Berlin: Mouton, 1984–
Hell	*Hellenica: Recueil d'épigraphie, de numismatique et d'antiquités grecques*
Hen	*Henoch*
Herm	*Hermanthena*
Hesperia	*Hesperia: Journal of the American School of Classical Studies at Athens*
Hethitica	*Hethitica*
HeyJ	Heythrop Journal
HibJ	Hibbert Journal
Historia	*Historia: Zeitschrift für alte Geschichte*
HKAT	Handkommentar zum Alten Testament
HKL	*Handbuch der Keilschriftliteratur*. Rykle Borger. 3 vols. Berlin: de Gruyter, 1967–1975
HKNT	Handkommentar zum Neuen Testament
HNT	Handbuch zum Neuen Testament
HNTC	Harper's New Testament Commentaries
HdO	Handbuch der Orientalistik
Hok	*Hokhma*
HolBD	*Holman Bible Dictionary*. Edited by Trent C. Butler. Nashville: Holman Bible Publishers, 1991
Hor	*Horizons*
HPMM	Hethitologie Portal Mainz–Materialien
HR	*History of Religions*
HRCS	Hatch, Edwin, and Henry A. Redpath. *Concordance to the Septuagint and Other Greek Versions of the Old Testament*. 2 vols. Oxford: Clarendon, 1897. 2nd ed. Grand Rapids: Baker, 1998
HS	*Hebrew Studies*
HSAO	Heidelberger Studien zum Alten Orient
HSAT	*Die Heilige Schrift des Alten Testaments*. Edited by Emil Kautzsch and Alfred Bertholet. 4th ed. Tübingen: Mohr Siebeck, 1922–1923
HSCP	*Harvard Studies in Classical Philology*
HSem	*Horae semiticae*. Margaret Dunlop Gibson et al. 9 vols. London: Clay; Cambridge: Cambridge University Press, 1903–1916

HSM	Harvard Semitic Monographs
HSS	Harvard Semitic Studies
HistTh	*History and Theory*
HT	*History Today*
HTB	Histoire du texte biblique. Lausanne, 1996–
HTh	*Ho Theológos*
HThKAT	Herders Theologischer Kommentar zum Alten Testament
HThKNT	Herders Theologischer Kommentar zum Neuen Testament
HTR	*Harvard Theological Review*
HTS	Harvard Theological Studies
HUCA	*Hebrew Union College Annual*
HUCM	Monographs of the Hebrew Union College
Hug	*Hugoye: Journal of Syriac Studies*
HumTeo	Biblioteca humanística e teológica
HUT	Hermeneutische Untersuchungen zur Theologie
HvTSt	*Hervormde teologiese studies*
HZL	*Hethitisches Zeichenlexikon: Inventar und Interpretation der Keilschriftzeichen aus den Bogazköy-Texten.* Christel Rüster and Erich Neu. Wiesbaden: Harrassowitz, 1989
IAR	*Iraq Archaeological Reports*
IATG[3]	*Internationales Abkürzungsverzeichnis für Theologie und Grenzgebiete.* Siegfried M. Schwertner. 3rd ed. Berlin: de Gruyter, 2014
IB	*Interpreter's Bible.* Edited by George A. Buttrick et al. 12 vols. New York, 1951–1957
IBC	Interpretation: A Bible Commentary for Teaching and Preaching
IBHS	*An Introduction to Biblical Hebrew Syntax.* Bruce K. Waltke and Michael O'Connor. Winona Lake, IN: Eisenbrauns, 1990
IBS	*Irish Biblical Studies*
ICAANE	International Congress on the Archaeology of the Ancient Near East
ICC	International Critical Commentary
ICMR	Islam and Christian-Muslim Relations
ICUR	*Inscriptiones christianae urbis Romae.* Edited by Giovanni B. de Rossi. Rome: Officina Libraria Pontificia, 1857–1888
IECOT	International Exegetical Commentary on the Old Testament
IDB	*The Interpreter's Dictionary of the Bible.* Edited by George A. Buttrick. 4 vols. New York: Abingdon, 1962
IDBSup	*Interpreter's Dictionary of the Bible: Supplementary Volume.* Edited by Keith Crim. Nashville: Abingdon, 1976
IDS	*In die Skriflig*
IEJ	*Israel Exploration Journal*
IEQ	*Integrated Encyclopedia of the Qurʾān.* Edited by Muzaffar Iqbal et al. Sherwood Park, AB: Center for Islamic Sciences, 2013–
IESS	*International Encyclopedia of the Social Sciences.* Edited by David L. Sills and Robert K. Merton. New York: Macmillan, 1968–

IF	*Indogermanische Forschungen*
IGNTP	International Greek New Testament Project
IG	*Inscriptiones Graecae. Editio Minor.* Berlin: de Gruyter, 1924–
IHC	Islamic History and Civilization: Studies and Texts
IHS	Ismaili Heritage Studies
IJMES	*International Journal of Middle East Studies*
IJT	*Indian Journal of Theology*
IKaZ	*Internationale katholische Zeitschrift*
IKZ	*Internationale kirchliche Zeitschrift*
ILCV	*Inscriptiones Latinae Christianae Veteres.* Edited by Ernst Diehl. 2nd ed. Berlin: Druckerei Hildebrand, 1961
ILS	*Islamic Law and Society*
Imm	*Immanuel*
INJ	*Israel Numismatic Journal*
Int	*Interpretation*
IOS	*Israel Oriental Studies*
IPN	*Die israelitischen Personennamen.* Martin Noth. Stuttgart: Kohlhammer, 1928. Repr., Hildesheim: Olms, 1980
IPTS	Islamic Philosophy, Theology, and Science: Studies and Texts
IQ	*Islamic Quarterly*
Iran	*Iran: Journal of the British Institute of Persian Studies*
IrAnt	*Iranica Antiqua*
Iraq	*Iraq*
Irén	*Irénikon*
IRT	Issues in Religion and Theology
IS	*Islamic Studies*
ISBE	*International Standard Bible Encyclopedia.* Edited by Geoffrey W. Bromiley. 4 vols. Grand Rapids: Eerdmans, 1979–1988
ISBL	Indiana Studies in Biblical Literature
Isd	*Isidorianum*
Istina	*Istina*
IstMitt	*Istanbuler Mitteilungen*
Itala	*Itala: Das Neue Testament in altlateinischer Überlieferung.* Adolf Jülicher, Walter Matzkow, and Kurt Aland. 4 vols. Berlin: de Gruyter, 1938–1963
ITC	International Theological Commentary
Iter	*Iter*
Itin (Italy)	*Itinerarium* (Italy)
Itin (Portugal)	*Itinerarium* (Portugal)
ITQ	*Irish Theological Quarterly*
ITT	Ismaili Texts and Translations
IU	Islamkundliche Untersuchungen
IVBS	International Voices in Biblical Studies
IZBG	*Internationale Zeitschriftenschau für Bibelwissenschaft und Grenzgebiete*

JA	*Journal Asiatique*
JAAL	*Journal of Afroasiatic Languages*
JAAR	*Journal of the American Academy of Religion*
JAARSup	Journal of the American Academy of Religion Supplements
JAC	*Jahrbuch für Antike und Christentum*
JACiv	*Journal of Ancient Civilizations*
Jahnow	Jahnow, Hedwig. *Das hebräische Leichenlied im Rahmen der Völkerdichtung*. Giessen: Töpelmann, 1923
JAIS	*Journal of Arabic and Islamic Studies*
JAL	Jewish Apocryphal Literature Series
JAL	*Journal of Arabic Literature*
JANER	*Journal of Ancient Near Eastern Religions*
JANESCU	*Journal of the Ancient Near Eastern Society of Columbia University*
JAOS	*Journal of the American Oriental Society*
JArSt	*Journal of Arabian Studies*
JAS	*Journal of Asian Studies*
JB	Jerusalem Bible
JBC	*Jerome Biblical Commentary*. Edited by Raymond E. Brown et al. Englewood Cliffs, NJ: Prentice-Hall, 1968
JBL	*Journal of Biblical Literature*
JBQ	*Jewish Bible Quarterly*
JBRec	*Journal of the Bible and Its Reception*
JBR	*Journal of Bible and Religion*
JBS	Jerusalem Biblical Studies
JCoptS	*Journal of Coptic Studies*
JCS	*Journal of Cuneiform Studies*
JCSCS	*Journal of the Canadian Society for Coptic Studies*
JCTR	*Journal of Christian Theological Research*
JdI	*Jahrbuch des deutschen archäologischen Instituts*
JDS	Judean Desert Studies
JDT	*Jahrbuch für deutsche Theologie*
JE	*The Jewish Encyclopedia*. Edited by Isidore Singer. 12 vols. New York: Funk & Wagnalls, 1925
JEA	*Journal of Egyptian Archaeology*
JECS	*Journal of Early Christian Studies*
Jeev	*Jeevadhara*
JEH	*Journal of Ecclesiastical History*
JEOL	*Jaarbericht van het Vooraziatisch-Egyptisch Gezelschap (Genootschap) Ex oriente lux*
JES	*Journal of Ecumenical Studies*
JESHO	*Journal of the Economic and Social History of the Orient*
JET	*Jahrbuch für Evangelische Theologie*
JETS	*Journal of the Evangelical Theological Society*
JFA	*Journal of Field Archaeology*

JFSR	*Journal of Feminist Studies in Religion*
JGRChJ	*Journal of Greco-Roman Christianity and Judaism*
JHebS	*Journal of Hebrew Scriptures*
JHI	*Journal of the History of Ideas*
JHNES	*The Johns Hopkins Near Eastern Studies*
JHS	*Journal of Hellenic Studies*
Jian Dao	*Jian Dao*
JIES	*Journal of Indo-European Studies*
JIS	*Journal of Islamic Studies*
JISMOR	*Journal of the Interdisciplinary Study of Monotheistic Religions*
JJA	*Journal of Jewish Art*
JJP	*Journal of Juristic Papyrology*
JJS	*Journal of Jewish Studies*
JJT	*Josephinum Journal of Theology*
JLA	*Jewish Law Annual*
JLCRS	Jordan Lectures in Comparative Religion Series
JMedHist	*Journal of Medieval History*
JMES	*Journal of Middle Eastern Studies*
JMS	*Journal of Mithraic Studies*
JNES	*Journal of Near Eastern Studies*
JNSL	*Journal of Northwest Semitic Languages*
JÖAI	*Jahreshefte des Österreichischen archäologischen Instituts*
JOTT	*Journal of Translation and Textlinguistics*
Joüon	Joüon, Paul. *A Grammar of Biblical Hebrew*. Translated and revised by T. Muraoka. 2 vols. Rome: Pontifical Biblical Institute, 1991
JPJ	*Journal of Progressive Judaism*
JPOS	*Journal of the Palestine Oriental Society*
JQR	*Jewish Quarterly Review*
JQRMS	Jewish Quarterly Review Monograph Series
JQS	*Journal of Qur'anic Studies*
JR	*Journal of Religion*
JRA	*Journal of Roman Archaeology*
JRAS	*Journal of the Royal Asiatic Society*
JRE	*Journal of Religious Ethics*
JRelS	*Journal of Religious Studies*
JRH	*Journal of Religious History*
JRitSt	*Journal of Ritual Studies*
JRS	*Journal of Roman Studies*
JRT	*Journal of Religious Thought*
JSAI	*Jerusalem Studies in Arabic and Islam*
JSem	*Journal of Semitics*
JSHRZ	Jüdische Schriften aus hellenistisch-römischer Zeit
JSJ	*Journal for the Study of Judaism in the Persian, Hellenistic, and Roman Periods*

JSNT	*Journal for the Study of the New Testament*
JSNTSup	Journal for the Study of the New Testament Supplement Series
JSOR	*Journal of the Society of Oriental Research*
JSOT	*Journal for the Study of the Old Testament*
JSOTSup	Journal for the Study of the Old Testament Supplement Series
JSP	*Journal for the Study of the Pseudepigrapha*
JSPSup	Journal for the Study of the Pseudepigrapha Supplement Series
JSQ	*Jewish Studies Quarterly*
JSS	*Journal of Semitic Studies*
JSSEA	*Journal of the Society for the Study of Egyptian Antiquities*
JSSR	*Journal for the Scientific Study of Religion*
JTC	*Journal for Theology and the Church*
JTISup	Journal for Theological Interpretation, Supplements
JTS	*Journal of Theological Studies*
JTSA	*Journal of Theology for Southern Africa*
Jud	*Judaica* (Buenos Aires)
JudChr	Judaica et Christiana
Judaica	*Judaica: Beiträge zum Verständnis des jüdischen Schicksals in Vergangenheit und Gegenwart* (Zurich: Zwingli)
Judaism	*Judaism*
JWSTP	*Jewish Writings of the Second Temple Period: Apocrypha, Pseudepigrapha, Qumran Sectarian Writings, Philo, Josephus.* Edited by Michael E. Stone. Assen: Van Gorcum: Philadelphia Fortress, 1984
K&D	Keil, Carl Friedrich, and Franz Delitzsch. *Biblical Commentary on the Old Testament.* Translated by James Martin et al. 25 vols. Edinburgh, 1857–1878. Repr., 10 vols., Peabody, MA: Hendrickson, 1996
KAH 1	*Keilschrifttexte aus Assur historischen Inhalts.* Leopold Messerschmidt. Vol. 1. Leipzig: Hinrichs, 1911
KAH 2	*Keilschrifttexte aus Assur historischen Inhalts.* Otto Schroeder. Vol. 2. Leipzig: Hinrichs, 1922
KAI	*Kanaanäische und aramäische Inschriften.* Herbert Donner and Wolfgang Röllig. 2nd ed. Wiesbaden: Harrassowitz, 1966–1969
Kairós	*Kairós*
KAR	*Keilschrifttexte aus Assur religiösen Inhalts.* Edited by Erich Ebeling. Leipzig: Hinrichs, 1919–1923
KAT	Kommentar zum Alten Testament
KB	*Keilinschriftliche Bibliothek.* Edited by Eberhard Schrader. 6 vols. Berlin: Reuther & Reichard, 1889–1915
KBANT	Kommentare und Beiträge zum Alten und Neuen Testament
KBL	Koehler, Ludwig, and Walter Baumgartner. *Lexicon in Veteris Testamenti libros.* 2nd ed. Leiden, 1958
KBo	*Keilschrifttexte aus Boghazköi.* Leipzig: Hinrichs, 1916–1923; Berlin: Gebr. Mann, 1954–
KD	*Kerygma und Dogma*

KEK	Kritisch-exegetischer Kommentar über das Neue Testament (Meyer-Kommentar)
Kerux	*Kerux*
KHC	Kurzer Hand-Commentar zum Alten Testament
KI	*Kanaanäische Inschriften (Moabitisch, Althebraisch, Phonizisch, Punisch)*. Edited by Mark Lidzbarski. Giessen: Töpelmann, 1907
KK	*Katorikku Kenkyu*
KlF	*Kleinasiatische Forschungen*
Klio	*Klio: Beiträge zur Alten Geschichte*
KlPauly	*Der kleine Pauly*
KlT	Kleine Texte
Konk.	*Konkordanz der hethitischen Keilschrifttafeln*. Silvin Košak. Wiesbaden: Harrassowitz, 2005–
KS	*Kirjath-Sepher*
Ktèma	*Ktèma: Civilisations de l'Orient, de la Grèce et de Rome antiques*
KTAH	Key Themes in Ancient History
KTU	*Die keilalphabetischen Texte aus Ugarit*. Edited by Manfried Dietrich, Oswald Loretz, and Joaquín Sanmartín. Münster: Ugarit-Verlag, 2013. 3rd enl. ed. of *KTU: The Cuneiform Alphabetic Texts from Ugarit, Ras Ibn Hani, and Other Places*. Edited by Manfried Dietrich, Oswald Loretz, and Joaquín Sanmartín. Münster: Ugarit-Verlag, 1995 (= *CTU*)
KUB	*Keilschrifturkunden aus Boghazköi*. Berlin: Akademie, 1921–
Kuhn	Kuhn, Karl G. *Konkordanz zu den Qumrantexten*. Göttingen: Vandenhoeck & Ruprecht, 1960
KVRG	Kölner Veroffentlichungen zur Religionsgeschichte
L&N	Louw, Johannes P., and Eugene A. Nida, eds. *Greek-English Lexicon of the New Testament: Based on Semantic Domains*. 2nd ed. New York: United Bible Societies, 1989
LÄ	*Lexikon der Ägyptologie*. Edited by Wolfgang Helck, Eberhard Otto, and Wolfhart Westendorf. Wiesbaden: Harrassowitz, 1972
LAI	Library of Ancient Israel
Lane	Lane, Edward W. *An Arabic-English Lexicon*. 8 vols. London: Williams & Norgate, 1863. Repr., Beirut: Libr. du Liban, 1980
LANE	*Languages of the Ancient Near East*
LAPO	Littératures anciennes du Proche-Orient
LASBF	*Liber Annuus Studii Biblici Franciscani*
Laur	*Laurentianum*
LB	*Linguistica Biblica*
LCC	Library of Christian Classics
LCI	*Lexikon der christlichen Ikonographie*. Edited by Engelbert Kirschbaum and Günter Bandmann. 8 vols. Rome: Herder, 1968–1976
LCL	Loeb Classical Library
LD	Lectio Divina
LEC	Library of Early Christianity

LEH	Lust, Johan, Erik Eynikel, and Katrin Hauspie, eds. *Greek-English Lexicon of the Septuagint*. Rev. ed. Stuttgart: Deutsche Bibelgesellschaft, 2003
Leö	*Leöonénu*
Levant	*Levant*
LexSyr	*Lexicon Syriacum*. Carl Brockelmann. 2nd ed. Halle: Niemeyer, 1928
LHBOTS	The Library of Hebrew Bible/Old Testament Studies
LIMC	*Lexicon Iconographicum Mythologiae Classicae*. Edited by H. Christoph Ackerman and Jean-Robert Gisler. 8 vols. Zurich: Artemis, 1981–1997
List	*Listening: Journal of Religion and Culture*
LJPSTT	Literature of the Jewish People in the Period of the Second Temple and the Talmud
LNTS	The Library of New Testament Studies
LQ	*Lutheran Quarterly*
LR	*Lutherische Rundschau*
LS	*Louvain Studies*
LSAWS	*Linguistic Studies in Ancient West Semitic*
LSB	La Sacra Bibbia
LSJ	Liddell, Henry George, Robert Scott, Henry Stuart Jones. *A Greek-English Lexicon*. 9th ed. with revised supplement. Oxford: Clarendon, 1996
LSS	Leipziger semitische Studien
LSTS	The Library of Second Temple Studies
LTK	Lexicon für Theologie und Kirche
LTP	*Laval théologique et philosophique*
LTQ	Lexington Theological Quarterly
LUÅ	Lunds universitets årsskrift
Lum	*Lumen*
LumVie	*Lumière et vie*
LW	*Living Word*
MAAR	Memoirs of the American Academy in Rome
Maarav	*Maarav*
MAD	Materials for the Assyrian Dictionary
MAMA	*Monumenta Asiae Minoris Antiqua*. Manchester and London, 1928–1993
MAOG	*Mitteilungen der Altorientalischen Gesellschaft*
MARI	*Mari: Annales de recherches interdisciplinaires*
Masāq	*Al-Masāq: Journal of the Medieval Mediterranean*
MasS	Masoretic Studies
MBE	Monumenta Biblica et Ecclesiastica
MBPF	Münchener Beiträge zur Papyrusforschung und antiken Rechtsgeschichte
MBS	Message of Biblical Spirituality
MC	Mesopotamian Civilizations

McCQ	*McCormick Quarterly*
MCom	*Miscelánea Comillas*
MCuS	*Manchester Cuneiform Studies*
MDAI	*Mitteilungen des Deutschen archäologischen Instituts*
MDB	*Mercer Dictionary of the Bible*. Edited by Watson E. Mills. Macon, GA: Mercer University Press, 1990
MdB	*Le Monde de la Bible*
MDOG	Mitteilungen der Deutschen Orient-Gesellschaft
ME	*Medieval Encounters: Jewish, Christian and Muslim Culture in Confluence and Dialogue*
MEAH	*Miscelánea de estudios arabes y hebraicos*
Med	*Medellin*
MEE	Materiali epigrafici de Ebla
MEFR	*Mélanges d'archéologie et d'histoire de l'école français de Rome*
MelT	*Melita Theologica*
MFOB	*Mélanges de la faculté orientale de l'Université St. Joseph de Beyrouth*
MGWJ	*Monatschrift für Geschichte und Wissenschaft des Judentums*
MH	*Museum Helveticum*
MIDEO	*Mélanges de l'institut dominicain d'études orientales du Caire*
Mid-Stream	*Mid-Stream*
MilS	*Milltown Studies*
MIOF	*Mitteilungen des Instituts für Orientforschung*
MM	Moulton, James H., and George Milligan. *The Vocabulary of the Greek Testament*. London, 1930. Repr., Peabody, MA: Hendrickson, 1997
Mnemosyne	*Mnemosyne: A Journal of Classical Studies*
MNTC	*Moffatt New Testament Commentary*
MPAIBL	Mémoires présentés à l'Academie des inscriptions et belles-lettres
MRS	Mission de Ras Shamra
MS	Mediaeval Studies
MScRel	Mélanges de science religieuse
MSJ	The Master's Seminary Journal
MSL	*Materialien zum sumerischen Lexikon/Materials for the Sumerian Lexikon*. 17 vols. Rome: Pontifical Biblical Institute, 1937–2004
MSS	Münchener Studien zur Sprachwissenschaft
MSU	Mitteilungen des Septuaginta-Unternehmens
MTSR	*Method and Theory in the Study of Religion*
MTZ	*Münchener theologische Zeitschrift*
Musurillo	Musurillo, Herbert, ed. and trans. *The Acts of the Christian Martyrs*. Oxford: Clarendon, 1972
Mus	*Muséon: Revue d'études orientales*
MUSJ	*Mélanges de l'Université Saint-Joseph*
MVAG	Mitteilungen der Vorderasiatisch-ägyptischen Gesellschaft
MW	*Muslim World* (formerly *Moslem World*)

MZL	*Mesopotamisches Zeichenlexikon*. Rykle Borger. Münster: Ugarit-Verlag, 2003
NABU	*Nouvelles assyriologiques brèves et utilitaires*
NAC	New American Commentary
NAWG	*Nachrichten (von) der Akademie der Wissenschaften in Göttingen*
NBD[3]	*New Bible Dictionary*. Edited by D. R. W. Wood, Howard Marshall, J. D. Douglas, and N. Hillyer. 3rd ed. Downers Grove, IL: InterVarsity Press, 1996
NBf	*New Blackfrairs*
NCB	New Century Bible
NCE	*New Catholic Encyclopedia*. Edited by William J. McDonald et al. 15 vols. New York: McGraw-Hill, 1967
NE	*Handbuch der nordsemitischen Epigraphik*. Edited by Mark Lidzbarski. Weimar: Felber, 1898. Repr., Hildesheim: Olms, 1962
NEA	*Near Eastern Archaeology*
NEAEHL	*The New Encyclopedia of Archaeological Excavations in the Holy Land*. Edited by Ephraim Stern. 4 vols. Jerusalem: Israel Exploration Society & Carta; New York: Simon & Schuster, 1993
NEchtB	Neue Echter Bibel
NedTT	*Nederlands theologisch tijdschrift*
Nem	*Nemalah*
Neot	*Neotestamentica*
NETR	*Near East School of Theology Theological Review*
NewDocs	*New Documents Illustrating Early Christianity*. Edited by Greg H. R. Horsley and Stephen Llewelyn. North Ryde, NSW: The Ancient History Documentary Research Centre, Macquarie University, 1981–
NFT	New Frontiers in Theology
NGTT	*Nederduitse gereformeerde teologiese tydskrif*
NHC	Nag Hammadi Codices
NHL	*Nag Hammadi Library in English*. Edited by James M. Robinson. 4th rev. ed. Leiden: Brill, 1996
NHS	*Nag Hammadi Studies*
NHScr	*The Nag Hammadi Scriptures: The International Edition*. Edited by Marvin Meyer. New York: HarperOne, 2007
NIB	*The New Interpreter's Bible*. Edited by Leander E. Keck. 12 vols. Nashville: Abingdon, 1994–2004
NIBCNT	New International Biblical Commentary on the New Testament
NIBCOT	New International Biblical Commentary on the Old Testament
NICNT	New International Commentary on the New Testament
NICOT	New International Commentary on the Old Testament
NIDB	*New Interpreter's Dictionary of the Bible*. Edited by Katharine Doob Sakenfeld. 5 vols. Nashville: Abingdon, 2006–2009
NIDBA	*New International Dictionary of Biblical Archaeology*. Edited by Edward M. Blaiklock and R. K. Harrison. Grand Rapids: Zondervan, 1983

NIDNTT — *New International Dictionary of New Testament Theology*. Edited by Colin Brown. 4 vols. Grand Rapids: Zondervan, 1975–1978
NIDOTTE — *New International Dictionary of Old Testament Theology and Exegesis*. Edited by Willem A. VanGemeren. 5 vols. Grand Rapids: Zondervan, 1997
NIGTC — New International Greek Testament Commentary
NJahrb — *Neue Jahrbücher für das klassiche Altertum (1898–1925); Neue Jahrbücher für Wissenschaft und Jugendbildung (1925–1936)*
NJBC — *The New Jerome Biblical Commentary*. Edited by Raymond E. Brown et al. Englewood Cliffs, NJ: Prentice-Hall, 1990
NKZ — *Neue kirchliche Zeitschrift*
Notes — *Notes on Translation*
NovT — *Novum Testamentum*
NovTSup — Supplements to Novum Testamentum
NPNF[1] — *Nicene and Post-Nicene Fathers*, Series 1
NPNF[2] — *Nicene and Post-Nicene Fathers*, Series 2
NRTh — *La nouvelle revue théologique*
NSKAT — Neuer Stuttgarter Kommentar, Altes Testament
NTA — *New Testament Abstracts*
NTAbh — Neutestamentliche Abhandlungen
NTApoc — *New Testament Apocrypha*. 2 vols. Revised ed. Edited by Wilhelm Schneemelcher. English trans. ed. Robert McL. Wilson. Cambridge: Clarke; Louisville: Westminster John Knox, 2003
NTD — Das Neue Testament Deutsch
NTF — Neutestamentliche Forschungen
NTG — New Testament Guides
NTGF — New Testament in the Greek Fathers
NTL — New Testament Library
NTM — New Testament Message
NTSI — New Testament and the Scriptures of Israel
NTOA — Novum Testamentum et Orbis Antiquus
NTS — *New Testament Studies*
NTT — *Norsk Teologisk Tidsskrift*
NTTS — New Testament Tools and Studies
NTTSD — New Testament Tools, Studies, and Documents
NumC — *Numismatic Chronicle*
Numen — *Numen: International Review for the History of Religions*
NuMu — *Nuevo mundo*
NV — *Nova et Vetera*
OAC — Orientis Antiqui Collectio
OBO — Orbis Biblicus et Orientalis
OBO.SA — Orbis Biblicus et Orientalis, Series Archaeologica
ÖBS — Österreichische biblische Studien
OBT — Overtures to Biblical Theology

OCD	*Oxford Classical Dictionary*. Edited by Simon Hornblower and Antony Spawforth. 4th ed. Oxford: Oxford University Press, 2012
OCM	Oxford Classical Monographs
OCP	*Orientalia Christiana Periodica*
OCT	Oxford Classical Texts/Scriptorum classicorum bibliotheca oxoniensis
OCuT	Oxford Editions of Cuneiform Texts
ODCC	*The Oxford Dictionary of the Christian Church*. Edited by F. L. Cross and E. A. Livingstone. 3rd ed. rev. Oxford: Oxford University Press, 2005
OEAE	*The Oxford Encyclopedia of Ancient Egypt*. Edited by Donald Redford. 3 vols. Oxford: Oxford University Press, 2001
OEANE	*The Oxford Encyclopedia of Archaeology in the Near East*. Edited by Eric M. Meyers. 5 vols. New York: Oxford University Press, 1997
OECS	Oxford Early Christian Studies
OECT	Oxford Early Christian Texts
OeO	Oriens et Occidens
OGIS	*Orientis Graeci Inscriptiones Selectae*. Edited by Wilhelm Dittenberger. 2 vols. Leipzig: Hirzel, 1903–1905
OiC	*One in Christ*
OIC	*Oriental Institute Communications*
OIMP	Oriental Institute Museum Publications
OIP	Oriental Institute Publications
OIS	Oriental Institute Seminars
OJA	*Oxford Journal of Archaeology*
OLA	Orientalia Lovaniensia Analecta
OLP	Orientalia Lovaniensia Periodica
OLZ	*Orientalistische Literaturzeitung*
Or	*Orientalia* (NS)
OrA	Orient-Archäologie
OrAnt	*Oriens Antiquus*
OrChr	*Oriens Christianus*
OrChrAn	Orientalia Christiana Analecta
Orient	*Orient: Report of the Society for Near Eastern Studies in Japan*
Orita	*Orita*
OrSyr	*L'orient syrien*
OSHT	Oxford Studies in Historical Theology
OTM	Old Testament Message
OTA	*Old Testament Abstracts*
OTE	*Old Testament Essays*
OTG	Old Testament Guides
ÖTK	Ökumenischer Taschenbuch-Kommentar
OTL	Old Testament Library
OTP	*Old Testament Pseudepigrapha*. Edited by James H. Charlesworth. 2 vols. New York: Doubleday, 1983, 1985
OTR	Old Testament Readings

OTS	Old Testament Studies
OtSt	*Oudtestamentische Studiën*
PAAJR	*Proceedings of the American Academy of Jewish Research*
Pacifica	*Pacifica*
PACS	Philo of Alexandria Commentary Series
PAe	Probleme der Ägyptologie
Palamedes	*Palamedes: A Journal of Ancient History*
PapyCast	*Papyrologica Castroctaviana, Studia et Textus*
Parab	*Parabola*
ParOr	*Parole de l'orient*
PaVi	*Parole di vita*
Payne Smith	*Thesaurus Syriacus*. Edited by R. Payne Smith et al. Oxford: Clarendon, 1879–1901
PBS	University of Pennsylvania, Publications of the Babylonian Section
PDM	*Papyri Demoticae Magicae*. Demotic texts in *PGM* corpus as collated in Hans Dieter Betz, ed. *The Greek Magical Papyri in Translation, including the Demotic Spells*. Chicago: University of Chicago Press, 1996
PEFQS	Palestine Exploration Fund Quarterly Statement
PEQ	*Palestine Exploration Quarterly*
Per	*Perspectives*
PerTeol	*Perspectiva teológica*
PG	Patrologia Graeca [= Patrologiae Cursus Completus: Series Graeca]. Edited by Jacques-Paul Migne. 162 vols. Paris, 1857–1886
PGL	*Patristic Greek Lexicon*. Edited by Geoffrey W. H. Lampe. Oxford: Clarendon, 1961
PGM	*Papyri Graecae Magicae: Die griechischen Zauberpapyri*. Edited by Karl Preisendanz. 2nd ed. Stuttgart: Teubner, 1973–1974
PhA	Philosophia Antiqua
Phasis	*Phasis, Greek and Roman Studies*
Phil	*Philologus*
Phon	*Phonetica*
PHSC	Perspectives on Hebrew Scriptures and Its Contexts
PIASH	Proceedings of the Israel Academy of Sciences and Humanities
PIHANS	Publications de l'Institut historique-archéologique néerlandais de Stamboul
PIBA	Proceedings of the Irish Biblical Association
PJ	*Palästina-Jahrbuch*
PL	Patrologia Latina [= *Patrologiae Cursus Completus:* Series Latina]. Edited by Jacques-Paul Migne. 217 vols. Paris, 1844–1864
PLO	Porta Linguarum Orientalium
PMLA	*Proceedings of the Modern Language Association*
Pneuma	*Pneuma: Journal for the Society of Pentecostal Studies*
PNTC	Pelican New Testament Commentaries
PO	Patrologia Orientalis

POut De Prediking van het Oude Testament
Presb *Presbyterion*
ProEccl *Pro Ecclesia*
Proof *Prooftexts: A Journal of Jewish Literary History*
Protest *Protestantesimo*
Proy *Proyección*
PRSt *Perspectives in Religious Studies*
PRU *Le palais royal d'Ugarit*
PS *Patrologia Syriaca*. Rev. ed. Ignatio Ortiz de Urbina. Rome: Pontifical Biblical Institute, 1965
PSB *Princeton Seminary Bulletin*
PSD *The Sumerian Dictionary of the University Museum of the University of Pennsylvania*. Edited by Åke W. Sjöberg with the collaboration of Hermann Behrens. Philadelphia: Babylonian Section of the University Museum, 1884–. Restructured into an online endeavor.
PSTJ *Perkins (School of Theology) Journal*
PTMS Pittsburgh Theological Monograph Series
PTS Patristische Texte und Studien
PTSDSSP Princeton Theological Seminary Dead Sea Scrolls Project
PVTG Pseudepigrapha Veteris Testamenti Graece
PW *Paulys Real-Encyclopädie der classischen Altertumswissenschaft*. New edition by Georg Wissowa and Wilhelm Kroll. 50 vols. in 84 parts. Stuttgart: Metzler and Druckenmüller, 1894–1980
PWSup Supplement to PW
PzB *Protokolle zur Bibel*
Qad *Qadmoniot*
Qanṭara *Al-Qanṭara: Revista de estudios árabes*
QC *Qumran Chronicle*
QD Quaestiones Disputatae
QDAP *Quarterly of the Department of Antiquities in Palestine*
QR *Quarterly Review*
Quasten Quasten, Johannes *Patrology*. 4 vols. Westminster, MD: Newman, 1953–1986
R&T *Religion and Theology*
RA *Revue d'assyriologie et d'archéologie orientale*
RAC *Reallexikon für Antike und Christentum*. Edited by Theodor Klauser et al. Stuttgart: Hiersemann, 1950–
RAI Rencontre assyriologique internationale
RAIS Resources in Arabic and Islamic Studies
RANE Records of the Ancient Near East
RÄR *Reallexikon der ägyptischen Religionsgeschichte*. Hans Bonnet. Berlin: de Gruyter, 1952
RAr *Revue archéologique*

RawlCu	*The Cuneiform Inscriptions of Western Asia*. Edited by H. C. Rawlinson. London, 1891
RB	*Revue biblique*
RBB	*Revista biblica brasileira*
RBén	*Revue bénédictine*
RBK	*Reallexikon zur byzantinischen Kunst*. Edited by Klaus Wessel and Marcell Restle. Stuttgart: Hiersemann, 1966–
RBL	*Review of Biblical Literature*
RBPH	*Revue belge de philologie et d'histoire*
RBS	Resources for Biblical Study
RC	*Religion Compass*
RCB	*Revista de cultura bíblica*
RCT	*Revista catalana de teología*
RdT	*Rassegna di teologia*
RE	*Realencyklopädie für protestantische Theologie und Kirche*
REA	*Revue des études anciennes*
REAug	*Revue des études augustiniennes*
REB	*Revista eclesiástica brasileira*
RechBib	Recherches bibliques
RechPap	*Recherches de papyrologie*
RefLitM	*Reformed Liturgy and Music*
RefR	*Reformed Review*
REg	*Revue d'égyptologie*
REG	*Revue des études grecques*
REI	*Revue des études islamiques*
REJ	*Revue des études juives*
RelArts	Religion and the Arts
RelEd	*Religious Education*
RelS	*Religious Studies*
RelSoc	*Religion and Society*
RelSRev	*Religious Studies Review*
RelStTh	*Religious Studies and Theology*
RES	*Répertoire d'épigraphie sémitique*
RES	Revue des études sémitiques
ResOr	Res Orientales
ResQ	*Restoration Quarterly*
RET	*Revista española de teología*
RevExp	*Review and Expositor*
RevistB	*Revista bíblica*
RevPhil	*Revue de philologie*
RevQ	*Revue de Qumran*
RevScRel	*Revue des sciences religieuses*
RGG	*Religion in Geschichte und Gegenwart*. Edited by Hans Dieter Betz. 4th ed. Tübingen: Mohr Siebeck, 1998–2007

RGRW	Religions in the Graeco-Roman World
RGTC	Répertoire géographique des textes cunéiformes
RHA	*Revue hittite et asianique*
RHE	*Revue d'histoire ecclésiastique*
RHPR	*Revue d'histoire et de philosophie religieuses*
RHR	*Revue de l'histoire des religions*
RIBLA	*Revista de interpretación bíblica latino-americana*
RIDA	*Revue internationale des droits de l'antiquité*
RIM	The Royal Inscriptions of Mesopotamia Project. Toronto
RIMA	The Royal Inscriptions of Mesopotamia, Assyrian Periods
RIMB	The Royal Inscriptions of Mesopotamia, Babylonian Periods
RIME	The Royal Inscriptions of Mesopotamia, Early Periods
RIMS	The Royal Inscriptions of Mesopotamia Supplements
RINAP	Royal Inscriptions of the Neo-Assyrian Period
RISA	*Royal Inscriptions of Sumer and Akkad*. Edited by George A. Barton. New Haven: Yale University Press, 1929
RivB	*Rivista biblica italiana*
RivSR	*Rivista di scienze religiose*
RlA	*Reallexikon der Assyriologie*. Edited by Erich Ebeling et al. Berlin: de Gruyter, 1928–
RLV	*Reallexikon der Vorgeschichte*. Edited by Max Ebert. Berlin: de Gruyter, 1924–1932
RNT	Regensburger Neues Testament
RO	*Rocznik orientalistyczny*
RocT	*Roczniki teologiczne*
RomBarb	*Romanobarbarica*
RoMo	Rowohlts Monographien
RPP	*Religion Past and Present: Encyclopedia of Theology and Religion*. Edited by Hans Dieter Betz et al. 14 vols. Leiden: Brill, 2007–2013
RQ	*Römische Quartalschrift für christliche Altertumskunde und Kirchengeschichte*
RR	*Review of Religion*
RRef	*La revue réformée*
RRelRes	*Review of Religious Research*
RS	Ras Shamra
RSC	*Rivista di studi classici*
RSém	*Revue de sémitique*
RSF	*Rivista di studi fenici*
RSO	*Rivista degli studi orientali*
RSP	*Ras Shamra Parallels*
RSPT	*Revue des sciences philosophiques et théologiques*
RSR	*Recherches de science religieuse*
RST	Regensburger Studien zur Theologie
RStB	*Ricerche storico bibliche*

RTAM	*Recherches de théologie ancienne et médiévale*
RThom	*Revue thomiste*
RTL	*Revue théologique de Louvain*
RTP	*Revue de théologie et de philosophie*
RTR	*Reformed Theological Review*
RUO	*Revue de l'université d'Ottawa*
RVV	Religionsgeschichtliche Versuche und Vorarbeiten
SA	Studia Anselmiana
SAA	State Archives of Assyria
SAAB	*State Archives of Assyria Bulletin*
SAACT	State Archives of Assyria Cuneiform Texts
SAALT	State Archives of Assyria Literary Texts
SAAS	State Archives of Assyria Studies
SAC	Studies in Antiquity and Christianity
SacEr	*Sacris erudiri: Jaarboek voor Godsdienstwetenschappen*
SAeg	*Studia Aegyptiaca*
Salm	*Salmanticensis*
SANE	Sources of the Ancient Near East
SANT	Studien zum Alten und Neuen Testaments
SAOC	Studies in Ancient Oriental Civilizations
Sap	*Sapienza*
SAQ	Sammlung ausgewählter Kirchen- und dogmen-geschichtlicher Quellenschriften
SB	*Sammelbuch griechischer Urkunden aus Aegypten*. Edited by Friedrich Preisigke et al. Vols. 1–21. Wiesbaden: Harrassowitz, 1915–2002
SB	Sources bibliques
SBA	Studies in Biblical Archaeology
SBAB	Stuttgarter biblische Aufsatzbände
SBAW	Sitzungsberichte der bayerischen Akademie der Wissenschaften
SBB	Stuttgarter biblische Beiträge
SBFA	Studium Biblicum Franciscanum Analecta
SBFCMa	Studium Biblicum Franciscanum, Collectio major
SBFCMi	Studium Biblicum Franciscanum, Collectio minor
SBFLA	*Studii Biblici Franciscani Liber Annus*
SBL	Society of Biblical Literature
SBLBAC	Society of Biblical Literature The Bible and American Culture
SBLCS	Society of Biblical Literature Commentary on the Septuagint
SBLDS	Society of Biblical Literature Dissertation Series
SBLHS	*Society of Biblical Literature Handbook of Style*. 2nd ed. Atlanta: SBL Press, 2014
SBLMS	Society of Biblical Literature Monograph Series
SBLSBS	Society of Biblical Literature Sources for Biblical Study
SBLSP	Society of Biblical Literature Seminar Papers
SBLStBL	Society of Biblical Literature Studies in Biblical Literature

SBLTT	Society of Biblical Literature Texts and Translations
SBM	Stuttgarter biblische Monographien
SBS	Stuttgarter Bibelstudien
SBT	Studies in Biblical Theology
SC	Sources chrétiennes
ScC	*La scuola cattolica*
SCCNH	Studies on the Civilization and Culture of Nuzi and the Hurrians
ScEccl	*Sciences ecclésiastiques*
ScEs	*Science et esprit*
SCH	Studies in Church History
SCHNT	Studia ad Corpus Hellenisticum Novi Testamenti
Schol	*Scholastik*
SCO	Studi classici e orientali
Scr	*Scripture*
SCR	*Studies in Comparative Religion*
ScrB	*Scripture Bulletin*
ScrC	*Scripture in Church*
ScrHier	Scripta Hierosolymitana
ScrTh	*Scripta Theologica*
ScrVict	*Scriptorium Victoriense*
SCS	Septuagint and Cognate Studies
SD	Studies and Documents
SDAW	Sitzungen der deutschen Akademie der Wissenschaften zu Berlin
SE	*Studia Evangelica I, II, III* (= TU 73 [1959], 87 [1964], 88 [1964], etc.)
SEÅ	*Svensk exegetisk årsbok*
SEAug	Studia Ephemeridis Augustinianum
SecCent	*Second Century*
Sef	*Sefarad*
SEG	Supplementum epigraphicum graecum
SEL	*Studi epigrafici e linguistici sul Vicino Oriente antico*
Sem	*Semitica*
Semeia	*Semeia*
SemeiaSt	Semeia Studies
SemeiaSup	Semeia Supplements
SEVO	Studi egei e vicinorientali
SFSHJ	South Florida Studies in the History of Judaism
SFulg	*Scripta fulgentina*
SHAJ	Studies in the History and Archaeology of Jordan
SHANE	Studies in the History of the Ancient Near East
SHAW	Sitzungen der heidelberger Akademie der Wissenschaften
SHBC	Smyth & Helwys Bible Commentary
Shofar	*Shofar*
SHR	Studies in the History of Religions (supplements to *Numen*)
SHT	Studies in Historical Theology

SIDIC	*SIDIC* (*Journal of the Service internationale de documentation judeo-chrétienne*)
SIG	*Sylloge Inscriptionum Graecarum*. Edited by Wilhelm Dittenberger. 4 vols. 3rd ed. Leipzig: Hirzel, 1915–1924
SILS	Studies in Islamic Law and Society
SIr	*Studia Iranica*
SIs	*Studia Islamica*
SJ	Studia Judaica
SJC	Studies in Jewish Civilization
SJLA	Studies in Judaism in Late Antiquity
SJOT	*Scandinavian Journal of the Old Testament*
SJT	*Scottish Journal of Theology*
SK	*Skrif en kerk*
SKKNT	Stuttgarter kleiner Kommentar, Neues Testament
SL	*Sumerisches Lexikon*. Edited by Anton Deimel. 8 vols. Rome: Pontifical Biblical Institute, 1928–1950
SLAEI	Studies in Late Antiquity and Early Islam
SLJT	*St. Luke's Journal of Theology*
SMBen	Série monographique de Benedictina: Section paulinienne
SMEA	*Studi Micenei ed Egeo-Anatolici*
SMNIA	Tel Aviv University Sonia and Marco Nadler Institute of Archaeology Monograph Series
SMS	Syro-Mesopotamian Studies
SMSR	*Studi e materiali di storia delle religioni*
SMT	*Studii Montis Regii*
SNT	Studien zum Neuen Testament
SNTA	Studiorum Novi Testamenti Auxilia
SNTSMS	Society for New Testament Studies Monograph Series
SNTSU	Studien zum Neuen Testament und seiner Umwelt
SNTW	Studies of the New Testament and Its World
SO	Symbolae Osloenses
SOA	Studia ad Orientem Antiquum
SÖAW	Sitzungen der österreichischen Akademie der Wissenschaften in Wien
Sobornost	*Sobornost*
SOTSMS	Society for Old Testament Studies Monograph Series
Sound	*Soundings*
SP	Sacra Pagina
SPap	*Studia Papyrologica*
SPAW	Sitzungsberichte der preussischen Akademie der Wissenschaften
Spec	*Speculum*
SPhA	Studies in Philo of Alexandria
SPhAMA	Studies in Philo of Alexandria and Mediterranean Antiquity
SPhilo	*Studia Philonica*
SPhiloA	Studia Philonica Annual

SPhiloM	Studia Philonica Monograph Series
SQAW	Schriften und Quellen der alten Welt
SR	*Studies in Religion*
SSEJC	Studies in Scripture in Early Judaism and Christianity
SSL	Spicilegium sacrum Lovaniense: Études et documents
SSN	Studia Semitica Neerlandica
SSS	Semitic Study Series
ST	*Studia Theologica*
St	*Studium*
StABH	Studies in American Biblical Hermeneutics
StBibLit	Studies in Biblical Literature (Lang)
StC	Studia Catholica
STDJ	Studies on the Texts of the Desert of Judah
SThU	*Schweizerische theologische Umschau*
SThZ	*Schweizerische theologische Zeitschrift*
STI	Studies in Theological Interpretation
STJ	*Stulos Theological Journal*
STK	*Svensk teologisk kvartalskrift*
StMed	Studia Mediterranea
StOr	Studia Orientalia
StOR	Studies in Oriental Religions
StPat	*Studia Patavina*
StPatr	Studia Patristica
StPB	Studia Post-biblica
StPohl	Studia Pohl
Str	*Stromata*
Str-B	Strack, H. L., and P. Billerbeck. *Kommentar zum Neuen Testament aus Talmud und Midrasch.* 6 vols. Munich, 1922–1961
STRev	*Sewanee Theological Review*
STSA	Studi e testi di storia antica
StSem	Studi semitici
StSin	Studia Sinaitica
StT	Studi e Testi, Biblioteca apostolica vaticana
StudBib	*Studia Biblica*
StudMon	Studia Monastica
StudNeot	Studia Neotestamentica
StudStor	*Studi storici: Rivista trimestrale dell'Istituto Gramsci*
StZ	Stimmen der Zeit
Su	*Studia Theologica Varsaviensia*
SubBi	Subsidia Biblica
Sumer	*Sumer: A Journal of Archaeology and History in Iraq*
SUNT	Studien zur Umwelt des Neuen Testaments
SVF	*Stoicorum Veterum Fragmenta.* Hans Friedrich August von Arnim. 4 vols. Leipzig: Teubne, 1903–1924

SVTP	Studia in Veteris Testamenti Pseudepigraphica
SVTQ	*St. Vladimir's Theological Quarterly*
SWBA	Social World of Biblical Antiquity
SwJT	*Southwestern Journal of Theology*
SymBU	Symbolae Biblicae Upsalienses
SymS	Symposium Series
T&K	*Texte &* Kontexte
TA	*Tel Aviv*
TAPA	*Transactions of the American Philological Association*
TAPS	Transactions of the American Philosophical Society
Tarbiz	*Tarbiz*
TAVO	Tübinger Atlas des Vorderen Orients
TB	Theologische Bücherei: Neudrucke und Berichte aus dem 20. Jahrhundert
TBC	Torch Bible Commentaries
TBei	*Theologische Beiträge*
TBl	*Theologische Blätter*
TBN	Themes in Biblical Narrative
TBT	*The Bible Today*
TCL	Textes cunéiformes. Musée du Louvre
TCSt	Text-Critical Studies
TCS	Texts from Cuneiform Sources
TCW	*Tydskrif vir Christelike Wetenskap*
TD	*Theology Digest*
TDNT	*Theological Dictionary of the New Testament.* Edited by Gerhard Kittel and Gerhard Friedrich. Translated by Geoffrey W. Bromiley. 10 vols. Grand Rapids: Eerdmans, 1964–1976
TDNTW	*The NIV Theological Dictionary of New Testament Words.* Edited by Verlyn D. Verbrugge. Grand Rapids: Zondervan, 2000
TDOT	*Theological Dictionary of the Old Testament.* Edited by G. Johannes Botterweck and Helmer Ringgren. Translated by John T. Willis et al. 8 vols. Grand Rapids: Eerdmans, 1974–2006
TdT	Themen der Theologie
TDV-EI	*TDV Encyclopedia of Islam* (*İslâm Ansiklopedisi*). Ahmet Topaloğlu, ed. Istanbul: Türkiye Diyanet Vakfı, 1988–.
TENTS	Texts and Editions for New Testament Study
Teol	*Teología*
Text	*Textus*
TF	*Theologische Forschung*
TGI	*Textbuch zur Geschichte Israels.* Edited by Kurt Galling. 2nd ed. Tübingen: Mohr Siebeck, 1968
TGl	*Theologie und Glaube*
TGST	Tesi Gregoriana, Serie Teologia
TGUOS	Transactions of the Glasgow University Oriental Society

THAT — *Theologisches Handwörterbuch zum Alten Testament.* Edited by Ernst Jenni, with assistance from Claus Westermann. 2 vols. Munich: Chr. Kaiser Verlag; Zürich: Theologischer Verlag, 1971–1976
THB — Text of the Hebrew Bible
Them — *Themelios*
Thf — *Theoforum*
Theo — *Theologika*
Theol — *Theologica*
THeth — Texte der Hethiter
ThH — Théologie historique
THKNT — Theologischer Handkommentar zum Neuen Testament
ThPQ — *Theologisch-praktische Quartalschrift*
ThSt — Theologische Studiën
ThT — *Theologisch tijdschrift*
ThTo — *Theology Today*
ThViat — *Theologia Viatorum*
ThWAT — *Theologisches Wörterbuch zum Alten Testament.* Edited by G. Johannes Botterweck and Helmer Ringgren. Stuttgart: Kohlhammer, 1970–
TI — *Teologia iusi*
TimesLitSupp — *Times Literary Supplement*
TJ — *Trinity Journal*
TJT — *Toronto Journal of Theology*
TK — Texte und Kommentare
TLG — *Thesaurus Linguae Graecae: Canon of Greek Authors and Works.* Edited by Luci Berkowitz and Karl A. Squitier. 3rd ed. New York: Oxford University Press, 1990
TLL — *Thesaurus Linguae Latinae*
TLNT — *Theological Lexicon of the New Testament.* C. Spicq. Translated and edited by J. D. Ernest. 3 vols. Peabody, MA: Hendrickson, 1994
TLOT — *Theological Lexicon of the Old Testament.* Edited by Ernst Jenni, with assistance from Claus Westermann. Translated by Mark E. Biddle. 3 vols. Peabody, MA: Hendrickson, 1997
TLZ — *Theologische Literaturzeitung*
TNTC — Tyndale New Testament Commentaries
TOTC — Tyndale Old Testament Commentaries
TP — *Theologie und Philosophie*
TPINTC — TPI New Testament Commentaries
TPQ — *Theologisch-praktische Quartalschrift*
TQ — *Theologische Quartalschrift*
Transeu — *Transeuphratène*
TRE — *Theologische Realenzyklopädie.* Edited by Gerhard Krause and Gerhard Müller. Berlin: de Gruyter, 1977–
TRev — *Theologische Revue*
TRSR — Testi e ricerche di scienze religiose

TRu	*Theologische Rundschau*
Trumah	*Trumah*
TS	Texts and Studies
TS	*Theological Studies*
TSAJ	Texte und Studien zum antiken Judentum
TSK	*Theologische Studien und Kritiken*
TSO	Texte und Studien zur Orientalistik
TSQ	Texts and Studies on the Qurʾān
TTE	*The Theological Educator*
TThSt	Trierer theologische Studien
TTJ	*Trinity Theological Journal*
TTKi	*Tidsskrift for Teologi og Kirke*
TTKY	Türk Tarih Kurumu Yayinları
TTZ	*Trierer theologische Zeitschrift*
TU	Texte und Untersuchungen
TUAT	*Texte aus der Umwelt des Alten Testaments*. Edited by Otto Kaiser. Gütersloh: Mohn, 1984–
TUGAL	Texte und Untersuchungen zur Geschichte der altchristlichen Literatur
TUMSR	Trinity University Monograph Series in Religion
TV	*Teología y vida*
TVM	Theologische Verlagsgemeinschaft: Monographien
TvT	*Tijdschrift voor theologie*
TWNT	*Theologische Wörterbuch zum Neuen Testament*. Edited by Gerhard Kittel and Gerhard Friedrich. Stuttgart: Kohlhammer, 1932–1979
TWOT	*Theological Wordbook of the Old Testament*. Edited by R. Laird Harris, Gleason L. Archer Jr., and Bruce K. Waltke. 2 vols. Chicago: Moody Press, 1980
TynBul	*Tyndale Bulletin*
TZ	*Theologische Zeitschrift*
UBL	Ugaritisch-biblische Literatur
UCOP	University of Cambridge Oriental Publications
UCPCP	University of California Publications in Classical Philology
UCPNES	University of California Publications, Near Eastern Studies
UCPSP	University of California Publications in Semitic Philology
UET	Ur Excavations: Texts
UF	*Ugarit-Forschungen*
UHP	*Ugaritic-Hebrew Philology*. Mitchell J. Dahood. 2nd ed. Rome: Pontifical Biblical Institute, 1989
UJEnc	*The Universal Jewish Encyclopedia*. Edited by I. Landman. 10 vols. New York: Universal Jewish Encyclopedia, 1939–1943
UNP	*Ugaritic Narrative Poetry*. Edited by Simon B. Parker. WAW 9. Atlanta: Society of Biblical Literature, 1997
UNT	Untersuchungen zum Neuen Testament
UrE	Ur Excavations

USFSJH	University of South Florida Studies in the History of Judaism
USQR	*Union Seminary Quarterly Review*
UT	*Ugaritic Textbook*. Cyrus H. Gordon. AnOr 38. Rome: Pontifical Biblical Institute, 1965
UUA	Uppsala Universitetsårskrift
VAB	Vorderasiatische Bibliothek
VAS	Vorderasiatische Schriftdenkmaler
VAT	Vorderasiatische Abteilung Tontafel. Vorderasiatisches Museum, Berlin
VC	*Vigiliae Christianae*
VCaro	*Verbum Caro*
VCS	Variorum Collected Studies (formerly Variorum Reprints)
VD	*Verbum Domini*
VDI	*Vestnik drevnej istorii*
VE	*Vox Evangelica*
VF	*Verkündigung und Forschung*
VH	*Vivens Homo*
Vid	*Vidyajyoti*
VL	Vetus Latina: Die Reste der altlateinischen Bibel
VoxS	*Vox Scripturae*
VR	*Vox Reformata*
VS	Vorderasiatische Schriftdenkmäler der (Königlichen) Museen zu Berlin
VS	*Verbum Salutis*
VSpir	*Vie spirituelle*
VT	*Vetus Testamentum*
VTSup	Supplements to Vetus Testamentum
WÄS	*Wörterbuch der ägyptischen Sprache*. Adolf Erman and Hermann Grapow. 5 vols. Leipzig: Hinrichs; Berlin: Akademie, 1926–1931. Repr., 1963
WAW	Writings from the Ancient World
WAWSup	Writings from the Ancient World Supplement Series
WBC	*The Women's Bible Commentary*. Edited by Carol A. Newsom, Sharon H. Ringe, and Jacqueline E. Lapsley. 3rd ed. Louisville: Westminster John Knox, 2012
WBC	Word Biblical Commentary
WC	Westminster Commentaries
WD	*Wort und Dienst*
WDB	*Westminster Dictionary of the Bible*
Wehr	Wehr, Hans. *A Dictionary of Modern Written Arabic*. Edited by J. Milton Cowan. 3rd ed. Ithaca: Spoken Languages Services, 1976. Repr., 4th enlarged and amended ed., Wiesbaden: Harrassowtiz, 1979
WGRW	Writings from the Greco-Roman World
WGRWSup	Writings from the Greco-Roman World Supplement Series
WHAB	*The Westminster Historical Atlas to the Bible*. George Ernest Wright and Floyd Vivian Filson. Rev. ed. Philadelphia: Westminster, 1974
WHJP	World History of the Jewish People

Wilbour Studies	Wilbour Studies in Egyptology and Ancient Western Asia
WI	*Die Welt des Islams*
WIW	Writings from the Islamic World
WKAS	*Wörterbuch der klassischen arabischen Sprache*. Edited by Jörg Kraemer, et al. Wiesbaden: Deutsche Morgenländische Gesellschaft, 1970–.
WLAW	Wisdom Literature from the Ancient World
WMANT	Wissenschaftliche Monographien zum Alten und Neuen Testament
WO	*Die Welt des Orients*
WOO	Wiener Offene Orientalistik
WTJ	*Westminster Theological Journal*
WTM	*Das Wörterbuch über die Talmudim und Midraschim*. Jacob Levy. 2nd ed. Berlin: Harz, 1924. Repr. 1963
WUANT	Wissenschaftliche Untersuchungen zum Alten und Neuen Testament
WUNT	Wissenschaftliche Untersuchungen zum Neuen Testament
WUS	*Das Wörterbuch der ugaritischen Sprache*. Joseph Aistleitner. Edited by Otto Eissfeldt. 4th ed. Berlin: Akademie, 1974
WVDOG	Wissenschaftliche Veröffentlichungen der deutschen Orient-Gesellschaft
WW	*Word and World*
WZ	*Wissenschaftliche Zeitschrift*
WZKM	*Wiener Zeitschrift für die Kunde des Morgenlandes*
WZKSO	*Wiener Zeitschrift für die Kunde Süd- und Ostasiens*
WZJ	*Wissenschaftliche Zeitschrift der Friedrich-Schiller-Universität Jena*
Xenia	Xenia, Konstanzer Althistorische Vorträge und Forschungen
YCS	Yale Classical Studies
YJS	Yale Judaica Series
YNER	Yale Near Eastern Researches
YOS	Yale Oriental Series, Texts
YOSR	Yale Oriental Series, Researches
ZA	*Zeitschrift für Assyriologie*
ZABeih	Zeitschrift für Assyriologie: Beihefte
ZABR	*Zeitschrift für altorientalische und biblische Rechtgeschichte*
ZAC	*Zeitschrift für Antikes Christentum/Journal of Ancient Christianity*
ZAH	*Zeitschrift für Althebräistik*
ZAL	*Zeitschrift für arabische Linguistik*
ZÄS	*Zeitschrift für ägyptische Sprache und Altertumskunde*
ZAW	*Zeitschrift für die alttestamentliche Wissenschaft*
ZB	Zürcher Bibel
ZBA	Zaberns Bildbände zur Archäologie
ZBK	Zürcher Bibelkommentare
ZDMG	*Zeitschrift der deutschen morgenländischen Gesellschaft*
ZDMGSup	Zeitschrift der deutschen morgenländischen Gesellschaft Supplementbände
ZDPV	*Zeitschrift des deutschen Palästina-Vereins*

ZEE	*Zeitschrift für evangelische Ethik*
ZHT	*Zeitschrift für historische Theologie*
ZIF	*Zeitschrift für Indogermanische Forschungen*
Zion	*Zion*
ZK	*Zeitschrift für Keilschriftforschung*
ZKG	*Zeitschrift für Kirchengeschichte*
ZKM	*Zeitschrift für de Kunde des Morgenlandes*
ZKT	*Zeitschrift für katholische Theologie*
ZKunstG	*Zeitschrift für Kunstgeschichte*
ZNW	*Zeitschrift für die neutestamentliche Wissenschaft und die Kunde der älteren Kirche*
Zorell	Zorell, Franz. *Lexicon Hebraicum et Aramaicum Veteris Testamenti.* Rome: Pontifical Biblical Institute, 1968
ZPE	*Zeitschrift für Papyrologie und Epigraphik*
ZPEB	*Zondervan Pictorial Encyclopedia of the Bible.* Edited by Merrill C. Tenney. 5 vols. Grand Rapids: Zondervan, 1975
ZRGG	*Zeitschrift für Religions- und Geistesgeschichte*
ZS	*Zeitschrift für Semitistik und verwandte Gebiete*
ZSS	*Zeitschrift der Savigny-Stiftung für Rechtsgeschichte*
ZST	*Zeitschrift für systematische Theologie*
ZTK	*Zeitschrift für Theologie und Kirche*
ZVS	*Zeitschrift für vergleichende Sprachforschung auf dem Gebiet der indogermanischen Sprachen*
ZWKL	*Zeitschrift für Wissenschaft und kirchliches Leben*
ZWT	*Zeitschrift für wissenschaftliche Theologie*

APPENDIX A: HEBREW BIBLE/OLD TESTAMENT CANONS

A.1 The Jewish Canon

The traditional number of books in the Jewish canon is twenty-four, since each of the following are understood to be a single book: 1–2 Samuel; 1–2 Kings; the Twelve; Ezra-Nehemiah; and 1–2 Chronicles. The italic titles in parentheses are transliterations of the Hebrew titles.

The Hebrew Bible (*Tanak*)

Torah (***Torah***)
- Genesis (*Bereshit*)
- Exodus (*Shemot*)
- Leviticus (*Wayyiqra'*)
- Numbers (*Bemidbar*)
- Deuteronomy (*Devarim*)

Prophets (***Nevi'im***)
- Former Prophets (*Nevi'im Rishonim*)
  - Joshua (*Yehoshu'a*)
  - Judges (*Shofetim*)
  - 1–2 Samuel (*Shemu'el 'aleph* and *bet*)
  - 1–2 Kings (*Melakim 'aleph* and *bet*)
- Latter Prophets (*Nevi'im 'Aharonim*)
  - Isaiah (*Yesha'yahu*)
  - Jeremiah (*Yirmeyahu*)
  - Ezekiel (*Yehezqe'l*)
  - The Twelve (*Tere 'Asar*)
    - Hosea (*Hoshe'a*)
    - Joel (*Yo'el*)
    - Amos (*'Amos*)
    - Obadiah (*'Ovadyah*)
    - Jonah (*Yonah*)
    - Micah (*Mikah*)
    - Nahum (*Nahum*)
    - Habakkuk (*Havaqquq*)
    - Zephaniah (*Tsefanyah*)
    - Haggai (*Haggay*)
    - Zechariah (*Zekaryah*)
    - Malachi (*Mal'aki*)

Writings (***Ketuvim***)
- Psalms (*Tehillim*)
- Proverbs (*Mishle*)
- Job (*'Iyyov*)
- Song of Songs (*Shir Hashirim*)
- Ruth (*Ruth*)
- Lamentations (*'Ekah*)
- Ecclesiastes (*Qoheleth*)
- Esther (*'Esther*)
- Daniel (*Daniyye'l*)
- Ezra (*'Ezra'*)
- Nehemiah (*Nehemyah*)
- 1–2 Chronicles (*Divre Hayyamim 'aleph* and *bet*)

A.2 The Roman Catholic Canon

The traditional number of books in the Roman Catholic canon is forty-nine. English titles in italic appear in the Roman Catholic canon but not in the Protestant canon. The order of books in Roman Catholic Bibles varies. The order below reflects current editions, such as the Jerusalem Bible and the New American Bible. The italic titles in parentheses are those found in the Latin Vulgate. The appendix of the Latin Vulgate contains 3 Esdras, 4 Esdras, and the Prayer of Manasseh.

Old Testament (*Vetus Testamentum*)

Pentateuch
Genesis (*Genesis*)
Exodus (*Exodus*)
Leviticus (*Leviticus*)
Numbers (*Numeri*)
Deuteronomy (*Deuteronomium*)

Historical Books
Joshua (*Josue*)
Judges (*Judices*)
Ruth (*Ruth*)
1 Samuel (*1 Samuel* [*1 Reges*])
2 Samuel (*2 Samuel* [*2 Reges*])
1 Kings ([3] *1 Reges*)
2 Kings ([4] *2 Reges*)
1 Chronicles (*1 Paralipomena*)
2 Chronicles (*2 Paralipomena*)
Ezra (*1 Esdras*)
Nehemiah (*2 Esdras*)
Tobit (*Tobias*)
Judith (*Judith*)
Esther [*with 6 additions*] (*Esther*)
1 Maccabees (*1 Macchabaei*)
2 Maccabees (*2 Macchabaei*)

Wisdom Books
Job (*Job*)
Psalms (*Psalmi*)
Proverbs (*Proverbia Salomonis*)
Ecclesiastes (*Ecclesiastes*)
Song of Songs (*Canticum canticorum*)
Wisdom of Solomon (*Sapientia*)
Ecclesiasticus (*Ecclesiasticus*)

Prophetic Books
Isaiah (*Isaias*)
Jeremiah (*Jeremias*)
Lamentations (*Lamentationes*)
Baruch [*chapter 6 = the Epistle of Jeremiah*] (*Baruch*)
Ezekiel (*Ezechiel*)
Daniel [*with 3 additions: the Prayer of Azariah and the Song of the Three Young Men, Susanna, and Bel and the Dragon*] (*Daniel*)
Hosea (*Osee*)
Joel (*Joel*)
Amos (*Amos*)
Obadiah (*Abdias*)
Jonah (*Jonas*)
Micah (*Michaeas*)
Nahum (*Nahum*)
Habakkuk (*Habacuc*)
Zephaniah (*Sophonias*)
Haggai (*Aggaeus*)
Zechariah (*Zacharias*)
Malachi (*Malachias*)

A.3 The Orthodox Canon

Orthodox here refers to the Greek and Russian Orthodox churches, the Slavonic Bible being the traditional text of the latter. In Orthodox Bibles, 4 Maccabees and the Prayer of Manasseh—and in Slavonic, 3 Esdras—are in an appendix.[1]

The Old Testament

Historical Books
Genesis (*Genesis*)
Exodus (*Exodos*)
Leviticus (*Leuitikon*)
Numbers (*Arithmoi*)
Deuteronomy (*Deuteronomion*)
Joshua (*Iēsous*)
Judges (*Kritai*)
Ruth (*Routh*)
1 Kingdoms (*Basileiōn A′*)[2]
2 Kingdoms (*Basileiōn B′*)
3 Kingdoms (*Basileiōn G′*)
4 Kingdoms (*Basileiōn D′*)
1 Chronicles (*Paraleipomenōn A′*)
2 Chronicles (*Paraleipomenōn B′*)
1 Esdras (*Esdras A′*)[3]
2 Esdras (*Esdras B′*)
Nehemiah (*Neemias*)
Tobit (*Tōbit*)
Judith (*Ioudith*)
Esther [*with 6 additions*] (*Esthēr*)
1 Maccabees (*Makkabaiōn A′*)
2 Maccabees (*Makkabaiōn B′*)
3 Maccabees (*Makkabaiōn G′*)

Poetic and Didactic Books
Psalms [*with Psalm 151*] (*Psalmoi*)
Job (*Iōb*)
Proverbs (*Paroimiai Solomōntos*)
Ecclesiastes (*Ekklēsiastēs*)
Song of Songs (*Asma*)
Wisdom of Solomon (*Sophia Solomōntos*)
Wisdom of Sirach (*Sophia Seirach*)

Prophetic Books
Hosea (*Ōsēe*)
Amos (*Amōs*)
Micah (*Michaias*)
Joel (*Iōēl*)
Obadiah (*Abdiou*)
Jonah (*Iōnas*)
Nahum (*Naoum*)
Habakkuk (*Abakoum*)
Zephaniah (*Sophonias*)
Haggai (*Aggaios*)
Zechariah (*Zacharias*)
Malachi (*Malachias*)
Isaiah (*Ēsaias*)
Jeremiah (*Ieremias*)
Baruch (*Barouch*)
Lamentations of Jeremiah (*Thrēnoi*)
Epistle of Jeremiah (*Epistolē Ieremiou*)
Ezekiel (*Iezekiēl*)
Daniel [*with the Prayer of Azariah, the Song of the Three Youths, Susanna, and Bel and the Dragon*] (*Daniēl*)

1. The editors thank Father Theodore Stylianopoulos for his assistance with this page.
2. 1 and 2 Kingdoms are the books of Samuel; 3 and 4 Kingdoms are the books of Kings
3. This 1 Esdras (= 1 Esdras in the Apocrypha of the NRSV) is called 2 Esdras in Slavonic Bibles. The 2 Esdras in this canon is equivalent to the bok of Ezra in the NRSV; in some Bibles it also includes Nehemiah.

A.4 The Protestant Canon

The Old Testament

Pentateuch
Genesis
Exodus
Leviticus
Numbers
Deuteronomy

Historical Books
Joshua
Judges
Ruth
1 Samuel
2 Samuel
1 Kings
2 Kings
1 Chronicles
2 Chronicles
Ezra
Nehemiah
Esther

Poetic Books
Job
Psalms
Proverbs
Ecclesiastes
Song of Songs

Prophetic Books
Isaiah
Jeremiah
Lamentations
Ezekiel
Daniel
Hosea
Joel
Amos
Obadiah
Jonah
Micah
Nahum
Habakkuk
Zephaniah
Haggai
Zechariah
Malachi

APPENDIX B: ENGLISH/HEBREW/GREEK VERSIFICATION

English	Hebrew	Greek
	Genesis	
	31:48a, 47, 51, 52a, 48b, 49, 50a, 52b	31:46b–52
31:55	32:1	
32:1–32	32:2–33	
	35:16 & 21, 17–20, 22a	35:16–21
	Exodus	
8:1–4	7:26–29	
8:5–32	8:1–28	
	20:14, 15, 13	20:13–15
22:1	21:37	
22:2–31	22:1–30	
	35:9–12, 17, 13–14, 16, 19, 15	35:8–11, 12, 15–16, 17, 18, 19b
	36:8–9	37:1–2
	36:20–34	37:18–20
	36:35–38	37:8–6
	37:1–24	38:1–17
	37:29	38:25
	38:1–7	38:21–24
	38:8	38:26
	38:9–23	37:7–21
	38:24–31	39:1–10
	39:1–31	36:8b–40
	39:32	39:11
	39:33–43	39:13–23
	40:8–10, 12–27, 29, 33, 38	40:6b–8, 10–25, 26, 27–32
	40:30–32	38:27
	Leviticus	
6:1–7	5:20–26	
6:8–30	6:1–23	
	Numbers	
	1:26–37, 24–25	1:24–37
	6:22, 23, 27, 24, 25, 26	6:22–26
16:36–50	17:1–15	
17:1–13	17:16–28	
26:1 (first clause)	25:19	
	26:19–27, 15–18, 44–47, 28–43	26:15–47
29:40	30:1	
30:1–16	30:2–17	

English	Hebrew	Greek
	Deuteronomy	
12:32	13:1	
13:1–18	13:2–19	
22:30	23:1	
23:1–25	23:2–26	
29:1	28:69	
29:2–29	29:1–28	
	Joshua	
	8:30–33; 9:3–27	9:3–33
	19:48, 47	19:47–48
	1 Samuel	
20:42 (last clause)	21:1	
21:1–15	21:2–16	
23:29	24:1	
24:1–22	24:2–23	
	2 Samuel	
18:33	19:1	
19:1–43	19:2–44	
	1 Kings (3 Kingdoms)	
	4:7–8, 2–4, 9–14	4:20–21, 22–24, 25–30
	4:18, 19, 17	4:17, 18, 19
	5:1a	10:30
4:21–34	5:1–14	
	5:15–30, 32b	5:1–16, 17
5:1–18	5:15–32	
	5:31–32a	6:2–3
	6:37–38, 2–3, 14, 4–10, 15–36	6:4–5, 6–7, 8, 9–15, 16–34
	7:13–18, 21, 19–20, 23–24, 26, 25	7:1–6, 7, 8–9, 10–11, 12–13
	7:27–51, 1–12	7:14–37, 38–50
	9:15, 17–19, 20–22	10:23–24a, 24b, 25
	10:23–26	10:26–29
	10:27–29	10:31–33
	11:4, 3, 7, 5, 8, 6	11:3–8
18:33 (last half)	18:34 (first half)	
20:2 (last half)	20:3 (first half)	
	21:20	20:21
22:22 (first clause)	22:21 (last clause)	
22:43 (last half)	22:44	
22:44–53	22:45–54	

English	Hebrew	Greek
2 Kings		
11:21	12:1	
12:1–21	12:2–22	
1 Chronicles		
6:1–15	5:27–41	
6:16–81	6:1–66	
12:4	12:4–5	
12:5–40	12:6–41	
2 Chronicles		
2:1	1:18	
2:2–18	2:1–17	
14:1	13:23	
14:2–15	14:1–14	
Nehemiah		
4:1–6	3:33–38	
4:7–23	4:1–17	
9:38	10:1	
10:1–39	10:2–40	
Job		
41:1–8	40:25–32	
41:9–34	41:1–26	
Psalms[1]		
3:title	3:1	
3:1–8	3:2–9	
4:title	4:1	
4:1–8	4:2–9	
5:title	5:1	
5:1–12	5:2–13	
6:title	6:1	
6:1–10	6:2–11	
7:title	7:1	
7:1–17	7:2–18	
8:title	8:1	
8:1–9	8:2–10	
9:title	9:1	
9:1–20	9:2–21	
	10:1–18	9:22–39
	11–113	**10–112**
11:title	11:1 (first clause)	
12:title	12:1	
12:1–8	12:2–9	
13:title	13:1	
13:1–5	13:2–6 (first half)	
13:6	13:6 (last half)	
14:title	14:1 (first clause)	
15:title	15:1 (first clause)	
16:title	16:1 (first clause)	
17:title	17:1 (first clause)	
18:title	18:1–2 (first clause)	
18:1–50	18:2 (last clause)–51	
19:title	19:1	
19:1–14	19:2–15	
20:title	20:1	
20:1–9	20:2–10	
21:title	21:1	
21:1–13	21:2–14	
22:title	22:1	
22:1–31	22:2–32	
23–29:title	23–29:1 (first clause)	
30:title	30:1	
30:1–12	30:2–13	
31:title	31:1	
31:1–24	31:2–25	
32:title	32:1 (first clause)	
34:title	34:1	
34:1–22	34:2–23	
35:title	35:1 (first word)	
36:title	36:1	
36:1–12	36:2–13	
37:title	37:1 (first word)	
38:title	38:1	
38:1–22	38:2–23	
39:title	39:1	
39:1–13	39:2–14	
40:title	40:1	
40:1–17	40:2–18	
41:title	41:1	
41:1–13	41:2–14	
42:title	42:1	
42:1–11	42:2–12	
44:title	44:1	
44:1–26	44:2–27	
45:title	45:1	
45:1–17	45:2–18	
46:title	46:1	
46:1–11	46:2–12	
47:title	47:1	
47:1–9	47:2–10	
48:title	48:1	
48:1–14	48:2–15	
49:title	49:1	
49:1–20	49:2–21	
50:title	50:1 (first clause)	
51:title	51:1–2	
51:1–19	51:3–21	
52:title	52:1–2	
52:1–9	52:3–11	
53:title	53:1	
53:1–6	53:2–7	
54:title	54:1–2	

1. Bold numbers refer to whole chapters and chapter ranges.

English	Hebrew	Greek
54:1–7	54:3–9	
55:title	55:1	
55:1–23	55:2–24	
56:title	56:1	
56:1–13	56:2–14	
57:title	57:1	
57:1–11	57:2–12	
58:title	58:1	
58:1–11	58:2–12	
59:title	59:1	
59:1–17	59:2–18	
60:title	60:1–2	
60:1–12	60:3–14	
61:title	61:1	
61:1–8	61:2–9	
62:title	62:1	
62:1–12	62:2–13	
63:title	63:1	
63:1–11	63:2–12	
64:title	64:1	
64:1–10	64:2–11	
65:title	65:1	
65:1–13	65:2–14	
66:title	66:1 (first clause)	
67:title	67:1	
67:1–7	67:2–8	
68:title	68:1	
68:1–35	68:2–36	
69:title	69:1	
69:1–36	69:2–37	
70:title	70:1	
70:1–5	70:2–6	
72:title	72:1 (first word)	
73:title	73:1 (first clause)	
74:title	74:1 (first clause)	
75:title	75:1	
75:1–10	75:2–11	
76:title	76:1	
76:1–12	76:2–13	
77:title	77:1	
77:1–20	77:2–21	
78:title	78:1 (first clause)	
79:title	79:1 (first clause)	
80:title	80:1	
80:1–19	80:2–20	
81:title	81:1	
81:1–16	81:2–17	
82:title	82:1 (first clause)	
83:title	83:1	
83:1–18	83:2–19	
84:title	84:1	
84:1–12	84:2–13	
85:title	85:1	
85:1–13	85:2–14	
86:title	86:1 (first clause)	
87:title	87:1 (first clause)	
88:title	88:1	
88:1–18	88:2–19	
89:title	89:1	
89:1–52	89:2–53	
90:title	90:1 (first clause)	
92:title	92:1	
92:1–15	92:2–16	
98:title	98:1 (first word)	
100:title	100:1 (first clause)	
101:title	101:1 (first clause)	
102:title	102:1	
102:1–28	102:2–29	
103:title	103:1 (first word)	
108:title	108:1	
108:1–13	108:2–14	
109, 110, 120–134, 138	**109, 110, 120–134, 138**	
139:title	139:1 (first clause)	
	114:1–8	113:1–8
	115:1–4	113:9–12
	116:1–9	114
	116:10–19	115
	117–147:11	**116–146**
140:title	140:1	
140:1–13	140:2–14	
141:title	141:1 (first clause)	
142:title	142:1	
142:1–7	142:2–8	
143:title	143:1 (first clause)	
144:title	144:1 (first word)	
145:title	145:1 (first clause)	
	147:12–20	147:1–9

Proverbs

English	Hebrew	Greek
	16:6; 15:28; 16:7; 15:29; 16:8–9; 15:30–33a; 16:5, 4a	15:27b–16:4, 6, 9
	20:20–22, 10–13, 23–30	20:10a–12, 13b–16, 17–24
	30:1–14; 24:23–34; 30:15–33; 31:1–9, 10–31	24:24–37, 38–49, 50–68, 69–77; 29:28–49

Ecclesiastes

English	Hebrew	Greek
5:1	4:17	
5:2–20	5:1–19	

Song of Songs

English	Hebrew	Greek
6:13	7:1	

English	Hebrew	Greek
7:1–13	7:2–14	

Isaiah

English	Hebrew	Greek
9:1	8:23	
9:2–21	9:1–20	
63:19	63:19a	
64:1	63:19b	
64:2–12	64:1–11	

Jeremiah

English	Hebrew	Greek
9:1	8:23	
9:2–26	9:1–25	
	25:15–38	32:1–24
	26	33
	27:2–22	34:1–18
	28	35
	29	36
	30	37
	31:1–34, 37, 35, 36, 38–40	38:1–34, 35–37, 38–40
	32	39
	33	40
	34	41
	35	42
	36	43
	37	44
	38	45
	39	46
	40	47
	41	48
	42	49
	43	50
	44:1–30; 45:1–5	51:1–30, 31–35
	46:2–28	26:2–28
	47:1–7	29:1–7
	48	31
	49:1–5, 28–33, 23–27	30:1–5, 6–11, 12–27
	49:7–22	29:8–23
	49:34a–39	25:14–19
	49:36b	26:1
	50	27
	51	28

Ezekiel

English	Hebrew	Greek
	7:6–9, 3–5	7:3–9
20:45–49	21:1–5	
21:1–32	21:6–37	

Daniel

English	Hebrew	Greek
4:1–3	3:31–33	
4:4–37	4:1–34	
5:31	6:1	
6:1–28	6:2–29	

Hosea

English	Hebrew	Greek
1:10–11	2:1–2	
2:1–23	2:3–25	
11:12	12:1	
12:1–14	12:2–15	
13:16	14:1	
14:1–9	14:2–10	

Joel

English	Hebrew	Greek
2:28–32	3:1–5	
3:1–21	4:1–21	

Jonah

English	Hebrew	Greek
1:17	2:1	
2:1–10	2:2–11	

Micah

English	Hebrew	Greek
5:1	4:14	
5:2–15	5:1–14	

Nahum

English	Hebrew	Greek
1:15	2:1	
2:1–13	2:2–14	

Zechariah

English	Hebrew	Greek
1:18–21	2:1–4	
2:1–13	2:5–17	

Malachi

English	Hebrew	Greek
4:1–6	3:19–24	

APPENDIX C: TEXTS FROM THE JUDEAN DESERT

by Emanuel Tov[1]

Introduction

This list revises three earlier versions:[2]

Emanuel Tov with the collaboration of Stephen J. Pfann, *Companion Volume to The Dead Sea Scrolls on Microfiche—A Comprehensive Facsimile Edition of the Texts from the Judean Desert* (Leiden: Brill and IDC, 1993).

Emanuel Tov with the collaboration of Stephen J. Pfann, *Companion Volume to The Dead Sea Scrolls Microfiche Edition* (2nd ed.; Leiden: Brill and IDC, 1995).

Emanuel Tov, "A List of the Texts from the Judaean Desert," in *The Dead Sea Scrolls after Fifty Years—A Comprehensive Assessment,* ed. Peter W. Flint and James C. VanderKam, 2 vols. (Leiden: Brill, 1999), 2:669–717.

The list contains the following data for all the texts from the Judean Desert:

Column 1. The sequential number in the list of the texts from the individual sites in the Judean Desert.

Column 2. The name of the composition as published in DJD or the most central publication outside that series (e.g., the large texts from Cave 1, as well as some texts from Cave 11, which were not scheduled to be included in DJD). In the nomenclature of DJD, a distinction is made between raised lowercase letters designating different copies of the same composition, such as 4QGen^{b} and 4QGen^{c}, and uppercase letters designating independent compositions within a certain literary genre, such as 4QTohorot A and 4QTohorot B. The names also contain references to the material (pap = papyrus), language (ar = Aramaic; gr = Greek; lat = Latin; nab = Nabatean; sem = Semitic), and script (paleo = Paleo-Hebrew; cr = cryptic [A or B]). All other documents are in Hebrew, written on leather.

Column 3. For Qumran texts (section 1): the siglum used in Raymon E. Brown, Joseph A. Fitzmyer, W. G. Oxtoby, and J. Teixidor, *A Preliminary Concordance to the Hebrew and Aramaic Fragments from Qumran Caves II–X, Including Especially, the Unpublished Material from Cave IV* (Göttingen: privately printed, 1988). For texts from sites other than Qumran (sections 2–13): the plate numbers in the early publication.

Column 4. The inventory number of the fragments in the Rockefeller Museum building (a number without details), the Shrine of the Book, Israel Museum (SHR), Biblio-

1. Emanuel Tov kindly provided the appendix of Texts from the Judean Desert. The Society is grateful to Professor Tov for allowing its publication. Citations of works that were listed as "in press" in the first edition of this handbook have been updated to provide the actual facts of publication. This edition has also revised the citations in column 6 to follow a modified author-date format that requires less space than the style used in the first edition, which allows for a larger font size throughout the appendix.

2. In the compilation and editing of this list over the years, I have been ably assisted first by Claire Pfann and then by Janice Karnis.

thèque nationale de Paris (BNP), Department of Antiquities of Jordan (DAJ), and others. An asterisked number (e.g., 216*) refers to a parallel series of numbers assigned to the documents from Naḥal Ḥever and Masada that were transferred from the Shrine of the Book to the Rockefeller Museum building in 1996.

Column 5. Previous sigla, such as C53 (C = Cross; M = Milik; Sl = Strugnell; Sn = Skehan; Sy = Starcky; Ul = Ulrich).

Column 6. Short bibliographical references identifying the names of the editors and publication year together with the plate number(s). Full references are provided in the Editors and Editions Cited section below.

The items in the List of Texts from the Judean Desert are grouped according to the sites at which they were found: first Qumran, and thereafter all other sites arranged from north to south:

No.	Site	No.	Site
1	Qumran	8	Wadi Sdeir
2	Wadi Daliyeh	9	Naḥal Ḥever
3	Ketef Jericho	10	Naḥal Ḥever/Seiyal
4	Khirbet Mird	11	Naḥal Mishmar
5	Wadi Nar	12	Naḥal Ṣeʾelim
6	Wadi Ghweir	13	Masada
7	Wadi Murabbaʿat		

Editors and Editions Cited

Aharoni, Yohanan. 1961. The Expedition to the Judean Desert, 1960, Expedition B. *IEJ* 11:11–24.

Aharoni 1962. Expedition B—"Cave of Horror." *IEJ* 12:186–99.

Alexander, Philip, and Géza Vermes. 1998. *Qumran Cave 4.XIX: 4QSerekh Ha-Yaḥad*. DJD XXVI. Oxford: Clarendon.

Allegro, John M. 1968. *Qumran Cave 4.I (4Q158–4Q186)*. DJDJ V. Oxford: Clarendon.

Attridge and Strugnell 1994. See Attridge et al. 1994.

Attridge, Harold W., et al. 1994. *Qumran Cave 4.VIII: Parabiblical Texts, Part 1*. DJD XIII. Oxford: Clarendon, 1994.

Avigad, Nahman, and Yigael Yadin. 1956. *A Genesis Apocryphon: A Scroll from the Wilderness of Judaea*. Jerusalem: Magnes and Heikhal Ha-Sefer.

Baillet 1962. See Baillet, Milik, and de Vaux 1962.

Baillet, Maurice. 1963. Un livret magique en christo-palestinien à l'université de Louvain. *Le Muséon* 76:375–401.

Baillet 1982. *Qumrân grotte 4.III (4Q482–4Q520)*. DJD VII. Oxford: Clarendon.

Baillet, Maurice, Józef T. Milik, and Roland de Vaux. 1962. *Les "petites grottes" de Qumrân*. DJDJ III. Oxford: Clarendon, 1962.

Bar Adon, Pessah. 1961. The Expedition to the Judean Desert 1960, Expedition C. *IEJ* 11:25–30.

Bar Adon 1977. Judean Desert Caves—The Nahal Mishmar Caves. Pages 683–90 in vol. 3 of *Encyclopedia of Archaeological Excavations in the Holy Land*. Edited by Michael Avi-Yonah and Ephraim Stern. Jerusalem: Israel Exploration Society and Massada.

Barthélemy 1955. See Barthélemy and Milik 1955.

Barthélemy, Dominique, and Józef T. Milik. 1955. *Qumran Cave 1*. DJD I. Oxford: Clarendon.

Baumgarten, Joseph M. 1996. *Qumran Cave 4.XIII: The Damascus Document (4Q266–273)*. DJD XVIII. Oxford: Clarendon.

Baumgarten 1999. See Baumgarten et al. 1999.

Baumgarten, Joseph M., et al. 1999. *Qumran Cave 4.XXV: Halakhic Texts*. DJD XXXV. Oxford: Clarendon.

Ben-Dov 2001. See Talmon, Ben-Dov, and Glessmer 2001.

Benoit 1961. See Benoit, Milik, and de Vaux 1961.

Benoit, Pierre, Józef T. Milik, and Roland de Vaux. *Les grottes de Murabbaʿât*. DJD II. Oxford: Clarendon, 1961.

Brooke 1996. See Brooke et al. 1996.

Brooke 1998. See Alexander and Vermes. 1998.

Brooke, George J., et al. 1996. *Qumran Cave 4.XVII: Parabiblical Texts, Part 3*. DJD XXII. Oxford: Clarendon.

Broshi 2000. See Pfann 2000.

Broshi and Yardeni 1995. See Broshi et al. 1995.

Broshi, Magen, et al. 1995. *Qumran Cave 4.XIV: Parabiblical Texts, Part 2*. DJD XIX. Oxford: Clarendon.

Burrows, Millar. 1950. *The Isaiah Manuscript and the Habakkuk Commentary*. Vol. 1 of *The Dead Sea Scrolls of St. Mark's Monastery*. New Haven: American Schools of Oriental Research.

Burrows 1951. *Plates and Transcription of the Manual of Discipline*. Vol. 2 of *The Dead Sea Scrolls of St. Mark's Monastery*. New Haven: American Schools of Oriental Research.

Charlesworth, James, et al. 2000. *Miscellaneous Texts from the Judaean Desert*. DJD XXXVIII. Oxford: Clarendon.

Chazon 1999. See Chazon et al. 1999.

Chazon 2000. See Pfann 2000.

Chazon, Esther G., et al. 1999. *Qumran Cave 4.XX: Poetical and Liturgical Texts, Part 2*. DJD XXIX. Oxford: Clarendon.

Cohen 2000. See Charlesworth et al. 2000.

Collins 1996. See Brooke et al. 1996.

Collins and Flint 1996. See Brooke et al. 1996.

Cotton 1997. See Cotton and Yardeni 1997.

Cotton 2000a. See Pfann 2000.

Cotton 2000b. See Charlesworth et al. 2000.

Cotton 2002. See Yadin et al. 2002.

Cotton, Hannah M., and Joseph Geiger. 1989. *Masada II, The Yigal Yadin Excavations 1963–1965, Final Reports: The Latin and Greek Documents*. Jerusalem: Israel Exploration Society.

Cotton, Hannah M., and Ada Yardeni. 1997. *Aramaic, Hebrew, and Greek Documentary Texts from Nahal Hever and Other Sites, with an Appendix Containing Alleged Qumran Texts*. DJD XXVII. Oxford: Clarendon.

Crawford 1995. See Ulrich et al. 1995.

Cross, Frank Moore. 1974. The Papyri and Their Historical Implications. Pages 17–29, 57–60 and pls. 59–63, 80, 81 in *Discoveries in the Wadi ed-Daliyeh*. Edited by Paul W. Lapp and Nancy L. Lapp. AASOR 41. Cambridge: American Schools of Oriental Research.

Cross 1994. See Ulrich and Cross 1994.

Cross 2000. See Ulrich et al. 2000.

Cross and Eshel 2000. See Pfann 2000.

Cross and Parry 2005. See Cross et al. 2005.

Cross, Frank Moore, et al. 2005. *Qumran Cave 4.XII:1–2 Samuel*. DJD XVII. Oxford: Clarendon.

Davila 1994. See Ulrich and Cross 1994.

Dimant, Devorah. 2001. *Qumran Cave 4.XXI: Parabiblical Texts, Part 4: Pseudo-Prophetic Texts*. DJD XXX. Oxford: Clarendon.

Duncan 1995. See Ulrich et al. 1995.

Elgvin 1996. See Brooke et al. 1996.

Elgvin 1997. See Elgvin et al. 1997.

Elgvin 1999a. See Chazon et al. 1999.

Elgvin 1999b. See Strugnell, Harrington, and Elgvin 1999.

Elgvin 1999c. See Baumgarten et al. 1999.

Elgvin 2000. See Pfann 2000.

Elgvin and Tov 1994. See Attridge et al. 1994.

Elgvin, Torleif, et al. 1997. *Qumran Cave 4.XV: Sapiential Texts, Part 1*. DJD XX. Oxford: Clarendon.

Ernst and Lange 2000. See Pfann 2000.

Eshel 1999a. See Chazon et al. 1999.

Eshel 1999b. See Baumgarten et al. 1999.

Eshel 2000a. See Pfann 2000.

Eshel 2000b. See Charlesworth et al. 2000.

Eshel and Broshi 2000. See Pfann 2000.

Eshel and Eshel 2000a. See Pfann 2000.

Eshel and Eshel 2000b. See Charlesworth et al. 2000.

Eshel and Kister 2000. See Pfann 2000.

Eshel and Misgav 2000. See Charlesworth et al. 2000.

Eshel, Esther, et al. 1998. *Qumran Cave 4.VI: Poetical and Liturgical Texts, Part 1*. DJD XI. Oxford: Clarendon.

Falk 1999. See Chazon et al. 1999.
Fitzmyer 1995. Broshi et al. 1995.
Fitzmyer 2000a. See Ulrich et al. 2000.
Fitzmyer 2000b. See Pfann 2000.
Flint 2000a. See Ulrich et al. 2000.
Flint 2000b. See Charlesworth et al. 2000.
Freedman, David Noel, and Kenneth A. Mathews. 1985. *The Paleo-Hebrew Leviticus Scroll*. Winona Lake, IN: American Schools of Oriental Research and Eisenbrauns.
Fuller 1997. See Ulrich et al. 1997.
García Martínez, Florentino, Eibert J. C. Tigchelaar, and Adam S. van der Woude. 1998. *Manuscripts from Qumran Cave 11 (11Q2–18, 11Q20–30)*. DJD XXIII. Oxford: Clarendon.
García Martínez et al. 1998. See García Martínez, Tigchelaar, and van der Woude 1998.
Glessmer 2001. See Talmon, Ben-Dov, and Glessmer 2001.
Greenfield, Jonas C., and Elisha Qimron. 1992. The Genesis Apocryphon Col. XII. *AbrN-Sup* 3:70–77.
Grohmann 1961. See Benoit, Milik, and de Vaux 1961.
Grohmann, Adolf. 1963. *Arabic Papyri from Hirbet el-Mird*. Bibliothèque du Muséon 52. Leuven: Publications Universitaires.
Gropp, Douglas M. 2001. *Wadi Daliyeh II: The Samaria Papyri for Wadi Daliyeh*; Eileen Schuller et al., *Qumran Cave 4.XXVIII: Miscellanea, Part 2*. DJD XXVIII. Oxford: Clarendon.
Haelst, Joseph van. 1991. Cinq textes provenant de Khirbet Mird. *Ancient Society* 22:297–317.
Herbert 1998. See García Martínez, Tigchelaar, and van der Woude 1998.
Jastram 1994. See Ulrich and Cross 1994.
Kister, Menahem. 1985–1987. Newly-Identified Fragments of the Book of Jubilees: Jub. 23:21–23, 30–31. *RevQ* 12:529–36.
Lange 2000a. See Pfann 2000.
Lange 2000b. See Charlesworth et al. 2000.
Larson 2000. See Pfann 2000.
Larson and Schiffman 1996. See Brooke et al. 1996.
Larson et al. 1995. See Broshi et al. 1995.
Larson et al. 1999. See Baumgarten et al. 1999.
Lemaire 2000. See Pfann 2000.
Lewis, Naphtali, ed. 1989. *The Documents from the Bar Kokhba Period in the Cave of the Letters*. JDS 2. Jerusalem: Israel Exploration Society, the Hebrew University of Jerusalem, and the Shrine of the Book.
Lifschitz, Baruch. 1961. The Greek Documents from Nahal Seelim and Nahal Mishmar. *IEJ* 11:53–62.
Lifschitz 1962. Papyrus grecs du desert de Juda. *Aegyptus* 42:240–56.
Lim 1997. See Elgvin et al. 1997.

Lim 2000. See Pfann 2000.

Milik, Józef T. 1953. Une inscription et une lettre en araméen christo-palestinien. *RB* 60:526–39.

Milik 1955. See Barthélemy and Milik 1955.

Milik 1961. See Benoit, Milik, and de Vaux 1961.

Milik 1962. See Baillet, Milik, and de Vaux 1962.

Milik, Józef T. 1976. *The Books of Enoch*. Oxford: Clarendon.

Milik 1977. See de Vaux and Milik 1977.

Morgenstern 2000. See Charlesworth et al. 2000.

Morgenstern, Matthew, Elisha Qimron, and Daniel Sivan. 1995. The Hitherto Unpublished Columns of the Genesis Apocryphon. *AbrN* 33:30–54.

Morgenstern and Segal 2000. See Charlesworth et al. 2000.

Morgenstern et al. 1995. See Morgenstern, Qimron, and Sivan 1995.

Muro, Ernest A., Jr. 1997. The Greek Fragments of Enoch from Qumran Cave 7 (7Q4, 7Q8 & 7Q12 = 7QEn gr = Enoch 103:3–4, 7–8). *RevQ* 70:307–12.

Murphy 2000. See Charlesworth et al. 2000.

Naveh 2000. See Pfann 2000.

Newsom 1995. See Broshi et al. 1995.

Newsom 1996. See Brooke et al. 1996.

Newsom 1998. See Eshel et al. 1998.

Nitzan 1997. See Elgvin et al. 1997.

Nitzan 1998. See Eshel et al. 1998.

Nitzan 1999. See Chazon et al. 1999.

Olyan 1994. See Attridge et al. 1994.

Perrot, Charles. 1963. Un fragment christo-Palestinien decouvert a Khirbet Mird. *RB* 70:506–55.

Pfann 1999. See Baumgarten et al. 1999.

Pfann, Stephen J. 2000. *Qumran Cave 4.XXVI: Cryptic Texts;* Philip S. Alexander et al., *Miscellanea, Part 1*. DJD XXXVI. Oxford: Clarendon.

Pfann 2001. See Gropp 2001.

Pfann and Kister 1997. See Elgvin et al. 1997.

Pike 2000. See Pfann 2000.

Puech, Émile. 1979–1981. Fragment d'un rouleau de la Genese provenant du Desert de Juda. *RevQ* 10:163–66.

Puech, Émile. 1989. Notes en marge de 11QpaléoLévitique: Le fragment L, des fragments inédits et une jarre de La grotte 11. *RB* 96:161–83.

Puech 1996. See Brooke et al. 1996.

Puech 1997. Sept fragments grecs de la *Lettre d'Hénoch* (1 Hén 100, 103 et 105) dans la grotte 7 de Qumrân. *RevQ* 18:313–23.

Puech 1998. *Textes Hebreux (4Q521–4Q528, 4Q576–4Q579): Qumran Cave 4.XVIII*. DJD XXV. Oxford: Clarendon.

Puech 2001. *Qumran Grotte 4.XXII: Textes araméens, première partie: 4Q529–549*. DJD XXXI. Oxford: Clarendon.

Puech 2009. *Qumran Grotte 4.XXVII: Textes araméens, deuxième partie: 4Q550–575a, 580–587*. DJD XXXVII. Oxford: Clarendon.

Qimron 1997. See Elgvin et al. 1997.

Qimron 1999. See Chazon et al. 1999.

Qimron, Elisha, and John Strugnell. 1994. *Qumran Cave 4.V: Miqsat Ma'ase ha-Torah*. DJD X. Oxford: Clarendon.

Sanders, James A. 1965. *The Psalms Scroll of Qumran Cave 11 (11QPs[a])*. DJDJ IV. Oxford: Clarendon.

Sanderson 1994. See Ulrich and Cross 1994.

Sanderson 1997. See Ulrich et al. 1997.

Schiffman 1997. See Elgvin et al. 1997.

Schuller 1998. See Eshel et al. 1998.

Schuller 1999. See Chazon et al. 1999.

Schuller and Bernstein 2000. See Pfann 2000.

Schuller and Bernstein 2001. See Gropp 2001.

Skehan and Ulrich 1995. See Ulrich et al. 1995.

Skehan and Ulrich 1997. See Ulrich et al. 1997.

Skehan, Patrick W., Eugene Ulrich, and Judith E. Sanderson. 1992. *Qumran Cave 4.IV: Palaeo-Hebrew and Greek Biblical Manuscripts*. DJD IX. Oxford: Clarendon.

Skehan et al. 1992. See Skehan, Ulrich, and Sanderson 1992.

Skehan et al. 2000. See Ulrich et al. 2000.

Smith 1995. See Broshi et al. 1995.

Sokoloff and Greenfield 2000. See Pfann 2000.

Starcky, Joseph. 1954. Un contrat Nabateen sur papyrus. *RB* 61:161–81.

Steudel 1997. See Elgvin et al. 1997.

Steudel 2000. See Pfann 2000.

Stone 1996. See Brooke et al. 1996.

Stone and Chazon 2000. See Pfann 2000.

Stone and Eshel 1995. See Broshi et al. 1995.

Stone and Greenfield 1996. See Brooke et al. 1996.

Strugnell 1995. See Broshi et al. 1995.

Strugnell and Harrington 1999. See Strugnell, Harrington, and Elgvin 1999.

Strugnell, John, Daniel J. Harrington, and Torleif Elgvin. 1999. *Sapiential Texts, Part 2: Cave 4.XXIV*. DJD XXXIV. Oxford: Clarendon.

Stuckenbruck 2000. See Pfann 2000.

Sukenik, Eleazar L. 1955. *The Dead Sea Scrolls of the Hebrew University*. Jerusalem: Magnes.

Talmon, Shemaryahu. 1999. Hebrew Fragments from Masada. Pages 1–149 in *Masada VI, The Yigal Yadin Excavations 1963–1965, Final Reports*. Edited by Shemaryahu Talmon and Yigael Yadin. Jerusalem: Israel Exploration Society, 1999.

Talmon with Ben-Dov 2001. See Talmon, Ben-Dov, and Glessmer. 2001

Talmon, Shemaryahu, Jonathan Ben-Dov, and Uwe Glessmer. 2001. *Qumran Cave 4.XVI: Calendrical Texts*. DJD XXI. Oxford: Clarendon.

Tanzer 2000. See Pfann 2000.

Tigchelaar, Eibert J. C. 1998. Some More Small 11Q1 Fragments. *RevQ* 18:325–30, pl. 2.

Tigchelaar 1999. See Chazon et al. 1999.

Tigchelaar 2000. See Pfann 2000.

Tigchelaar and García Martínez 2000. See Pfann 2000.

Tov, Emanuel. 1990. *The Greek Minor Prophets Scroll from Naḥal Ḥever (8HevXIIgr)*. DJD VIII. Oxford: Clarendon, 1990.

Tov 1994. See Ulrich and Cross. 1994.

Tov 1995. See Ulrich et al. 1995.

Tov 1997. See Ulrich et al. 1997.

Tov 2000a. See Ulrich et al. 2000.

Tov 2000b. See Pfann 2000.

Tov and White 1994. See Attridge et al. 1994.

Trebolle 1995. See Ulrich et al. 1995.

Trebolle 1996. See Brooke et al. 1996.

Trebolle 2000. See Ulrich et al. 2000.

Trever, John. 1964–1966. Completion of the Publication of Some Fragments from Qumran Cave I. *RevQ* 5:323–44.

Trever 1972. *Scrolls from Qumran Cave I* (= *Three Scrolls from Qumran*). Jerusalem: Albright Institute of Archaeology and the Shrine of the Book.

Ulrich 1994. See Ulrich and Cross. 1994.

Ulrich 1995. See Ulrich et al. 1995.

Ulrich 2000. See Ulrich et al. 2000.

Ulrich 2005. See Cross et al. 2005.

Ulrich, Eugene C., and Frank Moore Cross. 1994. *Qumran Cave 4.VII: Genesis to Numbers*. DJD XII. Oxford: Clarendon.

Ulrich and Flint 2000. See Pfann 2000.

Ulrich, Eugene C., et al. 1995. *Qumran Cave 4.IX: Deuteronomy to Kings*. DJD XIV. Oxford: Clarendon.

Ulrich, Eugene C., et al. 1997. *Qumran Cave 4.X: The Prophets*. DJD XV. Oxford: Clarendon.

Ulrich, Eugene C., et al. 2000. *Qumran Cave 4.XI: Psalms to Chronicles*. DJD XVI. Oxford: Clarendon.

VanderKam 2000. See Pfann 2000.

VanderKam and Milik 1994. See Attridge et al. 1994.

Vaux, Roland de, and Józef T. Milik. 1977. *Qumrân grotte 4.II*. DJD VI. Oxford: Clarendon.

Vermes and Alexander 2000. See Pfann 2000.

Weinfeld and Seely 1999. See Chazon et al. 1999.

Yadin, Yigael. 1962. Expedition D—The Cave of the Letters. *IEJ* 12:227–57, pls. 43–48.

Yadin 1965. *The Ben Sira Scroll from Masada*. Jerusalem: Israel Exploration Society and the Shrine of the Book.

Yadin 1969. *Tefillin from Qumran*. Jerusalem: Israel Exploration Society and the Shrine of the Book, 1969.

Yadin 1983. *The Temple Scroll*. 3 vols. Jerusalem: Israel Exploration Society.

Yadin and Greenfield 1989. See Lewis 1989.

Yadin, Yigael, Jonas C. Greenfield, and Ada Yardeni. 1994. Babatha's *Ketubba*. *IEJ* 44:87–98.

Yadin, Yigael, Jonas C. Greenfield, and Ada Yardeni. 1996. A Deed of Gift in Aramaic Found in Nahal Hever: Papyrus Yadin 7. *ErIsr* 25:383–403.

Yadin, Yigael, and Joseph Naveh. 1989 *Masada I: The Yigael Yadin Excavations 1963–1965, Final Reports: The Aramaic and Hebrew Ostraca and Jar Inscriptions*. Jerusalem: Israel Exploration Society and the Hebrew University of Jerusalem.

Yadin, Yigael, et al. 1994. See Yadin, Greenfield, and Yardeni 1994.

Yadin et al. 1996. See Yadin, Greenfield, and Yardeni 1996.

Yadin, Yigael, et al. 2002. *The Documents from the Bar Kokhba Period in the Cave of Letters: Hebrew, Aramaic and Nabatean-Aramaic Papyri*. JDS 3. 2 vols. Jerusalem: Israel Exploration Society, the Hebrew University of Jerusalem, and the Shrine of the Book.

Yardeni 1997. See Cotton and Yardeni 1997.

Yardeni 2000a. See Pfann 2000.

Yardeni 2000b. See Charlesworth et al. 2000.

Abbreviations of Texts from the Judean Desert

apGen	Genesis Apocryphon
apocr	apocryphon
D	Damascus Document
DibHam	Dibre Hame᾿orot (Words of the Luminaries)
DM	Dibre Moshe (Words of Moses)
En	Enoch
Enastr	Enoch, astronomical books
EnGiants	Enoch, Giants
EpJer	Epistle of Jeremiah
Flor	Florilegium
H(od)	Hodayot (Thanksgiving Scroll)
Hym/Pr	Hymns or Prayers
Hym/Sap	Sapiential or Hymnic fragments
JN	Jerusalem nouvelle (New Jerusalem)
Lit	Liturgy
M	Milḥamah (War Scroll)
Mez	Mezuza
MMT	Miqṣat Maᶜaśê ha-Torah (Some of the Torah Observations)
MSM	Midrash Sefer Moshe

Myst	Mysteries
NJ	New Jerusalem
Ord	Ordinances
p	pesher
par	paraphrase
Phyl	Phylactery
ps	pseudo-
Pr	Prayer(s)
PrFêtes	Prières pour les fêtes
PrQuot	Prières quotidiennes
RitMar	Rituel de mariage
RitPur	Rituel de purification
RP	Reworked Pentateuch (*olim* PP, Pentateuchal Paraphrase)
S	Serekh ha-Yaḥad (Manual of Discipline)
sap	sapiential
ShirShabb	Shirot ʿOlat Hashabbat (Songs of the Sabbath Sacrifice)
T	Temple Scroll
Tanḥ	Tanḥumim
Test	Testimonia
tg	targum
TLevi	Testament of Levi
TNaph	Testament of Naphtali
Unid.	unidentified

General Abbreviations

A	Allegro
A	in list of negatives of 11QT[a]: early reconstructions
ABMC	Ancient Biblical Manuscript Center, Claremont, California
ap	apocryphon
ar	Aramaic
arab	Arabic
bdl	bundle
BA	Babatha archive
BK	Bar Kokhba
BNP	Bibliothèque nationale de Paris
BT	Baillet
C	Cross
CNRS	Centre National de la Recherche Scientifique
col.	column
cpa	Christian Palestinian Aramaic
cr(ypt)	cryptic
D	in list of negatives of 11QT[a]: fragments with the "domino wad"
DAJ	Department of Antiquities of Jordan

E(B)	École Biblique
EG	Ein Gedi
frag.	fragment
G	Department of Antiquities of Jordan (purchased by the government)
gr	Greek
H	Hunzinger
Ḥev	Naḥal Ḥever
IAA	Israel Antiquities Authority
IDAM	Israel Department of Antiquities and Museums (now the IAA)
inv.	museum inventory number
ir	infrared
J	Palestine Archaeological Museum, Jerusalem
JWS	Jerusalem West Semitic Project
Kh.	Khirbet
lat	Latin
LB	Late Bronze Age
loc.	locus, loci
M	in list of negatives of 11QT^{a}: mirror image
M	Milik
Mas	Masada
MB	Middle Bronze Age
ms	manuscript
Mur	Murabbaʿat
nab	Nabatean
ostr	ostracon
paleo	Paleo-Hebrew
PAM	Palestine Archaeological Museum
pap	papyrus
Q	Qumran
R	in list of negatives of 11QT^{a}: infrared
r	recto
SBL	Society of Biblical Literature
Se	Seiyal
SHR	Shrine of the Book, Israel Museum, Jerusalem
SL	Strugnell
SN	Skehan
SY	Starcky
T	McCormick Theological Seminary
uv	ultraviolet
V	Vatican library
v	verso

ITEM NO.	COMPOSITION	CONC	INV	PREV	PUBLICATION
1Q1	Gen		BNP		Barthélemy 1955, pl. VIII
1Q2	Exod		BNP		Barthélemy 1955, pl. VIII
1Q3	paleoLev (and paleoNum?)		BNP		Barthélemy 1955, pls. VIII–IX
1Q4	Deut[a]		BNP		Barthélemy 1955, pl. IX
1Q5	Deut[b]		673		Barthélemy 1955, pl. X
1Q6	Judg		BNP		Barthélemy 1955, pl. XI
1Q7	Sam		BNP		Barthélemy 1955, pl. XI
1QIsa[a]	Isa[a]		SHR		Burrows 1950
	col. I (Isa 1:1–26)				Burrows 1950, pl. I
	col. II (Isa 1:26–2:21)				Burrows 1950, pl. II
	col. III (Isa 2:21–3:24)				Burrows 1950, pl. III
	col. IV (Isa 3:24–5:14)				Burrows 1950, pl. IV
	col. V (Isa 5:14–6:7)				Burrows 1950, pl. V
	col. VI (Isa 6:7–7:15)				Burrows 1950, pl. VI
	col. VII (Isa 7:15–8:8)				Burrows 1950, pl. VII
	col. VIII (Isa 8:8–9:11)				Burrows 1950, pl. VIII
	col. IX (Isa 9:11–10:14)				Burrows 1950, pl. IX
	col. X (Isa 10:14–11:12)				Burrows 1950, pl. X
	col. XI (Isa 11:12–14:1)				Burrows 1950, pl. XI
	col. XII (Isa 14:1–29)				Burrows 1950, pl. XII
	col. XIII (Isa 14:29–16:14)				Burrows 1950, pl. XIII
	col. XIV (Isa 16:14–18:7)				Burrows 1950, pl. XIV
	col. XV (Isa 18:7–19:23)				Burrows 1950, pl. XV
	col. XVI (Isa 19:23–21:15)				Burrows 1950, pl. XVI
	col. XVII (Isa 21:15–22:24)				Burrows 1950, pl. XVII
	col. XVIII (Isa 22:24–24:4)				Burrows 1950, pl. XVIII
	col. XIX (Isa 24:4–25:5)				Burrows 1950, pl. XIX
	col. XX (Isa 25:6–26:18)				Burrows 1950, pl. XX
	col. XXI (Isa 26:19–28:2)				Burrows 1950, pl. XXI
	col. XXII (Isa 28:2–24)				Burrows 1950, pl. XXII
	col. XXIII (Isa 28:24–29:21)				Burrows 1950, pl. XXIII
	col. XXIV (Isa 29:21–30:20)				Burrows 1950, pl. XXIV
	col. XXV (Isa 30:20–31:4)				Burrows 1950, pl. XXV
	col. XXVI (Isa 31:5–33:1)				Burrows 1950, pl. XXVI
	col. XXVII (Isa 33:1–24)				Burrows 1950, pl. XXVII
	col. XXVIII (Isa 34:1–36:2)				Burrows 1950, pl. XXVIII
	col. XXIX (Isa 36:3–20)				Burrows 1950, pl. XXIX
	col. XXX (Isa 36:20–37:24)				Burrows 1950, pl. XXX
	col. XXXI (Isa 37:24–38:8)				Burrows 1950, pl. XXXI
	col. XXXII (Isa 38:8–40:2)				Burrows 1950, pl. XXXII
	col. XXXIII (Isa 40:2–28)				Burrows 1950, pl. XXXIII
	col. XXXIV (Isa 40:28–41:23)				Burrows 1950, pl. XXXIV
	col. XXXV (Isa 41:23–42:17)				Burrows 1950, pl. XXXV
	col. XXXVI (Isa 42:18–43:20)				Burrows 1950, pl. XXXVI
	col. XXXVII (Isa 43:20–44:23)				Burrows 1950, pl. XXXVII
	col. XXXVIII (Isa 44:23–45:21)				Burrows 1950, pl. XXXVIII
	col. XXXIX (Isa 45:21–47:11)				Burrows 1950, pl. XXXIX
	col. XL (Isa 47:11–49:4)				Burrows 1950, pl. XL
	col. XLI (Isa 49:4–50:1)				Burrows 1950, pl. XLI
	col. XLII (Isa 50:1–51:13)				Burrows 1950, pl. XLII
	col. XLIII (Isa 51:13–52:12)				Burrows 1950, pl. XLIII
	col. XLIV (Isa 52:13–54:4)				Burrows 1950, pl. XLIV
	col. XLV (Isa 54:4–55:8)				Burrows 1950, pl. XLV
	col. XLVI (Isa 55:8–57:2)				Burrows 1950, pl. XLVI
	col. XLVII (Isa 57:2–58:6)				Burrows 1950, pl. XLVII
	col. XLVIII (Isa 58:6–59:17)				Burrows 1950, pl. XLVIII

ITEM NO.	COMPOSITION	CONC	INV	PREV	PUBLICATION
	col. XLIX (Isa 59:17–61:4)				Burrows 1950, pl. XLIX
	col. L (Isa 61:4–63:4)				Burrows 1950, pl. L
	col. LI (Isa 63:4–65:4)				Burrows 1950, pl. LI
	col. LII (Isa 65:4–18)				Burrows 1950, pl. LII
	col. LIII (Isa 65:19–66:14)				Burrows 1950, pl. LIII
	col. LIV (Isa 66:14–24)				Burrows 1950, pl. LIV
1Q8	Isa[b] (unopened scroll)				Sukenik 1955, pls. 1–15; figs. 10, 18–21
	frag. 1 (Isa 7:22–8:1)		677		Barthélemy 1955, pl. XII
	frag. 1 (Isa 10:17–19)		SHR		Sukenik 1955, pl. I
	frag. 2 (Isa 12:3–13:8)		677		Barthélemy 1955, pl. XII
	frag. 2 (Isa 13:16–19)		SHR		Sukenik 1955, pl. I
	frag. 3 (Isa 15:3–16:2)		677		Barthélemy 1955, pl. XII
	frag. 3 (Isa 16:7–11)		SHR		Sukenik 1955, pl. I
	frag. 4 (Isa 19:7–17)		677		Barthélemy 1955, pl. XII
	frag. 4 (Isa 19:20–20:1)		SHR		Sukenik 1955, pl. I
	frag. 5 (Isa 22:11–18)		677		Barthélemy 1955, pl. XII
	frag. 5 (Isa 22:24–23:4)		SHR		Sukenik 1955, pl. I
	frag. 6 (Isa 24:18–25:8)		677		Barthélemy 1955, pl. XII
	frag. 6 (Isa 26:1–5)		SHR		Sukenik 1955, pl. II
	frag. 6 bis (Isa 28:15–20)		SHR		Sukenik 1955, pl. II
	frag. 7 (Isa 29:1–8)		SHR		Sukenik 1955, pl. II
	frag. 8 (Isa 30:10–14)		SHR		Sukenik 1955, pl. II
	frag. 9 (Isa 30:21–26)		SHR		Sukenik 1955, pl. II
	frag. 10 (Isa 35:4–5)		SHR		Sukenik 1955, pl. II
	frag. 11 (Isa 37:8–12)		SHR		Sukenik 1955, pl. II
	col. I + frag. 12 (Isa 38:12–40:3)		SHR		Sukenik 1955, pl. III
	col. II (Isa 41:3–23)		SHR		Sukenik 1955, pl. IV
	col. III + frag. 13 (Isa 43:1–27)		SHR		Sukenik 1955, pl. V
	col. IV (Isa 44:21–45:13)		SHR		Sukenik 1955, pl. VI
	col. V (Isa 46:3–47:14)		SHR		Sukenik 1955, pl. VII
	col. VI (Isa 47:17–49:15)		SHR		Sukenik 1955, pl. VIII
	col. VII (Isa 50:7–51:10)		SHR		Sukenik 1955, pl. IX
	col. VIII (Isa 52:7–54:6)		SHR		Sukenik 1955, pl. X
	col. IX (Isa 55:2–57:4)		SHR		Sukenik 1955, pl. XI
	col. X (Isa 57:17–59:8)		SHR		Sukenik 1955, pl. XII
	col. XI (Isa 59:20–61:2)		SHR		Sukenik 1955, pl. XIII
	col. XII (Isa 62:2–64:8)		SHR		Sukenik 1955, pl. XIV
	col. XIII (Isa 65:17–66:24)		SHR		Sukenik 1955, pl. XV
	frag. 6		677		Barthélemy 1955, pl. XII
1Q9	Ezek		677		Barthélemy 1955, pl. XII
1Q10	Ps[a]				Barthélemy 1955, pl. XIII
1Q11	Ps[b]				Barthélemy 1955, pl. XIII
1Q12	Ps[c]				Barthélemy 1955, pl. XIII
1Q13	Phyl		DAJ		Barthélemy 1955, pl. XIV
1Q14	pMic		BNP		Milik 1955, pl. XV
1QpHab	pHab		SHR		Burrows 1950
	col. I				Trever 1972, 150–51
	col. II				Trever 1972, 150–51
	col. III				Trever 1972, 152–53
	col. IV				Trever 1972, 152–53
	col. V				Trever 1972, 154–55
	col. VI				Trever 1972, 154–55
	col. VII				Trever 1972, 156–57
	col. VIII				Trever 1972, 156–57
	col. IX				Trever 1972, 158–59

ITEM NO.	COMPOSITION	CONC	INV	PREV	PUBLICATION
	col. X				Trever 1972, 158–59
	col. XI				Trever 1972, 160–61
	col. XII				Trever 1972, 160–61
	col. XIII				Trever 1972, 162–63
1Q15	pZeph		BNP		Milik 1955, pl. XV
1Q16	pPs		BNP		Milik 1955, pl. XVI
1Q17	Jub[a]		DAJ		Milik 1955, pl. XVI
1Q18	Jub[b]		DAJ		Milik 1955, pl. XVI
1Q19	Noah		647, DAJ		Milik 1955, pl. XVI
1Q19bis	Noah		A. Samuel		Trever 1964–1966, 323–44
1Q20	apGen ar (unopened scroll)		SHR		Avigad and Yadin 1956
1QapGen	Excavated frags. from cave		DAJ		Milik 1955, pl. XVII
	col. I (frag. pulled from side of scroll)		A. Samuel, SHR		Morgenstern et al. 1995, 30–54
	col. II				Avigad and Yadin 1956
	col. III				Morgenstern et al. 1995, 30–54
	col. IV				Morgenstern et al. 1995, 30–54
	col. V				Morgenstern et al. 1995, 30–54
	col. VI				Morgenstern et al. 1995, 30–54
	col. VII				Morgenstern et al. 1995, 30–54
	col. VIII				Morgenstern et al. 1995, 30–54
	col. IX				Avigad and Yadin 1956
	col. X				Morgenstern et al. 1995, 30–54
	col. XI				Morgenstern et al. 1995, 30–54
	col. XII				Greenfield and Qimron 1992
	col. XIII				Morgenstern et al. 1995, 30–54
	col. XIV				Morgenstern et al. 1995, 30–54
	col. XV				Morgenstern et al. 1995, 30–54
	col. XVI				Morgenstern et al. 1995, 30–54
	col. XVII				Morgenstern et al. 1995, 30–54
	col. XVIII				Avigad and Yadin 1956
	col. XIX				Avigad and Yadin 1956
	col. XX				Avigad and Yadin 1956
	col. XXI				Avigad and Yadin 1956
	col. XXII				Avigad and Yadin 1956
1Q21	TLevi ar		647		Milik 1955, pl. XVII
1Q22	DM (apocrMoses[a]?)		DAJ		Milik 1955, pls. XVIII–XIX
1Q23	EnGiants[a] ar		DAJ		Milik 1955, pls. XIX–XX; re-edition: Stuckenbruck 2000
1Q24	EnGiants[b]? ar		BNP		Milik 1955, pl. XX; Stuckenbruck 2000
1Q25	Apocryphal Prophecy		BNP		Milik 1955, pl. XX
1Q26	Instruction (*olim* Wisdom Apocryphon)		BNP		Milik 1955, pl. XX; re-edition: Strugnell and Harrington 1999
1Q27	Myst		DAJ		Milik 1955, pls. XXI–XXII
1Q28	S title		663		Milik 1955, pl. XXII
1QS	S		SHR		Burrows 1951
	col. I				Trever 1972, 126–27
	col. II				Trever 1972, 128–29
	col. III				Trever 1972, 130–31
	col. IV				Trever 1972, 132–33
	col. V				Trever 1972, 134–35
	col. VI				Trever 1972, 136–37
	col. VII				Trever 1972, 138–39
	col. VIII				Trever 1972, 140–41
	col. IX				Trever 1972, 142–43
	col. X				Trever 1972, 144–45

ITEM NO.	COMPOSITION	CONC	INV	PREV	PUBLICATION
	col. XI				Trever 1972, 146–47
1Q28a	Sa		DAJ		Barthélemy 1955, pls. XXII–XXIV
1Q28b	Sb		662–664, 1000		Milik 1955, pls. XXV–XXIX
	Frag. of Sb		Schøyen, MS 1909		Brooke 1998, pl. XXIV
1Q29	Lit. of 3 Tongues of Fire (apocrMoses[b]?)		663		Milik 1955, pl. XXX
1Q30	Liturgical Text A?		BNP		Milik 1955, pl. XXX
1Q31	Liturgical Text B?		BNP		Milik 1955, pl. XXX
1Q32	NJ ar		BNP		Milik 1955, pl. XXXI
1Q33	M (unopened scroll)		SHR		Sukenik 1955, pls. XVI–XXXIV, 47; figs. 11–13, 26–28
	col. I				Sukenik 1955, pl. XVI
	col. II				Sukenik 1955, pl. XVII
	col. III				Sukenik 1955, pl. XVIII
	col. IV				Sukenik 1955, pl. XIX
	col. V				Sukenik 1955, pl. XX
	col. VI				Sukenik 1955, pl. XXI
	col. VII				Sukenik 1955, pl. XXII
	col. VIII				Sukenik 1955, pl. XXIII
	col. IX				Sukenik 1955, pl. XXIV
	col. X				Sukenik 1955, pl. XXV
	col. XI				Sukenik 1955, pl. XXVI
	col. XII				Sukenik 1955, pl. XXVII
	col. XIII				Sukenik 1955, pl. XXVIII
	col. XIV				Sukenik 1955, pl. XXIX
	col. XV				Sukenik 1955, pl. XXX
	col. XV inc. frags. 1 + 9				Sukenik 1955, fig. 27
	col. XVI				Sukenik 1955, pl. XXXI
	col. XVII				Sukenik 1955, pl. XXXII
	col. XVIII				Sukenik 1955, pl. XXXIII
	col. XIX				Sukenik 1955, pl. XXXIV
	frags. 1–10				Sukenik 1955, pl. XLVII
1Q34	LitPr[a]		DAJ		Milik 1955, pl. XXXI
1Q34bis	LitPr[b]		A. Samuel		Milik 1955
1QH[a]	H[a] (unopened scroll)		SHR		Sukenik 1955, pls. XXXV–LVIII; figs. 14–17, 29–30
	col. I				Sukenik 1955, pl. XXXV
	col. II				Sukenik 1955, pl. XXXVI
	col. III				Sukenik 1955, pl. XXXVII
	col. IV				Sukenik 1955, pl. XXXVIII
	col. V				Sukenik 1955, pl. XXXIX
	col. VI				Sukenik 1955, pl. XLVII
	col. VII				Sukenik 1955, pl. XLI
	col. VIII				Sukenik 1955, pl. XLII
	col. IX				Sukenik 1955, pl. XLIII
	col. X				Sukenik 1955, pl. XLIV
	col. XI				Sukenik 1955, pl. XLV
	col. XII				Sukenik 1955, pl. XLVI
	col. XIII				Sukenik 1955, pl. XLVII
	col. XIV				Sukenik 1955, pl. XLVIII
	col. XV				Sukenik 1955, pl. XLIX
	col. XVI				Sukenik 1955, pl. L
	col. XVII				Sukenik 1955, pl. LI
	col. XVIII				Sukenik 1955, pl. LII
	frag. 1				Sukenik 1955, pl. LIII

ITEM NO.	COMPOSITION	CONC	INV	PREV	PUBLICATION
	frag. 2				Sukenik 1955, pl. LIII
	frag. 3				Sukenik 1955, pl. LIV
	frag. 4				Sukenik 1955, pl. LIV
	frag. 5				Sukenik 1955, pl. LV
	frag. 6				Sukenik 1955, pl. LV
	frag. 7				Sukenik 1955, pl. LV
	frag. 8				Sukenik 1955, pl. LV
	frag. 9				Sukenik 1955, pl. LV
	frag. 10				Sukenik 1955, pl. LVI
	frag. 11				Sukenik 1955, pl. LVI
	frag. 12				Sukenik 1955, pl. LVI
	frag. 13				Sukenik 1955, pl. LVI
	frag. 14				Sukenik 1955, pl. LVI
	frag. 15				Sukenik 1955, pl. LVI
	frag. 15 bis				Sukenik 1955, pl. LVI
	frags. 16–44				Sukenik 1955, pl. LVII
	frags. 45–66				Sukenik 1955, pl. LVIII
1Q35	H[b]		DAJ		Milik 1955, pl. XXXI
1Q36	Hymns		DAJ		Milik 1955, pl. XXXII
1Q37	Hymnic Compositions?		DAJ		Milik 1955, pls. XXXII–XXXIII
1Q38	Hymnic Compositions?		BNP		Milik 1955, pls. XXXII–XXXIII
1Q39	Hymnic Compositions?		BNP		Milik 1955, pls. XXXII–XXXIII
1Q40	Hymnic Compositions?		BNP		Milik 1955, pls. XXXII–XXXIII
1Q41	Unclassified frags.		653		Milik 1955, pls. XXXIII–XXXV
1Q42	Unclassified frags.		653		Milik 1955, pls. XXXIII–XXXV
1Q43	Unclassified frags.		653		Milik 1955, pls. XXXIII–XXXV
1Q44	Unclassified frags.		653		Milik 1955, pls. XXXIII–XXXV
1Q45	Unclassified frags.		653		Milik 1955, pls. XXXIII–XXXV
1Q46	Unclassified frags.		653		Milik 1955, pls. XXXIII–XXXV
1Q47	Unclassified frags.		653		Milik 1955, pls. XXXIII–XXXV
1Q48	Unclassified frags.		653		Milik 1955, pls. XXXIII–XXXV
1Q49	Unclassified frags.		653		Milik 1955, pls. XXXIII–XXXV
1Q50	Unclassified frags.		BNP		Milik 1955, pls. XXXIII–XXXV
1Q51	Unclassified frags.		BNP		Milik 1955, pls. XXXIII–XXXV
1Q52	Unclassified frags.		BNP		Milik 1955, pls. XXXIII–XXXV
1Q53	Unclassified frags.		BNP		Milik 1955, pls. XXXIII–XXXV
1Q54	Unclassified frags.		BNP		Milik 1955, pls. XXXIII–XXXV
1Q55	Unclassified frags.		BNP		Milik 1955, pls. XXXIII–XXXV
1Q56	Unclassified frags.		BNP		Milik 1955, pls. XXXIII–XXXV
1Q57	Unclassified frags.		BNP		Milik 1955, pls. XXXIII–XXXV
1Q58	Unclassified frags.		BNP		Milik 1955, pls. XXXIII–XXXV
1Q59	Unclassified frags.		BNP		Milik 1955, pls. XXXIII–XXXV
1Q60	Unclassified frags.		BNP		Milik 1955, pls. XXXIII–XXXV
1Q61	Unclassified frags.		BNP		Milik 1955, pls. XXXIII–XXXV
1Q62	Unclassified frags.		BNP		Milik 1955, pls. XXXIII–XXXV
1Q63	Unclassified frags. ar		BNP		Milik 1955, pl. XXXV
1Q64	Unclassified frags. ar		BNP		Milik 1955, pl. XXXV
1Q65	Unclassified frags. ar		BNP		Milik 1955, pl. XXXV
1Q66	Unclassified frags. ar		BNP		Milik 1955, pl. XXXV
1Q67	Unclassified frags. ar		BNP		Milik 1955, pl. XXXV
1Q68	Unclassified frags. ar		BNP		Milik 1955, pl. XXXV
1Q69	papUnclassified frags.		652		Milik 1955, pl. XXXVI
1Q70	papUnclassified frags. (r + v)		DAJ		Milik 1955, pl. XXXVII
1Q70bis	papUnclassified frags.		A. Samuel		
1Q71	Dan[a]		A. Samuel		Trever 1964–1966; Barthélemy 1955, 150 (no pl.); Ulrich 2000

ITEM NO.	COMPOSITION	CONC	INV	PREV	PUBLICATION
1Q72	Dan[b]		MS 1926/4, Schøyen		Trever 1964–1966; Barthélemy 1955, 151 (no pl.)
2Q1	Gen		643		Baillet 1962, pl. X
2Q2	Exod[a]		643		Baillet 1962, pl. X
2Q3	Exod[b]		739		Baillet 1962, pl. XI
2Q4	Exod[c]		742		Baillet 1962, pl. XII
2Q5	paleoLev		742		Baillet 1962, pl. XII
2Q6	Num[a]		742		Baillet 1962, pl. XII
2Q7	Num[b]		742		Baillet 1962, pl. XII
2Q8	Num[c]		742		Baillet 1962, pl. XII
2Q9	Num[d]?		742		Baillet 1962, pl. XII
2Q10	Deut[a]		742		Baillet 1962, pl. XII
2Q11	Deut[b]		742		Baillet 1962, pl. XII
2Q12	Deut[c]		742		Baillet 1962, pl. XII
2Q13	Jer		741		Baillet 1962, pl. XIII
2Q14	Ps		741		Baillet 1962, pl. XIII
2Q15	Job		741		Baillet 1962, pl. XIII
2Q16	Ruth[a]		62		Baillet 1962, pl. XIV
2Q17	Ruth[b]		644		Baillet 1962, pl. XV
2Q18	Sir		644		Baillet 1962, pl. XV
2Q19	Jub[a]		644		Baillet 1962, pl. XV
2Q20	Jub[b]		644		Baillet 1962, pl. XV
2Q21	apocrMoses?		644		Baillet 1962, pl. XV
2Q22	apocrDavid?		644		Baillet 1962, pl. XV
2Q23	apocrProph		644		Baillet 1962, pl. XV
2Q24	NJ ar		645		Baillet 1962, pl. XVI
2Q25	Juridical Text		740		Baillet 1962, pl. XVII
2Q26	EnGiants ar (*olim* Fragment of Ritual?)		740		Baillet 1962, pl. XVII; re-edition: Stuckenbruck 2000
2Q27	Unclassified frags.		740		Baillet 1962, pl. XVII
2Q28	Unclassified frags.		740		Baillet 1962, pl. XVII
2Q29	Unclassified frags.		740		Baillet 1962, pl. XVII
2Q30	Unclassified frags.		740		Baillet 1962, pl. XVII
2Q31	Unclassified frags.		740		Baillet 1962, pl. XVII
2Q32	Unclassified frags.		740		Baillet 1962, pl. XVII
2Q33	Unclassified frags.		740		Baillet 1962, pl. XVII
2QX1	Debris in box		749		
3Q1	Ezek		648		Baillet 1962, pl. XVIII
3Q2	Ps		648		Baillet 1962, pl. XVIII
3Q3	Lam		648		Baillet 1962, pl. XVIII
3Q4	pIsa		648		Baillet 1962, pl. XVIII
3Q5	Jub (*olim* apProph)		648		Baillet 1962, pl. XVIII
3Q6	Hymn		648		Baillet 1962, pl. XVIII
3Q7	TJud?		648		Baillet 1962, pl. XVIII
3Q8	Text Mentioning Angel of Peace		745		Baillet 1962, pl. XIX
3Q9	Sectarian Text		745		Baillet 1962, pl. XIX
3Q10	Unclassified frags.		745		Baillet 1962, pl. XIX
3Q11	Unclassified frags.		745		Baillet 1962, pl. XIX
3Q12	Unclassified frags. ar		745		Baillet 1962, pl. XIX
3Q13	Unclassified frags. ar		745		Baillet 1962, pl. XIX
3Q14	Unclassified frags.		745		Baillet 1962, pl. XIX
3Q15	Copper Scroll (unopened scroll)		DAJ		Milik 1962, pl. XLIII
	col. I				Milik 1962, pls. XLVIII–XLIX
	col. II				Milik 1962, pls. L–LI

ITEM NO.	COMPOSITION	CONC	INV	PREV	PUBLICATION
	col. III				Milik 1962, pls. LII–LIII
	col. IV				Milik 1962, pls. LIV–LV
	col. V				Milik 1962, pls. LVI–LVII
	col. VI				Milik 1962, pls. LVIII–LIX
	col. VII				Milik 1962, pls. LX–LXI
	col. VIII				Milik 1962, pls. LXII–LXIII
	col. IX				Milik 1962, pls. LXIV–LXV
	col. X				Milik 1962, pls. LXVI–LXVII
	col. XI				Milik 1962, pls. LXVIII–LXIX
	col. XII				Milik 1962, pls. LXX–LXXI
3QX1	Largely uninscribed frags.		743		
3QX2	Uninscribed frags.		744		
3QX3	Uninscribed frags.		746		
3QX4	Leather knot in box		747		
3QX5	Debris in box		748		
3QX6	Squeeze of 3Q15 clay		1009		
4Q1	Gen–Exod[a]		169	C1	Davila 1994, pls. I–V
			397	C7a	
			391	C7b	
4Q2	Gen[b]		215	C2	Davila 1994, pls. VI–VIII
4Q3	Gen[c]		393	C3	Davila 1994, pl. IX
4Q4	Gen[d]		1071	C4	Davila 1994, pl. IX
4Q5	Gen[e]		420	C5	Davila 1994, pl. X
4Q6	Gen[f]		273	C2b	Davila 1994, pl. XI
4Q7	Gen[g]		275	C2a	Davila 1994, pl. XII
4Q8	Gen[h1]		275	C2a	Davila 1994, pl. XII
	Gen[h2]		275, 725	C2a	Davila 1994, pl. XII
	Gen[h-para]		275, 725	C2a	Davila 1994, pl. XII
	Gen[h-title]		1073	C4b	Davila 1994, pl. XII
4Q9	Gen[j]		1072	C4a	Davila 1994, pl. XIII
4Q10	Gen[k]		393	C5a	Davila 1994, pl. XII
4Q11	paleoGen–Exod[l]		402	Sn1b	Skehan et al. 1992, pls. I–VI
			204	Sn1b	
			422	Sn2	
			398	Sn3	
			395	Sn3b	
4Q12	paleoGen[m]		1125	Sn1a	Skehan et al. 1992, pl. VI
	for Gen[n] see 4Q576				
4Q13	Exod[b]		659	C6	Cross 1994, pls. XIV–XV
4Q14	Exod[c]		1075	C8a	Sanderson 1994, pl. XVI–XX
			1074	C8b	
			1076	C8c	
4Q15	Exod[d]		242	C9	Sanderson 1994, pl. XXI
4Q16	Exod[e]		396	C10a	Sanderson 1994, pl. XXI
4Q17	Exod–Lev[f]		1002	C11	Cross 1994, pl. XXII
4Q18	Exod[g]		1075	C10b	Sanderson 1994, pl. XXI
4Q19	Exod[h]		201	C15c	Sanderson 1994, pl. XXI
4Q20	Exod[j]		201	C15e	Sanderson 1994, pl. XXI
4Q21	Exod[k]		201	C15d	Sanderson 1994, pl. XXI
4Q22	paleoExod[m]		1005	Sn4	Skehan et al. 1992, pls. VII–XXXIII
			1126	Sn5	
			661	Sn6	
			1127	Sn7	
			1128	Sn8	
			1129	Sn9	

ITEM NO.	COMPOSITION	CONC	INV	PREV	PUBLICATION
			1130	Sn10	
			1131	Sn11	
			1132	Sn12	
			1133	Sn13	
			1134	Sn14	
			1135	Sn15	
			DAJ	Sn15a	
			1136	Sn16	
			1137	Sn16a	
			1155	Sn51	
			1156	Sn51a	
			1157	Sn51b	
			1154	Sn52	
			1158	Sn52	
			1158	Sn53	
			1160	Sn54	
			1159	Sn55	
			1161	Sn56	
			1162	Sn57	
			1163	Sn58	
4Q23	Lev–Num[a]		272	C12a	Ulrich 1994, pls. XXIII–XXX
			271	C12b	
			419	C16a	
			399	C16b	
			401	C17a	
			418	C17b	
4Q24	Lev[b]		1077	C13b	Ulrich 1994, pls. XXXI–XXXIV
			1078	C13c	
			1079	C13a	
4Q25	Lev[c]		316	C14	Tov 1994, pl. XXXV
4Q26	Lev[d]		198	C15b	Tov 1994, pl. XXXVI
4Q26a	Lev[e]		197	C15a	Tov 1994, pl. XXXVII
4Q26b	Lev[g]		197	C15a	Tov 1994, pl. XXXVII
	for Lev[h] see 4Q249j				
4Q27	Num[b]		1080	C19a	Jastram 1994, pls. XXXVIII–XLIX
			1081A	C19b	
			1081B	C19b	
			1082	C20a	
			1083	C20b	
			1084A	C21a	
			1084B	C21a	
			1085A	C21b	
			1085B	C21b	
			1086A	C22a	
			1086B	C22a	
			1087	C22b	
			1088	C22c	
4Q28	Deut[a]		256	C23	Crawford 1995, pl. I
4Q29	Deut[b]		1089	C24	Duncan 1995, pl. II
4Q30	Deut[c]		243	C25a	Crawford 1995, pls. III–IX
			237	C25b	
			238	C25c	
4Q31	Deut[d]		323	C26	Crawford 1995, pl. X
4Q32	Deut[e]		233	C27	Duncan 1995, pl. XI
4Q33	Deut[f]		322	C28a	Crawford 1995, pls. XII–XV
			317	C28b	

ITEM NO.	COMPOSITION	CONC	INV	PREV	PUBLICATION
4Q34	Deut^{g}		400	C31b	Crawford 1995, pl. XVI
4Q35	Deut^{h}		389	C29	Duncan 1995, pls. XVII–XVIII
4Q36	Deut^{i}		323		Crawford 1995, pl. XIX
4Q37	Deut^{j}		170	C30a	Duncan 1995, pls. XX–XXIII
			172	C30b	
			171	C30c	
4Q38	Deut^{k1}		1090	C31a	Duncan 1995, pls. XXIV
4Q38a	Deut^{k2}		1090	C31c	Duncan 1995, pl. XXV
4Q38b	Deut^{k3}		172		Duncan 1995, pl. XXV
4Q39	Deut^{l}		390	C32a	Duncan 1995, pl. XXVI
4Q40	Deut^{m}		255	C32b	Duncan 1995, pls. XXVII
4Q41	Deut^{n}		981	C32c	Crawford 1995, pls. XXVIII–XXIX
4Q42	Deut^{o}		1091	C32d	Crawford 1995, pl. XXX
			178	C32d	
4Q43	Deut^{p}		1091	C32d	Crawford 1995, pl. XXXI
4Q44	Deut^{q}		676	Sn19	Skehan and Ulrich 1995, pl. XXXI
4Q45	paleoDeut^{r}		1138	Sn17	Skehan et al. 1992, pls. XXXIV–XXXVI
			1139	Sn18	
4Q46	paleoDeut^{s}		1139	Sn58	Skehan et al. 1992, pl. XXXVII
4Q47	Josh^{a}		1092	C33a	Ulrich 1995, pls. XXXII–XXXIV
			1093	C33b	
4Q48	Josh^{b}		392	C34	Tov 1995, pl. XXXV
4Q49	Judg^{a}		305	C35a	Trebolle 1995, pl. XXXVI
4Q50	Judg^{b}		1123	C35b	Trebolle 1995, pl. XXXVI
4Q51	Sam^{a}		998	C36	Cross and Parry 2005
			1094	C37a	
			1095	C37b	
			1096	C38	
			1097	C39a	
			1098	C39b	
			1099	C40a	
			1100	C40b	
			1101	C41a	
			1102	C41b	
			1103	C42	
			1104	C43a	
			1105	C43b	
			1106	C44a	
			1107	C44b	
4Q52	Sam^{b}		206	C45a	Cross and Parry 2005
			195	C45b	
4Q53	Sam^{c}		405	C46a	Ulrich 2005
			406	C46b	
4Q54	Kgs		1108	C47	Trebolle 1995, pl. XXXVII
4Q55	Isa^{a}		266	Sn20	Skehan and Ulrich 1997, pls. I–II
			660	Sn20a	
4Q56	Isa^{b}		1140	Sn21	Skehan and Ulrich 1997, pls. III–VI
			1141	Sn21	
4Q57	Isa^{c}		363	Sn22	Skehan and Ulrich 1997, pls. VII–XII
			382	Sn22	
			387	Sn22	
4Q58	Isa^{d}		250	Sn23	Skehan and Ulrich 1997, pls. XIII–XV
			236	Sn24a	

ITEM NO.	COMPOSITION	CONC	INV	PREV	PUBLICATION
4Q59	Isa[e]		262	Sn27	Skehan and Ulrich 1997, pls. XVI–XVII
4Q60	Isa[f]		324	Sn28	Skehan and Ulrich 1997, pls. XVIII–XX
4Q61	Isa[g]		175	Sn29a	Skehan and Ulrich 1997, pl. XXI
4Q62	Isa[h]		262	Sn27	Skehan and Ulrich 1997, pl. XXI
			261	Sn29c	
4Q63	Isa[j]		1142	Sn29b	Skehan and Ulrich 1997, pl. XXII
4Q64	Isa[k]		250	Sn25	Skehan and Ulrich 1997, pl. XXII
4Q65	Isa[l]		262	Sn27	Skehan and Ulrich 1997, pl. XXII
			262	Sn27	
4Q66	Isa[m]		261	Sn29c	Skehan and Ulrich 1997, pl. XXII
4Q67	Isa[n]		261	Sn29c	Skehan and Ulrich 1997, pl. XXIII
4Q68	Isa[o]		261	Sn29c	Skehan and Ulrich 1997, pl. XXIII
4Q69	papIsa[p]		261	Sn29c	Skehan and Ulrich 1997, pl. XXIII
4Q69a	Isa[q]				Skehan and Ulrich 1997, pl. XXIII
4Q69b	Isa[r]				Skehan and Ulrich 1997, pl. XXIII
4Q70	Jer[a]		1109		Tov 1997, pls. XXIV–XXIX
			1110		
			1111	C48c	
4Q71	Jer[b]		152	C49	Tov 1997, pl. XXX
4Q72	Jer[c]		671	C50a	Tov 1997, pls. XXXI–XXXVII
			246	C50b	
			244	C52	
			232	C51a	
			245	C51b	
4Q72a	Jer[d]		152	C49	Tov 1997, pl. XXXVIII
4Q72b	Jer[e]		152	C49	Tov 1997, pl. XXXVIII
4Q73	Ezek[a]		1112	C53	Sanderson 1997, pl. XXXIX
4Q74	Ezek[b]		207	C54	Sanderson 1997, pl. XL
4Q75	Ezek[c]		207	C54bis	Sanderson 1997, pl. XL
4Q76	XII[a]		296	C55a	Fuller 1997, pls. XLI–XLIII
			1114	C55b	
			314	C56	
4Q77	XII[b]		1113	C57	Fuller 1997, pl. XLIV
4Q78	XII[c]		162	C58a	Fuller 1997, pls. XLV–XLVII
			161	C58b	
4Q79	XII[d]		410	C59	Fuller 1997, pl. XLVII
4Q80	XII[e]		258	C60	Fuller 1997, pl. XLVIII
4Q81	XII[f]		1115	C60bis	Fuller 1997, pl. XLVIII
4Q82	XII[g] (unopened scroll)		1143	Sn30	Fuller 1997, pls. XLIX–LVI
			1144	Sn31	
			1145	Sn32	
			1146	Sn33	
			1147	Sn34	
			1164	Sn59	
			1165	Sn60	
			1166	Sn61	
			1167	Sn62	
			1168	Sn63	
			1169	Sn64	
			1170	Sn65	
			1171	Sn65a	
4Q83	Ps[a]		1148	Sn35	Skehan et al. 2000, pls. I–II
4Q84	Ps[b]		383	Sn36	Skehan et al. 2000, pls. III–VI
			360	Sn37a	

ITEM NO.	COMPOSITION	CONC	INV	PREV	PUBLICATION
			999	Sn37	
4Q85	Ps[c]		312	Sn38	Skehan et al. 2000, pls. VII–IX
			312	Sn39	
4Q86	Ps[d]		225	Sn40	Skehan et al. 2000, pl. X
4Q87	Ps[e]		263	Sn41	Skehan et al. 2000, pls. XI–XII
4Q88	Ps[f]		1149	Sn42a	Skehan et al. 2000, pls. XIII–XIV
			436	Sn40	
4Q89	Ps[g]		1150	Sn43	Skehan et al. 2000, pl. XV
4Q90	Ps[h]		1150	Sn43	Skehan et al. 2000, pl. XV
4Q91	Ps[j]		1151	Sn43	Skehan et al. 2000, pl. XVI
4Q92	Ps[k]		1151	Sn43	Skehan et al. 2000, pl. XVII
4Q93	Ps[l]		1151	Sn43	Skehan et al. 2000, pl. XVII
4Q94	Ps[m]		1151	Sn43	Skehan et al. 2000, pl. XVII
4Q95	Ps[n]		1151	Sn43	Skehan et al. 2000, pl. XVIII
4Q96	Ps[o]		1151	Sn43	Skehan et al. 2000, pl. XVIII
4Q97	Ps[p] (*olim* 4Q237)		1151	Sn43	Skehan et al. 2000, pl. XVIII
4Q98	Ps[q]		Inst. Cath. Paris		Skehan et al. 2000, pl. XIX
4Q98a	Ps[r]		1151	Sn43	Skehan et al. 2000, pl. XIX
4Q98b	Ps[s]				Skehan et al. 2000, pl. XIX
4Q98c	Ps[t] (*olim* 4QPs[s] frag.		1151?		Skehan et al. 2000, pl. XIX
4Q98d	Ps[u] (*olim* 4QPs[r])		1151?		Skehan et al. 2000, pl. XIX
4Q98e	Ps[v]				
4Q98f	Ps[w]				Fitzmyer 2000a
4Q98g	Ps[x] (*olim* 4Q236)		304	M127	Skehan et al. 2000, pl. XVIII
4Q99	Job[a]		1116	C61	Ulrich 2000, pl. XXI
4Q100	Job[b]		1117	C61bis	Ulrich 2000, pl. XXII
4Q101	paleoJob[c]		1152	Sn44	Skehan et al. 1992, pl. XXXVII
4Q102	Prov[a]		1153	Sn45	Skehan, Ulrich 2000, pl. XXII
4Q103	Prov[b]		1153	Sn45	Skehan, Ulrich 2000, pl. XXIII
4Q104	Ruth[a]		410	C62a	Ulrich 2000, pl. XXIV
4Q105	Ruth[b]		1117	C62b	Ulrich 2000, pl. XXIV
4Q106	Cant[a]		1118	C64a	Tov 2000a, pl. XXIV
4Q107	Cant[b]		1119	C64	Tov 2000a, pl. XXV
4Q108	Cant[c]		1118	C64b	Tov 2000a, pl. XXV
4Q109	Qoh[a]		DAJ	C65a	Ulrich 2000, pl. XXVI
4Q110	Qoh[b]		1117	C65b	Ulrich 2000, pl. XXVI
4Q111	Lam		667	C66	Cross 2000, pls. XXVII–XXVIII
4Q112	Dan[a]		388	C67	Ulrich 2000, pl. XXX–XXXIII
			394	C68	
4Q113	Dan[b]		1120	C69	Ulrich 2000, pls. XXXIV–XXXV
			1121	C70	
4Q114	Dan[c]		224	C71	Ulrich 2000, pl. XXXVI
4Q115	Dan[d]		1122	C72	Ulrich 2000, pl. XXXVII
4Q116	Dan[e]		153	C76	Ulrich 2000, pl. XXXVIII
4Q117	Ezra		1124	C73	Ulrich 2000, pl. XXXIX
4Q118	Chr		1124	C74	Trebolle 2000, pl. XL
4Q119	LXXLev[a]		1004	Sn46	Skehan et al. 1992, pl. XXXVIII
4Q120	papLXXLev[b]		376	Sn47	Skehan et al. 1992, pls. XXXIX–XLI
			378	Sn48	
			379	Sn48a	
4Q121	LXXNum		265	Sn49	Skehan et al. 1992, pls. XLII–XLIII
4Q122	LXXDeut		265	Sn49	Skehan et al. 1992, pl. XLIII
4Q123	paleo paraJosh		1152	Sn44	Skehan et al. 1992, pl. XLVI
4Q124	paleoUnident. Text 1		1152	Sn44	Skehan et al. 1992, pls. XLIV–XLV
4Q125	paleoUnident. Text 2		1152	Sn44	Skehan et al. 1992, pl. XLVI

ITEM NO.	COMPOSITION	CONC	INV	PREV	PUBLICATION
4Q126	Unidentified Text gr		265	Sn49	Skehan et al. 1992, pl. XLVI
4Q127	pap paraExodus gr		374	Sn50	Skehan et al. 1992, pl. XLVII
			375	Sn50a	Skehan et al. 1992, pl. XLVII
4Q128	Phyl A			M1–4	Milik 1977, pls. VII, VIII, XXV
4Q129	Phyl B		211	M1–4	Milik 1977, pl. IX
4Q130	Phyl C		211	M1–4	Milik 1977, pls. X, XI
4Q131	Phyl D		173	M1–4	Milik 1977, pl. XII
4Q132	Phyl E		173	M1–4	Milik 1977, pls. XII, XIII
4Q133	Phyl F		173	M1–4	Milik 1977, pl. XIV
4Q134	Phyl G		809	M1–4	Milik 1977, pl. XV
4Q135	Phyl H		212	M1–4	Milik 1977, pl. XVI
4Q136	Phyl I		809	M1–4	Milik 1977, pl. XVII
4Q137	Phyl J			M1–4	Milik 1977, pl. XIX
4Q138	Phyl K		809	M1–4	Milik 1977, pl. XX
4Q139	Phyl L		211	M1–4	Milik 1977, pl. XXII
4Q140	Phyl M			M1–4	Milik 1977, pl. XXI
4Q141	Phyl N		212	M1–4	Milik 1977, pl. XXII
4Q142	Phyl O		211	M1–4	Milik 1977, pl. XXII
4Q143	Phyl P		809	M1–4	Milik 1977, pl. XXII
4Q144	Phyl Q		212	M1–4	Milik 1977, pl. XXIII
4Q145	Phyl R		212	M1–4	Milik 1977, pl. XXIII
4Q146	Phyl S		212	M1–4	Milik 1977, pl. XXIII
4Q147	Phyl T			M1–4	Milik 1977, pl. XXIV
4Q148	Phyl U		813	M1–4	Milik 1977, pl. XXV
4Q149	Mez A		813	M1–4	Milik 1977, pl. XXVI
4Q150	Mez B		210	M1–4	Milik 1977, pl. XXVI
4Q151	Mez C		174	M1–4	Milik 1977, pl. XXVII
4Q152	Mez D		174	M1–4	Milik 1977, pl. XXVI
4Q153	Mez E		174	M1–4	Milik 1977, pl. XXVI
4Q154	Mez F		813	M1–4	Milik 1977, pl. XXVI
4Q155	Mez G		173	M1–4	Milik 1977, pl. XXV
4Q156	tgLev	TgLev	299	M4a	Milik 1977, pl. XXVIII
4Q157	tgJob	TgJob	130	M4b	Milik 1977, pl. XXVIII
4Q158	BibPar (= 4QRP[a])	H–L	138		Allegro 1968, pl. I
4Q159	Ordinances[a]	Ordin	474	A17	Allegro 1968, pl. II
4Q160	VisSam	parSam	137	A14	Allegro 1968, pl. III
4Q161	pIsa[a]	pIsaa	583, 585	A5–5′	Allegro 1968, pls. IV–V
4Q162	pIsa[b]	pIsac	DAJ	A6?	Allegro 1968, pl. VI
4Q163	pap pIsa[c]	pIsa[b]	599, 584	A8a, b	Allegro 1968, pls. VII–VIII
4Q164	pIsa[d]	pIsa[d]	291	A7?	Allegro 1968, pl. IX
4Q165	pIsa[e]	pIsa[e]	587	A5′	Allegro 1968, pl. IX
4Q166	pHos[a]	pHos	675	A9, 9′	Allegro 1968, pl. X
4Q167	pHos[b]	pHos	354	A30	Allegro 1968, pls. X–XI
4Q168	pMic?		326		Allegro 1968, pl. XII
4Q169	pNah	pN	980	A10, 10′	Allegro 1968, pls. XII–XIV
4Q170	pZeph		600	A11	Allegro 1968, pl. XIV
4Q171	pPs[a]	pPs37, 45	600, 672	A11	Allegro 1968, pls. XIV–XVII
4Q172	pUnid		600	A12	Allegro 1968, pl. XVIII
4Q173	pPs[b]	pPs118, 127, 129	234, 290	A13	Allegro 1968, pl. XVIII
4Q174	Flor (= 4QMidrEschat[a]?)		281, 286	A2–3	Allegro 1968, pls. XIX–XX
4Q175	Test		DAJ	A1	Allegro 1968, pl. XXI
4Q176	Tanḥ	Tanḥ	285, 293	A27, 27′	Allegro 1968, pls. XXII–XXIII
4Q176 19–21	Jub? (instead of earlier 4Q176a)				Kister 1985–1987
4Q177	Catena A (= 4QMidrEschat[b]?)	Catena[a]	277, 289	A25	Allegro 1968, pls. XXIV–XXV

ITEM NO.	COMPOSITION	CONC	INV	PREV	PUBLICATION
4Q178	Unclassified frags. (= 4QMidr Eschat[d]?)		160		Allegro 1968, pl. XXV
4Q179	apocrLam A	Lament	235	A26	Allegro 1968, pl. XXVI
4Q180	AgesCreat A	Wisd[c]	468	A23	Allegro 1968, pl. XXVII
4Q181	AgesCreat B		473	A29?	Allegro 1968, pl. XVIII
4Q182	Catena B (= 4QMidrEschat[c]?)	Catena[b]	160	A25′	Allegro 1968, pl. XXVII
4Q183	MidrEschat[e]?		139	A16?	Allegro 1968, pl. XXVI
4Q184	Wiles of the Wicked Woman	Wisd[a]	287	A20–22	Allegro 1968, pl. XXVIII
4Q185	Sapiential Work		801	A31, 32?	Allegro 1968, pls. XXIX–XXX
4Q186	Horoscope	Cryp[a]	109	A18	Allegro 1968, pl. XXXI
4Q196	papTob[a] ar	Tb[a]	666	M5	Fitzmyer 1995, pls. I–V
			851	M6	
			852	M7	
			822	M8	
			808	M9	
4Q197	Tob[b] ar	Tb[b]	132	M10	Fitzmyer 1995, pls. VI–VII
			133	M11	
4Q198	Tob[c] ar	Tb[c]	231	M12	Fitzmyer 1995, pl. VIII
4Q199	Tob[d] ar		231	M12	Fitzmyer 1995, pl. VIII
4Q200	Tob[e]	Tb[h]	848	M13	Fitzmyer 1995, pls. IX–X
			850	M14	
4Q201	En[a] ar (recto of 4Q338)	Hen[a]	821	M25	Milik 1976, 139–63, 340–43, pls. I–V; re-edition: Stuckenbruck 2000
			904	M26	
4Q202	En[b] ar	Hen[c]	380	M29	Milik 1976, 164–78, 344–46, pls. VI–IX
4Q203	EnGiants[a] ar		188	M28	Milik 1976, 310–17, pls. XXX–XXXII; re-edition: Stuckenbruck 2000, pls. II–III
		Hen[b]	189	M28	
			906	M28a	
4Q204	En[c] ar	Hen[b]	199	M27	Milik 1976, 178–217, 346ff., pls. IX–XV
			200	M27a	
			191	M28	
			188	M28	
			189	M28′	
4Q205	En[d] ar	Hen[e]	142	M31	Milik 1976, 217–25, 353–55, pls. XVI–XVII
4Q206	En[e] ar	Hen[d]	359	M30	Milik 1976, 225–44, 355ff., pls. XVIII–XXI
			386	M30a	
			358	M30b	
4Q206 frags. 2–3	EnGiants[f]? ar		359		Milik 1976, 235–36; Stuckenbruck 2000, pl. III
4Q207	En[f] ar		143	M31a	Milik 1976, 244–45, 359, pl. XXI
4Q208	Enastr[a] ar	Ha[b]	823	M35	Tigchelaar and García Martínez 2000, pls. III–IV
			814	M35a	
4Q209	Enastr[b] ar	Ha[a]	846	M32	Milik 1976, 278–96, pls. XXV–XXVII, XXX; re-edition: Tigchelaar and García Martínez 2000, pls. VI–VIII
			847	M33	
			856	M34	
			857	M34	
4Q210	Enastr[c] ar	Ha[c]	229	M36	Milik 1976, 284–88, pls. XXVIII, XXX

ITEM NO.	COMPOSITION	CONC	INV	PREV	PUBLICATION
4Q211	Enastr[d] ar	Ha[d]	369	M36a	Milik 1976, 296–97, pl. XXIX
4Q212	En[g] ar (also = Letter of Enoch)	HenV	227	M37	Milik 1976, 245–72, 360–62, pls. XXI–XXIV
			228	M37a	
4Q213	Levi[a] ar	TL[a]	817	M41a	Stone and Greenfield 1996, pl. I
4Q213a	Levi[b] ar (*olim* part of Levi[a])		249	M41	Stone and Greenfield 1996, pl. II
4Q213b	Levi[c] ar (*olim* part of Levi[a])		816	M41b	Stone and Greenfield 1996, pl. III
4Q214	Levi[d] ar (*olim* part of Levi[b])	TL[b]	370	M42b	Stone and Greenfield 1996, pl. III
4Q214a	Levi[e] ar (*olim* part of Levi[b])		370	M42b	Stone and Greenfield 1996, pl. IV
4Q214b	Levi[f] ar (*olim* part of Levi[b])		370	M42b	Stone and Greenfield 1996, pl. IV
4Q215	TNaph	TN	368	M43	Stone 1996, pl. V
4Q215a	Time of Righteousness (*olim* part of TNaph)		371	M43a	Stone and Chazon 2000, pl. IX
4Q216	Jub[a]	Jb[a]	385	M 15	VanderKam and Milik 1994, pls. I–II
			385	M16	
			384	M17	
4Q217	papJub[b]?		586	M126	VanderKam and Milik 1994, pl. III
4Q218	Jub[c]	Jb[c]	849	M19	VanderKam and Milik 1994, pl. IV
4Q219	Jub[d]	Jb[b]	300	M18	VanderKam and Milik 1994, pl. IV
4Q220	Jub[e]		849	M19	VanderKam and Milik 1994, pl. V
4Q221	Jub[f]	Jb[d]	361	M20	VanderKam and Milik 1994, pl. VI
4Q222	Jub[g]	Jb[e]	230	M21	VanderKam and Milik 1994, pl. V
4Q223	papJub[h]	Jb[f]	134	M22	VanderKam and Milik 1994, pls. VII–IX
			135	M23	
4Q224	papJub[h]		136	M24	VanderKam and Milik 1994, pls. VII–IX
4Q225	psJub[a]	psJb[c]	311	M39a	VanderKam and Milik 1994, pl. X
4Q226	psJub[b]	psJb[a]	811	M40	VanderKam and Milik 1994, pl. XI
4Q227	psJub[c]?	psJb[b]	812	M39a	VanderKam and Milik 1994, pl. XII
4Q228	Text with a Citation of Jub	citJub	309	M124	VanderKam and Milik 1994, pl. XII
4Q229	Pseudep. work in mishnaic heb				(*sic* Milik's list; could not be located)
4Q230	Catalogue of Spirits[a]				(*sic* Milik's list; could not be located)
4Q231	Catalogue of Spirits[b]				(*sic* Milik's list; could not be located)
4Q232	NJ?				(*sic* Milik's list; could not be located; old name for 4Q365a)
4Q233	Frags. with place names				(*sic* Milik's list; could not be located)
4Q234	Exercitium Calami A		603		Yardeni 2000a, pl. X
4Q235	Unid. Text nab. (*olim* Book of Kings)		601	M129a	Yardeni 1997, pl. LV
4Q236	cancelled (= 4Q98g)		304	M127	Skehan et al. 2000, pl. XVIII
4Q237	cancelled (= 4Q97 Ps[p])				Skehan et al. 2000, pl. XVIII
4Q238	Hab 3				Ulrich and Flint 2000
4Q239	Pesher on the true Israel				(*sic* Milik's list; could not be located)
4Q240	Commentary on Canticles?				(*sic* Milik's list; could not be located)
4Q241	cancelled (now 4Q282 frags. h, i)				
4Q242	PrNab ar	sNab	248	M44	Collins 1996, pl. VI
			665		
4Q243	psDan[a] ar	psDan[a]	854	M45	Collins and Flint 1996, pls. VII–VIII
			908	M45a	
			855	M45b	
4Q244	psDan[b] ar	psDan[b]	853	M46	Collins and Flint 1996, pl. IX
4Q245	psDan[c] ar	psDan[c]	247	M46a	Collins and Flint 1996, pl. X
4Q246	apocrDan ar	psDan[d]	209	M132	Puech 1996, pl. XI
4Q247	Pesher on the Apocalypse of Weeks	PsHistC	377	M47a	Broshi 2000, pl. X

ITEM NO.	COMPOSITION	CONC	INV	PREV	PUBLICATION
4Q248	Historical Text A	PsHistE?	815	M47b	Eshel and Broshi 2000, pl. X
4Q249	pap cryptA Midrash SeferMoshe (= recto of 4Q250) (title on verso of frag. 1 in square script)		589r	M108	Pfann 1999, pls. I–III
			589v		
			590	M109	
			598	M110	
			597	M111	
			596	M112	
			593	M113a	
4Q249a	pap cryptA Serekh ha-ʿEdah^{a}		598		Pfann 2000
4Q249b	pap cryptA Serekh ha-ʿEdah^{b}		596, 598		Pfann 2000
4Q249c	pap cryptA Serekh ha-ʿEdah^{c}		598		Pfann 2000
4Q249d	pap cryptA Serekh ha-ʿEdah^{d}		590		Pfann 2000
4Q249e	pap cryptA Serekh ha-ʿEdah^{e}		598		Pfann 2000
4Q249f	pap cryptA Serekh ha-ʿEdah^{f}				Pfann 2000
4Q249g	pap cryptA Serekh ha-ʿEdah^{g}				Pfann 2000
4Q249h	pap cryptA Serekh ha-ʿEdah^{h}				Pfann 2000
4Q249i	pap cryptA Serekh ha-ʿEdah^{i}				Pfann 2000
4Q249j	pap cryptA Lev^{h}?		590		Pfann 2000
4Q249k	pap cryptA Text Quoting Leviticus A		590		Pfann 2000
4Q249l	pap cryptA Text Quoting Leviticus B		590, 598		Pfann 2000
4Q249m	pap cryptA Hodayot-like Text D				Pfann 2000
4Q249n	pap cryptA Liturgical Work E?		590		Pfann 2000
4Q249o	pap cryptA Liturgical Work F?				Pfann 2000
4Q249p	pap cryptA Prophecy?				Pfann 2000
4Q249q	pap cryptA Frag. Mentioning Planting		589, 590		Pfann 2000
4Q249r	pap cryptA Unid. Text A		598		Pfann 2000
4Q249s	pap cryptA Unid. Text B		598		Pfann 2000
4Q249t	pap cryptA Unid. Text C				Pfann 2000
4Q249u	pap cryptA Unid. Text D				Pfann 2000
4Q249v	pap cryptA Unid. Text E				Pfann 2000
4Q249w	pap cryptA Unid. Text F				Pfann 2000
4Q249x	pap cryptA Unid. Text G				Pfann 2000
4Q249y	pap cryptA Unid. Text H				Pfann 2000
4Q249z	pap cryptA Miscellaneous Frags.				Pfann 2000
4Q250	pap cryptA Text Concerning Cultic Service A		593	M113a	Pfann 2000
4Q250a	pap cryptA Text Concerning Cultic Service B (r + v)		593	M113a	Pfann 2000
4Q250b	pap cryptA Text Related to Isa 11 (r + v)		593		Pfann 2000
4Q250c	pap cryptA Unid. Text J (recto of 4Q250d)				Pfann 2000
4Q250d	pap cryptA Unid. Text K (verso of 4Q250c)				Pfann 2000
4Q250e	pap cryptA Unid. Text L (recto of 4Q250f)				Pfann 2000
4Q250f	pap cryptA Unid. Text M (verso of 4Q250e)				Pfann 2000
4Q250g	pap cryptA Unid. Text N (r+v)				Pfann 2000
4Q250h	pap cryptA Unid. Text O (r+v)				Pfann 2000
4Q250i	pap cryptA Unid. Text P (r+v)				Pfann 2000
4Q250j	pap cryptA Misc. Texts (r+v)				Pfann 2000
4Q251	Halakha A	Hlk^{a}	702	M80	Larson et al. 1999, pls. III–IV
			711	M81	

ITEM NO.	COMPOSITION	CONC	INV	PREV	PUBLICATION
4Q252	CommGen A (*olim* PBless; pGen)	pGen B	668	M38	Brooke 1996, pls. XII–XIII
			670	M131	
4Q253	CommGen B	pGenVI[b]	819	M38a	Brooke 1996, pl. XIV
4Q253a	CommMal (*olim* part of CommGen B)	pGenVI[b]	819	M38a	Brooke 1996, pl. XIV
4Q254	CommGen C	pGen A	113	M125	Brooke 1996, pl. XV
4Q254a	CommGen D	pGenVI[a]	820	M38	Brooke 1996, pl. XVI
4Q255	papS[a] (= verso [?] of 4Q433a)	S[a]	177	M49	Alexander and Vermes 1998, pl. I
4Q256	S[b] (*olim* S[d])	S[b]	907	M50	Alexander and Vermes 1998, pls. II–V
			905	M50a	
4Q257	papS[c]	S[c]	858	M51	Alexander and Vermes 1998, pls. VI–IX
			859	M51a	
				M51′	
4Q258	S[d] (*olim* S[b])	S[d]	140	M52	Alexander and Vermes 1998, pls. X–XIII
			141	M53	
4Q259	S[e]	S[e]	810, 818	M54	Alexander and Vermes 1998, pls. XIV–XVI
4Q260	S[f]	S[f]	366	M55	Alexander and Vermes 1998, pl. XVII
4Q261	S[g]	S[g]	705	M56	Alexander and Vermes 1998, pls. XVIII–XIX
4Q262	S[h]	S[h]	105	M57	Alexander and Vermes 1998, pl. XX
4Q263	S[i]	S[i]	251	M57a	Alexander and Vermes 1998, pl. XXI
4Q264	S[j]	S[j]	297	M57b	Alexander and Vermes 1998, pl. XXI
4Q264a	Halakha B (*olim* S[z])	S[z]	110		Baumgarten 1999, pl. V
4Q265	Miscellaneous Rules (*olim* Serekh Damascus)	SD	306		Baumgarten 1999, pls. V–VIII
			307	M78′	
			308		
4Q266	D[a] (*olim* D[b])	D[b]	701	M59a	Baumgarten 1996, pls. I–XVII
			680	M60	
			699	M60	
			704+	M61	
			700	M62	
			686	M63	
			687	M63	
			707	M64	
			688	M59, 65	
			706	M65	
			689	M66	
4Q267	D[b] (*olim* D[d])	D[d]	106	M69	Baumgarten 1996, pls. XVIII–XXI
			107	M70	
4Q268	D[c] (*olim* D[a])	D[a]	373	M58	Baumgarten 1996, pl. XXII
4Q269	D[d] (*olim* D[f])	D[f]	220	M75	Baumgarten 1996, pls. XXIII–XXV
			221	M75	
4Q270	D[e]	D[e]	698	M71	Baumgarten 1996, pls. XXVI–XXXVI
			685	M72	
			690	M73	
			697	M74	
			703	M74	

ITEM NO.	COMPOSITION	CONC	INV	PREV	PUBLICATION
4Q271	D^{f} (*olim* D^{e})	D^{e}	357	M67	Baumgarten 1996, pls. XXXVII–XXXIX
			362	M68	
4Q272	D^{g}	D^{g}	219	M76a	Baumgarten 1996, pl. XL
4Q273	papD^{h}	D^{h}	108	M77	Baumgarten 1996, pls. XLI–XLII
4Q274	Tohorot A	ThrA	182	M82a	Baumgarten 1999, pl. VIII
4Q275	Communal Ceremony (*olim* Tohorot B^{a})	ThrB^{a}/S^{x}	679	M79b	Alexander and Vermes 1998, pl.
4Q276	Tohorot B^{a} (*olim* B^{b})	ThrB^{b}	111	M82a	Baumgarten 1999, pl. IX
4Q277	Tohorot B^{b} (*olim* B^{c})	ThrB	111	M82a	Baumgarten 1999, pl. IX
4Q278	Tohorot C	ThrC	111	M82a	Baumgarten 1999, pl. IX
4Q279	Four Lots (*olim* Tohorot D?)	Sy	111	M82b	Alexander and Vermes 1998, pl. XXIII
4Q280	Curses (*olim* Ber^{f})	Brk^{z}	223	M76c	Nitzan 1999, pl. I
4Q281a–f	Unidentified Fragments A, a–f		304		Fitzmyer 2000b, pl. XI
4Q282a–t	Unidentified Fragments B, a–t (frags. h, i: *olim* 4Q241)		303		Fitzmyer 2000b, pls. XI–XII
4Q283	cancelled				
4Q284	Purification Liturgy	Sndt	239	M83	Baumgarten 1999, pl. X
4Q284a	Harvesting (*olim* Tohorot G + Leqet)	Lqt	679	M79b	Baumgarten 1999, pl. XI
4Q285	Sefer ha-Milḥamah (*olim* Serekh ha-Milḥamah)	BM	301	M48	Vermes and Alexander 2000, pls. XIII–XIV
4Q286	Ber^{a}	B^{a}	709	M84	Nitzan 1998, pls. I–IV
			691	M85	
			692	M85a	
4Q287	Ber^{b}	B^{b}	381	M86	Nitzan 1998, pls. V–VI
4Q288	Ber^{c}	B^{c}	222	M85b	Nitzan 1998, pl. VII
4Q289	Ber^{d}	B^{d}	222	M87a	Nitzan 1998, pl. VII
4Q290	Ber^{e}				Nitzan 1998, pl. VII
4Q291	Work Containing Prayers A	B^{w}	222	M87d	Nitzan 1999, pl. I
4Q292	Work Containing Prayers B	B^{x}	223	M87c	Nitzan 1999, pl. I
4Q293	Work Containing Prayers C	B^{y}	222	M87b	Nitzan 1999, pl. I
4Q294	Sapiential-Didactic Work C		618		Tigchelaar 2000, pl. XV
4Q295	cancelled				
4Q296	cancelled				
4Q297	cancelled				
4Q298	cryptA Words of the Maskil to All Sons of Dawn	DS	898	M113	Pfann and Kister 1997, pls. I–II
4Q299	Myst^{a}	Myst^{a}	605	M117	Schiffman 1997, pls. III–VII
			604	M117a	
			594	M118	
			595	M119	
			592	M120	
4Q300	Myst^{b}	Myst^{b}	591	M116	Schiffman 1997, pl. VIII
4Q301	Myst^{c}?	Myst^{c}	582	M121	Schiffman 1997, pl. IX
4Q302	papAdmonitory Parable (*olim* Praise of God)	SapA	356	M122	Nitzan 1997, pls. X–XII
4Q302a	cancelled (now part of 4Q302) (*olim* Parable of the Tree)		333	M123	
4Q303	Meditation on Creation A (*olim* MedCreat A^{a})	SapC	350	M124b	Lim 1997, pl. XIII
4Q304	Meditation on Creation B (*olim* MedCreat A^{b})		295	M124b	Lim 1997, pl. XIII
4Q305	Meditation on Creation C (*olim* MedCreat B)		295	M124	Lim 1997, pl. XIII
4Q306	Men of People Who Err (*olim* SapB)	SapB	350		Lim 2000, pl. XV

ITEM NO.	COMPOSITION	CONC	INV	PREV	PUBLICATION
4Q307	Text Mentioning Temple (*olim* SapWork E)		295?	Msap frag.	Lim 2000, pl. XV
4Q308	Sapiential frags.?				(*sic* Milik's list; could not be located)
4Q309	Cursive work ar				(*sic* Milik's list; could not be located)
4Q310	papText ar				(*sic* Milik's list; could not be located)
4Q311	papUnclassified text				(*sic* Milik's list; could not be located)
4Q312	Heb text in Phoenician cursive?				(*sic* Milik's list; could not be located)
4Q313	cryptA Miqṣat Maʿaśê ha-Torah^{g}?				Pfann 2000
4Q313a	cryptA Cal. Doc. E				Pfann 2000
4Q313b	cryptA Unid. Text Q				Pfann 2000
4Q313c	cryptA Unid. Text R				Pfann 2000
4Q314	cancelled				
4Q315	cancelled				
4Q316	cancelled				
4Q317	cryptA Phases of the Moon (*olim* AstrCrypt)		896	M101	Milik 1976, 68–69; Pfann 2001
			899	M101a	
			903	M102	
			902	M103	
			897	M104	
			900	M105	
4Q318	Zodiology and Brontology ar	Br	805	M100	Sokoloff and Greenfield 2000, pls. XVI–XVII
4Q319	Otot (*olim* 4QS^{b} + 4QS^{c}; 4Q260b)		683	M97	Milik 1976, 62; Ben-Dov 2001
			695	M97a	
			696	M98	
			708	M99	
4Q320	Cal. Doc. Mishmarot A (*olim* Mishmarot A)	Mish A	681	M90	Talmon with Ben-Dov 2001
			682	M91	
4Q321	Cal. Doc. Mishmarot B (*olim* Mishmarot B^{a})	Mish B^{a}	372	M88	Talmon with Ben-Dov 2001
			365	M89	
4Q321a	Cal. Doc. Mishmarot C (*olim* Mishmarot B^{b})	Mish B^{b}	190	M92a	Talmon with Ben-Dov 2001
4Q322	Mishmarot A (*olim* Mishmarot C^{a})	MishC^{a}	694	M94a	Talmon with Ben-Dov 2001
4Q323	Mishmarot B (*olim* Mishmarot C^{b})	MishC^{b}	694	M95a	Talmon with Ben-Dov 2001
4Q324	Mishmarot C (*olim* Mishmarot C^{c}; recto of 4Q355)	Mish C^{c}	694	M95b	Talmon with Ben-Dov 2001
4Q324a	Mishmarot D (*olim* Mishmarot C^{d})	MishC^{d}	684	M95c	Talmon with Ben-Dov 2001
4Q324b	papCal. Doc.? A (*olim* Mishmarot C^{e})	Mish C^{e}	302	M95′a	Talmon with Ben-Dov 2001
4Q324c	cryptA Cal. Doc. B		240	M107	Talmon with Ben-Dov 2001
			241	M106	
4Q324d	Mishmarot E				Pfann 2001
4Q325	Cal. Doc. Mishmarot D (*olim* Mishmarot D)	Mish D	226	M93a	Talmon with Ben-Dov 2001
4Q326	Cal. Doc. C (*olim* Mishmarot E^{a})	MishE^{a}	693	M96b	Talmon with Ben-Dov 2001
4Q327	cancelled (see 4Q394 frags. 1–2)				
4Q328	Mishmarot F (*olim* Mishmarot F^{a})	MishF^{a}	693	M92b	Talmon with Ben-Dov 2001
4Q329	Mishmarot G (*olim* Mishmarot F^{b})	MishF^{b}	710	M93b	Talmon with Ben-Dov 2001
4Q329a	Mishmarot H (*olim* Mishmarot G)	Mish G	710	M94b	Talmon with Ben-Dov 2001

ITEM NO.	COMPOSITION	CONC	INV	PREV	PUBLICATION
4Q330	Mishmarot I (*olim* Mishmarot H)	Mish H	710	M94c	Talmon with Ben-Dov 2001
4Q331	papHistorical Text C		302	M95a	Fitzmyer 2000b, pl. XVIII
4Q332	Historical Text D		694	M95a	Fitzmyer 2000b, pl. XVIII
4Q333	Historical Text E		694	M95b	Fitzmyer 2000b, pl. XIX
4Q334	Ordo	Ordo	710	M94d	Glessmer 2001
4Q335–336	Astronomical frags.?				(*sic* Milik's list; could not be located)
4Q337	Cal. Doc. F		710	M96c	Glessmer 2001
4Q338	Genealogical List? (= verso of 4Q201)		821		Tov 2000b, pl. XX
4Q339	List of False Prophets ar		377	M47a	Broshi and Yardeni 1995, pl. XI
4Q340	List of Netinim		346	M130	Broshi and Yardeni 1995, pl. XI
4Q341	Exercitium Calami C (*olim* 4QTher; List of Proper Names)		346	M130a	Naveh 2000, pl. XIX
4Q342	Letter? ar (r + v)		602	M129e	Yardeni 1997, fig. 28, pl. LIV
4Q343	Letter nab (r + v)		601	M129a	Yardeni 1997, fig. 28, pl. LV
4Q344	Debt Acknowledgement ar		602	M129b	Yardeni 1997, fig. 29, pl. LVI
4Q345	Deed A ar or heb (r + v)		602	M129c	Yardeni 1997, fig. 29, pl. LVI
4Q346	Deed of Sale ar		603		Yardeni 1997, fig. 30, pl. LVII
4Q346a	Unidentified Fragment (A)		603		Yardeni 1997, fig. 30, pl. LVII
4Q347	papDeed F ar (= part of XḤev/Se 32)		184		Yardeni 1997, fig. 19, pl. XXI
4Q348	Deed B heb? (r + v)		602	M129d	Yardeni 1997, fig. 29, pl. LVIII
4Q349	cancelled				
4Q350	Account gr (= v of 4Q460 frag. 9)		254		Cotton 2000a, pl. XXI
4Q351	Account of Cereal A ar		603		Yardeni 1997, fig. 30, pl. LIX
4Q352	papAccount of Cereal B ar or heb		184		Yardeni 1997, fig. 31, pl. LIX
4Q352a	papAccount A ar or heb		184		Yardeni 1997, fig. 31, pl. LIX
4Q353	papAccount of Cereal or Liquid ar or heb		184		Yardeni 1997, fig. 30, pl. LX
4Q354	Account B ar or heb		603		Yardeni 1997, fig. 30, pl. LX
4Q355	Account C ar or heb (= verso of 4Q324)		694		Yardeni 2000a, pl. XXI
4Q356	Account D ar or heb		603		Yardeni 1997, fig. 30, pl. LX
4Q357	Account E ar or heb		603		Yardeni 1997, fig. 30, pl. LX
4Q358	papAccount F? ar or heb		184		Yardeni 1997, fig. 30, pl. LX
4Q359	papDeed C? ar or heb		184		Yardeni 1997, fig. 30, pl. LX
4Q360	Exercitium Calami B		603	M130c	Yardeni 2000a, pl. XXI
4Q360a	papUnidentified Fragments ar (B)		184		Yardeni 1997, fig. 31, pl. LXI
4Q360b	Unidentified Fragment C		603		Yardeni 1997, fig. 30, pl. LXI
4Q361	papUnidentified Fragment gr		184		Cotton 1997, pl. LXI
4Q362	cryptB undeciphered frags. A		901	M114	Pfann 2000
4Q363	cryptB undeciphered frags. B		367	M115	Pfann 2000
			364	M115a	
4Q363a	cryptC Text		112	M115b	Pfann 2000
4Q364	RP[b]		483	SL	Tov and White 1994, pls. XIII–XXI
		SL1	484	SL1	
			477	SL2	
			482	SL2′	
			459	SL3	
			458	SL	
4Q365	RP[c]	SL2	800	SL4	Tov and White 1994, pls. XXII–XXXII
			807	SL7	
			480	SL21	

ITEM NO.	COMPOSITION	CONC	INV	PREV	PUBLICATION
			475	SL11?	
			460	SL6	
4Q365a	T[a]?	JNh	475		Tov and White 1994, pls. XXXIII–XXXIV
			480		
4Q366	RP[d]		257	SL7	Tov and White 1994, pl. XXXV
4Q367	RP[e]		467	SL7	Tov and White 1994, pl. XXXV
4Q368	apocrPent. A	SL5	268	SL5	Vanderkam 2000
4Q369	Prayer of Enosh (Prayer Concerning God and Israel?)	SL6	264	SL78+9a	Attridge and Strugnell 1994, pl. XXXVII
4Q370	AdmonFlood (*olim* apocrFlood)	SL8	341	SL28	Newsom 1995, pl. XII
4Q371	apocrJoseph[a]	SL9	176	SL97, Sy49a	Schuller and Bernstein 2001
4Q372	apocrJoseph[b]	SL10	337	SL10	Schuller and Bernstein 2001
4Q373	apocrJoseph[c]	SL16	469	SL16	Schuller and Bernstein 2000
4Q374	Exod/Conq. Trad. (*olim* apocrMoses A)	SL11	476	SL11?	Newsom 1995, pl. XIII
4Q375	apocrMoses[a] (*olim* apocrMoses B)	SL13	122a	SL12	Strugnell 1995, pl. XIV
4Q376	apocrMoses[b]? (*olim* 3 Tongues of Fire)	SL45	355	SL46	Strugnell 1995, pl. XV
4Q377	apocrPent. B (*olim* apocrMoses C)	SL12	122b	SL12′	Vanderkam 2000
4Q378	apocrJosh[a] (*olim* Psalms of Joshua[a])	SL14	167	SL15′	Newsom 1996, pls. XVII–XX
			168	SL15	
4Q379	apocrJosh[b] (*olim* Psalms of Joshua[b])	SL15	479	SL13	Newsom 1996, pls. XXI–XXV
		Flag. (frag. 1)			
			481	SL14	
4Q380	Non-Canonical Psalms A	SL17	283	S17	Schuller 1998, pl. VIII
4Q381	Non-Canonical Psalms B	SL18	472	SL18	Schuller 1998, pls. IX–XV
			471	SL18b	
			478	SL19	
			470	SL19a	
4Q382	pap paraKings et al. (*olim* papTehilot Ha-'Avot)	SL19	351	SL20	Olyan 1994, pls. XXXVIII–XLI
			339	SL20a	
			338	SL21b	
			340	SL7	
4Q383	apocrJer A	SL20	519	SL24b, c	Dimant 2001
			519	SL30b	
4Q384	papApocrJer B?	SL21	120	SL29	Smith 1995, pl. XVI
4Q385	psEzek[a]	SL22	270	SL22	Dimant 2001
			274	SL22	
4Q385a	apocrJer C[a] (*olim* psMos[a])	SL22	274	SL22a	Dimant 2001
4Q385b	psEzek[c] (*olim* 4Q385 frag. 24, apocrJer C)	SL22	267	SL23	Dimant 2001
4Q386	psEzek[b]	SL23	269	SL48	Dimant 2001
4Q387	Jer C[b] (*olim* psMos[b])	SL24	525	SL24a	Dimant 2001
4Q387a	apocrJer D	SL24	525	SL24a	Dimant 2001
4Q388	psEzek[d]	SL25	125	SL25	Dimant 2001
4Q388a	Jer C[c] (*olim* psMos[c])	SL25	125	SL25	Dimant 2001
4Q389	Jer C[d] (*olim* psMos[d]) ??	SL27	349	SL27	Dimant 2001
4Q389a	Jer E (*olim* apocrMos[e]) ??	SL27	349	SL27	Dimant 2001
4Q390	apocrJer E (psMos[e])	SL26	524	SL30	Dimant 2001
4Q391	pap psEzek[e]		454	SL94.1	Smith 1995, pls. XVII–XXV
			523	SL94	

ITEM NO.	COMPOSITION	CONC	INV	PREV	PUBLICATION
			453	SL95.1	
			455	SL95	
4Q392	Works of God (*olim* liturgical work)	SL30	126	SL25a	Falk 1999, pls. II–III
4Q393	Communal Confession (*olim* liturgical work)	SL29	124	SL26	Falk 1999, pls. II–III
4Q394	MMT[a]	SL31	336	SL32	Qimron and Strugnell 1994, pls. I–III
			335	SL32	
4Q394 1–2	Cal. Doc. D (*olim* 4Q327; Mishmarot E[b])	Mish E[b]	693	M96a	Talmon with Ben-Dov 2001
4Q395	MMT[b]	SL32	187	SL35a	Qimron and Strugnell 1994, pl. III
4Q396	MMT[c]	SL33	520	SL33	Qimron and Strugnell 1994, pl. IV
			526	SL33	
4Q397	MMT[d]	SL34	121b	SL34	Qimron and Strugnell 1994, pls. V–VI
			157a	SL35b	
			121a	SL34	
4Q398	papMMT[e]	SL35	157b	SL72	Qimron and Strugnell 1994, pls. VII–VIII
			157c	SL72	
4Q399	MMT[f]	SL36	292	SL82a	Qimron and Strugnell 1994, pl. VIII
4Q400	ShirShabb[a]	SL37	674	SL40	Newsom 1998, pl. XVI
4Q401	ShirShabb[b]	SL37	491	SL40′	Newsom 1998, pls. XVII–XVIII
				43	
4Q402	ShirShabb[c]	SL41	282	SL41	Newsom 1998, pl. XVIII
4Q403	ShirShabb[d]	SL39	155	SL42	Newsom 1998, pl. XX
4Q404	ShirShabb[e]	SL38	517	SL43b	Newsom 1998, pl. XXI
4Q405	ShirShabb[f]	SL40	669	SL37b	Newsom 1998, pls. XXII–XXX
			506	SL36	
			518	SL37	
			507	SL38	
			497	SL37a	
			504	SL39	
			503	SL39a	
4Q406	ShirShabb[g]		155	SL42	Newsom 1998, pl. XXXI
4Q407	ShirShabb[h]	SL41	127	SL49d	Newsom 1998, pl. XXXI
4Q408	apocrMoses[c]?	SL84	253	SL84	Steudel 2000, pl. XXII
4Q409	Liturgical Work A	SL47	292	SL43a	Qimron 1999, pl. IV
4Q410	Vision and Interpretation (*olim* sap. work)	SL46	510	SL46	Steudel 2000, pl. XXII
4Q411	Sapiential Hymn (*olim* sap. work)		292	SL82c	Steudel 1997, pl. XIV
4Q412	Sapiential-Didactic Work A (*olim* sap. work)	SL82	292	SL82b	Steudel 1997, pl. XIV
4Q413	Comp. conc. Div. Provid. (*olim* sap. work)	SL50	127	SL42d	Qimron 1997, pl. XIV
4Q414	RitPur A (*olim* Baptismal Liturgy) (= verso of 4Q415)	SL51	488	SL47	Eshel 1999b, pls. XI–XII
			487	SL47a	
4Q415	Instruction[a] (*olim* Sap.Work A[d]) (= recto of 4Q414)	SL52	488	SL47	Strugnell and Harrington 1999, pls. I–II
			487	SL47a	
4Q416	Instruction[b] (*olim* Sap. Work A[b])	SL53	181	SL53	Strugnell and Harrington 1999, pls. III–VII
			180	SL48a	
4Q417	Instruction[c] (*olim* Sap. Work A[c])	SL54	329	SL50	Strugnell and Harrington 1999, pls. VIII–XI
			331	SL50′	

ITEM NO.	COMPOSITION	CONC	INV	PREV	PUBLICATION
			321	SL51	
4Q418	Instruction[d] (*olim* Sap. Work A[a])	SL55	505	SL53	Strugnell and Harrington 1999, pls. XII–XXVII
			486	SL53a	
			493	SL54	
			489	SL55	
			494	SL56	
			495	SL56a	
			500	SL57	
			499	SL57a	
			496	SL58	
			498	SL58a	
			502	SL59a	
4Q418a	Instruction[e]	SL59b	511		Strugnell and Harrington 1999, pls. XXVIII–XXIX
4Q418b	Text with Quotation from Psalm 107?				Strugnell and Harrington 1999, pl. XXIX
4Q418c	Instruction[f]?				Strugnell and Harrington 1999, pl. XXIX
4Q419	Sap. Work B	SL56	509	SL52	Tanzer 2000, pl. XXIII
4Q420	Ways of Righteousness[a] (*olim* Sap. Work D[a])	SL58	509	SL52, 61b	Elgvin 1997, pl. XV
4Q421	Ways of Righteousness[b] (*olim* Sap. Work D[b])	SL57	512	SL61a	Elgvin 1997, pl. XVI
4Q422	Paraphrase of Gen and Exod	SL59	165, 166	SL62′	Elgvin and Tov 1994, pls. XLII–XLIII
				62	
4Q423	Instruction[g] (*olim* Sap. Work A[e] and E; *olim* Tree of Knowledge)	SL60	183	SL60′	Elgvin 1999a, pls. XXX–XXXI
			185	SL60	
4Q424	Instruction-like Work	SL61	123	SL61	Tanzer 2000, pls. XXIII–XXIV
4Q425	Sapiential-Didactic Work B (*olim* Sap. Work C)	SL62	501	SL14b	Steudel 1997, pl. XVII
4Q426	Sapiential-Hymnic Work A (*olim* sap. work)	SL63	276	SL63	Steudel 1997, pl. XVIII
4Q427	H[a]	H[a]	115	SL65	Schuller 1999, pls. IV–VI
			116	SL65	
4Q428	H[b]	H[b]	515	SL68	Schuller 1999, pls. VII–XI
			514	SL69	
			514	SL69	
			521	SL68′	
			514	SL69	
4Q429	H[c]	H[c]	522	SL64	Schuller 1999, pls. XI–XII
			522	SL64	
4Q430	H[d]	H[d]	352	SL66	Schuller 1999, pl. XII
4Q431	H[e]	H[f]	513	SL69′, 11b, 67	Schuller 1999, pls. XII, XXVIII
4Q432	papH[f]	H[e]	117	SL70	Schuller 1999, pls. XIII–XIV
			118	SL71, 72	
4Q433	Hodayot-like Text A	SL70	513	SL69′, 11b, 67	Schuller 1999, pl. XV
4Q433a	papHodayot-like Text B (= recto[?] of 4Q255)	4	177		Schuller 1999, pl. XV
4Q434	Barkhi Nafshi[a]	SL71	156	SL93	Weinfeld and Seely 1999, pls. XVII–XIX
				SL93a	
4Q435	Barkhi Nafshi[b]	SL73	327	SL73b	Weinfeld and Seely 1999, pl. XX
4Q436	Barkhi Nafshi[c]	SL72	325	SL73a	Weinfeld and Seely 1999, pl. XXI

ITEM NO.	COMPOSITION	CONC	INV	PREV	PUBLICATION
4Q437	Barkhi Nafshi[d]	SL74	325	SL73a	Weinfeld and Seely 1999, pls. XXII–XXIII
			516	SL74	
4Q438	Barkhi Nafshi[e]	SL87	259	SL87	Weinfeld and Seely 1999, pls. XXIII–XXIV
4Q439	Lament by a Leader (*olim* Work Similar to Barkhi Nafshi)	SL76	334	SL76	Weinfeld and Seely 1999, pl. XXIV
4Q440	Hodayot-like Text C	SL77	508	SL77	Schuller 1999, pl. XVI
4Q440a	Hodayot-like Text D (*olim* 4QH[a] frag. 14)				Lange 2000a, pl. XXV
4Q440b	Fragment Mentioning a Court		196		Lange 2000a, pl. XXV
4Q441	Individual Thanksgiving A	SL78	492	SL78	Chazon 1999, pl. XXV
4Q442	Individual Thanksgiving B	SL79	492	SL79, 71′	Chazon 1999, pl. XXV
4Q443	Personal Prayer	SL80	345	SL80a	Chazon 1999, pl. XXV
4Q444	Incantation	SL81	194	SL81a	Chazon 1999, pl. XXVI
4Q445	Lament A	SL82	490	SL83a	Tigchelaar 1999, pl. XXVI
4Q446	Poetic Text A	SL83	490	SL83b	Tigchelaar 1999, pl. XXVI
4Q447	Poetic Text B		490	SL83c	Tigchelaar 1999, pl. XXVI
4Q448	Apocr. Psalm and Prayer	SL85	490	SL85	Eshel et al. 1998, pl. XXXII
4Q449	Prayer A	SL112	186	SL81	Chazon 1999, pl. XXVII
4Q450	Prayer B?		186	SL81	Chazon 1999, pl. XXVII
4Q451	Prayer C	SL108	186	SL81	Chazon 1999, pl. XXVII
4Q452	Prayer D?		186	SL81	Chazon 1999, pl. XXVII
4Q453	Lament B	SL105	186	SL81	Chazon 1999, pl. XXVII
4Q454	Prayer E?		186	SL81	Chazon 1999, pl. XXVII
4Q455	Didactic Work C (*olim* Prayer F)		186	SL81	Chazon 2000, pl. XXVII
4Q456	Halleluyah		186	SL81	Chazon 1999, pl. XXVII
4Q457a	Creation?	SL44	355	SL42b	Chazon 1999, pl. XXVII
4Q457b	Eschatological Hymn (*olim* prayer)	SL44	355	SL42b	Chazon 1999, pl. XXVII
4Q458	Narrative A	SL90	442	SL90	Larson 2000, pl. XXV
4Q459	Narr. Work Ment. Lebanon (*olim* pseud. work)	SL103	254	SL103	Larson 2000, pl. XXV
4Q460	Narr. Work and Prayer (*olim* pseud. work) (frag. 9 = recto of 4Q350)	SL75	254	SL75	Larson 2000, pl. XXVI
4Q461	Narrative B	SL113	441	SL89b	Larson 2000, pl. XXVII
4Q462	Narrative C	SL89	163	SL89a	Smith 1995, pl. XXVI
4Q463	Narrative D	SL111–112	441	SL89c	Smith 1995, pl. XXVII
4Q464	Exposition on the Patriarchs	SL7	264	SL78+9a	Stone and Eshel 1995, pl. XXVIII
4Q464a	Narrative E		264		Stone and Eshel 1995, pl. XXIX
4Q464b	Unclassified Frags.		264		Stone and Eshel 1995, pl. XXIX
4Q465	papText Mentioning Samson?		268	SL81	Larson 2000, pl. XXVII
4Q466	Text Ment. the Congregation of the Lord		203		Pike 2000, pl. XXVII
4Q467	Text Mentioning "Light to Jacob"		203		Pike 2000, pl. XXVII
4Q468a–d	Unidentified Fragments C, a–f		304		Broshi 2000, pl. XXVIII
4Q468e	Historical Text F		303		Broshi 2000, pl. XXVIII
4Q468f	Historical Text G		131		Lange 2000a, pl. XXVIII
4Q468g	Eschatological Work A		131		Lange 2000a, pl. XXVIII
4Q468h	Hymnic Text A		492		Lange 2000a, pl. XXIX
4Q468i	Sectarian Text		239		Lange 2000a, pl. XXIX
4Q468j	papUnclass. frags.				Lange 2000a, pl. XXIX
4Q468k	Hymnic Text B?				Lange 2000a, pl. XXIX
4Q468l	Frag. Mentioning Qoh 1:8–9				Lange 2000a, pl. XXIX
4Q468m–bb	Unidentified Fragments D				Ernst and Lange 2000a, pls. XXIX–XXX

ITEM NO.	COMPOSITION	CONC	INV	PREV	PUBLICATION
4Q469	Narrative I	SL	519	SL30b	Larson 2000
4Q470	Text Mentioning Zedekiah	SL470	519	SL24c	Larson et al. 1995, pl. XXIX
4Q471	War Scroll-like Text B (*olim* Mh)	SL86	129	SL86	Eshel and Eshel 2000a, pl. XXX
4Q471a	Polemical Text	SL86	129	SL86	Eshel and Kister 2000
4Q471b	Self-Glorification Hymn (= 4QHe?) (*olim* Prayer of Michael)	SL86	129	SL86	Eshel 1999a, pl. XXVIII
4Q471c	Prayer Concerning God and Israel				Eshel 1999b, pl. XXVIII
4Q472	Eschatological Work B		129	SL86′	Elgvin 2000
4Q472a	Halakha C		129	SL86′	Elgvin 1999c, pl. XII
4Q473	The Two Ways	SL109	444	SL92A	Elgvin 1996, pl. XXVI
4Q474	Text Concerning Rachel and Joseph (*olim* apocrJosephA; sap. work)	SL106	444	SL92B	Elgvin 2000, pl. XXXI
4Q475	Renewed Earth (*olim* sap. work)		Flag.	SL106	Elgvin 2000, pl. XXXI
4Q476	Liturgical Work B	SL91	128	SL91	Elgvin 1999a, pl. XXVIII
4Q476a	Liturgical Work C	SL91	128	SL91	Elgvin 1999a, pl. XXVIII
4Q477	Rebukes Reported by the Overseer (*olim* decrees)	SL88	443	SL88	Eshel 2000a, pl. XXXII
4Q478	papFrag. Mentioning Festivals (*olim* Tobit?)		194	SL81	Larson and Schiffman 1996, pl. XXVI
4Q479	Text Mentioning Descendants of David		186	SL	Larson and Schiffman 1996, pl. XXVII
4Q480	Narrative F		186	SL	Larson and Schiffman 1996, pl. XXVII
4Q481	Text Mentioning Mixed Kinds		186	SL	Larson and Schiffman 1996, pl. XXVII
4Q481a	apocrElisha (*olim* Frag. Ment. Elisha)		194	SL	Trebolle 1996, pl. XXVIII
4Q481b	Narrative G	SL101	194	SL	Larson and Schiffman 1996, pl. XXVIII
4Q481c	Prayer for Mercy	SL10b	194	SL	Larson and Schiffman 1996, pl. XXVIII
4Q481d	Frags. with Red Ink		194	SL	Larson and Schiffman 1996, pl. XIX
4Q481e	Narrative H		194	SL	Larson and Schiffman 1996, pl. XIX
4Q481f	Unclassified Frags.				Pike 2000
4Q482	papJub^{i}?		13		Baillet 1982, pl. I
4Q483	papGen or papJub^{j}?		13		Baillet 1982, pl. I
4Q484	papTJud?		15		Baillet 1982, pl. I
4Q485	papProph		13		Baillet 1982, pl. II
4Q486	papSap A?		13		Baillet 1982, pl. I
4Q487	papSap B?		9, 10		Baillet 1982, pls. III–IV
4Q488	papApocryphon ar		15		Baillet 1982, pl. II
4Q489	papApocalypse ar		15		Baillet 1982, pl. II
4Q490	papFrags. ar		15		Baillet 1982, pl. II
4Q491	M^{a}		457, 1001	H1–2	Baillet 1982, pls. V–VI
4Q492	M^{b}		284	H3a	Baillet 1982, pl. VII
4Q493	M^{c}		344	H3c	Baillet 1982, pl. VIII
4Q494	M^{d}		344	H3b	Baillet 1982, pl. VIII
4Q495	M^{e}		344	H3b	Baillet 1982, pl. VIII
4Q496	papM^{f} (= verso of 4Q505 and 4Q509)		20–25		Baillet 1982, pls. X, XII, XIV, XVI–XVIII, XXII, XXIV
4Q497	papWar Scroll-like Text A (*olim* papM^{g}?; = verso of 4Q499)		28		Baillet 1982, pl. XXVI
4Q498	papSap/Hymn		12		Baillet 1982, pl. XXVII
4Q499	papHymns/Prayers (= recto of 4Q497)		28		Baillet 1982, pls. XV, XIX, XXV
4Q500	papBened		11	Bt8	Baillet 1982, pl. XXVII

ITEM NO.	COMPOSITION	CONC	INV	PREV	PUBLICATION
4Q501	apocrLam B	Bt 8	279		Baillet 1982, pl. XXVIII
4Q502	papRitMar		1–6		Baillet 1982, pls. XXI, XXIV, XXIX–XXXIV
4Q503	papPrQuot (= recto of 4Q512)		461–466, 463a		Baillet 1982, pls. XXXV, XXXVII, XXXIX, XLI, XLIII, XLV–XLVIII
4Q504	DibHam[a]	Bt 3	30, 421, 982	Bt3	Baillet 1982, pls. XLIX–LIII
4Q505	papDibHam[b] (= r of 4Q496, 4Q506)		20		Baillet 1982, pl. XXIII
4Q506	papDibHam[c] (= v of 4Q505, 4Q509)		20, 25–26		Baillet 1982, pls. XVIII, XX, XXIV
4Q507	PrFêtes[a]	Bt 7	179	Bt7	Baillet 1982, pl. XXVIII
4Q508	PrFêtes[b]	Bt 6	298	Bt6	Baillet 1982, pls. LIV, LXXII
4Q509	papPrFêtes[c] (= recto of 4Q496 and 4Q506)		16, 17, 20–26,		Baillet 1982, pls. IX, XI, XIII, XV, XVII, XIX, XXI, XXII
4Q510	Shir[a]	Bt 5	280	Bt5	Baillet 1982, pl. LV
4Q511	Shir[b]	Bt 4	403–404, 407–409, 411–417	Bt4	Baillet 1982, pls. LVI–LXIII, LXV, LXVII–LXXI
4Q512	papRitPur B (= verso of 4Q503)		461–466, 463a		Baillet 1982, pls. XXXVI, XXX-VIII, XL, XLII, XLIV–XLVIII
4Q513	Ordinances[b]	Bt 1	310, 315	Bt1	Baillet 1982, pls. LXXII–LXXIII
4Q514	Ordinances[c]	Bt 2	154	Bt2	Baillet 1982, pl. LXXIV
4Q515	papUnclassified frags.		14		Baillet 1982, pl. LXXV
4Q516	papUnclassified frags.				Baillet 1982, pls. LXXV, LXXVII
4Q517	papUnclassified frags.		31, 33		Baillet 1982, pls. LXXVI, LXXVII
4Q518	papUnclassified frags. (= recto of 4Q519)		31, 34		Baillet 1982, pl. LXXVIII
4Q519	papUnclassified frags. (= verso of 4Q518)		31, 34		Baillet 1982, pl. LXXIX
4Q520	papUnclassified frags. (verso)		35		Baillet 1982, pl. LXXX
4Q521	Messianic Apocalypse		330	Sy37	Puech 1998, pls. I–III
4Q522	Prophecy of Joshua (apocrJosh[c]?) (*olim* Work with Place Names)		425	Sy16	Puech 1998, pls. IV, V; Skehan et al. 2000, pl. XX
4Q523	Jonathan (*olim* Heb. frag. B)		288	Sy49b	Puech 1998, pl. VI
4Q524	T[b] (*olim* halakhic text)		320	Sy48	Puech 1998, pls. VI–VIII
4Q525	Beatitudes (*olim* Wisdom Text with Beatitudes)	Beat	423	Sy38	Puech 1998, pls. IX–XIII
			424	Sy39	
			432	Sy39b	
4Q526	Testament? (*olim* Heb. frag. C)		252	Sy49c	Puech 1998, pl. XIV
4Q527	Liturgical Work D? (*olim* Heb. frag. D)		252	Sy49c	Puech 1998, pl. XIV
4Q528	Hymnic or Sapiential Work B (*olim* Heb. frag. E)		252	Sy49c	Puech 1998, pl. XIV
4Q529	Words of Michael ar	kM	164	Sy1	Puech 2001
4Q530	EnGiants[b] ar	psHenA	437	Sy2	Milik 1976, 304–6; Puech 2001
4Q531	EnGiants[c] ar	psHenB	328	Sy3	Milik 1976, 307–8; Puech 2001
			342	Sy4	
4Q532	EnGiants[d] ar	psHenC	148	Sy5	Puech 2001
4Q533	EnGiants[e] ar (Eschat. Vision?)	arT/arU	428	Sy53b	Puech 2001
4Q534	Noah[a] ar (*olim* Elect of God ar)	Mess ar	1006	Sy50	Puech 2001
				Sy51	
4Q535	Noah[b] (*olim* Aramaic N)	mN	348	Sy4b	Puech 2001
4Q536	Noah[c] (*olim* Aramaic C)	arC	451	Sy54a	Puech 2001
4Q537	TJacob? ar	arN	260	Sy25	Puech 2001
4Q538	TJud ar	TB	450	Sy8	Puech 2001
4Q539	TJoseph ar (*olim* aJo ar)	arM	433	Sy55b	Puech 2001

ITEM NO.	COMPOSITION	CONC	INV	PREV	PUBLICATION
4Q540	apocrLevi^{a}? ar (*olim* AhA [bis] = TLevi^{g}? ar)	arA	150	Sy13b	Puech 2001
4Q541	apocrLevi^{b}? ar (*olim* AhA = TLevi^{h}? ar)	AhA	149	Sy12	Puech 2001
			147	Sy13	
4Q542	TQahat ar	TQ	193	Sy7b	Puech 2001
4Q543	Visions of Amram^{a} ar	h'A^{a}	347	Sy10a	Puech 2001
		h'A^{b}	343	Sy10b	
4Q544	Visions of Amram^{b} ar	h'A^{c}	431	Sy11	Puech 2001
4Q545	Visions of Amram^{c} ar	h'A^{d}	192	Sy9	Puech 2001
4Q546	Visions of Amram^{d} ar	h'A^{e}	434	Sy14	Puech 2001
4Q547	Visions of Amram^{e} ar		144	Sy7	Puech 2001
4Q548	Visions of Amram^{f} ar	arB	427	Sy53	Puech 2001
4Q549	Visions of Amram^{g}? ar (*olim* Work Ment. Hur and Miriam ar)	AhC	447	Sy15	Puech 2001
4Q550	PrEsther^{a} ar	DCP	430	Sy17b	Puech 2009
4Q550a	PrEsther^{b} ar	DCP	430	Sy17b	Puech 2009
4Q550b	PrEsther^{c} ar	DCP	430	Sy17b	Puech 2009
4Q550c	PrEsther^{d} ar	DCP	426/430	Sy17	Puech 2009
4Q550d	PrEsther^{e} ar	DCP	426	Sy17	Puech 2009
4Q550e	PrEsther^{f} ar	DCP	260		Puech 2009
4Q551	DanSuz? ar	arO	?	Sy18	Puech 2009
4Q552	Four Kingdoms^{a} ar	QR^{a}	278	Sy19	Puech 2009
4Q553	Four Kingdoms^{b} ar	QR^{b}	353	Sy20	Puech 2009
4Q554	NJ^{a} ar	Jna	319	Sy22	Puech 2009
			318	Sy23–24	
4Q555	NJ^{b} ar		205	Sy57	Puech 2009
4Q556	Vision^{a} ar		446	Sy2b	Puech 2009
4Q557	Vision^{c} ar	arQ	313	Sy29a	Puech 2009
4Q558	papVision^{b} ar		448	Sy26	Puech 2009
			452	Sy27	
			449	Sy28a	
			440	Sy28b	
4Q559	papBibChronology ar	ChrB	438	Sy30	Puech 2009
4Q560	Exorcism ar	OC	445	Sy36	Puech 2009
4Q561	Physiognomy/Horoscope ar	Hor ar	439	Sy52	Puech 2009
4Q562	Aramaic D	arD	332	Sy54b	Puech 2009
4Q563	Aramaic E	arE	159	Sy55a	Puech 2009
4Q564	Aramaic F	arF	433	Sy55b	Puech 2009
4Q565	Aramaic G	arG	433	Sy55b	Puech 2009
4Q566	Aramaic H	arH	433	Sy55b	Puech 2009
4Q567	Aramaic I	arI	433	Sy55b	Puech 2009
4Q568	Aramaic K	arK	433	Sy55b	Puech 2009
4Q569	Aramaic L	arL	433	Sy55b	Puech 2009
4Q570	Aramaic R	arR	429	Sy55c	Puech 2009
4Q571	Aramaic V	arV	435	Sy56	Puech 2009
4Q572	Aramaic W	arW	435	Sy56	Puech 2009
4Q573	Aramaic X	arX	435	Sy56	Puech 2009
4Q574	Aramaic Y	arY	435	Sy56	Puech 2009
4Q575	Aramaic Z	arZ1/ arZ2	435	Sy56	Puech 2009
4Q576	Gen^{n} (*olim* part of 4Q524)		320	Sy48	Puech 1998, pl. XV
4Q577	Text Mentioning the Flood		320	Sy48	Puech 1998, pl. XV
4Q578	Historical Text B		320	Sy48	Puech 1998, pl. XV
4Q579	Hymnic Work?		330		Puech 1998, pl. XV
5Q1	Deut		97		Milik 1962, pl. XXXVI

ITEM NO.	COMPOSITION	CONC	INV	PREV	PUBLICATION
5Q2	Kgs		98		Milik 1962, pl. XXXVI
5Q3	Isa		99		Milik 1962, pl. XXXVI
5Q4	Amos		100		Milik 1962, pl. XXXVI
5Q5	Ps		98, 100, 104		Milik 1962, pl. XXXVII
5Q6	Lam[a]		100		Milik 1962, pls. XXXVII–XXXVIII
5Q7	Lam[b]		100		Milik 1962, pl. XXXVIII
5Q8	Phyl.		100		Milik 1962, pl. XXXVIII
5Q9	Work with Place Names (apocrJosh?)				Milik 1962, pl. XXXVIII
5Q10	apocrMal				Milik 1962, pl. XXXVIII
5Q11	S		101		Milik 1962, pl. XXXVIII
5Q12	D		101		Milik 1962, pl. XXXVIII
5Q13	Rule				Milik 1962, pls. XXXIX–XL
5Q14	Curses		101		Milik 1962, pl. XL
5Q15	NJ ar				Milik 1962, pls. XL–XLI
5Q16	Unclassified frags.				Milik 1962, pls. XLI–XLII
5Q17	Unclassified frags.				Milik 1962, pls. XLI–XLII
5Q18	Unclassified frags.		102		Milik 1962, pls. XLI–XLII
5Q19	Unclassified frags.		102		Milik 1962, pls. XLI–XLII
5Q20	Unclassified frags.		102		Milik 1962, pls. XLI–XLII
5Q21	Unclassified frag.		102		Milik 1962, pls. XLI–XLII
5Q22	Unclassified frag.		102		Milik 1962, pls. XLI–XLII
5Q23	Unclassified frag.				Milik 1962, pls. XLI–XLII
5Q24	Unclassified frag. ar				Milik 1962, pls. XLI–XLII
5Q25	Unclassified frags.		102		Milik 1962, pl. XLII
5QX1	Uninscribed leather frag.		50		
6Q1	paleoGen		894		Baillet 1962, pl. XX
6Q2	paleoLev		894		Baillet 1962, pl. XX
6Q3	papDeut?		894		Baillet 1962, pl. XX
6Q4	papKgs		894		Baillet 1962, pls. XX–XXII
			895		
			738		
6Q5	papPs?		646		Baillet 1962, pl. XXIII
6Q6	Cant		646		Baillet 1962, pl. XXIII
6Q7	papDan		646		Baillet 1962, pl. XXIII
6Q8	papEnGiants ar (*olim* apocrGen)		785		Baillet 1962, pls. XXIV, XXIX; reedition: Stuckenbruck 2000
6Q9	pap apocrSam–Kgs		785, 892		Baillet 1962, pls. XXIV–XXV
6Q10	papProph		649		Baillet 1962, pl. XXVI
6Q11	Allegory of the Vine		649		Baillet 1962, pl. XXVI
6Q12	apocrProphecy		649		Baillet 1962, pl. XXVI
6Q13	Priestly Prophecy		649		Baillet 1962, pl. XXVI
6Q14	Apoc ar		649		Baillet 1962, pl. XXVI
6Q15	D		649		Baillet 1962, pl. XXVI
6Q16	papBened		737		Baillet 1962, pl. XXVII
6Q17	papCalendrical Doc.		737		Baillet 1962, pl. XXVII
6Q18	papHymn		737		Baillet 1962, pl. XXVII
			29		unpublished
6Q19	Text Related to Genesis ar		893		Baillet 1962, pl. XXVIII
6Q20	Deut?		893		Baillet 1962, pl. XXVIII
6Q21	Prophetic Text?		893		Baillet 1962, pl. XXVIII
6Q22	papUnclassified frags.		893		Baillet 1962, pl. XXVIII
6Q23	papUnclassified frags. ar (Words of Michael?)		893		Baillet 1962, pl. XXVIII

ITEM NO.	COMPOSITION	CONC	INV	PREV	PUBLICATION
6Q24	papUnclassified frags.		893		Baillet 1962, pl. XXVIII
6Q25	papUnclassified frags.		893		Baillet 1962, pl. XXVIII
6Q26	papAccount or contract		784		Baillet 1962, pl. XXIX
6Q27	papCursive unclassified frags.		784		Baillet 1962, pl. XXIX
6Q28	papCursive unclassified frags.		784		Baillet 1962, pl. XXIX
6Q29	papCursive unclassified frag.		784		Baillet 1962, pl. XXIX
6Q30	papCursive unclassified frags.		784		Baillet 1962, pl. XXIX
6Q31	papUnclassified frags.		784		Baillet 1962, pl. XXIX
6QX1	papUnclassified frags.		786		
6QX2	Unclassified frags.		787		
7Q1	papLXXExod		789		Baillet 1962, pl. XXX
7Q2	papEpJer gr		789		Baillet 1962, pl. XXX
7Q3	papBiblical Text? gr		789		Baillet 1962, pl. XXX
7Q4	papBiblical Text? gr (papEn gr?)		789		Baillet 1962, pl. XXX; Muro 1997
7Q5	papBiblical Text? gr		789		Baillet 1962, pl. XXX
7Q6	papUnclassified frags. gr		789		Baillet 1962, pl. XXX
7Q7	papUnclassified frags. gr		789		Baillet 1962, pl. XXX
7Q8	papUnclassified frags. gr (papEn gr?)		789		Baillet 1962, pl. XXX; Muro 1997
7Q9	papUnclassified frags. gr		789		Baillet 1962, pl. XXX
7Q10	papUnclassified frags. gr		789		Baillet 1962, pl. XXX
7Q11	papUnclassified frags. gr (papEn gr?)		789		Baillet 1962, pl. XXX; Puech 1997
7Q12	papUnclassified frags. gr (papEn gr?)		789		Baillet 1962, pl. XXX; Puech 1997
7Q13	papUnclassified frags. gr (papEn gr?)		789		Baillet 1962, pl. XXX; Puech 1997
7Q14	papUnclassified frags. gr (papEn gr?)		789		Baillet 1962, pl. XXX; Puech 1997
7Q15	papUnclassified frags. gr		789		Baillet 1962, pl. XXX
7Q16	papUnclassified frags. gr		789		Baillet 1962, pl. XXX
7Q17	papUnclassified frags. gr		789		Baillet 1962, pl. XXX
7Q18	papUnclassified frags. gr		789		Baillet 1962, pl. XXX
7Q19	papImprint gr		789A		Baillet 1962, pl. XXX
8Q1	Gen		788		Baillet 1962, pl. XXXI
8Q2	Ps		788		Baillet 1962, pl. XXXI
8Q3	Phyl		914		Baillet 1962, pls. XXXII–XXXIII
8Q4	Mez		916		Baillet 1962, pl. XXXIV
8Q5	Hymn		917		Baillet 1962, pl. XXXV
8QX1	Reinforcing tabs		56		
8QX2–3	Thongs		57, 58		
9Q	papUnclassified frag.		917		Baillet 1962, pl. XXXV
10Q	ostr?		918		Baillet 1962, pl. XXXV
11Q1	paleoLev[a]				Freedman and Mathews 1985
	frag. A (Lev 4:24–26)		1039		Freedman and Mathews 1985, pl. 1; Puech 1989, 176 bis
	frag. B (Lev 10:4–7)		1039		Freedman and Mathews 1985, pl. 1
	frag. C (Lev 11:27–32)		1039		Freedman and Mathews 1985, pls. 1, 12
	frag. D (Lev 13:3–9)		1039		Freedman and Mathews 1985, pl. 1; Puech 1989, 176 bis
	frag. E (Lev 13:39–43)		1039		Freedman and Mathews 1985, pls. 2, 12

ITEM NO.	COMPOSITION	CONC	INV	PREV	PUBLICATION
	frag. F (Lev 14:16–21)		1039		Freedman and Mathews 1985, pls. 2, 12; Puech 1989, 176 bis
	frag. G (Lev 14:52–15:5/ 16:2–4)		1039		Freedman and Mathews 1985, pl. 2
	frag. H (Lev 16:34–17:5)		1039		Freedman and Mathews 1985, pls. 3, 12; Puech 1989, 176 ter
	frag. I (Lev 18:27–19:4)		1039		Freedman and Mathews 1985, pls. 3, 13
	frag. J (Lev 20:1–6)		1039		Freedman and Mathews 1985, pls. 4, 13; Puech 1989, 176 ter
	frag. K (Lev 21:6–11)		1039		Freedman and Mathews 1985, pls. 4, 14
	frag. L (Lev 21a–27a, Lev. 21:7a–12a)		Paris		Freedman and Mathews 1985, pl. 5; Puech 1989, 176 quat
	frag. M (Lev 16:1–6)		1039		Freedman and Mathews 1985, pl. 6; Puech 1989, 176 bis
	col. 1 (Lev 22:21–27)		1039		Freedman and Mathews 1985, pls. 6, 14, 20
	col. 2 (Lev 23:22–29)		1039		Freedman and Mathews 1985, pls. 7, 15, 20
	col. 3 (Lev 24:9–14)		1039		Freedman and Mathews 1985, pls. 8, 16, 20
	col. 4 (Lev 25:28–36)		1039		Freedman and Mathews 1985, pls. 9, 17, 20
	col. 5 (Lev 26:17–26)		1039		Freedman and Mathews 1985, pls. 10, 18, 20
	col. 6 (Lev 27:11–19)		1039		Freedman and Mathews 1985, pls. 11, 19, 20
	frags. a–f		1022		Puech 1989, 176 bis
	frags.		614		Puech 1989, 176 ter
	frags.		567		Puech 1989
	frags. aa–ai		988		Tigchelaar 1998
11Q2	Lev[b]				
	frag. 1 (Lev 7:34–35)		577		García Martínez et al. 1998, pl. I
	frags. 2, 8 (Lev 9:23–10:2)		566		
	frag. 3 (Lev 13:58–59)		615		
	frag. 4 (Lev 14:16–17)		1032		
	frags. 5 + 6 (Lev 15:18–19)		567, 577		
	frag. 7 (Lev 25:31–33)		567, 1016		
	frag. 9 (?)		567		
11Q3	Deut				García Martínez et al. 1998, pl. II
	frag. 1 (Deut 1:4–5)		576		
	frag. 2 (Deut 2:28–30)		1016		
	frag. 3 (?)		1016		
11Q4	Ezek (unopened scroll)				Herbert 1998, pl. II
	scroll frags. after unsuccessful opening		1010		
	frag. 1 (Ezek 1:8–10)		1013–1013A		
	frag. 2 (Ezek 4:3–5)		1013–1013A		
	frag. 3a (Ezek 4:6)		1013–1013A		
	frags. 4–5 (Ezek 4:9–10)		1013–1013A		
	frags. 3b + 6 (Ezek 5:11–17)		1013–1013A		
	frag. 7 (Ezek 7:9–12)		1013–1013A		
	frag. 8		1013–1013A		
	frag. 9		1013–1013A		
11Q5	Ps[a] (unopened scroll)		977		Sanders 1965, pls. I–II
	frag. A (Ps 101:1–8; 102:1–2)		977		Sanders 1965, pl. III
	frag. B (Ps 101:1–8; 102:1–2)		977		Sanders 1965, pl. III
	frag. C I (Ps 101:1–8; 102:1–2)		977		Sanders 1965, pl. III

ITEM NO.	COMPOSITION	CONC	INV	PREV	PUBLICATION
	frag. C II (Ps 102:18–29; 103?; 104)		977		Sanders 1965, pl. III
	frag. D (Ps 109:21–31)		976		Sanders 1965, pl. III
	frag. E (Ps 118:25–29; 104:1–6, 21–35; 147:1–2, 18–20; 105:1–11)		976?		García Martínez et al. 1998, pls. IV–V
	frag. F (Ps 147:3?)		614B		García Martínez et al. 1998, pl. V
	col. I (Ps 105:25–45)		979		Sanders 1965, pl. IV
	col. II (Ps 146:9?–10; 148:1–12)		979		Sanders 1965, pl. IV
	col. III (Ps 121:1–8; 122:1–9; 123:1–2)		979		Sanders 1965, pl. IV
	col. IV (Ps 124:7–8; 125:1–5; 126:1–6; 127:1)		979		Sanders 1965, pl. V
	col. V (Ps 128:3–6; 129:1–8; 130:1–8)		979		Sanders 1965, pl. V
	col. VI (Ps 132:8–18; 119:1–6)		979		Sanders 1965, pl. VI
	col. VII (Ps 119:15–28)		979		Sanders 1965, pl. VI
	col. VIII (Ps 119:37–49)		979		Sanders 1965, pl. VII
	col. IX (Ps 119:59–73)		979		Sanders 1965, pl. VII
	col. X (Ps 119:82–96)		979		Sanders 1965, pl. VIII
	col. XI (Ps 119:105–20)		979		Sanders 1965, pl. VIII
	col. XII (Ps 119:128–42)		979		Sanders 1965, pl. IX
	col. XIII (Ps 119:150–64)		975		Sanders 1965, pl. IX
	col. XIV (Ps 119:171–6; 135:1–9)		975		Sanders 1965, pl. X
	col. XV (Ps 135:17–21; 136:1–16)		975		Sanders 1965, pl. X
	col. XVI (Ps 136:26b; 118:1?, 15, 16, 18, 19, ?, 29; 145:1–7)		975		Sanders 1965, pl. XI
	col. XVII (Ps 145:13–21+?)		975		Sanders 1965, pl. XI
	col. XVIII (Syriac Ps II)		975		Sanders 1965, pl. XII
	col. XIX (Plea for Deliverance)		978		Sanders 1965, pl. XII
	col. XX (Ps 139:8–24; 137:1)		978		Sanders 1965, pl. XIII
	col. XXI (Ps 137:9; 138:1–8; Sirach 51:13ff.)		978		Sanders 1965, pl. XIII
	col. XXII (Sirach 51:30; Apostr. to Zion; Ps 93:1–3)		978		Sanders 1965, pl. XIV
	col. XXIII (Ps 141:5–10; 133:1–3; 144:1–7)		978		Sanders 1965, pl. XIV
	col. XXIV (Ps 144:15; Syriac Ps III)		978		Sanders 1965, pl. XV
	col. XXV (Ps 142:4–8; 143:1–8)		974		Sanders 1965, pl. XV
	col. XXVI (Ps 149:7–9; 150:1–6; Hymn to the Creator)		974		Sanders 1965, pl. XVI
	col. XXVII (2 Sam 23:7; David's Comps; Ps 140:1–5)		974		Sanders 1965, pl. XVI
	col. XXVIII (Ps 134:1–3; 151A; 151B)		576		Sanders 1965, pl. XVII
11Q6	Ps^b				García Martínez et al. 1998, pl. III
	frag. 1 (Ps 77:18–78:1)		606		
	frag. 2 (Ps 119:163–165)		614		
	frag. 3 (Ps 118:1, 15–16)		613		
	frags. 4 + 5 (Plea for Deliverance)		576		
	frag. 6 (Apostrophe to Zion)		621B		
	frag. 7 (Ps 141:10; 133; 144:1–2)		576, 621B		
	frag. 8 (Ps 109:3–4?)		1032		
	frag. 9 (?)		1032		

ITEM NO.	COMPOSITION	CONC	INV	PREV	PUBLICATION
11Q7	Ps[c]				García Martínez et al. 1998, pl. VI
	frags. 1 + 2 (Ps 2:1–8)		606		
	frag. 3 (Ps 9:3–7)		606		
	frags. 4 + 6 + 7 (Ps 12:5–14:6)		606		
	frag. 5 (Ps 12:6–9)		614		
	frag. 8 (Ps 17:9–18:12)		606		
	frag. 9 (Ps 18:15–17?)		614		
	frag. 10 (Ps 19:4–8)		621B		
	frag. 11 (Ps 25:2–7)		1027		
11Q8	Ps[d]				
	frag. 1 (Ps 6:2–4)		?		García Martínez et al. 1998, pl. VII
	frag. 2 (Ps 9:3–6)		1025		García Martínez et al. 1998, pl. VII
	frag. 3 (Ps 18:26–29; *olim* Mas1g?; XQPs)		78–79*		Flint 2000a; García Martínez et al. 1998, pl. VII
	frag. 4 (Ps 18:39–42)		619		García Martínez et al. 1998, pl. VII
	frag. 5 (Ps 36:13–37:4)		621B		García Martínez et al. 1998, pl. VII
	frag. 6 (Ps 39:13–40:2)		569		García Martínez et al. 1998, pl. VII
	frag. 7 (Ps 43:1–3)		569		García Martínez et al. 1998, pl. VII
	frag. 8 (Ps 45:6–8)		621B		García Martínez et al. 1998, pl. VII
	frag. 9 (Ps 59:5–8)		569		García Martínez et al. 1998, pl. VII
	frag. 10 (Ps 68:1–5)		569		García Martínez et al. 1998, pl. VII
	frag. 11 (Ps 68:14–18)		569		García Martínez et al. 1998, pl. VII
	frag. 12 (Ps 78:5–12)		569, 621B		García Martínez et al. 1998, pl. VII
	frag. 13 (Ps 81:4–9)		569		García Martínez et al. 1998, pl. VII
	frag. 14 (Ps 86:11–14)		621B		García Martínez et al. 1998, pl. VIII
	frag. 15 (Ps 115:16–116:1)		581A		García Martínez et al. 1998, pl. VIII
	frag. 16 (Ps 78:36–37?)		580		García Martínez et al. 1998, pl. VIII
	frag. 17 (Ps 60:9?)		1032		García Martínez et al. 1998, pl. VIII
11Q9	Ps[e]? (Ps 50:3–7)		1016		García Martínez et al. 1998, pl. VIII
11Q10	tgJob (unopened scroll)				
	col. I (Job 17:14–18:4)		635		García Martínez et al. 1998, pl. IX
	col. II (Job 19:11–19)		627		García Martínez et al. 1998, pl. IX
	col. III (Job 19:29–20:6)		627		García Martínez et al. 1998, pl. IX
	col. IV (Job 21:2–10)		628		García Martínez et al. 1998, pl. IX
	col. V (Job 21:20–27)		628		García Martínez et al. 1998, pl. IX
	col. VI (Job 22:3–9)		636		García Martínez et al. 1998, pl. X
	col. VII (Job 22:16–22)		636		García Martínez et al. 1998, pl. X
	col. VIIA (Job 23:1–8)				García Martínez et al. 1998, pl. X
	col. VIII (Job 24:12–17)		636		García Martínez et al. 1998, pl. X
	col. IX (Job 24:24–26:2)		633		García Martínez et al. 1998, pl. X
	col. X (Job 26:10–27:4)		633		García Martínez et al. 1998, pl. XI
	col. XI (Job 27:11–20)		637		García Martínez et al. 1998, pl. XI
	col. XII (Job 28:4–13)		637		García Martínez et al. 1998, pl. XI
	col. XIII (Job 28:20–28)		637		García Martínez et al. 1998, pl. XI
	col. XIV (Job 29:7–16)		632		García Martínez et al. 1998, pl. XII
	col. XV (Job 29:24–30:4)		632		García Martínez et al. 1998, pl. XII
	col. XVI (Job 30:13–20)		631		García Martínez et al. 1998, pl. XII
	col. XVII (Job 30:25–31:1)		567, 631		García Martínez et al. 1998, pl. XII
	col. XVIII (Job 31:8–16)		624, 631		García Martínez et al. 1998, pl. XII
	col. XIX (Job 31:26–32)		624		García Martínez et al. 1998, pls. XII–XIII
	col. XX (Job 31:40–32:3)		624		García Martínez et al. 1998, pl. XIII
	col. XXI (Job 32:10–17)		634		García Martínez et al. 1998, pl. XIII
	col. XXII (Job 33:6–16)		634		García Martínez et al. 1998, pl. XIII
	col. XXIII (Job 33:24–32)		629, 635		García Martínez et al. 1998, pl. XIV
	col. XXIV (Job 34:6–17)		621, 629		García Martínez et al. 1998, pl. XIV

ITEM NO.	COMPOSITION	CONC	INV	PREV	PUBLICATION
	col. XXV (Job 34:24–34)		621		García Martínez et al. 1998, pl. XIV
	col. XXVI (Job 35:6–15)		626		García Martínez et al. 1998, pl. XV
	col. XXVII (Job 36:7–16)		626, 630		García Martínez et al. 1998, pl. XV
	col. XXVIII (Job 36:23–33)		623, 630		García Martínez et al. 1998, pl. XV
	col. XXIX (Job 37:10–19)		635, 638		García Martínez et al. 1998, pl. XVI
	col. XXX (Job 38:3–13)		638		García Martínez et al. 1998, pl. XVI
	col. XXXI (Job 38:23–34)		638		García Martínez et al. 1998, pl. XVII
	col. XXXII (Job 39:1–11)		638		García Martínez et al. 1998, pl. XVII
	col. XXXIII (Job 39:20–29)		638		García Martínez et al. 1998, pl. XVIII
	col. XXXIV (Job 40:5–14[15?])		638		García Martínez et al. 1998, pl. XVIII
	col. XXXV (Job 40:23–31)		638		García Martínez et al. 1998, pl. XIX
	col. XXXVI (Job 41:7–17)		638		García Martínez et al. 1998, pl. XIX
	col. XXXVII (Job 41:25–42:2; 40:5; 42:4–6)		638		García Martínez et al. 1998, pl. XX
	col. XXXVIII (Job 42:9–12)		638		García Martínez et al. 1998, pl. XX
	frags. A1, A3, A5		635		García Martínez et al. 1998, pl. XXI
	frags. A7, A9, A10		567		García Martínez et al. 1998, pl. XXI
	frag. A8		581		García Martínez et al. 1998, pl. XXI
	frags. A11–19		625		García Martínez et al. 1998, pl. XXI
	frag. G		---		García Martínez et al. 1998, pl. XXI
	frags. N, O		---		García Martínez et al. 1998, pl. XXI
	frag. P		---		García Martínez et al. 1998, pl. XXI
11Q11	apocrPs (unopened scroll; *olim* apocrPs[a])				García Martínez et al. 1998, pl. LIII
	frags. 1 + 2		619		García Martínez et al. 1998, pl. XXII
	frags. 3 + 4		1032		García Martínez et al. 1998, pl. XXII
	col. I		612		García Martínez et al. 1998, pl. XXII
	col. II		61		García Martínez et al. 1998, pl. XXIII
	col. III		61		García Martínez et al. 1998, pl. XXIII
	col. IV		61		García Martínez et al. 1998, pl. XXIV
	col. V (Ps 91)		61		García Martínez et al. 1998, pl. XXIV
	col. VI		61, 612		García Martínez et al. 1998, pl. XXIV
	handle sheet and wooden handle		612		García Martínez et al. 1998, pl. XXII
11Q12	Jub				García Martínez et al. 1998, pl. XXVI
	frag. 1 (Jub 4:6–11)		619, 621B		
	frag. 2 (Jub 4:13–14)		606		
	frag. 3 (Jub 4:16–17 [4:11–12?])		?		
	frag. 4 (Jub 4:17–18?)		621B		
	frag. 5 (Jub 4:29–30)		619		
	frag. 6 (Jub 4:31)		621B		
	frag. 7 (Jub 5:1–2)		619		
	frag. 8 (Jub 12:15–17)		619		
	frag. 9 (Jub 12:28–29)		619		
	frag. 10?		621B		
	frag. 11?		614		

ITEM NO.	COMPOSITION	CONC	INV	PREV	PUBLICATION
	frag. 12?		614B		
	frag. 13?		619		
11Q13	Melch				García Martínez et al. 1998, pl. XXVII
	frags. 1a, 1b, 2–9		579		
	frag. 1c		1031		
	frag. 10		621B		
	frag. 11		1032		
11Q14	Sefer ha-Milḥamah (*olim* Ber)				García Martínez et al. 1998, pl. XXVIII
	frags. 1a, 1b, 1e, 3		607		
	frag. 1c		?		
	frag. 1d		567		
	frag. 1f		607		
	frag. 2		614		
	frag. 4		615		
11Q15	Hymns[a]				García Martínez et al. 1998, pl. XXIX
	frag. 1		576		
	frag. 2		1025		
	frags. 3, 4		621B		
11Q16	Hymns[b]		614		García Martínez et al. 1998, pl. XXIX
11Q17	ShirShabb (unopened scroll)				García Martínez et al. 1998, pl. LIII
	frag. 1		567		García Martínez et al. 1998, pl. XXX
	frags. 2–4, 6, 8, 10–12, 14–15, 28–29, 34		565		García Martínez et al. 1998, pls. XXX, XXXI, XXXIV
	frags. 5, 26b, 27, 30, 31		---		García Martínez et al. 1998, pls. XXX, XXXIV
	frag. 26a		1032		García Martínez et al. 1998, pl. XXXIV
	frags. 7, 9, 13, 23, 24		618		García Martínez et al. 1998, pls. XXX–XXXI, XXXIII
	frags. 21a, 22		618		García Martínez et al. 1998, pl. XXXII
	frag. 25		618		García Martínez et al. 1998, pl. XXXIII
	frag. 16		609		García Martínez et al. 1998, pl. XXXI
	frags. 17–19, 33		609		García Martínez et al. 1998, pls. XXXI–XXXII
	frag. 20		609		García Martínez et al. 1998, pl. XXXII
	frag. 32		621B		García Martínez et al. 1998, pl. XXXIV
	frag. 35		614		García Martínez et al. 1998, pl. XXXIV
	frags. 36, 42		1032		García Martínez et al. 1998, pl. XXXIV
	frag. 37		1034		García Martínez et al. 1998, pl. XXX
	frags. 38–41		1030		García Martínez et al. 1998, pl. XXXIII
11Q18	NJ ar (unopened scroll)				García Martínez et al. 1998, pl. LIII
	frags. 1–4, additional frags.		578A		García Martínez et al. 1998, pls. XXXV, XL
	frags. 5–9		578		García Martínez et al. 1998, pls. XXXV–XXXVI

ITEM NO.	COMPOSITION	CONC	INV	PREV	PUBLICATION
	frags. 10–11		574, 572, 615		García Martínez et al. 1998, pl. XXXVI
	frags. 12–13		564, 572		García Martínez et al. 1998, pls. XXXVI, XXXVII
	frags. 14–15		564, 568		García Martínez et al. 1998, pl. XXXVII
	frags. 16, 21		572, 617		García Martínez et al. 1998, pls. XXXVII, XXXVIII
	frags. 17–18		611		García Martínez et al. 1998, pls. XXXVII, XXXVIII
	frags. 19–20		575		García Martínez et al. 1998, pl. XXXVIII
	frags. 22–24		573, 572, 615		García Martínez et al. 1998, pl. XXXVIII
	frags. 25–27		570, 572, 615		García Martínez et al. 1998, pl. XXXXIX
	frags. 28–31		571, 572, 614B		García Martínez et al. 1998, pl. XXXXIX
	frags. 32–37 petrified remnants of scroll		572, 1030		García Martínez et al. 1998, pl. XXXXIX
11Q19	T[a] (unopened scroll)		SHR		Yadin 1983
	col. I		SHR		Yadin 1983, pl. 16
	col. II		SHR		Yadin 1983, pl. 17
	col. III		SHR		Yadin 1983, pl. 18
	col. IV		SHR		Yadin 1983, pl. 19
	col. V		SHR		Yadin 1983, pl. 20
	col. VI		SHR		Yadin 1983, pl. 21
	col. VII		SHR		Yadin 1983, pl. 22
	col. VIII		SHR		Yadin 1983, pl. 23
	col. IX		SHR		Yadin 1983, pl. 24
	col. X		SHR		Yadin 1983, pl. 25
	col. XI		SHR		Yadin 1983, pl. 26
	col. XII		SHR		Yadin 1983, pl. 27
	col. XIII		SHR		Yadin 1983, pl. 28
	col. XIV		SHR		Yadin 1983, pl. 29
	col. XV		SHR		Yadin 1983, pl. 30
	col. XVI		SHR		Yadin 1983, pl. 31
	col. XVII		SHR		Yadin 1983, pl. 32
	col. XVIII		SHR		Yadin 1983, pl. 33
	col. XIX		SHR		Yadin 1983, pl. 34
	col. XX		SHR		Yadin 1983, pl. 35
	col. XXI		SHR		Yadin 1983, pl. 36
	col. XXII		SHR		Yadin 1983, pl. 37
	col. XXIII		SHR		Yadin 1983, pl. 38
	col. XXIV		SHR		Yadin 1983, pl. 39
	col. XXV		SHR		Yadin 1983, pl. 40
	col. XXVI		SHR		Yadin 1983, pl. 41
	col. XXVII		SHR		Yadin 1983, pl. 42
	col. XXVIII		SHR		Yadin 1983, pl. 43
	col. XXIX		SHR		Yadin 1983, pl. 44
	col. XXX		SHR		Yadin 1983, pl. 45
	col. XXXI		SHR		Yadin 1983, pl. 46
	col. XXXII		SHR		Yadin 1983, pl. 47
	col. XXXIII		SHR		Yadin 1983, pl. 48
	col. XXXIV		SHR		Yadin 1983, pl. 49
	col. XXXV		SHR		Yadin 1983, pl. 50
	col. XXXVI		SHR		Yadin 1983, pl. 51
	col. XXXVII		SHR		Yadin 1983, pl. 52

ITEM NO.	COMPOSITION	CONC	INV	PREV	PUBLICATION
	col. XXXVIII		SHR		Yadin 1983, pl. 53
	col. XXXIX		SHR		Yadin 1983, pl. 54
	col. XL		SHR		Yadin 1983, pl. 55
	col. XLI		SHR		Yadin 1983, pl. 56
	col. XLII		SHR		Yadin 1983, pl. 57
	col. XLIII		SHR		Yadin 1983, pl. 58
	col. XLIV		SHR		Yadin 1983, pl. 59
	col. XLV		SHR		Yadin 1983, pl. 60
	col. XLVI		SHR		Yadin 1983, pl. 61
	col. XLVII		SHR		Yadin 1983, pl. 62
	col. XLVIII		SHR		Yadin 1983, pl. 63
	col. XLIX		SHR		Yadin 1983, pl. 64
	col. L		SHR		Yadin 1983, pl. 65
	col. LI		SHR		Yadin 1983, pl. 66
	col. LII		SHR		Yadin 1983, pl. 67
	col. LIII		SHR		Yadin 1983, pl. 68
	col. LIV		SHR		Yadin 1983, pl. 69
	col. LV		SHR		Yadin 1983, pl. 70
	col. LVI		SHR		Yadin 1983, pl. 71
	col. LVII		SHR		Yadin 1983, pl. 72
	col. LVIII		SHR		Yadin 1983, pl. 73
	col. LIX		SHR		Yadin 1983, pl. 74
	col. LX		SHR		Yadin 1983, pl. 75
	col. LXI		SHR		Yadin 1983, pl. 76
	col. LXII		SHR		Yadin 1983, pl. 77
	col. LXIII		SHR		Yadin 1983, pl. 78
	col. LXIV		SHR		Yadin 1983, pl. 79
	col. LXV		SHR		Yadin 1983, pl. 80
	col. LXVI		SHR		Yadin 1983, pl. 81
	col. LXVII		SHR		Yadin 1983, pl. 82
11Q20	T^b frags. 1a, 1c, 1e, 2, 9, 10b, 11b, 15a–b, 20, 26, 28b		577		García Martínez et al. 1998, pls. XLI–XLIV, XLVI
	frag. 7		577		García Martínez et al. 1998, pl. XLII
	frags. 1b, 4a, 11a, 21, 22, 23a–c, 25, 30a		580		García Martínez et al. 1998, pls. XLI–XLIII, XLV, XLVII
	frag. 30b		580		
	frags. 8a–b, 10a, 10c, 10e–f		608, 1031		García Martínez et al. 1998, pls. XLII, XLIII
	frag. 10g		608		
	frags. 10d, 41		607		García Martínez et al. 1998, pls. XLIII, XLVII
	frag. 13		610		García Martínez et al. 1998, pl. XLIV
	frag. 17		566		García Martínez et al. 1998, pl. XLIV
	frags. 1d, 6b, 28a, 36, 37		614		García Martínez et al. 1998, pls. XLI, XLII, XLVI, XLVII
	frags. 3, 18, 29		567		García Martínez et al. 1998, pls. XLII, XLIV, XLVI
	frags. 4b, 42		1032		García Martínez et al. 1998, pls. XLII, XLVII
	frags. 5, 27, 33, 40		621B		García Martínez et al. 1998, pls. XLII, XLVII
	frags. 6a, 6c, 12, 15c, 16, 24, 38, 39		614B		García Martínez et al. 1998, pls. XLII–XLV, XLVII
	frag. 14		1020		
	frags. 19, 23d, 34, 35		613		García Martínez et al. 1998, pls. XLIV, XLV, XLVII
	frag. 31		606, 615		García Martínez et al. 1998, pl. XLVII

ITEM NO.	COMPOSITION	CONC	INV	PREV	PUBLICATION
	frag. 32		1016		García Martínez et al. 1998, pl. XLVII
11Q21	T[c]?				García Martínez et al. 1998, pl. XLVIII
	frag. 1		619		
	frag. 2		614		
	frag. 3		567		
11Q22	paleoUnidentified Text				García Martínez et al. 1998, pl. XLVIII
	frag. 1		?		
	frag. 2		?		
	frags. 3, 4		614		
	frag. 5		?		
	frag. 6		1020		
	frag. 7		1032		
11Q23	CryptA Unidentified Text		613		García Martínez et al. 1998, pl. XLVIII
11Q24	Unidentified Text ar		567		García Martínez et al. 1998, pl. XLIX
11Q25	Unidentified Text A				García Martínez et al. 1998, pl. XLIX
	frags. 1, 2		567		
	frag. 3		621B		
	frag. 4		614		
	frag. 5		1032		
	frags. 6–8		581A		
11Q26	Unidentifed Text B				García Martínez et al. 1998, pl. XLIX
	frag. 1		621B		
	frags. 2, 3		567		
11Q27	Unidentified Text C		614B		García Martínez et al. 1998, pl. XLIX
11Q28	papUnidentified Text D		988		García Martínez et al. 1998
11Q29	Frag. Related to Serekh ha-Yaḥad		615		García Martínez et al. 1998, pl. L
11Q30	Unclassified Fragments		567		García Martínez et al. 1998, pls. L–LI
			581A		
			615		
			621B		
			988		
			1016		
			1031		
			1032		
			1034		
11Q31	Unidentified wads		563		García Martínez et al. 1998, pl. LII
XQ1–4	Phyl. 1–4		SHR		Yadin 1969
XQ6	Offering ar		Private		Lemaire 2000, pl. XXXII
XQ7			SHR		Lange 2000b
Kh.Q	Ostracon 1				Cross and Eshel 2000, pl. XXXIII
Kh.Q	Ostracon 2				Cross and Eshel 2000, pl. XXXIV

2. Wadi Daliyeh

ITEM NO.	COMPOSITION	INV	PUBLICATION
WDSP 1	papDeed of Slave Sale A ar	554r	Gropp 2001
WDSP 2	papDeed of Slave Sale B ar	555	Gropp 2001
WDSP 3	papDeed of Slave Sale C ar	558	Gropp 2001
WDSP 4	papDeed of Slave Sale D ar	553	Gropp 2001
WDSP 5	papDeed of Slave Sale E ar	559	Gropp 2001
WDSP 6	papDeed of Slave Sale F ar	548	Gropp 2001
WDSP 7	papDeed of Slave Sale G ar	549r, 549v	Gropp 2001
WDSP 8	papDeed of Slave Sale H ar	755r ,755v	Gropp 2001
WDSP 9	papDeed of Slave Sale I ar (r + v)	552r, 552v	Gropp 2001
WDSP 10	papLoan with Pledge of Slave A? ar	551r 551v	Gropp 2001
WDSP 11	papDeed of Slave Sale J? ar (recto)	754r	Gropp 2001
WDSP 11a	papSettlement of Dispute? ar (verso)	754v	
WDSP 12	papLoan with Pledge of Slave B? ar	920	Gropp 2001
WDSP 13	papPledge of Slave C? ar (recto)	757r	Gropp 2001
WDSP 13a	papRelease of Pledged Slave? ar (verso)	757v	
WDSP 14	papDeed of Conveyance of Public Rooms ar	562	Gropp 2001
WDSP 15	papDeed of House Sale ar	560	Gropp 2001
WDSP 16	papDeed of Pledge of Vineyard? ar	561	Gropp 2001
WDSP 17	papReceipt of Payment in Relation to a Pledge ar	751	Gropp 2001
WDSP 18	papDeed of Slave Sale K ar	750	Gropp 2001
WDSP 19	papDeed of Slave Sale L ar	557	Gropp 2001
WDSP 20	papDeed of Slave Sale M ar	919C	Gropp 2001
WDSP 21	papDeed of Sale A ar	919B	Gropp 2001
WDSP 22	papDeed of Slave Sale N? ar	556	Gropp 2001
WDSP 23	papDeed of Settlement? ar (r + v)	752r, 752v	Gropp 2001
WDSP 24	papDeed of Sale B? ar	756	Gropp 2001
WDSP 25	papDeed of SaleC ? ar	756	Gropp 2001
WDSP 26	papDeed of Slave Sale O? ar	756	Gropp 2001
WDSP 27	papPledge of Slave D? ar	758	Gropp 2001
WDSP 28	papMiscellaneous Fragments A ar	759B	
WDSP 29	papMiscellaneous Fragments B ar (r + v)	544r, 544v	
WDSP 30	papMiscellaneous Fragments C ar	545	
WDSP 31	papMiscellaneous Fragments D ar	546	
WDSP I.3	papFrag. Nos 26–29 ar	547	Cross 1974, pl. 60; Gropp 2001
WDSP 32	papMiscellaneous Fragments E ar	550	
WD pap 33	papMiscellaneous Fragments F ar	557 (757?)	
WDSP 34	papMiscellaneous Fragments G ar	753	
WDSP 35	papMiscellaneous Fragments H ar (recto)	759r	Gropp 2001
WDSP 35a	papMiscellaneous Fragments I ar (verso)	759v	
WDSP 36	papMiscellaneous Fragments ar	919A	

3. Ketef Jericho

ITEM NO.	COMPOSITION	INV	PUBLICATION
Jer 1	papList of Loans ar		Eshel and Eshel 2000b
Jer 2	papDeed of Sale A ar		Eshel and Eshel 2000b
Jer 3	Deed of Sale B ar		Eshel and Eshel 2000b
Jer 4–5d	papUnidentified Text(s) gr		Cohen 2000
Jer 4	papDeed of Sale or Lease? gr	K28556	Cohen 2000
Jer 5a–d	pap gr		Cohen 2000
Jer 5e	papTransaction Concerning Seeds gr		Cohen 2000
Jer 6	papUnidentified Text		Eshel 2000b
Jer 7	papSale of Date Crop		Eshel and Misgav 2000

ITEM NO.	COMPOSITION	INV	PUBLICATION
Jer 8–30	papUnidentified Texts		Charlesworth et al. 2000
Jer 31	papDeed of Sale? gr		Cotton 2000b
Jer 32	papDeed of Sale? gr		Cotton 2000b
Jer 33	papTreasury Receipt gr		Cotton 2000b
Jer 34–34g	pap gr		Cohen 2000
Jer 34	papWritten Order? gr		Cohen 2000
Jer 34a	papUnidentified Text gr		Cohen 2000
Jer 34b	papList of Witnesses? gr		Cohen 2000
Jer c–g	papUnidentified Texts gr		Cohen 2000

4. Khirbet Mird

ITEM NO.	COMPOSITION	OLD PLATE	INV	PUBLICATION
APHM 1	papByzantine Protocols arab	A33a1	1201	Grohmann 1963
APHM 2	papByzantine Protocols arab	A1a1	1183	Grohmann 1963
APHM 3	papByzantine Protocols arab	A23a1	1179	Grohmann 1963
APHM 4	papByzantine Protocols arab	A23a2	1179	Grohmann 1963
APHM 5	papProtocols arab	A30b2	1218	Grohmann 1963
APHM 6	papProtocols arab	38r	1177r	Grohmann 1963
APHM 7	papProtocols arab	A30b1	1218	Grohmann 1963
APHM 8	papSignatures of Witnesses arab	A27.3	1258	Grohmann 1963
APHM 9	papConclusion of Contract of Sale arab	28.5r	1212	Grohmann 1963
APHM 10	papGalil-script Letter Frags. arab	36	1203	Grohmann 1963
APHM 11	papGalil-script Letter Frags. arab	37	1261	Grohmann 1963
APHM 12	papGalil-script Letter Frags. arab	4A	1174	Grohmann 1963
APHM 13	papGalil-script Letter Frags. arab	4B	1192	Grohmann 1963
APHM 14	papGalil-script Letter Frags. arab	4C	1192	Grohmann 1963
APHM 15	papGalil-script Letter Frags. arab	4D	1192	Grohmann 1963
APHM 16	papGalil-script Letter Frags. arab	A32a1	1260	Grohmann 1963
APHM 17	papGalil-script Letter Frags. arab	A11a1	1187	Grohmann 1963
APHM 18	papReply Re: An Act of Violence arab	35	1249	Grohmann 1963
APHM 19	papOrder for Investigation of Robbery arab	12.1v	1209	Grohmann 1963
APHM 20	papFrag. of Official Letter arab	26.1r	1222	Grohmann 1963
APHM 21	papFrag. of Official Letter arab	2.2	1196	Grohmann 1963
APHM 22	papConclusion of Official Letter? arab	A4	1257	Grohmann 1963
APHM 23	papLetter to the Governor arab	11	1259	Grohmann 1963
APHM 24	papFrag. of Report of an Official arab	17.4	1245	Grohmann 1963
APHM 25	papFrag. of Official Letter arab	29	1212	Grohmann 1963
APHM 26	papFrag. of Official Letter arab	28.4r	1212	Grohmann 1963
APHM 27	papFrag. of Official Letter arab	28.4v	1246	Grohmann 1963
APHM 28	papFrag. of Official Letter arab	A31a1	1212	Grohmann 1963
APHM 29	papFrag. of Official Letter arab	28.3v	1209	Grohmann 1963
APHM 30	papFrag. of Official Letter arab	28.3r	1252	Grohmann 1963
APHM 31	papFrag. of Official Letter arab	10.1	1213	Grohmann 1963
APHM 32	papFrag. of Official Letter arab	4.1r	1240	Grohmann 1963
APHM 33	papAdministrative List arab	A34a2	1240	Grohmann 1963
	papAdministrative List arab	A35.1,4		Grohmann 1963
APHM 34	papAdministrative List arab	18.6	1216	Grohmann 1963
APHM 35	papEconomic Text arab	26a3v	1209	Grohmann 1963
APHM 36	papEconomic Text arab	A14a1	1188r	Grohmann 1963
APHM 37	papEconomic Text arab	A14b1	1188v	Grohmann 1963
APHM 38	papEconomic Text arab	28.1	1212	Grohmann 1963
APHM 39	papEconomic Text arab	A22a	1185r	Grohmann 1963
APHM 40	papEconomic Text arab	A22b3	1185v	Grohmann 1963

ITEM NO.	COMPOSITION	OLD PLATE	INV	PUBLICATION
APHM 41	papEconomic Text arab	A27a1	1258	Grohmann 1963
APHM 42	Private Letter arab	32	1176	Grohmann 1963
APHM 43r	Private Letter arab	A34a1	1251	Grohmann 1963
APHM 43v	Private Letter arab	A34b1	1251	Grohmann 1963
APHM 44	Private Letter arab	38v	1177v	Grohmann 1963
APHM 45	Private Letter arab	13a1	1244	Grohmann 1963
APHM 46	Private Letter arab	13.1	1244	Grohmann 1963
APHM 47	Private Letter arab	5.2	1194	Grohmann 1963
APHM 48r	Private Letter arab	A34a4r	1251	Grohmann 1963
APHM 48v	Private Letter arab	A34a4v	1251	Grohmann 1963
APHM 49	Private Letter arab	40	1254	Grohmann 1963
APHM 50	Private Letter arab	6	1250	Grohmann 1963
APHM 51	Private Letter arab	33	1248	Grohmann 1963
APHM 52	Private Letter arab	34	1248	Grohmann 1963
APHM 53	Private Letter arab	18.3	1216	Grohmann 1963
APHM 54	Private Letter arab	3	1172	Grohmann 1963
APHM 55	Private Letter arab	22Bgr	Louvain	Grohmann 1963
APHM 56	Private Letter arab	15.1r	1206	Grohmann 1963
APHM 57	Private Letter arab	15.2		Grohmann 1963
APHM 58	Private Letter arab	15.3r	1206	Grohmann 1963
APHM 59	Private Letter arab	15.1v	1206	Grohmann 1963
APHM 60	Private Letter arab	14.2r	1217	Grohmann 1963
APHM 61	Private Letter arab	14.2v	1217	Grohmann 1963
APHM 62	Private Letter arab	14a3v	1217	Grohmann 1963
APHM 63	Private Letter arab	A3a2v	1181	Grohmann 1963
APHM 64	Private Letter arab	14.5		Grohmann 1963
APHM 65	Private Letter arab	14a5		Grohmann 1963
APHM 66r	Private Letter arab	18.4	1216	Grohmann 1963
APHM 66v	Private Letter arab	18a4	1216	Grohmann 1963
APHM 67	Private Letter arab	18.1r	1216	Grohmann 1963
APHM 68	Private Letter arab	26.24	1209	Grohmann 1963
APHM 69	Private Letter arab	5.1r	1194	Grohmann 1963
APHM 70	Private Letter arab	7.2	1213	Grohmann 1963
APHM 71	Literary Text arab	28.11r	1212	Grohmann 1963
APHM 72	Literary Text arab	37	1261	Grohmann 1963
APHM 73	Literary Text arab	A19.1	1230	Grohmann 1963
APHM 74	Frags. of Protocol Texts	A17a1	1219	Grohmann 1963
APHM 75	Frags. of Protocol Texts	A23a3	1179	Grohmann 1963
APHM 76	Frags. of Protocol Texts	A17a4	1219	Grohmann 1963
APHM 77	Frags. of Protocol Texts	A17a3	1219	Grohmann 1963
APHM 78	Frags. of Protocol Texts	A30.3	1218	Grohmann 1963
APHM 79	Frag. of Official Letter	A33.2	1201	Grohmann 1963
APHM 80	Frag. of List	A10a1	1226	Grohmann 1963
APHM 81r	Frag. of List	A34.3	1251	Grohmann 1963
APHM 81v	Frag. of List		1251	Grohmann 1963
APHM 82	Frag. of Economic Text	30.3	1207	Grohmann 1963
APHM 83	Frag. of Economic Text	17.2	1259	Grohmann 1963
APHM 84	Frag. of Private Letter	41	1247	Grohmann 1963
APHM 85	Frag. of Private Letter	A13a	1180r	Grohmann 1963
APHM 86	Frag. of Private Letter	A13b	1180v	Grohmann 1963
APHM 87	Frag. of Private Letter	A15a1	1229	Grohmann 1963
APHM 88	Frag. of Private Letter	A35.34	1253	Grohmann 1963
APHM 89	Frag. of Private Letter	A19a5	1230	Grohmann 1963
APHM 90	Frag. of Private Letter	12.2	1249	Grohmann 1963
APHM 91	Frag. of Private Letter	2.5	1222	Grohmann 1963
APHM 92	Frag. of Private Letter	30.1r	1207	Grohmann 1963

ITEM NO.	COMPOSITION	OLD PLATE	INV	PUBLICATION
APHM 93	Frag. of Private Letter	18.2v	1216	Grohmann 1963
APHM 94	Frag. of Private Letter	13B1gr	Louvain	Grohmann 1963
APHM 95	Frag. of Private Letter	12.5	1249	Grohmann 1963
APHM 96	Frag. of Private Letter	A27.2	1258	Grohmann 1963
APHM 97	Frag. of Private Letter	3.1r	1181	Grohmann 1963
APHM 98	Frag. of Private Letter	28.7	1212	Grohmann 1963
APHM 99	Frag. of Private Letter	13B2gr	Louvain	Grohmann 1963
APHM 100	Frag. of Drawing	A23a4	1179	Grohmann 1963
	Aland p83 (Matt 20:23–25)	16gr	Louvain	
	Aland p83 (Matt 20:30–31?)	16Bgr	Louvain	
	Aland p83	29gr	Louvain	
	Aland p83	29Bgr	Louvain	
	Aland p84 (Matt 2:3–5; John 17:3)	26gr	Louvain	
	Aland p84 (Matt 2:8–9; John 17:7–8)	26Bgr	Louvain	
	Aland p84 (Matt 6:30–31, 33–34)	27gr	Louvain	
	Aland p84 (Matt 6:36–37, 39–41)	27Bgr	Louvain	
	Aland p84	4gr	Louvain	
	Aland p84	4Bgr	Louvain	
	Aland p84	11gr	Louvain	
	Aland p84	11Bgr	Louvain	
	Uncial 0244 (Acts 11:29–12:1)	8gr	Louvain	
	Uncial 0244 (Acts 12:2–5)	8Bgr	Louvain	
	Josh 22:6–7, 9–10 cpa		1238	
	Matt 21:30–34 cpa		1238	
	Luke 3:1, 3–4		1238	
Mird Acts cpa	Acts cpa		657	Perrot 1963, pl. XIX
			657	Perrot 1963, pl. XIX
			657	Perrot 1963, pl. XVIII
	Col 1:16–18, 20b–21 cpa		1238	Perrot 1963, pl. XIX
papMird A	papLetter from Monk Gabriel to Abbot		656	Milik 1953, pl. XIX
MirdAmul cpa			Louvain	Baillet 1963, 375–401
	Plaster with Syriac Inscription	S2	1234	
	papFrag.	S3	1227	
	Alphabet gr	G1a	Louvain	van Haelst 1991, 306–15, pl. III
	Tropologion gr	G1b	Louvain	van Haelst 1991, 306–15, pl. III
	Tropologion gr	G2a	Louvain	van Haelst 1991, 306–15, pl. IV
	Tropologion gr	G2b	Louvain	van Haelst 1991, 306–15, pl. V
	Alphabet (joined with G4b) gr	G3a	Louvain	van Haelst 1991, 316, pl. VII
	Greek papyri	G3b	Louvain	
	Greek papyri	G4a	Louvain	
	Alphabet (joined with G3a) gr	G4b	Louvain	van Haelst 1991, 316, pl. VII
	Greek papyri	G5a	Louvain	
	Greek papyri	G5b	Louvain	
	Greek papyri	G6a	Louvain	
	Greek papyri	G6b	Louvain	
	Greek papyri	G7a	Louvain	
	Greek papyri	G7b	Louvain	
	Greek papyri	G8a	Louvain	
	Ecclesiastical Letter gr	G8b	Louvain	van Haelst 1991, 305–6, pl. II
	Greek papyri	G9a	Louvain	
	Greek papyri	G9b	Louvain	
	Greek papyri	G10a	Louvain	
	Greek papyri	G10b	Louvain	
	Greek papyri	G11a	Louvain	
	Greek papyri	G11b	Louvain	

ITEM NO.	COMPOSITION	OLD PLATE	INV	PUBLICATION
	Greek papyri	G12	Louvain	
	Greek papyri	G13	Louvain	
	Greek papyri	G14a	Louvain	
	Greek papyri	G14b	Louvain	
	Greek papyri	G15a	Louvain	
	Greek papyri	G15b	Louvain	
	Greek papyri	G16a	Louvain	
	Greek papyri	G16b	Louvain	
	Greek papyri	G17a	Louvain	
	Greek papyri	G17b	Louvain	
	Greek papyri	G18	Louvain	
	Greek papyri	G19	Louvain	
	Greek papyri	G20a	Louvain	
	Greek papyri	G20b	Louvain	
	Greek papyri	G21a	Louvain	
	Greek papyri	G21b	Louvain	
	Monastic Letter gr	G22a	Louvain	van Haelst 1991, 302–5, pl. I
	Doxastica gr	G22b	Louvain	van Haelst 1991, 315–16, pl. VI
	Greek papyri	G23a	Louvain	
	Greek papyri	G23b	Louvain	
	Greek papyri	G24a	Louvain	
	Greek papyri	G24b	Louvain	
	Greek papyri	G25a	Louvain	
	Greek papyri	G25b	Louvain	
	Greek papyri	G26a	Louvain	
	Greek papyri	G26b	Louvain	
	Greek papyri	G27a	Louvain	
	Greek papyri	G27b	Louvain	
	Greek papyri	G28a	Louvain	
	Greek papyri	G28b	Louvain	
	Greek papyri	G31a	Louvain	
	Greek papyri	G31b	Louvain	

5. Wadi Nar

ITEM NO.	COMPOSITION	INV	PUBLICATION
Nar 1	papFrag. gr	1015	
Nar 2	papFrags. sem	1018	
Nar 3	Frag. gr	1023	
Nar 4	papUnclass. frags.	1054	
Nar 5	Leather and linen frags.	1055	

6. Wadi Ghweir

ITEM NO.	COMPOSITION	INV	PUBLICATION
Ghweir? 1	papCursive frag. gr	1019	
Ghweir? 2	paperFrag. sem	1019	

7. Wadi Murabbaʿat

ITEM NO.	COMPOSITION	INV	PUBLICATION
Mur 1 frags. 1–3	Gen	806	Milik 1961, pl. XIX

ITEM NO.	COMPOSITION	INV	PUBLICATION
Mur 1 frags. 4–5	Exod	824	Milik 1961, pl. XX
Mur 1 frags. 6–7	Num	832	Milik 1961, pl. XXI
Mur 2	Deut	832	Milik 1961, pl. XXI
Mur 3	Isa	833	Milik 1961, pl. XXII
Mur 4	Phyl	650	Milik 1961, pls. XXII–XXIV
Mur 5	Mez	792	Milik 1961, pl. XXIV
Mur 6	Unidentified Literary Text	792	Milik 1961, pl. XXV
Mur 7	Contract?	793	Milik 1961, pl. XXV
Mur 8	Account of Cereals and Vegetables ar	793	Milik 1961, pl. XXV
Mur 9	Account	830	Milik 1961, pl. XXVI
Mur 10A	Account (palimpsest)	830	Milik 1961, pl. XXVI
Mur 10B	Abecedary (palimpsest)	830	Milik 1961, pl. XXVI
Mur 11	Abecedary	830	Milik 1961, pl. XXVII
Mur 12	Unclassified frag.	874	Milik 1961, pl. XXVII
Mur 13	Unclassified frag.	874	Milik 1961, pl. XXVII
Mur 14	Unclassified frag.	874	Milik 1961, pl. XXVII
Mur 15	Unclassified frag.	874	Milik 1961, pl. XXVII
Mur 16	Unclassified frag.	874 r + v	Milik 1961, pl. XXVII
Mur 17A	papLetter (palimpsest)	835	Milik 1961, pl. XXVIII
Mur 17B	papList of Personal Names (palimpsest)	835	Milik 1961, pl. XXVIII
Mur 18	papAcknowledgement of Debt ar	834 r + v	Milik 1961, pl. XXIX
Mur 19	papWrit of Divorce ar	879 r + v	Milik 1961, pls. XXX–XXXI
Mur 20	papMarriage Contract ar	879 r + v	Milik 1961, pls. XXX–XXXI
Mur 21	papMarriage Contract ar	875 r + v	Milik 1961, pls. XXXII–XXXIII
Mur 22	papDeed of Sale of Land	882 r + v	Milik 1961, pls. XXXIII–XXXIV
Mur 23	papDeed of Sale? ar	840 r + v	Milik 1961, pl. XXXIV
Mur 24	papFarming Contracts	825, 828	Milik 1961, pls. XXXV–XXXVII
Mur 25	papDeed of Sale of Land ar	r + v	Milik 1961, pl. XXXVIII
Mur 26	papDeed of Sale ar	725	Milik 1961, pls. XXXIX–XL bis
Mur 27	papDeed of Sale ar	797	Milik 1961, pls. XXXIX–XL bis
Mur 28	papDeed of Sale ar	884 r + v	Milik 1961, pls. XXXIX–XL bis
Mur 29	papDeed of Sale	836 r + v	Milik 1961, pls. XLI–XLI bis
Mur 30	papDeed of Sale of Plot	791 r + v	Milik 1961, pls. XLI bis–XLII bis
Mur 31	papFrags. of Deeds of Sale	790 r + v	Milik 1961, pl. XLII bis
Mur 32	papDeed Concerning Money ar	883	Milik 1961, pl. XLIII
Mur 33	papDeed Concerning Money ar	878	Milik 1961, pl. XLIII
Mur 34	papContract ar	798	Milik 1961, pl. XLIII
Mur 35	papContract ar	798	Milik 1961, pl. XLIII
Mur 36	papContract	837	Milik 1961, pl. XLIII
Mur 37	papContracts and Signatures	878	Milik 1961, pls. XLIII–XLIV
Mur 38	papContracts and Signatures	837	Milik 1961, pls. XLIII–XLIV
Mur 39	papContracts and Signatures	837	Milik 1961, pls. XLIII–XLIV
Mur 40	papContracts and Signatures	794	Milik 1961, pls. XLIII–XLIV
Mur 41	papList of Personal Names	837	Milik 1961, pl. XLIV
Mur 42	papLetter from Beit-Mashiko to Yeshua b. Galgula	639	Milik 1961, pl. XLV
Mur 43	papLetter from Shimʿon b. Kosba to Yeshua b. Galgula	640	Milik 1961, pl. XLVI
Mur 44	papLetter from Shimʿon b. Kosba to Yeshua b. Galgula	720	Milik 1961, pl. XLVI
Mur 45	papLetter	829	Milik 1961, pl. XLVII
Mur 46	papLetter Sent from Ein Gedi	829	Milik 1961, pl. XLVII
Mur 47	papLetter	873	Milik 1961, pl. XLVIII
Mur 48	papLetter	837	Milik 1961, pl. XLVIII
Mur 49	papLetter	873	Milik 1961, pl. XLVIII

ITEM NO.	COMPOSITION	INV	PUBLICATION
Mur 50	papLetter?	837	Milik 1961, pl. XLVIII
Mur 51	papLetter?	873	Milik 1961, pl. XLVIII
Mur 52	papLetter?	831	Milik 1961, pl. XLVIII
Mur 53	papUndeciphered Text	826	Milik 1961, pls. XLIX–LI
Mur 54	papUndeciphered Text	880	Milik 1961, pls. XLIX–LI
Mur 55	papUnclassified frags.	826	Milik 1961, pls. XLIX–LI
Mur 56	papUnclassified frags.	794	Milik 1961, pls. XLIX–LI
Mur 57	papUnclassified frags.	826	Milik 1961, pls. XLIX–LI
Mur 58	papUnclassified frags.	826	Milik 1961, pls. XLIX–LI
Mur 59	papUnclassified frags.	826	Milik 1961, pls. XLIX–LI
Mur 60	papUnclassified frags.	826	Milik 1961, pls. XLIX–LI
Mur 61	papUnclassified frags.	826	Milik 1961, pls. XLIX–LI
Mur 62	papUnclassified frag.	798	Milik 1961, pls. XLIX–LI
Mur 63	papUnclassified frag.	798	Milik 1961, pls. XLIX–LI
Mur 64	papUnclassified frag.	798	Milik 1961, pls. XLIX–LI
Mur 65	papUnclassified frag.	798	Milik 1961, pls. XLIX–LI
Mur 66	papUnclassified frag.	798	Milik 1961, pls. XLIX–LI
Mur 67	papUnclassified frag.	798	Milik 1961, pls. XLIX–LI
Mur 68	papUnclassified frag.	798	Milik 1961, pls. XLIX–LI
Mur 69	papUnclassified frag.	798	Milik 1961, pls. XLIX–LI
Mur 70	papUnclassified frag.	794	Milik 1961, pls. XLIX–LI
Mur 71	papFrag. nab	881	Milik 1961, pl. LI
Mur 72	ostr ar	1066	Milik 1961, pl. LII
Mur 73	ostrAbecedary and List of Personal Names	1033	Milik 1961, pl. LII
Mur 74	ostrList of Personal Names	1049	Milik 1961, pl. LIII
Mur 75	ostrPersonal Name	1037	Milik 1961, pls. LIII–LIV
Mur 76	ostrPersonal Name	1052	Milik 1961, pls. LIII–LIV
Mur 77	ostrPersonal Name	1052	Milik 1961, pls. LIII–LIV
Mur 78	ostrAbecedary	1014	Milik 1961, pls. LIV–LV
Mur 79	ostrAbecedary	1049	Milik 1961, pls. LIV–LV
Mur 80	ostrAbecedary	1036	Milik 1961, pls. LIV–LV
Mur 81	ostrUnclassified	1050	Milik 1961, pl. LV
Mur 82	ostrUnclassified	1037	Milik 1961, pl. LV
Mur 83	ostrUnclassified	1037	Milik 1961, pl. LV
Mur 84	ostrUnclassified	1037	Milik 1961, pl. LV
Mur 85	ostrUnclassified	1028, 1037	Milik 1961, pl. LV
Mur 86	ostrUnclassified	1028	Milik 1961, pl. LV
Mur 87	ostrPersonal Name	1035	Milik 1961, pl. LV
Mur 88	XII (unopened scroll)		
	col. I (Joel 2:20)	?	Milik 1961, pl. LVI
	col. II (Joel 2:26–4:16)	?	Milik 1961, pl. LVI
	col. III (Amos 1:5–2:1)	?	Milik 1961, pl. LVI
	col. VI (Amos)	64	Milik 1961, pl. LVII
	col. VII (Amos 7:3–8:7)	64	Milik 1961, pl. LVII
	col. VIII (Amos 8:11–9:15)	64	Milik 1961, pl. LVIII
	col. IX (Obad 1–21)	64	Milik 1961, pl. LIX
	col. X (Jonah 1:1–3:2)	64, 213	Milik 1961, pl. LX
	col. XI (Jonah 3:2–Mic 1:5)	65, 213	Milik 1961, pl. LXI
	col. XII (Mic 1:5–3:4)	65	Milik 1961, pl. LXII
	col. XIII (Mic 3:4–4:12)	65	Milik 1961, pl. LXIII
	col. XIV (Mic 4:12–6:7)	65	Milik 1961, pl. LXIV
	col. XV (Mic 6:11–7:17)	65	Milik 1961, pl. LXV
	col. XVI (Mic 7:17–Nah 2:12)	65, 66	Milik 1961, pl. LXVI
	col. XVII (Nah 2:13–3:19)	66	Milik 1961, pl. LXVII
	col. XVIII (Hab 1:3–2:11)	66	Milik 1961, pl. LXVIII
	col. XIX (Hab 2:18–Zeph 1:1)	66	Milik 1961, pl. LXIX

ITEM NO.	COMPOSITION	INV	PUBLICATION
	col. XX (Zeph 1:11–3:6)	66, 67	Milik 1961, pl. LXX
	col. XXI (Zeph 3:8–Hag 1:11)	67	Milik 1961, pl. LXXI
	col. XXII (Hag 1:12–2:10)	67	Milik 1961, pl. LXXII
	col. XXIII (Hag 2:12–Zech 1:4)	67	Milik 1961, pl. LXXII
	Unidentified frags.	540	Milik 1961, pl. LXXIII
Mur 89	Account of Money gr	728	Benoit 1961, pl. LXXIV
Mur 90	Account of Cereals and Vegetables gr	728	Benoit 1961, pl. LXXV
Mur 91	Account of Cereals and Vegetables gr	841	Benoit 1961, pl. LXXVI
Mur 92	Account of Cereal gr	841	Benoit 1961, pl. LXXVI
Mur 93	Account? gr	841	Benoit 1961, pl. LXXVI
Mur 94	Resume of Accounts gr	843	Benoit 1961, pl. LXXVII
Mur 95	List of Personal Names gr	723	Benoit 1961, pl. LXXVIII
Mur 96	Account of Cereals gr	723	Benoit 1961, pl. LXXVIII
Mur 97	Account of Cereals gr	723	Benoit 1961, pl. LXXVIII
Mur 98	Accounts? gr	911	Benoit 1961, pl. LXXIX
Mur 99	Accounts? gr	911	Benoit 1961, pl. LXXIX
Mur 100	Accounts? gr	911	Benoit 1961, pl. LXXIX
Mur 101	Accounts? gr	911	Benoit 1961, pl. LXXIX
Mur 102	Accounts? gr	911	Benoit 1961, pl. LXXIX
Mur 103	List of Personal Names gr	727	Benoit 1961, pl. LXXX
Mur 104	Corners and Edges of Leather gr	727	Benoit 1961, pl. LXXX
Mur 105	Corners and Edges of Leather gr	727	Benoit 1961, pl. LXXX
Mur 106	Corners and Edges of Leather gr	727	Benoit 1961, pl. LXXX
Mur 107	Corners and Edges of Leather gr	727	Benoit 1961, pl. LXXX
Mur 108	papPhilosophical Text gr	713	Benoit 1961, pl. LXXXI
Mur 109	papLiterary Text gr	712 r	Benoit 1961, pls. LXXXII–LXXXIII
Mur 110	papLiterary Text gr	712 v	Benoit 1961, pls. LXXXII–LXXXIII
Mur 111	papLiterary Text gr	712 r + v	Benoit 1961, pls. LXXXII–LXXXIII
Mur 112	papLiterary Text gr	910 r	Benoit 1961, pls. LXXXII–LXXXIII
Mur 113	papProceedings of Lawsuit gr	910 v	Benoit 1961, pl. LXXXIV
Mur 114	papRecognition of Debt gr	641 r + v	Benoit 1961, pl. LXXXV
Mur 115	papRemarriage Contract gr	716 r + v	Benoit 1961, pls. LXXXVI–LXXXVIII
Mur 116	papMarriage Contract gr	715 r	Benoit 1961, pl. LXXXIX
Mur 117	papExtracts from Official Ordinances gr	839 r + v	Benoit 1961, pl. XC
Mur 118	papAccount gr	712 r + v	Benoit 1961, pls. XCI–XCIV
Mur 119	papAccount gr	712 r + v	Benoit 1961, pls. XCI–XCIV
Mur 120	papAccount gr	845	Benoit 1961, pls. XCI–XCIV
Mur 121	papAccount gr	722	Benoit 1961, pls. XCI–XCIV
Mur 122	papAccount gr	722	Benoit 1961, pls. XCI–XCIV
Mur 123	papAccount gr	722	Benoit 1961, pls. XCI–XCIV
Mur 124	papAccount gr	724	Benoit 1961, pls. XCI–XCIV
Mur 125	papAccount gr	719	Benoit 1961, pls. XCI–XCIV
Mur 126	papLiterary or Notarial Writing gr	717	Benoit 1961, pl. XCV
Mur 127	papLiterary or Notarial Writing gr	722	Benoit 1961, pl. XCV
Mur 128	papLiterary or Notarial Writing gr	724	Benoit 1961, pl. XCV
Mur 129	papLiterary or Notarial Writing gr	722	Benoit 1961, pl. XCV
Mur 130	papLiterary or Notarial Writing gr	712 r + v	Benoit 1961, pl. XCV
Mur 131	papLiterary or Notarial Writing gr	712 r + v	Benoit 1961, pl. XCV
Mur 132	papLiterary or Notarial Writing gr	717	Benoit 1961, pl. XCV
Mur 133	papCursive Text gr	909	Benoit 1961, pls. XCVI–XCVIII
Mur 134	papCursive Text gr	909	Benoit 1961, pls. XCVI–XCVIII
Mur 135	papCursive Text gr	909	Benoit 1961, pls. XCVI–XCVIII
Mur 136	papCursive Text gr	909	Benoit 1961, pls. XCVI–XCVIII
Mur 137	papCursive Text gr	909	Benoit 1961, pls. XCVI–XCVIII
Mur 138	papCursive Text gr	909	Benoit 1961, pls. XCVI–XCVIII
Mur 139	papCursive Text gr	909	Benoit 1961, pls. XCVI–XCVIII

ITEM NO.	COMPOSITION	INV	PUBLICATION
Mur 140	papCursive Text gr	909	Benoit 1961, pls. XCVI–XCVIII
Mur 141	papCursive Text gr	909	Benoit 1961, pls. XCVI–XCVIII
Mur 142	papCursive Text gr	909	Benoit 1961, pls. XCVI–XCVIII
Mur 143	papCursive Text gr	909 r + v	Benoit 1961, pls. XCVI–XCVIII
Mur 144	papCursive Text gr	909	Benoit 1961, pls. XCVI–XCVIII
Mur 145	papCursive Text gr	717	Benoit 1961, pls. XCVI–XCVIII
Mur 146	papCursive Text gr	712 r + v	Benoit 1961, pls. XCVI–XCVIII
Mur 147	papCursive Text gr	719	Benoit 1961, pls. XCVI–XCVIII
Mur 148	papCursive Text gr	717	Benoit 1961, pls. XCVI–XCVIII
Mur 149	papCursive Text gr	717	Benoit 1961, pls. XCVI–XCVIII
Mur 150	papCursive Text gr	724	Benoit 1961, pls. XCVI–XCVIII
Mur 151	papCursive Text gr	722	Benoit 1961, pls. XCVI–XCVIII
Mur 152	papCursive Text gr	724	Benoit 1961, pls. XCVI–XCVIII
Mur 153	papCursive Text gr	724	Benoit 1961, pls. XCVI–XCVIII
Mur 154	papCursive Text gr	722	Benoit 1961, pls. XCVI–XCVIII
Mur 155	papDocument gr	913	Benoit 1961, pl. XCIX
Mur 156	Christian Liturgical Text gr	718 r + v	Benoit 1961, pl. C
Mur 157	Magical Text gr	721	Benoit 1961, pl. C
Mur 158	Unclassified frags. lat	844	Benoit 1961, pl. CI
Mur 159	Cursive Text lat	838	Benoit 1961, pl. CI
Mur 160	Unclassified frags. lat	838	Benoit 1961, pl. CII
Mur 161	Unclassified frags. lat	838	Benoit 1961, pl. CII
Mur 162	Unclassified frags. lat	838	Benoit 1961, pl. CII
Mur 163	Unclassified frags. lat	838	Benoit 1961, pl. CII
Mur 164	Document in Shorthand gr	802	Benoit 1961, pls. CIII–CV
Mur 164a	Document in Shorthand gr	802	
Mur 164b	Document in Shorthand gr	802	
Mur 165	ostr gr	1051	Benoit 1961, pl. CV
Mur 166	ostr gr	1051	Benoit 1961, pl. CV
Mur 167	ostr gr	1051	Benoit 1961, pl. CV
Mur 168	ostr lat	1051	Benoit 1961, pl. CV
Mur 169	Receipt arab	721	Grohmann 1961, pl. CVI
Mur 170	Sales Contract arab	730	Grohmann 1961, pl. CVI
Mur 171	Magical Text arab	721 r + v	Grohmann 1961, pl. CVI
Mur 172	Religious or Magical Text arab	721	Grohmann 1961, pl. CVI
Mur 173	Amulet arab	642 r + v	Grohmann 1961, pl. CVII
Mur?	Gen (Gen 33:18–34:3)		Puech 1979–1981, 163–66

8. Wadi Sdeir

ITEM NO.	COMPOSITION	INV	PUBLICATION
Sdeir 1	Gen	984	Murphy 2000
Sdeir 2	papPromissory Note? ar	985 r + v	Yardeni 2000b
Sdeir 3	Unidentified Text A gr	986 r + v	Charlesworth et al. 2000
Sdeir 4	Unidentified Text B gr	983 r + v	Charlesworth et al. 2000

9. Naḥal Ḥever

ITEM NO.	COMPOSITION	INV	PUBLICATION
5/6Ḥev 1a	Num[a] (*olim* 5/6Ḥev 41)	534	Flint 2000b
5/6Ḥev 1b	Ps (*olim* 5/6 Ḥev 40) (+ XḤev/Se 4)	888	Flint 2000b
		890	
		891	
5/6Ḥev 1	papDowry Settlement? nab [P.Yadin 1] (BA bdl. 15)	r	Yadin et al. 2002
		v	

ITEM NO.	COMPOSITION	INV	PUBLICATION
5/6Ḥev 2	papSale of Property nab [P.Yadin 2] (BA bdl. 16)	216* r	Yadin et al. 2002
		v	
5/6Ḥev 3	papSale of Property nab [P.Yadin 3] (BA bdl. 14a)	r	Yadin et al. 2002
		v	
5/6Ḥev 4	papFragmentary Deed nab [P.Yadin 4] (BA bdl. 14b)	r	Yadin et al. 2002
		v	
5/6Ḥev 5	papDeposit gr [P.Yadin 5] (BA bdl. 11c1, 11c2)	104*	Lewis 1989, pl. 1
5/6Ḥev 6	papLease of Land? nab [P.Yadin 6] (BA bdl. 11b)	142*	Lewis 1989, pl. 2
5/6Ḥev 7	papDeed of Gift ar [P.Yadin 7] (BA bdl. 6)	207* r	Yadin et al. 1996, 383–403
		v	
5/6Ḥev 8	papSale of Donkeys ar [P.Yadin 8] (BA bdl. 11a1)	144*	Yadin et al. 2002
5/6Ḥev 9	papQuittance nab [P.Yadin 9] (BA bdl. 11a2)	145*	Yadin et al. 2002
5/6Ḥev 10	papMarriage Contract ar [P.Yadin 10] (BA bdl. 7c)	205* r	Yadin et al. 1994, 75–101
		v	
5/6Ḥev 11	papLoan on Hypothec gr [P.Yadin 11] (BA bdl. 13)	134* r	Lewis 1989, pl. 3
		v	Lewis 1989, pl. 4
5/6Ḥev 12	papExtract from Council Minutes gr [P.Yadin 12] (BA bdl. 5f)	137* r	Lewis 1989, pl. 5
		v	Lewis 1989, pl. 6
5/6Ḥev 13	papPetition to Governor gr [P.Yadin13] (BA bdl. 11d)	139*	Lewis 1989, pl. 7
5/6Ḥev 14	papSummons gr [P.Yadin 14] (BA bdl. 10c)	141* r	Lewis 1989, pl. 8
		v	Lewis 1989, pl. 9
5/6Ḥev 15	papDeposition gr [P.Yadin 15] (BA bdl. 2)	215* r	Lewis 1989, pls. 10, 11
		v	Yadin and Greenfield 1989, pl. 12
5/6Ḥev 16	papRegistration of Land gr [P.Yadin 16] (BA bdl. 7b)	123* r	Lewis 1989, pl. 13
		v	Yadin and Greenfield 1989, pl. 14
5/6Ḥev 17	papDeposit gr [P.Yadin 17] (BA bdl. 7a)	140* r	Lewis 1989, pl. 15
		v	Yadin and Greenfield 1989, pl. 16
5/6Ḥev 18	papMarriage Contract gr [P.Yadin 18] (BA bdl. 1)	r	Lewis 1989, pls. 17, 18
		v	Yadin and Greenfield 1989, pl. 19
5/6Ḥev 19	papDeed of Gift gr [P.Yadin 19] (BA bdl. 8b)	108* r	Lewis 1989, pl. 20
		v	Yadin and Greenfield 1989, pl. 21
5/6Ḥev 20	papConcession of Rights gr [P.Yadin 20] (BA bdl. 8a)	r	Lewis 1989, pls. 22, 23
		v	Yadin and Greenfield 1989, pl. 24
5/6Ḥev 21	papPurchase of a Date Crop gr [P.Yadin 21] (BA bdl. 3)	105* r	Lewis 1989, pl. 25
		v	Lewis 1989, pl. 26
5/6Ḥev 22	papSale of a Date Crop gr [P.Yadin 22] (BA bdl. 10d)	r	Lewis 1989, pl. 27
		v	Lewis 1989, pl. 28
5/6Ḥev 23	papSummons gr [P.Yadin 23] (BA bdl. 10a)	110* r	Lewis 1989, pls. 29, 30
		v	Lewis 1989, pl. 31
5/6Ḥev 24	papDeposition gr [P.Yadin 24] (BA bdl. 10e)	116*	
5/6Ḥev 25	papSummons, Countersum. gr [P.Yad. 25] (BA bdl. 10b)	206*	Lewis 1989, pls. 32, 33
5/6Ḥev 26	papSummons and Reply gr [P.Yadin 26] (BA bdl. 9)	124* r	Lewis 1989, pl. 34
		v	Lewis 1989, pl. 35
5/6Ḥev 27	papReceipt gr [P.Yadin 27] (BA bdl. 4)		Lewis 1989, pl. 36
5/6Ḥev 28	papJudiciary Rule gr [P.Yadin 28] (BA bdl. 5a)	121*	Lewis 1989, pl. 37
5/6Ḥev 29	papJudiciary Rule gr [P.Yadin 29] (BA bdl. 5a bis)	122*	Lewis 1989, pl. 38
5/6Ḥev 30	papJudiciary Rule gr [P.Yadin 30]	120*	
5/6Ḥev 31	papContract? gr [P.Yadin 31] (BA bdl. 14c)	136*	
5/6Ḥev 32	papContract? gr [P.Yadin 32] (BA bdl. 18)		
5/6Ḥev 32a	papContract? gr [P.Yadin 32a] (BA bdl. 17)		
5/6Ḥev 33	Petition gr [P.Yadin 33] (BA bdl. 5b)	118* r	Lewis 1989, pl. 39
		v	
5/6Ḥev 34	papPetition gr [P.Yadin 34] (BA bdl. 12)	208*	
5/6Ḥev 35	papSummons? gr [P.Yadin 35] (BA bdl. 11e)	109*	

ITEM NO.	COMPOSITION	INV	PUBLICATION
5/6Ḥev 36	papFragment nab [P.Yadin 36] (= XḤev/Se Nab. 1)	99*	Yadin et al. 2002
		654	
		655	
		867	
5/6Ḥev 37	papMarriage Contract gr (= XḤev/Se gr 65) indent [P.Yadin 37] (BA bdl. 9/10)	138*	Lewis 1989, pl. 40
5/6Ḥev 38	papUnclassified Text nab [P.Yadin 38] (BA bdl. 4[a])	r	Yadin et al. 2002
		v	
5/6Ḥev 39	papUnclassified Frag. nab [P.Yadin 39] (BA bdl. 4[b])	115*	Yadin et al. 2002
5/6Ḥev 40	Ps [P.Yadin 40] (= 5/6Ḥev 1b)		
5/6Ḥev 41	Num [P.Yadin 41] (= 5/6Ḥev 1a)	27*, 103*	
5/6Ḥev 42	papLease Contract ar [P.Yadin 42] (EG bdl. 2)	102*	Yadin et al. 2002
5/6Ḥev 43	papReceipt ar [P.Yadin 43] (EG bdl. 1)	129* r	Yadin et al. 2002
		v	
5/6Ḥev 44	papLease of Land [P.Yadin 44] (EG bdl. 5)		Yadin 1962, pl. 48C; Yadin et al. 2002
5/6Ḥev 45	papLease of Land [P.Yadin 45] (EG bdl. 6)	126*	Yadin et al. 2002
5/6Ḥev 46	papLease of Land [P.Yadin 46] (EG bdl. 7)		Yadin et al. 2002
5/6Ḥev 47a, b	papDeed of Sale of Half of a Garden ar I [P.Yadin 47 I, II]	117* r	Yadin et al. 2002
		v	
5/6Ḥev 48	Uninscribed Leather [P.Yadin 48]		
5/6Ḥev 49	papLetter [P.Yadin 49] (BK bdl. 11)		Yadin et al. 2002
5/6Ḥev 50	papLetter [P.Yadin 50] (BK bdl. 7)		Yadin et al. 2002
5/6Ḥev 51	papLetter [P.Yadin 51] (BK bdl. 4)	128*	Yadin et al. 2002
5/6Ḥev 52	papLetter gr [P.Yadin 52] (BK bdl. 2)		Lifschitz 1962, 240ff.; Cotton 2002
5/6Ḥev 53	papLetter ar [P.Yadin 53] (BK bdl. 3)	100*	Yadin et al. 2002
5/6Ḥev 54	woodLetter ar [P.Yadin 54]	119*	Yadin et al. 2002
5/6Ḥev 55	papLetter ar [P.Yadin 55] (BK bdl. 13)		Yadin et al. 2002
5/6Ḥev 56	papLetter ar [P.Yadin 56] (BK bdl. 10)	114*	Yadin et al. 2002
5/6Ḥev 57	papLetter ar [P.Yadin 57] (BK bdl. 14)		Yadin et al. 2002
5/6Ḥev 58	papLetter ar [P.Yadin 58] (BK bdl. 9)	107*	Yadin et al. 2002
5/6Ḥev 59	papLetter gr [P.Yadin 59] (BK bdl. 5)	213*	Lifschitz 1962, 258ff.; Cotton 2002
5/6Ḥev 60	papLetter ar? [P.Yadin 60] (BK bdl. 8)		Yadin et al. 2002
5/6Ḥev 61	papLetter [P.Yadin 61] (BK bdl. 6)	127*, 131*	Yadin et al. 2002
5/6Ḥev 62	papLetter ar? [P.Yadin 62] (BK bdl. 12)	133*	Yadin et al. 2002
5/6Ḥev 63	papPalimpsest Letter ar [P.Yadin 63]	125*	Yadin et al. 2002
5/6Ḥev 64	papFrag. gr [P.Yadin 64]	106*	Cotton 2002
8Ḥev 1	8ḤevXII gr		Tov 1990
	col. 2 (Jon 1:14–2:7)	539	Tov 1990, pls. I, II
	col. 3 (Jon 3:2–5, 7–10; 4:1–2, 5)	539, 539A	Tov 1990, pls. I, III
	col. 4 (Mic 1:1–7a)	539	Tov 1990, pls. I, IV
	col. 5 (Mic 1:7b–8)	532	Tov 1990, pl. IV
	col. 6 (Mic 2:7–8; 3:5–6)	529, 532	Tov 1990, pl. V
	col. 7 (Mic 4:3–5)	529, 531	Tov 1990, pl. V
	col. 8 (Mic 4:6–10; 5:1–4[5])	530, 531	Tov 1990, pl. VI
	col. 9 (Mic 5:4[5]–6[7])	530	Tov 1990, pl. VII
	col. 13 (Nah 1:13–14)	539A	Tov 1990, pl. VII
	col. 14 (Nah 2:5–10, 14)	535, 539A	Tov 1990, pl. VIII
	col. 15 (Nah 3:6–17)	535, 539A	Tov 1990, pl. IX
	col. 16 (Hab 1:5–11)	528	Tov 1990, pl. X
	col. 17 (Hab 1:14–17; 2:1–8a)	63, 530	Tov 1990, pls. XI, XVIII
	col. 18 (Hab 2:13–20)	63	Tov 1990, pls. XII, XVIII
	col. 19 (Hab 3:9–15)	63	Tov 1990, pls. XIII, XVIII
	col. 20 (Zeph 1:1–6a)	63	Tov 1990, pls. XIV, XVIII
	col. 21 (Zeph 1:13–18)	63	Tov 1990, pls. XV, XVIII

ITEM NO.	COMPOSITION	INV	PUBLICATION
	col. 22 (Zeph 2:9–10)	63	Tov 1990, pls. XV, XVIII
	col. 23 (Zeph 3:6–7)	63	Tov 1990, pls. XV, XVIII
	col. 28 (Zech 1:1–4)	530	Tov 1990, pl. XVI
	col. 29 (Zech 1:12–15)	530	Tov 1990, pl. XVI
	col. 30 (Zech 1:19–2:4, 7–12)	530, 539A	Tov 1990, pl. XVII
	col. 31 (Zech 2:16–3:7)	530, 539A	Tov 1990, pl. XVII
	col. B1 (Zech 8:19–23a)	538	Tov 1990, pl. XIX
	col. B2 (Zech 8:23b–9:5)	538	Tov 1990, pl. XIX
	Unclassified Frags. 1–6	537–539	Tov 1990, pl. XX
8Ḥev 2	Prayer	223*, 225*	Aharoni 1962, pl. 30F; Morgenstern 2000
8Ḥev 3	papFrags.	222*	Aharoni 1962, pl. 30E
8Ḥev 4	papUnidentified Text gr	221*	Cotton 2000b
8Ḥev 5	ostr	IAA	Aharoni 1962, pl. 29A
8Ḥev 6	ostr	IAA	Aharoni 1962, pl. 29B
8Ḥev	ostrFrags.	IAA	Aharoni 1962, pl. 31A–D

10. Naḥal Ḥever/Seiyal

ITEM NO.	COMPOSITION	INV	PUBLICATION
XḤev/Se 1	Num[a] (= part of 5/6Ḥev 1a)		Flint 2000b
XḤev/Se 2	Num[b]	534	Flint 2000b
XḤev/Se 3	Deut	534	Flint 2000b
XḤev/Se 4	Ps (= part of 5/6Ḥev 1b)		
XḤev/Se 5	Phylactery	886	Morgenstern and Segal 2000
XḤev/Se 6	Eschatological Hymn	889	Morgenstern 2000
XḤev/Se 7	Deed of Sale A ar (r + v)	889	Yardeni 1997, fig. 1, pl. I
XḤev/Se 8	papDeed of Sale B ar and heb	533	Yardeni 1997, figs. 2–3, pl. II
XḤev/Se 8a	papDeed of Sale C ar	651	Yardeni 1997, figs. 4–5, pl. III
XḤev/Se 9	papDeed of Sale D ar	543	Yardeni 1997, figs. 6–8, pls. IV–V
XḤev/Se 9a	papUnclassified Fragment A ar	543	Yardeni 1997, fig. 9, pl. VI
XḤev/Se 10	papReceipt for Payment of a Fine? ar	736	Yardeni 1997, fig. 9, pl. VII
XḤev/Se 11	papMarriage Contract? ar	736	Yardeni 1997, fig. 9, pl. VII
XḤev/Se 12	papReceipt for Dates ar	736	Yardeni 1997, fig. 10, pls. VIII–IX
XḤev/Se 13	papWaiver of Claims? Ar	736	Yardeni 1997, fig. 11, pls. VIII–IX
XḤev/Se 14	papFragment of a Deed ar?	542	Yardeni 1997, fig. 12, pl. X
XḤev/Se 15	papUnclassified Fragment B	542	Yardeni 1997, fig. 12, pl. X
XḤev/Se 16–17	papUnclassified Fragments C–D	542	Yardeni 1997, fig. 12, pl. X
XḤev/Se 18	papUnclassified Fragment E	542	Yardeni 1997, fig. 12, pl. X
XḤev/Se 19	papUnclassified Fragment F	542	Yardeni 1997, fig. 12, pl. X
XḤev/Se 20	(cancelled)		
XḤev/Se 21	papDeed of Sale E ar	527	Yardeni 1997, figs. 12–13, pls. XI–XII
XḤev/Se 22	papDeed of Sale F? ar	735	Yardeni 1997, fig. 14, pl. XIII
XḤev/Se 23	papDeed of Sale G ar	536	Yardeni 1997, fig. 15, pl. XIV
XḤev/Se 24	papDeed A ar	536	Yardeni 1997, fig. 15, pl. XV
XḤev/Se 24a	papDeed B ar	536	Yardeni 1997, fig. 15, pl. XVI
XḤev/Se 25	papDeed C ar	542	Yardeni 1997, fig. 16, pl. XVII
XḤev/Se 26	papText Dealing with Deposits and Barley ar	542	Yardeni 1997, fig. 16, pl. XVII
XḤev/Se 27	papDeed D ar	542	Yardeni 1997, fig. 16, pl. XVIII
XḤev/Se 28	papUnclassified Fragment G ar	536	Yardeni 1997, fig. 17, pl. XIX
XḤev/Se 29	papUnclassified Fragments H	732, 733	Yardeni 1997, fig. 17, pl. XIX
XḤev/Se 30	papLetter to Shimʿon ben Kosibah	542	Yardeni 1997, fig. 18, pl. XX
XḤev/Se 31	papDeed E ar	734	Yardeni 1997, fig. 19, pl. XXI
XḤev/Se 32	papDeed F ar (+ 4Q347)	184, 734	Yardeni 1997, fig. 19, pl. XXI

ITEM NO.	COMPOSITION	INV	PUBLICATION
XḤev/Se 33	papUnclassified Fragment I ar	734	Yardeni 1997, fig. 19, pl. XXII
XḤev/Se 34	papDeed G ar	734	Yardeni 1997, fig. 19, pl. XXII
XḤev/Se 35	papUnclassified Fragment J ar	734	Yardeni 1997, fig. 19, pl. XXII
XḤev/Se 36	papUnclassified Fragment K	734	Yardeni 1997, fig. 19, pl. XXII
XḤev/Se 37	papDeed H ar?	734	Yardeni 1997, fig. 20, pls. XXIII–XXIV
XḤev/Se 38	papUnclassified Fragments L	865	Yardeni 1997, fig. 20, pl. XXV
XḤev/Se 39	papUnclassified Fragment M	865	Yardeni 1997, fig. 20, pl. XXV
XḤev/Se 40	papUnclassified Fragment N	865	Yardeni 1997, fig. 20, pl. XXV
XḤev/Se 41	papUnclassified Fragment O	865	Yardeni 1997, fig. 20, pl. XXV
XḤev/Se 42	papUnclassified Fragment P	865	Yardeni 1997, fig. 21, pl. XXV
XḤev/Se 43	papUnclassified Fragment Q	865	Yardeni 1997, fig. 21, pl. XXV
XḤev/Se 44	papUnclassified Fragment R	865	Yardeni 1997, fig. 21, pl. XXV
XḤev/Se 45	papUnclassified Fragment S	865	Yardeni 1997, fig. 21, pl. XXV
XḤev/Se 46	papUnclassified Fragment T	865	Yardeni 1997, fig. 21, pl. XXV
XḤev/Se 47a	papUnclassified Fragment U	865	Yardeni 1997, fig. 21, pl. XXVI
XḤev/Se 47b	papUnclassified Fragment V	865	Yardeni 1997, fig. 21, pl. XXVI
XḤev/Se 47c	papUnclassified Fragment W	865	Yardeni 1997, fig. 21, pl. XXVI
XḤev/Se 47d	papUnclassified Fragment X	865	Yardeni 1997, fig. 21, pl. XXVI
XḤev/Se 47e	papUnclassified Fragment Y	865	Yardeni 1997, fig. 21, pl. XXVI
XḤev/Se 47f	papUnclassified Fragment Z	865	Yardeni 1997, fig. 21, pl. XXVI
XḤev/Se 47g	papUnclassified Fragment AA	865	Yardeni 1997, fig. 21, pl. XXVI
XḤev/Se 47h	papUnclassified Fragment BB	865	Yardeni 1997, fig. 21, pl. XXVI
XḤev/Se 48	(cancelled)		
XḤev/Se 49	Promissory Note	Priv. Coll.	Yardeni 1997, figs. 22–23, pl. XXVII
XḤev/Se 50	papDeed of Sale H ar (= part of Mur 26)	725, BTS 7163	Yardeni 1997, figs. 24–26, pls. XXVII–XXX
XḤev/Se 60	papTax (or Rent) Receipt from Mahoza gr	866	Cotton 1997, fig. 27, pls. XXXI–XXXII
XḤev/Se 61	papConclusion to a Land Declaration gr	866	Cotton 1997, pls. XXXI, XXXIII
XḤev/Se 62	papLand Declaration gr		Cotton 1997, pls. XXXIV–XXXVII
XḤev/Se 63	papDeed of Renunciation of Claims gr	866	Cotton 1997, pls. XXXI and XXXVIII
XḤev/Se 64	papDeed of Gift gr	869	Cotton 1997, fig. 27, pls. XXXIX–XL
XḤev/Se 65	papMarriage Contract gr	99	Cotton 1997, pl. XLI
XḤev/Se 66	papLoan with Hypothec gr	732	Cotton 1997, pl. XLII
XḤev/Se 67	papText Mentioning Timber gr	866	Cotton 1997, pls. XXXI, XLIII
XḤev/Se 68	papText Mentioning a Guardian gr	866	Cotton 1997, pls. XXXI, XLIV
XḤev/Se 69	papCancelled Marriage Contract gr	870	Cotton 1997, pls. XLV–XLVI
XḤev/Se 70	papUnidentified Fragment A gr	866	Cotton 1997, pls. XXXI, XLVII
XḤev/Se 71	papUnidentified Fragment B gr	866	Cotton 1997, pls. XXXI, XLVII
XḤev/Se 72	papUnidentified Fragment C gr	866	Cotton 1997, pls. XXXI, XLVII
XḤev/Se 73	papEnd of a Document gr	731	Cotton 1997, pl. XLVII
XḤev/Se 74–139	papUnidentified Fragments gr	732	Cotton 1997, pl. XLVIII
XḤev/Se 140–169	papUnidentified Fragments gr	731	Cotton 1997, pl. XLIX
XḤev/Se Nab. 1	papContract nab (= 5/6Ḥev 36)	654	Starcky 1954, 161–81, pls. I–III; Yadin et al. 2002
		655	
		867	
XḤev/Se Nab. 2	papContract nab	862 r	Yadin et al. 2002
		v	
XḤev/Se Nab. 3	papContract nab	863 r	Yadin et al. 2002

ITEM NO.	COMPOSITION	INV	PUBLICATION
		v	
XḤev/Se Nab. 4	papContract nab	868	Yadin et al. 2002
XḤev/Se Nab. 5	papContract nab	864 r	Yadin et al. 2002
		v	
XḤev/Se Nab. 6	papFrag. nab (*olim* "Wadi Habara")	860	Yadin et al. 2002
		860A	
Ḥev/Se? 1–12	papUnidentified Fragments gr	3001	Cotton 1997, pl. L
Ḥev/Se? 13–14	papUnidentified Fragments gr	3004	Cotton 1997, pl. LI
Ḥev/Se? 15–23	papUnidentified Fragments gr	3005	Cotton 1997, pl. LI
Ḥev/Se? 24–35	papUnidentified Fragments gr	3006	Cotton 1997, pl. LII
Ḥev/Se? 36–57	papUnidentified Fragments gr	3007	Cotton 1997, pl. LIII

11. Naḥal Mishmar

ITEM NO.	COMPOSITION	PUBLICATION
1Mish 1	papOfficial Document	Bar Adon 1961 pl. 13E
1Mish 2	papList of Names and	Lifschitz 1961, pl. 23H (cf. 13D)
	Account gr (recto)	Cotton 2000b
	(verso)	Lifschitz 1961, pl. 23I
1Mish 3	papPromissory Note?	Bar Adon 1977, 3:690
1Mish 4	ostrUnclassified	Bar Adon 1977, 3:690
1Mish 5	ostrUnclassified	Bar Adon 1977, 3:690
1Mish 6	ostrUnclassified	Bar Adon 1977, 3:690
1Mish 7	ostrUnclassified	Bar Adon 1977, 3:690
1Mish 8	ostrUnclassified gr	Bar Adon 1977, 3:690

12. Naḥal Ṣe'elim

ITEM NO.	COMPOSITION	INV	PUBLICATION
34Ṣe 1	Phylactery	220*	Aharoni 1961, pl. 11
34Ṣe 2	Num		Aharoni 1961, pl. 11; Morgenstern 2000
34Ṣe 3a	papDeed A		Morgenstern 2000
34Ṣe 3b	Deed B		Morgenstern 2000
34Ṣe 4	papCensus List from Judaea or Arabia gr	226, 229	Cotton 2000b
34Ṣe 5	papAccount gr	226	Cotton 2000b

13. Masada

ITEM NO.	COMPOSITION	INV	PUBLICATION
Mas1	Gen (*olim* Mas1i Jub)	91*	Talmon 1999, ill. 2
Mas1a	Lev^{a}	195*	Talmon 1999, ill. 3
Mas1b	Lev^{b}	198*	Talmon 1999, ill. 4
Mas1c	Deut	196*	Talmon 1999, ill. 6
Mas1d	Ezek	197*	Talmon 1999, ill. 8
Mas1e	Ps^{a}	237*	Talmon 1999, ill. 9
Mas1f	Ps^{b}	81*	Talmon 1999, ill. 10
Mas1g	(cancelled; see 11QPs^{d})		
Mas1h	Sir	238*	Yadin 1965, pls. 1–9
Mas1j	Jub or psJub	236*	Talmon 1999, ill. 14

ITEM NO.	COMPOSITION	INV	PUBLICATION
Mas1k	ShirShabb	232*	Newsom 1998, pl. XIX; Talmon 1999, ill. 15
Mas1l	apocrJosh (*olim* paraJosh)	90*	Talmon 1999, ill. 13
Mas1m	apocrGen (*olim* apEsther?)	82-83*	Talmon 1999, ill. 12
Mas1n	Qumran-type Frag. (*olim* sectarian? frag.)	92*	Talmon 1999, ill. 16
Mas1o r	pap paleoText of Sam. Origin (recto)	235*	Talmon 1999, ill. 18
Mas1o v	pap paleoUnidentified Text (verso)	235*	Talmon 1999, ill. 18
Mas1p	Unclassified frag. ar?	93*	Talmon 1999, ill. 17
Mas1–553	ostrLetters		Yadin and Naveh 1989
Mas554	ostrLetter		Yadin and Naveh 1989, pl. 45
Mas555	ostrLetter		Yadin and Naveh 1989, pl. 45
Mas556	ostrLetter		Yadin and Naveh 1989, pl. 45
Mas557–720	ostrMisc.		Yadin and Naveh 1989
Mas721 r	papVirgil lat (recto)	70*	Cotton and Geiger 1989, pl. 1
Mas721 v	papVirgil lat (verso)	70*	Cotton and Geiger 1989, pl. 1
Mas722	papLegionary Pay Record lat	64*	Cotton and Geiger 1989, pl. 2
Mas723	papMedical Care in the Roman Army lat	59*	Cotton and Geiger 1989, pl. 4
Mas724 r	papLetter to Iulius Lupus lat (recto)	212*	Cotton and Geiger 1989, pl. 4
Mas724 v	papLetter to Iulius Lupus lat (verso)	212*	Cotton and Geiger 1989, pl. 4
Mas725	papThe Balsam Trade lat	233*	Cotton and Geiger 1989, pl. 5
Mas726	papLetter Concerning a Centurion lat	67-68*	Cotton and Geiger 1989, pl. 5
Mas727	papMilitary Document lat	67-68*	Cotton and Geiger 1989, pl. 5
Mas728	papLetter lat	77*	Cotton and Geiger 1989, pl. 5
Mas728a	papLetter lat	50-53*	Cotton and Geiger 1989, pl. 6
Mas729	papMilitary Document lat	71*	Cotton and Geiger 1989, pl. 6
Mas730	papMilitary Document? lat	61*	Cotton and Geiger 1989, pl. 6
Mas731	papMilitary Document? lat (r + v)	46*	Cotton and Geiger 1989, pl. 6
Mas732	papFrag. lat	56-58*	Cotton and Geiger 1989, pl. 7
Mas733	papFrag. lat	57*	Cotton and Geiger 1989, pl. 7
Mas734	papFrag. lat	50-53*	Cotton and Geiger 1989, pl. 7
Mas735	papFrag. lat	47-49*	Cotton and Geiger 1989, pl. 7
Mas736	papFrag. lat		Cotton and Geiger 1989, pl. 7
Mas737	papFrag. lat	55*	Cotton and Geiger 1989, pl. 7
Mas738	Frag. lat	63*	Cotton and Geiger 1989, pl. 7
Mas739	papLiterary Text? gr	54*	Cotton and Geiger 1989, pl. 8
Mas740	papDocuments? gr	60*	Cotton and Geiger 1989, pl. 8
Mas741	papLetter of Abakantos to Judas gr	45*	Cotton and Geiger 1989, pl. 8
Mas742	papByzantine Document gr	69*	Cotton and Geiger 1989, pl. 9
Mas743	woodTablet gr	65*	Cotton and Geiger 1989, pl. 9
Mas744	papList of Names? gr	50-53*	Cotton and Geiger 1989, pl. 9
Mas745	papLetter gr	50-53*	Cotton and Geiger 1989, pl. 9
Mas746	papLetter(s) gr	47-49*	Cotton and Geiger 1989, pl. 9
Mas747	papFrag. gr	66*	Cotton and Geiger 1989, pl. 10
Mas748	papBilingual List of Names lat-gr	62*	Cotton and Geiger 1989, pl. 10
Mas749	papFrags. lat or gr	43*, 233*	Cotton and Geiger 1989, pl. 10
Mas750–927	ostrMisc. lat and gr		Cotton and Geiger 1989
Mas928–945	Graffiti		Cotton and Geiger 1989
Mas946–951	Amphora stamps lat		Cotton and Geiger 1989

APPENDIX D: SHEPHERD OF HERMAS

As noted at §8.3.11, citing the Shepherd of Hermas is complicated by the fact that two numbering systems are sometimes used: an older, tripartite system that numbers the mandates, similitudes, and visions, then divides each into the anticipated chapter and verse (this system would suggest a reference with periods, e.g., Herm. Vis. 4.1.4); and a more recent system introduced by Molly Whittaker (*Der Hirt des Hermas*, GCS 48, Apostolischen Väter 1 [Berlin: Akademie, 1967]) that disregards the three divisions of the Shepherd and renumbers the whole into 114 chapters (allowing the above reference to become Herm. 22.4 [or 22:4]). For the Shepherd, we recommend composite references such as Herm. Vis. 4.1.4 (22.4). The chart below can be used to create or check the accuracy of such composite references.

	older numbering	Whittaker numbering		older numbering	Whittaker numbering
Visions	1.1	1	Mandates	1	26
	1.2	2		2	27
	1.3	3		3	28
	1.4	4		4.1	29
	2.1	5		4.2	30
	2.2	6		4.3	31
	2.3	7		4.4	32
	2.4	8		5.1	33
	3.1	9		5.2	34
	3.2	10		6.1	35
	3.3	11		6.2	36
	3.4	12		7	37
	3.5	13		8	38
	3.6	14		9	39
	3.7	15		10.1	40
	3.8	16		10.2	41
	3.9	17		10.3	42
	3.10	18		11	43
	3.11	19		12.1	44
	3.12	20		12.2	45
	3.13	21		12.3	46
	4.1	22		12.4	47
	4.2	23		12.5	48
	4.3	24		12.6	49
	5	25			

	older numbering	Whittaker numbering	older numbering	Whittaker numbering
Similitudes	1	50	9.6	83
	2	51	9.7	84
	3	52	9.8	85
	4	53	9.9	86
	5.1	54	9.10	87
	5.2	55	9.11	88
	5.3	56	9.12	89
	5.4	57	9.13	90
	5.5	58	9.14	91
	5.6	59	9.15	92
	5.7	60	9.16	93
	6.1	61	9.17	94
	6.2	62	9.18	95
	6.3	63	9.19	96
	6.4	64	9.20	97
	6.5	65	9.21	98
	7	66	9.22	99
	8.1	67	9.23	100
	8.2	68	9.24	101
	8.3	69	9.25	102
	8.4	70	9.26	103
	8.5	71	9.27	104
	8.6	72	9.28	105
	8.7	73	9.29	106
	8.8	74	9.30	107
	8.9	75	9.31	108
	8.10	76	9.32	109
	8.11	77	9.33	110
	9.1	78	10.1	111
	9.2	79	10.2	112
	9.3	80	10.3	113
	9.4	81	10.4	114
	9.5	82		

INDEX